REVIEW OF
CIVIL LITIGATION COSTS

Review of Civil
Litigation Costs:
Final Report

December 2009

information & publishing solutions

Published by TSO (The Stationery Office) and available from:
Online
www.tsoshop.co.uk

Mail, Telephone, Fax & E-mail
TSO
PO Box 29, Norwich, NR3 1GN
Telephone orders/General enquiries: 0870 600 5522
Fax orders: 0870 600 5533
E-mail: customer.services@tso.co.uk
Textphone 0870 240 3701

TSO@Blackwell and other Accredited Agents

Customers can also order publications from:
TSO Ireland
16 Arthur Street, Belfast BT1 4GD
Tel 028 9023 8451 Fax 028 9023 5401

Published with the permission of the Ministry of Justice on behalf of the Controller of Her Majesty's Stationery Office.

First published 2010

ISBN 9780117064041

Printed in the United Kingdom for The Stationery Office.

P002341871   c7   01/10   860   19585

FOREWORD

In some areas of civil litigation costs are disproportionate and impede access to justice. I therefore propose a coherent package of interlocking reforms, designed to control costs and promote access to justice.

21st December 2009   Rupert Jackson

| REVIEW OF |
| CIVIL LITIGATION COSTS |

FINAL REPORT

By the Right Honourable Lord Justice Jackson

December 2009

PART 8. CONCLUSION

GLOSSARY

Where I refer in the Final Report to paragraphs of the Preliminary Report I do so in the following manner:

PR paragraph [chapter number].[paragraph number].[sub-paragraph number]

For example, a reference to paragraph 3.1 of chapter 6 of the Preliminary Report would be set out as PR paragraph 6.3.1.

Word or expression	Meaning or description
Aarhus Convention	The Convention on Access to Information, Public Participation in Decision-Making and Access to Justice in Environmental Matters, signed in Aarhus, Denmark, on 25th June 1998.
ABI	The Association of British Insurers.
ABS	Alternative Business Structure.
ACCC	The Advisory Committee on Civil Costs.
access to justice	The ability of a person to obtain legal advice and representation, and to secure the adjudication through the courts of their legal rights and obligations.
ACSG	The Accident Compensation Solicitors Group.
ACTAPS	The Association of Contentious Trust and Probate Specialists.
additional liabilities	Collectively, CFA success fees and ATE insurance premiums.
ADR	Alternative Dispute Resolution – ways of attempting to resolve disputes so as to avoid litigation. Mediation is the primary form of ADR. See chapter 36.
after-the-event ("ATE") insurance	Insurance by one party against the risk of it having to pay its opponent's legal costs, where the insurance policy is taken out after the event giving rise to court proceedings (e.g. an accident involving personal injury).
AJF	The Access to Justice Fund, established in October 2009 as the charitable body to receive monies recovered pursuant to an order made under section 194 of the Legal Services Act 2007.
ALCD	The Association of Law Costs Draftsmen.
AMRO	The Association of Medical Reporting Organisations.

ANM	The Association of Northern Mediators.
APIL	The Association of Personal Injury Lawyers.
assessment	The process by which the amount of costs payable by one person to another is determined by a judicial officer (usually a judge or a costs judge). Assessment was formerly known as "taxation". An assessment may be a detailed assessment or a summary assessment.
ATE insurance.	See after-the-event insurance.
AvMA	Action against Medical Accidents.
before-the-event ("BTE") insurance	Insurance, protecting a claimant or defendant, that was in place before the occurrence of an event giving rise to a legal claim (eg. a motor vehicle accident) that covers the claimant's or defendant's legal fees, and possibly also those of its opponent (in the event of the insured being ordered to pay their opponent's costs). See generally chapter 8.
Birmingham form	The template form for parties to submit their costs budgets under the Birmingham pilot scheme (referred to in paragraph 3 of the Guidelines for the Birmingham pilot). See chapter 40.
Birmingham seminar	The Costs Review seminar organised by the Master of the Rolls' office and held in Birmingham on 26th June 2009.
Birmingham pilot (scheme)	The costs management pilot in the Birmingham Mercantile Court and the Birmingham TCC which began during Phase 2 of the Costs Review. See chapter 40.
Birmingham TCC	The Birmingham Technology and Construction Court.
BTE insurance	See before-the-event insurance.
CAB	A Citizens Advice Bureau.
CAJE	The Coalition for Access to Justice for the Environment.
CAP	Claims Against Professionals, a body of leading professional indemnity insurers.
Cardiff seminar	The Costs Review seminar organised by the Master of the Rolls' office and held in Cardiff on 19th June 2009.
CBI	The Confederation of British Industry.
CCBC	The County Courts Bulk Centre. This is a facility attached to Northampton County Court for the filing of vast numbers of straightforward claims. Also known as the Claims Production Centre.

CCF	See charitable contingent fund.
CCIT	The Commercial Court IT project.
CEDR	The Centre for Effective Dispute Resolution.
CFA	See conditional fee agreement.
charitable contingent fund ("CCF")	A not-for-profit CLAF as described by the CLAF Group.
ChBA	The Chancery Bar Association.
Citizens Advice	The National Association of Citizens Advice Bureaux.
Civil Procedure Rules 1998 ("CPR")	The primary rules of court for civil litigation in England and Wales, introduced as a consequence of the Woolf reforms.
CJC	The Civil Justice Council.
CLAF	See contingency (or contingent) legal aid fund.
CLAF Group	The Bar Council's CLAF Group.
Claims Outcome Advisor ("COA")	One of two main software systems currently used by insurers in England and Wales for assessing general damages for pain, suffering and loss of amenity. The second is Colossus.
Claims Standards Council ("CS Council")	The trade association which represents claims management companies.
CLAN	The Commercial Litigation Association.
CLASC	The Civil Legal Aid Sub-Committee of the Bar Council.
CLLSLC	The City of London Law Society's Litigation Committee.
CM Council	The Civil Mediation Council.
CMC	Case management conference.
CN	Clinical negligence.
COA	See Claims Outcome Advisor.
Colossus	One of two main software systems currently used by insurers in England and Wales for assessing general damages for pain, suffering and loss of amenity. The second is COA.
COMBAR	The Commercial Bar Association.

conditional fee agreement ("CFA")	An Agreement pursuant to which a lawyer agrees with his or her client to be paid a success fee in the event of the client's claim succeeding, where the success fee is not calculated as a proportion of the amount recovered by the client. A typical example of a CFA is where is retained on a "no win, no fee" basis. See generally PR chapter 16.
contingency fee	A lawyer's fee calculated as a percentage of monies recovered, with no fee payable if the client loses.
contingency (or contingent) legal aid fund ("CLAF")	A fund which grants funding to chosen applicants, where the receipt of funding is conditional on the applicant agreeing to pay a percentage of any amount awarded (e.g. as damages) back into the fund. CLAFs attempt to be self-financing and operate on a not-for profit basis. See generally chapter 13.
costs	The costs incurred by a party through engaging lawyers to act for it. These costs may include the costs of expert witnesses, barristers, photocopying and other disbursements. Costs may be distinguished from fees which are payable to the court in civil litigation.
costs capping	A mechanism whereby judges impose limits on the amount of future costs that the successful party can recover from the losing party.
costs judge	A judicial officer, usually a master of the court, who decides the amount of costs payable by one party to another should the amount be disputed.
Costs PD	See Costs Practice Direction.
Costs Practice Direction	The Practice Direction about Costs, which supplements Parts 43 to 48 of the CPR.
costs shifting	The ordering that one person is to pay another's costs. Costs shifting usually operates on a "loser pays" basis, so that the unsuccessful party is required to pay the successful party's recoverable costs.
CPD	Continuing Professional Development.
CPR	The Civil Procedure Rules.
CRU	The Compensation Recovery Unit.
CS Council	See Claims Standards Council.
CSC	The provider of Colossus.
defamation pilot	The mandatory pilot costs management pilot in defamation cases which is proceeding in London and Manchester for the 12 month period commencing 1st October 2009.

detailed assessment	An assessment of costs which is carried out by a costs officer or judge (as appropriate). A detailed assessment is more involved than a summary assessment.
disclosure	The process in litigation by which relevant documents are made available to an opponent. Prior to the Woolf reforms disclosure was referred to as "discovery" (and it is still known by that name in many common law jurisdictions).
DJ	District Judge.
Docketing	The system of assigning a case to one judge from issue up to and including trial. See PR paragraph 43.5.9.
DWP	The Department of Work and Pensions.
EAT	The Employment Appeal Tribunal.
ECHR	The European Convention on Human Rights.
e-disclosure	The disclosure of electronic material.
e-working	Electronic working. Provides an electronic filing system for court users and an electronic case file for judges and court staff plus the listing component from CCIT.
EL	Employers' liability.
ELA	Employers' liability accident.
ELD	Employers' liability disease.
ELF	The Environmental Law Foundation.
ESI	Electronically stored information.
ET	The Employment Tribunal.
fixed costs	Costs which are fixed in amount by rules of court, especially CPR Part 45. See generally Part 3 of this Final Report.
fixed recoverable costs ("FRC") scheme	The regime for fixed recoverable costs in low value RTA cases, contained in section II of CPR Part 45. Also known as the "predictable costs regime" or "PCR").
FOCIS	The Forum of Complex Injury Solicitors.
FoE	Friends of the Earth.
FOIL	The Forum of Insurance Lawyers.
Form H	Precedent H, which is annexed to the Costs PD.
Form N260	The format for statements of costs for summary assessment.

FRC scheme	See fixed recoverable costs scheme.
FSA	The Financial Services Authority.
FSB	The Federation of Small Businesses.
Funding Code	The set of rules used by the LSC to determine which cases to fund through civil legal aid.
GC100 Group	The Association of General Counsel and Company Secretaries of the FTSE 100 companies.
general protocol	Sections III and IV of the PDPAC.
GHRs	Guideline hourly rates for solicitors.
HD	Housing disrepair.
HLPA	The Housing Law Practitioners Association.
HMCS	Her Majesty's Courts Service.
HMRC	HM Revenue & Customs.
hot tubbing	A colloquial term for the Australian procedure of concurrent evidence. See PR paragraph 42.14.2 and chapter 38 of this report.
IBA	The International Bar Association.
IFB	The Insurance Fraud Bureau.
ILA	The Insolvency Lawyers' Association.
indemnity basis	The assessment of a party's legal costs, made on the basis that the party may recover its reasonable costs that were reasonably incurred and which are reasonable in their amount. However, there is no specific requirement that costs recovered on such a basis be proportionate to the amount or issues in dispute. See further chapter 3, paragraph 5.14.
indemnity principle	The indemnity principle holds that a successful party cannot recover from an unsuccessful party more by way of costs than the successful party is liable to pay his or her legal representatives.
interim hearing	Any hearing before trial, including a CMC or PTR.
IP	Intellectual property.
IPCUC	The Intellectual Property Court Users' Committee.
IPCUC Working Group	A working group set up by the IPCUC to formulate proposals for the reform of the Patents County Court.

IPLA	The Intellectual Property Lawyers Association.
IPO	The Intellectual Property Office.
IPR	Intellectual property rights.
IPWP	The Intellectual Property Working Party which provided the Law Society's comments on IP issues.
ISO	The provider of COA.
ISTC	An Independent Sector Treatment Centre.
IT	Information technology.
ITAC	The Information Technology and the Courts Committee.
IUA	The International Underwriting Association of London.
JAC	The Judicial Appointments Commission.
JSB	The Judicial Studies Board.
LCLCBA	The London Common Law and Commercial Bar Association.
legal expenses insurance ("LEI")	Insurance that covers a person against his own legal costs and/or the legal costs of an opponent in litigation. LEI includes both BTE insurance and ATE insurance.
LEI	See legal expenses insurance.
LEIG	The Legal Expenses Insurance Group.
LFA	The Litigation Funders Alliance.
LMA	The Lloyd's Market Association.
London seminar	The Costs Review seminar organised by the Master of the Rolls' office and held in London on 10th July 2009.
LSB	The Legal Services Board.
LSC	The Legal Services Commission.
LSLA	The London Solicitors Litigation Association.
LTWP	The Commercial Court Long Trials Working Party.
Manchester seminar	The Costs Review seminar organised by the Master of the Rolls' office and held in Manchester on 3rd July 2009.
MASS	The Motor Accidents Solicitors Society.

MCOL	Money Claims Online. An electronic system which allows litigants to issue simple, straightforward claims for money claims online. See also PCOL.
MDU	The Medical Defence Union.
menu option	The fifth out of the eight options for disclosure rules set out in PR chapter 41.
MIB	Motor Insurers' Bureau.
MINELA	Middle Income No Entitlement to Legal Aid.
MLA	Media Lawyers Association.
MoJ	The Ministry of Justice.
MPS	The Medical Protection Society.
MRO	Medical Reporting Organisation.
MRO Agreement	The Medical Reporting Organisation Agreement, dated 2nd April 2009, made between liability insurers and "compensators" on the one hand and MROs on the other. It provides for capped recoverable costs in respect of certain expert medical reports in RTA, EL and PL claims where general damages do not exceed £15,000.
Multi-Track Code	The Personal Injury Multi-Track Code for handling personal injury claims above £250,000, agreed between APIL, FOIL and a number of insurers.
NAH	The National Accident Helpline.
NCCBA	Northern Circuit Commercial Bar Association.
new process	The new process being developed by the MoJ for handling personal injury claims arising out of RTAs up to £10,000 where liability is admitted.
NHSLA	The National Health Service Litigation Authority.
NMH	The National Mediation Helpline.
"no win, no fee"	An agreement between a client and a lawyer that the lawyer will only be entitled to payment should the client be successful in its claim. In England and Wales such agreements are usually in the form of CFAs.
NUT	The National Union of Teachers.
OFT	The Office of Fair Trading.

One way costs shifting	A regime under which the defendant pays the claimant's costs if its claim is successful, but the claimant does not pay the defendant's costs if the claim is unsuccessful.
Ontario model	The contingency fees regime which operates in Ontario, Canada, as described in PR paragraphs 61.2.5, 61.2.6, 61.4.3 and 61.4.4.
P&I Club	See Protection and Indemnity Club.
Part 36	Part 36 of the CPR.
partial CFA	A "no win, low fee" agreement.
PBA	The Property Bar Association.
PCC	The Patents County Court.
PCO	A protective costs order.
PCOL	Possession Claims Online. An electronic system which allows litigants to issue simple, straightforward claims for possession claims online. See also MCOL.
PDF	Portable Document Format.
PDPAC	The Practice Direction – Pre-Action Conduct which came into effect on 6th April 2009.
PI	Personal injury.
PI small claims limit	The upper limit for personal injury claims on the small claims track in respect of general damages.
PIBA	The Personal Injuries Bar Association.
PL	Public liability.
PLA	Public liability accident.
PLP	The Public Law Project, a national charity whose central aim is to improve access to public law remedies for those who are poor or otherwise disadvantaged.
PNBA	The Professional Negligence Bar Association.
PNLA	The Professional Negligence Lawyers' Association.
PR	The Review of Civil Litigation Costs: Preliminary Report published on 8th May 2009.
Protection and Indemnity Club ("P&I Club")	An insurance mutual which provides collective self insurance to its members, with the members pooling their risks in order to obtain "at cost" insurance cover.

PSLA	Pain, suffering and loss of amenity, consequential upon personal injury.
PTR	Pre-trial review.
QB	Queen's Bench.
QBD	The Queen's Bench Division.
qualified one way costs shifting	A system of one way costs shifting which may become a two-way costs shifting system in certain circumstances, e.g. if it is just that there be two way costs shifting given the resources available to the parties.
RCJ	The Royal Courts of Justice in London.
Referral fee	A fee paid by a solicitor to obtain the referral of a case to him or her. See chapter 20.
RSC	The Rules of the Supreme Court, the predecessor to the CPR.
RTA	Road traffic accident.
Rule Committee	The Civil Procedure Rule Committee.
SABIP	The Strategic Advisory Board for Intellectual Property Policy.
SCCO	The Senior Courts Costs Office, formerly known as the Supreme Court Costs Office.
SLAS	See supplementary legal aid scheme.
SMART Evaluate	A claimant solicitor focused online quantum assessment tool developed by SMART Online Ltd.
SME	A small or medium enterprise.
SRA	The Solicitors Regulation Authority.
standard basis	The assessment of a party's legal costs, made on the basis that the party may recover its reasonable and proportionate costs.
summary assessment	The assessment of costs by a judge at the end of a hearing, as set out in chapter 44.
supplementary legal aid scheme ("SLAS")	Similar to a CLAF, in that it is a legal fund which aims to be self-funding, and the granting of funding is conditional upon the applicant agreeing to pay a percentage of any amounts recovered back into the fund. A SLAS is different from a CLAF in that it is usually operated by a legal aid body, and is intended to provide funding to persons who are not of sufficient means to afford legal representation for their case. See generally chapter 13.

TCC	The Technology and Construction Court.
TECBAR	The Technology and Construction Bar Association.
TeCSA	The Technology and Construction Solicitors Association.
third party funding	The funding of litigation by a party who has no pre-existing interest in the litigation, usually on the basis that (i) the funder will be paid out of the proceeds of any amounts recovered as a consequence of the litigation, often as a percentage of the recovery sum; and (ii) the funder is not entitled to payment should the claim fail.
TML	Trust Mediation Ltd, a specialist provider of fixed costs mediations in personal injury cases.
TUC	The Trades Union Congress.
UKELA	The UK Environmental Lawyers Association.
Ungley order	Master Ungley's direction on ADR. See chapter 36, paragraphs 2.7 and 3.4.
Woolf Inquiry	The review of the civil justice system conducted by Lord Woolf, concluding with his final report "*Access to Justice*" in July 1996.
Woolf reforms	Reforms arising out of the review of the civil justice system conducted by Lord Woolf, concluding with his final report "*Access to Justice*" in July 1996. The CPR were brought in as a result of Lord Woolf's recommendations.

EXECUTIVE SUMMARY

1. INTRODUCTION

1.1   <u>Terms of reference.</u> The terms of reference require me to review the rules and principles governing the costs of civil litigation and to make recommendations in order to promote access to justice at proportionate cost. They also require me to review case management procedures; to have regard to research into costs and funding; to consult widely; to compare our costs regime with those of other jurisdictions; and to prepare a report setting out recommendations with supporting evidence by 31st December 2009.

1.2   <u>Evidence and review of overseas jurisdictions.</u> I gathered most of the relevant evidence and data during Phase 1 of the Costs Review and set that evidence out in a Preliminary Report[1] published on 8th May 2009. My review of overseas jurisdictions is also contained in the Preliminary Report. The evidence and data gathered since 8th May is set out in this report or its appendices.

1.3   <u>Recommendations.</u> My recommendations are set out in this report, since all opinions expressed in the Preliminary Report were provisional only. In some areas of litigation costs are neither excessive nor disproportionate, so I do not recommend substantial changes. In other areas costs are excessive or disproportionate and I do recommend substantial changes. I also make recommendations in respect of funding regimes, in order to promote access to justice at proportionate cost. The funding regimes affect costs and the costs rules impact upon funding. Neither topic can be considered in isolation.

2. MAJOR RECOMMENDATIONS

2.1   <u>"No win, no fee" agreements.</u> Conditional fee agreements ("CFAs"), of which "no win, no fee" agreements are the most common species, have been the major contributor to disproportionate costs in civil litigation in England and Wales. There are two key drivers of cost under such agreements, being (i) the lawyer's success fee; and (ii) the after-the-event ("ATE") insurance premium that is usually taken out when a CFA is entered into (to cover the claimant against the risk of having to pay the defendant's costs). Both the success fee and the ATE insurance premium are presently recoverable from an unsuccessful defendant.

2.2   <u>Success fees and ATE insurance premiums should cease to be recoverable.</u> I recommend that success fees and ATE insurance premiums should cease to be recoverable from unsuccessful opponents in civil litigation. If this recommendation is implemented, it will lead to significant costs savings, whilst still enabling those who need access to justice to obtain it. It will be open to clients to enter into "no win, no fee" (or similar) agreements with their lawyers, but any success fee will be borne by the client, not the opponent.

2.3   <u>Consequences for personal injuries litigation.</u> The importance of ensuring that successful claimants are properly compensated for their injuries or losses was rightly emphasised to me during the Costs Review. Indeed, it must be acknowledged that one of the benefits of the current CFA regime is that it is geared towards ensuring that claimants receive proper compensation. This, however, comes at a

---

[1] Most of the evidence and data are contained in the appendices to the Preliminary Report.

heavy price for defendants, who often have to bear a disproportionate costs burden. If the current regime is reformed along the lines I have proposed, so that success fees are no longer recoverable from an opponent in litigation, lawyers will still be able to agree CFAs with their clients, but any success fee will be payable by the client. This is likely to mean that the success fee comes out of the damages awarded to the client.

2.4   Increase in general damages. In order to ensure that claimants are properly compensated for personal injuries, and that the damages awarded to them (which may be intended to cover future medical care) are not substantially eaten into by legal fees, I recommend as a complementary measure that awards of general damages for pain, suffering and loss of amenity be increased by 10%, and that the maximum amount of damages that lawyers may deduct for success fees be capped at 25% of damages (excluding any damages referable to future care or future losses). In the majority of cases, this should leave successful claimants no worse off than they are under the current regime, whilst at the same time ensuring that unsuccessful defendants only pay normal and proportionate legal costs to successful claimants. It will also ensure that claimants have an interest in the costs being incurred on their behalf.

2.5   Referral fees. It is a regrettably common feature of civil litigation, in particular personal injuries litigation, that solicitors pay referral fees to claims management companies, before-the-event ("BTE") insurers and other organisations to "buy" cases. Referral fees add to the costs of litigation, without adding any real value to it. I recommend that lawyers should not be permitted to pay referral fees in respect of personal injury cases.

2.6   Qualified one way costs shifting. ATE insurance premiums add considerably to the costs of litigation. Litigation costs can be reduced by taking away the need for ATE insurance in the first place. This can occur if qualified one way costs shifting is introduced, at least for certain categories of litigation in which it is presently common for ATE insurance to be taken out. By "qualified" one way costs shifting I mean that the claimant will not be required to pay the defendant's costs if the claim is unsuccessful, but the defendant will be required to pay the claimant's costs if it is successful. The qualifications to this are that unreasonable (or otherwise unjustified) party behaviour may lead to a different costs order, and the financial resources available to the parties may justify there being two way costs shifting in particular cases.

2.7   If it is accepted in principle that CFA success fees and ATE insurance premiums should cease to be recoverable, and qualified one way costs shifting should be introduced, there will need to be further consultation on which categories of litigation should involve qualified one way costs shifting. I can certainly see the benefit of there being qualified one way costs shifting in personal injuries litigation. It seems to me that a person who has a meritorious claim for damages for personal injuries should be able to bring that claim, without being deterred by the risk of adverse costs. The same could be said of clinical negligence, judicial review and defamation claims. There may be other categories of civil litigation where qualified one way costs shifting would be beneficial.

2.8   Overall result. If the package of proposed reforms summarised above is introduced, there will be five consequences:

- Most personal injury claimants will recover more damages than they do at present, although some will recover less.

xvii

- Claimants will have a financial interest in the level of costs which are being incurred on their behalf.

- Claimant solicitors will still be able to make a reasonable profit.

- Costs payable to claimant solicitors by liability insurers will be significantly reduced.

- Costs will also become more proportionate, because defendants will no longer have to pay success fees and ATE insurance premiums.

2.9   Fixed costs in fast track litigation. Cases in the fast track are those up to a value of £25,000, where the trial can be concluded within one day. A substantial proportion of civil litigation is conducted in the fast track. I recommend that the costs recoverable for fast track personal injury cases be fixed. For other types of case I recommend that there be a dual system (at least for now), whereby costs are fixed for certain types of case, and in other cases there is a financial limit on costs recoverable (I propose that £12,000 be the limit for pre-trial costs). The ideal is for costs to be fixed in the fast track for all types of claim.

2.10   There are several advantages to the fixing of costs in lower value litigation. One is that it gives all parties certainty as to the costs they may recover if successful, or their exposure if unsuccessful. Secondly, fixing costs avoids the further process of costs assessment, or disputes over recoverable costs, which can in themselves generate further expense.   Thirdly, it ensures that recoverable costs are proportionate. There is a public interest in making litigation costs in the fast track both proportionate and certain.

2.11   Costs Council. If a fixed costs regime is adopted for the fast track, the costs recoverable for the various types of claim will need to be reviewed regularly to make sure that they are reasonable and realistic. I propose that a Costs Council be established to undertake the role of reviewing fast track fixed costs, as well as other matters.

3. OTHER FUNDING ISSUES

3.1   BTE insurance (chapter 8). BTE insurance (or "legal expenses insurance") is insurance cover for legal expenses taken out before an event which gives rise to civil litigation. It is under-used in England and Wales. If used more widely, it could produce benefits for small and medium enterprises ("SMEs") and individuals who may become embroiled in legal disputes.

3.2   Contingency fees (chapter 12). A contingency fee agreement may be described as one under which the client's lawyer is only paid if his or her client's claim is successful, and then the lawyer is paid out of the settlement sum or damages awarded, usually as a percentage of that amount.   Lawyers are not presently permitted to act on a contingency fee basis in "contentious" business.

3.3   It is my recommendation that lawyers should be able to enter into contingency fee agreements with clients for contentious business, provided that:

- the unsuccessful party in the proceedings, if ordered to pay the successful party's costs, is only required to pay an amount for costs reflecting what would be a conventional amount, with any difference to be borne by the successful party; and

- the terms on which contingency fee agreements may be entered into are regulated, to safeguard the interests of clients.

Permitting the use of contingency fee agreements increases the types of litigation funding available to litigants, which should thereby increase access to justice. This will be of especial importance if (as proposed) the current CFA regime is reformed.

3.4   Contingency Legal Aid Fund ("CLAF") and Supplementary Legal Aid Scheme ("SLAS") (chapter 13). CLAFs and SLASs are self-funding and usually not-for-profit forms of litigation funding. They are used overseas (e.g. in Australia, Canada and Hong Kong), but on a relatively small scale. CLAFs or a SLAS could play a role in funding litigation, especially if the current CFA regime is reformed along the lines I have proposed. However, one of the critical matters for any CLAF or SLAS is whether a self-funding scheme is economically viable for any significant number of cases. The information I have reviewed during the Costs Review does not provide any strong indication of financial viability. I would, nevertheless, recommend that the use of CLAFs and SLASs as a form of legal funding for civil litigation be kept under review.

4. PERSONAL INJURIES LITIGATION

4.1   Assessment of general damages for pain, suffering and loss of amenity (chapter 21). The majority of personal injury claims settle before trial. Computer software systems, which calculate the level of general damages based on the type of injury and other factors, already influence settlement offers. Defendants' lawyers and liability insurers currently operate and maintain the principal extant types of software used in the calculation of general damages. The complaint is sometimes made by claimant representatives that computer-generated assessments of claims for general damages are too low. This is said to have two adverse effects: (i) settlement may be delayed, thus increasing costs; (ii) alternatively, there may be under-settlement.

4.2   During the Costs Review I explored the possibility of producing a transparent and "neutral" calibration of existing software systems to assist in calculating general damages,[2] which could encourage the early settlement of personal injury claims for acceptable amounts. I believe that this is indeed possible, and suggest that a working group be set up consisting of representatives of claimants, defendants, the judiciary and others to take this matter further.

4.3   Process and procedure (chapter 22). In recent times progress has been made to develop new processes for personal injuries litigation. The Ministry of Justice has developed a process for handling personal injury claims arising out of road traffic accidents where the amount in dispute is up to £10,000 and liability is admitted. I recommend that this new process be monitored, to see whether it leads to costs being kept proportionate, or whether costs in fact increase due to satellite litigation. I also encourage a productive engagement, under the aegis of the Civil Justice Council, between claimant and defendant representatives to see whether a similar procedure can be applied in other fast track personal injuries litigation.

4.4   Clinical negligence (chapter 23). One of the principal complaints that was made during the Costs Review about clinical negligence actions was that pre-action costs were often being racked up to disproportionately high levels. There may be a number of reasons for this (which I mention in chapter 23). The recommendations I

---

[2] Up to £10,000.

have made here include increasing the response time for defendants to pre-action letters from three months to four months (to give more time for a thorough investigation of the claim), and that where the defendant is proposing to deny liability it should obtain independent expert evidence on liability and causation within that period. I also recommend that case management directions for clinical negligence claims be harmonised across England and Wales and that costs management of clinical negligence cases be piloted.

5. SOME SPECIFIC TYPES OF LITIGATION

5.1   <u>Intellectual property litigation (chapter 24).</u>   The creation and use of intellectual property ("IP") rights play a crucial role in economic activity and the owners of IP rights must be able to assert or defend them in the courts. The cost to SMEs (and larger enterprises) of resolving IP disputes can be significant. To reduce the costs of IP litigation, and particularly the cost to SMEs, I recommend that the Patents County Court (the "PCC"), which deals with lower value IP disputes, be reformed to provide a cost-effective environment for IP disputes. These reforms include (i) allowing costs to be recovered from opponents according to cost scales; and (ii) capping total recoverable costs to £50,000 in contested actions for patent infringement, and £25,000 for all other cases. I also recommend that there be a fast track and a small claims track in the PCC.

5.2   <u>Small business disputes (chapter 25).</u>   Much attention is often given to large, high-profile disputes in the High Court (particularly the Commercial Court). Yet the vast majority of business disputes that turn into civil court proceedings are between SMEs, or are for lower value amounts which are nevertheless significant to the businesses involved. These proceedings are brought in the Mercantile Courts and other courts. It is important that the litigation environment for such cases is streamlined, accessible to non-lawyers and cost-effective.

5.3   To assist bringing about such an environment for these disputes, I recommend that a High Court judge should be appointed as judge in charge of the Mercantile Courts, whose role will include streamlining procedures and preparing a court guide for users of all Mercantile Courts. I also recommend that HMCS[3] prepare a "small business disputes" guide for business people who wish to conduct lower value county court cases on the small claims track. The limits of the small claims track could be extended in cases where the parties on both sides are businesses.

5.4   <u>Housing claims (chapter 26).</u>   The cost of housing claims is to some extent a function of the complexity of the substantive law concerning housing. A simplification of the law, along the lines recommended by the Law Commission in its reports of 2003, 2006 and 2008, should therefore be considered. I have set out other recommendations of a fairly specific nature in chapter 26.

5.5   <u>Large commercial claims (chapter 27).</u>   Much large commercial litigation is conducted in the Commercial Court. The feedback that I received during the Costs Review indicated that there was a strong general level of satisfaction amongst court users with the current workings of the Commercial Court, and that it generally deals with proceedings in a time and cost efficient manner. Advances in Commercial Court procedure have been made as a result of the efforts of the Commercial Court Long Trials Working Party (the "LTWP"). Many of the recommendations of the LTWP are reflected in the Admiralty & Commercial Courts Guide (8th edition, 2009). I do not

---

[3] Her Majesty's Courts Service.

recommend that any major changes be made to the specific workings of the Commercial Court, although I have made certain recommendations in relation to disclosure, the use of lists of issues as a case management tool and docketing of cases to judges.

5.6   Chancery litigation (chapter 28).   I make a number of specific recommendations in relation to chancery litigation. One is that CPR Part 8 should be amended to enable actions to be assigned to the fast track at any time. This would enable smaller value chancery cases to be dealt with under the economical model that applies in the fast track. Another recommendation is that there should be developed a scheme of benchmark costs for routine bankruptcy and insolvency cases.

5.7   Technology and Construction Court litigation (chapter 29).   Litigation in the Technology and Construction Court (the "TCC") is often conducted in a proportionate manner, and I make only modest recommendations concerning the operation of that court. I do, however, recommend that there be a fast track in the TCC.

5.8   Judicial review (chapter 30).   Perhaps the main issue in relation to judicial review cases is the question of whether there should be qualified one way costs shifting. This is covered in the "major recommendations" section, above. Qualified one way costs shifting would ensure compliance with the Aarhus Convention[4] in relation to environmental judicial review claims. Also, judicial review proceedings have the benefit of a "permission" stage, which filters out unmeritorious cases (thus reducing the need for two way costs shifting as a deterrent).

5.9   Nuisance cases (chapter 31).   Statutory nuisance proceedings in the magistrates' courts provide affordable redress for many claimants. I recommend that a greater take-up of BTE insurance be encouraged, particularly for households. This would help to meet the costs of private nuisance litigation in the civil courts.

5.10   Defamation and related claims (chapter 32).   One principal concern that has been expressed in relation to the costs of defamation proceedings and privacy cases is the widespread use of CFAs with ATE insurance, which can impose a disproportionate costs burden on defendants. I have recommended that lawyers' success fees and ATE insurance premiums should cease to be recoverable for all types of civil litigation. If this recommendation is adopted, it should go a substantial distance to ensuring that unsuccessful defendants in such proceedings are not faced with a disproportionate costs liability. However, such a measure could also reduce access to justice for claimants of slender means.

5.11   To overcome this potential problem, I recommend complementary measures for defamation and related proceedings, namely:

- increasing the general level of damages in defamation and breach of privacy proceedings by 10%; and

- introducing a regime of qualified one way costs shifting, under which the amount of costs that an unsuccessful claimant may be ordered to pay is a reasonable amount, reflective of the means of the parties and their conduct in the proceedings.

---

[4] The Convention on Access to Information, Public Participation in Decision-Making and Access to Justice in Environmental Matters, signed in Aarhus, Denmark, on 25th June 1998.

xxi

I also make a number of specific recommendations in respect of defamation and related proceedings.

5.12   Collective actions (chapter 33). Collective actions are used to provide a means of legal redress to claimants who have a shared or common legal grievance. It is often cost-effective if such claims are dealt with collectively, in a single action, rather than by each claimant bringing his or her individual claim. One of the major issues concerning collective actions is costs shifting, and whether claimants (who individually may be of modest means) should be required to pay the defendant's costs in the event that the claim fails. Costs shifting can reduce access to justice, but it may also have the effect of weeding out unmeritorious claims. My recommendation is that costs shifting should remain for collective actions (with the exception of personal injury collective actions), but that the court should have a discretion to order otherwise if this will better facilitate access to justice.

5.13   Appeals (chapter 34). Any changes to the costs rules affecting appeals should await (and follow) changes to the costs rules affecting lower courts. Having said this, one interim measure which I recommend is that where an appeal comes from a court or tribunal in which there is no costs shifting, the appellate court should have the power to order (i) that each party bear its own costs of the appeal; or (ii) that recoverable costs be capped at a specified sum.

6. CONTROLLING THE COSTS OF LITIGATION

6.1   Pre-action protocols (chapter 35). There are ten pre-action protocols for specific types of litigation. By-and-large they perform a useful function, by encouraging the early settlement of disputes, which thereby leads (in such cases) to the costs of litigation being avoided. I recommend that these specific protocols be retained, albeit with certain amendments to improve their operation (and to keep pre-action costs proportionate).

6.2   On the other hand, the Practice Direction – Pre-Action Conduct, which was introduced in 2009 as a general practice direction for all types of litigation, is unsuitable as it adopts a "one size fits all" approach, often leading to pre-action costs being incurred unnecessarily (and wastefully). I recommend that substantial parts of this practice direction be repealed. Were this to occur, however, it would not give carte blanche to claimants to whom no specific protocol applied to act unreasonably, e.g. by commencing proceedings with no prior warning to the defendant of the claim or the nature of the claim. Cost sanctions will apply to curb unreasonable behaviour.

6.3   Alternative dispute resolution (chapter 36). Alternative dispute resolution ("ADR") (particularly mediation) has a vital role to play in reducing the costs of civil disputes, by fomenting the early settlement of cases. ADR is, however, under-used. Its potential benefits are not as widely known as they should be. I therefore recommend that:

- There should be a serious campaign to ensure that all litigation lawyers and judges are properly informed of how ADR works, and the benefits that it can bring.

- The public and small businesses who become embroiled in disputes are also made aware of the benefits of ADR. An authoritative handbook for ADR should be prepared, explaining what ADR is and how it works, and listing reputable providers of ADR services. This handbook should be used as the standard work for the training of judges and lawyers.

Nevertheless ADR should not be mandatory for all proceedings. The circumstances in which it should be used (and when it should be used) will vary from case to case, and much will come down to the judgment of experienced practitioners and the court.

6.4   Disclosure (chapter 37). Disclosure is an exercise which is necessary in many types of litigation, to ensure that all relevant evidence is brought before the court. The extent of disclosure has increased in recent times with the widespread use of electronic communications and electronic records. Disclosure can be an expensive exercise (particularly in higher value, complex cases), and it is therefore necessary that measures be taken to ensure that the costs of disclosure in civil litigation do not become disproportionate.

6.5   E-disclosure in particular has emerged as a new and important facet of disclosure generally, and I recommend that solicitors, barristers and judges alike be given appropriate training on how to conduct e-disclosure efficiently.

6.6   I also recommend that there be a "menu" of disclosure options available for large commercial and similar claims, where the costs of standard disclosure are likely to be disproportionate. I would, however, exclude large personal injury and clinical negligence claims from this "menu" option, as standard disclosure usually works satisfactorily in those cases.

6.7   Witness statements and expert evidence (chapter 38). There is nothing fundamentally wrong with the manner in which evidence is currently adduced in civil litigation, by way of witness statements and expert reports. The only substantial complaint which is made is that in some cases the cost of litigation is unnecessarily increased because witness statements and expert reports are unduly long. I recommend two measures (in appropriate cases) for curbing litigants' over-enthusiasm for prolixity, being (i) case management measures to place controls on the content or length of statements; and (ii) cost sanctions.

6.8   Case management (chapter 39). One of the points that was impressed upon me during the Costs Review was that judges should take a more robust approach to case management, to ensure that (realistic) timetables are observed and that costs are kept proportionate. Case management can and should be an effective tool for costs control.

6.9   I recommend a number of measures to enhance the courts' role and approach to case management, including:

- where practicable allocating cases to judges who have relevant expertise;

- ensuring that, so far as possible, a case remains with the same judge;

- standardising case management directions; and

- ensuring that case management conferences and other interim hearings are used as effective occasions for case management, and do not become formulaic hearings that generate unnecessary cost (e.g. where directions could easily have been given without a hearing).

xxiii

6.10　Costs management (chapter 40). Costs management is an adjunct to case management, whereby the court, with input from the parties, actively attempts to control the costs of cases before it. The primary means by which costs management is effected is for the parties to provide budgets of their own costs, with those budgets being updated from time to time and submitted for approval to the court. The court then formulates the directions and orders which it makes with a view to ensuring that costs do not become disproportionate. It may do this, for example, by limiting disclosure, or limiting the number of witnesses.

6.11　Effective costs management has the potential to lead to the saving of costs (and time) in litigation. I recommend that lawyers and judges alike receive training in costs budgeting and costs management. I also recommend that rules be drawn up which set out a standard costs management procedure, which judges would have a discretion to adopt if the use of costs management would appear to be beneficial in any particular case.

6.12　Part 36 offers (chapter 41). Most cases settle, rather than go to trial and judgment. It is manifestly beneficial that cases should settle, so as to avoid the further incurring of legal costs. Part 36 of the Civil Procedure Rules plays an important role in incentivising parties to make settlement offers. However, Part 36 does not go far enough in terms of incentivising defendants to accept offers made by claimants. In order to provide greater incentives for defendants to accept settlement offers, I recommend that where a defendant fails to beat a claimant's offer, the claimant's recovery should be enhanced by 10%.

6.13　IT (chapter 43). IT plays an important role in modern litigation and court management. It certainly has the potential to lower the costs of litigation, when it is implemented and operating smoothly across the courts. I recommend that e-working, which is currently used only in the TCC and the Commercial Court, be rolled out across the High Court in London and (suitably adapted) across all county courts and district registries. The future development and use of IT in civil litigation (which I would encourage) is a matter that will require the oversight and input of court users, courts administration staff and judges alike.

6.14　Summary and detailed assessments (chapters 44 and 45). The procedure for the summary assessment of costs generally works well, and should be retained. I do, however, recommend a number of specific improvements to the process. For detailed assessments, I recommend that a new format for bills of costs be developed. I also recommend the streamlining of the procedure for detailed assessment through the use of IT.

PART 1. INTRODUCTION

CHAPTER 1. THE CIVIL JUSTICE COSTS REVIEW

INDEX

1. INTRODUCTION

1.1   <u>Setting up of the Civil Justice Costs Review.</u> The background to the setting up of the Civil Justice Costs Review is set out in PR paragraphs 1.1 to 1.2.   On 3rd November 2008 Sir Anthony Clarke MR announced the setting up of the review in the following terms:

"The Master of the Rolls has appointed Lord Justice Jackson to lead a fundamental review into the costs of civil litigation.

The review will commence in January 2009, and the findings are due to be presented to the Master of the Rolls in December 2009. Lord Justice Jackson will be the sole author of the final report, but he will be assisted in the review by a small group of 'assessors', drawn from the judiciary, legal profession and an economist. The review group are due to meet monthly to discuss issues and findings.

The review is being undertaken as the Master of the Rolls, Sir Anthony Clarke, is concerned at the costs of civil litigation and believes that the time is right for a fundamental and independent review of the whole system."

1.2   <u>Terms of reference.</u> The terms of reference for the review were set out as follows in an appendix to the Master of the Rolls' announcement:

"With the support of the Ministry of Justice, the Master of the Rolls has asked Lord Justice Jackson to conduct a wide ranging review into civil costs.

Objective

To carry out an independent review of the rules and principles governing the costs of civil litigation and to make recommendations in order to promote access to justice at proportionate cost.

Terms of reference:

In conducting the review Lord Justice Jackson will:

- Establish how present costs rules operate and how they impact on the behaviour of both parties and lawyers.

- Establish the effect case management procedures have on costs and consider whether changes in process and/or procedure could bring about more proportionate costs.

- Have regard to previous and current research into costs and funding issues; for example any further Government research into Conditional Fee Agreements - 'No win, No fee', following the scoping study.

- Seek the views of judges, practitioners, Government, court users and other interested parties through both informal consultation and a series of public seminars.

- Compare the costs regime for England and Wales with those operating in other jurisdictions.

- Prepare a report setting out recommendations with supporting evidence by 31 December 2009."

1.3   Organisation of the review. The review commenced on 1st January 2009 with an allotted span of one year. I have divided this year into three phases:

- Phase 1 (January to April): Fact finding, preliminary consultation and preparation of Preliminary Report ("PR").

- Phase 2 (May to July): Consultation.

- Phase 3 (September to December): Analysis of material received and preparation of Final Report.

1.4   Assessors. Throughout the year I have been assisted by the following panel of assessors:

- Mr Justice Cranston.

- Professor Paul Fenn.

- Senior Costs Judge Master Peter Hurst.

- Jeremy Morgan QC.

- Michael Napier CBE, QC (Hon).

- Andrew Parker.

- Colin Stutt.

2. PHASE 1 AND PUBLICATION OF PRELIMINARY REPORT

2.1   <u>Work carried out during Phase 1.</u> The work carried out during Phase 1 is set out in PR paragraphs 1.5.3 to 1.5.9. Essentially, the work consisted of attending meetings, conferences and seminars; considering written submissions; a number of overseas visits and drafting the Preliminary Report.

2.2   <u>Late Phase 1 submissions.</u> The deadline for making submissions for Phase 1 of the Costs Review was 31st January 2009. Written submissions received after that date, but during Phase 1, were treated as Phase 2 submissions. These are listed in annex 1.

2.3   <u>Publication of Preliminary Report.</u> The Preliminary Report was published on 8th May 2009. In that report I endeavoured to marshal the available facts and evidence, to identify the issues for consideration and to set out the relevant factors and competing arguments. Where I had formed tentative opinions, I set these out in the Preliminary Report. I invited those who disagreed to explain why such opinions were wrong. Many respondents accepted this invitation with alacrity.

2.4   <u>Role of the Preliminary Report.</u> The Preliminary Report provided background material for the consultation exercise during Phase 2. That report also provides background material and data for the present report. The Preliminary Report is available online[1] and I shall take it as read. In this Final Report I shall cross-refer as necessary to the Preliminary Report, without repeating the contents.

3. PHASE 2

(i) Written submissions, conferences, meetings and seminars

3.1   <u>Written submissions.</u> During Phase 2 I received a large number of written submissions. These are listed in annex 2. Emails sent in following seminars elaborating points made by the various speakers (although gratefully received and extremely helpful) have not been listed as Phase 2 submissions.

3.2   <u>Conferences, seminars and meetings.</u> During Phase 2 I attended a large number of conferences, seminars and meetings. These are listed in annex 3. I am most grateful to all of the organisers and hosts of those events.

3.3   The seminars included four major seminars organised by the Master of the Rolls' office. These were held at the following venues:

- Cardiff: 19th June 2009 (the "Cardiff seminar").

- Birmingham: 26th June 2009 (the "Birmingham seminar").

- Manchester: 3rd July 2009 (the "Manchester seminar").

- London: 10th July 2009 (the "London seminar").

3.4   The seminars also included eight informal seminars devoted to specific topics. The informal seminars were advertised on the Costs Review website. Anyone who wished to come to any of those seminars was given a place. The informal seminars were as follows:

---

[1] http://www.judiciary.gov.uk/about_judiciary/cost-review/preliminary-report.htm.

- After-the-event insurance, success fees and conditional fee agreements (Monday 20th July, hosted by Reynolds Porter Chamberlain) (the "CFA seminar").

- CLAFs,[2] SLASs[3] and contingency fees (Tuesday 21st July, hosted by the Chartered Institute of Arbitrators) (the "contingency fees seminar").

- Fixed costs (a) in the fast track and (b) above the fast track (Wednesday 22nd July, hosted by Eversheds LLP) (the "fixed costs seminar").

- Chancery litigation (Friday 24th July, hosted by Clifford Chance LLP) (the "chancery seminar").

- Judicial review and environmental claims (Monday 27th July, hosted by Herbert Smith LLP) (the "judicial review seminar").

- Business disputes involving SMEs[4] (Tuesday 28th July, hosted by Holman Fenwick Willan LLP) (the "SMEs seminar").

- Case management and costs management (Wednesday 29th July, hosted by Mayer Brown International LLP) (the "case management seminar").

- The assessment of costs (Thursday 30th July, hosted by the Supreme Court Costs Office[5] Costs Practitioners' Group and Reed Smith LLP) (the "costs assessment seminar").

3.5   In later chapters of this report I quite often summarise what was said at seminars. I do this, so that readers can see the competing arguments which I am evaluating. It should be noted that in paragraphs which summarise what was said at seminars I am not setting out my own opinions or endorsing what was said.

(ii) Pilot exercises

3.6   A pilot exercise on costs management commenced at the Birmingham Mercantile Court and the Birmingham Technology and Construction Court ("TCC") on 1st June 2009. The court users agreed in principle to participate in the pilot at a joint meeting of the Birmingham Mercantile Court Users Committee and the Birmingham TCC Users Committee on 26th May 2009.[6] Participation in the pilot was voluntary. The pilot will run for a year.

3.7   My judicial assistant has monitored the pilot by regular liaison with the Birmingham court manager and judges, by sitting in on certain case management conferences and by talking to solicitors who had participated.

3.8   A second pilot exercise on costs management was set up for defamation proceedings in London and Manchester. This pilot commenced on 1st October 2009.

---

[2] Contingent Legal Aid Funds.

[3] Supplementary Legal Aid Schemes.

[4] Small and medium enterprises.

[5] Now the Senior Courts Costs Office.

[6] The meeting was well attended. The specialist judges of both courts were present, together with a substantial number of solicitors and counsel. I outlined the purpose of the pilot and answered question. The details of the costs management pilot were amended at the end of the meeting, in order to take account of points which had been made.

(iii) Working groups

3.9   In the course of Phase 2 a number of working groups were set up to consider particular issues in depth.

3.10   <u>Calibration of software systems for assessing personal injury general damages.</u> On 29th June 2009 a working group was set up to endeavour to agree calibration instructions which could be adopted by all existing software systems for the valuation of general damages in personal injury claims up to £10,000 in respect of pain, suffering and loss of amenity. The calibration was intended to reflect the levels of general damages currently awarded by the courts for personal injuries. The members of the working group were:

- John Spencer (Motor Accident Solicitors Society).

- David Bott (Association of Personal Injury Lawyers).

- Ashton West (Motor Insurers' Bureau).

- Ray Fisher (Zurich).

- Joe Pendle (ISO).

- Gill Manley (CSC Limited).

The working group subsequently appointed Davinder Singh as a facilitator in order to assist the working group. The working group reported on 5th November 2009

3.11   <u>Fixed costs of insolvency proceedings.</u> On 15th July 2009 a working group was set up with the following terms of reference:

> "To recommend (a) categories of insolvency proceedings for which fixed costs would be appropriate and (b) figures or bases for fixed costs in respect of each of those categories of proceedings."

The members of the working group were:

- Chief Registrar Stephen Baister.

- Stephen Davies QC.

- Christopher Berry (Edwin Coe).

- Master Colin Campbell.

- District Judge Robert Jordan.

The working group reported on 19th October 2009.

3.12   <u>Costs management of insolvency proceedings.</u> On 31st July 2009 a working group was set up with the following terms of reference:

> "To consider, in relation to insolvency proceedings, and in particular insolvency proceedings in which an office-holder is a party, whether and how it would be beneficial and cost effective for the court to manage (a) the recoverable costs as between the parties and (b) the costs and remuneration of the office-holder as between the office-holder and the insolvent estate."

The members of the working group were:

- Sir Gavin Lightman.

- Chief Registrar Stephen Baister.

- Stephen Davies QC.

The working group reported on 27th October 2009.

3.13   Disclosure.   On 18th June 2009 a working group was set up to consider the fifth[7] out of the eight options for disclosure rules set out in PR chapter 41. This has been referred to as the "menu option". The members of the working group were:

- Robin Knowles QC.

- Andrew King (Travers Smith LLP).

- Ted Greeno (Herbert Smith LLP).

- Gary Milner-Moore (Herbert Smith LLP).

- Will Luker (RBS Group).

- Raj Parker (Freshfields Bruckhaus Deringer LLP).

The working group was also assisted by Janice Wong and Rajesh Singh of Freshfields Bruckhaus Deringer LLP. The working group reported on 25th June, setting out their proposed draft together with comments. This draft was tabled for discussion at a seminar on 13th July organised by the City of London Law Society and the Commercial Litigators' Forum and hosted by Freshfields Bruckhaus Deringer LLP (the "commercial litigators seminar").

3.14   Libel.   On 21st July 2009 I attended a meeting of libel lawyers (principally but not exclusively acting for defendants) hosted by Farrer & Co. The question arose at that meeting as to whether the media would be willing to fund the establishment of a Contingent Legal Aid Fund for libel claims. A working group was set up to look into this issue. The members were:

- Alastair Brett (Times Newspapers Ltd).

- Colin Stutt (Legal Services Commission).

- Gill Phillips (Guardian Media Group).

- Alisdair Pepper (Carter-Ruck).

- Razi Mireskandari (Simons Muirhead & Burton).

- Redvers Cunningham (Thomas Miller & Co Ltd).

The working group subsequently appointed Jacob Dean of 5 Raymond Buildings as a seventh member of the group. Jacob Dean joined the working group at its second meeting on 16th September 2009. The working group reported on 5th October 2009.

3.15   Assessment of costs. At the costs assessment seminar a working party was set up to consider possible revisions to the format for bills of costs. The members of the working group were:

---

[7] See PR paragraph 41.6.6.

- Costs Judge Jonathan Simons.

- District Judge Ian Besford.

- Matthew Harman (costs lawyer, costs draftsman).

The working group reported on 19th October 2009.

3.16 <u>Costs management.</u> In order to provide me with the views of third party funders on costs management, at my request three third party funders set up a working group to report on that issue. The working group was set up on 23rd June 2009 and reported on 21st July 2009. The members of the working group were Allianz ProzessFinanc GmbH, Harbour Litigation Funding and Calunius Capital LLP.

4. PHASE 3

4.1 <u>Work done in Phase 3.</u> My principal task during Phase 3 (September to December 2009) has been to analyse the evidence and the arguments gathered during Phase 2 and to prepare this report. The deadline for submissions has passed and I have not accepted "late" submissions during Phase 3. Nevertheless, I have reserved the right to seek further information or clarification during Phase 3.[8] As and when I have needed further information or clarification, I have approached legal practitioners, judges and others for help. They have all responded generously to such requests.

4.2 <u>Visits to solicitors.</u> On 14th September I visited the costs departments of Irwin Mitchell LLP and Beachcroft LLP (in Sheffield and Birmingham respectively) in order to gain some first hand experience of how costs draftsmen work and what their role involves. On 27th November and 4th December I visited the London office of Olswang LLP to learn how that firm undertook costs budgeting.

4.3 <u>Meetings and seminars attended.</u> For obvious reasons there were few such events during Phase 3. On 22nd September I attended the annual conference of the Civil Court Users Association. On 28th September I attended a meeting with the Legal Services Board. On 30th September I attended a meeting with representatives of the Judicial Studies Board, in order to discuss judicial training in respect of e-disclosure and costs. On 19th October I attended s seminar in Glasgow for the launch of Lord Gill's "*Report of the Scottish Civil Courts Review*".[9] On 11th November I attended a seminar at University College London on "*The Future of Patent Litigation*".

4.4 <u>Citizens Advice Bureaux.</u> I did not receive any written submission from Citizens Advice Bureaux ("CABs") during Phase 2. Their input to the Costs Review would obviously be important. I therefore held a meeting on 25th November 2009 with the Policy Officer for Legal Affairs of the National Association of Citizens Advice Bureaux ("Citizens Advice"). The information which he provided and the views which he expressed may be summarised as follows:

---

[8] See my introductory statement at the London seminar on 10th July 2009:
http://www.judiciary.gov.uk/about_judiciary/cost-review/london.htm.
[9] September 2009.

(i)   36% of the adult population of England and Wales have unresolved legal problems.[10] Citizens Advice is concerned that in many small debt claims the costs which debtors have to pay far exceed the primary debt (especially if conflated with debt collector/debt collection charges and other enforcement costs).

(ii)   Citizens Advice is concerned about conditional fee agreements ("CFAs"), which many consumers simply do not understand.[11] Percentage based contingency fees would be better than CFAs. These would be easier to understand. After-the-event ("ATE") insurance is unsatisfactory. In many instances clients have had to repay loans taken out to cover ATE insurance. Sometimes those repayments can exceed the damages received. Citizens Advice considers that one way costs shifting of the kind that already exists in legal aid cases would be better than ATE insurance as a means of dealing with the adverse costs risk in personal injury cases.

(iii)   Regulation of fees chargeable by solicitors would be far more effective than the process of retrospective assessment in individual cases.[12] Neither the Legal Services Board nor any regulator has the power to regulate solicitors' fees. In Citizens Advice's view, that is a big gap. In Citizens Advice's experience, CAB clients complain of firms' added costs. For example, Citizens Advice is aware of some firms of solicitors charging £200 to assess if a client is eligible for legal aid, a task that should only take couple of minutes with the aid of the Legal Services Commission's eligibility calculator.

(iv)   Citizens Advice agrees with the comments in chapter 7 of the Preliminary Report about levels of court fees. There is a particular problem in relation to the remission scheme. For example, in order to obtain remission of court fees, a client who is on benefits has to produce a letter from the Department of Work and Pensions (the "DWP") dated within the last month. However, the DWP is not usually prepared to provide such letters.

(v)   In relation to possession proceedings there is a serious problem of (a) private landlords not complying with the rent arrears protocol and (b) mortgagees not complying with the mortgage protocol.[13] The language of the protocols should be tightened, so that "must" is used in place of "should". Judges should be more ready to impose sanctions upon lenders and mortgagees who do not comply with the protocols. Citizens Advice would like to see a regime of fixed costs for all possession proceedings, whether brought by landlords or by mortgagees and whether based on arrears or on any other ground.

(vi)   Citizens Advice regrets the declining availability of legal aid. Citizens Advice proposes that there should be a provision in the Funding Code,[14] entitling a judge to make an order for legal aid in any case where this would be in the public interest: for example, a person of limited means is in court and there may be an Article 6 issue.

4.5   Contact with DWP. My judicial assistant has contacted the DWP about the matter raised in paragraph 4.4 (iv) above. She has been informed that the DWP has

---

[10] See *"Civil Justice in England and Wales: Report of the 2007 English and Welsh Civil and Social Justice Survey"*, LSRC Research Paper No. 22, available on the Legal Services Research Centre website at http://www.lsrc.org.uk/publications.htm.

[11] See *"No win, no fee, no chance"*, a report by Citizens Advice dated December 2004, available online at http://www.citizensadvice.org.uk/no_win_no_fee_no_chance-2.

[12] See *Callery v Gray* [2002] UKHL 28 at [33] – [35]; [2002] 1 WLR 2000 at pages 2010-2011.

[13] These protocols are discussed in chapter 26 below.

[14] The Funding Code is the set of rules used by the Legal Services Commission to determine which cases to fund through civil legal aid.

no policy against the provision of letters for clients who are seeking remission of court fees. The DWP regards it as appropriate for such letters to be written. I revert to this issue in chapter 4 below.

4.6   Civil Justice Council facilitative meetings. During September and October the Civil Justice Council (the "CJC"), at my request, held a series of facilitative meetings with stakeholders in connection with fixed costs. These meetings are described in chapter 15 below. I did not attend the meetings but received a report from the CJC concerning the meetings and their outcome.

4.7   Preparation of this report. This report has been drafted during September to December 2009. As required by the terms of reference, I am delivering a copy of this report to the Master of the Rolls before the end of December. In order to allow time for printing and distribution, the report will be published on 14th January 2010.

5. THANKS

5.1   The 2009 Costs Review has been a major collaborative exercise. Very many individuals and organisations have given of their time to send in written submissions, respond to my queries, furnish information or data, look at draft paragraphs in confidence (to see if I have got the facts right), comment on issues, organise or attend meetings and so forth. As the year draws to a close, and I draft this report against a looming deadline, it is not practicable for me, individually and by name, to thank everyone who has helped. The following paragraphs are by no means comprehensive.

5.2   Those who helped with Phase 1. In PR paragraphs 1.4.1 to 1.4.14 I have set out the names of those who assisted in Phase 1 of the Costs Review and the respects in which they assisted. I repeat my thanks to all of them for their help. Their work is of enduring assistance, not least because the material and data set out in the Preliminary Report are adopted and relied upon in this Final Report.

5.3   Assessors. I am extremely grateful to the assessors for their considerable assistance with all aspects of the Costs Review. I am also grateful to David Hunt (Lord Hunt of Wirral),[15] who stood in for Andrew Parker at the assessors meeting on 1st July 2009. It is not possible for the assessors to agree with each other or with me on every point. The role of the assessors has been to debate the issues, to expose the conflicting arguments and to give me the benefit of their immense experience. This they have done in full measure.

5.4   Judicial assistants. My judicial assistant during Phase 2 was Ilona Groark of Herbert Smith LLP, who came to the Costs Review in the latter part of Phase 1 and remained until mid-August. My judicial assistant during Phase 3 is Hannah Piper of Lovells LLP, who came on 1st September and will remain until the end of December. Both Ilona and Hannah have worked immensely hard on all aspects of the review, often late into the night or at weekends. They have done much legal research. They have accompanied me to meetings or represented me at meetings and checked my various drafts with an eagle eye. I thank them for all that they have done.

5.5   Accountant judicial assistants. Since 27th July Deloitte LLP has very kindly seconded a forensic accountant to work full time on the Costs Review as my accountant judicial assistant. Initially Lucy Harrison fulfilled that role. Lucy went on

---

[15] Lord Hunt was originally appointed an assessor, but was unable to serve through ill health. Andrew Parker, his partner at Beachcroft LLP, took his place.

maternity leave in early October and was replaced by Chris Tune. Both Lucy and Chris have given me an enormous amount of assistance in analysing the data contained in appendices to the Preliminary Report; liaising with outside organisations to obtain further data; preparing the various tables in this report and discussing the accountancy issues with me. I am most grateful to both of them.

5.6   Julian Bailey. Julian Bailey of CMS Cameron McKenna LLP is the one assistant who has been involved throughout the Costs Review. His role is described in PR paragraph 1.4.2. Although based at his own office, he is always available to investigate and advise upon specific issues. He has researched a number of matters with meticulous care, often at weekends. In recent weeks he has given up a huge amount of time to reviewing draft chapters and correcting at least some of my errors. My thanks to Julian for all his hard work.

5.7   Clerks. The clerk to the Costs Review during Phase 2 was Abigail Pilkington: see PR paragraph 1.4.3. Abi continued to give sterling support to the Costs Review, as she had done during Phase 1. When necessary she worked all night. Clare Smith replaced Abi in mid September and faced the formidable task of picking up the reins. Clare has done so with enthusiasm and has given me much help. She acts as stenographer when required, puts my chaotic files into good order and is currently formatting this report. I am most grateful to both my clerks.

5.8   Working groups. As can be seen from section 3 above a number of working groups have, at my request, explored particular issues in depth. Their reports have been enlightening and have influenced many chapters of this report. My thanks go to all members of the working groups.

5.8   Civil Justice Council. The CJC has given a huge amount of support to the Costs Review, in particular organising the facilitative meetings referred to in paragraph 4.6 above. Bob Musgrove, chief executive of the CJC, is always available to discuss points and has given me much helpful advice. I am most grateful to Bob and all his team at the CJC.

5.9   Organisers of Costs Review seminars. Phase 2 involved a total of twelve Costs Review seminars. The details of those seminars and their respective organisers are set out in section 3 above. I am most grateful to the organisers for their hard work and their hospitality.

5.10   Organisers of other seminars and meetings. As can be seen from paragraph 4.3 above and annex 3 below, I have attended a large number of meetings and seminars organised by others. These events have been immensely helpful occasions to debate the issue with experts in many areas of litigation.

5.11   Judges involved in pilot exercises. I do not normally thank judges for assistance, because they are accustomed to supporting law reform projects and do not expect public thanks. I must, however, thank the Birmingham specialist judges, in particular Judge Brown and Judge Grant, for their support over the last six months in conducting the Birmingham costs management pilot. I must also thank Mr Justice Eady, Senior Master Whitaker and their respective colleagues for supporting the costs management pilot in relation to defamation proceedings.

5.12   Lawyers who have assisted on specific issues. Many lawyers have responded to my requests for help, research and advice on specific issues. These include Alison

Potter,[16] Kate Wilson,[17] Andrew Higgins, Nick Bacon,[18]Andrew Francis,[19] Martin Farber and Tony Guise. Those mentioned have spent many hours gathering material, preparing background papers, checking my drafts and so forth. A number of judges, legal practitioners and others have kindly read and commented upon various chapters in draft. I am most grateful to all the lawyers who have given me assistance.

5.13　Speakers at seminars. Those who presented papers[20] at seminars have made an invaluable contribution to the Costs Review. So also have the legal practitioners, judges and court users who gave up time to attend the seminars. As can be seen from later chapters of this report, I have taken due note of what was said at all the seminars and of the votes taken on specific issues. The clash of argument during the seminars has been enormously helpful to me in deciding which way to go on particular issues.

5.14　Contributors of written submissions. The written submissions during Phase 3 run to several thousand pages. They are immensely helpful. I have read and taken into account all of those submissions, even though it is not practicable in this report to rehearse all the arguments advanced.

5.15　Oxford University. The Centre for Socio-Legal Studies and the Institute for European and Comparative Law at Oxford University have carried out a comparative study of costs and funding of litigation across 34 different jurisdictions. They have kindly done this within a timeframe that coincides with my own Costs Review. They organised a most enlightening two day seminar on this subject at Oxford in July, which I attended. They have subsequently produced their report "*Costs and Funding of Civil Litigation: a Comparative Study.*"[21] This report gives an invaluable insight into many jurisdictions which I did not have time to visit during my own study tour.[22] I commend that report to all who seek a comprehensive review of overseas costs rules. I am most grateful to Professor Stefan Vogenauer, Dr Christopher Hodges and Dr Magdalena Tulibacka of Oxford University for carrying out a project which has been of such timely assistance to my own review.

5.16　Distinguished academic lawyers. From time to time I have sought the views of distinguished academic lawyers on specific issues. They include Professor Dame Hazel Genn, Professor Michael Zander, Professor Adrian Zuckerman and Professor John Peysner. I am most grateful for their advice.

5.17　President of the Law Society and Chairman of the Bar. From time to time I have consulted the President of the Law Society or the Chairman of the Bar on particular points. They and the officials have been most helpful in dealing with my queries and I am grateful to them.

5.18　Surveys carried out. At my request, the Federation of Small Businesses (the "FSB") carried out a survey of members' views in relation to fixed recoverable costs.[23] At my request, the Strategic Advisory Board for Intellectual Property Policy ("SABIP") commissioned internet surveys of freelancers and SMEs in relation to

---

[16] See PR paragraph 1.4.4. Alison also organised the e-disclosure demonstration referred to at chapter 37 below, paragraph 2.2.

[17] See PR paragraph 1.4.4.

[18] See PR paragraph 1.4.4.

[19] See PR paragraph 1.4.4.

[20] The papers for the four main seminars can be seen on the Costs Review website at http://www.judiciary.gov.uk/about_judiciary/cost-review/timetable.htm.

[21] Oxford, November 2009.

[22] See PR paragraph 1.5.6.

[23] See chapter 16 below, section 2.

proposed reforms of intellectual property litigation.[24] The results of these surveys are revealing. I am most grateful to the FSB and SABIP for undertaking this work.

5.19   Ministry of Justice and HMCS representatives.   I have had a number of meetings with Ministry of Justice ("MoJ") officials and HMCS representatives during Phases 2 and 3 of the Costs Review. They have responded to my queries most helpfully. I am grateful for their assistance.

5.20   I alone am responsible.   Despite the wealth of assistance and advice which has come in from all sides, I alone am responsible for the contents of this report. Those who advise or assist me often take radically different views upon major issues. It is my task to choose between those different views. Therefore none of those named and thanked above has any responsibility for the contents of this report or the heresies which they may perceive within it.

6. IS A YEAR SUFFICIENT TIME FOR THE COSTS REVIEW?

6.1   Some respondents have suggested that one year is insufficient time for the civil justice Costs Review and have commented that Lord Woolf's review took four years.

6.2   Comparison with Woolf Inquiry.   Factually the above assertion about the Woolf Inquiry is not correct. Lord Woolf's "Access to Justice" Inquiry ran for two years. Lord Woolf commenced his inquiry in mid 1994 and produced his final report in July 1996. There was then a further period of two years whilst Lord Woolf's recommendations were evaluated before being taken forward by means of primary and secondary legislation. Lord Woolf's terms of reference were substantially wider than my mine and included, in effect, re-writing the entire White Book. The present project is, essentially a matter of building upon Lord Woolf's work and proposing reforms where (after ten years experience) these appear to be appropriate.

6.3   The assessors and I have now spent 12 months debating and considering the issues raised by the present terms of reference. There have been five months of fairly intense consultation and meetings (January, February, May, June and July). The assessors and I have received and considered many thousands of pages of written submissions from stakeholders and interested parties. Although the Preliminary Report was lengthy, it did not come like a thunderbolt from the blue. The stakeholder groups were well familiar with the factual background set out in that report. The issues raised by the Preliminary Report have been a matter of detailed and earnest debate within and between the stakeholder groups throughout the last decade. During the course of the 2009 Costs Review all of the relevant arguments have been rehearsed and little would be gained by extending this review for a further period. Indeed, extending the review would compound the difficulties of the exercise, because the review is focused upon a moving target. In the space of just 12 months, there have been major developments in relation to civil litigation costs.[25]

---

[24] See chapter 24 below, section 1.

[25] For example, the introduction of costs capping rules in April 2009; other major rule amendments in April and October 2009; the MoJ consultation re libel costs between February and May 2009; the publication of the MoJ's new process for personal injuries litigation (designed to reduce costs in low value uncontested claims); the Law Society's consultation exercise re contingency fees; the report of Senior Master Whitaker's working party on e-disclosure; the revision of the Commercial Court Guide following the pilot exercise in respect of the recommendations of the Long Trials Working Party; the consultation exercise by the IP Court Users Committee on proposals for reform of the Patents County Court; the introduction of the new Practice Direction – Pre-Action Conduct in April 2009.

6.4   The stakeholders are deeply divided on all major issues. Whether the present review lasts for one year or for many years, I could never hope to achieve agreement or common ground[26] between the myriad stakeholders upon the main topics. People have a natural tendency to perceive the public interest as residing in a state of affairs which is closely aligned with their own commercial interests. This is not to say that the submissions made during Phase 1 or Phase 2 are disingenuous. Far from it. The reality is that the different stakeholder groups hold radically different views as to where the public interest lies. I must choose between those rival views, or where appropriate, alight upon some middle ground with which everybody may disagree.

6.5   I believe that one year is a sufficient period of time for a judge (with the immense assistance of the assessors and the others thanked in section 5 above) to reach a considered opinion upon the issues set out in the terms of reference for this review. The opinion which I have formed is set out in the following chapters of this report.

6.6   Whether a further period of consultation is required in respect of funding issues (as proposed by the Bar Council) or in respect of the proposals in this report generally must be for others to decide.

---

[26] Except in relation to court fees, as discussed in PR chapter 7.

CHAPTER 2. THE COSTS OF CIVIL LITIGATION

INDEX

1. INTRODUCTION

1.1   The Preliminary Report contains a substantial quantity of data concerning costs currently being incurred in different categories of civil litigation. Some of the data are to be found in chapters on individual topics.[27] I have also set out substantial blocks of data in PR appendices 1 to 28 and have provided a (hopefully helpful) "guided tour" of those appendices in PR chapter 11. I shall not repeat those data in the present report, but instead will focus on parts of the data which merit further analysis.

1.2   For reasons explained in the Preliminary Report, the surveys of district judges and circuit judges yielded more data than the surveys of High Court judges and masters. Accordingly, I shall concentrate in section 2 of this chapter on costs in lower value cases. I shall then turn to the data obtained from insurers and the data which are specific to personal injury cases, defamation cases and intellectual property ("IP") cases. In relation to other areas of litigation, readers are referred to the data in the Preliminary Report and in PR appendices 3, 4, 5, 6, 7, 11, 13, 14 and 15.

1.3   The tables referred to in this chapter are set out in appendix 1 to this report.

1.4   Accountancy input. All calculations in this chapter have been undertaken with the assistance of my accountant judicial assistants. Likewise all the tables in appendix 1 to this report have been prepared with their assistance.

---

[27] For example, chapter 25 (on one way costs shifting in personal injuries litigation) contains data from a major insurer on (i) the sums which it pays out on after-the-event ("ATE") insurance premiums in cases which it loses and (ii) the costs which it recovers in cases where it is successful.

2. REVIEW OF DATA FROM JUDICIAL SURVEYS

(i) Results of judicial surveys

2.1   The surveys. As set out in PR chapter 11, every first instance judge was asked to record details of every case in which he or she made an assessment of costs[28] during the four week period 19th January to 13th February 2009 (the "survey period"). In respect of the West Midlands the survey was expanded to cover a five month period, namely November 2008 to March 2009. The results of these surveys are set out in PR appendices 1, 2 and 8.

2.2   Comments of Professor Dame Hazel Genn. Professor Genn pointed out at the Birmingham seminar on 26th June 2009 that the data in PR appendices 1 and 2 relate to a thin subset of all civil litigation, because the great majority of civil cases settle either before issue or before they come to a hearing. On the other hand, the data from insurers in PR appendices 18 and 23 are more representative of all cases, since those data include both litigated and the more numerous non-litigated cases.

2.3   Professor Genn's seminar paper is available online.[29] She analyses the data from circuit judges and district judges in some detail and represents the relationship between costs and damages graphically. She then conducts a similar analysis on the insurance company data. Professor Genn concludes in her Addendum Note on Data:[30]

> "Despite the differences in sources and the extent to which the data are representative of all cases, there is a considerable degree of consistency in, for example, median claim values, median costs and the relationship between costs and claim value."

2.4   In addition to the considerable degree of consistency between (a) the data on adjudicated cases and (b) the data on all cases, Professor Genn also ascribes significance to adjudicated cases for a different reason. In her 2008 Hamlyn lectures[31] she stated:

> "It is arguable that for civil justice to perform its public role – to cast its shadow – adjudication and public promulgation of decisions are critical. This is the public role of the judge. Adjudication provides the framework for settlements – the shadow in which settlements can be reached. That it is underpinned by coercive power provides the background threat that brings unwilling litigants to the negotiating table. While the reality is that most cases settle, a flow of adjudicated cases is necessary to provide guidance on the law and, most importantly, to create the credible threat of litigation if settlement is not achieved."

(ii) District judges' survey

2.5   Cases dealt with by district judges. PR appendix 1 contains details of 699 cases dealt with by district judges and deputy district judges during the survey period. It is helpful to analyse the data contained in PR appendix 1 in a number of ways.

---

[28] Either summary or detailed assessment.
[29] http://www.judiciary.gov.uk/docs/costs-review/analysis-costs-data.pdf.
[30] Which was added to reflect her oral comments at the seminar.
[31] Hazel Genn, The Hamlyn Lectures 2008, "Judging Civil Justice", page 21.

2.6   Personal injury cases. Out of the 699 cases in PR appendix 1, it can be seen that 280 relate to personal injury claims in which damages were awarded to the claimant. PR appendix 1A is a summary of those personal injury cases. The figures are discussed PR paragraph 11.2.5. It can be seen that for every £1 which the liability insurers paid out in damages, they paid out £1.80[32] in claimant costs.

2.7   Cases won by claimants. The cases won by claimants can be divided into those where there was a conditional fee agreement (a "CFA") and those where there was not a CFA. The claimants' costs were substantially higher in the CFA cases. Table 1 sets out details of CFA cases won by claimants. Table 2 sets out details of non-CFA cases won by claimants.

2.8   In CFA cases the total costs paid to claimants were on average 158% of the damages paid to the claimants. In non-CFA cases the total costs paid to claimants were on average 51% of the damages paid to claimants. Although this difference must in part be due to the types of cases which attract CFAs, the difference also shows the substantial effect which the CFA regime exerts upon recoverable costs in fully contested cases.

2.9   Cases won by defendants or where defendants were awarded costs. Of the cases identified as won by defendants in the tables below, none of the defendants had CFAs. It is however, helpful to look at the overall levels of costs incurred by defendants. As can be seen from table 3, the average costs awarded to defendants in these cases was £4,105.08. This is substantially less than the average costs awarded to claimants in tables 1 and 2.

2.10   It is not easy to correlate defendants' costs with the sums which were in issue, because in most cases where defendants were awarded costs the court did not quantify the claim. However, it is possible to compare the defendants' costs with the sums which were claimed in the particulars of claim. This comparison is undertaken in table 4. It can be seen that in cases won by defendants, the defendants' costs were approximately 15% of the sums in issue in the proceedings.

2.11   Overall picture. Subject to all the caveats set out above, the overall picture which emerges from the district judges survey is as follows. In CFA cases won by claimants, claimant costs amounted to approximately 158% of damages. In non-CFA cases, claimant costs amounted to approximately 51% of damages. In cases won by defendants, defendant costs amounted to approximately 15% of the sums in issue.

(iii) Circuit judges' survey

2.12   Cases dealt with by circuit judges. PR appendix 2 contains details of 128 cases dealt with by circuit judges and recorders during the survey period.

2.13   Cases won by claimants. The cases won by claimants can be divided into those where there was a CFA and those where there was not a CFA. The claimants' costs were substantially higher in the CFA cases. Table 5 sets out details of CFA cases won by claimants. Table 6 sets out details of non-CFA cases won by claimants.

2.14   In CFA cases the total costs paid to claimants were on average 203% of the damages paid to the claimants. In non-CFA cases the total costs paid to claimants were on average 55% of the damages paid to claimants. Although this difference must in part be due to the types of cases which attract CFAs, the difference also

---

[32] This figure includes VAT. It should be noted that VAT is excluded in tables 2.1 to 2.11 below.

shows the substantial effect which the CFA regime exerts upon recoverable costs in fully contested cases.

(iv) West Midlands survey

2.15   <u>West Midlands cases.</u> PR appendix 8 sets out details of 143 cases dealt with by circuit judges, recorders, district judges and deputy district judges sitting in the West Midlands between November 2008 and March 2009. These cases have all been excluded from appendices 1 and 2, so that there is no overlap between the data discussed here and the data discussed above.

2.16   <u>Cases won by claimants.</u> The cases won by claimants can be divided into those where there was a CFA and those where there was not a CFA. The claimants' costs were substantially higher in the CFA cases. Table 7 sets out details of CFA cases won by claimants. Table 8 sets out details of non-CFA cases won by claimants.

2.17   In CFA cases the total costs paid to claimants were on average 177% of the damages paid to the claimants. In non-CFA cases the total costs paid to claimants were on average 47% of the damages paid to claimants. Although this difference must in part be due to the types of cases which attract CFAs, the difference also shows the substantial effect which the CFA regime exerts upon recoverable costs in fully contested cases.

2.18   <u>Cases won by defendants or where defendants were awarded costs.</u> In the West Midlands survey one defendant had a CFA for a counterclaim. It is helpful to look at the overall levels of costs incurred by defendants in the cases where defendants were successful. As can be seen from table 9, the average costs awarded to defendants in these cases was £2,538.48. This is materially less than the average costs awarded to claimants in tables 7 and 8.

(v) Overall picture in respect of litigated cases

2.19   As Professor Genn pointed out at Birmingham, the judicial surveys only relate to cases which are fully litigated. To that extent the cases are far from typical, although there is a similar pattern in the data from both litigated and non-litigated cases. Furthermore, as Professor Genn pointed out in her 2008 Hamlyn Lectures, litigated cases play a crucial role in the civil justice process. They provide the shadow under which all other cases are settled.[33] Following up Professor Genn's comments, I would add that the costs liabilities in cases which are litigated provide a framework of incentives for other cases.[34] In so far as potential costs liabilities have a deterrent effect upon prospective litigants, they may inhibit access to justice.

2.20   The overall picture which emerges from the judicial surveys is this. First, claimant costs are substantially higher than defendant costs. Secondly, claimant costs in CFA cases are substantially higher than in non-CFA cases. Subject to the various caveats set out above, claimant costs in the CFA cases, which have been analysed, range between 158% and 203% of the damages awarded. Claimant costs in the non-CFA cases, which have been analysed, range between 47% and 55% of the damages awarded.

---

[33] See paragraph 2.4 above.
[34] This is part of the "shadow" to which Professor Genn refers.

3. REVIEW OF DATA FROM INSURERS

3.1   <u>PR appendix 18.</u> This schedule sets out details of all cases resolved in favour of claimants by one liability insurer during the week 2nd to 6th February 2009. This coincides with the third week of the four week judicial survey. There were 989 cases in which the insurer's costs liability was resolved during that week. In two of those cases the costs liability was resolved by judicial decision. In the other 987 cases the costs liability was resolved by agreement between the parties. In other words, the overlap is miniscule between (a) the appendix 18 data and (b) the judicial surveys data. Collectively, appendix 18 on the one hand and the judicial surveys on the other hand present an overall picture of costs liabilities[35] which were being incurred during the relevant period in relation to lower value claims.

3.2   The data in respect of 46 cases in appendix 18 contain anomalies which cause the insurer to question whether the data have been captured correctly.[36] I shall therefore confine the present analysis to the remaining 943 cases. Those 943 cases can be divided into 494 cases where the claimant had a CFA and 449 cases where the claimant did not have a CFA.

3.3   Details of the 494 CFA cases are set out in table 10. It can be seen that 415 CFA cases (84%) settled before issue. 78 CFA cases (15.8%) settled between issue and trial. One case (0.2%) went to trial. It can be seen that in the CFA cases claimant costs on average equalled 59% of damages.[37]

3.4   Details of the 449 non-CFA cases are set out in table 11. It can be seen that 356 non-CFA cases (79.3%) settled before issue. 92 non-CFA cases (20.5%) settled between issue and trial. One case (0.2%) went to trial. It can be seen that in the non-CFA cases claimant costs on average equalled 39% of damages.[38]

3.5   <u>PR appendix 23.</u> This appendix sets out details of all personal injury cases settled by one liability insurer during 2007 and 2008. The claims relate to employers' liability and public liability. The first page of the appendix shows that, in 2007, there were 182 cases up to £15,000 (previously the fast track upper limit). The costs in these cases amounted on average to 227% of the damages. In 2008 there were 247 cases up to £15,000 and the costs as a percentage of damages were, on average, 218%. As for cases between £15,001 and £100,000, the data shows that, in the 15 cases in 2007, the costs amounted on average to 77% of damages. This compares to 78% in the 35 cases in 2008.

3.6   <u>PR appendix 24.</u> The data in this appendix are a summary of all personal injury claims resolved by one liability insurer in 2008. Again, the claims relate to employers' liability and public liability. One point to note about this sample of cases is that over two thirds of claims up to £5,000 settled before proceedings were issued. On the other hand, no cases were settled before issue where the value of the claim exceeded £50,000. Average costs in cases below £5,000 which were settled post-issue amounted to almost three times the average damages. Average costs also exceeded average damages in claims between £5,000 and £15,000. In the very high

---

35 It should be noted neither the district judges survey nor PR appendix 18 includes details of cases dropped by the claimant before trial. It is not unusual in such cases for the parties to agree each to bear their own costs.

36 A number of people were involved in collecting the data in February. It is not now practicable to go back and investigate the anomalous cases.

37 The defendants also had to meet their own costs, but the amount of these is not recorded.

38 The defendants also had to meet their own costs, but the amount of these is not recorded.

value claims (over £100,000), however, costs were more proportionate, amounting to just over 20% of damages on average.

3.7   PR appendix 26. This schedule sets out the details of all the cases of one liability insurer in respect of which costs payable to claimants were resolved during the year 1st December 2007 to 30th November 2008. These data show that the costs of 11,185 cases were resolved during that year (both litigated and non-litigated). The total costs claimed amounted to £73,403,336.76 which was approximately 67% of the £108,844,998.10 damages paid. The total costs agreed were just under 49% of the damages paid. 1,023 (12.94%) cases went to costs only proceedings. The total costs claimed for these cases amounted to £7,120,760.94 which was approximately 73% of the £9,758,610.45 paid. Total costs agreed were 56% of the damages paid.

4. LOW VALUE PERSONAL INJURY CLAIMS

4.1   The data in PR appendix 1A (discussed above) relate specifically to low value personal injury claims. So also do most of the data in PR appendices 2, 8 and 18 (also discussed above).

4.2   In the course of Phase 2, I received further helpful data in respect of the costs of low value personal injury claims.

4.3   Liability insurer. One liability insurer in its Phase 2 submission supplies data concerning all low value personal injury claims in which it paid out damages during 2008. I set these data out in table 12.

4.4   It can be seen that in the great majority of cases in table 12 costs substantially exceeded damages. It can also be seen that defendant costs were substantially less than claimant costs, the ratio often being in the region of 1:3.

4.5   Major supermarket. One major supermarket has supplied data in respect of personal injury claims against itself. The supermarket states that despite its continuous efforts to improve safety in its stores and workplaces it receives a substantial number of personal injury claims per year. Where the compensation paid is between £2,000 and £3,000, the claimant's costs (including disbursements) amount to 160% of the compensation. The costs to damages ratio reduces to 115% where the compensation amounts to between £3,000 and £5,000. The costs to damages ratio reduces to 85% where compensation amounts to between £5,000 and £10,000.

4.6   Cardiff district judges. The six Cardiff district judges are particularly concerned about costs, especially in low value personal injury claims. As district judges, of course they only see cases which are fully contested either at trial or at assessment of costs. Nevertheless their perception is as follows:

> "1   We all feel that the issue of costs is out of control and that the costs incurred in pursuing a claim are invariably wholly disproportionate to the amount in issue. This applies to both fast track and multi track cases but is more pronounced in fast track cases because of the amounts involved.
>
> 2   In standard fast track cases, where the facts are uncomplicated and straight forward it is not uncommon for the claimant's bill to be 10 or 15 times the amount of the damages recovered. Eg damages of £2,500 with the claimant's bill being £30,000.

3   The amount of base costs claimed in summary assessments is often unreasonably high, and when added to these is a 100% success fee (allowable for road traffic and employer's liability cases) and an expensive insurance premium, very high costs are claimed.

4   We regret to say that in far too many instances, we suspect that the bill is seen as a costs building exercise. Eg in a straightforward road traffic accident with no police proceedings or independent witnesses, a claim being made for perusal of documents of 13 hours and this is when solicitors are probably aiming at 6.5 chargeable hours a day!"

4.7   The Cardiff district judges state that costs are a particular problem in hand arm vibration syndrome and vibration white finger cases. They state that where the claimant is successful, the settlement figure or damages award is usually between £4,000 and £7,000. The claimants' costs are generally between £20,000 and £30,000, whereas the defendants' costs are generally one third of the claimants' costs.[39]

4.8   Liverpool district judges. During Phase 1 of the Costs Review, the Liverpool district judges made very similar comments about the high costs of low value personal injury cases: see PR paragraphs 10.17.2 to 10.17.9.

4.9   PR appendix 26. As stated in paragraph 3.7 above, this schedule sets out the details of all the cases of one liability insurer in respect of which costs payable to claimants were resolved during the year 1st December 2007 to 30th November 2008. The low value personal injury cases in PR appendix 26 were split between fast track cases and predictable cost regime ("PCR")[40] cases.[41] The data related to these cases are shown in tables 13 to 17 below.

4.10   Fast track cases (excluding PCR cases). The average costs to damages ratio for litigated cases in the fast track was 130%. Non-litigated cases in the fast track had costs of 90% of damages. There was a wide variation in the amount of costs as a proportion of damages for different kinds of cases with occupational health (disease) having costs which were 154% of damages in litigated cases and 156% in non-litigated cases. Motor cases showed a significant reduction in costs for non-litigated cases being 46% of damages in non-litigated cases compared to 116% in litigated cases, this figure rose to 72% for cases which resulted in costs only proceedings. Interestingly occupational health (disease) cases had lower average costs compared to damages in the cases which went to costs only proceedings. However, it should be noted that there were relatively few cases of this type (57 litigated, 74 non-litigated of which 15 were costs only proceedings).

4.11   PCR cases. Costs in PCR cases were on average 76% of damages. Although this is higher than the costs for non-litigated motor cases in the fast track, one should bear in mind that PCR cases relate to lower value cases (under £10,000), which do tend to have much higher costs in relation to damages. PCR cases which went to costs only proceedings (8% of all the PCR cases in PR appendix 26) had higher levels of costs at 104% of damages.

---

[39] This claimant to defendant costs ratio of 3:1 in contested cases is similar to that appearing in the insurer data quoted in paragraph 4.4 above, which relate principally to settled cases.
[40] These are cases falling within the fixed recoverable costs scheme in CPR Part 45. In this chapter the abbreviation "PCR" is adopted, as this is how the cases are described in PR appendix 26. However, in the rest of the report the scheme is known as the fixed recoverable costs ("FRC") scheme.
[41] See PR paragraphs 21.3.1 to 21.3.8 for details of the PCR.

4.12   Whether the high costs of low value personal injuries litigation are (a) attributable to the conduct of claimant lawyers or (b) attributable to the conduct of liability insurers and their lawyers or (c) a necessary consequence of the work involved in such litigation will be discussed later in this report.

5. PERSONAL INJURY CLAIMS IN THE MULTI-TRACK

5.1   PR appendix 26. The data in PR appendix 26 include high value multi-track cases (where the damages claimed were over £100,000) and low value multi-track cases (where the damages claimed were between £25,000 and £100,000).

5.2   High value multi-track cases. Data relating to high value multi-track cases are set out in tables 18 and 19 below. In high value multi-track litigated cases (where claims were issued), the average costs were 11% of the damages, this compares to 9% for non-litigated cases. There were variations depending on the type of case with a cost to damages ratio for litigated cases of 16% for employers' liability cases, 8% for motor cases and 17% for public liability cases. Non-litigated cases show a costs to damages ratio of 8%, 11%[42] and 6% for employers' liability cases, motor cases and public liability cases respectively. A subset of the non-litigated cases which went to costs only proceedings had average costs of 9% of damages for employers' liability cases and 11% for motor cases.

5.3   The average damages awarded ranged between £185,450 and £458,186 for litigated cases and £115,000 and £200,773 for non-litigated cases. The non-litigated cases which went to costs only proceedings actually had lower average damages than the total population of non-litigated cases: £173,023 compared to £200,773 for employers' liability cases and £110,000 compared to £144,237 for motor cases. No public liability cases went to costs only proceedings.

5.4   Low value multi-track cases. Data relating to low value multi-track cases are set out in tables 20 and 21. These cases show a much higher level of costs compared to damages than the high value multi-track cases. Litigated cases had average costs of 40% of damages and non-litigated cases had average costs of 22% of damages. The average costs as a percentage of damages for the different categories of cases were as follows: employers' liability 39%, motor cases 39%, occupational health (disease) 49%, public liability 48%. In non-litigated cases costs were a lower percentage of damages: employers' liability 22%, motor cases 21%, occupational health (disease) 23%, public liability 23%. The subset of non-litigated cases which went to costs only proceedings had costs as a percentage of damages as follows: employers' liability 26%, motor cases 28%, occupational health (disease) 34% and public liability 27%.

5.5   The average damages awarded ranged between £30,803 and £38,752 for litigated cases and £25,794 and £33,699 for non-litigated cases. Average damages for those non-litigated cases which went to costs only proceedings were higher for all types of cases apart from public liability cases. Average base costs in the costs only proceedings were always higher than in general non-litigated cases, but not as high as in the fully litigated cases.

---

[42] The total claimant costs as a percentage of damages for non-litigated motor cases are higher than for litigated cases. This apparent anomaly is most likely due to the very small subset of data as there are only ten non-litigated motor cases in this category.

6. CLINICAL NEGLIGENCE CLAIMS

6.1   <u>Appendix 2.</u> The data in appendix 2 to this report include a sample (chosen at random)[43] of 1,000 clinical negligence cases closed or settled by the NHSLA[44] in the period from 1st April 2008 to 31st March 2009. Of these 1,000 cases, 443 were closed with nil damages paid (the claim being dropped or successfully defended) and damages were paid in 557 cases ranging from £80 to £4.2 million. Table 22 summarises these 557 cases. The cases where damages were paid have been split between high value (damages over £100,000), medium value (damages of £25,000 or more but less than £100,000) and low value (damages less than £25,000).

6.2   The total amount paid in damages on these 557 cases was £76,974,504, an average of £138,195. Included in the 557 cases are 14 high value structured settlements in which total damages of £18,419,168 were paid in the period.[45] The average damages paid figure is £107,837 if these structured settlements are excluded.

6.3   <u>The 443 unsuccessful cases.</u> A breakdown of when the 443 unsuccessful cases were dropped is not available. However, I am informed by the NHSLA that the great majority of these cases would have been dropped by the claimant pre-issue.

6.4   <u>Funding of claims.</u> Data relating to how the 1,000 clinical negligence claims were funded are set out in table 23. Damages were paid or a structured settlement reached in 70% of cases funded by a CFA, compared to 61% for cases funded by the Legal Services Commission (the "LSC"), 50% for self-funded cases and 78% for cases funded by before-the-event ("BTE") insurance. CFA and LSC funding was used in the same number of cases (306). Of the 14 cases where a structured settlement was entered into, 13 were funded by the LSC and only one via a CFA.

6.5   <u>High value cases.</u> Data relating to high value cases are set out in tables 24 and 25. In high value cases the claimant costs as a percentage of damages ranges from 16% for LSC funded cases to 32% for CFA funded cases. This range widens to 14% for LSC funded cases to 37% for CFA funded cases when structured settlements are excluded. In high value CFA funded cases the total costs incurred by claimants were approximately four times those incurred by defendants. By comparison, in high value LSC funded cases the total costs incurred by claimants were approximately double those incurred by defendants.

6.6   <u>Medium value cases.</u> Data relating to medium value cases are set out in table 26. In medium value cases the claimant costs as a percentage of damages ranges from 30% for self-funded cases to 75% for CFA funded cases. In medium value CFA funded cases the total costs incurred by claimants were approximately four times those incurred by defendants, a similar pattern to the high value cases. By comparison, in medium value LSC funded cases the total costs incurred by claimants were approximately two and a half times those incurred by defendants.

6.7   <u>Low value cases.</u> Data relating to low value cases are set out in table 27. These cases show a much higher level of costs compared to damages than the high and medium value cases, with the claimant costs as a percentage of damages ranging from 47% for self-funded cases to 140% for CFA funded cases. The low value cases also show a higher ratio of claimant costs compared to defendant costs. In low value CFA funded cases the total costs incurred by claimants were approximately five times

---

[43] The sample excludes cases where the claimant costs (if any) were paid after 30th June 2009.
[44] The National Health Service Litigation Authority.
[45] The capitalised value of future payments which will be made under these structured settlements has not been included in the figures quoted.

those incurred by the defendants. By comparison, in low value LSC funded cases the total costs incurred by claimants were just under three times those incurred by defendants.

7. LIBEL AND PRIVACY CASES

7.1 <u>PR appendix 17.</u> PR appendix 17 is a schedule of libel and privacy claims against nine media organisations, which were resolved by settlement or judgment during 2008. The nine media organisations fall into the following categories: national newspaper groups, broadcasters, news agencies and local newspaper publishers. As can be seen from PR appendix 17, there are far more claims against the media for libel than for breach of privacy.

7.2 In the analysis which follows I exclude cases which resulted in a global settlement, as the relationship between damages and costs cannot be disentangled in such cases. The remaining cases comprise 27 cases where the claimant had a CFA and 120 cases where the claimant did not have a CFA.

7.3 Table 28 contains an analysis of the 27 CFA cases. It can be seen that in the CFA cases claimant costs were on average 314% of damages, whereas defendant costs were on average 125% of damages.

7.4 Table 29 contains an analysis of the 120 non-CFA cases. It can be seen that in non-CFA cases claimant costs were on average 296% of damages, whereas defendant costs were on average 209% of damages.

7.5 It may be thought that the average figures in tables 28 and 29 have been distorted by the very high figures attributed to cases 1 and 2 in PR appendix 17. In order to test this I now set out, as tables 30 and 31, revised versions of the two previous tables omitting cases 1 and 2.

7.6 In interpreting the above data it must be borne in mind that media organisations have a capacity to deal in-house with some of the work which claimants entrust to solicitors. It must also be borne in mind that the figures for claimant costs will often include VAT, whereas defendant costs presumably do not (since defendants can reclaim VAT).[46]

7.7 It may also be helpful to repeat the above analyses, but excluding cases where the defendants' costs were shown as nil. I presume that in these cases the defendants accepted liability at an early stage and dealt with the matter in-house. I now set out, as tables 32, 33, 34 and 35, revised versions of the four previous tables omitting cases where the defendants' costs are shown as nil.

7.8 It can be seen from table 34 that after all the above adjustments are made, there are 20 CFA cases to consider. In these cases claimant costs were on average 230% of damages; defendant costs were on average 107% of damages.

7.9 It can be seen from table 35 that after all the above adjustments are made, there are 47 non-CFA cases to consider. In these cases claimant costs were on average 184% of damages; defendant costs were on average 124% of damages.

---

[46] In most other appendices to the Preliminary Report, costs figures on both sides have been quoted net of VAT.

8. INTELLECTUAL PROPERTY CASES

8.1   Appendix 3. The data in appendix 3 to this report include a sample of 15 large intellectual property cases settled or taken to first instance trial by a leading IP department from a City law firm in the period from 1999 to 2007. Of these 15 cases, the firm acted for the claimant in ten cases and the defendant in five cases. The cases covered disputes over patents, trademarks, design and copyright. Of the 15 cases, three settled and 12 went to trial.

8.2   The adjusted costs incurred on these cases up to first instance judgment or settlement range from £196,957 to £1,540,933, with an average cost incurred per case of £696,742. The costs have been adjusted from actual costs to current costs by reference to the hours spent on the case at current hourly rates.

8.3   The data show the total costs incurred (profit costs and disbursements) up to various standardised stages in the litigation process (service of claim, defence, disclosure, witness statements, trial etc). This assists the law firm to estimate potential costs for clients up to various stages of the litigation process. The costs incurred up to a particular stage are cumulative, including the costs for all work up to that stage, not merely the costs incurred on performing tasks for that stage.

8.4   The data also include the number of weeks each case took to reach the various stages outlined above. The cases ranged between 36 weeks and 111 weeks from start to first instance judgement or settlement, with the average length being 66 weeks.

8.5   The law firm is also able to calculate the average monthly cost of the IP cases. The cases in the sample incurred average monthly costs ranging from £18,376 to £104,615, with the average being £45,542.

8.6   The costs incurred from the start of trial to judgment or settlement averaged nearly 20% of the total costs of the cases. The trial costs were a large proportion of the total costs due to the cross examination of the expert witnesses.

9. FURTHER DATA ON CFA FUNDED CASES AGAINST PUBLICLY FUNDED BODIES

9.1   Phase 3. During Phase 3 of the Costs Review I sought and obtained further data from both the NHSLA and the Treasury Solicitor in respect of claims where CFAs were used.

(i) Data from the NHSLA

9.2   The NHSLA provided costs data for a four week period (from 12th October 2009 to 6th November 2009) in respect of clinical negligence claims where (a) costs were settled in the period and (b) the claimants were bringing their claims using a CFA. There were 109 such claims settled in the period. The claims settled in a four week period should be representative of the cases brought against the NHSLA.

9.3   The total success fees claimed on the 109 cases amounted to £1,961,203, an average success fee of £17,993 per case. The success fees ranged between £704 and £251,184. Where the NHSLA has negotiated a settlement on costs, it has apportioned the settlement figure against the various components of the claimants' total costs. The NHSLA estimates that in the 109 cases the amount paid out for success fees was approximately £1,200,000.

9.4   If the level of success fees claimed on the cases settled in the period is representative of the cases brought against the NHSLA, then the total annual amount of success fees claimed (arrived at by extrapolation from the four week period) would amount to £25,495,634.   The total amount of success fees paid (arrived at by extrapolation) would amount to approximately £15,600,000.

9.5   In 61 of the 109 cases the claimant also claimed for ATE insurance premiums. The total amount claimed for ATE insurance premiums was £610,771, an average premium of £10,013 for the 61 cases. The ATE insurance premiums ranged between £274 and £31,364. Where the NHSLA has negotiated a settlement on costs, it has apportioned the settlement figure against the various components of the claimants' total costs. The NHSLA estimates that in the 61 cases the amount paid out for ATE insurance premiums was approximately £511,000.

9.6   If the level of ATE insurance premiums claimed on the cases settled in the period is representative of the cases brought against the NHSLA then the total annual cost of ATE insurance premiums claimed (arrived at by extrapolation of the four week period) would amount to £7,940,020. The total amount of ATE insurance premiums paid (arrived at by extrapolation) would amount to approximately £6,643,000.

9.7   The NHSLA paid out a total £103,632,000 to claimant solicitors in respect of claimant costs incurred on cases settled in the year to 31st March 2009. [47] Success fees and ATE insurance premiums paid to claimant solicitors therefore make up a significant part of the legal costs paid out by the NHSLA.

(ii) Data from the Treasury Solicitor

9.8   The Treasury Solicitor provided cost data on claims settled between July and October 2009 where the claimants were bringing their claims using either a CFA or ATE insurance (or in some instances, both). There were 38 such claims settled in the period, comprising 37 personal injury claims and one unlawful detention claim.

9.9   In these 38 claims, the total costs (including profit costs, disbursements, success fees and VAT) claimed by the claimant amounted to £1,089,162. The total amount paid out by the Treasury Solicitor on these cases amounted to £799,574, a reduction of approximately 27% to the amount claimed.

9.10   The Treasury Solicitor costs department (or external costs draftsmen) will review the costs claimed on each case, reviewing the hours claimed, the rates used and the level of disbursements. The success fee claimed will also be reviewed as part of the process. An assessment is made as to the level of success fee the Treasury Solicitor believes to be appropriate. The Treasury Solicitor will then make an offer to the claimant for costs based on what he assesses to be reasonable.

9.11   I have used the data provided to calculate approximate amounts for costs settled in each of the various categories as set out in table 36. For profit costs, counsel fees and the respective success fees, ATE insurance premiums and other disbursements I have based this approximation on the assessment by the Treasury Solicitor. For VAT I have assumed the average reduction of approximately 27%.

9.12   The data shows that the average solicitor success fee claimed is approximately 70% of base costs and that the average success fee settled is 40% of base costs.

---

[47] See chapter 23 below, paragraph 1.3 for further detail on the NHSLA.

Success fees of 100% were claimed in 23 out of the 38 claims. Solicitor success fees make up 28% of the total costs claimed and 19.5% of the total costs settled.

9.13   In those cases where counsel was used, counsel was sometimes instructed on a disbursement basis and sometimes on a CFA.

CHAPTER 3. PROPORTIONATE COSTS

INDEX

1. INTRODUCTION

1.1   <u>Abbreviations.</u> In this chapter I refer to the Costs Practice Direction as the "Costs PD". I refer to the former Rules of the Supreme Court as the "RSC". I refer to the Civil Procedure Rule Committee as the "Rule Committee".

1.2   <u>Plan for this chapter.</u> I shall first review the principles upon which recoverable costs are assessed. Next, I shall review the principle of proportionality in relation to civil procedure. I shall then review the judicial guidance on the meaning of "proportionate" costs since April 1999, when that concept was introduced. Finally, I shall discuss the principles governing recoverable costs and state how, in my view, the principle of proportionality should be formulated and should be applied in relation to recoverable costs.

1.3   <u>The wider debate about proportionality of costs.</u> There is a debate amongst law reformers and commentators across the Commonwealth as to whether it is appropriate to limit costs by reference to proportionality: see "*Civil Justice Review*", Report 14 published by the Victorian Law Commission in 2008, pages 656 to 658.[48] The luxury of this debate is not open to myself and the assessors, because the objective of the Costs Review (as stated in the terms of reference) is "*to make*

---

[48] See
http://www.lawreform.vic.gov.au/wps/wcm/connect/Law+Reform/Home/Completed+Projects/Civil+Justice/.

recommendations in order to promote access to justice at proportionate cost". The Civil Procedure Rules already include a requirement for costs to be proportionate. It would not be appropriate for me to recommend any departure from that principle. The central question to be explored in this chapter is: what does the requirement that costs be "proportionate" mean?

2. THE PRINCIPLES UPON WHICH RECOVERABLE COSTS ARE ASSESSED

(i) History

2.1   <u>1883 to 1959.</u> Under the RSC 1883 the test applied upon assessment of costs was as follows:

> "On every taxation the Taxing Master shall allow all such costs, charges and expenses as shall appear to him to have been necessary or proper for the attainment of justice or for defending the rights of any party, but save as against the party who incurred the same no costs shall be allowed which appear to the Taxing Master to have been incurred or increased through over caution, negligence or mistake or by payment of special fees to counsel or special charges or expenses to witnesses or other persons, or by other unusual expenses."

2.2   <u>1959 to 1986.</u> Between 1959 and 1986, the test was reformulated, but continued to include the key phrase "necessary or proper for the attainment of justice". Costs taxed on the party and party basis entitled the receiving party to:

> "All such costs as were necessary or proper for the attainment of justice or for enforcing or defending the rights of the party whose costs are being taxed."

2.3   <u>1986 to 1999.</u> In 1986 the concepts of the "standard basis" and the "indemnity basis" were first introduced into the rules. On the standard basis, the receiving party was entitled to "a reasonable amount in respect of all costs reasonably incurred". On the indemnity basis, the test was similar but any doubt was resolved in favour of the receiving party.

2.4   <u>1999 to now.</u> In April 1999 the CPR were introduced. The concepts of standard basis and indemnity basis were retained in the CPR, but they were redefined. The methods by which costs are assessed on each of those bases under the CPR are explained in chapter 3 of the Preliminary Report at paragraphs 4.17 to 4.24. Since April 1999 the standard basis for assessing costs (but not the indemnity basis) has included a requirement of proportionality.

(ii) The current rules

2.5   <u>CPR rule 44.4.</u> CPR rule 44.4(1) provides that the court will not allow costs which have been unreasonably incurred or are unreasonable in amount. Rule 44.4(2) provides:

> "Where the amount of costs is to be assessed on the standard basis, the court will –
>
> (a)   only allow costs which are proportionate to the matters in issue; and

(b)   resolve any doubt which it may have as to whether costs were reasonably incurred or reasonable and proportionate in amount in favour of the paying party."

Rules 51(1) and (2) of the Supreme Court Rules 2009 are to similar effect.

2.6   <u>Factors to be taken into account when the court is assessing costs on the standard basis.</u> CPR rule 44.5(1) provides that the court will have regard to all the circumstances when deciding whether costs were (i) proportionately and reasonably incurred and (ii) proportionate and reasonable in amount. Rule 44.5(3) provides that the court must also have regard to:

"(a)   the conduct of all the parties, including in particular –

(i)   conduct before, as well as during, the proceedings; and

(ii)   the efforts made, if any, before and during the proceedings in order to try to resolve the dispute;

(b)   the amount or value of any money or property involved;

(c)   the importance of the matter to all the parties;

(d)   the particular complexity of the matter or the difficulty or novelty of the questions raised;

(e)   the skill, effort, specialised knowledge and responsibility involved;

(f)   the time spent on the case; and

(g)   the place where and the circumstances in which work or any part of it was done."

2.7   <u>Section 11 of the Costs PD.</u> Paragraphs 11.1 to 11.3 and 11.6 of the Costs PD provide:

"11.1 In applying the test of proportionality the court will have regard to rule 1.1(2)(c). The relationship between the total of the costs incurred and the financial value of the claim may not be a reliable guide. A fixed percentage cannot be applied in all cases to the value of the claim in order to ascertain whether or not the costs are proportionate.

11.2 In any proceedings there will be costs which will inevitably be incurred and which are necessary for the successful conduct of the case. Solicitors are not required to conduct litigation at rates which are uneconomic. Thus in a modest claim the proportion of costs is likely to be higher than in a large claim, and may even equal or possibly exceed the amount in dispute.

11.3 Where a trial takes place, the time taken by the court in dealing with a particular issue may not be an accurate guide to the amount of time properly spent by the legal or other representatives in preparation for the trial of that issue.

...

11.6 In deciding whether base costs are reasonable and (if relevant) proportionate, the court will consider the factors set out in rule 44.5."

2.8   Paragraphs 11.4, 11.5 and 11.7 to 11.11 relate to success fees under conditional fee agreements ("CFAs") and after-the-event insurance premiums (collectively "additional liabilities"). The effect of these paragraphs is that if the base costs are proportionate, then the total of the base costs plus additional liabilities will not be regarded as disproportionate.

3. THE PRINCIPLE OF PROPORTIONALITY IN RELATION TO CIVIL PROCEDURE

(i) Emergence of the principle

3.1   The Evershed Report. The Committee on Supreme Court Practice and Procedure, chaired by Lord Evershed, published its report (the "Evershed Report") in 1953.[49] The Evershed Report stated the principle that "extravagant" costs should not be recovered. Lord Evershed's concept of extravagance was related to both the sum in issue and the complexity of the case. Lord Evershed's concept of what was and what was not extravagant may be seen, perhaps, as the forerunner of proportionality.

3.2   The Woolf Inquiry and Lord Woolf's Interim Report. The principle of proportionality, which has long been a feature of European law,[50] came to the fore during the Woolf Inquiry into Access to Justice between 1994 and 1996. Proportionality became one of the key principles underpinning the Woolf reforms. In his Interim Report on Access to Justice[51] Lord Woolf identified eight basic principles which should be met by the civil justice system. The third principle was stated to be:

> "Procedures and cost should be *proportionate* to the nature of the issues involved."

(ii) Lord Woolf's Final Report

3.3   Discussion of proportionality. In chapter 2 of his Final Report[52] Lord Woolf explained proportionality as follows. The new rules which he proposed would require the court to deal with cases in ways proportionate to the amount involved, the importance or complexity of the issues and the parties' financial position. Proportionality underlay the whole concept of the fast track. The argument against proportionality was put by the Association of Personal Injury Lawyers ("APIL"). First, APIL argued that it was impossible to investigate and prove personal injury claims in a way that was proportionate to the compensation eventually awarded, because insurers were prepared to throw unlimited sums of money into the defence of quite small claims. Lord Woolf accepted that this argument would have weight in a minority of cases, but in the majority of cases the insurers would have little scope to deploy excessive resources even if they wanted to do so because of the limited procedure. APIL's second argument was that disproportionate cost was immaterial since the majority of personal injury claims succeeded and the costs of litigating the action were in any event reimbursed to the claimant by the defendant. Lord Woolf considered that this point went to the root of his Inquiry and was not to be accepted.

---

[49] Report of the Committee on Supreme Court Practice and Procedure (1953) Cmnd 8878.

[50] The principle of proportionality has underpinned the European Community since it was established in 1957. The fourth paragraph of Article 5 of the Treaty on the European Union provides: "*Under the principle of proportionality, the content and form of Union action shall not exceed what is necessary to achieve the objectives of the Treaties.*" This is widely accepted as enshrining the proportionality principle.

[51] June 1995, Lord Chancellor's Department.

[52] July 1996, HMSO.

-30-

3.4   Lord Woolf stated that a system which usually paid those who litigated cases as much as, and sometimes more than, the victims received in compensation simply failed to command public confidence. Even where the individual litigants received back the full cost of achieving their compensation, that cost had to be borne in the first place by the insurers, in the second place by the insured and in the third place by society generally.   Further, the pattern of high spending on personal injury contaminated other areas of litigation where costs were less likely to be borne by insurers. The whole concept of the fast track was intended to increase access to justice by removing the uncertainty over excessive cost which deterred people from litigating.

3.5   <u>Discussion of costs.</u> In his discussion on costs Lord Woolf aimed to secure a regime in which costs would be proportionate. In chapter 7 at paragraph 20 he stated that the aim of the new procedural rules was to *"ensure that litigation is conducted less expensively than at present and to achieve greater certainty as to costs"*.

3.6   <u>Formulation of the principle of proportionality.</u>   The principle of proportionality was formulated in the "overriding objective", which appeared in the draft rules appended to Lord Woolf's Final Report. It is now embodied in Part 1 of the CPR. Rule 1.1(2) provides:

> "Dealing with a case justly includes, so far as is practicable...
>
> (c)   dealing with the case in ways which are proportionate –
>
> > (i)   to the amount of money involved;
> >
> > (ii)   to the importance of the case;
> >
> > (iii)   to the complexity of the issues; and
> >
> > (iv)   to the financial position of each party..."

3.7   As stated above, a requirement of proportionality was incorporated into the test for assessing costs on the standard basis.

4. JUDICIAL GUIDANCE ON THE MEANING OF PROPORTIONATE COSTS SINCE 1999

(i) The guideline cases

4.1   In *Jefferson v National Freight Carriers plc* [2001] EWCA Civ 2082; [2001] 2 Costs LR 313 at [39] – [41] Lord Woolf MR stated:

> "...proportionality is a very important feature of the assessment of costs on the standard basis. This is particularly true in relation to the fast track, and if a claimant is going to seek to recover a sum which is as substantially in excess of the amount recovered, as was being sought to be recovered in this case, the legal representatives of the Claimant at the hearing have to be in a position to help the Judge further than was the case here. They first of all must bear in mind that if they are going to conduct litigation of a modest nature, of the sort which was being conducted here, where the likely sum which was to be recovered, even on their own Part 36 offer, was a sum below £3000, they are under a heavy duty to conduct that litigation in as economic a manner as possible.

There is no decision which has been placed before this Court indicating precisely what approach should be adopted in exercising the jurisdiction which the Judge was exercising. However, we have been shown a decision of the Birmingham County Court on the 22 June of last year, when Judge Alton dealt with the issue, and if I may say so dealt with the issue in a manner which I regard as of considerable assistance. The Judge said, in particular:

> 'In modern litigation, with the emphasis on proportionality, it is necessary for parties to make an assessment at the outset of the likely value of the claim and its importance and complexity, and then to plan in advance the necessary work, the appropriate level of person to carry out the work, the overall time which would be necessary and appropriate to spend on the various stages in bringing the action to trial, and the likely overall cost. While it was not unusual for costs to exceed the amount in issue, it was, in the context of modest litigation such as the present case, one reason for seeking to curb the amount of work done, and the cost by reference to the need for proportionality.'

I would respectfully endorse every word of those comments of Judge Alton."

4.2   In *Lownds v Home Office* [2002] EWCA Civ 365; [2002] 1 WLR 2450 Lord Woolf MR, delivering the judgment of the court, gave further guidance on the meaning of proportionality at [1] – [10] and [23] – [40]. The key paragraphs read as follows:

> "[10] Because of the central role that proportionality should have in the resolution of civil litigation, it is essential that courts attach the appropriate significance to the requirement of proportionality when making orders for costs and when assessing the amount of costs. What has however caused practitioners and the members of the judiciary who have to assess costs difficulty is how to give effect to the requirement of proportionality. In particular there is uncertainty as to the relationship between the requirement of reasonableness and the requirement of proportionality. Where there is a conflict between reasonableness and proportionality does one requirement prevail over the other and, if so, which requirement is it that takes precedence? There is also the question of whether the proportionality test is to be applied globally or on an item by item basis, or both globally and on an item by item basis. These are the questions which directly arise on this appeal and explain why this judgment is so important...

> [31] In other words what is required is a two-stage approach. There has to be a global approach and an item by item approach. The global approach will indicate whether the total sum claimed is or appears to be disproportionate having particular regard to the considerations which CPR r 44.5(3) states are relevant. If the costs as a whole are not disproportionate according to that test then all that is normally required is that each item should have been reasonably incurred and the cost for that item should be reasonable. If on the other hand the costs as a whole appear disproportionate then the court will want to be satisfied that the work in relation to each item was necessary and, if necessary, that the cost of the item is reasonable. If, because of lack of planning or due to other causes, the global costs are disproportionately high, then the requirement that the costs should be proportionate means that no more should be payable than would have been payable if the litigation had been conducted in a proportionate manner. This is turn means that

reasonable costs will only be recovered for the items which were necessary if the litigation had been conducted in a proportionate manner...

[37] Although we emphasise the need, when costs are disproportionate, to determine what was necessary, we also emphasise that a sensible standard of necessity has to be adopted. This is a standard which takes fully into account the need to make allowances for the different judgments which those responsible for litigation can sensibly come to as to what is required. The danger of setting too high a standard with the benefit of hindsight has to be avoided. While the threshold required to meet necessity is higher than that of reasonableness, it is still a standard that a competent practitioner should be able to achieve without undue difficulty. When a practitioner incurs expenses which are reasonable but not necessary, he may be able to recover his fees and disbursements from his client, but extra expense which results from conducting litigation in a disproportionate manner cannot be recovered from the other party.

[38] In deciding what is necessary the conduct of the other party is highly relevant. The other party by co-operation can reduce costs, by being unco-operative he can increase costs. If he is uncooperative that may render necessary costs which would otherwise be unnecessary and that he should pay the costs for the expense which he has made necessary is perfectly acceptable. Access to justice would be impeded if lawyers felt they could not afford to do what is necessary to conduct the litigation. Giving appropriate weight to the requirements of proportionality and reasonableness will not make the conduct of litigation uneconomic if on the assessment there is allowed a reasonable sum for the work carried out which was necessary."

4.3   A significant feature of *Lownds* is this: the concept of necessity, which was embodied in rules of court for over a century before being dropped in 1986, has been re-introduced. It now forms a crucial part of the exegesis of proportionality.

(ii) Recent application of proportionality principle in tribunals

4.4   The decision of the Competition Appeal Tribunal (the "Tribunal") in *Tesco plc v Competition Commission* [2009] CAT 26 illustrates the operation of the proportionality principle in the context of tribunals. The applicant incurred costs of £1,391,904 in bringing judicial review proceedings. The respondent incurred costs of £242,605. The applicant succeeded in its claim and obtained an order for costs. The Tribunal held that the applicant's costs were disproportionate. In the circumstances of that case, the costs incurred by the respondent provided a benchmark for what level of costs was proportionate. However, £100,000 should be added to take account of the additional burdens on the applicant. The Tribunal assessed the applicant's recoverable costs at £342,000. It should be noted that the Tribunal did not adopt the same approach in *Barclays Bank plc v Competition Commission* [2009] CAT 31,[53] because additional justification was put forward for the discrepancy between the claimant's costs and the respondent's costs. In *Barclays Bank* the Tribunal ordered that the claimant's costs be assessed by a costs officer of the Senior Courts.

---

[53] A case in which the claimant's costs (£790,000) were three and a half times as much as the respondent's costs (£225,000).

(iii) Comments on *Lownds*

4.5   Professor Zuckerman's commentary. Professor Adrian Zuckerman discusses *Lownds* and the decisions which followed it in *Civil Procedure: Principles of Practice*[54] at paragraphs 26.74 to 26.87. He considers that the Court of Appeal's decision in *Lownds* has not satisfactorily clarified the difference between proportionality and reasonableness. Nor, as the law now stands, is the proportionality test effective in reducing costs which have been established to be reasonable.

4.6   In *Willis v Nicolson* [2007] EWCA Civ 199 the Court of Appeal noted that the proportionality test had not proved effective in controlling costs. At paragraphs 18 – 19 Buxton LJ, delivering the judgment of the court, said:

> "The very high costs of civil litigation in England & Wales is a matter of concern not merely to the parties in a particular case, but for the litigation system as a whole. While disputants should be given every encouragement to settle their differences without going to court, that encouragement should not include the making of litigation prohibitively costly so that litigants are deterred irrespective of the merits of their case. One element in the present high cost of litigation is undoubtedly the expectations as to annual income of the professionals who conduct it. The costs system as it at present operates cannot do anything about that, because it assesses the proper charge for work on the basis of the market rates charged by the professions, rather than attempting the no doubt difficult task of placing an objective value on the work. When the Civil Procedure Rules replaced the Rules of the Supreme Court, and encouraged active intervention by the court and the application of public values and not merely those values with which the parties were comfortable, it was hoped that that practice might change; and that hope was reinforced when this court said, in [2] of its judgment in *Lownds v Home Office* [2002] 1 WLR 2450:
>
> > 'Proportionality played no part in the taxation of costs under the Rules of the Supreme Court. The only test was that of reasonableness. The problem with that test, standing on its own, was that it institutionalised, as reasonable, the level of costs which were generally charged by the profession at the time when professional services were rendered. If a rate of charges was commonly adopted it was taken to be reasonable and so allowed on taxation even though the result was far from reasonable.'
>
> However, in the event nothing seems to have changed. That is because, as explained in [29] of the same judgment, 'proportionality' is achieved by determining whether it was necessary to incur any particular item of costs. And then 'When an item of costs is necessarily incurred then a reasonable amount for the item should normally be allowed': and the reasonable amount per hour of the professional's time continues to be determined by the market."

4.7   Cardiff seminar. At the Cardiff seminar on 19th June 2009 Sir Anthony May, President of the Queen's Bench Division ("QBD"), expressed concern about the effect of *Lownds*. He said:

---

[54] 2nd edition, Thomson Sweet & Maxwell, 2006.

"Thus as I understand the judgment, the court has to ask whether the costs claimed are proportionate. If on the face of it they are not, the court has to examine on an item by item basis whether the work which they represent was necessary and whether the amounts claimed are reasonable. Reductions in cost resulting from this process may reduce or eliminate the apparent disproportion. But they may not. If it is determined that all items were both necessary and reasonable in amount, they are, as I understand it, recoverable even though the result may be disproportionate. I may have missed it, but I do not think you can find in this judgment a yardstick of reasonableness. Take counsel's fees. A brief fee of (say) £10,000 may be a reasonable amount for this job and it may be reasonable for the party engaging this barrister to pay this amount. It does not follow that it is necessarily reasonable, let alone proportionate, that an opposing party ordered to pay costs should be saddled with the full fee...

I do not for a moment question the correctness of the *Lownds* decision as an application of the law and Civil Procedure Rules as they now stand. But the tension remains. I do think we should ask whether, in the expensive world of adversarial litigation, a litigant should be able to recover from a losing opponent costs which it was reasonable and necessary for the winner to spend, even though the resulting amount may be out of all proportion to the amount claimed or the amount recovered? Assessments which have to concentrate retrospectively on what the winning party has spent will always risk producing a disproportionate result.

In my experience, there is no doubt at all but that costs are assessed with nodding respect only to proportionality. An application of rule 44.5 of the Civil Procedure Rules and section 11 of the Costs Practice Direction can scarcely expect to do better than that."

4.8   The President of the QBD went on to argue that the application of *Lownds* should be reversed. The rules should provide that costs which are disproportionate to the amount involved and the nature of the claim are irrecoverable against the paying party. This exercise should be carried out both on an item by item basis and globally. Judges should be able to stand back and make broad judgments about proportionality. He added:

"It is more important that a defendant should not be at risk of a grotesquely disproportionate costs order than that claimants should be enabled to conduct risk free litigation."

5. DISCUSSION

(i) Two relevant principles

5.1   <u>The two relevant principles.</u> To what extent should the winning party in litigation recover the costs which it has incurred against the losing party? Two principles are relevant to the debate which this question has generated. They are compensation and proportionality.

5.2   <u>Compensation.</u> The principle of compensation is embedded both in common law and in equity. The essence of compensation is that a wrongdoer should restore the innocent party to the position in which he would have been, if the wrong had not occurred. The principle of compensation underlies the law of contract, the law of tort, the law of damages and the remedies of equity.[55]

5.3   Proportionality. As explained in section 3 of this chapter, proportionality is a more recent arrival on the scene. Proportionality is an open-textured concept. It now pervades many areas of the law, both substantive and adjectival. The essence of proportionality is that the ends do not necessarily justify the means. The law facilitates the pursuit of lawful objectives, but only to the extent that those objectives warrant the burdens thereby being imposed upon others.

(ii) Impact upon litigation costs

5.4   Interaction of the two principles. The principle of compensation requires that a party whose claim or defence is vindicated should be made whole. In other words, that party's costs should be paid by the other side.[56] However, the principle of proportionality requires that the costs burden cast upon the other party should not be greater than the subject matter of the litigation warrants. The focus of this chapter is upon the extent to which the second principle limits the operation of the first principle.

5.5   Proportionality of costs. Proportionality of costs is not simply a matter of comparing the sum in issue with the amount of costs incurred, important though that comparison is. It is also necessary to evaluate any non-monetary remedies sought and any rights which are in issue, in order to compare the overall value of what is at stake in the action with the costs of resolution.

5.6   The comparison exercise set out in the previous paragraph produces a strong indication of whether the costs of a party are proportionate. Before coming to a final conclusion, however, it is also necessary to look at the complexity of the litigation. There can be complex low value claims where the costs of litigation (if conducted properly) are bound to exceed the sum at stake. Equally, there can be high value, but straightforward, commercial claims[57] where the costs are excessive, despite representing only a small proportion of the damages. It is also relevant to consider conduct and any wider factors, such as reputational issues or public importance.

5.7   It is therefore necessary to consider proportionality of costs by reference to (a) the sums at stake, (b) the value of any non-monetary remedies claimed and any rights in issue, (c) the complexity of the litigation, (d) conduct and (e) any wider factors, such as reputational issues or public importance.

5.8   Professor Zuckerman pithily summarises proportionality as follows:

"The aim of the proportionality test is to maintain a sensible correlation between costs, on the one hand, and the value of the case, its complexity and importance on the other hand."[58]

5.9   In borderline cases it will be a matter of subjective opinion whether the costs in any particular case are disproportionate. Nevertheless, despite the difficulty of

---

[55] See e.g. *Erlanger v New Sombrero Phosphate Company* (1878) 3 App Cas 1218 at 1278-1279; *Newbigging v Adam* (1886) 34 Ch D 582 at 595; *Livingstone v Rawyards Coal Company* (1880) 5 App Cas 25 at 39. This principle is sometimes referred to as *restitutio in integrum*.

[56] The indemnity principle discussed in chapter 5 below is a manifestation of the principle of compensation.

[57] E.g. turning upon the interpretation of one clause in a charterparty

[58] *"Civil Procedure: Principles of Practice"*, 2nd edition (2006) at paragraph 26.88.

determining in borderline cases whether or not costs are proportionate, there are many cases where it is readily apparent that costs are or are not proportionate, having regard to all the circumstances of the case.

5.10   <u>Disproportionate costs do not become proportionate because they were necessary.</u> If the level of costs incurred is out of proportion to the circumstances of the case, they cannot become proportionate simply because they were "necessary" in order to bring or defend the claim. It will be recalled from chapter 12 of the Preliminary Report that the Legal Services Commission applies a cost / benefit test when deciding whether to support a case with public funds.[59] Any self funding litigant would do the same. The fact that it was necessary to incur certain costs in order to prove or disprove a head of claim is obviously relevant, but it is not decisive of the question whether such costs were proportionate.

5.11   At the time when *Lownds* was decided, it seemed to myself and others that this decision[60] was a neat way of applying the proportionality test, which would bring costs under proper control. Experience, however, has taught otherwise. In my view, the time has now come to say that the guidance given by the Court of Appeal in *Lownds* is not satisfactory, essentially for the reasons given by the President of the QBD at the Cardiff seminar. The effect of *Lownds* was to insert the Victorian test of necessity into the modern concept of proportionality.

5.12   <u>Disproportionate costs should be disallowed in an assessment of costs on the standard basis.</u> If a judge assessing costs concludes that the total figure, alternatively some element within that total figure, was disproportionate, the judge should say so. It then follows from the provisions of CPR rule 44.4(3) that the disproportionate element of costs should be disallowed in any assessment on the standard basis. In my view, that disproportionate element of the costs cannot be saved, even if the individual items within it were both reasonable and necessary.

5.13   In other words, I propose that in an assessment of costs on the standard basis, proportionality should prevail over reasonableness and the proportionality test should be applied on a global basis.[61] The court should first make an assessment of reasonable costs, having regard to the individual items in the bill, the time reasonably spent on those items and the other factors listed in CPR rule 44.5(3). The court should then stand back and consider whether the total figure is proportionate. If the total figure is not proportionate, the court should make an appropriate reduction.[62] There is already a precedent for this approach in relation to the assessment of legal aid costs in criminal proceedings: see *R v Supreme Court Taxing Office ex p John Singh and Co* [1997] 1 Costs LR 49.

5.14   <u>Assessment of costs on the indemnity basis.</u> Rule 44.4 does not lay down any test of proportionality to be applied when the court is assessing costs on the indemnity basis. However, by reason of rule 1.1(2)(c) (the overriding objective), the principle of proportionality exerts a degree of influence even over assessment of costs upon the indemnity basis. In my view, the contrast between the descriptions of the standard basis and the indemnity basis in rule 44.4 is so stark, that a direct

---

[59] See PR paragraph 12.2.13.
[60] In accordance with the provisions of section 11 of the Costs PD set out above.
[61] This is my proposed answer to the two "puzzling questions" posed by Professor Zuckerman at "*Civil Procedure: Principles of Practice*", 2nd edition (2006) paragraph 26.74.
[62] The test of proportionality does not, however, replace the requirement for the court to consider the bill in detail on an item by item basis. The application of any reduction for proportionality should only take place when each item on the bill has been assessed individually.

application of the proportionality principle cannot have been intended.[63] Although the court will bear proportionality in mind when dealing with individual items, it will not cut down the total sum by reference to the principle of proportionality.

<u>(iii) Proposed amendments to the rules and the Costs Practice Direction</u>

 <u>(a) Proposed rule changes</u>

5.15   I propose that the CPR be amended to include a definition of proportionate costs along the following lines:

> "Costs are proportionate if, and only if, the costs incurred bear a reasonable relationship to:
>
> (a)   the sums in issue in the proceedings;
>
> (b)   the value of any non-monetary relief in issue in the proceedings;
>
> (c)   the complexity of the litigation;
>
> (d)   any additional work generated by the conduct of the paying party; and
>
> (e)   any wider factors involved in the proceedings, such as reputation or public importance."

The precise formulation of the rule must be for the Rule Committee.

5.16   <u>Reversal of effect of *Lownds*.</u> The rules should also provide that the fact that costs were necessarily incurred does not make them proportionate. This should be stated explicitly, if the Rule Committee sees fit to reverse the effect of *Lownds*.

5.17   <u>Policy.</u> The policy which underlies the proposed new rule is that cost benefit analysis has a part to play, even in the realm of civil justice.[64] If parties wish to pursue claims or defences at disproportionate cost, they must do so, at least in part, at their own expense.

5.18   <u>Effect of the proposed rule in multi-track cases.</u> In relation to multi-track cases, the proposed rule should act as a long stop. In the first instance, the court should assess costs by applying the test of reasonableness, as required by CPR rule 44.4(1).[65] In applying the test of reasonableness, the court will have regard to the factors set out in rule 44.5(3).[66] That process will usually result in a total sum which is "proportionate", as defined above. However, if the process of assessment on the standard basis (whether summary or detailed) results in a figure which is not "proportionate", then the receiving party's entitlement to costs will be limited to such sum as is proportionate.

5.19   <u>Effect of proposed rule in fast track cases.</u> In relation to fast track cases, the proposals for fixed costs in chapter 15 below should secure that recoverable costs are always "proportionate" in accordance with the definition proposed in this chapter. However, for fast track cases which come within the proposed "escape clause",[67] it

---

[63] See *ARM Asset-Backed Securities SA v Lewinsohn*, a decision of Barling J dated 13th November 2009. At the time of writing no neutral citation number has been assigned to this judgment.

[64] See e.g. *AB v John Wyeth and Brothers Ltd*, CAT 13th December 1996.

[65] Either in its present form or in its amended form, as proposed in chapter 5 below.

[66] Although the list of relevant factors is lengthy, in practice the total amount of time reasonably spent on all of the individual items plays a dominant part in determining what sum is reasonable: see factor (f).

[67] See chapter 15 paragraph 5.18.

may be necessary to apply the principle of proportionality as a long stop. The principle of proportionality should also be applied to fast track cases for which no matrix of fixed costs has been devised.

5.20　Terms of reference for the Costs Review. The terms of reference require me to make recommendations "in order to promote access to justice at proportionate cost". The CPR currently state that, when assessing costs on the standard basis, the court will only allow "proportionate" costs. In order to give that rule "teeth", it is necessary that the CPR should give guidance as to what constitutes "proportionate" costs. If a definition along the lines proposed above is incorporated into the CPR, this will fulfil one limb of my terms of reference.

5.21　Safeguard against unreasonable conduct. The proposed new rule will not be a charter for wealthy litigants to put their opponents to excessive and disproportionate costs by tactical manoeuvring. The sanction for such oppressive conduct will be an order for indemnity costs. Such an order will substantially (although not entirely)[68] free the receiving party from the shackles of the requirement for proportionality. Furthermore, even where there is no order for indemnity costs, the definition of "proportionality" which I propose protects a receiving party who has been put to extra expense by the tactics of the opposition.

(b) Proposed practice direction amendments

5.22　Provisions relating to proportionality. If proportionality is defined as suggested above, then *Lownds* will have been reversed by rule change. Consequential amendments will also be required to paragraphs 11.1, 11.2, 11.3 and 11.6 of the Costs PD. It should be made clear that, in an assessment of costs on the standard basis, proportionality prevails over reasonableness and the proportionality test must be applied on a global basis.

5.23　Provisions relating to additional liabilities. The provisions in paragraphs 11.4, 11.5 and 11.7 to 11.11 of the Costs PD relate to additional liabilities. They have the effect that recoverable costs are liable to be disproportionate in every case brought under a CFA. This is because additional sums are added to that which is reasonable and proportionate (viz the base costs) without regard to the proportionality of the total figure. If the recommendations made in chapters 9 and 10 below are accepted, then those paragraphs of the Costs PD will have to be repealed.

6. RECOMMENDATION

6.1　I recommend that "proportionate costs" be defined in the CPR by reference to sums in issue, value of non-monetary relief, complexity of litigation, conduct and any wider factors, such as reputation or public importance; and that the test of proportionality should be applied on a global basis.

6.2　The consequential amendments which will be required have been set out above, but these do not need to be the subject of a separate recommendation.

---

[68] See paragraph 5.14 above.

CHAPTER 4. THE CAUSES OF DISPROPORTIONATE COSTS AND HOW THEY SHOULD BE TACKLED WHILST PROMOTING ACCESS TO JUSTICE

INDEX

1. INTRODUCTION

1.1   The present Costs Review was established because of a perception that the costs of civil litigation are too high: see section 1 of chapter 1 of the Preliminary Report. Litigation is a labour intensive process carried out by professionals in the face of skilled opposition. The costs of such process will always be substantial. It is not my function to devise ways of slashing costs as an end in itself, but to make recommendations *"to promote access to justice at proportionate cost"*.

1.2   "Excessive" and "disproportionate". In this chapter I use the term "excessive" to mean costs which are too high. I use the term "disproportionate" to mean costs which are not proportionate, as defined in the previous chapter. In practice, excessive costs may well be disproportionate. In sections 3 and 4 below I shall concentrate upon what causes costs to be too high, without constantly repeating that such costs may also be disproportionate.

1.3   Abbreviations. In this chapter I refer to the Civil Procedure Rule Committee as the "Rule Committee". I refer to the Ministry of Justice as the "MoJ".

2. ACCESS TO JUSTICE, FUNDING AND PROPORTIONATE COSTS

2.1   Civil justice. In chapter 4 of the Preliminary Report I summarised the functions of the civil courts and set out what I see as the crucial role of civil justice in society. Although much of the Preliminary Report has come in for some robust criticism during Phase 2 of the Costs Review, chapter 4 has survived unscathed. The views expressed in that chapter concerning civil justice and the role of the civil courts remain my views, but they will not be repeated in this report.

2.2   The present Governor of the Bank of England (following litigation in which the Bank was vindicated) has stated:

> "A legal framework for enforcing contracts and resolving disputes is not just an arcane process which allows professionals to earn vast fees, but an integral part of the infrastructure of a successful market economy. It matters that there are simple, clear and timely ways of resolving disputes."[69]

I agree with those comments.

2.3   Access to justice. Access to justice entails that those with meritorious claims (whether or not ultimately successful) are able to bring those claims before the courts for judicial resolution or post-issue settlement, as the case may be. It also entails that those with meritorious defences (whether or not ultimately successful) are able to put those defences before the courts for judicial resolution or, alternatively, settlement based upon the merits of the case.

2.4   Funding makes access to justice possible. Access to justice is only possible if both parties have adequate funding. If neither party has adequate funding, the litigation will not happen. If only one party has adequate funding, the litigation will be a walk over.

2.5   Proportionate costs make access to justice practicable. Access to justice is only practicable if the costs of litigation are proportionate. If costs are disproportionate, then even a well-resourced party may hesitate before pursuing a valid claim or maintaining a valid defence. That party may simply drop a good claim or capitulate to a weak claim, as the case may be.

2.6   Funding methods and costs rules impact upon each other. It is wrong to regard "funding" and "costs" as separate topics which must be tackled individually, in order to provide access to justice. They impact upon each other. Some methods of funding tend to drive up costs and some methods of funding have the opposite effect. Some costs regimes reduce the need for funding (e.g. one way costs shifting). Some costs regimes increase the need for funding (e.g. a regime that requires one party to pay double costs if it loses). Indeed the costs rules themselves constitute one form of funding regime, namely that the loser funds the winner.

---

[69] Speech by Mervyn King at the Lord Mayor's Banquet for Bankers and Merchants of the City of London at the Mansion House on 21st June 2006.

2.7   Three linked concepts. Accordingly, the three concepts of access to justice, costs and funding are interlinked. It is unsurprising, indeed inevitable, that they are conjoined in my terms of reference.

2.8   The supposed antithesis. It has sometimes been suggested during the Costs Review that there is an antithesis between controlling costs and promoting access to justice. I accept that if litigation becomes uneconomic for lawyers, so that they cease to practise, there is a denial of access to justice. But, for the most part, achieving proportionate costs and promoting access to justice go hand in hand. If costs on both sides are proportionate, then (i) there is more access to justice and (ii) such funding as the parties possess is more likely to be sufficient.

2.9   Actual costs and recoverable costs. Both forms of costs are crucial to this review.

(i)   Actual costs. The total actual costs of both sides in a case represent the true costs of the litigation, which are distributed between the parties and sometimes fall upon the general public. For example, the total legal costs which the National Health Service Litigation Authority (the "NHSLA") incurred (over the duration of the claim) on cases which were settled in the last financial year (2008/09) were some £143 million.[70] Of that sum it paid 72% to claimant lawyers and 28% to its own lawyers. The taxpayer bears the entirety of that sum. The taxpayer also bears the costs of unsuccessful claims brought against the NHSLA on legal aid.

(ii)   Recoverable costs. Recoverable costs represent a source of funding for the winning party and thus promote access to justice. From that point of view, there is an interest in narrowing the gap between actual and recoverable costs. On the other hand, recoverable costs represent a burden upon the losing party and thus inhibit access to justice. From that point of view, there is an interest in controlling recoverable costs below actual costs. From the point of view of someone who does not know whether he will be winner or loser, i.e. a litigant in the "original position" as defined by Rawls,[71] there is also an interest in controlling recoverable costs below actual costs. This is because the total actual costs tend to rise when the stakes for winning are raised.[72]

2.10   In some areas of litigation, both the recoverable costs and the actual costs are excessive. The reform advocated in the previous chapter (namely limiting recoverable costs to a "proportionate" sum) is only part of the answer. It is also necessary to identify the causes of excessive costs and to prescribe how those causes should be tackled. I shall attempt this task, in outline, in the remainder of this chapter.

3. GENERAL CAUSES OF EXCESSIVE COSTS AND HOW THEY SHOULD BE TACKLED

3.1   In my view there are sixteen general causes which, in differing combinations (and according to the particular circumstances), give rise to excessive costs. The order in which I set them out is a matter of convenience, not an indication of the potency or importance of individual causes.

---

[70] See chapter 23 below.
[71] This is the best position from which to make an evaluation. See John Rawls, "*A Theory of Justice*", OUP (1976) chapter III.
[72] See PR chapter 9.

(i)   The rules of court require parties to carry out time consuming procedures involving professional skill.

(ii)   In some areas of litigation, the complexity of the law causes parties to incur substantial costs.

(iii)   The costs rules are such as to generate satellite litigation.

(iv)   Too few solicitors, barristers and judges have a sufficient understanding of the law of costs or how costs may be controlled.

(v)   Lawyers are generally paid by reference to time spent, rather than work product.

(vi)   The recoverable hourly rates of lawyers are not satisfactorily controlled.

(vii)   The preparation of witness statements and expert reports can generate excessive costs.

(viii) The costs shifting rule creates perverse incentives.

(ix)   The conditional fee agreement ("CFA") regime has had unfortunate unintended consequences, namely (a) litigants with CFAs have little interest in controlling the costs which are being incurred on their behalf and (b) opposing litigants face a massively increased costs liability.

(x)   The advent of emails and electronic databases means that, in substantial cases, the process of standard disclosure may be prohibitively expensive.

(xi)   There is no effective control over pre-issue costs; certain pre-action protocols lead to magnification of these costs and duplication of effort.

(xii)   In some instances there is ineffective case management, both by the parties and by the court.

(xiii) Some cases which ought to settle early settle too late or not at all.

(xiv)   The procedures for detailed assessment are unduly cumbersome, with the result that (a) they are unduly expensive to operate and (b) they frequently discourage litigants from securing a proper assessment.

(xv)   The current level of court fees is too high and the current policy of full cost pricing is wrong in principle.

(xvi)   Despite the growth of court fees in recent years, the civil courts remain under-resourced in terms of both staff and IT.

<u>Factor (i): Requirements of the rules of procedure</u>

3.2   A number of respondents during the Costs Review comment upon the complexity of the procedural rules as being one cause of high costs.   The Civil Committee of the Council of Her Majesty's Circuit Judges states:

"The Woolf reforms aimed to achieve three things: greater speed, greater simplicity, and lower cost.   The first of these has been achieved.   The second two plainly have not, and are interconnected.   The more work the rules require to be done, the more it will cost.   There is now much more work to be done, especially before proceedings are started, as the Report has analysed.   The reticulation of protocols   (which are ever being increased and never simplified) mean that even in cases which are going quickly to settle much more work will be done than it was pre CPR.   The more sophistication is introduced into the Rules (notable examples of this are the costs rules themselves), the more work will be involved, the more time will be taken, and the more satellite litigation will increase. Since the CPR were introduced the size of the White Book has grown considerably and inexorably. There has manifestly not been the simplification which Lord Woolf called for, whereby the rules should be comprehensible to ordinary litigants. Quite the reverse in some cases. This, in part, is responsible for the unacceptable increases in costs which have taken place. There needs to be a very determined drive for simplification."

3.3　There is here an irreconcilable tension. On the one hand litigants and their advisers desire certainty. They need to know what steps have to be taken and when, in order to deal with the ever burgeoning issues in civil litigation. Extensive new civil remedies are created by Parliament every year, for which the Rule Committee is asked to make provision. Litigants wish to know the criteria upon which applications will be dealt with, so that they can predict as accurately as possible how the court will exercise its discretion in every situation. Furthermore, many submissions during the Costs Review have emphasised that "one size does not fit all". The Bar Council, for example, states:

> "What is abundantly clear, from Jackson LJ's Preliminary Report and from the Bar Council's review, is that 'One size does not fit all.' Particular types of litigation give rise to particular issues, be they funding issues, case management issues or otherwise."

If the rules are to provide the requisite degree of predictability in this situation, they are bound to be lengthy and detailed. On the other hand, lengthy and detailed rules take time to digest and generate high costs of compliance.

3.4　The Rule Committee, the MoJ drafting team, the authors of practice directions, protocols and court guides have to strike a balance on every rule making occasion between the need for predictability on the one hand and the need for simplicity on the other hand. I am bound to say that as I survey (for the purpose of the Costs Review) the vast mass of rules, practice directions, protocols, court guides and so forth, I do wonder whether we are getting the balance right. It is not easy to identify specific provisions which could safely be repealed.[73] On the other hand, the total corpus of procedural rules is of daunting size and complexity.

3.5　This problem does not admit of any simplistic solution, such as taking an axe to the existing structure and starting all over again. That exercise occurs approximately once every century and was last undertaken in 1998. I do not recommend any radical overhaul of that nature. I do, however, recommend that in future the Rule Committee, the MoJ drafting team and the authors of practice directions, protocols and court guides should accord higher priority to the goal of simplicity when striking the balance described above. In particular, as each part of the CPR comes up for review, the opportunity should be taken to delete those provisions in practice directions which merely duplicate the rules, so that practice directions will comprise and only comprise genuinely supplementary material.

3.6　It must, however, be accepted that however skilfully the rules may be drafted, civil procedure is bound to be complex and the process of civil litigation is bound to be costly. As Professor Dame Hazel Genn observed at the Birmingham seminar,

---

[73] However, I do recommend a number of repeals in the course of this report.

"there appears to be an irreducible amount of work that must be done even to recover damages of £2,000 or less".[74]

Factor (ii): Complexity of the law

3.7   In some areas of litigation the complexity or uncertainty of the law is itself a contributory cause of disproportionate costs. For example, the complexity of the law governing rented housing was identified as a cause of additional costs in chapter 31 of the Preliminary Report, dealing with housing claims: see PR paragraphs 31.1.3 to 31.1.5. The reform of substantive law lies outside my terms of reference, although I draw attention to the issue where appropriate.

Factor (iii): The costs rules are such as to generate satellite litigation

3.8   The history of the "Costs War" has been narrated in PR chapter 3. Cumulatively, there has been a vast mass of litigation about costs, which represents a shocking waste of resources. This is due in large part to the existence of the indemnity rule, which gives rise to numerous technical defences and endless legal argument. It is also due in large part to the "recoverability" regime,[75] which is fraught with complications and imposes inequitable costs burdens. It is also due to the complexity of the costs rules.

3.9   In relation to these matters, I propose that both the indemnity principle and the recoverability of additional liabilities be abolished: see chapters 5, 9 and 10 below. I also propose that, as and when the costs rules come to be amended, high priority should be accorded to simplicity and clarity. Attempting to legislate for every single permutation of events is a hopeless endeavour. If my recommendations in respect of additional liabilities are accepted, there will be a welcome thinning out of the costs rules and the Costs Practice Direction in that regard.

Factor (iv): Insufficient understanding of costs

3.10   <u>Can the court undertake costs management?</u>   One of the proposals in this report is that the court should undertake costs management as an adjunct to case management. Many respondents who support this proposal express concern that it may be impracticable, because lawyers lack the requisite skills. It is often said that neither barristers nor judges (most of whom are ex-barristers) know much about costs or possess the skills required for effective costs management. Solicitors know about costs, but only a minority appear to be skilled in costs budgeting for litigation.

3.11   <u>Judges.</u>   Judges now have ten years' experience of carrying out summary assessments of costs. Therefore their knowledge base is materially greater than it was in 1999, when the Woolf reforms were introduced. Nevertheless, the fact remains that "costs" is not a topic which interests all judges. Some judges frankly confess their lack of familiarity with this aspect of litigation. In my view, this approach is no longer acceptable. In a very large number of civil cases the question of costs is the most important single issue. If the culture change which I advocate elsewhere in this report is to be achieved, judges must become as skilled at assessing costs as they are skilled at assessing damages. Also judges must acquire a thorough understanding of the costs consequences of the case management directions which they give.

---

[74] Professor Genn's seminar paper, 26th June 2009, paragraph 10 which can be found at http://www.judiciary.gov.uk/docs/costs-review/analysis-costs-data.pdf.
[75] In respect of "additional liabilities", i.e. success fees and after-the-event ("ATE") insurance premiums.

3.12   <u>Litigation as a project.</u> Many respondents during the Costs Review have made the point that litigation is, in essence, a project. All participants in a project must be aware of the budget for the project and aware of the budgetary consequences of what they do. This analogy has limitations. Litigation is more unpredictable than a construction project. Neither an architect nor a contractor is battling against an opponent who is trying to knock their building down. On the other hand, this element of adversity is not a licence to disregard costs. Just as an architect or engineer giving variation instructions must take account of the costs involved, so must a lawyer making case management decisions. To take one example, in a commercial dispute which is solely about money (not issues of principle or reputation), if £1 million is at stake, it does not make sense to embark upon a disclosure exercise costing twice that amount. In the course of the Costs Review I have learnt of a number of instances in which case management directions (given with the best of intentions) gave rise to costs out of all proportion to the benefits.

3.13   <u>Barristers.</u> One member of the Bar in his Phase 2 submission stated:

> "In my view it would be helpful if members of the Bar were encouraged to be far more aware of the significance and relevance of costs (perhaps by a requirement of including costs as part of the CPD[76] requirements each year in addition to core areas of practice)."

3.14   I see force in that observation. Barristers ought to be up to date in relation to the law of costs, because costs are an issue in every single case. Barristers ought to be aware of the likely costs of each step which they recommend should or must be taken. In my view, both the assessment of costs and costs budgeting should form part of Continuing Professional Development ("CPD") for barristers.

3.15   <u>Solicitors.</u> Some solicitors are highly skilled at costs budgeting. At meetings during the Costs Review I have encountered experienced solicitors who tell me that they can estimate the likely costs of a complex case at the outset with reasonable accuracy.[77] They cannot foretell the precise course of the litigation, but they can make a reasonable allowance for contingencies on the basis of past experience.[78] On the other hand many solicitors are not proficient at costs budgeting. Indeed some profess that the task is impossible because of the uncertainties of litigation.

3.16   The in-house solicitor of one third party funder states in their Phase 2 submission:

> "The elements of case and costs management are still pitifully absent from the formal education of solicitors and barristers...
>
> It remains our view that much better training about assessing the elements of a dispute, its likely timing and costs are matters which much be addressed in training – most are still learning by osmosis. To inject that sense of project and costs management at an early stage will eventually filter through the profession. The best solicitor we deal with is one who used to work in the construction industry, then trained first as a legal executive and then as a solicitor and his organizational, financial and strategic and planning skills make him the best litigator we encounter whose bills are always eminently reasonable. So it is possible."

---

[76] Continuing Professional Development.
[77] See e.g. PR paragraph 10.7.10.
[78] Sometimes with the assistance of costs budgeting software.

3.17   In the case of solicitors, the obligation to give competent advice about likely costs is enshrined in paragraph 2.03 of the Solicitors' Code of Conduct. In my view, costs budgeting for litigation should form part of CPD for solicitors who practise in the field of litigation.

3.18   My recommendations about costs management and the training of judges and lawyers in costs budgeting are developed in chapter 40 below.

Factor (v): Method of remuneration

3.19   Litigation solicitors and (save in respect of brief fees) counsel are generally paid by reference to the number of hours worked.[79] It is not easy for a costs judge long after the end of a case, or even for a trial judge immediately after a trial, to look back over the course of the proceedings and determine how efficiently each member of the team was working. Thus the system of remuneration tends to reward inefficiency and to penalise efficiency.

3.20   In chapters 15, 16 and 40 below I discuss how the rules may be changed in order to remunerate lawyers by reference to work done, rather than by reference to "billable hours" recorded and retrospectively justified.

Factor (vi): The recoverable hourly rates of lawyers are not satisfactorily controlled

3.21   The Guideline Hourly Rates for solicitors ("GHRs") for summary assessment are often, in practice, applied in detailed assessments as well. The present mechanism for setting and reviewing those GHRs is not satisfactory. In chapter 6 below I propose that a Costs Council be set up for this purpose. In chapter 44 below I advocate a new approach to the setting of GHRs.

Factor (vii): Factual and expert evidence

3.22   Factual and expert evidence is sometimes the cause of excessive costs in "heavy" cases. Even in modest claims expert evidence may generate excessive costs. In chapter 38 below I discuss how the costs of factual and expert evidence might be controlled, whilst ensuring that each party's case is properly disclosed before trial and presented at trial.

Factor (viii): Costs shifting rule

3.23   <u>Tendency to increase overall costs.</u> The costs shifting rule creates perverse incentives in two situations.

(i)   Sometimes the consequence of the costs shifting rule is that while each party is running up costs, it does not know who will be paying the bill. In some instances a litigant may believe that the more he or she spends in costs, the less likely he or she is to foot the ultimate bill because the costs liability will be shifted. If both parties take this view, then costs escalate upwards without any proper control and ultimately result in one or other party[80] picking up an enormous and disproportionate bill. I have seen this phenomenon both in small domestic or neighbour disputes and in major High Court litigation.

(ii)   Sometimes both parties know that the defendant will be paying costs, for example where there is no defence on liability (or liability has been admitted)

---

[79] Indeed by reference to six minute units, a system which itself is open to abuses.
[80] Occasionally both parties.

and no Part 36 offer has been made. In such a situation the claimant has no incentive to control costs. The only restraint upon the claimant's lawyers will be their perception of what may be disallowed on assessment.

Academic research confirms that the costs shifting rule tends to drive up the costs of litigation.[81]

3.24 <u>Effect on access to justice.</u> The conflicting effects of the costs shifting rule upon access to justice and the relevant academic research are discussed in chapters 9 and 46 of the Preliminary Report.

3.25 Having considered the wealth of submissions during Phases 1 and 2, I accept that the arguments of policy and principle which underlie the costs shifting rule justify the general retention of that rule in civil proceedings. However, there are some respects in which I consider that the operation of the rule should be modified. Some modifications are required in order to prevent parties from recovering disproportionate costs. Some modifications are required in order to protect vulnerable parties against adverse costs liability. The purpose of all such modifications is to promote access to justice. I shall discuss these modifications in later chapters.

Factor (ix): The CFA regime

3.26 The CFA regime, with recoverable success fees and recoverable after-the-event ("ATE") insurance premiums, was designed to promote access to justice following the retraction of legal aid in April 2001. That regime has had unfortunate unintended consequences, which I address in chapters 9 and 10 below. Indeed the CFA regime has emerged as one of the major drivers of excessive costs. I recommend that success fees and ATE insurance premiums should cease to be recoverable.

Factor (x): Disclosure in the electronic age

3.27 The traditional rules of disclosure generate massively increased costs in a world where the great majority of communications and records are preserved electronically. In chapter 37 below, I recommend modifications to the disclosure rules in substantial cases. I also recommend that legal practitioners and judges should receive specific training in relation to e-disclosure, so that they can deal with the process more efficiently and economically.

Factor (xi): Pre-action costs and procedures

3.28 <u>Pre-action protocols.</u> Pre-action protocols were designed to promote constructive discussion and, where possible, settlement, before proceedings were issued. Protocols have in large measure achieved that objective. But in certain respects they have had the unintended consequence of duplicating costs to no useful purpose. I address this issue in chapter 35 below.

3.29 <u>Pre-action costs management.</u> In some areas of litigation a party may run up substantial costs before issuing proceedings. In the event that liability is admitted, at least some of those costs may prove to be unnecessary. If a regime of costs management is introduced for litigation post-issue, there will also have to be some control over the recoverable costs which may be incurred pre-issue. Otherwise there

---

[81] See the research papers discussed in PR chapter 9, in particular at paragraphs 2.1 to 3.3.

will be a temptation to incur costs at an earlier stage. I discuss this question in chapters 23 and 40 below.

Factor (xii): Case management

3.30 Case management by the court, with the assistance of the parties, was one of the cornerstones of the Woolf reforms. It is clear from the submissions and seminars during the Costs Review that in some areas case management works extremely well, for the benefit of all parties. In other areas case management is not satisfactory and reforms are called for. I discuss this issue in chapter 39 below.

Factor (xiii): Late settlements

3.31 A number of cases, which ought to settle early, in fact settle late in the day. Occasionally these cases go to trial. The cause of such futile litigation is (a) the failure by one or both parties to get to grips with the issues in good time or (b) the failure of the parties to have any effective dialogue.

3.32 In my view, there are two reforms which will tackle this haemorrhage of wasted costs. First, there are many cases which are suitable for alternative dispute resolution ("ADR"), but in which ADR is not attempted. Whilst I readily accept that those litigants who wish the court to resolve their disputes are fully entitled to press on to trial, I believe that there are many parties who would be amenable to mediation and who would benefit from it. Mediation can bring about earlier resolution in cases which are destined to settle and can, on occasions, identify common ground which conventional negotiation does not reach. I address ADR in chapter 36 below. The second reform which will promote earlier settlement is to amend Part 36, so that (a) there is greater certainty about the effect of offers and (b) claimant offers have more "teeth". I address these issues in chapter 41 below.

Factor (xiv): Procedures for detailed assessment of costs

3.33 The current procedures for detailed assessment of costs, which we have largely inherited from the Victorians (despite CPR amendments), have been much criticised during the Costs Review. The procedures are cumbersome and expensive to operate. They are seldom resorted to in practice. This can result in large payments of costs, if paying parties regard it as prohibitively expensive to challenge bills of costs.

3.34 I discuss in chapter 45 below how the procedures for detailed assessment may be reformed.

Factor (xv): Court fees

3.35 In chapter 7 of the Preliminary Report I expressed the view that court fees were too high and that the principle of full cost pricing was wrong in principle. During Phase 2 of the Costs Review there has been almost universal agreement with the views expressed in PR chapter 7. The Association of Personal Injury Lawyers states:

> "We do not support the Government's policy of full cost pricing when setting court fees. We believe the civil court system should be funded by the taxpayer, with a contribution from court users, as providing access to the courts, and therefore to justice, is fundamental for a fair society."

HM Revenue & Customs states:

> "HMRC supports the conclusion of Phase one of the review that the MoJ proposals to achieve full cost pricing should be reconsidered."

The Law Society in its Phase 2 submission repeats and adopts its response to the MoJ consultation on this issue in 2008, as follows:

> "The Law Society continues to be fundamentally opposed to the Government's policy of full cost recovery. We accept that there is a cost to running the court system and that it is appropriate for litigants to be charged a fee towards that cost, if only to discourage frivolous litigation. However, it must be set at a level which enables there to be proper access to justice for all in society. We are concerned that any policy which seeks to obtain full recovery of the costs will undermine this by potentially setting a level of fee that will discourage people from bringing legitimate disputes. This applies particularly for those on low incomes but who, nevertheless, do not qualify for fee concessions. The impact of the continuing policy of full cost recovery is therefore likely to exclude more people from the civil justice system."

3.36   Other responses were to the same effect as those set out in the previous paragraph. These confirm my provisional view as expressed in the Preliminary Report.

3.37   I am further fortified in my provisional view by the Segmental Analysis Reports published by the MoJ. These show that the fee recovery "gross v expenditure" over the last four years was as follows:

Year 2005-6	115%
Year 2006-7	108%
Year 2007-8	104%
Year 2008-9	103%

3.38   This shows that over the last four years HMCS[82] has set court fees for civil work at a level above full cost pricing.

3.39   I recognise that, at least in the present economic climate, it is unrealistic to propose a reduction in court fees, even though such a reduction would be welcome and would be very much in the public interest. Instead I shall limit myself to the recommendation that there be no further increases in civil court fees, save increases which are in line with the Retail Price Index rate of inflation. All receipts from civil court fees should be ploughed back into the civil justice system, not used to subsidise other parts of the legal system.

3.40   <u>Remission of court fees.</u> I draw the attention of DWP local offices to the fact that letters from those offices are required, in order to enable clients who are on benefits to obtain remission of court fees: see chapter 1 above, paragraph 4.4 (iv). I do not make this the subject of a specific recommendation, but stress the fact that (a) such letters are needed in order to facilitate access to justice and (b) the DWP regards it as appropriate for such letters to be written: see chapter 1 above, paragraph 4.5.

---

[82] Her Majesty's Courts Service.

3.41   The civil courts remain under-resourced, particularly the county courts. This materially increases the costs of litigation. I address this issue in chapter 42 below.

3.42   The IT systems of our civil courts are some way behind those of certain overseas jurisdictions. If court IT is improved (as originally recommended by Lord Woolf), this will yield substantial costs savings for the parties. I address this issue in chapter 43 below.

4. SPECIFIC CAUSES OF EXCESSIVE COSTS AND HOW THEY SHOULD BE TACKLED

4.1   Many of the causes of excessive costs are specific to particular areas of litigation, for example the impact of referral fees upon the costs of personal injury cases.

4.2   I deal with those specific causes and how they should be tackled in chapters 18 to 34 below. I do not here attempt to summarise those chapters or to extract any common themes.

5. SHOULD LEGAL FEES BE REGULATED?

5.1   This issue arose at a late stage of the Costs Review as a result of my meeting with the Policy Officer for Legal Affairs of the National Association of Citizens Advice Bureaux ("Citizens Advice"). Citizen's Advice's arguments in support of regulation are set out in chapter 1 above at paragraph 4.4.

5.2   I have consulted both the Solicitors Regulation Authority (the "SRA") and the Legal Services Board (the "LSB") about this matter. Officers of both bodies have responded to the effect that regulation of solicitors' fees might be anti-competitive. The SRA points out that a client can complain about overcharging to the Legal Complaints Service (soon to be replaced by the Office for Legal Complaints). The Director of Strategy and Research at the LSB writes as follows:

> "We understand the concern that Citizens Advice have about the problem of costs of and access to legal services. It is our view however that to seek to regulate it is not the best means of addressing the matter. Opening up the legal services market to more competition will bring new entrants with more innovative products which will in turn drive existing law firms to respond by focusing more on what clients want and being ever more efficient in the way services are delivered. Our expectation is that the net effect will be consumers having greater choice about how they access legal services and increased flexibility from the market regarding price and quality. Regulating solicitors' costs will stifle a market that is already insufficiently responsive to the needs of consumers. I think that it is fair to say that were such a proposal to be made to the LSB it is very likely that we would reject it."

5.3   I see force in the points raised by the SRA and the LSB. Therefore, despite the arguments of Citizens Advice, I do not recommend the regulation of legal fees.

6. RECOMMENDATIONS

6.1 <u>Recommendations.</u> In respect of factors (i) and (xv) identified above, I make the following recommendations:

(i) When striking the balance between the need for predictability and the need for simplicity, the Rule Committee, the MoJ drafting team and the authors of practice directions, protocols and court guides should accord higher priority in future to the goal of simplicity.

(ii) There should be no further increases in civil court fees, save for increases which are in line with the Retail Price Index rate of inflation. All receipts from civil court fees should be ploughed back into the civil justice system.

6.2 <u>Conclusion.</u> In the course of the Costs Review I have identified sixteen general causes of excessive costs and a large number of specific causes. With the exception of the two matters dealt with in the preceding paragraph, my recommendations for dealing with those causes of excessive costs are set out in the following chapters of this report.

6.3 If the causes of excessive costs are tackled effectively, this will promote access to justice at proportionate cost.

CHAPTER 5. THE INDEMNITY PRINCIPLE

INDEX

1. INTRODUCTION

1.1   <u>Common law principle.</u> The indemnity principle, a creature of the common law, is set out in PR paragraph 3.4.13. In essence the principle prevents a party recovering more by way of costs from an opponent than it is obliged to pay to its own lawyers. A number of exceptions have been carved out of the indemnity principle by legislation or case law. There are conflicting views as to whether this principle (a) now serves any valuable purpose or (b) should be abolished. See PR paragraphs 3.4.14, 3.5.48, 10.14.4 and 53.1.8. The issue is of importance because in recent years the indemnity principle has generated extensive and expensive satellite litigation. It sometimes enables unsuccessful parties to escape liability for costs on what may be seen as technical grounds.

1.2   <u>What the indemnity principle must not be confused with.</u> There are two areas of confusion to be avoided:

(i)   The costs shifting rule or "loser pays" rule is sometimes referred to as the "indemnity rule" or even the "indemnity principle". This is something entirely different from the indemnity principle which is under discussion in the present chapter. The terminology has sometimes given rise to confusion during the Costs Review. Indeed during one of the seminars I noted that some speakers were using the term "indemnity principle" to mean the common law principle under discussion in this chapter, whereas others were using the term to mean costs shifting.

(ii)   The "indemnity basis" is also a concept entirely separate from the indemnity principle discussed in this chapter. The indemnity basis for assessing costs is explained in chapter 3 above and in PR paragraph 3.4.21.

1.3   <u>Legislation.</u> Section 60(3) of the Solicitors Act 1974 provides that where there is a *"contentious business agreement"* between solicitor and clients, *"a client shall not be entitled to recover from any other person under an order for the payment of any costs to which a contentious business agreement relates more than the amount payable by him to his solicitor in respect of those costs under the agreement"*. Section 51(2) of the Senior Courts Act 1981 (the "1981 Act") enables the Civil Procedure Rule Committee to make provision *"for securing that the amount awarded to a party in respect of costs to be paid by him to such representatives is not limited to what would have been payable to them if he had not been awarded costs"*.

1.4   <u>The Government's position in 1999.</u> Section 51(2) was added to the 1981 Act by section 31 of the Access to Justice Act 1999 (the "1999 Act"). The explanatory notes to the 1999 Act[83] stated that section 31 was a general provision allowing rules of court to limit or abolish the indemnity principle. The explanatory notes refer to the exceptions which have been carved out of the indemnity principle and conclude:

> "The Government believes that the partial survival of the principle is anomalous; section 31 is intended to rationalise the position."

1.5   Civil Justice Council. At the various costs forums held by the Civil Justice Council (the "CJC") since 2001, most attendees have favoured abolition of the indemnity principle.

2. VIEWS EXPRESSED DURING PHASE 2

2.1   During Phase 2, as during Phase 1, forceful submissions have been made on both sides of this debate.

2.2   Personal injury lawyers. Most, but not all, personal injury lawyers appear to favour abolition. In the Personal Injury Bar Association survey of members, there were 146 votes for abolition and 120 votes for retention. The Association of Personal Injury Lawyers ("APIL") has consistently campaigned for abolition. APIL points out that the principle has led to confusion and has provided the basis for technical challenges by liability insurers, whilst affording no benefit or protection to claimants. APIL argues that there are other mechanisms to control costs. One firm of personal injury solicitors with a substantial claimant and defendant practice argues that the indemnity principle is directed at the wrong target: "*it is solely directed at the receiving party's liability to pay rather than the question of whether the work was actually done*".

2.3   The Law Society. The Law Society states:

> "The indemnity principle was, in the Law Society's view, the main cause of the 'costs wars'. This principle has, in effect, led insurers to challenge the terms of solicitors' retainers and, in effect, to gain a windfall if those are, for some reason, technically defective. Their attempts to do have resulted in the many hundreds of 'costs only' litigation cases which have plagued the civil justice system for several years and which have unnecessarily taken up the resources of the county courts, the SCCO[84] and the Court of Appeal.

> In the Law Society's view, it is inherently wrong and contrary to the public interest for the unenforceability of a solicitor's retainer to result in a windfall for the unsuccessful defendant. The work has been done by the solicitor perfectly legitimately and he or she should be paid for it."

The Chester and North Wales Law Society[85] argues that the indemnity principle should be abolished, at least in relation to personal injury cases.

2.4   Supporters of the principle. The City of London Law Society's Litigation Committee (the "CLLSLC") argues that the indemnity principle is necessary in order to prevent the injustice of winning parties recovering a windfall. The CLLSLC adds that recent case law has largely disposed of the technical arguments that were being

---

[83] Prepared by the Lord Chancellor's Department (the predecessor to the Ministry of Justice).
[84] The Senior Courts Costs Office.
[85] Adopting the Phase 2 submission of its former president.

used. The Chancery Bar Association (the "ChBA") argues that the indemnity principle should be retained, as follows

> "While it might be tempting to some to get rid of the indemnity principle, such a step would be detrimental. It is evident from common experience (and as a matter of common sense) that the most effective control on costs is personal liability, or potential personal liability, for costs. This can only be achieved by the existence of the indemnity principle.
>
> The indemnity principle has or should have a function as a 'control' over costs – the facts that someone is legally liable to pay the costs gives some prospect of the costs being controlled at a reasonable amount. As the courts have commented, notoriously in CFA/BTE/ATE[86] insurance cases, costs and success fees appear to run out of control where the client has no real liability for costs.
>
> The indemnity principle also has or should have a valuable function as a measure of judging what is a reasonable amount of costs – if there is a legal liability then there is some prospect that the receiving party would have kept costs to what someone in his position can afford and considers to be reasonable and proportionate in the context of the litigation."

The ChBA then points out that, absent the indemnity principle, parties could enter into retrospective retainers at more favourable rates after the outcome of the litigation was known.

2.5 <u>Views of district judges.</u> The Association of Her Majesty's District Judges argues for abolition, as do some individual district judges in their separate submissions. District Judge Mackenzie writes:

> "I know that many are wedded to the idea that the indemnity principle should remain. I believe that is wrong. The Indemnity principle has long since had its day. It causes far more problems than it solves. As a check on costs claimed inter partes it is useless except in those cases where solicitors and others fall foul of it by error and opposing parties take legally successful but pretty unmeritorious advantage of the slip. It has already been abrogated in a number of ways via CFAs and otherwise. The way solicitors have been forced to artificially construct their retainers so as not to fall foul of the indemnity principle is something which in my view brings lawyers into disrepute. It is time it went completely."

2.6 <u>Work by in-house lawyers.</u> The managers of a P&I Club[87] offering Freight, Defence and Demurrage ("FD&D") insurance cover submit that the indemnity principle operates to their members' detriment. This is because their members have access to the assistance of in-house lawyers of the FD&D department in return for their annual membership subscription. However, despite successfully pursuing or defending a claim, their members may face difficulties in recovering costs in respect of the work done by those lawyers. Nevertheless, those same members remain at risk of adverse costs in cases which they lose. The managers believe that this unequal positioning of the parties is unjust.

---

[86] Conditional fee agreement/before-the-event/after-the-event.
[87] A Protection and Indemnity Club: an insurance mutual which provides collective self insurance to its members, with the members pooling their risks in order to obtain "at cost" insurance cover.

2.7   Manchester seminar. At the Manchester seminar on 3rd July 2009 there was a debate about the indemnity principle during the panel session at the end of the day. At the conclusion of the debate 12 people voted in favour of retaining the indemnity principle, 36 voted for abolition and 12 abstained. Those present at the panel session included 21 claimant solicitors and 17 defendant solicitors.

2.8   Cook on Costs. His Honour Michael Cook in his well known textbook on costs[88] argues forcefully for abolition of the indemnity principle. See chapter 17, paragraphs 17.12 to 17.13. The nub of the argument is in the first part of paragraph 17.13, where Mr Cook states:

> "The method of financing litigation should be a privileged matter between the client and the solicitor. Funding may or may not be under a conditional fee agreement, which itself may be 'no win, no fee' or 'no win, lesser fee' or some other formula, it may be by a trade union or a maiden aunt and it may involve after-the-event insurance or be covered by legal expenses insurance ('before-the-event insurance'), none of which should be of concern to the court or other party.
>
> Costs recoverable between the parties should be such sum as is reasonable and proportionate having regard to the subject matter of the litigation regardless of the terms under which those services have been provided."

3. ASSESSMENT

3.1   The indemnity principle has assumed a totemic character. Supporters maintain that the indemnity principle is vital in the battle to control excessive costs and they rally round it as their standard. Opponents see the indemnity principle not only as a relic of the nineteenth century, but also as the root cause of satellite litigation and wastage of costs; they maintain that it must be abolished.

3.2   I have (intermittently) spent three months debating this issue with experts on both sides of the fence. I have attempted on a number of occasions to find some middle ground or to arrive at a compromise which the distinguished lawyers and judges in both camps would find acceptable. The quest is hopeless. I must come down firmly on one or other side of the fence.

3.3   My conclusion. In my view, provided that CPR rule 44.4 is amended so as to constitute an effective control on recoverable costs, the indemnity principle should be abrogated.

3.4   Reasons. I reach this conclusion for seven reasons:

(i)   Over the last two decades the indemnity principle has generated much satellite litigation at huge cost to the civil justice system and with no perceptible benefit either to court users or to society.[89]

(ii)   On occasions the indemnity principle has enabled liability insurers to gain windfalls. They have knocked out altogether claims for costs in respect of work properly and competently done on behalf of successful claimants.[90]

---

[88] Cook on Costs by His Honour Michael J Cook, LexisNexis, 2010.
[89] See the history of the Costs War set out in PR chapter 3.
[90] See PR chapter 3.

(iii)   It is clear from all the submissions made and the evidence received during the Costs Review that despite the repeal of the Conditional Fee Agreements Regulations 2000, technical arguments based upon the indemnity principle still abound at costs assessment hearings. Given the ingenuity of lawyers, so long as the indemnity principle is there to tempt them, such unedifying battles are likely to continue into the future.

(iv)   Although the indemnity principle has an obvious appeal, both in logic and justice, history supports the view that the courts can assess costs properly without it. Although the principle has been recognised for two centuries, in the latter half of the twentieth century it was rarely raised on taxation or detailed assessment until the early 1990s. In the experience of Jeremy Morgan QC (who is one of my assessors) it was the Divisional Court decision in *British Waterways Board v Norman*[91] that revived it. Once this decision had been circulated amongst costs draftsmen, indemnity principle challenges became commonplace: see PR paragraphs 3.5.3 and 3.5.4.

(v)   A set of rules exists to ensure that receiving parties do not recover more by way costs than reasonable and proportionate remuneration for the work which has been done. There is no need for any additional common law principle to hover in the background.

(vi)   The indemnity principle does not provide an effective longstop to prevent over-recovery in cases where such protection may be appropriate: see e.g. chapter 28 below, paragraph 3.5. Nor has it prevented claimants from recovering windfalls in cases such as *Lamont v Burton*[92] and *Crane v Canons Leisure*.[93]

(vii)   The indemnity principle has been eroded over the years by a series of statutory exceptions. Examples are the legal aid scheme, CFA Lites[94], the fixed recoverable costs scheme and the *pro bono* costs rules.[95] It must be questioned whether a principle which is so frequently overridden continues to serve any valuable purpose.

3.5   In my view, it is better that the rules should clearly set out what costs are recoverable in any situation, rather than rely upon a somewhat shadowy principle derived from case law, which is subject to an ever growing number of exceptions.

3.6   <u>Amendment to CPR rule 44.4(1).</u> I recommend that CPR rule 44.4 be amended by substituting a new sub-paragraph (1) along the following lines:[96]

> "When assessing the amounts of recoverable costs, the court will, subject to the following provisions of this rule, allow reasonable amounts in respect of work actually and reasonably done and services actually and reasonably supplied for the benefit of the receiving party. The court will assess those amounts on either the standard basis or the indemnity basis."

I make no reference in this suggested draft to "proportionate", because that concept is dealt with elsewhere, namely in rule 1.1(2)(c) and rule 44.4(2).[97] Consequential

---

[91] [1993] 26 HLR 232.
[92] [2007] EWCA Civ 429; [2007] 1 W.L.R. 2814.
[93] [2007] EWCA Civ 1352; [2008] 1 W.L.R. 2549.
[94] As to which, see PR paragraph 3.5.28 and CPR rule 43.2(3).
[95] See chapter 33 below at paragraphs 4.8 to 4.10.
[96] I say "along the following lines", because the precise wording must be a matter for the Rule Committee.
[97] See chapter 3 above.

amendments will also be required to rule 44.4(2) and 44.4(3) in order to remove any reference to costs having been "incurred".

3.7   There is no reason why the court should not have regard to the contract of retainer between the receiving party and its solicitors.[98] The rules should probably make this clear. Provision must also be made in the rules for cancellation fees, which are sometimes reasonably incurred, but do not relate to work actually done. Counsel's brief fee in a case which settles the night before trial falls into the same category. It seems to me, however, that these are all matters which should be dealt with explicitly in the rules or the Costs Practice Direction. Reliance upon the indemnity principle or upon exceptions carved out of the indemnity principle does not assist.

3.8   <u>Abrogation of indemnity principle.</u> Once CPR rule 44.4(1) has been amended to provide proper protection for the paying party, I recommend that the common law indemnity principle be abrogated.

3.9   Views differ as to what measures are necessary in order to achieve abolition of the indemnity principle. It has been pointed out that a number of statutory provisions proceed upon the basis that the indemnity principle exists. A comprehensive review of all primary and secondary legislation must be carried out, in order to ensure that any statutory provisions which go beyond the proposed new rule 44.4(1) are either repealed or are amended appropriately. The technical details of how, as a matter of mechanics, to achieve abrogation are complex and lie beyond the scope of this review.

4. RECOMMENDATION

4.1   I recommend that the common law indemnity principle be abrogated.

---

[98] For example, it is unlikely that the court will regard as reasonable any hourly rates which are higher than the rates which that party has agreed to pay to its own lawyers.

CHAPTER 6. COSTS COUNCIL

INDEX

1. INTRODUCTION

1.1   Definitions. In this chapter I refer to the Civil Justice Council as the "CJC", the Ministry of Justice as the "MoJ", the Advisory Committee on Civil Costs as the "ACCC", the Senior Courts Costs Office[99] as the "SCCO" and guideline hourly rates for solicitors as "GHRs". I refer to the Civil Procedure Rule Committee as the "Rule Committee".

1.2   CJC recommendation. In its report *"Improved Access to Justice - Funding Options and Proportionate Costs"*[100] the CJC recommended at recommendation 20:

> "A Costs Council should be established to oversee the introduction, implementation and monitoring of the reforms we recommend and in particular to establish and review annually the recoverable fixed fees in the fast track and guideline hourly rates between the parties in the multi-track. Membership of the Costs Council should include representatives of the leading stakeholder organisations involved in the funding and payment of costs and should be chaired by a member of the judiciary."

1.3   This recommendation gained the support of both practitioners and senior judges at the CJC Costs Forum held on 1st and 2nd March 2006. Following that forum Senior Costs Judge Peter Hurst wrote a paper dated 27th March 2006, entitled *"Costs Council Recommendation"*. In that paper he proposed that a Costs Council be set up with powers to publish authoritative guideline rates. The Senior Costs Judge proposed that the Costs Council should have the following constitution:

- The Costs Council should be chaired by a member of the judiciary with experience of the law relating to legal costs.

- The members of the Costs Council should include representatives of the Bar, the Law Society, legal practitioners, the insurance industry, both after-the-event and liability insurers; the Association of British Insurers, trade unions and one or more academics with expertise in economics and/or statistics.

---

[99] Formerly the Supreme Court Costs Office.
[100] CJC, August 2005.

- The Costs Council should be given the power to co-opt other persons with special expertise to assist with particular aspects of its work.

1.4   The Senior Costs Judge proposed that the remit of the Costs Council should include:

- Making recommendations to the Lord Chancellor on the appropriate structure for the payment of costs, and figures for any predictable or guideline rates.

- Reviewing economic criteria for determining predictable or guideline rates.

- Establishing a review mechanism for predictable or guideline rates.

- Undertaking discussions with representative groups of civil justice stakeholders to assist and inform the recommendations.

1.5   The CJC repeated the recommendation that a Costs Council should be established in Appendix 1 to its June 2007 paper entitled "*Improved Access to Justice – Funding Options and Proportionate Costs; The Future Funding of Litigation – Alternative Funding Structures*" at recommendation 20.

1.6   In the event the recommendation of the CJC and the Senior Costs Judge was not implemented. Instead, during 2007, the ACCC was set up. The functions and work of the ACCC are summarised in PR paragraphs 52.2.6 to 52.2.12.

1.7   Similar recommendation made in Victoria.   The Victorian Law Reform Commission has recently come to conclusions similar to those of the CJC. In its recent Civil Justice Review Report[101] the Victorian Law Reform Commission recommends as follows:

> "A specialist Costs Council should be established, as a division of the Civil Justice Council. The Costs Council, in consultation with stakeholder groups, would: (a) review the impact of the commission's implemented recommendations about costs; (b) investigate the additional matters in relation to costs referred to in the commission's report, including those matters raised in submissions; (c) carry out or commission further research in relation to costs; and (d) consider such other reforms in relation to costs as the council considers appropriate."

The reasoning which underlies this recommendation, as set out in chapter 11 of the report, is the need to provide a rational mechanism for the control of litigation costs.

1.8   Recent paper by the Costs and Funding Committee of the Civil Justice Council.   I have been looking more closely at the question of a Costs Council during Phase 3 of the Costs Review, in the light of (a) the emerging recommendations for fast track fixed costs and (b) concerns expressed during Phase 2 concerning the mechanism for setting GHRs. In response to my inquiries, the Costs and Funding Committee of the CJC formed a sub-group (the "sub-group") to give further consideration to the possibility of a Costs Council. In a paper for the Costs Review dated 19th November 2009, the sub-group reinforces the CJC's recommendation set out at paragraph 1.2 above. The sub-group considers that, as a standing body, a Costs Council should be able to provide "*continuity of treatment of subjects within its*

---

[101] "*Civil Justice Review*", Report 14 published by the Victorian Law Commission in 2008, at page 692. This is discussed in PR paragraph 58.4.13.

remit, and to develop expertise over time". However, this potential will depend on a number of factors, including the calibre and experience of membership, solid arrangements for monitoring and research, and the supply of reliable data on a timely basis. The view of the sub-group is that the area of fixed and predictable costs would alone give a "*clear role*" for a Costs Council.

2. PROPOSAL FOR A COSTS COUNCIL

(i) Need for an independent body

2.1   If the recommendations later in this report are accepted, some independent and authoritative body will need to undertake the following tasks every year:

(i)   set GHRs for summary assessments and detailed assessments;[102]

(ii)   review the matrices of fixed costs for the fast track; and

(iii)   review the overall upper limit for fast track costs.

2.2 The above tasks will, collectively, be a far more onerous operation than that currently undertaken by the ACCC. The ACCC's current role is limited to setting GHRs for summary assessments.

2.3   It would, of course, be possible for the ACCC to undertake the expanded role set out in paragraph 2.1 above. However, in my view and in the view of all seven of my assessors, it would be far better if that expanded role were undertaken by a Costs Council, rather than the ACCC. The present ACCC has a small number of members, some of whom represent particular interest groups. The chairman is an economist of outstanding ability and expertise in matters of finance, but with no intimate experience of litigation costs. I am told that the proceedings of the ACCC tend to be dominated by "trench warfare".

2.4   If a Costs Council is set up, it should be chaired by a judge or other senior person, who has long experience of the operation of the costs rules and costs assessment. It is appropriate for the Costs Council to include representatives of stakeholder groups. However, its membership should not be dominated by vested interests. It is important that all members be of high calibre and appropriate experience, so that the recommendations of the Costs Council will be authoritative. The Costs Council, like the Civil Procedure Rule Committee, should include a consumer representative. It should also, in my view, include an economist and a representative of the MoJ. It is unrealistic to expect the Costs Council to act on the basis of consensus, because of the conflicting interests which will be represented within it. The chairman will sometimes act as mediator and sometimes as arbitrator between opposing views, so as to ensure that fair and consistent recommendations are made on costs levels.

2.5   If a Costs Council is established, it will be able to take on wider functions. In particular, the Costs Council could set or give guidance upon recoverable fees for counsel. Whether it should deal with these on the basis of fixed fees or hourly rates or a combination of both would be a matter for the Costs Council to consider. The Costs Council could also set or give guidance upon recoverable fees for experts.

---

[102] GHRs at the moment are applicable only to summary assessment: see PR chapter 52, section 2. In chapters 44 and 45 below I recommend that GHRs be set for both summary and detailed assessment.

(ii) Review of guideline hourly rates

2.6 It must now be accepted that the level of GHRs is a critical element in the civil justice system, because solicitors' profit costs account for a high percentage of total litigation costs: see the first of Professor Kritzer's slides at the London seminar.[103] It will be the function of the Costs Council to strike a proper balance between the interests of lawyers and litigants. It will also be the function of the Costs Council to ensure that the GHRs for both detailed and summary assessment are set at proportionate levels, in order to do justice as between paying parties and receiving parties.

2.7 If the above recommendation is accepted, the Costs Council will have to make some robust decisions in order to redress existing anomalies. Some of the matters which will have to be addressed are identified in chapter 44 below.

(iii) Review of fast track fixed costs

2.8 Many respondents during Phase 2 have stressed the importance of there being regular reviews of fast track costs. I agree that such reviews are important, indeed essential to a regime of fixed costs in the fast track. Even if the review concludes that no change in fixed costs is required in a particular year (e.g. because fixed costs are linked to damages which rise with inflation), it is necessary that the review should take place.

2.9 If the reviews of fixed costs are going to be credible and authoritative, it is necessary they be carried out by a well informed and independent body, which commands the respect of all parties. In my view, a Costs Council of the kind proposed above would be such a body and would be able to maintain a credible and effective fixed costs regime over the years to come.

2.10 The recommendation in this chapter for the establishment of a Costs Council should be seen as closely linked to the recommendations in chapter 15 below for introducing fixed costs in the fast track.

(iv) Review of other matters

2.11 Litigants in person. In chapter 14 below it is recommended that the hourly rate for litigants in person should be increased to £20 and that such rate should be subject to periodic review. If this recommendation is accepted, then the periodic review should fall within the remit of the Costs Council.

2.12 Medical reports in fast track cases. In chapter 15 below it is recommended that the sums recoverable for obtaining medical reports and medical records should be capped at the levels currently specified in the Medical Reporting Organisation Agreement.[104] It is further recommended that those fixed maximum costs should be

---

[103] See Professor Kritzer's slides, entitled "The American Contingency Fee Regime: Misperceptions and Realities", from the London seminar on 10th July 2009. The slides can be viewed on the Costs Review website at http://www.judiciary.gov.uk/about_judiciary/cost-review/london.htm. The first slide is a pie chart presentation of PR appendices 1, 2, 8 and 26. This shows that lawyers' fees (solicitors and counsel combined) account for between 76% and 89% of legal costs. Of the lawyers' fees in appendices 1, 2 and 8, solicitors' fees account for approximately 80% to 85% and counsel's fees account for the remainder (i.e. 15% to 20%). There is no separate figure for counsel's fees in appendix 26, but counsel's fees in appendix 26 are likely to be materially lower because most of those cases would have settled without going to a court hearing.
[104] See chapter 15 below paragraph 5.22.

regularly reviewed. If these recommendations are accepted, then the Costs Council would be an appropriate body to carry out such reviews.

2.13 <u>Counsel's fees.</u> The Costs Council should also regularly review the recoverable fees of counsel.

2.14 If the costs of civil litigation are going to be brought under control, in a manner which is fair to all parties, further issues requiring review by the Costs Council may arise from time to time.

(v) Structure and administration

2.15 <u>Nature of the Costs Council.</u> The Costs Council could either be set up as a free standing body or, alternatively, as an adjunct to the CJC. I would support either approach. The latter course, however, may be preferred as involving less expense.

2.16 <u>To whom should the Costs Council report?</u> In my view, it would be appropriate for the Costs Council to report to the Master of the Rolls as Head of Civil Justice, Chairman of the Rule Committee and Chairman of the CJC. In so far as the Costs Council makes recommendations on matters within the remit of the Secretary of State, the Costs Council should report to the Secretary of State.

2.17 <u>Implementation of the Costs Council's recommendations.</u> The Rule Committee, acting on the advice of the Costs Council, should make whatever changes may be required to the fixed costs set out in CPR Part 45[105] with effect from the 1st April in each year. That would dovetail in with the normal date for amendments to the CPR.

2.18 The Master of the Rolls, as Head of Civil Justice and Chairman of the Rule Committee, currently issues new GHRs each year, acting on the advice of the ACCC. I recommend that in future years he should do so, acting on the advice of the Costs Council. In order to harmonise the dates when changes occur, I recommend that the new GHRs should come into effect on 1st April in each year. This date will coincide with the date of the CPR amendments.

3. RESOURCE IMPLICATIONS

(i) Costs saved

3.1 <u>Savings on ACCC.</u> The current administration of the ACCC is funded by the MoJ (Civil Law and Justice Division). The MoJ provides the secretariat for the ACCC, as well as any research requested by the ACCC.

3.2 <u>Fewer detailed assessments.</u> If there is a complete fixed costs regime in the fast track, there will be a reduced number of detailed assessments. The only cases where detailed assessment will be required will be exceptional cases, where the fixed costs regime does not apply: for example, cases falling within the escape clause or cases where indemnity costs are ordered. It is estimated within the SCCO that this will cause a reduction of about 700 detailed assessments per year at the SCCO. This reduction would free up the time of costs judges and costs officers. There would also be a significant drop in the number of detailed assessments undertaken by district

---

[105] If the recommendations set out in chapter 15 are accepted, CPR Part 45 will provide fixed costs for all fast track cases.

judges and regional costs judges at court centres outside London, but no estimate is currently available of what that saving might be.

3.3   Fewer costs only proceedings. If there is a complete fixed costs regime in the fast track, there will be a greatly reduced number of costs only proceedings. The numbers of costs only proceedings currently brought in the county courts are not collected within the Judicial Statistics published by the MoJ. However, it is clear to me that a very large number of costs only proceedings are currently being brought in fast track cases. This is illustrated by PR appendix 26, which records details of all cases resolved by one insurer during the year ended 30th November 2008. There were 11,185 such cases, the vast majority of which were fast track personal injury cases. Out of those 11,185 cases, 1,023 cases (12.94%) went to costs only proceedings. If my proposals for fixed costs in respect of fast track personal injury cases[106] are accepted, such costs only proceedings will not be required. For further analysis of the data in PR appendix 26, see chapter 2 above and the tables in appendix 1 to this report.

3.4   If my recommendations for costs management in respect of multi-track cases[107] are accepted, costs judges and regional costs judges whose time has been freed up could be redeployed to assist in costs management. For example, they could sit as assessors at costs management hearings.

3.5   Savings to the public purse. In a large number of cases where the defendant is a public body, there will be significant savings in costs liabilities if there is an effective Costs Council performing the above functions. None of the data provided or collected during the Costs Review makes it possible to quantify those savings to the public purse.

(ii) Additional costs

3.6   Secretarial and administration. The new Costs Council would require secretarial and administrative support. This could be funded by the MoJ. Alternatively, the Costs Council could be established as an adjunct of the CJC and so could make use of the CJC's secretariat and facilities.

3.7   Members' expenses. Members of the Costs Council would expect their travel and incidental expenses to be met. However, they would not be paid for the time which they devote to the business of the Costs Council. They would be in a similar position to members of the Rule Committee and members of the CJC, who freely give up their time to this form of public service. In the case of judicial members, arrangements will have to be made to cover cases which would have been listed before them on days when they are attending Costs Council meetings.

3.8   There would be no accommodation costs. The Costs Council could meet in the rooms currently used for Rule Committee meetings or CJC meetings.

3.9   Monitoring and gathering information. This will be an important ongoing task for the staff who serve the Costs Council. The Costs Council will have to gather information, with the assistance of the Law Society, the Solicitors Regulation Authority and the Bar Council, as to what it costs lawyers to run their practices.

---

[106] Set out in chapter 15 below.
[107] Set out in chapter 40 below.

4. RECOMMENDATION

4.1　　I recommend that the ACCC be disbanded and that a Costs Council be established.

REVIEW OF
CIVIL LITIGATION COSTS

PART 2. FUNDING CIVIL LITIGATION

CHAPTER 7. LEGAL AID

INDEX

1. INTRODUCTION

1.1   Preliminary Report. Chapter 12 of the Preliminary Report summarises the history of legal aid and the current statutory regime under which the Legal Services Commission (the "LSC") operates.[1]

1.2   In this chapter I refer to the legal aid scheme which has existed under successive statutes since the Legal Aid and Advice Act 1949 as the "Scheme".

1.3   Recent and current reviews of legal aid. In 2005 and 2006 Lord Carter carried out a review of legal aid procurement, publishing his final report entitled "*Legal aid: A market-based approach to reform*"[2] on 13th July 2006. Sir Ian Magee is currently undertaking a review of legal aid delivery, and is due to report in January 2010.

2. SUBMISSIONS DURING PHASE 2

2.1   Legal Services Commission. In a letter dated 20th July 2009 the LSC stated that it would not be submitting a formal response. However, it welcomes the current review of civil litigation costs and notes that any reforms consequent upon this review will impact upon the context in which the legal aid scheme operates. The LSC then adds:

---

[1] The Supreme Court has recently held that where the LSC funds a litigant who is successful, that decision must ordinarily be seen to carry with it something close to an assurance that the LSC will continue to support him in any subsequent appeal by the unsuccessful party: see *R (E) v Governing Body of JFS* [2009] UKSC 1; [2009] 1 WLR 2353.

[2] Available online at http://www.legalaidprocurementreview.gov.uk/publications.htm.

"On the other hand, financial pressures on the legal aid budget, like all other areas of public expenditure, are particularly intense at the moment. We would have concerns over any wider reforms, which might result in an increase in pressures on the legal aid fund, especially in areas like clinical negligence where both legal aid and private funding mechanisms are currently available. Any such pressures could lead to the need to make savings in other areas."

2.2   Law Society. The Law Society states:

"The Society opposed the removal of legal aid for the majority of civil work. Regrettably, it also recognizes that, particularly in the present economic circumstances, it is inconceivable that it will ever be replaced.

Legal aid is an important way of providing access to justice to those who could not afford it. However, the proportion of the population eligible for public funding and the types of cases for which such funding is available have decreased significantly since 2000."

2.3   The Law Society notes two criticisms, which were of legal aid: (i) a substantial portion of middle England[3] were financially not eligible for legal aid, yet could not afford to litigate; (ii) in most cases there was one way costs shifting, which meant that successful defendants did not get their costs.

2.4   Civil liberties solicitors.   The head of the Civil Liberties Department and Police Actions Team at a major firm of solicitors states that most of his department's cases are publicly funded, because conditional fee agreements as a form of funding are not well suited to civil rights work. In relation to legal aid rates, he comments:

"The litigation charging rates recommended by the Supreme Court Costs Office are considerably more than double the rates recoverable from the Legal Services Commission even for a junior solicitor. As a consequence, my department relies for its financial survival on its ability to recover *inter partes* costs in cases where the claimant has been successful in litigation...

My submission in essence is that <u>Cost-shifting on successful cases subsidises legal aid work, and legal aid work is essential in terms of access to justice, holding public authorities to account and to the bringing of cases that clarify/develop the law.</u> A department conducting primarily publicly funded civil litigation (whether against the police, in housing matters, clinical negligence, etc) could simply not survive at the rates paid by the Legal Services Commission."

2.5   The head of the Civil Liberties Department and Police Actions Team also draws attention to the gap between legal aid lawyers and those in other forms of private practice. He adds:

"Legal aid lawyers earn less [than lawyers in other forms of private practice] and are in a precarious position due to the sustainability pressures placed on the practices in which they choose to work. I sincerely hope that the final report will reflect this."

---

[3] I.e. MINELAs; see chapter 10 paragraph 1.5 below.

2.6   Housing practitioners. A number of housing practitioners, both in their submissions and at the fixed costs seminar, have drawn my attention to the low hourly rates paid by the LSC for advice, assistance and representation in connection with housing matters. They maintain that costs orders which they obtain in successful cases against local authorities or other landlords subsidise their other work.

2.7   "Legal Help" in housing cases. One experienced housing solicitor writes:

> "Although this is a review of litigation costs, any analysis of legal aid must recognise the part played by the *Legal Help* system in solving disputes before the need for proceedings to be issued or by solving them, after issue, without a lawyer going on the court record as acting for a party. Thus, many possession actions are dealt with by practitioners without the issue of public funding and many disrepair cases are disposed of, with or without the issue of public funding but without the issue of proceedings."

2.8   Citizens Advice. I did not receive any written submission from Citizens Advice Bureaux during Phase 2 but I did hold a meeting with the National Association of Citizens Advice Bureaux ("Citizens Advice") on 25th November 2009. A summary of the meeting is set out in chapter 1 paragraph 4.4 above. One proposal made by Citizens Advice at that meeting was that a provision should be added to the Funding Code[4] whereby judges would have the power to make an order for legal aid in any civil case where this would be in the public interest,[5] for example where there is a potential issue under article 6 of the European Convention on Human Rights (the "ECHR").[6]

3. COMMENT

3.1   Financial eligibility for legal aid. The Law Society's point about the diminishing financial eligibility for civil legal aid is well made. When the legal aid scheme was set up, approximately 80% of the population was eligible for civil legal aid. In 1986 some 63% of the population was eligible for civil legal aid. By 2000 that figure had dropped to 50%. By 2007 the figure had dropped to 29%. In other words more than two thirds of the population were ineligible for legal aid on financial grounds.[7] The subsequent downturn in the economy and resulting changes to people's income and capital has however lead to an increase in the eligible population figure to 36%.[8]

3.2   Legal aid is still available for some key areas of litigation, in particular clinical negligence, housing cases and judicial review. It is vital that legal aid remains in these areas. However, the continued tightening of financial eligibility criteria, so as to exclude people who could not possibly afford to litigate, inhibits access to justice in those key areas. In my view any further tightening of the financial eligibility criteria would be unacceptable. It is not within my terms of reference to make recommendations about eligibility for legal aid and I do not do so. However, I place on record my firm view that it would be quite wrong to tighten the eligibility criteria

---

[4] The Funding Code is the set of rules used by the LSC to determine which cases to fund through civil legal aid.
[5] See chapter 1 paragraph 4.4(vi) above.
[6] Article 6 protects the right to a fair trial.
[7] See "*The Justice Gap. Whatever Happened to Legal Aid?*" by Steve Hynes and Jon Robins, LAG 2009 at pages 70-71.
[8] Ministry of Justice models of civil eligibility based on the Family Resources Survey, 2009.

further, so that an even larger percentage of the population falls outside the legal aid net.

3.3   Positive features. Having set out my concerns, I should also draw attention to the positive features of our legal aid system. Whilst eligibility levels restrict funding to the poorest members of society, the number of people helped by the Scheme has held up well. In 2008/09, the 60th anniversary year for the Scheme, the LSC funded 1.16 million civil acts of assistance, a significant increase over the previous year. A total civil spend of £887 million reflects the fact that it remains one of the most comprehensive schemes in the world, as confirmed by recent studies.[9]

3.4   Cross-subsidisation. The fact that legal aid lawyers use costs orders in successful cases as a means of subsidising legal aid work is an important matter, which does impact directly upon my terms of reference. At the fixed costs seminar held on 22nd July 2009, a number of housing lawyers relied upon the fact of cross-subsidisation as an argument against fixing costs in housing cases. In my view, it would not be right to exempt housing cases from the fast track fixed costs regime, which was recommended by Lord Woolf 13 years ago and which should now be implemented. Whilst I accept that there is cross subsidy in the sense that legal aid lawyers depend on the recoverability of *inter partes* costs to make their business as a whole profitable, it does not follow that *inter partes* costs should be artificially inflated in response to the level of legal aid remuneration. First, there are no areas where legal aid does or should act as the sole means of funding a case. *Inter partes* rates as recommended in this review must provide fair and proportionate remuneration for public and privately funded cases alike. Secondly, concerns about the availability of legal aid providers is not a reason for holding back the move to fixed costs in the fast track. Fixed costs could be implemented in principle for the fast track at a level which is on average no less attractive for claimant firms. However, for some categories of case covered by legal aid, in particular housing, the provider base may be less robust than mainstream personal injury, and we should therefore proceed with caution.

3.5   It is certainly my view that legal aid remuneration rates should be set at a level which, in light of the levels of *inter partes* costs available and all other circumstances, enables competent and well organised lawyers to carry out such work. Whether such rates are currently set at a sufficient level is not for me to judge within the scope of this review. Although practitioners argue the case powerfully, the LSC reports that it is able to secure contracts for housing providers across the country under existing remuneration rules whenever gaps in supply are identified. Indeed, in 2008/09 the number of providers with housing contracts increased by 4% while housing acts of assistance rose 10% and legal aid certificates by 7.5%.[10] To get to the bottom of this debate I would need to conduct the sort of economic analysis of profitability of legal aid work which was undertaken as part of the Carter Review.[11] To undertake that form of exercise again is outside the practical scope of this review.

3.6   The proposal by Citizens Advice. The proposal made by Citizens Advice is set out in paragraph 2.8 above. I have considered this proposal with the assistance of my assessors and I have come to the conclusion that such a measure is neither viable nor necessary. First, the amount of money available to the LSC for the funding of legal aid is limited. If judges were given a power to order legal aid in any civil case (or even in any civil case raising a potential article 6 issue), there could be no effective control

---

[9] International Comparison of Publicly Funded Legal Services and Justice Systems, Ministry of Justice Research Series 14/9, October 2009.
[10] LSC Statistical Information 2008/09.
[11] Lord Carter's Review of Legal Aid Procurement, July 2006.

over the funds which the LSC would be required to expend in order to comply with such orders. Decisions about whether to grant legal aid in a particular case have to be made by the LSC in the light of the funds available. Secondly, the present legal aid scheme already has safeguards in place. Cases raising article 6 issues are generally ones which are within the scope of legal aid in any event (family cases, cases where an individual's liberty is at stake etc). The existing legal aid scheme is designed to be ECHR compliant and the LSC already takes into account any potential breaches of article 6 when deciding whether to fund a particular case.

3.7   Comments of the Master of the Rolls. Lord Neuberger of Abbotsbury MR, in his speech to the Law Society and Bar Council Opening of the Legal Year Seminar on 30th September 2009, said:

> "Today, not least because of the effects of the credit crunch, many countries are finding it difficult to fund legal aid. Economic reality must, of course, play a part. It must play a part in any future reform. But we should still ask how we manage to find ourselves in the situation that the total (criminal and civil) legal aid budget for 2008 came to no more than the total NHS budget for two weeks.[12] Reverting to Heber Smith,[13] the rule of law and the defence of the realm are the most fundamental and well-established duties of government: if either fails, the more recently developed, high-profile and expensive government services, such as the provision of health, education and social security, become impossible or of little value. Why some might ask, as a society, are we willing to invest so little on legal aid, when both the unacceptably unfair effects on individuals and the fundamental risks to society of the denial of justice to many citizens are so profound?"

I entirely agree with those comments of the Master of the Rolls.

4. CONCLUSION

4.1   Some respondents during the Costs Review have urged me to recommend that legal aid be restored to at least the pre-2000 levels.[14] Whilst I would welcome such a restoration, I do not regard such a recommendation (if made) as having any realistic chance of implementation. Also a review of the legal aid system does not fall within my terms of reference.

4.2   I do not make any recommendation in this chapter for the expansion or restoration of legal aid. I do, however, stress the vital necessity of making no further cutbacks in legal aid availability or eligibility. The legal aid system plays a crucial role in promoting access to justice at proportionate costs in key areas. The statistics set out elsewhere in this report demonstrate that the overall costs of litigation on legal aid are substantially lower than the overall costs of litigation on conditional fee agreements. Since, in respect of a vast swathe of litigation, the costs of both sides are ultimately borne by the public, the maintenance of legal aid at no less than the present levels makes sound economic sense and is in the public interest.

---

[12] Hynes & Robins, ibid, at page 34.
[13] Heber Smith, "*Economics of the Legal Profession*" (ABA, 1938) at pages 119 and 120.
[14] The restriction of legal aid to key areas was introduced in April 2000.

CHAPTER 8. BEFORE-THE-EVENT INSURANCE

INDEX

1. INTRODUCTION

1.1   Nature of before-the event insurance. In chapter 13 of the Preliminary Report I set out a description of before-the-event ("BTE") insurance, which is sometimes described as legal expenses insurance ("LEI"). The majority of respondents during Phase 2 accepted that description, including the distinction which I drew between BTE1 and BTE2.[15] However some respondents disagreed, arguing that many policies are a mix of BTE1 and BTE2 or that the true nature of BTE insurance is opaque.

1.2   Right to choose own lawyer. The EU Council Directive 87/344 provides that a person with the benefit of LEI must be able to choose the lawyer who acts for him.[16] That Directive is implemented in England and Wales by means of the Insurance Companies (Legal Expenses Insurance) Regulations 1990 (the "1990 Regulations"). Regulation 6 of the 1990 Regulations provides:

> "6   (1) Where under a legal expenses insurance contract recourse is had to a lawyer (or other person having such qualifications as may be necessary) to defend, represent or serve the interests of the insured in any inquiry or proceedings, the insured shall be free to choose that lawyer (or other person).
>
> (2) The insured shall also be free to choose a lawyer (or other person having such qualifications as may be necessary) to serve his interests whenever a conflict of interests arises.
>
> (3) The above rights shall be expressly recognised in the policy."

1.3   Regulation 6 is interpreted both by BTE insurers and the Financial Ombudsman Service as meaning that the insured has a right to choose his or her lawyer at the moment when proceedings are issued, but not earlier. By that stage, of course, it is not normally practicable for the claimant suddenly to switch lawyers.

---

[15] See PR paragraphs 13.4.2 to 13.4.4.
[16] The Directive is discussed by Willem van Boom in "*Juxtaposing BTE and ATE – on the role of the European insurance industry in funding civil litigation*" (2010) Oxford U Comparative L Forum 1 at ouclf.iuscomp.org. The European Court of Justice recently affirmed the insured's right under the Directive to choose his own lawyer, even where a large number of other insureds have also suffered loss as a result of the same event and wish to make claims: see *Eschig v UNIQA*, Case C-199/08.

2. THE BAR CLAF GROUP'S PROPOSAL

2.1   The proposal made by the Bar CLAF Group (the "CLAF Group") is set out in PR paragraph 13.4.6.

2.2   <u>Amplification during Phase 2.</u>   In its Phase 2 submission the CLAF Group cites the following case:

> "The following actual case dating from 1996/97 illustrates one way in which existing BTE policies can fund civil litigation.
>
> C was the passenger in a vehicle being driven by D.   D had a legal expenses insurance policy covering both himself and his passengers, bought as an optional add-on with his car insurance policy.   There was an accident and C was badly injured.   The police prosecuted D for driving without due care and he was convicted.   C then sued D for damages for having caused her injuries by his negligent driving.   C's claim against D was entirely funded by <u>D's</u> legal expenses insurance.   C won her claim against D.   It cost her not a penny in legal costs.   Neither legal aid nor a CFA[17] was required."

2.3   The CLAF Group points out that it is not expensive to purchase legal expenses cover which includes passengers in the insured's car.   The CLAF Group proposes that such cover should become compulsory.   The CLAF Group goes on to propose that tortfeasors in other areas should be compelled to have LEI in place for the benefit of those whom they might injure.

2.4   The CLAF Group identifies a number of advantages of the scheme which it proposes, including the following:

(i)   It is building on an existing arrangement that is long established and works.

(ii)   Premiums will be gathered from all drivers, employers, occupiers and professionals and thus the risks will be widely spread and individual premiums can be kept low.

(iii)   Where a driver, employer, occupier or professional is a bad risk, higher premiums can be charged to reflect this.   This will provide an incentive for greater care and safety.

(iv)   The policies will provide, as at present, that cover will only be provided if the claim satisfies and continues to satisfy the insurer's "merits test".   Thus bad claims will be weeded out.   This will be welcomed by those insuring defendants.

(v)   The conduct and costs of pursuing the case will be closely monitored by the insurer, who will have the expertise and resources to do this effectively.

(vi)   Such policies will fund only legal expenses, not (potentially enormous) damages.   Moreover, because of the merits test, the insurer will expect most of the cases that it funds to be winning cases, where its costs will be substantially recovered.   Accordingly, the overall cost of such policies to the insurer, and hence the premiums charged to the driver, employer, occupier and professional should remain modest.

---

[17] Conditional fee agreement.

2.5   Response to CLAF Group's proposal.   Although some respondents during Phase 2 expressed support for the CLAF Group's proposal, most opposed it.   The principal arguments advanced were:

(i)   Premiums would rise substantially if BTE1 were introduced on a wide scale.

(ii)   A general scheme whereby the tortfeasor's insurer funds both sides of litigation will give rise to unacceptable conflicts of interest.

(iii)   BTE insurers appoint their own panel solicitors to act, who are often far removed from the claimant. This affects the quality of service. It would be wrong in principle to make such extended BTE insurance cover mandatory.

2.6   The Commercial Litigation Association in its submission states:

"The existing BTE arrangement simply could not work for the CLAF proposal. Such proposals naively assume that BTE is what it appears to be. The true cost of existing BTE is considerable and the cost of the CLAF proposal would be such as to meet with serious resistance in particular from employers and motorists faced with significant premiums out of all recognition to existing levels."

2.7   Conclusion.   Although I was originally attracted by the CLAF Group's proposal, I have been persuaded by the arguments advanced against that proposal during Phase 2.[18]   Therefore I do not recommend that motorists or any other potential tortfeasors be compelled to take out BTE insurance on behalf of those whom they might injure.

3. BTE INSURANCE FOR PERSONAL INJURY CLAIMS

3.1   In this section I use the term "personal injury" in the narrow sense, excluding claims for personal injury caused by clinical negligence.

(i) Response during Phase 2

3.2   A number of respondents during Phase 2 expressed strong hostility to the effects of BTE insurance upon personal injuries litigation.   They rejected the suggestion in the Preliminary Report that a substantially more extensive take-up of BTE insurance should be promoted.[19]

3.3   Trade unions. Trade unions argue that BTE insurance is far from beneficial and should neither be promoted nor encouraged. The Trades Union Congress (the "TUC") submission, which encapsulates the views of individual unions expressed in other Phase 2 submissions, reads as follows:

"It has been suggested that it would *be in the public interest to promote a substantial extension of BTE insurance*. In fact this is certainly not the case and BTE is, in effect, a vehicle for 3rd party capture. It is cheap because people do not use it, if they know they have it at all. It is also being mis-sold in the sense that it is added on to motor and household and other insurance without a positive election to buy it. If it was not so, it would be a much more expensive product, which people would not buy. Hence the statement by First

---

[18] See the reasoning of the Court of Appeal in *Sarwar v Alam* [2001] EWCA Civ 1401; [2002] 1 WLR 125.
[19] See PR paragraph 13.4.8 (iii).

Assist that they do offer one stand-alone policy for individuals, but the take-up of this policy is miniscule.

...

The TUC believes that they are far from comprehensive and many lead to a costs shortfall to be paid by the claimant. There are controls exercised by the BTE insurer and there are problems with their panel lawyers, who may be encouraged to keep costs down. The quality of service generally is suspect."

3.4   Solicitors. A number of solicitors firms express similar concerns about BTE insurance. Several make the point that legal expenses cover is limited, usually to £50,000. They also observe that if referral fees are banned,[20] this would cause a further escalation of BTE insurance premiums.

3.5   The alternative view. On the other side of the fence BTE insurance has its champions. The Forum of Insurance Lawyers ("FOIL") advocates greater use of BTE insurance to fund claims. Consistently with this view FOIL supports the introduction of compulsory BTE insurance for drivers.

3.6   Council of Her Majesty's Circuit Judges. The Council of Her Majesty's Circuit Judges in its Phase 2 submission discusses the options for funding litigation following the retraction of legal aid. The Council concludes as follows:

"By far the most attractive of the various possibilities dealt with in the Report is Before the Event legal insurance of one sort or another. Equipped with this, an individual or small company can go through life confident that should there be a need to bring or defend proceedings it will be possible to do so. We are not in a position to deal in any detail with the likely cost of this, but note that it is widespread already in litigation connected with motoring, and is also provided for in some contexts in many householder insurance policies. It is already common in Europe, and it has the great benefit of simplicity. Another form of before the event insurance is membership of trade unions, now in decline, which traditionally funded their members' personal injuries litigation against employers (and met defendant's costs orders if they lost). There is a further advantage in Before the Event insurance, which is that the litigation will be carried out, generally, by large scale professional litigators who will be in a position to stipulate effectively for economical representation.

For these reasons we very strongly favour Before the Event insurance. It could readily be encouraged by making the premiums tax deductible expenditure. As there is a very large potential market, and purchasers would be insuring only against the possibility, not the actuality, of litigation, it might reasonably be thought that the premiums in a competitive insurance market would be low."

3.7   BTE insurers. BTE insurers are, of course, strongly supportive of their product. However, they do not advocate compulsory BTE insurance. The Legal Expenses Insurance Group (the "LEIG"), which represents twelve substantial legal expenses insurers and intermediaries, states in its submission that it disagrees with any suggestion that BTE insurance should be compulsory.

---

[20] As is proposed in chapter 20 of this report.

(ii) Assessment

3.8   <u>The new world in which BTE insurers may operate.</u> If the recommendations made elsewhere in this report are accepted, the world in which BTE insurers operate in the future will be very different from the present world. BTE insurers will not be permitted to receive referral fees. Success fees and after-the-event ("ATE") insurance premiums will be irrecoverable. General damages will be 10% higher for personal injuries. Personal injury claimants will have the benefit of qualified one way costs shifting. Costs in the fast track will be fixed.

3.9   <u>BTE insurance will adapt.</u> BTE insurers will no doubt adapt their products to suit that new world. BTE insurance will continue to be offered as an add-on to motor insurance policies, but hopefully some of the features which have generated complaint during Phase 2 will be absent. For those personal injury claimants who do not have BTE insurance cover, the proposals made elsewhere in this report will, in my view, promote access to justice.

3.10   I do not make any specific recommendations in respect of BTE insurance for personal injury claims.

4. BTE INSURANCE FOR SMALL BUSINESS DISPUTES

4.1   <u>View expressed in Preliminary Report.</u>   I expressed the view in my Preliminary Report that litigation costs are a particular problem for small businesses and that BTE insurance may offer one solution to this problem. See PR chapter 13, section 3 and chapter 29, section 3(iii).

4.2   <u>Federation of Small Businesses.</u> On 20th May 2009 I had a meeting with representatives of the Federation of Small Businesses (the "FSB"). They made the point that BTE insurance was beneficial for small businesses, when they could afford it, but that it was expensive.   In its subsequent written submission the FSB commented that most of its members are at the smaller end of SMEs[21] and may be described as micro businesses. The FSB wrote in relation to BTE insurance:

> "The FSB agrees with the suggestion in the report that overall SMEs will be better protected if BTE insurance cover was extended across the SME community. The FSB insurance package does cover BTE legal expenses insurance chiefly for the defence of employment claims against business but also in respect of limited other areas. All members have the defence package of BTE insurance as it is embedded within the subscription. The FSB legal team confirm that the reach of BTE insurance is increasing, either through the growth of the FSB and similar organisations, or purchased as a 'stand alone' offering through commercial brokers. The FSB package is one of the most cost effective ways of purchasing BTE insurance. However, there are barriers to the increased take up of BTE insurance by FSB and SMEs, namely the combination of cost and product or benefit awareness, particularly in the current, difficult, economic climate. Cost alone may exclude many smaller FSB members from extending their BTE cover and such cover may always be limited in scope because of the enormous variety of business derived disputes making standardised cover difficult for insurers to package."

---

[21] Small and medium enterprises.

4.3   BTE insurers. During Phase 2 a number of BTE insurers sent to me details of the BTE insurance cover available to small businesses. I selected one of these insurers and challenged it to give me examples of cases which its insured had pursued or defended with the benefit of BTE cover. The insurer duly sent in details of a number of commercial contract cases in which the insured was claimant or defendant, where the legal costs had been covered by BTE insurance. In each of these cases the premium which the insured had paid for such cover was modest.

4.4   A number of other respondents agreed with the view that a greater uptake of BTE insurance would be beneficial for SMEs. For example, the Commercial Bar Association ("COMBAR") agrees that the availability of BTE insurance should be more widely publicised to businesses, although COMBAR doubts that many SMEs would be willing to pay the premiums involved. One respondent advocated that there be a Government initiative to publicise the availability of BTE cover similar to the campaign for stakeholder pensions.[22]

4.5   Conclusion. I remain of the opinion, expressed in the Preliminary Report, that BTE insurance is beneficial for small businesses. The average small business is better able to negotiate with insurers than the average personal injury claimant and will have a better understanding of its rights under the policy. A substantial extension of BTE cover for small businesses, in respect of litigation costs as well as tribunal costs, would in my view be highly beneficial. On the basis that the many pay for the few and that most small businesses do not get embroiled in litigation in any given year, the premiums ought to be affordable at least by some small businesses, if they are prepared to attach sufficient priority to LEI.

4.6   It is, of course, no business of mine what overheads small businesses choose to incur. I do, however, recommend that both insurers and the Department for Business, Innovation and Skills should make serious efforts to draw to the attention of SMEs, and especially micro businesses, the forms of BTE insurance available and the costs. In my view, a greater take-up of BTE by small businesses would be one way of promoting access to justice. In other words, in relation to BTE insurance for small businesses, I agree with the sentiments expressed by the Council of Circuit Judges quoted above.

5. BTE AS AN ADD-ON TO HOUSEHOLD INSURANCE

5.1   Take up of BTE insurance is already extensive. There are approximately 25 million households in the UK.[23] Approximately 10-15 million households have BTE insurance as an add-on to house or contents insurance.[24]

5.2   Cover afforded. I am told that BTE insurance as an add-on to household insurance typically covers the following:

•   Death or personal injury (including clinical negligence).

---

[22] In January 2001, the Government launched a campaign to promote low-cost stakeholder pensions, reportedly spending around £6.5m on advertising the scheme. Stakeholder pensions became available in April 2001 and they were aimed at people earning between £9,000 and £20,000 a year who had not made provision for their retirement.

[23] Estimate by the Office of National Statistics in 2008: see chapter 2 of "*Social Trends 39 Full Report*", available online at http://www.statistics.gov.uk/StatBase/Product.asp?vlnk=5748.

[24] See PR paragraph 13.2.3.

- Contract disputes arising out of the sale, purchase or hire of goods or services (including holidays).

- Property disputes such as boundary disputes, noisy neighbours, sale of property and tenancy disputes.

- Employment disputes and related tribunal proceedings.

I understand that the cover afforded is usually BTE1, rather than BTE2, as defined in PR paragraph 13.4.2.

5.3   The cover is effective when required. The vast majority of householders never become embroiled in litigation. So this insurance, unlike ATE insurance, operates on the basis that the many pay for the few. On the evidence that I have received during Phase 2, the cover does appear to be effective when required. See, for example, chapter 31 below at paragraph 2.1, where it is recorded that many claimants in private nuisance claims proceed with the support of BTE insurance.

5.4   Clinical negligence claims supported by BTE insurance. It can be seen from PR paragraph 11.4.2 and PR appendix 21, graphs A6 to A10, that BTE insurance supports a significant number of clinical negligence claims. A similar picture emerges from section 6 of chapter 2 above and the accompanying tables (set out in appendix 1 to this report). It can be seen that clinical negligence claims funded by BTE insurance have a reasonable success rate.[25] It can also be seen that in clinical negligence claims supported by BTE insurance, costs are significantly lower than in clinical negligence claims supported by CFAs: see PR appendix 21, graph A7 and appendix 1 table 22 to this report.

5.5   Insured unaware of cover? The point is often made that people with BTE insurance are unaware of the cover which they have purchased. I do not believe that this should be an obstacle to the use of BTE insurance. The first question which any litigation solicitor should, and would, ask of a client with a claim in the categories mentioned in paragraph 5.2 above is whether the client has household insurance and, if so, what are its terms. Indeed solicitors are required, as a matter of professional conduct, to discuss with their clients at the outset whether the client's costs are covered by insurance.[26]

5.6   Conclusion. In my view, BTE insurance as an add-on to household insurance is a beneficial product at an affordable price, established on the basis that the many pay for the few. If the reforms advocated in chapter 9 below are implemented, BTE insurance will have an increasingly important role in promoting access to justice. Therefore the uptake of BTE insurance by householders should be actively encouraged.

6. RIGHT TO CHOOSE OWN LAWYER

6.1   The relevant EU directive and UK regulation have been set out in section 1 above. There has been considerable debate during Phase 2 about the proper application of these provisions.

6.2   Law Society's view. The Law Society in its Phase 2 submission acknowledges both the strengths and weaknesses of BTE insurance. The Law Society writes:

---

[25] The rate is 78% in table 23 of appendix 1 to this report.
[26] Paragraph 2.03 (1) (d) (ii) of the Solicitors' Code of Conduct 2007.

"The Law Society agrees that BTE insurance has an important role to play in the funding of litigation. We also accept the distinction made by Jackson LJ between what he calls 'BTE1' and 'BTE2' and that 'BTE1' is the preferable model.

The report does not however give, in our view, adequate attention to the way in which the market is manipulated by BTE insurers so that clients are not free to choose the solicitor of their choice. Their role as funders and gatekeepers gives insurers significant power in their relations with solicitors and clients. Claimants wishing to take advantage of his BTE policy either instruct their own solicitors and are refused funding unless they agree to instruct a panel solicitor, often in a different part of the country, or are referred direct their by their insurer. The Association of District Judges has made known to the Law Society, during 2008, its concerns that this system frequently operates as a denial of justice to claimants who lose, under-settle or do not pursue cases as a result of the nature of representation provided.

The problem arises out of section 6 of the Insurance Companies (Legal Expenses Insurance) Regulations 1990 (the '1990 Regulations'). This appears to enshrine freedom of choice by clients; but this is available only in respect of 'any enquiry or proceedings'. Insurers take the view that proceedings do not commence until a claim is actually issued; even the protocol procedure is deemed by them not to be 'proceedings'...

The three BTE issues which need to be resolved are:

i) The insured has no say in the terms of the contract between the insurer and the panel solicitor and therefore has less influence in the handling of the case than a client who does not have the benefit of BTE.

ii) The solicitor panels are restricted by insurers and there are frequently issues regarding the lack of freedom of choice of a client's own solicitor. The Law Society considers that freedom of choice of solicitor is important in the public interest. It is essential that the litigant should feel confidence in his or her legal advisers and will enhance the integrity of the system. Secondly, the litigant will be able to assess the competence of the firm directly and take action if dissatisfied.

iii) The definition of proceedings in the Regulations and how this is interpreted. The Law Society's view is that any extension of BTE should be subject to the agreement by insurers that the definition of 'proceedings' under the 1990 Regulations includes the pre-action protocol procedure or by clarification of those Regulations."

6.3 I see considerable force in the three specific concerns raised by the Law Society. In my view those concerns would all, in substance, be met if regulation 6 of the 1990 Regulations were amended to provide that the insured's right to choose a lawyer arises when a letter of claim is sent on his or her behalf to the opposing party.[27] However, before any such amendment of regulation 6 is considered, the effect upon BTE insurance premiums must first be considered. BTE insurers maintain that the present panel arrangements are beneficial in keeping costs down. I

---

[27] Insurers may still use their own panel solicitors to investigate and assess the merits of claims. In practice, no doubt many insureds would be content to proceed thereafter using the same panel solicitors.

do not make this issue the subject matter of a recommendation. However, I place on record my support for making an amendment to regulation 6, as suggested above, if the impact of such an amendment on premiums turns out to be modest.

7. RECOMMENDATION

7.1　　I recommend that positive efforts should be made to encourage the take up of BTE insurance by SMEs in respect of business disputes and by householders as an add-on to household insurance policies.

7.2　　My views on other BTE issues have been set out in the course of this chapter, but are not the subject of recommendations.

CHAPTER 9. AFTER-THE-EVENT INSURANCE AND HOW TO DEAL WITH THE LIABILITY FOR ADVERSE COSTS

INDEX

1. INTRODUCTION

1.1   <u>Preliminary Report.</u>   After-the-event ("ATE") insurance is described in chapter 14 of the Preliminary Report. The principal function (but not the only function)[28] of ATE insurance is to provide the insured with a fund to meet the opponent's costs in the event that the insured is ordered to pay those costs. The question whether ATE insurance premiums should continue to be recoverable under costs orders is discussed in PR chapter 47. The Preliminary Report also discusses whether, if ATE insurance premiums become irrecoverable, there should be one way costs shifting.[29]

1.2   <u>Number of ATE insurers.</u> In PR paragraph 14.1.2 I recorded the statement from an informed source that there were 36 ATE insurers. A number of respondents during Phase 2 have stated that the figure of 36 is too high. The number of separate insurers offering ATE insurance cover is lower. Different respondents have quoted different figures, but it appears that the total number of substantial ATE insurers currently operating is somewhat less than 20.

1.3   <u>ATE insurance is usually for claimants.</u> In the majority of cases where ATE insurance exists, it is the claimant who has taken out such insurance.[30] The paradigm

---

[28] ATE may also provide cover for own disbursements, in the event that these are not recovered from the opponent.

[29] PR chapter 25 generally, also PR paragraphs 35.4.5, 35.4.6, 36.3.7, 36.3.8, and 38.6.1 to 38.6.6.

[30] In a smaller number of cases defendants take out ATE insurance. In a very few cases, where opposing insurers take a very different view of the merits, both parties may have ATE insurance.

case, which is assumed in most financial modelling, is one in which a claimant with ATE insurance is litigating against a defendant who has no such cover. For convenience, in this chapter when I refer to "claimant" I am referring to a claimant with ATE insurance; when I refer to "defendant" I am referring to a defendant without ATE insurance. However, I have been told that certain defendants in professional liability cases have recently started taking out ATE insurance. Whilst in most cases the reason for taking out ATE insurance will be to provide protection against adverse costs liabilities, it can also be used by either claimants or defendants as a tactical measure.

1.4   Plan for this chapter. In this chapter I shall first review the debate about ATE insurance which followed publication of the Preliminary Report. I shall then set out my conclusions on the question whether ATE insurance premiums should continue to be recoverable. I shall then consider the two follow-on questions, namely (i) what measures should be taken to protect claimants if ATE insurance premiums become irrecoverable and (ii) what measures should be taken to protect opposing parties if ATE insurance premiums remain recoverable.

2. DEBATE DURING PHASE 2

2.1   The question of principle. The main debate during Phase 2 has revolved around a single question of principle. That is whether ATE insurance premiums should continue to be recoverable from an opposing party under a costs order (the "recoverability" issue).

2.2   Follow-on questions. If the answer to the question of principle is "yes", then the next issue is whether any steps should be taken to lessen the burden which the present regime places upon defendants. If the answer to the question of principle is "no", then the next issues are (a) whether any measures, and if so what measures, should be taken to protect claimants against adverse costs orders and (b) how those disbursements which are currently funded by ATE insurers should be met.

2.3   Meeting with clinical negligence defence solicitors. On 22nd May 2009 I attended a meeting with clinical negligence defence solicitors. General support was expressed for a qualified one way costs shifting regime, coupled with ATE insurance premiums being irrecoverable. "Qualified one way costs shifting" in this context means a one way costs shifting regime, which carries a costs penalty for failing to beat a defendant's Part 36 offer[31] or other unreasonable conduct.

2.4   Professional Negligence and Liability Forum. At the Professional Negligence and Liability Forum held on 11th June 2009 there was some debate about the merits of recoverability of ATE insurance premiums and differing views were expressed. One member of the Bar outlined a case of his in which the damages claimed were £8 million and the claimant was taking out ATE insurance at a premium between £4 million and £5 million. The threat of that additional liability (together with the success fee under a conditional fee agreement (a "CFA")) was a major cause of settlement in a case which otherwise might have been fought on the evidence. The barrister suggested that high ATE insurance premiums and CFAs with significant uplifts are being used as a tactical device by claimants to force settlement in cases which turn on the evidence and which might otherwise properly be fought to trial on their merits. Other speakers pointed out that ATE insurance acts as a filter against

---

[31] Possibly along the lines of the matrix proposed by the Forum of Insurance Lawyers at PR paragraph 10.10.8 (table 10.1).

unmeritorious claims, because insurers rigorously vet the risks which they are taking on.

2.5   Meeting with clinical negligence claimant solicitors. On 12th June 2009 I attended a meeting with clinical negligence claimant solicitors. They could see the attractions of substituting one way costs shifting for recoverable ATE insurance premiums, but were concerned about how disbursements would be met in that scenario. Furthermore, if ATE insurance were only required for disbursements this may seriously damage the ATE insurance market.

2.6   Cardiff seminar. At the Cardiff seminar on 19th June 2009 Professor Richard Moorhead presented a paper on *"Regulated one way costs-shifting".*[32] Professor Moorhead proposed that recoverability of ATE insurance premiums should be abolished; instead there should be one way costs shifting in all personal injury cases which were registered by claimants with a regulator. In the discussion which followed this presentation, there was some support for one way costs shifting. There was also concern that such a system may lead to more unmeritorious or fraudulent claims. A representative of one local authority, who supported one way costs shifting in place of recoverability, cited a tripping case in which the damages were £5,000 and the ATE insurance premium was £38,000. Another speaker pointed out that an individual uninsured defendant who defeated a personal injuries claim would be penalised if there were one way costs shifting. Sir Anthony May, President of the Queen's Bench Division (the "QBD"), spoke next and delivered a powerful attack on the recoverability principle.[33] I set out the relevant extract from his speech in chapter 10 below.

2.7   Commercial Litigation Funding Conference. At the Commercial Litigation Funding Conference organised by No5 Chambers on 23rd June 2009 there was general support for the principle of recoverability. Speakers referred to ATE insurance premiums ranging between 30% and 50% of the level of costs insured. One speaker said that on occasions the fact of ATE insurance caused the other side to capitulate. Examples were given of attractive packages which could be put together, enabling clients to bring commercial claims with the combined benefit of a CFA and ATE insurance.

2.8   Herbert Smith meeting. At a meeting of practitioners and clients hosted by Herbert Smith on 29th June 2009 there was general opposition to the recoverability of both success fees and ATE insurance premiums. One attendee recounted a case where the parties wanted to settle, but were hampered by the enormous ATE insurance premium incurred by the claimant. By reason of the ATE insurance premium, coupled with the success fee, costs became huge in comparison to the claim and were a real issue in relation to settlement.

2.9   London seminar. At the London seminar on 10th July 2009 Professor Herbert Kritzer presented two written papers to supplement his oral presentation. In the first paper, entitled *"Fee regimes and the cost of civil justice",*[34] Professor Kritzer suggested that the regime of recoverable ATE insurance premiums is a form of one

---

[32] This paper is on the Costs Review website at http://www.judiciary.gov.uk/docs/costs-review/regulated-one-way-costs-shifting.pdf.

[33] See the President of the QBD's paper on the Costs Review website at http://www.judiciary.gov.uk/docs/costs-review/pqbd-costs-conference-190609.pdf.   For logistical reasons Sir Anthony's keynote address was delivered after Professor Moorhead's presentation and the ensuing discussion.

[34] This paper is on the Costs Review website at http://www.judiciary.gov.uk/docs/costs-review/fee-regimes.pdf. It was also published in the Civil Justice Quarterly, Volume 28, Issue 3, 2009 at page 344.

way costs shifting.[35] Senior Costs Judge Peter Hurst presented an overview of costs regimes overseas. In none of the regimes reviewed is there a recoverability regime. In the discussion following that presentation the point was made that there is much less use of ATE insurance overseas. A legal expenses underwriter stated that a small number of ATE insurance policies are taken out in Scotland, even though there is no recoverability. Another speaker pointed out that in Australia solicitors doing cases on a contingency fee basis often give their client an indemnity against adverse costs.

2.10   CFA seminar. At the CFA seminar on 20th July 2009 there was debate about ATE insurance premiums, and whether or not market forces held down premium levels. There was also debate about the principle of recoverability. At the end of that debate there were 39 votes in favour of ATE insurance premiums being recoverable, 13 votes against and two votes in favour of only half the ATE insurance premium being recoverable.

2.11   Chancery litigation seminar. At the chancery litigation seminar held on 24th July 2009, one solicitor said that premiums quoted to him by ATE insurers were often in the region of 90% of costs. He added that in one current case he has been offered ATE insurance at a premium of 95%. That premium is assessed by reference to his own likely total base costs up to trial (currently estimated at £100,000), even though in practice such a case is unlikely to go to trial. This is a professional negligence claim where the sum at issue is £60,000.

3. WRITTEN SUBMISSIONS DURING PHASE 2

3.1   There was a profusion of detailed written submissions in relation to the issues identified in paragraphs 2.1 and 2.2 above. It is not practicable within the confines of this chapter to summarise all those submissions individually. Instead I shall outline the principal arguments which have been advanced.

3.2   Trade unions. A number of trade unions forcefully argue that recoverability should continue. The trade unions maintain that ATE insurance is the best way of ensuring that in unsuccessful cases (a) any adverse costs order is met and (b) the claimant's own disbursements are paid without making any financial demands upon the claimant.

3.3   The Association of Personal Injury Lawyers. The Association of Personal Injury Lawyers ("APIL") argues that ATE insurance premiums should continue to be recoverable. However, APIL accepts that a "true" one way costs shifting regime, whereby the claimant is never at risk on costs, could work for personal injury cases. This would, of course, render at least part of ATE insurance redundant.

3.4   Personal Injuries Bar Association. The Personal Injuries Bar Association ("PIBA") argues firmly that ATE insurance premiums should be recoverable, but accepts that the Court of Appeal's decision in *Rogers v Merthyr Tydfil CBC*[36] makes it very difficult for defendants to challenge the level of ATE insurance premiums. PIBA adds:

> "Even staged premiums, whose use was approved in *Rogers*, do little to ameliorate the position, because the end-stage premiums are generally very high and impose on the Defendant with a viable case on liability an

---

[35] See pages 22 to 23.
[36] [2006] EWCA 1134 (Civ); [2007] 1 WLR 808, see PR paragraphs 14.2.6 and 14.4.4.

unreasonable additional burden (we know of Fast Track cases where the premium sought after a trial has been as high as £25,000), far outstripping the costs risk faced by the Claimant."

3.5   PIBA then goes on to argue that additional liabilities at this level cannot be excluded by reference to any overall proportionality test. On the contrary they are *"the price, paid as things stand by losing defendants, of achieving access to justice"*. PIBA concludes:

"Subject to fixing uplifts, allowing some discretion in the event of Claimant's (mis)conduct and fixing a scale of ATE premiums in fast track claims (see below), that price seems to us to be not only proper but unavoidable so long as the CFA regime remains."

3.6   <u>Personal injury solicitors.</u>   Numerous firms of claimant personal injury solicitors have written in, arguing that recoverability of ATE insurance premiums should be retained in order to promote access to justice for injured claimants. They point out that even if one way costs shifting were introduced, it would still be necessary to fund disbursements and that ATE insurance may not be possible for disbursements alone. They also stress that ATE insurance benefits defendants in those cases which claimants lose, because defendants recover their costs in such cases and pay no ATE insurance premium.

3.7   <u>Personal injury liability insurers.</u> Liability insurers argue that recoverability of ATE insurance premiums should end. Many accept that there should be a regime of one way costs shifting in its place. One liability insurer writes:

"The cost of ATE is spiralling out of control, not least because the approach to ATE established by the Court of Appeal in *Rogers* makes it incredibly difficult for defendants to challenge ATE premiums. The type of evidence that can be used is severely restricted; the courts will not accept material from Litigation Funding or the Judge website, for instance. Defendants must then try to obtain information from ATE providers themselves, which they are reticent to provide as it may curb the amount that they are able to recover. There is a conspiracy of silence...

[We believe] that ending the recoverability of success fees and ATE would overnight rectify many of the problems with the costs regime, as it would re-introduce consumer based market forces to regulate the level of claimant costs."

3.8   <u>Clinical negligence.</u> Claimant solicitors and representative bodies argue for recoverability of ATE insurance premiums. However, Action against Medical Accidents ("AvMA") acknowledges the problems posed by ATE insurance. AvMA states:

"AvMA supports the idea of one way costs shifting which has long been a familiar mechanism in clinical negligence where cases are funded by legal aid. AvMA does not support an unnecessary burden on the public purse of recoverability of large ATE premiums if another costs mechanism could apply."

3.9   Clinical defence organisations oppose recoverability. The Medical Defence Union (the "MDU") states that one way costs shifting would be preferable, but only in cases supported by CFAs. The MDU adds that it is not unusual for the MDU under the current regime to pay out ATE insurance premiums in the region of £50,000; it is difficult to challenge such premiums and there is no real competition in the ATE insurance market. One major firm of solicitors acting for the National Health Service Litigation Authority considers that recoverability of ATE insurance premiums should end and should be replaced by qualified one way costs shifting.

3.10   <u>Commercial practitioners.</u>   My overall impression is that the majority of commercial practitioners, but by no means all such practitioners, believe that recoverability has no place in commercial and similar litigation. The Commercial Bar Association states:

> "Our overall view is that, so far as we can see, there is no reason why a commercial litigant should be prevented from taking out ATE insurance if it so wishes (if such insurance can be found at a reasonable price), but no plausible justification why the premium that he pays should be recoverable from the other party in the event that he succeeds.

> Indeed, once again it seems to us that were there to be an intensification in the use of CFAs and ATE insurance in large commercial cases, and were the existing rules on the recovery of success fees and ATE premiums to remain, then there would be significant racheting up of costs in commercial cases – with a potentially serious effect on the attraction of London as a forum for international dispute resolution."

3.11   On the other hand, the Commercial Litigation Association believes that ATE insurance premiums should be recoverable in non-personal injuries litigation. A number of solicitors firms support recoverability of ATE insurance premiums and have developed business models which take advantage of this for the benefit of their clients in commercial and similar litigation. One of the firms which favours retaining recoverability in commercial litigation helpfully annexes some of its cases as illustrations. In one of those illustrative cases the claimant's profit costs were £425,000, disbursements were £561,000 and the ATE insurance premium was £976,000. In other words the ATE insurance premium was about as much as all the other costs and disbursements put together.

3.12   <u>Chancery Bar Association.</u>   The Chancery Bar Association (the "ChBA") maintains that ATE insurance premiums ought not to be recoverable. In practice, the ChBA argues, the effect of the authorities in this area is that any insurer following the industry norm in its approach to calculating premiums is acting reasonably and the premium is therefore reasonable. This means that paying parties have no basis on which to challenge the amount of ATE insurance premiums and costs judges are *"powerless"* to reduce them. However, if ATE insurance premiums were wholly or partly irrecoverable, then market forces would operate to drive down premiums. The ChBA also objects to the recovery of ATE insurance premiums as a matter of principle, because the premium is not a true item of "legal costs" and only "legal costs" are recoverable in law. Further, it does not accept that the current form of ATE insurance "premium" (not payable if the case is lost when the insurance is needed; payable only if the case is won when the insurance is not needed and then payable by the other side) constitutes a "premium" in law.

3.13   <u>Environmental private law claims.</u>   The UK Environmental Lawyers Association ("UKELA") supports the continuation of recoverability. UKELA argues that one way costs shifting would not suffice as an alternative, because of the claimant's need to meet its own disbursements. A firm of solicitors specialising in environmental nuisance claims puts forward similar arguments in its Phase 2 submission.

3.14   Repudiation of ATE insurance policy. A number of respondents during Phase 2 state that the injustice of having to pay ATE insurance premiums is compounded by the possibility that if the defendant wins a case the ATE insurers may repudiate. Such repudiation, if and when it occurs, is commonly based upon the facts as found by the judge in the course of dismissing the claimant's action. In other words, the event which triggers entitlement under the policy also triggers the insurers' repudiation. The solicitors for one major construction company cite the following example. They were instructed by the construction company to defend a contractual claim relating to a development. The claimant took out ATE insurance and its lawyers were all acting on CFAs. The defendant was concerned about the financial standing of the claimant and considered making an application for security for costs. The claimant's solicitors stated that they and the insurers would resist on the basis that the ATE insurance policy was adequate security. Accordingly, no application was made for security. The defendant was ultimately successful at trial. The insurers then avoided liability on grounds of non-disclosure. The defendant then became embroiled in litigation against the ATE insurers.

3.15   The solicitors for the construction company argue in their submission that ATE insurers should not be able to put themselves in a position where they can claim the premium from the opponent if the action is successful but avoid liability under the policy if it is unsuccessful.

3.16   ATE insurers. ATE insurers argue vigorously for the retention of recoverability of ATE insurance premiums. One ATE insurer states that none of its premiums has ever been reduced by the courts upon assessment of costs. Another ATE insurer helpfully gives a breakdown of ATE insurance premiums into their component elements. The build up of the premium is said to be approximately as follows: 65% risk premium, 15 to 20% brokerage and 15 to 20% administration and profit. This may be illustrated:

Approximate breakdown of an ATE premium

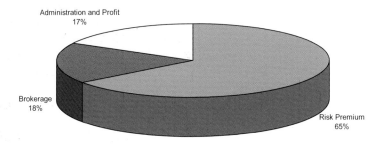

3.17   Law Society. The Law Society maintains that ATE insurance premiums should continue to be recoverable. It points out that the insurers who complain about paying ATE insurance premiums also receive those payments, as providers of ATE insurance.

3.18   Judiciary.   The majority of judges are opposed to ATE insurance premiums being recoverable. This is the position of The Association of Her Majesty's District Judges. The Council of Her Majesty's Circuit Judges has "*major reservations*" about whether ATE insurance premiums should be recoverable.

4. THE RECOVERABILITY ISSUE

4.1   As Professor Kritzer has pointed out, the regime of ATE insurance with recoverable premiums is a form of one way costs shifting. Indeed, I would add, it is an extremely expensive form of one way costs shifting. Even if one disregards that portion of the premium which is referable to own disbursements, the present ATE insurance regime is substantially more expensive for defendants than one way costs shifting. It would be substantially cheaper for defendants to bear their own costs in every case, whether won or lost, than to pay out ATE insurance premiums in those cases which they lose. This can be demonstrated on the figures: see chapter 19 below. Also it is self evident. As set out in section 3 above, only about 65 % of the premium is referable to the risk accepted by ATE insurers. The remainder of the premium is referable to the administration costs, brokerage and profit of the ATE insurers.

4.2   The question whether ATE insurance premiums should be recoverable from an opposing party under a costs order raises very similar policy issues to the question whether CFA success fees should be recoverable from an opposing party under a costs order. Almost everyone who has contributed to the Costs Review, on either side of the debate, maintains that both questions should be answered in the same way.

4.3   I shall therefore discuss the question of recoverability in relation to both ATE insurance premiums and CFA success fees in chapter 10 below, after all the arguments on both sides of this question have been summarised.

4.4   For the reasons which will be set out in chapter 10 below, my conclusion is that ATE insurance premiums ought not to be recoverable under a costs order. The regime of recoverable ATE insurance premiums is based upon the premise that certain claimants need to be protected against the risk of having to pay adverse costs. In other words, for policy reasons those claimants should be allowed to benefit from the costs shifting rule when they win, but be protected against its adverse effects when they lose. The flaw in the present regime is that it is not targeted upon those who merit such protection. Any person who finds a willing insurer can take out ATE insurance,[37] whether that person is rich or poor, human or corporate, deserving or undeserving.   Furthermore, the protection which a claimant derives from ATE insurance is total. The claimant is not required to make a modest contribution towards adverse costs (as was the case under the legal aid regime, which the recoverability regime replaced in April 2000), even if he can afford to do so.

4.5   Professor Willem van Boom has delivered a forceful attack upon the regime of recoverable ATE insurance premiums in his article "*Juxtaposing BTE and ATE on the role of the European insurance industry in funding civil litigation*".[38]   He concludes:

---

[37] Subject to satisfying the insurer as to prospects of success.
[38] (2010) Oxford University Comparative Law Forum 1 at http://ouclf.iuscomp.org.

"So, the upshot of all this is that a prevailing claimant can fully shift the costs of his solicitor and his ATE premium onto the defendant and a defeated claimant doesn't pay anything. The CFA+ATE industry justifies this on the basis that the policy is 'self-insured', which actually implies that the insurer pools all risks and funds all the unsuccessful cases from premiums charged to defendant in successful cases. So, what 'self-insured' really means is allowing claimants and insurers to design an aleatory contract through which the costs of both parties can be fully externalized on third parties."

4.6   In my view, the present regime of recoverable ATE insurance premiums is (a) unfair to opposing parties (usually but not always defendants) and (b) an unsatisfactory way of achieving the intended social objective. I therefore recommend that section 29 of the Access to Justice Act 1999 (the "1999 Act") and the rules made thereunder be repealed.

5. IF RECOVERABILITY IS ABOLISHED, HOW SHOULD CLAIMANTS' LIABILITY FOR ADVERSE COSTS BE DEALT WITH?

(i) The question of principle

5.1   <u>The question.</u> If the recoverability regime is abolished, the question arises as to how the law should protect those claimants who, as a matter of social policy should be protected, against the risk of adverse costs.

5.2   <u>The answer.</u> In my view, there is only one sensible way to give effect to that social policy, namely by introducing one way costs shifting. The advantage of this solution is that costs protection can be targeted upon those who need it, rather than offered as a gift to the world at large.

5.3   <u>The best formula for one way costs shifting.</u> The best formula for one way costs shifting is that contained in section 11(1) of the 1999 Act.[39] This is the formula which has been used for 60 years to protect legally aided parties against the risk of adverse costs. It contains mechanisms to protect both parties and it provides for conduct to be taken into account when assessing costs liability. I shall develop this point in chapter 19 below, when discussing one way costs shifting for personal injury claims. The formula in section 11(1) of the 1999 Act is so structured that if the relevant party turns out to be wealthy, or subsequently becomes wealthy, the order for costs may be enforced; likewise if the party fails to beat a Part 36 offer, the order for costs may be enforced. It would be more apt to describe the regime created by section 11 of the 1999 Act as qualified one way costs shifting.

5.4   The next question to consider is which categories of litigant should receive the benefit of qualified one way costs shifting. This question is best addressed by reference to different categories of litigation.

(ii) Commercial, construction and similar litigation

5.5   In my view there is no place either for qualified one way costs shifting or for recoverable ATE insurance premiums in the context of commercial, construction or similar litigation. The parties are generally in a contractual relationship and there is

---

[39] "*Costs ordered against an individual...shall not exceed the amount (if any) which is a reasonable one for him to pay having regard to all the circumstances including – (a) the financial resources of all parties to the proceedings and (b) their conduct in connection with the dispute...*"

symmetry in their legal positions. It is often a matter of chance which party is claimant.

5.6   The present ability of a party involved in commercial litigation to insure against adverse costs at the expense of the other side is, I would suggest, neither logical nor grounded in any discernible social policy. Indeed the ability of one party to so insure subverts the purpose of the costs shifting rule.[40] It may be argued that when a small or medium enterprise (an "SME") is litigating against a multi-national, recoverable ATE insurance will strengthen the hands of the SME. However, the flaw in this argument is that the present "recoverability" rules give the multi-national just as much right as the SME to take out ATE insurance. ATE insurance with recoverable premiums is a trump card which may be taken into the hand of either player.

5.7   It would, in theory, be possible to devise procedural rules to shield smaller companies from costs liabilities to larger companies, but such a quest would be fraught with difficulties and unintended consequences. I most certainly do not recommend that approach. In my view, in ordinary commercial, construction and similar litigation there should be no special rules to protect weaker parties against adverse costs orders. If any party wishes to obtain insurance against adverse costs liability, it should do so at its own expense, as was the position before April 2000.

(iii) Personal injuries litigation

5.8   In personal injuries litigation it must be accepted that claimants require protection against adverse costs orders. Otherwise injured persons may be deterred from bringing claims for compensation. I recommend a form of qualified one way costs shifting in personal injury cases, as set out in chapter 19 below.

5.9   In chapter 19 I also address the question how and by whom disbursements in personal injury cases should be paid.

(iv) Other categories of litigation

5.10   <u>Further consultation required if my recommendations are accepted in principle.</u> The essential thrust of the present chapter is that recoverability of ATE insurance premiums should be abolished and that this should be replaced by qualified one way costs shifting, targeted upon those who merit such protection on grounds of public policy. The question then arises as to which categories of litigant should benefit from qualified one way costs shifting. This is a question upon which further consultation will be required, in the event that the recommendations made in this chapter are accepted as a matter of principle.

5.11   <u>Areas where qualified one way costs shifting may be appropriate.</u> In my view qualified one way costs shifting may be appropriate on grounds of social policy, where the parties are in an asymmetric relationship. Examples of parties who are generally in an asymmetric relationship with their opponents are claimants in housing disrepair cases, claimants in actions against the police, claimants seeking judicial review and individuals making claims for defamation or breach of privacy against the media. If protection modelled upon section 11(1) of the 1999 Act is extended to claimants in such cases, it will not avail those who bring frivolous claims (because unreasonable conduct is taken into account). Nor will it avail those whose resources are such that they can afford to pay adverse costs if they lose.

---

[40] The purpose of the costs shifting rule is discussed in PR chapter 46.

5.12   I discuss more fully in chapter 19 below how the section 11 model might be adapted and applied to non-legally aided parties, in the event that it is decided to confer upon such parties the benefit of qualified one way costs shifting.   See in particular paragraphs 4.5 to 4.11 of that chapter.

5.13   Professional negligence litigation. Whether qualified one way costs shifting should be introduced for any (and if so which) categories of professional negligence litigation should be the subject of consultation. My own view is that this may be difficult to justify outside clinical negligence. Most persons who employ solicitors, accountants, architects etc could afford to take out before-the-event ("BTE") insurance, if they chose to do so.[41]

5.14   Private nuisance claims. I accept that private nuisance claims sometimes involve parties in an asymmetric relationship: for example local householders suing a sewage works. However, this is not always the case.[42] Furthermore householders can take out BTE insurance against the costs of such claims, if they choose to do so. I would not positively support qualified one way costs shifting for private nuisance claims, but others may take a different view. If qualified one way costs shifting were introduced in the manner suggested in paragraph 5.3 above, it would only in practice avail persons of limited means suing well resourced defendants. Also it would be possible to provide that only human claimants (as opposed to corporate claimants) would benefit from qualified one way costs shifting in private nuisance cases.

(v) Effect upon the insurance industry

5.15   Effect on ATE insurance. If ATE insurance premiums cease to be recoverable under costs orders, that does not prevent parties taking out ATE insurance, if they choose to do so at their own expense. ATE insurance existed in England and Wales in the period before April 2000, when the premiums were not recoverable under costs orders. ATE insurance currently exists in Scotland, even though the premiums are not recoverable under costs orders: see paragraph 2.9 above and chapter 14 of Lord Gill's recent report[43] at paragraphs 96 and 97.

5.16   Despite the points made in the previous paragraph, it must be accepted that if my recommendations are implemented, the ATE insurance industry will suffer a significant loss of business. It is perfectly understandable that, during Phase 2 of the Costs Review, ATE insurers have opposed so vigorously any suggestion that recoverability of ATE insurance premiums should be abolished. Nevertheless it is my firm view that the present regime of recoverable ATE insurance premiums is one of the factors that have driven up litigation costs. I do not believe that this element of the costs regime should be maintained in order to support one sector of the insurance industry.

5.17   Effect on BTE insurance.   At the moment about ten to fifteen million households have BTE insurance.[44]   One possible consequence of the reforms proposed in this chapter (if implemented) may be a growth in BTE insurance[45] and possibly a widening of the cover offered. I appreciate that BTE insurance premiums may rise, but they will be far below the level of ATE insurance premiums, if only because the many pay for the few. The insured under a BTE policy is highly unlikely

---

[41] Normally as an add-on to household insurance.

[42] Private nuisance claims between neighbours are not unusual. I have acted as counsel in such claims.

[43] Report of the Scottish Civil Courts Review (September 2009) ISBN: 978-0-9552511-2-2.

[44] See PR paragraph 13.2.3.

[45] The insurance would have to be BTE1, not BTE 2, as defined in PR paragraph 13.4.2.

to become involved in litigation. Quite the reverse is true of the insured under an ATE insurance policy.

5.18   The publicity consequent upon any repeal of section 29 of the 1999 Act may possibly alert people or their professional advisers to the desirability of taking out such insurance. It is, however, a matter for individuals whether or not they choose to take out BTE insurance as an add-on to household or other insurance.

6. IF RECOVERABILITY IS NOT ABOLISHED, WHAT MEASURES SHOULD BE TAKEN TO PROTECT THE OPPOSING PARTIES?

(i) Introduction

6.1   I regard the recommendation that recoverability of ATE insurance premiums be abolished as important and not one to be watered down. England and Wales is out of step with all the other jurisdictions which I have visited or considered in permitting the winning party's method of funding litigation to influence the price which the losing party has to pay.[46]

(ii) Measures to control the premiums which are recoverable

6.2   If it is concluded that it is not possible to repeal section 29 of the 1999 Act, then the circumstances in which incurring the cost of a policy should be recoverable as a reasonable step should be more closely controlled.

6.3   Amnesty period. The defendant facing a case funded by ATE insurance may have very little opportunity to avoid the cost of the premium. If premiums are to remain recoverable, then there should be a limited period in which the defendant has the opportunity to admit liability and avoid the cost of an ATE insurance policy. This should be no longer than the relevant protocol period and there may be a case for a more restricted window of opportunity, akin to the period of 42 days allowed in the new CPR rule 44.12B in respect of publication proceedings.

6.4   Part 36 risks. Cover is currently extended to Part 36 risks: that is the risk that the claimant is found to have acted unreasonably by failing to accept a defendant's offer. I do not accept that claimants should be divorced from the consequences of their own behaviour in this way. A claimant with such insurance has less incentive to accept settlement offers. Whilst claimants may choose to buy such cover, the cost of that element of cover should not be recoverable from the defendant.

6.5   Assuming that policies are "sold" at a single premium to meet all aspects of cover, it may not be easy to judge how much of the premium relates to the Part 36 risk. I would not encourage a factual enquiry in every case as to the relative cost of the two aspects or the ATE insurer's experience of claims payment. The costs judge may simply have to take a view as to the extent to which Part 36 cover was important to the parties to the contract.

6.6   Cap on recoverable premiums. Several examples were quoted to me during Phase 2 of ATE insurance premiums which seemed unreasonably high when

---

[46] See further Christopher Hodges, Stefan Vogenauer and Magdalena Tulibacka, 'Costs and Funding of Civil Litigation: A Comparative Study' (December 02, 2009), Oxford Legal Studies Research Paper No. 55-2009, available at SSRN: http://ssrn.com/abstract=1511714, forthcoming in C Hodges, S Vogenauer and M Tulibacka (eds), /Costs and Funding of Civil Litigation/.

compared with the sums at stake in the litigation. Whilst there may be valid underwriting reasons for high premiums, particularly when taken out at a late stage before trial and where the premium itself is insured, I do not think it is appropriate to leave premiums uncontrolled in this way. Other elements of costs are subject to caps or guideline rates. In my view the same approach should be adopted towards ATE insurance premiums.

6.7   As the law now stands, in many cases the claimant is not concerned as to the cost of ATE insurance, since there is an expectation that the premium will be recovered from the losing party (or borne by the ATE insurer if the claimant loses). It seems to me that a reasonable claimant would not commit more than 50% of the sum at stake in the litigation to meet the cost of buying insurance cover. I recommend that recoverable ATE insurance premiums be capped at 50% of damages, with any shortfall being a matter for negotiation between the claimant and their insurer. Claimants would be represented in such matters by their solicitors and there should be no difficulty in such a process. It may well be that the ATE insurance industry will come forward with some arbitration or other dispute resolution process in such cases.

(iii) Protection of opposing parties when the ATE insurer is entitled to repudiate

6.8   One recurring complaint about ATE insurance is the difficulty in enforcing claims for costs on behalf of successful defendants. This is a critical point: if premiums are to remain recoverable from defendants in winning cases, there should be no obstacles created for payment of claims for costs on those policies.

6.9   I accept that, like any policy of insurance, an ATE insurance policy will have terms and conditions and that the insurer will have rights to repudiate the policy for material non-disclosure. However, there is a balance to be struck, particularly in a market where the claimant typically does not pay a premium at the start of the policy.

6.10   Although ATE insurance is not a compulsory class of insurance business, there is a useful parallel to be drawn with those classes. In such cases the insurer will pay out but will then have a right to recover any payments from the policyholder. It seems to me that this is a useful model to apply to ATE insurance as well. The provision could either be applied by statute or by a voluntary code of conduct amongst ATE insurers. The latter is obviously preferable and I imagine some of the larger players would be prepared to sign up to such a code.

(iv) Summary of fallback recommendations

6.11   My alternative proposals, if ATE insurance premiums remain recoverable are:

- no ATE insurance premium to be recovered if liability is admitted within protocol period;

- no ATE insurance premium to be recovered for Part 36 risks;

- cap premiums at 50% of damages awarded; and

- in cases where the ATE insurer is entitled to avoid, allow recovery from the insurer with rights against the policyholder preserved.

7. RECOMMENDATIONS

7.1   I make the following recommendations:

(i)   Section 29 of the 1999 Act and all rules made pursuant to that provision should be repealed.

(ii)   Those categories of litigants who merit protection against adverse costs liability on policy grounds should be given the benefit of qualified one way costs shifting.

7.2   If the recommendations in this chapter are rejected, then alternative proposals to limit the impact of section 29 of the 1999 Act have been set out in section 6 of this chapter.

CHAPTER 10. CONDITIONAL FEE AGREEMENTS

INDEX

1. INTRODUCTION

1.1   Preliminary Report. Conditional fee agreements ("CFAs") are described in chapter 16 of the Preliminary Report. The question whether success fees under CFAs should continue to be recoverable under costs orders is discussed in PR chapter 47.

1.2   Success fees recoverable. Under section 58A(6) of the Courts and Legal Services Act 1990 (the "CLSA 1990"), success fees payable under a CFA are recoverable under a costs order. This has been the position since 1st April 2000: see section 27 of the Access to Justice Act 1999 (the "1999 Act"), which amended the CLSA 1990.

(i) The position of solicitors prior to April 2000

1.3   The former professional conduct rules of solicitors and "speccing". Until 1995, it was widely accepted that, at common law, barristers and solicitors could not agree to conduct litigation on the basis that they would only be paid if the action was successful. The common law position in respect of solicitors was reinforced by the Solicitors' Practice Rules 1990, the effect of which was that a solicitor was not permitted to agree to receive remuneration which was related to the outcome of an action. This rule became increasingly detached from the general perception of what was ethically acceptable. A number of solicitors have told me that they turned a blind eye to this rule and engaged in "speccing". In other words, they conducted cases for clients on the explicit or implicit understanding that if the case was won, they would charge their normal fee (or at least what was recovered from the other side); if the case was lost, they would charge nothing. There were two situations in which solicitors commonly engaged in "speccing". First, the solicitor might regard a case as so strong that there was no real risk of losing; thus a "speccing" arrangement made good sense, in order to ensure that the solicitor got the business. Secondly, a solicitor might desire to help an impecunious client, whose case was meritorious but not certain of success. In the first situation, the solicitor was essentially making a commercial decision. In the second situation the solicitor, although making a commercial decision, was also taking a deliberate risk in order to promote access to justice.

1.4   The essence of "speccing" was that solicitors were paid only their normal fee (or what was recovered from the other side) if they won. There was no question of either the clients or the opponents making any additional payment as reward for the risks which the solicitors had taken.

1.5   Style 1 CFAs. On 5th July 1995 style 1 CFAs, as described in PR paragraphs 16.3.1 to 16.3.3 came into use in respect of certain types of work.[47] Style 1 CFAs had two principal consequences. First, the former practice of "speccing" became legalised. Secondly, solicitors became entitled to charge success fees for the risk which they ran in speccing. As stated in PR paragraph 16.3.2, style 1 CFAs made a major contribution to justice. They enabled the so-called MINELAs[48] (individuals whose means were above legal aid limits, but who could not afford to litigate) to gain access to justice.

(ii) The position of barristers prior to April 2000

1.6   The former professional conduct rules of barristers. Until 4th July 1998, the Bar's Code of Conduct prohibited barristers from conducting litigation on the basis that they would only be paid if the action was successful. "Speccing" was generally not possible, because the Bar's Code of Conduct required counsel's brief fee to be agreed in advance. This had the consequence that if (out of concern for the client) counsel intended to charge either no brief fee or a much reduced fee in the event of defeat, counsel's clerk had to agree a nil brief fee or a much reduced brief fee at the outset.[49] This state of affairs inured to the benefit of the other side and served no obvious social purpose.

1.7   As set out in paragraph 1.5 above, on 5th July 1995 style 1 CFAs, as described in PR paragraphs 16.3.1 to 16.3.3, came into use. As from July 1998, style 1 CFAs had two principal consequences for the Bar. First they enabled barristers to act on a "no win, no fee" basis. Secondly, they enabled barristers to charge success fees in cases which they won, as recompense for the risk that they might have been paid nothing. These success fees were paid by the client, not by the other side.

---

[47] The scope of style 1 CFAs was extended on 30th July 1998 by the Conditional Fee Agreements Order 1998; see PR paragraph 16.2.4.
[48] Middle Income No Entitlement to Legal Aid.
[49] As most barristers of my generation have experienced.

(iii) Analysis of reforms implemented prior to April 2000

1.8   Although many people formerly regarded it as an anathema for lawyers to have a financial stake in the outcome of litigation which they were conducting, this is no longer the case. In the course of the Costs Review I have encountered no tenable arguments for returning to the position which existed before style 1 CFAs were permitted.[50] In my view, there can be no objection in principle to lawyers agreeing to forego or reduce their fees if a case is lost. Nor can there be any objection to clients paying something extra in successful cases as compensation for the risks undertaken by their lawyers, provided that the extra payment is reasonable. Therefore I do not recommend that the clock should be put back, so as to prohibit "no win, no fee" agreements. Nor do I recommend any ban upon style 1 CFAs, which remain perfectly lawful.[51]

(iv) The position since April 2000

1.9   In April 2000 style 2 CFAs, as described in PR paragraphs 16.4.1 to 16.4.4, came into use. Under style 2 CFAs, success fees became payable by the opposing party, rather than by the lawyers' own client. This was a massive reform, which has had widespread unintended consequences. This reform set England and Wales apart from all other jurisdictions. See chapters 54 to 62 of the Preliminary Report and also the report by Professor Stefan Vogenauer, Dr Chris Hodges and Dr Magdalena Tulibacka of Oxford University.[52] During 2009 Professor Vogenauer, Dr Hodges and Dr Tulibacka have undertaken a massive review of the costs rules of 33 overseas jurisdictions. They have not found any jurisdictions under which CFA success fees are recoverable from opposing parties.

(v) General observations

1.10   It must be frankly admitted that the conclusions reached in this chapter will cause dismay to many lawyers. It is, of course, congenial for claimant lawyers to see their clients provided with comprehensive funding and insulated from all risk of adverse costs. It is congenial for both claimant and defendant lawyers to have a constant stream of work passing across their desks. Indeed, it is congenial for judges to know that the claimants who appear before them are not putting their personal assets at risk, whatever the outcome of the individual case. But these undoubted benefits have been achieved at massive cost, especially in cases which are fully contested. That cost is borne by taxpayers, council tax payers, insurance premium payers and by those defendants who have the misfortune to be neither insured nor a large and well resourced organisation.

2. DEBATE DURING PHASE 2

2.1   <u>The question of principle.</u> The main debate during Phase 2 has revolved around a single question of principle. That is whether success fees should continue to be recoverable from an opposing party under a costs order (the "recoverability" issue).

---

[50] See PR paragraphs 16.3.1 to 16.3.4.

[51] Although generally no longer used, because of the availability of style 2 CFAs.

[52] Christopher Hodges, Stefan Vogenauer and Magdalena Tulibacka, "*Costs and Funding of Civil Litigation: A Comparative Study*" (December 02, 2009), Oxford Legal Studies Research Paper No. 55-2009, the abstract of which is available at SSRN: http://ssrn.com/abstract=1511714, forthcoming in C Hodges, S Vogenauer and M Tulibacka (eds), /Costs and Funding of Civil Litigation/.

2.2   <u>Follow-on questions.</u> If the answer to the question of principle is "yes", then the next issue is whether any steps should be taken to lessen the burden which the present regime places upon defendants. If the answer to the question of principle is "no", then the next issue is whether any measures, and if so what measures, should be taken to assist claimants who will have to pay success fees out of the damages or other sums recovered.

2.3   <u>Conditional Fee Agreements Conference.</u> At Sweet and Maxwell's Conditional Fee Agreements Conference on 14th May 2009 there was general support for the principle of recoverability. One speaker explained the two constituents of a success fee, namely the risk element and the fee deferment element, and also how it was possible for success fees to be staged. There was much discussion of the technicalities of CFAs and also an explanation of how CFAs could be used by a party to a commercial dispute.

2.4   <u>Meeting with clinical negligence defence solicitors.</u> On 22nd May 2009 I attended a meeting with a group of clinical negligence defence solicitors. There was general opposition to the principle of recoverability. Concern was expressed that success fees were always claimed at 100% and that this element placed a huge burden on defendants (whether recovered in full or reduced on assessment).

2.5   <u>Professional Negligence and Liability Forum.</u> At the Professional Negligence and Liability Forum organised by IBC Legal and held on 11th June 2009, there was some debate about the merits of recoverability. Opinion was divided as to whether the present recoverability regime was satisfactory. In answer to my query, the delegates at this forum indicated that in the general run of professional negligence cases it was now normal practice for claimants to proceed on CFAs. On the claimants' side, the point was made that defendants could avoid paying high success fees and high after-the-event ("ATE") insurance premiums by settling early. On the defence side, concern was expressed about disproportionate costs. One solicitor said that he was dealing with a series of cases where CFAs had been signed after the defendant had admitted liability. Nevertheless success fees of 65% were being claimed and costs were generally two or three times the settlement value. He was critical of detailed assessment as a mechanism to control success fees.

2.6   <u>Meeting with clinical negligence claimant solicitors.</u> On 12th June 2009 I attended a meeting with a group of clinical negligence claimant solicitors. The meeting proceeded on the basis that recoverable success fees were essential. Those present maintained that detailed assessments were an effective check on levels of success fees. Costs judges took seriously the exercise of assessing prospects of success on the information originally available.

2.7   <u>Cardiff seminar.</u> At the Cardiff seminar on 19th June 2009, Sir Anthony May, President of the Queen's Bench Division ("QBD"), speaking after Professor Richard Moorhead's presentation, delivered a powerful attack on the recoverability principle.[53] He stated:

> "Is it right in principle that a losing party should have to pay an additional amount, in excess of the proper and reasonable costs of the litigation, to cover the winning party's lawyer's costs of losing other cases on behalf of other clients? Is it in principle right that an eventual losing party to litigation should be at risk of paying a greater uplift if he has a strongly arguable case

---

[53] See the President of the QBD's paper on the Costs Review website at
http://www.judiciary.gov.uk/docs/costs-review/pqbd-costs-conference-190609.pdf.

which he nevertheless loses, whereas, if he has a rotten case, the justifiable uplift will be less? So too with the after the event insurance premium. This has insured the winning party against the costs he would have been ordered to pay if he had lost, including the costs he would have paid to the eventual losing party. Is it right in principle that a party to litigation should be ordered to pay costs referable to an insurance policy which would have covered his own costs if he had been successful? I do not here question the appropriateness of agreements providing for success fees nor the sense of insuring against potential liabilities in costs. What I do question is whether the other party should in principle be ordered to pay these elements. After all, we do start from the position that the base costs are the proper reasonable costs of conducting the litigation. Why should the losing party additionally finance the costs of other litigation of which he is not a party or of an insurance premium to cover the risk that his own defence might succeed. And the stronger his own defence, the more he has to pay if nevertheless he loses. He may have been negligent or in breach of contract, but his negligence or breach of contract did not generate these expenses."

2.8   A debate on recoverability followed Sir Anthony's speech, at the end of which I took a straw poll. In relation to success fees, there were 21 votes in favour of recoverability, 23 votes against and 12 abstentions. In relation to ATE insurance premiums, there were 17 votes in favour of recoverability, 24 votes against and 18 abstentions. In his subsequent presentation His Honour Judge Nicholas Chambers QC, the Cardiff mercantile judge, stated that CFAs with recoverability can have damaging effects in Mercantile Court litigation. This can produce exposure to costs out of all proportion to what the defendant should pay, if it fights and loses. Sometimes the parties are evenly matched and it is perfectly reasonable for the losing party to have contested the case.

2.9   <u>Meeting with practitioners and clients of a City firm.</u> In June 2009 I attended a meeting with practitioners and clients organised by a City firm. The partners gave a demonstration of business models which they had (perfectly properly) developed in order to take advantage of the recoverability regime. The client is offered a package comprising CFA (on a no win, low fee basis), ATE insurance (premium ranging between 20 and 65% of costs) and third party funding. This package enables the client to hedge much of the risk of commercial litigation and to pursue its claim at relatively modest cost. At the same time the other side will face a potentially crushing costs burden, namely (i) its own costs, (ii) the ATE insurance premium (up to 65% of its own costs), (iii) the other side's base costs (at full hourly rates, not the "low fee" rate) and (iv) a success fee (100% of the other side's base costs). The partners in their presentations, not unreasonably, described the client with such a package as a "super-claimant". The super-claimant has modest exposure to costs liability, whereas the opponent has a very substantial exposure to costs risk. This should incentivise the opponent to settle early, while the ATE insurance premium and success fee remain at a low level.

2.10   <u>Birmingham seminar.</u> The Birmingham seminar on 26th June 2009 was primarily focused on personal injuries litigation. Recoverability was not the subject of a specific presentation or voted upon, but my impression was that most participants supported the principle of recoverability.

2.11   <u>Herbert Smith LLP meeting.</u> At a meeting of practitioners and clients hosted by Herbert Smith LLP on 29th June 2009, there was general opposition to recoverability. One speaker pointed out that the regime was open to abuse. Any party may take advantage of the recoverability regime, regardless of whether that party required financial support. For example, a wealthy party suing a publisher may proceed on a CFA. A representative from an oil company said that CFAs are still rare in his field; the malign and unfair consequences of CFAs in commercial litigation have not yet been appreciated. An experienced solicitor said that the effect of the recoverability regime was (a) that a disproportionate burden was imposed on defendants and (b) that claimants had no incentive to control costs.

2.12   Meeting with Civil Justice Committee of the Law Society. On 9th July 2009 I attended a meeting with the Civil Justice Committee of the Law Society. The committee expressed the strong view that both ATE insurance premiums and success fees should continue to be recoverable, in order to promote access to justice. The committee pointed out, using a flip chart, that in many instances insurers were both the payers and recipients of ATE insurance premiums. Thus the money goes round in a circle and insurers can hardly complain. One member of the committee suggested that the effect might be ameliorated if there were a limited initial period during which a defendant could settle without incurring liability for any success fee or ATE insurance premium.

2.13   King's College conference. At the construction law conference held at King's College on 9th July 2009 I invited debate on a number of issues, including recoverability of success fees. There was strong hostility to the use of CFAs with recoverability in construction litigation. One speaker said that CFAs were used for easy cases to swell costs. Another speaker said that the use of a CFA with recoverability had proved a sticking point in a case which he mediated. On the other hand the recoverability regime could be beneficial when an individual was suing an insurer. At the end of this debate there were nine votes in favour of recoverability and 45 votes against.

2.14   London seminar. At the London seminar on 10th July 2009 Mr Bob Satchwell of the Society of Editors argued with some fervour that the CFA regime was oppressive and unjust in publication cases. He said:

> "Access to justice may well have been improved but there have been too many other unintended and potentially damaging and dangerous consequences.
>
> What was meant as a system to help the less well off has been used by the rich and famous who could well afford to finance actions themselves. Among many others they have included Hollywood actress Sharon Stone, footballer Ashley Cole, supermodel Naomi Campbell, boxing promoter Frank Warren and former Prime Minister's wife Cherie Blair...None of these were being denied justice on financial grounds.
>
> To those of us on the receiving end of what was supposed to be a safety net to compensate lawyers for no win, no fee, cases which their clients lost, the system has become a gravy train financed by the media to reward lawyers who in reality face little serious risk."

2.15   There was a discussion about the principle of recoverability during the panel session at the end of the London seminar. Mr John Foy QC of the Personal Injuries Bar Association ("PIBA") argued powerfully that in personal injury cases the ATE insurance premium and the success fee should fall upon the defendant as wrongdoer, not upon the claimant as victim. Most cases settle early when both success fees and ATE insurance premiums are low. Most defendants are insured and can recover the additional liabilities through premiums. Mr Foy argued that this approach is so obviously right as to be a *"no brainer"*. Professor Michael Zander and Professor

Kritzer argued the opposite case. Professor Zander stated that profit costs broadly comprise 70% overheads and 30% profit; therefore a 100% success fee provides the solicitor with an additional 300% profit. He argued that going down this road ten years ago was a huge mistake; the detailed assessment process cannot properly control the level of success fee. In relation to assessment, Senior Costs Judge Peter Hurst stated that costs judges did their best in relation to success fees, but they were always looking back across the "*smoking ruins*" of the litigation; it was not easy to determine what success fee was reasonable and proportionate; ATE insurance premiums were even more difficult for a costs judge to control, because there must be evidence upon which the costs judge bases his or her decision. Andrew Francis pointed out the difficulty of assessing success fees or ATE insurance premiums retrospectively in chancery litigation. His Honour Michael Cook pointed out that old style CFAs worked satisfactorily.[54] Professor Kritzer pointed out that England and Wales were unique amongst all jurisdictions in insisting that claimants should retain 100% of damages without suffering any deduction in respect of costs. No vote was taken at the end of this panel session, but the majority of speakers both from the floor and the panel were opposed to recoverability.

2.16   CFA seminar. At the CFA seminar on 20th July 2009 there was debate about success fees, with some speakers maintaining that they are too high. There was also debate about the principle of recoverability. At the end of that debate there were 36 votes in favour of success fees being recoverable, nine votes against and nine votes in favour of only half the success fee being recoverable.

2.17   Meeting with a firm of clinical negligence solicitors. One firm of clinical negligence solicitors sent me a summary of its results since 1993. It maintained that "*the existing mechanism of conditional fee agreements (CFAs), with recoverability of additional liabilities, has been outstandingly successful in delivering unfettered access to justice for Claimants in clinical negligence cases*". The firm stated that since 1993 it had won 263 CFA cases and lost 306. The senior partner asked to see me in order to enlarge upon his letter. At our meeting he stated that the great majority of "lost" cases are abandoned before a letter of claim is sent, but after incurring the costs of investigation. Of the cases which the firm pursued after investigating and sending a letter of claim, 92% succeeded. His firm has lost two CFA cases at trial, one of which went to the Court of Appeal. His firm and the ATE insurers have borne substantial costs in respect of the 8% of cases which failed (including the two unsuccessful cases which went to trial).

3. WRITTEN SUBMISSIONS DURING PHASE 2

3.1   There was a profusion of detailed written submissions in relation to the issues identified in paragraphs 2.1 and 2.2 above. It is not practicable within the confines of this chapter to summarise those submissions individually. Instead I shall outline the principal arguments which have been advanced.

3.2   Trade unions. A number of trade unions forcefully argue that recoverability for personal injury claims should continue. The trade unions are principally concerned about the personal injury claims brought by their members. They argue that damages for personal injuries are sacrosanct and no deductions should be permitted.

---

54 Style 1 CFAs, as defined in the Preliminary Report, under which there was no recoverability.

3.3   The Association of Personal Injury Lawyers. The Association of Personal Injury Lawyers ("APIL") argues that success fees should continue to be recoverable. APIL calls for an urgent review of fixed success fees for asbestos related claims. It advocates an extension of fixed success fees in further areas of personal injuries litigation.

3.4   Personal Injuries Bar Association. PIBA, as foreshadowed at the London seminar, put in a powerful submission supporting recoverability. In a survey of its members, 247 supported recoverability and only three opposed. PIBA argues that success fees are essential to enable both solicitors and counsel to take on cases which appear meritorious but ultimately fail. Absent success fees lawyers would only take on "*sure fire certainties*". PIBA accepts that in commercial litigation it may well be right that the party with a CFA should pay the success fee; but personal injuries litigation is different and a personal injury claimant should not suffer any deduction from damages in respect of a success fee.

3.5   PIBA proposes an extension of the fixed success fee rules along the following lines:

- 25% if the case settles more than 21 days before the fixed date of trial or commencement of the warned period for trial.

- 50% in a fast track and 75% in a multi track if there is settlement between that time and the commencement of the trial. (This middle tier should apply only to counsel, thus maintaining the symmetry of the present fixed uplift regime.)

- 100% if the trial has commenced.

3.6   PIBA also accepts that success fees should be restricted in cases where liability is admitted and it recognises the "*apparent injustice*" of *Lamont v Burton*.[55] However, it is argued that every case has some risk.

3.7   Personal injury solicitors. Numerous firms of personal injury solicitors have written in arguing that recoverability of success fees should be retained, in order to promote access to justice for injured claimants. By way of example, one claimant firm writes:

> "We cannot conceive why what can only be an insurance drive to abolish recoverability of success fees and ATE premiums should be given credence.
>
> Recoverable success fees and insurance premiums were the government's answer to doing away with legal aid in PI cases. To now make them non recoverable must mean that Claimants will end up having to make deductions from their damages. Why should a victim of someone else's negligence not get 100% of their compensation?"

3.8   The Forum of Complex Injury Solicitors ("FOCIS") argues that the current regime of recoverability should be maintained. It provides access to justice for seriously injured claimants. FOCIS states:

> "The principle of recoverability.
>
> This is an extension of the 'polluter pays' doctrine which was debated and approved in Parliament. Primary legislation following democratic debate

---

[55] [2007] EWCA 429; [2007] 1 WLR 2814, see PR paragraph 21.6.1.

would be required to reverse this government policy. However, in such a debate all should remember the clear promises by government to the poorest in society who lost the benefit of legal aid that they would not suffer reduction in compensation as a result of the abolition of legal aid."

FOCIS goes on to argue that defendants can protect themselves by Part 36 offers. FOCIS cites example cases of catastrophic cases which were settled and where the success fee was modest. FOCIS concludes:

"The present CFA/ATE regime presents a potential claimant with arguably the best funding option of any jurisdiction. What is so wrong with that given that:

- the regime has largely met the MINELA problem identified in the pre CFA era;

- the Defendants (in practice insurers) have not demonstrated any significant financial difficulty; indeed insurers collect premiums at various stages of the process and return profit for their shareholders;

- we have only just reached a mature marketplace where all sides understand the dynamics so it does not make sense to change it again so quickly."

3.9   A number of trade unions and claimant personal injury solicitors make the point that damages are already too low, since the Law Commission's 1998 recommendations[56] were not implemented. Therefore abolishing recoverability will simply make matters worse. Also there is a risk that claimant solicitors will cherry pick only the most promising cases.

3.10   Personal injury liability insurers. Liability insurers argue that recoverability should end. One major insurer suggests that the success fee, capped, should be deducted from damages, excluding any damages referable to future care or future losses. To illustrate the anomalies of the present regime, one insurer appends details of a tripping case which it defended with good reason and only just lost. Damages totalled £9,028. The claimant's costs (including 100% success fee and ATE insurance premium of £51,466) totalled £141,840.

3.11   Clinical negligence. Claimant solicitors and representative bodies argue for recoverability, essentially on the same grounds as put forward by personal injury solicitors. One firm which represents claimants in clinical negligence cases states:

"The perceived problems with recoverability of Success Fees and ATE premiums are far outweighed by the benefits, particularly for our seriously injured clients of:

(i)   Access to justice for all litigants, resolving the previous MINELA problem;

(ii)   Preserving the 100% compensation principle so that damages serve their intended purpose."

3.12   Defence organisations and their solicitors maintain the opposite. One major firm of defence solicitors states:

---

[56] In Law Com No. 257, 15th December 1998, which can be found online at http://www.lawcom.gov.uk/docs/lc257.pdf.

"We share the view expressed by many others that claimants' solicitors are 'cherry picking' the best cases, particularly in clinical negligence and personal injury, and therefore the notion that success fees are necessary to subsidise the cases which fail is a fallacy."

The Medical Defence Union states:

"We would support the abolition of recovery of success fees from defendants in clinical negligence actions. This may result in some adjustment to damages to accommodate additional costs borne by claimants. Research would need to be undertaken in order to determine the appropriate level of any adjustment. Future losses should be ring fenced from the calculation of any success fee payable."

3.13   One clinical negligence defence firm has done some research into its own records and writes as follows:

"The rationale for success fees is to facilitate access to justice by providing Claimant solicitors with a fund to investigate claims, a proportion of which will not succeed. Essentially success fees should fund the losers. The reality is that there are very few losers and the success fee fund has become pure profit for Claimant solicitors. It is difficult to find the evidence to prove this assertion as the Claimant's solicitors do not publish details of their success rates. However, an analysis of our case data shows that since December 2008 we have closed 114 clinical negligence files. Of those claims 29 were unsuccessful and the Claimants failed to recover any damages. None of those 29 unsuccessful claims was funded by way of a CFA.

In addition, one leading Claimant clinical negligence firm has told us that they always charge a success fee of 100% but have lost only one case after proceedings have been served. The Claimant clinical negligence specialists have become very adept at selecting cases which will succeed but it is common to hear Claimant solicitors saying that they work for free and have to drop cases every day. They use these losers as examples of why a 'success fee or claims investigation' fund is required and the system is working as it should be. Not taking a case on because you do not think it will proceed is very different from taking a case on and losing.

Given that we do not see these CFA losers in our cases (and understand from other NHSLA[57] panel firms that their experience is the same) we believe that if the claim is funded by a CFA the 'losers' are identified by the Claimant's solicitors at a very early stage and claims are not pursued. There will be some cost to the Claimant solicitors but we suggest that this will be limited in most cases with a substantial profit overall after success fees paid for the winners are taken into account."

3.14   <u>Professional negligence solicitors.</u>   Claimant solicitors argue that in the general run of professional negligence cases CFAs with recoverability are necessary for access to justice. The Professional Negligence Lawyers' Association (the "PNLA") states:

---

[57] National Health Service Litigation Authority.

"We can now say to a claimant with a claim of £150,000 that if their case is assessed at over 60% chance of success that they could get most of the money they have lost back. There will be a shortfall on costs – perhaps typically 30% of the profit costs...which they are liable to pay depending on the amount of recoveries. In practice most claimant firms negotiate the shortfall depending on the outcome...So eg if a settlement of £120,000 was agreed then the client will probably recover £100,000 or so in practice.

If success fees and ATE premiums were not recoverable then the assessment changes radically. If a settlement was obtained at £120,000 then the PNLA member would have to explain that the maximum recovery would be £120,000 less (£50,000 plus VAT success fee plus the ATE Premium at say £30,000 – being £87,500) = £32,500. In addition there might be a shortfall of 30% on the base costs."

3.15   Professional Negligence Bar Association. The Professional Negligence Bar Association ("PNBA") offers a balanced assessment of the recoverability issue. It acknowledges the problems of the present regime as follows:

"We recognise that:

a.   the recoverability of success fees and after the event insurance premiums have given rise to an expectation amongst many, which claimants' solicitors competing for business have to take on board, that litigants should never have to pay any costs, win or lose.

b.   the recoverability of success fees and after the event insurance premiums also means that there are few incentives on the CFA-funded (and usually claimant's) side to keep costs down, as (in contrast to the traditional model of a paying client), the client does not have any costs and thus has no interest in the costs, and the solicitors of course has an interest to recover as much as they reasonably can. We recognise that this is a disadvantage in the present system.

c.   the recoverability of additional liabilities has increased the paying party's (normally the defendant's) liability for costs significantly, and that this is another disadvantage of the present system."

3.16   Having acknowledged those problems, the PNBA concludes that, on balance, recoverability should continue for four main reasons, namely:

(i)   The claimant's costs are subject to detailed assessment.

(ii)   The extra costs are paid by a tortfeasor.

(iii)   Abolition of CFAs would decimate professional negligence cases.

(iv)   Abolition would offend against the principle of full recovery.

The PNBA places particular emphasis on the third and fourth reasons in its subsequent exegesis. It argues that better policing of the present regime is the preferable response to a perception of high costs in professional negligence litigation.

3.17   Professional liability insurers. Professional liability insurers are opposed to recoverability. Claims Against Professionals ("CAP"), a body of leading professional indemnity insurers, has surveyed its members for the purpose of responding to the Preliminary Report. The majority of CAP members, but not all CAP members, believe that neither ATE insurance premiums nor CFA success fees should be recoverable.

3.18   Commercial practitioners.   My overall impression is that the majority of commercial practitioners, but by no means all such practitioners, believe that recoverability has no place in commercial and similar litigation. This view has been expressed by a number of City firms, by the London Solicitors Litigation Association and by the City of London Law Society's Litigation Committee.

3.19   The Commercial Bar Association states:

> "...there is no reason why a commercial defendant should have to pay an enhanced (and disproportionate) fee to the claimant because of the agreement which the claimant has reached with his lawyers. If a claimant wishes to reward his lawyers for their success in pursuing his claim, then that should not be done at the expense of the defendant. Of the respondents to our questionnaire who addressed the question of whether success fees should be recoverable, all bar one expressed the view that they should not be recoverable. We agree.
>
> We also take the view that the use of CFAs, if they are recoverable from the other party, may diminish the attraction of London to foreign litigants. If a party may have to pay not only the other party's (substantial) costs, but also an equally substantial uplift, then that party may decide that other jurisdictions which do not pose that risk are more attractive."

3.20   On the other hand the Commercial Litigation Association believes that any part of the success fee which exceeds 25% of the damages should be recoverable. A number of solicitors firms support recoverability of success fees and have developed business models which take advantage of this for the benefit of their clients in commercial and similar litigation.

3.21   Chancery Bar Association.   The Chancery Bar Association (the "ChBA") argues that success fees ought not to be recoverable. The ChBA notes that under the present CFA regime, the CFA party has no interest in controlling costs. If success fees were borne in part or whole by the party entering into the CFA, that party would have reason to negotiate the success fee down. This would operate as a "*natural brake*" on success fees and perhaps make CFAs a more attractive option for funding higher risk chancery and commercial cases. The ChBA argues further that shifting the burden of paying the success fee back onto the CFA party would give the CFA party reason to control hourly rates and the base costs. In the case of a simplified CFA,[58] there would also be a powerful disincentive to lawyers to incur excessive or unreasonable costs because the client is not liable for the portion not recovered on assessment. If success fees were irrecoverable, this would cut back on speculative and weak claims.

3.22   Property Bar Association.   The Property Bar Association (the "PBA") believes that the manner in which a litigant funds litigation is a matter between the litigant and his lawyers. It should not affect the amount of costs recoverable from the other party. Success fees should not be recoverable. The PBA states that its members do not have the same objection as other sections of the Bar to a litigant's damages being reduced by reason of having to pay a success fee or similar sum.

---

[58] Sometimes known as a "CFA Lite"; see PR paragraph 3.5.28.

3.23   Environmental private law claims. The UK Environmental Lawyers Association ("UKELA") supports the continuation of recoverability. UKELA points out that in many environmental claims the client cannot afford to pay the success fee and it is not practicable to deduct the success fee from the damages. In some instances the defendant is well resourced and will pursue its defence without regard to commercial considerations. In the alternative, UKELA argues that the claimant should recover its success fee when it obtains a result more advantageous than its Part 36 offer.

3.24   A firm of solicitors specialising in environmental nuisance claims puts forward similar arguments in its Phase 2 submission:

> "In our experience, Claimants in environmental nuisance cases are primarily interested in obtaining injunctive relief, but general damages in these cases, in particular in respect of transitory nuisances, are typically small and are likely to be awarded by reference to the cost of a modest holiday. Our experience shows that damages in loss of amenity cases are assessed at around £1,500 - £2,000 per annum in transitory nuisance cases.
>
> In these circumstances, it would be impossible for a success fee (whether capped at 25% or otherwise) realistically to be recovered out of the client's damages."

3.25   Tree root claims. One specialised, but certainly not uncommon, form of private nuisance action is a claim for damage by tree roots. Typically, the house owners recover the costs of underpinning and remedial works on their household insurance policy; the insurers then bring a subrogated claim against the local authority. Self-evidently the household insurers can afford to fund their own litigation and there is no conceivable reason why they should not abide by the normal costs rules.[59] Nevertheless, I have received a submission sent in on behalf of sixteen councils in the London area, stating:

> "Insurance companies are increasingly engaging the services of solicitors under CCFAs[60] to handle recovery actions for costs incurred in subsidence claims where local authorities trees are implicated as the cause of the damage. This practice, however, is having a detrimental effect on public finances by significantly increasing claim costs unnecessarily."

The councils state that the costs of these cases have risen greatly and are inflated by 100% success fees.[61]

3.26   The Local Government Association shares the concern of the sixteen councils. It states:

> "We share [the councils'] concern that, at a time when councils and the wider public sector are facing increased pressure on resources, the existing rules enable commercial firms to inflate the costs of these cases, despite local authorities typically being willing to settle these claims pre-litigation. It seems to us that the benefits of using solicitors acting under CCFAs accrue almost entirely to the firms themselves, through excessive legal fees, rather than to the claimants, and that this is to the detriment of local taxpayers."

---

[59] As they did when I conducted such actions as a barrister.
[60] Collective conditional fee agreements.
[61] I cite the tree roots cases merely as an example. During Phase 2, I was told of many other subrogated claims which insurers bring on CCFAs, thus inflating costs to no useful purpose.

3.27   ATE insurers.   ATE insurers generally support recoverability.   One ATE insurer offers a pithy explanation for the introduction of recoverability:

> "Recoverability was introduced partly to facilitate the reduction of Legal Aid but also to deal with the fact that Access to Justice was harder for 'middle England' than for those eligible for Legal Aid.   Its removal would undermine that public policy objective."

3.28   Law Society and Manchester Law Society.   The Law Society maintains that success fees should continue to be recoverable.   It states that the "*100% recovery of damages principle*" must be maintained.   The Manchester Law Society takes a similar view.

3.29   Bar organisations.   The Bar Council acknowledges that there are strongly conflicting views within the Bar on CFAs and recoverability, but does not address those issues in its Phase 2 submission.   The Bar Council believes that funding issues should be the subject of separate consultation.   The CFA Panel, a sub-committee of the Bar's Remuneration Committee, identifies a number of problems in administering the CFA regime.   It points out that barristers face greater risks than solicitors.   It believes that CFA funding is particularly unsuitable to fund claims brought on behalf of children or patients or large and complex claims which will run for many years.   It favours an extension of fixed success fees.   At least implicitly, the CFA Panel supports the continuation of recoverability.   On the other hand, the Contingency Legal Aid Fund Group (set up by the Bar Council, but independent of the Bar Council) takes a more unfavourable view of recoverability.   It states:

> "The current recoverability regime in CFAs has operated to the serious disadvantage of defendants who, as Lord Justice Jackson identifies, end up paying for all claimants' costs (winners and losers) through success fees and ATE premiums.   Claimants have little if any interest in the costs incurred in their names.   There is no downward pressure on claimants' costs.   There is no true market in costs or ATE premiums; the cost judges accept that they have effectively no control on the general level of PI and clinical negligence costs as a result.[62]"

3.30   Judiciary.   The majority of judges are strongly opposed to ATE insurance premiums being recoverable.   This is the position of Her Majesty's District Judges. The Council of Her Majesty's Circuit Judges states:

> "The concept of a losing defendant in any particular case having to subsidise the costs which the opposing solicitor has notionally or actually lost in other cases is manifestly unfair, and could indeed be called grotesque. It means that defendants pay for everything, and claimants can litigate entirely risk free whatever the lack of merit in their claims.   It is especially unfair when claimants' solicitors do their best not to take on cases which they may lose anyway. CFAs have themselves led to considerable satellite litigation."

3.31   The Chief Chancery Master states in his comments on the Preliminary Report:

> "My strong view is that success fees and ATE premiums visited on the losing side are, quite simply, an iniquity in a civilized society.   It is in principle wrong for the paying party to replace legal aid."

---

[62] As explained by the Senior Costs Judge, Peter Hurst, at the London seminar on 10th July 2009.

4. THE RECOVERABILITY ISSUE

(i) Background

4.1   Scope of this section. In this section I shall discuss whether success fees and ATE insurance premiums should be recoverable under costs orders from losing parties. The issues of policy and principle in respect of (a) success fees and (b) ATE insurance premiums are very similar. The relevant facts and arguments in respect of ATE insurance premiums are set out in chapter 9 above. The relevant facts and arguments in respect of success fees are set out in sections 1 to 3 of this chapter.

4.2   The policy reasons for introducing recoverability. Recoverability was introduced by the 1999 Act with effect from 1st April 2000, to coincide with the substantial retraction of legal aid and the establishment of a new system of public funding which occurred on that date. The stated intention of recoverability was fourfold:[63]

- To ensure that the compensation awarded to a successful party was not eroded by any uplift or premium – the party in the wrong would bear the full burden of costs.

- To make conditional fees more attractive, in particular to defendants and to claimants seeking non-monetary redress.

- To discourage weak cases and encourage settlements.

- To provide a mechanism for regulating the uplifts that solicitors charge.

In its White Paper, *"Modernising Justice"*,[64] the Government had recognised that the civil law tended to be accessible only to those who could afford to pay the high and unpredictable costs of litigation or to those who were so poor that they qualified financially for legal aid. The so-called MINELAs, sometimes described as middle England, were people who had means above the legal aid threshold but who could not afford to litigate without putting their homes and their assets at risk. Introducing recoverability would provide support not only for those who would previously have qualified for legal aid, but also for the MINELAs.

4.3   Costs transferred from taxpayers to opposing litigants. One effect of sections 27 and 29 of the 1999 Act[65] was that the burden of financing a huge swathe of litigation was transferred from taxpayers[66] to opposing litigants.[67] Ironically, those opposing litigants are, in many cases, funded by taxpayers or council taxpayers: for example, the NHS Litigation Authority, local authorities, police authorities, etc. It is beyond the resources of this Costs Review to calculate the overall effect on the public purse. It is, however, plain that the savings made by the Legal Services Commission (the "LSC") are but one part of the picture. The additional costs which the recoverability regime has cast upon those who pay taxes or insurance premiums are very substantial. See, for example, the appendices to the Preliminary Report, chapter 2 above and chapter 23 below.

---

[63] See the Explanatory Notes to the 1999 Act.
[64] December 1998, which can be found online at http://members.lycos.co.uk/lawnet/MODJUST.PDF.
[65] Section 27 of the 1999 Act amended the Courts and Legal Services Act 1990, by amending section 58 and inserting section 58A. Section 58A(6) provides for CFA success fees to be recoverable, subject to rules of court. Section 29 of the 1999 Act provides for ATE insurance premiums to be recoverable, subject to rules of court.
[66] As contributors to the Legal Aid Fund.
[67] It should be noted, however, that opposing litigants have always borne part of the burden by reason of one way costs shifting, described in paragraph 4.5 below.

4.4   Costs transferred from trade unions to opposing litigants. Trade unions traditionally support personal injury claims brought by their members. Before the present CFA regime was introduced trade unions bore the costs of unsuccessful actions.[68] As a result of the recoverability regime, trade unions and their solicitors are reimbursed the costs of unsuccessful actions by opposing parties in successful actions.[69] Thus at a stroke a substantial costs burden has been transferred from trade unions to liability insurers. Indeed personal injury actions have now become a source of profit for trade unions. Some unions receive referral fees for referring personal injury claims to solicitors, whereas others receive free legal services in return for such referrals: see chapter 20 below, paragraphs 2.3 and 3.7. Also, in successful cases, trade unions recover from opposing parties an additional amount not exceeding the equivalent ATE insurance premium.

4.5   The legal aid regime which recoverability replaced. Prior to 1st April 2000 the Legal Aid Fund financed personal injury and other litigation, in that it met the assisted party's costs initially and only recouped its own costs later if and when a favourable costs order was made. However, in unsuccessful cases neither the Legal Aid Fund[70] nor the assisted party[71] was normally ordered to pay the other side's costs. Thus a regime of one way costs shifting has always existed in legal aid cases and, indeed continues to exist,[72] although the ambit of legal aid is now much reduced.

4.6   Two crucial features of the legal aid regime. The legal aid regime possesses two crucial features. First, legal aid is targeted upon persons who merit financial support with their litigation. The Legal Aid Board used to apply, and the LSC now applies, both a means test and a merits test before agreeing to assist a party. Secondly, the assisted party is required to make a contribution towards costs, in accordance with his means.[73]

(ii) Flaws in the recoverability regime

4.7   The recoverability regime does not possess either of the two crucial features of the legal aid regime which it replaces. In my view these omissions are two of its flaws. The third flaw is that the burden placed upon opposing parties is simply too great. The fourth flaw is that it presents an opportunity for some lawyers to make excessive profits. The consequence of these four flaws is to generate disproportionate costs.

(a) First flaw

4.8   Any person, whether rich or poor and whether human or corporate, is entitled to enter into a CFA and take out ATE insurance. All that such a person needs to do is to find willing solicitors and willing insurers. This gives rise to anomalies and

---

[68] The arrangements which trade unions made with their solicitors for dealing with the costs of unsuccessful cases varied from one trade union to another.

[69] They recover the costs of unsuccessful actions through the mechanisms of (a) success fees and (b) additional amounts not exceeding the equivalent ATE insurance premiums.

[70] In respect of first instance proceedings, the unassisted party had to demonstrate that it would suffer "severe financial hardship" in order to recover costs against the Legal Aid Board: see section 18(4)(b) of the Legal Aid Act 1988. Orders against the Legal Aid Board were more common in appeal proceedings since the requirement of severe financial hardship did not apply.

[71] See section 17(1) of the Legal Aid Act 1988.

[72] See section 11 of the 1999 Act.

[73] Subject to recovering those costs from the other side if the case was successful.

unintended consequences on a grand scale. I will give three examples in the next three paragraphs.[74]

4.9   The tree root claims. It is, in my view, absurd that insurance companies can bring claims against local authorities using CCFAs (as described in paragraphs 3.25 and 3.26 above), thereby doubling the costs burden upon council tax payers. The insurance companies can well afford to fund such litigation themselves and should do so.

4.10   Commercial claims. It is also, in my view, absurd that one party to commercial litigation can become a "super-claimant" (as described in paragraph 2.9 above) and thereby transfer most of the costs burden to the other party. Two arguments have been pressed upon me by defenders of recoverability in such cases: first, that recoverability enables SMEs[75] to take on larger companies; secondly that the opposing party can avoid the crushing costs burden by settling early. As to the first argument, the recoverability provisions are of universal application. They are just as likely to be used by a large company against an SME as vice versa. As to the second argument, as Judge Chambers pointed out at the Cardiff seminar, some business disputes are evenly balanced. It is perfectly reasonable for the companies on both sides to decide to fight. It is quite wrong for one or other party to be pressurised into settling by a gross imbalance in the costs liabilities of the parties. If party A has a CFA and ATE insurance and party B does not, party A may be litigating at virtually no costs risk, whereas party B may face liability for quadruple[76] costs if it loses. This is not the level playing field which the courts ought to provide for such litigation.

4.11   Consumer dispute. County court litigation sometimes involves disputes between suppliers of goods and customers or consumers. Where such litigation is above the level of the small claims track, it is not unknown for the supplier to have a CFA and for the individual on the other side not to have a CFA. It all depends upon the terms which each party manages to agree with its own solicitors. In some cases the recoverability regime will give the consumer a "free ride" against the supplier. In other cases it will have precisely the opposite effect. It is perfectly possible for the recoverability regime to give the supplier a free ride and to expose the consumer to a massively increased costs liability.

4.12   The first flaw in the recoverability regime is that it is unfocused. There is no eligibility test for entering into a CFA, provided that a willing solicitor can be found.

(b) Second flaw

4.13   The second flaw is that the party with a CFA generally has no interest in the level of costs being incurred in his or her name. Whether the case is won or lost, the client will usually pay nothing. If the case is lost, the solicitors waive their costs and pay the disbursements, in so far as not covered by ATE insurance. If the case is won, the lawyers will recover whatever they can from the other side either (a) by detailed or summary assessment or (b) by negotiation based upon the likely outcome of such an assessment.

---

[74] Such examples could be multiplied: see e.g. *Campbell v MGN Ltd* [2005] UKHL 61, [2005] 4 All ER 793.
[75] Small and medium enterprises.
[76] Own costs plus other side's costs plus ATE insurance premium (which in some commercial cases drawn to my attention goes up to 100%) plus other side's success fee.

4.14   This circumstance means that the client exerts no control (or, in the case of a no win, low fee agreement, little control) over costs when they are being incurred. The entire burden falls upon the judge who assesses costs retrospectively at the end of the case, when it is too late to "control" what is spent.

(c) Third flaw

4.15   The third flaw in the recoverability regime is that the costs burden placed upon opposing parties is excessive and sometimes amounts to a denial of justice. If one takes any large block of cases conducted on CFAs, the opposing parties will end up paying more than the total costs of both parties in every case, regardless of the outcome of any particular case.

4.16   If the opposing party contests a case to trial (possibly quite reasonably) and then loses, its costs liability becomes grossly disproportionate. Indeed the costs consequences of the recoverability rules can be so extreme as to drive opposing parties to settle at an early stage, despite having good prospects of a successful defence. This effect is sometimes described as "blackmail", even though the claimant is using the recoverability rules in a perfectly lawful way.

(d) Fourth flaw

4.17   If claimant solicitors and counsel are successful in only picking "winners", they will substantially enlarge their earnings. As Professor Zander pointed out at the London seminar, if the claimant solicitor wins a case with a 100% success fee, he or she receives an additional 300% profit.[77] As the Senior Costs Judge explained at the same seminar, it is not possible for costs judges effectively to control success fees retrospectively.

4.18   Of course, not all lawyers are good at picking winners and some suffer losses on that account. Nevertheless, one repeated criticism of the recoverability regime, which I have heard throughout the Costs Review, is that some claimant lawyers "cherry pick". In other words they generally conduct winning cases on CFAs, they reject or drop at an early stage less promising cases and thus generate extremely healthy profits. Obviously the financial records of individual solicitors firms and barristers are confidential. Moreover, even if one such set of accounts were made public, that would tell us nothing about all the others. Nevertheless, the one point that can be made about the CFA regime is that it presents the *opportunity* to cherry pick. If lawyers succumb to that temptation, they will greatly increase their own earnings and they will do so in a manner which is entirely lawful.

4.19   Having worked in the legal profession for 37 years, I have a high regard for my fellow lawyers, both solicitors and counsel. The fact remains, however, that lawyers are human. As Professor Adrian Zuckerman has forcefully pointed out both during the Woolf Inquiry and during the present Costs Review, work tends to follow the most remunerative path. In my view, it is a flaw of the recoverability regime that it presents an opportunity to lawyers substantially to increase their earnings by cherry picking. This is a feature which tends to demean the profession in the eyes of the public.[78]

---

[77] The counter-argument to this is that success fees replace both overheads and profits on cases that are lost. However, for this mechanism to work effectively it is necessary that solicitors should lose a sufficient number of cases.
[78] See the extensive press comment about the effects of the CFA regime throughout 2009.

4.20   In my view the proper course is to abolish recoverability and to revert to style 1 CFAs, as they existed before April 2000. Those arrangements were satisfactory and opened up access to justice for many individuals who formerly had no such access: see PR paragraph 16.3.2. During 1996 APIL confirmed that those arrangements provided access to justice for personal injury claimants and that those arrangements were satisfactory: see paragraph 25 of chapter 2 of Lord Woolf's Final Report on Access to Justice.[79]

5. FOLLOW-ON QUESTIONS

(i) If my recommendation to abolish recoverability is accepted

5.1   The follow-on question which arises is whether any measures and, if so, what measures ought to be taken to assist claimants to meet the success fees which they will have to pay in successful cases out of damages or other sums recovered.

5.2   The measures which I propose are set out below.

(a) Personal injuries litigation

5.3   In order to assist personal injury claimants in meeting the success fees out of damages, I recommend that:

(i)   The level of general damages for pain, suffering and loss of amenity be increased by 10% across the board.

(ii)   The amount of success fee which lawyers may deduct be capped at 25% of damages, excluding any damages referable to future care or future losses.

(iii)   The reward for making a successful claimant's offer under CPR Part 36 (i.e. an offer which the defendant fails to beat at trial) be enhanced.

5.4   I am advised by Professor Paul Fenn (economist assessor) that such an increase in general damages will in the great majority of cases leave claimants no worse off. Indeed the great majority of claimants (whose claims settle early) will be better off. At the same time proper incentives for all parties to personal injuries litigation will have been restored.

5.5   In this regard, it is significant that in Scotland personal injury cases are conducted satisfactorily on CFAs, despite the fact that success fees are not recoverable.[80] Indeed at the Glasgow seminar on 19th October 2009,[81] a number of speakers made the point that personal injuries litigation, which is currently being conducted under the new procedures developed by the Court of Session, is the most successful part of the Scottish civil justice system.

(b) Other litigation brought by individuals

5.6   I recommend that the level of general damages for nuisance, defamation and any other tort which causes suffering to individuals be increased by 10%. This will

---

[79] HMSO (1996) ISBN 0 11 380099 1.
[80] See paragraphs 96, 97 and 106 of chapter 14 of Lord Gill's "*Report of the Scottish Civil Courts Review*" published in September 2009.
[81] To mark the publication of Lord Gill's Report.

assist those claimants who proceed on CFAs to meet the success fees. Such an increase may appear to be a windfall for claimants who are not on CFAs. On the other hand, the level of general damages in England and Wales is not high at the moment.[82] The abolition of "recoverability" would be an opportune moment for raising the level of such damages generally.

(c) Claimants' offers

5.7 In chapter 41 below I shall be recommending reforms to CPR Part 36. One of these reforms will be that, where the claimant makes a Part 36 offer which the defendant fails to beat at trial, the claimant's reward is substantially enhanced. The proposed enhancement is that the court awards to the claimant an additional 10%. That will be 10% of (a) any financial sum awarded and (b) the best assessment that the judge can make of the financial value of any non-monetary relief granted, such as an injunction or vindication of reputation.

5.8 Such an enhancement (which will be open to any claimant who is litigating against an obdurate or unreasonable defendant) will substantially assist claimants to pay success fees in those few cases which go to trial and thus generate success fees substantially above the norm. See chapter 41 below, paragraph 3.16.

(d) Level of success fees

5.9 If success fees become payable by the solicitors' and counsel's own clients rather than opposing parties, I anticipate that lower success fees will be agreed. No evidence has been produced to me during the Costs Review to demonstrate that success fees at the levels currently charged are necessary to cover the costs of "lost" cases. Indeed the Libel CLAF Group (which included both claimant and defendant representatives)[83] frankly accepted that the present level of success fees was too high and was getting the whole system a bad name.

5.10 The accounts of solicitors who do CFA work are confidential and, unsurprisingly, the relevant data are not in the public domain.

5.11 In relation to the points raised at the CFA conference on 14th May 2009, I would question whether success fees ought to contain any fee deferment element. This is because deferred payment is one of the factors relied upon by claimant solicitors in order to justify their hourly rates being above defence hourly rates. The success fee is of course a proportion of base costs calculated upon those hourly rates.

(ii) If my recommendation to abolish recoverability is not accepted

5.12 I regard my recommendation that recoverability of success fees be abolished as an important one and not one to be lightly discarded. However, if it is concluded that it is not possible to "turn back the clock" to a pre-April 2000 regime, then the level of recoverable success fees will need to be rigorously controlled.

5.13 Personal injuries litigation has been the focus for most of the initial litigation on success fee levels. As a result of that litigation, fixed success fees were introduced

---

[82] See the Law Commission's report "*Damages for personal injury: non pecuniary loss*", Law Com 257 (1998).
[83] This working group was set up following the meeting of libel lawyers on 21st July 2009 in order to consider the possible establishment of a contingent legal aid fund for libel cases. See chapter 1 paragraph 3.14 above and chapter 32 below.

between 2003 and 2005 for road traffic accident ("RTA") cases, employers' liability ("EL") claims and industrial disease cases (see sections II to V of CPR Part 45).

5.14   The reason for introduction of fixed success fees was simple. It was easy to demonstrate that the risks of an individual case were significantly higher than the overall risk of a particular type of case. For example it is known that RTA and EL claims are broadly likely to succeed, but individual success fees tended to be set at levels that suggested otherwise. Even in the period before recoverability was introduced, surveys showed that solicitors were naturally cautious in setting the level of success fee and erred on the high side: see the report of Stella Yarrow in 1997, "*The Price of Success*".[84]

5.15   Fixed success fees should be introduced into all areas of litigation where CFAs are commonly used. The responses cited in sections 2 and 3 above give a guide as to the likely areas to be considered. Such success fees should be based on research into the likely outcomes from CFA backed cases in particular areas or generally, as happened with the personal injuries success fees now contained in CPR Part 45.

5.16   The model for a two-stage success fee used in Part 45 has been found to be broadly acceptable. A relatively low level of success fee is set throughout the life of the case and increases if a trial or final hearing commences. However, although the model is broadly successful, it does produce some anomalies.

5.17   There is a strong argument for saying that there should be a period in which the defendant has the opportunity to admit liability before a success fee is chargeable or recoverable, particularly in those cases which are governed by pre-action protocols. For the pre-action protocols to serve a useful purpose, they should be designed to permit behaviour which has the effect of reducing costs and speeding up settlement. Although case law has determined that a CFA can be entered into at the outset of a case before the defendant has even been notified of the claim,[85] I recommend that no success fee should be recoverable from the paying party (or chargeable to the client) for the protocol period.

5.18   A further anomaly arises in the treatment of CPR Part 36. The original model CFA drafted by the Law Society in 2000 provided that if the client rejected a Part 36 offer on advice and that offer was not beaten, the solicitor would charge base costs but not a success fee for the period after the offer was rejected. It is now commonplace for solicitors to agree with their client that they will bear the Part 36 risk completely, that is, that the solicitor will not charge the client base costs or a success fee if the claimant fails to beat an offer rejected on advice. This has led to the risks of Part 36 being included in the risk assessment and forming the basis of the level of recoverable success fee sought from the defendant.

5.19   The effect of permitting such success fees to be recovered is circular and risks undermining the effectiveness of Part 36. The client is in effect guaranteed a satisfactory protection against the Part 36 risk and has correspondingly less interest in accepting an offer.[86] A defendant who makes a good Part 36 offer faces the risk of paying a correspondingly high success fee for the risk of the claimant rejecting that offer.

---

[84] Grantham Books (1997).
[85] See *Callery v Gray* [2002] UKHL 28; [2002] 1 WLR 2000.
[86] ATE insurance has developed to meet the same demand for protection against risk of adverse costs: see the previous chapter.

5.20   The purpose of Part 36 is to encourage parties to accept reasonable offers and, by implication, to apply sanctions to those who do not act reasonably in accepting such offers. The claimant with such a funding regime is in effect protected from the consequences of his own unreasonable behaviour.

5.21   The ability of solicitors to calculate high success fees based on Part 36 risks is neatly illustrated by the 2008 Court of Appeal decision of *C v W*.[87] In this case a success fee of 83% was "negotiated" with the client even after liability was admitted.[88]

5.22   I would recommend that any element of a success fee which provides for protection against the risk of the claimant not accepting a good Part 36 offer should not be recoverable from the paying party. This change could be achieved by the Civil Procedure Rules.

5.23   There are also some anomalous decisions around the effect of fixed success fees in cases where Part 36 offers are rejected (*Lamont v Burton*)[89], as to the application of success fees to costs assessment proceedings (*Crane v Canons Leisure*)[90] and entitling the receiving party to a success fee even where there is some doubt as to the existence of a retainer (*Kilby v Gawith*).[91]

5.24   I recommend that where a two-stage success fee model is applied and a Part 36 offer is made and not beaten at trial, the receiving party should be limited to the level of success fee that applies at the last date when he could have accepted the offer. So in an RTA case for example with 12.5% success fee for the period up to trial and 100% at trial, a claimant who proceeds to trial and does not beat a pre-trial Part 36 offer is limited to a success fee of 12.5% and is not entitled to 100%. This overturns the decision in *Lamont v Burton*.

5.25   I see no justification for a success fee being allowed in detailed assessment proceedings, where the receiving party is normally entitled to their costs by virtue of the Civil Procedure Rules. The Rules should be amended to make it clear that fixed recoverable success fees do not apply to assessment proceedings and that no success fee is recoverable, overturning the decision in *Crane v Canons Leisure*.

5.26   Where a fixed success fee is claimed by the receiving party, the paying party is entitled to be shown evidence that a CFA was in place for the material period so as to justify the charge of a success fee. Where the claimant could have used other funding which would not have resulted in a CFA being used, that should be a valid reason for disallowing any claim for a success fee, but should not otherwise invalidate the retainer or prevent recovery of base costs. This would amend the effect of the decision in *Kilby v Gawith*.

5.27   All the above recommendations could be achieved by changes to the Civil Procedure Rules and would not require primary legislation. Inevitably there would be a need for research as to fair levels of success fee to be set. If the funds and resources of the Civil Justice Council allow for further industry wide agreements (based on research data) to be reached, that would be valuable. If not, the fixed

---

[87] [2008] EWCA Civ 1459; [2009] 4 All ER 1129; [2009] C.P. Rep. 20.
[88] The success fee allowed by the district judge was 70%. This was reduced by the circuit judge on appeal to 50% and by the Court of Appeal to 20%.
[89] [2007] EWCA Civ 429; [2007] 1 WLR 2814.
[90] [2007] EWCA Civ 1352; [2008] 1 WLR 2549.
[91] [2008] EWCA Civ 812; [2009] 1 WLR 853.

success fees could be set by the Civil Procedure Rule Committee or the Costs Council[92] on the basis of research carried out.

5.28   One further fallback option which has been suggested is this: ATE insurance premiums could cease to be recoverable under costs orders, but success fees[93] could remain recoverable. If this option is pursued, two way costs shifting would remain. In a regime where defendants are liable to pay success fees when they lose, they would expect to recover their costs when they win. If my primary recommendations are not accepted, then this fallback option would merit consideration. The advantage of this fallback position is that market forces would cause ATE insurance premiums (paid by claimants) to reduce.

6. RECOMMENDATIONS

6.1   I make the following recommendations:

(i)   Section 58A(6) of the CLSA 1990 and all rules made pursuant to that provision should be repealed.

(ii)   The level of general damages for personal injuries, nuisance and all other civil wrongs to individuals should be increased by 10%.

6.2   If the recommendations in this chapter are rejected, then alternative proposals to limit the impact of section 58A(6) of the 1990 Act have been set out in section 5 of this chapter.

---

[92] If my recommendations in chapter 6 above are accepted.
[93] Subject to the restrictions discussed above.

CHAPTER 11. THIRD PARTY FUNDING

INDEX

1. INTRODUCTION

1.1   <u>Background.</u> The nature of third party funding, the manner in which funders operate and the legal background are set out in PR chapter 15.

1.2   <u>Benefits of third party funding.</u> In PR paragraph 15.1.1 I expressed the view that the institution of third party funding was beneficial in that it promoted access to justice.[94] The majority of contributors to the debate in Phase 2 of the Costs Review supported that view both at meetings and in written submissions.[95] I remain of the view that, in principle, third party funding is beneficial and should be supported, essentially for five reasons:

(i)   Third party funding provides an additional means of funding litigation and, for some parties, the only means of funding litigation. Thus third party funding promotes access to justice.

(ii)   Although a successful claimant with third party funding foregoes a percentage of his damages, it is better for him to recover a substantial part of his damages than to recover nothing at all.

(iii)   The use of third party funding (unlike the use of conditional fee agreements ("CFAs")) does not impose additional financial burdens upon opposing parties.

(iv)   Third party funding will become even more important as a means of financing litigation if success fees under CFAs become irrecoverable.

(v)   Third party funding tends to filter out unmeritorious cases, because funders will not take on the risk of such cases. This benefits opposing parties.

1.3   <u>Recent example.</u> A recent and well known case in which, seemingly, third party funding operated satisfactorily is *Stone & Rolls Ltd (in Liquidation) v Moore Stephens* [2009] UKHL 39; [2009] 3 WLR 455. The claimant company brought a substantial claim for professional negligence against its former auditors, with the benefit of third party funding. The Court of Appeal, reversing Langley J, held that on

---

[94] The Civil Justice Council (the "CJC") has expressed a similar view: see the CJC report "*Improved Access to Justice – Funding Options and Proportionate Costs*", June 2007, recommendation 3 and chapter C.

[95] This view was not universal. In particular, the Young Barristers Committee argued that third party funding should be prohibited in all circumstances on public policy grounds.

the facts alleged the auditors had a defence of *ex turpi causa non oritur actio* and accordingly struck out the claim.[96] The House of Lords dismissed the claimant's appeal. According to press reports, the funder, which had stood to receive some 40% of the proceeds if the action succeeded, duly accepted liability for the auditors' costs. Those costs were reported as being in the region of £2.5 million. It was also reported that there was no after-the-event ("ATE") insurance. In an interview with the Law Society Gazette following the House of Lords decision a legal director of the funder said that the funder currently had a portfolio of 10 to 12 ongoing cases with a success rate of 80%. These facts illustrate that third party funders can operate satisfactorily in the absence of ATE insurance and they can accept liability for any adverse costs orders. The risk undertaken by the funder is reflected in the percentage of damages which the funder is entitled to receive in the event of success.

1.4   It should also be noted that third party funding is commonly used in some overseas jurisdictions: see PR chapters 55 to 61.

1.5   Limitations of third party funding. Although third party funding is beneficial, in that it promotes access to justice for certain litigants, its limitations must also be recognised. Third party funding is not usually feasible where non-monetary relief, such as an injunction or declaration, is the main remedy sought. Third party funding is most readily obtained for high value cases with good prospects of success.

1.6   Matters for consideration. The matters which arise for consideration now may be formulated as follows:

(i)   Whether third party funders should be regulated or should subscribe to a voluntary code.

(ii)   Measures to ensure the capital adequacy of third party funders.

(iii)   Liability for adverse costs.

(iv)   Maintenance and champerty.

2. SHOULD THIRD PARTY FUNDERS BE REGULATED OR SUBSCRIBE TO A VOLUNTARY CODE?

2.1   The general view (but not universal view) expressed during Phase 2 was that there should be some form of restriction upon the activities of third party funders. The central issue which emerged was whether a voluntary code would suffice or whether there should be statutory regulation.[97]

2.2   Law Society's comments. The Law Society believes that third party funding may well assist access to justice, but that proper regulation is required. The Law Society is particularly concerned about two matters:

(i)   The litigation funding agreement is likely to allow the funder to withdraw funding in circumstances which would be contrary to the client's interest or unreasonable.

(ii)   There is no guarantee against the funder becoming insolvent, with all the consequences which would flow from that.

---

[96] From a bad cause no action arises. This principle of public policy means that a claim cannot be based on the illegal actions or wrongful conduct of the claimant, nor can he benefit from his own wrongdoing.
[97] Both views were expressed in the written submissions. At the Commercial Litigation Funding Conference on 23rd June 2009, the majority of those present indicated support for regulation.

2.3   Voluntary code. The draft voluntary code referred to in PR paragraph 15.4.3 was not in the public domain when I published my Preliminary Report. Now, however, the draft voluntary code is in the public domain and can be found upon the Civil Justice Council ("CJC") website.[98] It has been developed by the Third Party Litigation Funders Association in conjunction with the CJC. Support for this voluntary code was expressed by a number of respondents. The point was made that third party funding is still nascent in England and Wales at the moment and that nothing more formal is required. The point was also made that third party funding is not regulated in the overseas jurisdictions studied.[99]

2.4   I accept that third party funding is still nascent in England and Wales and that in the first instance what is required is a satisfactory voluntary code, to which all litigation funders subscribe. At the present time, parties who use third party funding are generally commercial or similar enterprises with access to full legal advice. In the future, however, if the use of third party funding expands, then full statutory regulation may well be required, as envisaged by the Law Society.

2.5   I turn now to the contents of the draft voluntary code. Section 1 is introductory. Section 2 sets out criteria for the selection of cases. Section 3 sets out what the funding agreement should contain.   Section 4.1 sets out the funder's commitments of fair dealing. Section 5 sets out some key obligations of both parties, including the client's obligation to support the litigation and the funder's obligation to pay out adverse costs. Section 6 sets out the funder's entitlement to costs and a share of the proceeds in the event of success. Section 7 deals with the role of the client's solicitor. Section 8 protects confidential information. The remaining sections deal with disclosure of terms, complaints, enforcement of the code and so forth. The appendix to the draft code sets out key terms which should be included in any litigation funding agreement.

2.6   The detailed wording of the draft code is now the subject of debate under the aegis of the CJC and I do not enter into that debate, save in respect of two matters which I believe to be of particular concern.

2.7   Withdrawal by funder. Paragraph 2.7.1 of the appendix to the draft code proposes that the following key term be included in a litigation funding agreement:

> "The Funder may terminate the Litigation Funding Agreement at any time subject to paying all the accrued obligations. The Funder will give 21 days' notice of termination, unless agreed otherwise in the Litigation Funding Agreement. The Funder will terminate if it is no longer satisfied of the merits of your claim and/or has determined that the proceedings are no longer viable."

2.8   I do not regard this as satisfactory. In my view the funder should be obliged to continue to provide whatever funding it originally contracted to provide, unless there are proper grounds to withdraw. The precise definition of proper grounds for withdrawal will require some careful drafting.

---

[98] Annex D to the CJC's submission to the Costs Review which can be found at http://www.civiljusticecouncil.gov.uk/files/Submission_to_the_Review_of_Civil_litigation_Costs.pdf.
[99] It should be noted, however, that in Australia a litigation funding agreement may be subject to regulation as a derivative under the Corporations Act 2001, in which case the funder must hold a financial services licence under the Act. In order to obtain such a licence the funder must satisfy capital adequacy requirements and similar matters. IMF (Australia) Ltd, the most well established funder in Australia, has obtained such a licence.

2.9   Section 4.2.   Section 4.2 of the draft code deals with capital adequacy requirements. That section (in the version current at the time of drafting this chapter) provides:

> "4.2.1 A Member complies with the capital adequacy requirements under this Code, if the Member
>
> (a) (i)   is able to pay all its debts as and when they become due and payable;
>
> (ii)   has total assets that exceed total liabilities as shown in the most recent balance sheet of the Member;
>
> (iii) has no reason to believe that its total assets would not exceed its total liabilities on a current balance sheet;
>
> (iv)   reasonably expects that it will have adequate resources of cash or cash equivalent (when needed) to meet its liabilities for at least the next three months (including any additional liabilities it might incur during that period), taking into account all commercial contingencies for which the Member should reasonably plan; and
>
> (v)   has ensured that a responsible officer of the Member has documented that the officer has the reasonable expectation for at least the following three month period together with the reasons for forming that expectation, the contingencies for which the Member considers it is reasonable to plan, the assumptions made concerning the contingencies and the basis for selecting those assumptions; or
>
> (b)   the Member is covered by an agreement for the current calendar year by virtue of which the Member's (ultimate) parent company shall compensate any annual net loss incurred by the Member during the term of the agreement to the extent that such loss is not compensated by withdrawing amounts from the profit reserves which were transferred to such reserves during the term of the agreement and the (ultimate) parent company is a regulated insurance company that is covered by EU capital adequacy requirements or is otherwise the holder of a financial services license issued by a national regulator approved by the Association."

2.10   Bearing in mind that litigation supported by a third party funder may last for years, section 4.2 of the draft code does not in my view afford adequate protection for the client. How such protection may be achieved is discussed in section 3 below.

2.11   One further point which merits mention concerns paragraph 7.3.2 of the draft code, which states: "*Whilst the Funder may assert some measure of control over the litigation funding, your solicitor must not cede control of his or her firm or the conduct of your case to the Funder.*" As presently drafted the phrase "*some measure of control*" is ambiguous and might benefit from clarification. In particular, the code might set out what rights the funder should have in relation to settlement negotiations.

2.12   Conclusion. I support the approach of the CJC in trying to establish, in the first instance, a voluntary code for third party funding. Provided that a satisfactory code is established and that all funders subscribe to that code, then at this stage, subject to my concern about capital adequacy requirements, I see no need for statutory regulation. However, if the use of third party funding expands, there may well be a need for full statutory regulation.

3. MEASURES TO ENSURE THE CAPITAL ADEQUACY OF THIRD PARTY FUNDERS

3.1   My initial view was that capital adequacy was matter of such pre-eminent importance that it should be the subject of statutory regulation. The natural body to undertake such regulation is the Financial Services Authority (the "FSA").

3.2   Indications from the FSA. I have made contact with the FSA to ascertain whether that body is the appropriate body to monitor the capital adequacy of third party funders. I understand that the FSA would not be able to deal with capital adequacy alone. If the FSA takes on a regulatory role, it would undertake full regulation of third party funders, the costs of which would need to be outweighed by the benefits. Hitherto the FSA, as a risk based regulator, has been holding a general watching brief in relation to this area and, on the basis of liaison with the Ministry of Justice, is not aware of any significant risk to consumers.

3.3   Given the low volume of third party funding at the moment and the fact that most clients are commercial parties with access to full legal and financial advice, I do not think it appropriate to recommend full regulation by the FSA at the present time. Also, I doubt that any such recommendation (involving substantial costs) would be accepted.

3.4   After some hesitation, in the short term I think that capital adequacy requirements are best dealt with by a substantial tightening up of section 4.2 of the draft code. In the long term, however, this matter must be revisited. Regard must be had to the nature of the funders entering the market. Also regard must be had to the nature of the cases and the nature of the claimants that they are funding. If funders are supporting group actions brought by consumers on any scale, then this would be a ground for seriously re-considering the question of statutory regulation of third party funders by the FSA.

4. LIABILITY FOR ADVERSE COSTS

4.1   _Arkin._ In _Arkin v Borchard Lines Ltd_ [2005] EWCA Civ 655 Lord Phillips MR, delivering the judgment of the court, said this at [39] to [43]:

> "39   If a professional funder, who is contemplating funding a discrete part of an impecunious claimant's expenses, such as the cost of expert evidence, is to be potentially liable for the entirety of the defendant's costs should the claim fail, no professional funder will be likely to be prepared to provide the necessary funding. The exposure will be too great to render funding on a contingency basis of recovery a viable commercial transaction. Access to justice will be denied. We consider, however, that there is a solution that is practicable, just and that caters for some of the policy considerations that we have considered above.

41   We consider that a professional funder, who finances part of a claimant's costs of litigation, should be potentially liable for the costs of the opposing party to the extent of the funding provided. The effect of this will, of course, be that, if the funding is provided on a contingency basis of recovery, the funder will require, as the price of the funding, a greater share of the recovery should the claim succeed. In the individual case, the net recovery of a successful claimant will be diminished. While this is unfortunate, it seems to us that it is a cost that the impecunious claimant can reasonably be expected to bear. Overall justice will be better served than leaving defendants in a position where they have no right to recover any costs from a professional funder whose intervention has permitted the continuation of a claim which has ultimately proved to be without merit.

42   If the course which we have proposed becomes generally accepted, it is likely to have the following consequences. Professional funders are likely to cap the funds that they provide in order to limit their exposure to a reasonable amount. This should have a salutary effect in keeping costs proportionate. In the present case there was no such cap, and it is at least possible that the costs that MPC had agreed to fund grew to an extent where they ceased to be proportionate. Professional funders will also have to consider with even greater care whether the prospects of the litigation are sufficiently good to justify the support that they are asked to give. This also will be in the public interest.

43   In the present appeal we are concerned only with a professional funder who has contributed a part of a litigant's expenses through a non-champertous agreement in the expectation of reward if the litigant succeeds. We can see no reason in principle, however, why the solution we suggest should not also be applicable where the funder has similarly contributed the greater part, or all, of the expenses of the action. We have not, however, had to explore the ramifications of an extension of the solution we propose beyond the facts of the present case, where the funder merely covered the costs incurred by the claimant in instructing expert witnesses."

4.2   The High Court of Australia has recently taken a different view concerning the liability of third party funders for adverse costs. See *Jeffery & Katauskas Pty Ltd v SST Consulting Pty Ltd* [2009] HCA 43 in which, by a majority, the funder was held not liable to pay adverse costs.

4.3   <u>Comments during Phase 2.</u> This reasoning of the Court of Appeal attracted some criticism during Phase 2. In their Response to the Preliminary Report the City of London Law Society's Litigation Committee wrote:

"We consider that the court should have the ability to order the third party funder in an unsuccessful case to pay all of the successful defendant's costs (subject to assessment in the usual way) and its ability to do so should not be circumscribed by the principle in *Arkin*."

It should be noted that the facts of *Arkin* were unusual. MPC, the funder in that case, had funded only the claimant's expert evidence and the cost of organising the documents.

4.4   The Commercial Litigation Association commented that the *Arkin* approach creates an uneven playing field. The balance is tilted in favour of third party funding, in that the funder is only liable for costs up to the amount of its investment.

4.5   <u>My view.</u> In my view, the criticisms of *Arkin* are sound. There is no evidence that full liability for adverse costs would stifle third party funding or inhibit access to justice. No evidence to this effect is mentioned in the judgment. Experience in Australia is to the opposite effect. See, for example, the summary of my meeting with IMF on 1st April 2009.[100] IMF have funded approximately 200 cases in Australia. In approximately five of those cases costs orders were made against IMF's clients. IMF duly complied with those adverse costs orders. It is perfectly possible for litigation funders to have business models which encompass full liability for adverse costs. This will remain the case, even if ATE insurance premiums (in those cases where ATE insurance is taken out) cease to be recoverable under costs orders. This is illustrated by the *Stone & Rolls* case discussed in paragraph 1.3 above.

4.6   In my view, it is wrong in principle that a litigation funder, which stands to recover a share of damages in the event of success, should be able to escape part of the liability for costs in the event of defeat. This is unjust not only to the opposing party (who may be left with unrecovered costs)[101] but also to the client (who may be exposed to costs liabilities which it cannot meet).

4.7   I recommend that either by rule change or by legislation third party funders should be exposed to liability for adverse costs in respect of litigation which they fund. The extent of the funder's liability should be a matter for the discretion of the judge in the individual case. The funder's potential liability should not be limited by the extent of its investment in the case.

5. MAINTENANCE AND CHAMPERTY

5.1   <u>The issue.</u> The uncertain ambit of the law of maintenance and champerty has on occasions caused doubt as to the precise boundaries of proper conduct in relation to litigation funding.[102] In PR paragraph 15.4.2 I raised the question whether (provided that third party funding is satisfactorily controlled by other means) section 14(2) of the Criminal Law Act 1967 (the "1967 Act") should be repealed. A similar question has recently been raised in New Zealand: see PR paragraph 59.4.10.

5.2   <u>Views expressed during Phase 2.</u> Unsurprisingly, views differed on this question. A number of respondents pointed out that abolishing the common law doctrine of maintenance and champerty could have unintended consequences. Significantly, the Litigation Funders Alliance (the "LFA")[103] states in its comments on the Preliminary Report:

---

[100] See PR paragraph 58.4.6.
[101] It will inhibit access to justice for the defendant, if (a) it faces a claimant supported by third party funding and (b) the defendant is in the position that – win or lose – it will have to bear its own costs.
[102] The common law position is summarised in PR paragraph 15.1.2.
[103] The LFA states that its members include "*the main professional providers of third party funding in the UK*".

"We have no desire for the rule against champerty to be repealed. We feel that this is a useful mechanism to ensure the balance of power between claimant and professional funder remains appropriate."

5.3   My view. In my view, section 14(2) of the 1967 Act should not be repealed. It should, however, be made clear either by statute or by judicial decision that if third party funders comply with whatever system of regulation emerges from the current consultation process, then the funding agreements will not be overturned on grounds of maintenance and champerty. The law of maintenance and champerty has a wider impact, which goes beyond third party litigation funding of the kind discussed above. The abolition of this common law doctrine may have unforeseen and adverse consequences. Furthermore, such a drastic step is not necessary in order to protect the legitimate interests of third party funders.

6. RECOMMENDATIONS

6.1   I do not consider that full regulation of third party funding is presently required. I do, however, make the following recommendations:

(i)   A satisfactory voluntary code, to which all litigation funders subscribe, should be drawn up. This code should contain effective capital adequacy requirements and should place appropriate restrictions upon funders' ability to withdraw support for ongoing litigation.

(ii)   The question whether there should be statutory regulation of third party funders by the FSA ought to be re-visited if and when the third party funding market expands.

(iii)   Third party funders should potentially be liable for the full amount of adverse costs, subject to the discretion of the judge.

CHAPTER 12. CONTINGENCY FEES

INDEX

1. INTRODUCTION

(i) General

1.1   Definition. As discussed in the Preliminary Report, the phrase "contingency fees" is ambiguous.[104] As before, I shall use the term in its narrower sense to denote fees which (a) are payable if the client wins and (b) are calculated as a percentage of the sum recovered. On this definition, neither solicitors nor barristers are presently permitted to charge contingency fees in contentious business.

1.2   Discussion in the Preliminary Report. The issues surrounding contingency fees and whether they should be permitted are set out in chapter 20 of the Preliminary Report. In that chapter I set out the competing arguments and review the experience of other jurisdictions where contingency fees are permitted.

(ii) Use of contingency fees overseas

1.3   Jurisdictions discussed in Preliminary Report. The extent to which contingency fees are permitted overseas is reviewed in chapters 54 to 62 of the Preliminary Report. In particular, the experience of contingency fees in the USA is set out in PR chapter 60. PR appendix 29 sets out the wide variety of restrictions upon contingency fees which different US states have imposed by regulation. PR chapter 61 sets out the experience of contingency fees in Canada, with particular reference to Ontario. I shall refer to the contingency fees regime which operates in Ontario[105] as the "Ontario model".

1.4   Other jurisdictions. Professor Stefan Vogenauer and Dr Christopher Hodges of, respectively, the Institute of European and Comparative Law and the Centre for Socio-Legal Studies, both at Oxford University, have conducted a study of costs and funding in a number of overseas jurisdictions. In relation to jurisdictions not discussed in the Preliminary Report, they report that contingency fees are permitted in the following jurisdictions: Estonia, Finland,[106] Hungary, Italy, Japan, Lithuania, Slovakia, Slovenia, Spain and Taiwan; contingency fees are banned in Austria,

---

[104] See PR paragraph 20.1.1
[105] As described in PR paragraphs 61.2.5, 61.2.6, 61.4.3 and 61.4.4.
[106] Contingency fee agreements, although permitted, are rarely used in practice in Finland.

Belgium, Cyprus, Czech Republic, Denmark, Greece, Ireland, Luxembourg, Malta, Norway, Portugal, Romania, Singapore and Switzerland.[107]

2. THE DEBATE AT MEETINGS AND SEMINARS DURING PHASE 2

2.1   Meeting with Herbert Smith LLP.   I debated the issues concerning contingency fees at a meeting with practitioners and clients organised by Herbert Smith LLP on 29th June 2009. The great majority favoured the use of contingency fees in commercial litigation on the Ontario model.

2.2   Meeting with CMS Cameron McKenna LLP.   I debated the issues concerning contingency fees at a meeting with practitioners and clients organised by CMS Cameron McKenna LLP on 30th June 2009. The majority favoured the use of contingency fees in commercial litigation, provided that costs shifting is retained on the conventional basis. At the end of the discussion, there were 38 votes in favour of permitting contingency fees and 24 votes in favour of retaining the ban on contingency fees.

2.3   Oxford conference.   At the International Conference on Litigation Costs and Funding held at Oxford University on 6th and 7th July 2009 Dr Hodges presented the preliminary findings of the study referred to in section 1 above. A speaker from the USA stated that contingency fees do not cause frivolous litigation, because lawyers do not take on frivolous cases, but some disagreed, although more so in relation to court-approved fees in class actions. Every lawyer has a portfolio of cases. A speaker from Italy said that contingency fees have been permitted since 2006. However, in the event of success the client only recovers the "tariff fee" from the other side; thus the client has to pay the balance of the contingency fee. A speaker from Germany said that as contingency fees had only been permitted since July 2008,[108] no real experience had yet accumulated and they were expected to be rarely used. Two speakers from Canada said that contingency fees were mainly used in personal injury actions; the client paid the contingency fee out of damages and recovered reasonable costs from the other side.[109] This arrangement was satisfactory.

2.4   London seminar.   At the London seminar held on 10th July 2009 Professor Herbert Kritzer[110] gave a talk on the operation of contingency fee agreements in the USA. He stated that, outside routine road traffic accident cases, lawyers are very selective about the cases which they take on. The risk of failing on liability is low in the cases which they accept, but there is often considerable uncertainty about the level of recovery. The biggest uncertainty is how much work the lawyer will have to do. This depends upon factors such as whether the other side is willing to settle early. The most common contingency fee is one third of the damages recovered. However, some agreed contingency fees are above one third and an equal number are below one third. In some cases the contingency fee is on a sliding scale. Quite often lawyers agree to take less than the contingency fee which is due to them. US lawyers are careful to preserve their reputations. Also they have an incentive to negotiate up

---

[107] See Christopher Hodges, Stefan Vogenauer and Magdalena Tulibacka, "*Costs and Funding of Civil Litigation: A Comparative Study*" (December 02, 2009), Oxford Legal Studies Research Paper No. 55-2009, available at SSRN: http://ssrn.com/abstract=1511714, forthcoming in C Hodges, S Vogenauer and M Tulibacka (eds), /Costs and Funding of Civil Litigation/.

[108] See PR paragraph 55.2.9.

[109] See PR paragraph 61.4.3.

[110] Professor Kritzer is Professor of Law and Public Policy at the University of Minnesota Law School. He is also the author of many of the academic papers referred to in PR chapter 9. Copies of the slides with which Professor Kritzer illustrated his talk can be seen on the Costs Review website at http://www.judiciary.gov.uk/docs/costs-review/fee-regimes.ppt.

settlements as high as possible. In Professor Kritzer's view, contingency fee agreements encourage efficiency, whereas conditional fee agreements ("CFAs") encourage inefficiency.

2.5   In the debate which followed, one solicitor argued that we have *"crossed the Rubicon"* with CFAs and we should now permit contingency fees agreements, albeit on the Ontario model (i.e. only normal costs recoverable from the other side). Another solicitor observed that there will come a point with a contingency fee agreement when the work done wipes out all profits and so there is pressure to settle rapidly. Professor Kritzer did not accept this view. He responded that a portfolio of cases is like a portfolio of investments. The lawyer accepts that he will make money on some cases, but lose money on others. A member of the Bar Council staff suggested that, whatever is decided, the position should be the same for barristers and solicitors. It is anomalous at the moment that in employment tribunals solicitors can act on contingency fees, but barristers cannot.[111] In answer to questions, Professor Kritzer said that some US firms under-settled, but most did not for the sake of their reputations. The biggest source of work for lawyers comprised referrals from other lawyers. I took a vote at the end of this debate. On the question of principle, 22 people voted for the proposition that contingency fee agreements were objectionable in principle; 52 people voted for the proposition that contingency fees agreements were not objectionable in principle; and there were 15 abstentions. Of the 52 people who supported contingency fee agreements in principle, 30 thought that it was acceptable to use them for personal injury cases; 13 thought that it was not acceptable to use contingency fee agreements for personal injury cases and nine abstained on this issue. Following this vote, a solicitor stated that if contingency fee agreements are used for personal injury cases, it is important that damages for future care costs should be ring fenced.

2.6   <u>Commercial litigators seminar.</u> At the seminar organised by the City of London Law Society and the Commercial Litigators Forum and hosted by Freshfields Bruckhaus Deringer on 13th July 2009, there was debate about permitting contingency fees on the Ontario model after a presentation by an experienced commercial solicitor who supported such a reform. One speaker made the point that there was little impetus for law firms to undertake work on a contingency fee basis. Another speaker feared that contingency fees would bring the worst excesses of US litigation. A solicitor who tends to defence work expressed support for contingency fees, which he believes act as an effective filter. He said that when the unsuccessful Benzodiazepine litigation was being run in England (on legal aid) that was not picked up in the US, because *"bad cases don't get run"*. One speaker suggested that solicitors should be licensed to do work on a contingency fee basis and should lose their licences if they abused the system. I took a vote on the issue of principle. There were 39 votes in favour of permitting contingency fees and 25 votes against.

3. WRITTEN SUBMISSIONS DURING PHASE 2

3.1   The written submissions during Phase 2 revealed a wide spread of strongly held views on the issue of contingency fees. As with so many issues, I can only summarise a cross-section of the submissions.

3.2   <u>Ministry of Justice.</u> The Ministry of Justice (the "MoJ"), although not making any submission to the Costs Review, in relation to the contingency fees issue has

---

[111] Following the seminar a member of the Bar wrote in to disagree with these comments. He considered that contingency fees would pose greater difficulties for counsel than for solicitors.

drawn my attention to its consultation paper *"Regulating Damages Based Agreements"*.[112] In that consultation paper the MoJ notes that contingency fees are permitted in tribunals. It notes that there are concerns about (i) failures to inform claimants about alternative methods of funding their claims and (ii) lack of clarity and understanding of the fee arrangements and the costs which claimants are likely to pay. Accordingly, the Government proposes to introduce regulations to address these issues. The proposed regulations will introduce requirements in respect of the following elements:

(i)   The provision of clear and transparent advice and information provided to consumers, on (a) costs; (b) other expenses (such as VAT, counsel's fees, expert reports etc); and (c) other methods of funding available.

(ii)   The maximum percentage of the damages that can be recovered in fees from the award.

(iii)   Controlling the use of unfair terms and conditions (such as penalty and settlement clauses).

Following that consultation paper, section 154 of the Coroners and Justice Act 2009 (which received Royal Assent on 12th November 2009) (the "2009 Act") allows for the regulation of damages-based agreements relating to employment matters only. "Damages-based agreement" is the term used in the 2009 Act to refer to an agreement for contingency fees, as defined in paragraph 1.1 above.

3.3   <u>Law Society.</u> The Law Society states in its Phase 2 submission that it is currently reviewing the issue, following consultation with its members. The Law Society adds:

> "It is notable that contingency fees have been operating, broadly successfully in employment and similar Tribunal cases. While the Society recognizes that there have been a number of concerns about how these operate, particularly by unregulated providers, we believe that these can be dealt with by appropriate regulation."

3.4   <u>Personal injury lawyers.</u> Personal injury lawyers are generally opposed to contingency fees. The Association of Personal Injury Lawyers ("APIL") is opposed to contingency fees, because these would eat into the claimant's damages. APIL adds that if contingency fees are introduced, damages will have to be substantially increased over and above the previous recommendation of the Law Commission. The Personal Injuries Bar Association ("PIBA") also opposes contingency fees. Indeed in a survey conducted by PIBA, members voted against this reform by 316 votes to five. PIBA argues in its submission that contingency fees would not work in small cases or big cases and that the best profit for solicitors would be on the basis of minimum work. PIBA maintains that contingency fees do not work well in employment cases or criminal injuries compensation appeals. PIBA fears that under contingency fees the Bar would be instructed less than it now is for advice and representation before trial; this would be contrary to the public interest.

3.5   <u>Trade unions.</u> Trade unions are also opposed to contingency fees. The Trades Union Congress (the "TUC") states:

---

[112] Consultation Paper CP 10/09, published on 1st July 2009, which can be found online at http://www.justice.gov.uk/consultations/docs/regulating-damages-based-agreements.pdf. The website has recently been updated to include a summary of responses, as well as the MoJ's consultation letter dated December 2009.

"The TUC's position is that the current cost regime the unions rely on, CCFA[113] agreement together with success fees and either ATE[114] insurance or union self-insurance, with those additional liabilities being fully recoverable, leads to access to justice for all and ensures claimants keep their whole entitlement to compensation."

The TUC fears that conflicts of interest would arise between client and solicitor under a contingency fees regime, and that clients would suffer deduction from their damages. The TUC adds that it welcomes the Government's proposal to regulate contingency fees in employment tribunals, because of problems which members have encountered under those arrangements. If contingency fees are permitted for personal injuries litigation, then detailed regulations will be required. In the TUC's view, such regulations would not be dissimilar to those outlined in the Government's current consultation.

3.6 _Professional Negligence Bar Association._ The Professional Negligence Bar Association (the "PNBA") states that its members are overwhelmingly opposed to contingency fee agreements for three principal reasons. First, they increase the risk of conflict between lawyer and client. Secondly, there is a danger of clients being under-compensated. Thirdly, there is a danger of lawyers being over-compensated. The PNBA challenges some of the arguments in support of contingency fees identified in PR paragraph 20.3.2. The PNBA believes that if contingency fees are permitted, then (a) the entire contingency fee should be recoverable in a successful action and (b) there should be safeguards to prevent abuse.

3.7 _Medical Defence Union._ The Medical Defence Union (the "MDU") opposes contingency fees. It believes that these would only be viable in clinical negligence if there were a significant increase in levels of damages, which the MDU would not welcome. The MDU points out that if contingency fees co-existed with CFAs, then solicitors would choose whichever system gave them the better return.

3.8 _Consumer Focus._ Consumer Focus takes a more favourable view of contingency fees. It states:

"Consumer Focus understands and accepts as valid the motivations for considering the expansion of contingency fees in civil cases. We appreciate that some of the motivations are born out of the need for greater access to justice, particularly for plaintiffs who are outside of legal aid, but who would find it difficult to fund a claim, and indeed for defendants opposing a weak claim by a wealthy and oppressive claimants. Although we are not opposed to contingency fees in principle, we are keen to ensure that any proposal has inbuilt safeguards which protects the interest of consumers."

3.9 Based on the experience of countries where contingency fees are permitted, Consumer Focus does not believe that these cause problems of conflict of interest. However, Consumer Focus believes that regulation is necessary to protect consumers. The list of matters proposed for regulation is, essentially, the same as the MoJ's list. However, Consumer Focus believes that personal injury claims should be exempt from contingency fee agreements. This is because Consumer Focus believes that general damages are too low and accident victims should retain 100% of their compensation.

---

[113] Collective conditional fee agreement.
[114] After-the-event.

3.10   <u>Third party funders.</u>   Third party funders are generally supportive of contingency fees. One funder supports contingency fees on grounds of freedom of contract. It argues that this provides another funding option and so widens choice for the litigant. It believes that clients would be protected if there were a requirement for review of every contingency fee agreement by an independent solicitor.

3.11   <u>GC100 Group.</u>   The GC100 Group strongly opposes the introduction of contingency fee agreements. It sees no evidence that warrants such a fundamental change. The GC100 Group believes that this reform would increase rewards for lawyers, who would select either CFAs or contingency fees according to which one would yield greater profit in any given case. Finally, the GC100 Group states that if a contingency fees system is introduced, it should be strictly regulated.

3.12   <u>Commercial lawyers.</u>   Commercial lawyers are divided in their views. The Costs Sub-Committee of the Commercial Court Users Committee believes that the introduction of contingency fees would be a retrograde step. It believes that this reform would damage the professional culture of Commercial Court practitioners, to the detriment of that court. The Sub-Committee believes that the benefits in terms of access to justice would be outweighed by the risks involved. It sees no strong evidence of demand for contingency fee arrangements amongst commercial litigants. However, it adds that if contingency fees are introduced, they should be properly regulated. On the other hand, the City of London Law Society's Litigation Committee (the "CLLSLC") is cautiously in favour of contingency fees. It notes that the "conflict of interest" issue has existed for some time in relation to CFAs and therefore finds it difficult to see any objection in principle to contingency fees. The CLLSLC supports costs shifting on the basis set out in PR paragraph 20.2.5. It believes that the size of the contingency fee should be a matter for negotiation between the solicitor and client, subject to review by the trial judge or challenge before the costs judge.

3.13   A firm of City solicitors states that it cautiously supports the introduction of contingency fees on the Ontario model, so long as proper safeguards are put in place. It conducted a survey of its clients on this issue. Those who thought that contingency fees were objectionable in principle amounted to 37.5%, whereas 50% thought that contingency fees were not objectionable in principle. The remainder were undecided.

3.14   <u>Commercial Litigation Association.</u>   The Commercial Litigation Association opposes contingency fees with the following argument:

> "It is difficult to see any reason for contingency fees in litigation where costs shifting remains. If the success fee under a CFA ceases wholly or partly to be recoverable and some form of statutory cap is placed on the portion of damages that can be taken then it must be assumed that that percentage would be the same under a contingency fee scheme. The theory of success fees is that the fee pays no more than is needed to fund losing cases of the same prospects. A different rationale for a contingency fee has not been made out. Assuming contingency fees are only designed to serve the same function as a success fee there is no justification in that for contingency fees. We do not support a proposal that the level of contingency fee should exceed that needed to fund losing cases. The suggestion that contingency fees are needed in group litigation because other funding is not available is difficult to support given the availability of CFAs which are often used in such cases and the emergence of TPF.[115] To enable contingency fees as yet another form of funding is not supported."

---

[115] Third party funding.

3.15   Commercial Bar Association. The Commercial Bar Association ("COMBAR") reports that the views of its members were mixed. A small majority favoured permitting both solicitors and counsel to act on contingency fees. However, the COMBAR executive remains concerned about introducing contingency fees. The executive believes that moving from CFAs to contingency fees is a descent down the slippery slope. It does not believe that even sophisticated clients should have freedom to enter into contingency fee agreements. The executive points out that although the contingency fee may always be proportionate to the sum recovered, it may be disproportionate to the amount of work carried out. It is also concerned about the potential for conflicts of interest.

4. MY CONCLUSION

(i) Issue of principle

4.1   Having weighed up the conflicting arguments, I conclude that both solicitors and counsel should be permitted to enter into contingency fee agreements with their clients on the Ontario model. In other words, costs shifting is effected on a conventional basis and in so far as the contingency fee exceeds what would be chargeable under a normal fee agreement, that is borne by the successful litigant.[116]

4.2   In my view the arguments in favour of contingency fees set out in PR paragraph 20.3.2 outweigh the arguments against, as set out in PR paragraph 20.3.3. Furthermore, it is desirable that as many funding methods as possible should be available to litigants. This will be particularly important if my earlier recommendations are accepted, that CFA success fees and ATE insurance premiums should become irrecoverable.[117] I also see particular force in the freedom of contract argument, despite its rejection by COMBAR. It seems to me that this is self-evident in the case of commercial litigants. In the case of private litigants, such as personal injury claimants, in my view a requirement for independent advice together with effective regulation will provide sufficient safeguards.[118] If the client wishes to enter into a contingency fee agreement, after having received independent advice, he should be free to do so.

4.3   Although personal injury claimant lawyers and a number of other groups are strongly opposed to contingency fees, I suspect that this opposition arises, at least in part, from their satisfaction with the present CFA regime. If that regime is changed radically by the abolition of "recoverability" and at the same time general damages are raised by 10% across the board,[119] there may be some claimants whom it would suit to enter into contingency fee agreements. They should not be prohibited by law from doing so.

4.4   A number of opponents of contingency fees fear that solicitors would exploit the new regime by selecting the arrangement most favourable to themselves. There is always a danger that solicitors will negotiate retainer terms which are favourable to themselves, but I do not accept that the danger is greater in this situation. If the solicitor is willing to proceed on either a CFA or a contingency fee basis, then he has a duty to advise the client of the implications of each. If the solicitor is only willing to

---

[116] This recommendation is consistent with my proposals in respect of conditional fee agreements. The success fee, which by definition is an excess over the normal fee, is borne by the client, not the opposing party.
[117] See chapters 9 and 10 above.
[118] See section (ii) below.
[119] As recommended in chapter 10 above and chapter 22 below.

proceed on one or other basis, then no question of selection arises. However, if the independent solicitor (proposed in paragraph 4.10 below) considers that a contingency fee agreement is inappropriate and that a CFA ought to be on offer, no doubt he or she will say so.

4.5　　The PNBA highlights the risk that lawyers may be over-compensated under a contingency fee regime. In my view, this risk could be controlled by regulations limiting the percentage of damages that can be taken in fees.[120] Furthermore, the risk of over-compensation currently exists under the CFA regime with 100% success fees.

(ii) Safeguards

4.6　　Regulation. I agree with the comment made by many respondents that if contingency fees are to be introduced into litigation, they must be properly regulated. The three matters identified by the MoJ in its consultation paper CP 10/9 are the principal matters which will require regulation. In my view the regulations which the MoJ is planning to introduce in respect of contingency fees in tribunal proceedings[121] should be suitably adapted for the purpose of court proceedings. The regulations should (i) introduce a requirement that clear and transparent advice and information be provided to consumers on costs, other expenses and other methods of funding available; (ii) provide a maximum percentage of the damages that can be recovered in fees from the award; and (iii) control the use of unfair terms and conditions.

4.7　　Potential liability for adverse costs. There is one important difference between tribunal proceedings (in which contingency fee agreements are currently used) and litigation, namely the potential liability for adverse costs.[122] Agreement must be reached at the outset as to how any adverse order for costs will be met.[123] If it is agreed that the solicitors will meet any such order (as quite often happens in Canada),[124] then this additional risk should be reflected in the percentage recovery to which the solicitors will be entitled in the event of success.

4.8　　Counsel's fees. If solicitors are acting on a contingency fee, then counsel's fees could be dealt with in one of two ways: (i) those fees could be a disbursement to be paid by the solicitors in any event; or (ii) counsel could be on a contingency fee as well and entitled to a specified percentage of any sums recovered. The arrangement with counsel should be clearly set out in any contingency fee agreement.

4.9　　Other disbursements. There are two ways in which other disbursements might be met: (i) they might be paid by the client; or (ii) they might be funded by the solicitors as part of the contingency arrangement. If the latter course is taken, then the risk accepted by the solicitors should be reflected in the percentage recovery to which they are entitled in the event of success.

4.10　　Independent advice. As an additional safeguard, I recommend that no contingency fee agreement should be valid unless it is countersigned by an independent solicitor, who certifies that he or she has advised the client about the terms of that agreement. If the regulations prescribe a simple form of certificate and a simple definition of "independent solicitor", I do not believe that these should generate satellite litigation. It would be a matter for discussion between solicitor and

---

[120] See paragraph 4.6 below.
[121] See paragraphs 30 to 40 of the MoJ's consultation paper CP 10/9.
[122] I.e. there is no costs shifting in tribunal proceedings.
[123] Where qualified one way costs shifting applies, presumably it will be agreed that any liability for adverse costs will be borne by the client.
[124] See PR paragraph 61.4.4.

client as to who should pay for the independent advice. If the client lacks the means to do so and the solicitor pays the adviser,[125] this would not undermine the independence of the advice.

4.11   <u>Personal injuries litigation.</u>   Having considered the satisfactory Canadian experience of contingency fee agreements in personal injury cases, I do not think that this category of litigation should be exempted. However, the cap on deductions from damages should be the same for CFAs and contingency fee agreements. I therefore recommend that no contingency fee deducted from damages should exceed 25% of the claimant's damages, excluding damages referable to future costs or losses.[126]

5. RECOMMENDATIONS

5.1   I make the following recommendations:

(i)   Both solicitors and counsel should be permitted to enter into contingency fee agreements with their clients. However, costs should be recoverable against opposing parties on the conventional basis and not by reference to the contingency fee.

(ii)   Contingency fee agreements should be properly regulated and they should not be valid unless the client has received independent advice.

---

[125] Which would make good commercial sense in many cases.
[126] This cap in relation to personal injury damages should be included in the more general regulations proposed in paragraph 4.6 above.

CHAPTER 13. CLAF OR SLAS

INDEX

1. INTRODUCTION

(i) General

1.1   Definitions. A Contingent Legal Aid Fund ("CLAF") or Supplementary Legal Aid Scheme ("SLAS") are self funding schemes, which have been proposed as means of funding litigation in the event that the present regime for conditional fee agreements ("CFAs") is changed. The normal beneficiary of such a scheme is the claimant, although it could on occasion be used by a defendant (e.g. where a contractor sues a householder for payment and the householder raises a counterclaim for defects). In this chapter I shall always refer to the party supported by a CLAF or SLAS as "claimant", without repeating this qualification.

1.2   Discussion in Preliminary Report. In chapter 18 of the Preliminary Report I described the essential features of both a CLAF and a SLAS. I summarised the views of the Civil Justice Council (the "CJC") on these options. I also described the SLAS which operates in Hong Kong and the various CLAFs which operate in Australia and Canada.[127] In chapter 19 I discussed whether either a SLAS or a CLAF should be established in this jurisdiction and set out some relevant considerations.

(ii) Proposal of the Bar Council's CLAF Group

1.3   Original proposal. The Bar Council's CLAF Group (the "CLAF Group") set out its original proposal in a paper dated 27th February 2009. This paper is summarised in the Preliminary Report.[128] It can read in full on the Bar Council's website.[129]

1.4   CLAF Group's amplification of its original proposal. The CLAF Group has amplified its original proposal in a "second discussion paper", dated 31st July 2009. This paper can be read in full on the Bar Council's website.[130] In its second discussion

---

[127] The information about Hong Kong, Australia and Canada is up to date as at March/April 2009 when I visited those jurisdictions.
[128] See PR paragraphs 19.3.1 to 19.3.10.
[129] http://www.barcouncil.org.uk/assets/documents/CCF%20Paper%202%20April%202009.pdf.
[130] http://www.barcouncil.org.uk/assets/documents/CLAF%20Second%20Report%20Jul%2009.pdf.

paper the CLAF Group states that its principal focus is upon not-for-profit CLAFs, which it calls "Charitable Contingent Funds" or "CCFs". The CLAF Group accepts that, at least for the time being, CLAFs or CCFs could not take over from CFAs as the principal means of funding litigation. In paragraph 15 the Group states:

> "We do <u>not</u> for our part envisage a new start up CLAF having the capacity – to step in to fund the vast body of personal injuries litigation (some 750,000 cases a year). The capital required would be very substantial; it would be a venture with many unknowns; the skills to run it need first to be developed on more modest scale. A CLAF cannot in the short term stand as a replacement for CFAs."

1.5 The CLAF Group raises a number of specific issues for consideration in its second discussion paper. The first issue concerns "funding costs". Should losing defendants pay (in addition to damages and normal costs[131]) any funding costs to CCFs, alternatively to all CLAFs? In relation to this issue, it must be borne in mind that in so far as defendants do not pay the totality of funding costs, those costs will be a deduction from the claimant's damages. The CLAF Group opines that, outside personal injury and clinical negligence litigation, it is acceptable for claimants to contribute a sum from their damages to pay for the provision of funding. The CLAF Group identifies three possible models:

(i)   The defendant pays all funding costs.

(ii)   The claimant pays all funding costs.

(iii)   Each party bears a proportion of the funding costs, possibly 50% each.

1.6 The second issue is whether a CCF or CLAF should be liable for adverse costs in those cases which the claimant loses. The members of the CLAF Group are divided on this issue. If liability for adverse costs is accepted, it is suggested that this might be met by a block after-the-event ("ATE") insurance policy.

1.7 A third issue raised by the CLAF Group is whether the defendant should be exempted from the obligation to pay the claimant's ATE insurance premium in cases where the defendant agrees at the outset not to claim costs if it is successful. In my view, this issue does not arise, essentially for two reasons. First, for the reasons set out in chapter 9 above it is my view that ATE insurance premiums should cease to be recoverable. Secondly, even if that recommendation is rejected, I doubt that the "election" proposal is viable. It would have the effect that ATE insurance is only sought in those cases which defendants expect to win. This circumstance would have an adverse impact upon ATE insurance premiums.

1.8 The CLAF Group proposes that any CLAF or CCF should apply a strict merits test before taking on any case. The CLAF Group acknowledges the difficulties of means testing. A substantial CLAF might be able to do this. But a smaller CLAF probably could not. However, it could exclude the "positively wealthy" or those with other means of funding, such as trade union membership or before-the-event insurance.

1.9 The CLAF Group suggests a number of variants of the above, including a possible hybrid regime. Under the hybrid regime defendants would pay to the CLAF funding costs equal to (i) success fees under the present regime and (ii) (absent any election at the outset by the defendant not to claim costs) ATE insurance premiums.

---

[131] By "normal costs" I mean the claimant's costs excluding success fee and ATE insurance premium.

1.10   In relation to the provision of seed corn funding, the CLAF Group has had discussion with a director of a well known Protection and Indemnity Club[132] ("P&I Club"), directors of a major investment bank and a senior lawyer from a large City firm of solicitors, who has expertise in raising finance for projects. It reports that the responses have been positive and that the expertise for running a CLAF clearly exists. The CLAF Group's present view is that a CLAF's potential use is as an additional resource rather than as an immediate alternative to all the perceived problems of CFAs.

1.11   The CLAF Group states that detailed work on a CLAF cannot start until the costs landscape is known following the publication of my Final Report and any subsequent legislative changes. The CLAF Group considers that modelling can only sensibly be done once it is known what provisions will be made for CFAs. Any prospective CLAF will need to do the following:

(i)   estimate what its cost will be to run a particular portfolio of cases;

(ii)   ascertain likely base legal costs to be met and hopefully recovered together with what percentages of cases would be lost with concomitant costs not recovered;

(iii)   know whether it will have to meet opponent's costs and estimate the number of such cases and the amounts at stake;

(iv)   be able to estimate what return it needs to take per annum;

(v)   produce models based on those figures; and

(vi)   be able to indicate what primary legislative changes will be needed and what matters should be addressed in statutory instruments.

Arguably any CLAF that is established should first be of a moderate size. It must be large enough to have economies of scale and finance overheads, but with tight control and oversight until the business model is tried and tested.

1.12   On the basis of the discussions mentioned above, the CLAF Group considers that seed corn funding is a real possibility, provided there is a viable business model. There seem to be at least three possible models for raising the money: (i) some sort of bond issue; (ii) a drawdown facility; or (iii) a limited partnership of the sort popular with private equity investors. In all models, a dividend would have to be given to those investors with a realistic promise to repay capital over time.

1.13   The CLAF Group has also, at my request, specifically considered the possibility of a CLAF to fund defamation cases. This is a distinct sub-set of cases, with approximately 200 cases being issued each year.[133] The CLAF Group believes that a defamation CLAF may be viable on the principles discussed above. The Group notes that costs in defamation cases tend to be high relative to damages, not least because the most important remedy sought is non-monetary, namely a public apology. Accordingly, the claimant may need to make a higher contribution to the CLAF than in other forms of litigation.

---

[132] An insurance mutual which provides collective self insurance to its members, with the members pooling their risks in order to obtain "at cost" insurance cover. See paragraphs 93 to 95 of the CLAF Group's original paper.
[133] See PR paragraphs 5.3.4 and 37.3.2.

2. DEBATE DURING PHASE 2

(i) Discussion at seminars

2.1   Manchester seminar.   At the Manchester seminar on 10th July 2009 Sir Andrew Morritt, Chancellor of the High Court, surveyed the intractable problems of funding civil litigation and concluded that a CLAF may be the best way forward. He expressed the hope that this option would receive serious consideration.

2.2   Contingency fees seminar.   At the contingency fees seminar on 21st July 2009[134] the merits of a CLAF or SLAS were discussed. Concern was expressed about importing a bureaucratic scheme of the kind that is absent from the present CFA regime. The possibility of a hybrid scheme was ventilated. The point was made that defamation cases should not be treated differently from other civil cases. Michael Napier QC (assessor) outlined the four models of SLAS considered by the CJC. There was also reference to the uncertainty about what a SLAS or CLAF would cost. A straw poll was taken at the end. Seven people voted in favour of the principle of a CLAF or SLAS replacing the present CFA regime. One person voted against. The majority abstained.

2.3   British Institute of International and Comparative Law seminar.   On 1st October 2009 the British Institute of International and Comparative Law hosted a seminar entitled *"CLAF: Towards a self-funding scheme for civil litigation?"*. Although this date fell outside the consultation period, my judicial assistant attended the seminar. One of the speakers was Guy Mansfield QC, who had recently chaired the CLAF Group. Mr Mansfield accepted that a CLAF could not compete in a world with recoverable success fees and ATE insurance premiums. However, he expressed his belief (and that of the CLAF Group) that it could offer an additional resource if the general costs terrain is suitable (i.e. if recoverability is abolished). Although a CLAF could not enter the mass market of high volume / low value cases, as the administration costs would be too high, it could support higher value cases whose prospects are good. The legal manager of a national newspaper thought that the idea of a CLAF was *"wholly meritorious"* provided the pool of cases was sufficiently large, but a CLAF would not be suitable for publication proceedings (libel and privacy) as there were too few cases and because the damages were low and the costs extremely high. However, some scepticism was expressed by other attendees. Professor Mark Mildred pointed out that the CLAFs operating overseas, such as in Ontario and Québec, are highly conservatively run and support very few cases. The law needs marginal cases and there is a worry that a CLAF would not improve the ability of lawyers to take on "adventurous" cases. If the CLAF was only suitable for high value cases (a floor of £1 million had been mooted), he questioned whether there would be sufficient cases every year to keep the fund in business. Another speaker stated that defendants would benefit from a CLAF scheme but there is nothing in it for claimants. He questioned why the structure of a CLAF was needed and thought that contingency fees could do the job. In response to this, Professor Martin Chalkley pointed out that a CLAF would have the advantage of pooling risk, further, CFAs encourage cost inflation which a CLAF would not.

(ii) Written submissions

2.4   Civil Legal Aid Sub-Committee of the Bar Council.   The Civil Legal Aid Sub-Committee of the Bar Council ("CLASC") states that its members, in common with

---

[134] This was one of the less well attended seminars. 27 people were present (excluding assessors and my "team"), but they were all well informed and specifically interested in funding issues.

many practitioners and Bar Associations, have real concerns about the CLAF Group's proposals. CLASC makes three principal points:

(i) A claimant should not suffer a deduction from damages in order to fund a CLAF/CCF.

(ii) There is a real danger that the establishment of a CLAF/CCF for clinical negligence would lead to withdrawal of legal aid from that category of litigation.

(iii) The establishment of a CLAF/CCF in substitution for the present means of funding litigation will reduce rather than increase access to justice, because a CLAF/CCF will only support strong cases.

CLASC supports these three contentions with detailed arguments and cross-reference to the overseas experience, as recorded in PR chapter 18.

2.5   Law Society. The Law Society also opposes the establishment of a CLAF or SLAS. It considers that a CLAF would not be viable in the context of the present CFA regime, because of the inevitable *"cherry-picking"*. The Law Society considers that the present CFA regime should be continued. The Law Society states that it has canvassed stakeholders about the possibility of establishing a SLAS. Their overwhelming view was, and still is, that the Government would use the assets of the SLAS to supplement the Legal Aid fund.

2.6   Bar Associations. The Personal Injuries Bar Association ("PIBA") doubts that a CLAF is workable. The PIBA does recognise, however, that CLAFs may be viable in high value cases, group actions and other exceptional cases. The Professional Negligence Bar Association (the "PNBA") also opposes the establishment of a CLAF or SLAS for similar reasons to those set out above.

2.7   The Chancery Bar Association (the "ChBA") takes a different view. The ChBA supports the principle of a CLAF, although noting that the details need to be worked out. The ChBA accepts the basic tenet that a successful claimant must make a contribution to the fund, but adds that this must be subject to exceptions. There should be no deduction from a money award calculated to provide future subsistence or care. The ChBA rejects the suggestion that the defendant should make any additional contribution[135] as *"unprincipled and objectionable"*.

2.8   Other legal associations. Action against Medical Accidents ("AvMA") cautiously supports the proposal for a CLAF or SLAS, provided that it is modified to exclude support from damages. AvMA believes that this could support access to justice for those with modest claims. AvMA would support a pilot exercise. The Association of Personal Injury Lawyers ("APIL") opposes the proposal for a CLAF or SLAS, principally because it would lead to deductions from damages. APIL also sees a number of practical objections. The Motor Accidents Solicitors Society ("MASS") does not believe that the CLAF Group's proposals are practicable. Also MASS opposes any deductions from the claimant's damages.

2.9   The Forum of Complex Injury Solicitors ("FOCIS") comments that the CLAF has a long history of being debated. FOCIS notes the substantial practical difficulties in getting a CLAF off the ground, including the need for massive initial investment. FOCIS accepts that a CLAF might have a role to play in a minority of cases, such as

---

[135] I.e. "funding costs" in the language of the CLAF Group.

group actions, but adds that this should not drive policy considerations for the bulk of personal injury cases.

2.10   A number of firms of solicitors have responded on this issue, broadly reflecting the range of views above. One specialist personal injury firm comments that at best a CLAF or SLAS could provide a useful alternative for some group actions; the CLAF Group's proposals would at best be an additional, rather than alternative, method of funding.

2.11   The Libel CLAF Working Group. At my request a working group was convened to consider the viability of a CLAF for libel and other publication proceedings.[136] The Group was chaired by Alastair Brett[137] and contained representatives from claimant and defendant firms and insurers. However, at an early stage in their discussions, that Group formed the unanimous view that a CLAF would not be viable in this area. Broadly this was for the following reasons:

(i)   There is a much lower volume of publication proceedings than proceedings in other areas like personal injury, in particular far fewer simple and successful claims to provide positive funding for a CLAF (even assuming they could be brought within its remit).

(ii)   The average costs of publication proceedings are particularly high set against other areas, and the damages relatively low by comparison, such that a convincing economic case for a CLAF could not be made out.

2.12   Having dismissed the CLAF option, the Libel CLAF Working Group proceeded to make recommendations as to procedural and funding reforms for publication proceedings which are considered further at chapter 32 below.

3. ANALYSIS

(i) CLAF or SLAS as "the only game in town"

3.1   Most of the Phase 2 submissions on CLAFs and SLASs propose such options as a supplementary means of funding in addition to CFAs or other funding mechanisms, or for specialist areas. Adverse selection in favour of CFAs is often raised as the Achilles' heel of a CLAF or SLAS. Therefore consideration should be given to the more radical option of abolishing CFAs entirely and relying on a CLAF or SLAS as the exclusive or dominant funding option for damages claims in England and Wales.

3.2   Whilst this option has some superficial attraction, I do not consider it to be a serious and viable reform proposal for a number of reasons:

(i)   Such an approach would require vast start up costs which neither the state nor any private funder would be likely to make available in these or any other economic circumstances.

(ii)   It would place reliance on a novel method of funding which has never been tried anywhere else in the world on such a scale. Even if theoretically such a

---

[136] The Bar's CLAF Group looked into this at my request and suggested that this area might possibly be suitable for a "niche" CLAF.
[137] Legal Manager of Times Newspapers Ltd.

scheme could be viable, in my view it would be taking far too great a risk of loss of access to justice if the system did not prove to be viable.

(iii)   Even without CFAs it would be very difficult to model such a system financially, not least because it would be almost impossible to prevent high volume straightforward personal injury claims being dealt with "on spec" by lawyers or claims managers.

(iv)   The need for such an approach largely disappears if the other reforms recommended in this review proceed and deal with the perceived evils of the current CFA regime.

(ii) CLAF as an additional funding mechanism

3.3   The most fully developed proposal for a CLAF is that put forward by the Bar Council's CLAF Group. The proposal has obvious attractions in the event that my recommendations in chapters 9 and 10 above are accepted.[138] However, the proposal also has certain difficulties, in particular the following:

(i)   The investment bank to whom the CLAF Group spoke would no doubt be looking for a commercial return on its investment. So would any third party funder, which put up money for the CLAF.

(ii)   People with expertise to administer the CLAF would require remuneration commensurate with their skills and experience.

(iii)   The CLAF may not be able to cover the costs of funding, administration and "lost" cases out of deductions taken from claimant damages.

3.4   I have looked at the data with the assistance of my accountant judicial assistant, but have not been able myself to produce any viable model for a large scale CLAF. However, the CLAF Group has indicated its willingness to take this matter forward once the recommendations of the present Costs Review upon the key issues are known.

3.5   In principle, I support the creation of one or more CLAFs or CCFs, if a viable financial model for such bodies can be created. All the indications are, and indeed the CLAF Group accepts, that at least in the short term CLAFs or CCFs could only function as an alternative means of funding a minority of cases. That is no reason not to take the project forward, once decisions have been made by Government as to which recommendations in this report will be implemented. Any additional means of funding litigation, which promote access to justice for at least some claimants with meritorious cases, should be encouraged. However, the difficulty with a CLAF remains the risks of adverse selection by lawyers and clients choosing to proceed under CFAs or (if my recommendations in chapter 12 above are accepted) contingency fees. If stronger cases pursue that route, a CLAF may not be viable. Assessing the extent of this risk to any CLAF proposal is not simply a matter of statistics and economic modelling, but also involves an estimation of likely behaviour based on incentives. This leads me to be cautious about the potential of a CLAF to make a significant contribution to access to justice.

---

[138] Namely that ATE insurance premiums and CFA success fees should cease to be recoverable under costs orders.

<u>(iii) SLAS as an additional funding mechanism</u>

3.6   <u>Civil Justice Council view.</u> The CJC in its report "*Improved Access to Justice – funding Options and Proportionate Costs*", dated August 2007, recommended that a SLAS should be established and operated by the Legal Services Commission. The CJC advanced a number of arguments in support of this recommendation.   In particular:

(i)   A SLAS would have no need for seed funding.

(ii)   A SLAS could incorporate the statutory protection against adverse costs orders already enjoyed be parties with legal aid.

(iii)   A SLAS could be grafted onto the existing Legal Services Commission, which would greatly reduce administrative costs.

3.7   Whether the first point is right depends on how the SLAS would be set up. The Hong Kong SLAS was grafted on to an existing legal aid scheme, but still required initial seed funding: see PR paragraph 18.2.1.   That was because the additional clients helped under that SLAS were outside normal eligibility limits so that the funding of the additional cases was strictly ring-fenced.

3.8   During Phase 2 the SLAS proposal received less detailed attention than the CLAF proposal. However, the point made by the Law Society is important. In my view no SLAS should be established unless the assets of the SLAS are ring fenced, so that no assets of the SLAS are redirected into the general legal aid fund.

3.9   An alternative way to develop a SLAS is to build recovery mechanisms into legal aid for some or all existing clients and then extend eligibility only when income is generated under the system.   Such an approach would clearly concern the Law Society and others who fear that a SLAS mechanism would be used solely to support the general Legal Aid Fund rather than to extend access to justice. However, in the context of group actions, which were the main focus of the CJC report, these are currently funded out of a limited central budget. Therefore anything which reduces the net cost of such actions to the Legal Aid Fund has the potential to allow more cases to be funded.

3.10   Having considered all the evidence and discussed it with my assessors, I conclude that a SLAS could only ever be a supplementary means of funding for a minority of cases. Whether there is need for a SLAS depends upon whether there exist gaps in access to justice. This will depend upon the wider costs and funding regime, as reformed in the light of this review. Once the Government has determined how those wider reforms should proceed, any gaps in access to justice must be identified. If there is a possibility that a SLAS can meet those needs, then financial modelling should be carried out along the lines recommended by the CJC.

4. RECOMMENDATION

4.1   I recommend that financial modelling be undertaken to ascertain the viability of one or more CLAFs or a SLAS, after and subject to, any decisions announced by Government in respect of the other recommendations of this report.

CHAPTER 14. LITIGANTS IN PERSON

INDEX

1. INTRODUCTION

1.1   Preliminary Report and response. Chapter 17 of the Preliminary Report sets out the basis on which litigants in person are entitled to recover costs, and some concerns expressed during Phase 1 on the amounts recoverable by litigants in person. The submissions received in Phase 2 on this issue, albeit few in number, amplified those concerns.

1.2   Relevant provisions of the CPR. The provisions of the CPR upon which debate has focused are those contained in rule 48.6(2) and (4). These provide:

> "(2)   The costs allowed under this rule must not exceed, except in the case of a disbursement, two-thirds of the amount which would have been allowed if the litigant in person had been represented by a legal representative...

> (4)   The amount of costs to be allowed to the litigant in person for any item of work claimed shall be –

>> (a)   where the litigant can prove financial loss, the amount that he can prove he has lost for time reasonably spent on doing the work; or

>> (b)   where the litigant cannot prove financial loss, an amount for the time reasonably spent on doing the work at the rate set out in the practice direction."

Rule 46.3(5) contains provisions to similar effect in respect of fast track trial costs.

2. PHASE 2 SUBMISSIONS

2.1   Low hourly rate. The principal concern expressed during Phase 2 was that the amount presently recoverable by litigants in person (when in a costs-shifting forum), in circumstances where the litigant cannot prove that it has suffered financial loss through spending time on legal work, is too low. The current rate is £9.25 per hour.[139]

2.2   Federation of Small Businesses. The Federation of Small Businesses (the "FSB") states the following in its Phase 2 submission:

---

[139] Costs Practice Direction, paragraph 52.4.

"...the FSB firmly believes that the time for a review of litigant in person costs is long overdue. Some businesses have in-house expertise and they are in general reasonably well equipped to conduct a straightforward case. They should not be penalised for doing so by being unable to recover the costs and losses incurred by the business in conducting its own case. It is time to redress the balance."

2.3   The FSB's view is that litigants in person should be able to recover their "*true costs and losses*", subject to the current ceiling of two thirds of solicitors' costs rates. It should be assumed that, by conducting its own case, a business will incur loss, as the time spent will displace other productive work. If, however, a maximum hourly rate for litigants in person is appropriate, the FSB draws attention to the fact that this rate (£9.25 per hour) has not been reviewed since 1998.[140] By comparison, solicitors' recoverable charging rates increase annually as overheads increase.

2.4   Solicitors and insurers. One national firm of solicitors, which undertakes defendant work in a variety of practice areas, agrees that the hourly rate of £9.25 is too low. It would support an increase of that rate to no more than two thirds of the amount which would have been allowed if the litigant in person had been legally represented.[141] One major insurance company expresses similar views.

2.5   International Underwriting Association. The International Underwriting Association of London (the "IUA") does not believe that a litigant in person should be able to recover its own internal costs which could not be recovered by a represented litigant. It does, however, recognise that there is an "*imbalance*" where one side has legal representation and the other does not. The IUA states:

"We would therefore only support a payment to the litigant in person on a lump sum basis that is set out in a schedule, with the principle set out that a litigant in person should not be put in a better position than a represented litigant."

2.6   Judges. The Association of Her Majesty's District Judges makes the following suggestion in its submission:

"Perhaps there could be a clearer definition of 'financial loss' when considering when a litigant in person is entitled to recover more that the fixed rate of £9.25 per hour. Perhaps also, there should be a modest (inflation) increase in that fixed rate."

2.7   One experienced circuit judge writes:

"The assessment of costs for litigants in person is antiquated and over-complicated. Difficult issues can arise as to whether the litigant is able to show that he has suffered financial loss. This distinction should be abolished, as should the tie to two thirds of what a solicitor can recover. The litigant in person's recovery should be limited to what it is reasonable in all the circumstances. (In my experience most litigants in person are content with loss of earnings and travel to court for themselves and any witnesses.)"

---

[140] In fact the rate was set with effect from 1st December 1995.
[141] The current system for the recovery of costs by litigants in person attempts to maintain proportionality so that the recoverable costs do not exceed two thirds of the amount that would have been allowed had the litigant in person been legally represented: see PR paragraph 17.3.6 and CPR rules 46.3(5)(a) and 48.6(2).

3. ASSESSMENT

3.1   There is some force in the argument that a successful litigant in person should be compensated for the time that it spends performing work in litigation which would otherwise be performed by a legal representative, on the basis of the actual cost, or opportunity cost, to the litigant. There is also force in the argument that there is an unfair inequality of arms, when the litigant in person is at risk of swingeing adverse costs, but the represented opponent is not. On the other hand, it is the policy of the law to encourage parties to be represented, because this assists the just and expeditious management and resolution of civil litigation.

3.2   <u>Correct approach.</u> Having weighed up the conflicting arguments, I consider that the present approach strikes the right balance. For sound policy reasons, the costs recoverable by litigants in person[142] should never be more than two thirds of the costs which would be recoverable if that party were represented. If all costs in the fast track are fixed, as proposed in chapter 15 below, then the amount recoverable by litigants in person in fast track cases[143] should never be more than two thirds of the level of fixed costs that would have been recovered if they had been legally represented.

3.3   <u>Financial loss.</u> I note the suggestion that there should be a clearer description in the CPR of the "financial loss" that a litigant in person may recover under CPR rule 48.6(4)(a) if proven. In my view, however, it is sufficiently clear that the phrase means a proven and quantifiable loss (such as income foregone) that a litigant has suffered as a consequence of having to devote his or her time to litigation. The Court of Appeal proceeded on this basis in *Greville v Sprake* [2001] EWCA Civ 234. Some litigants in person will be able to prove financial loss as a consequence of time devoted to litigation. For example, a professional person in sole practice with an abundant supply of work may be able to prove such loss. Likewise a litigant in person, who pays another to mind the shop or act as *locum tenens* for the day of a fast track trial, may be able to prove such loss.

3.4   In my view, CPR rule 48.6(4)(a) performs an important function and it should not be repealed. Equally, however, it should not be expanded. If the test in rule 48.6(4)(a) is extended beyond financial loss which has been proved, this could lead to prolonged argument or even satellite litigation about the appropriate amount or rate of recovery.

3.5   <u>Hourly rate.</u> The recoverable hourly rate is essentially an arbitrary figure. It is applicable to all litigants in person who cannot prove any specific financial loss. For some litigants the rate will be too high and for others it will be too low. It should be noted, incidentally, that whatever rate is set will constitute yet another exception to the indemnity principle.

3.6   Many litigants in person, whose time is valuable, cannot prove any specific financial loss as a result of time spent preparing their case or presenting it in court. For example, an employee may take a day's holiday for the purpose of a court hearing, with the result that earnings are unaffected but a more pleasurable day's holiday is foregone. A self-employed person may make up for time lost to his business by working at weekends. The claimant in *Greville v Sprake* is a good example of a person for whom time was valuable, but who could not prove any specific financial loss. Kennedy LJ observed at paragraph 37:

---

[142] Except in respect of disbursements.
[143] Except in respect of disbursements.

"Mr Sprake's position, dealing with the matter entirely frankly this morning, is that he is not in a position to prove financial loss because he is part of a farming partnership and, in a sense, his absence is covered; what is not done today will have to be done another day."

3.7   In my view, the prescribed rate of £9.25 per hour, having been set more than a decade ago, is now too low. Remuneration at this rate under-compensates very many litigants in person and over-compensates very few. The rate should now be raised to a more realistic level. The level should not, however, be such as would positively encourage litigants to act in person.

3.8   The question then arises as to what the new rate should be. The hourly rate allowed to litigants in person in employment tribunals increases by £1 per year and is currently £29.[144] However, costs orders are only made in exceptional circumstances in employment tribunals and usually as a sanction for unreasonable conduct.[145] I do not consider that the courts should be constrained to adopt employment tribunal rates.

3.9   The rate of £9.25 per hour was set with effect from 1st December 1995. If one applies the average earnings index for private sector services, the equivalent figure now (December 2009) would be £15.32. In my view, a reasonable rate to set would be £20 per hour. That produces a round figure for what is essentially an arbitrary rate. This allows slightly more than a simple adjustment for inflation would require. It will, I hope, go some way to meet the concerns expressed during Phase 2, without giving undue encouragement to litigants to act in person.

4. RECOMMENDATION

4.1   I recommend that the prescribed rate of £9.25 per hour recoverable by litigants in person be increased to £20 per hour. The prescribed rate should be subject to periodic review.

---

144 See PR paragraph 50.2.15.
145 See PR paragraphs 50.2.8 to 50.2.9 and 50.3.2 to 50.3.14.

REVIEW OF
CIVIL LITIGATION COSTS

PART 3. FIXED COSTS

CHAPTER 15. FAST TRACK FIXED COSTS

1. INTRODUCTION

1.1   Preliminary Report. In chapter 22 of the Preliminary Report I stated that it was the unanimous view of my panel of assessors that we should try to achieve a fixed costs system for all fast track cases. PR chapter 22 also set out set out a possible matrix of fixed costs for consideration.

1.2   Definitions. In this chapter I use the following abbreviations for certain categories of claims: "RTA" for road traffic accident; "ELA" for employers' liability accident; "ELD" for employers' liability disease; "EL" for employers' liability generally; "PLA" for public liability accident, "PL" for public liability generally and "HD" for housing disrepair. I refer to the Civil Justice Council as the "CJC". I use the phrase "fixed costs" as a general term to embrace (a) costs for which figures are specified and (b) costs which can be calculated by a predetermined means, such as the formulae in CPR Part 45. I refer to the new process for lower value personal injury claims proposed by the Ministry of Justice (the "MoJ"), discussed in PR chapter 26 and chapter 22 below, as the "new process". I use "FRC" to mean the fixed recoverable costs set out in CPR Part 45, section II.

1.3   MRO Agreement. I refer to the Medical Reporting Organisation Agreement as the "MRO Agreement". This agreement, dated 2nd April 2009, was made between liability insurers and "compensators" on the one hand and medical reporting organisations ("MROs") on the other. It provides for capped recoverable costs in respect of certain expert medical reports in RTA, EL and PL claims where general damages do not exceed £15,000.

1.4   The reforms recommended in this chapter (if the recommendations are accepted) could all be implemented fairly rapidly by the Civil Procedure Rule Committee, without any need for primary legislation. Therefore the recommendations in this chapter differ from the reforms recommended in chapters 9 and 10 above, which would require primary legislation. In this chapter, I shall assume that the present rules concerning conditional fee agreements ("CFAs"), after-the-event ("ATE") insurance and the recoverability of success fees and ATE insurance premiums remain in place. In chapter 17 below I shall discuss how the fixed costs rules will need to be amended in the event that success fees and ATE insurance premiums cease to be recoverable.

1.5   In this chapter I make proposals for introducing a regime of fixed costs, which will apply in any fast track case where costs fall to be assessed (whether by order of the court or by agreement between the parties) on the standard basis. The proposed fixed costs will not apply in a case where a party acts so unreasonably that the court makes an order for indemnity costs against that party.

2. SEMINARS DURING PHASE 2

(i) Birmingham seminar

2.1   Range of views expressed. The Birmingham seminar on 26th June 2009 was focused primarily on personal injuries litigation. During the floor discussion, one speaker argued that costs should not be fixed, because that limits the quality of investigation and presentation. Another speaker argued in favour of fixed costs. He maintained that this does not lower the quality of work; defence solicitors work on fixed costs and to a satisfactory standard. A claimant solicitor said that the costs of clinical negligence cases should not be fixed. Another claimant solicitor argued that it was difficult to fix costs because of the effect of delays on the defendant side. There should at least be an escape clause. The President of the Forum of Insurance Lawyers argued that the data showed sufficient consistency, so that fixed costs were feasible. Most claimant firms do large volumes of work, so that the "swings and roundabouts" principle would apply. There should be no escape clause. A union representative made the point that claimant solicitors turn some cases down after consideration. Defendant solicitors never have to do that. They take on every case sent to them and are paid for every case. One speaker suggested that fixed costs might be disapplied for a party whose opponent did not comply with the pre-action protocol.

(ii) Fixed costs seminar

2.2   The seminar. A seminar on fixed costs (a) in the fast track and (b) above the fast track was held on 22nd July 2009, hosted by Eversheds LLP (the "fixed costs seminar"). A partner of Eversheds opened the debate, urging that the proposal for fixed costs should be maintained. He said that defence solicitors were dismayed when fixed fees were first introduced by insurers, but in fact the solicitors can still operate profitably under such a system. It has forced them to become more efficient without any drop in standards. He believes that the same would be true for claimant solicitors. The Vice-President of the Association of Personal Injury Lawyers ("APIL") spoke against fixing costs in the fast track. He stated that claimant solicitors (unlike defendant solicitors) do not have a consistent volume of work, with payment for every case. He pointed out that the upper limit for the fast track has been increased to £25,000 and that the fast track cases can embrace some complex cases. Commercial considerations should not be the main driver of reform in personal injuries litigation. The new process will achieve fixed costs for a large swathe of fast track cases and there should be no further extension. Indeed, fixed costs do not work well where they have been introduced. The figures have not been increased since October 2003. A member of the Bar reviewed the pros and cons of fixed costs. Professor Dominic Regan urged that the parasitic activity which surrounds personal injuries litigation in the fast track (referral fees, medical agencies etc) should be removed. In Professor Regan's view, it is inevitable that we will see fixed costs in the fast track, but they must be based upon research and solid foundations. Fees must be staged, in order to prevent the temptation to under-settle. There should be penalties for unreasonable conduct and Part 36 should be extended to provide real incentives to settle.

2.3   Personal injury cases. Following the initial prepared speeches, a wide range of views were expressed by those attending. Some speakers argued that ELD cases should come out of any fixed costs regime, because of the difficulty of tracing who to sue and the complex causation issues which arise. On the other hand it was pointed out that if such cases are complex, they take more than a day to try and so come out of the fast track anyway. A trade union legal officer stated that her union did not welcome fixed costs. Furthermore, in claims above £10,000 the statistics are less reliable anyway. A member of the Bar suggested that if one party behaved unreasonably the case could be re-allocated to the multi-track. A solicitor suggested that the remedy for unreasonable conduct should be to disapply fixed costs. Another solicitor urged that damages should be increased by 25%, where the claimant made an offer which was rejected but not beaten.

2.4   Housing cases. In relation to housing cases, a number of claimant solicitors spoke against fixed costs. They pointed out that legal aid rates for advice and assistance are very low. Therefore tenants' solicitors survive on recovered costs in cases which they win. In other words, there is cross-subsidisation. It is difficult to apply fixed costs in housing cases, because the redress is often non-monetary; also the procedures are not process driven. There are no success fees in housing cases, because they are usually done on legal aid.[1] Concern was expressed about the low number of solicitors firms and law centres doing legal aid housing work.

2.5   Vote. I took a straw poll at the end of the meeting. In relation to fast track personal injury cases, there were 33 votes in favour of fixed costs and seven votes against. In relation to fixing all costs on the fast track, there were 11 votes in favour and nine votes against. The number of abstentions was not counted.

---

[1] But see *Birmingham CC v Forde* [2009] EWHC 12 (QB); [2009] 1 WLR 2732; [2009] N.P.C. 7; and paragraph 4.7 below.

3. WRITTEN SUBMISSIONS DURING PHASE 2

3.1   A large volume of submissions have been received on this issue. They are divided very much along "party lines". Claimant solicitors (in agreement with APIL) and trade unions oppose any extension of fixed costs in the fast track beyond (a) those which have been agreed as part of the new process for personal injury claims and (b) those in the FRC scheme in CPR Part 45. Defendant solicitors and liability insurers support the fixing of costs across the whole fast track. Many of the arguments in the written submissions are along the same lines as those advanced at the seminars, summarised above. It is not practicable to embark upon a summary of all those written submissions.

3.2   Law Society. The Law Society states that it agreed to the present fixed costs regime for RTA claims and supports the principle. However, it comments that the figures have never been reviewed, which is contrary to the original agreement. The escape clause has rarely succeeded or even been invoked, because the exceptionality test is high. Furthermore fixed costs are not usually paid within 14 days of settlement, as they should be. The Law Society then discusses whether there should be a comprehensive fixed costs regime in the fast track. I shall quote this passage at length, because it encapsulates the views of many who have reservations about fixing costs across the whole fast track:

> "The principle of fixed costs
>
> The Law Society is not opposed in principle to fixed costs in the fast track, providing that there is the option to apply to remove the case from such a scheme if significant costs are envisaged at any stage. We also consider that it is too ambitious to try to fix costs for all PI[2] cases and all other fast track cases at this stage. Any proposal to do so should be delayed until the proposed RTA streamlined claims process has been evaluated. To extend the principle of fixed costs could adversely affect access to justice or increase the number of unrepresented litigants bringing claims.
>
> It also needs to be made clear that any fixing must take account of the processes. In the Law Society's view, fixed costs will only reduce overall costs if changes to the process are made. If reductions are made without such changes then the likely effect may well be that solicitors will seek to recover any shortfall from the client. This means that there is likely to be further pressure on the principle, which the Law Society supports, that the client should not lose money from their damages.
>
> Housing cases
>
> Historically, housing cases have always been treated differently to personal injury claims. Illegal eviction and housing disrepair matters below £5,000 have not been allocated to the small claims track for the simple reason that those drafting the CPR were aware of the very real complexity of housing matters. The review does not appear to have considered this history and focuses attention on a one size fits all solution. The Law Society does not believe that you can compare accidents at work with 'all other forms of housing litigation'.

---

[2] Personal injury.

Housing cases relate to a person's home. They can be very complex, especially when they may result in a client losing their home. Whilst some forms of housing disrepair cases can be relatively straight-forward, many cases arise by way of counter-claim in possession proceedings and the issues become far more complex. Equally, homelessness appeals are very difficult pieces of litigation which are invariably handled by specialists.

Table 22.3 in the review[3] seems to take a too simplistic approach to housing litigation and we believe this to be the wrong approach.

<u>Key elements of fixed costs</u>

If, despite the above, it is determined that a fixed cost regime should be introduced for fast track claims, the key elements must be as follows:

i) The costs must be fair and must represent the current cost of doing the work. This will require careful evidence gathering and surveys.

ii) There must be an annual review (this is conceded in para 2.17 of chapter 22 of the preliminary report).

iii) Proportionality appears to be the starting point for the proposed matrices and this will cause considerable problems for cases where the value may be relatively small but, where, as Hazel Genn has suggested, there is an irreducible minimum of work, it would be unacceptable for consumers effectively to be deprived of a remedy because the level of the claim was low.

iv) There must be a fair 'escape clause' which provides the right to recover costs actually incurred where the issues in the case and the interests of justice so require. Also, either party should have the right to apply at any stage if the circumstances of the case requires.

v) The scheme must ensure that a fair amount of costs is recovered so that claimants get their damages and their solicitors are paid fairly for the effort in achieving this. As most cases are driven largely by defendant insurers to their conclusion, the amount of work done will be dictated by them. It will be unfair if such work is not paid for because of a restrictive scheme. The current emphasis seems to be weighted towards savings for defendants and insurers.

vi) There needs to be careful provision for additional factors which can include:

- Multi defendants
- Language difficulties
- A child or patient client
- Multi experts required
- Cases involving psychiatric as well as physical injury
- Self employed claimants
- Numbers of witnesses
- Contributory negligence
- Fatal cases and inquest costs"

---

[3] This is a reference to Table 22.3 in PR chapter 22.

3.3   Bar Council. The Bar does not support extension of the fixed costs regime. However, if the regime is to be extended the Bar Council states that there needs to be a degree of flexibility to allow for the more difficult and time consuming points. The Bar Council adds:

> "The points that justify the instruction of counsel (in preparation and in advocacy) are, by definition, points that are more complex than the usual. The level of expertise provided and the responsibility undertaken by a barrister (often in cases where the solicitor is junior and inexperienced) is considerable and justifies recognition and reward."

3.4   The Bar Council goes on to propose that there should be a range of recoverable fees for preparation and advocacy, say three scales distinguishing cases as simple, moderate and complex. Above that costs should be in the discretion of the court. The Bar Council proposes that pre-trial work and advocacy by barristers should form a separate category of costs from the costs allowed to solicitors. It adds:

> "In any event, a system whereby the solicitor apportions a single allowance between the solicitor and barrister may not operate fairly and should be rejected. Advocacy fees must be ring fenced and not rolled into general litigation costs."

3.5   Bar Associations. Bar Associations present a range of views. The Chancery Bar Association (the "ChBA") states that any fixed costs regime must have flexibility to allow for the varied nature of chancery work and the inherent complexity of some low value chancery claims. There must be exceptions for cases with no money value. The judge must have a discretion to award costs above the scale figures in appropriate cases. The ChBA points out that many categories of chancery litigation were excluded from the former county court scales. Pre-trial work done by barristers must form a separate category from solicitors' work for which costs are fixed. The Property Bar Association can see the attraction in principle of fixed recoverable costs in the fast track, but believes that in practice there would be insuperable problems in achieving this.

3.6   The Professional Negligence Bar Association (the "PNBA") points out that most professional negligence cases are allocated to the multi-track. Such cases involve issues of reputation, as well as money. The PNBA believes that there should be greater flexibility to award higher recoverable costs than is contained in the fixed costs provisions which currently exist in CPR Parts 45 and 46. The PNBA strongly endorses the suggestion that any system of fixed costs should have built into it an adequate mechanism for regular review. Also allowance must be made for counsel's fees.

3.7   The Personal Injuries Bar Association ("PIBA") states that three matters are particularly important if the present fixed costs regime is to be extended:

(i)   There should be distinctions between the fixed costs allowed in RTA, EL, disease and other personal injury cases. These different types of case require different levels of knowledge and expertise which should be reflected in the fees.

(ii)   Counsel's fees should be ring fenced. Otherwise counsel will not be instructed, and claimants will be deprived of independent advice and the court of specialist advocates.

(iii)   There should be provision for regular inflationary increases in any fixed cost regime.   The length of time that advocates' fees in the fast track were unchanged is unacceptable.

3.8   <u>Comments of one liability insurer.</u> One major liability insurer states that the predictive costs regime[4] has worked well. The defendant insurers get certainty, while claimant solicitors seem able to generate healthy profits. The insurer believes that fixed costs should be extended to the whole fast track, and indeed to multi-track cases. It states that clear rules are necessary to prevent claimant lawyers exploiting the regime. The insurer suggests that allowance should be made for the following additional factors: multiple defendants; cases where the correct defendant to a PL claim was not immediately apparent; work required in attending a mediation, whether before or after issue. Incentives to issue proceedings, rather than settle pre-issue, must be removed.

3.9   <u>Association of Law Costs Draftsmen.</u> The Association of Law Costs Draftsmen states:

> "We agree in principle that all costs of cases determined on the fast track should be capable of being fixed in amount by a consistent and regularly reviewed tariff system albeit judges should retain the power in exceptional cases to refer cases to detailed assessment."

3.10   <u>Professor Zuckerman.</u>   Professor Adrian Zuckerman, in his review of the Preliminary Report,[5] argues that a system of fixed recoverable costs is the only way of achieving access to justice at predictable and proportionate cost (unless costs shifting is abolished altogether). He is, however, critical of the approach to fast track fixed costs which is set out in PR chapter 22. After reviewing the detail, he summarises his criticisms as follows:

> "The real problem lies in the position that Jackson LJ seems to have adopted, that fixed costs must be the product of a genuine attempt to estimate the actual (reasonable) costs of the winning party. As already observed, any such estimation will inevitably be made by reference to current practice and current levels of costs, which have been the product of a system that allows unpredictable and disproportionate costs to be incurred. Consequently, a fixed costs system which is founded on the present costs level and which, in addition, permits the level to be exceeded in "exceptional" circumstances, will be in the end self-defeating. For a system of fixed costs to succeed, it must be robust, free standing and cap the expenses at a level which is proportionate to the amount in dispute and possibly to its importance, leaving litigants free to spend disproportionate costs at their own expense, if they so wish."

3.11   <u>Housing cases – tenant view.</u> A number of housing firms which act for tenants very strongly argue against fixed costs, essentially for the reasons outlined at the fixed costs seminar.   The Housing Law Practitioners Association is firmly opposed to fixing costs for fast track housing cases for the following main reasons:

- Implementing fixed costs would accelerate what has already been a marked decline in suppliers of advice and representation in housing cases.

---

[4] This is a reference to the FRC scheme.

[5] *"Lord Justice Jackson's Review of Civil Litigation Costs - Preliminary Report"*, (2009) 28 C.J.Q. 435; for the contrary view, see Neil Andrews, chapter on costs, European Casebook on Civil Procedure (IUS COMMUNE Series) (Hart, Oxford, forthcoming) (edited by Remco van Rhee and Paul Overhammer).

- There are sufficient existing mechanisms to control costs (e.g. landlords making realistic Part 36 offers and complying with orders for repairs) and more use should be made of them.

- No empirical research (or inadequate research) has been carried out to justify the proposals and to consider their likely effects.

- Housing cases are not comparable with personal injury cases.

- There has been a failure to consult properly with housing practitioners.

3.12 A member of the Bar, who practises in the North East and also sits as a deputy district judge, writes:

> "The levels of factual complexity to be found in contested disrepair cases (and they all seem to be contested to a greater extent than RTA cases), similarly usually dwarf those of Fast Track RTA cases. Most FT[6] RTA cases, even with PI, are relatively straightforward factually, and require the Court to accept one version of facts over another on usually only one or two issues. In disrepair cases, there is usually an expert on both sides, whose reports may deal with 20 to 40 issues each, and fast track trial bundles usually run to between 200 and 700 pages. There is often a PI element in disrepair cases, and more complex (in terms of items and causation) special damages claims than are found in RTA cases. It also needs to be borne in mind that interim and final repairing orders are often sought, which mean that the relief sought is not just monetary."

He is concerned that if the fixed costs are too low, tenants' representatives will be encouraged to settle too early and too low. He is concerned about the dwindling number of housing practitioners in the North East and that this would be exacerbated by the introduction of fixed costs. He is also worried about extending fixed costs to anti-social behaviour injunctions and homelessness appeals, where the same access to justice considerations arise.

3.13 <u>Housing cases – landlord view.</u> Birmingham City Council ("BCC") states that it is concerned about the high costs of HD cases. It welcomes the proposals for fixed costs in the fast track. However, if that is not possible, BCC proposes that success fees for HD cases should be fixed. A member of the Bar with recent experience of housing litigation writes that the nature of HD claims is such that they are among the most straightforward types of case; it is extremely rare for a disrepair claim to be lost by a claimant. He argues that costs in HD cases should be limited either by way of fixed costs or by an upper threshold by which costs can exceed damages.[7]

3.14 <u>The Association of Her Majesty's District Judges.</u> The Association of Her Majesty's District Judges states:

> "We strongly believe that a fixed costs regime should apply to all cases that are allocated to the Fast Track. With hindsight, so much litigation would have been avoided if such a regime had been put in place at or soon after the commencement of the Civil Procedure Rules 1998. If the core principles that we espouse under paragraph 1.4[8] of this response are to be applied to Fast

---

[6] Fast track.

[7] Presumably "damages" in this context includes the value of any repairs which the court orders the landlord to carry out.

[8] These "core principles" are: (i) the promotion and enhancement of access to the justice through the court system; (ii) simplicity of the costs rules; (iii) the avoidance of a regime that allows for "satellite"

Track cases, a fixed costs regime is the only practical way forward. We do not share the view that such a scheme will deny access to the courts since, whatever funding source a litigant chooses to use, there would still be an ultimate benefit to a successful litigant."

The Association believes that there should be costs reduction for early admission of liability. The Association would prefer not to see counsel's fees absorbed within the solicitors' matrix fee. It also proposes that experts' fees should be fixed, after appropriate consultation.

3.15   Need for regular review. A large number of submissions emphasise the need for regular review of any fixed costs set for the fast track. Many respondents draw attention to the failure to review the FRC in CPR Part 45 section II and the delays in reviewing the fixed fast track trial costs in CPR Part 46.

4. THE CIVIL JUSTICE COUNCIL FACILITATIVE MEETINGS

4.1   The meetings. During autumn 2009 the CJC hosted a series of five facilitative meetings (a) between claimant representatives and defendant representatives in relation to personal injury claims and (b) between landlord representatives and tenant representatives in relation to HD claims. The meetings were chaired by Michael Napier QC, who is one of my assessors. A substantial quantity of data was assembled and provided by Professor Paul Fenn, another of my assessors, for the assistance of all present. Tim Wallis of the CJC acted as mediator, when required. His Honour Judge Nic Madge assisted Mr Napier in chairing the HD meetings. Bob Musgrove, chief executive of the CJC, was the overall organiser. A list of all those who participated in the facilitative meetings is attached as appendix 4 to this report. It should be noted that APIL representatives withdrew from the process after the first meeting, but rejoined the process for the last two meetings.

4.2   Data produced by Professor Fenn. At each facilitation meeting Professor Fenn produced in chart form a series of alternative figures and fixed fee models based on data provided to him by the parties involved in the facilitation process. The chart was modelled on the first matrix set out in chapter 22 of the PR with additional columns to reflect fixed costs already in place namely:

(i)   the new MoJ streamlined process in RTA cases that settle below £10,000 where liability is admitted, due to be introduced in 2010;

(ii)   the fixed recoverable costs regime already in place in CPR Part 45 for RTA cases up to £10,000, which settle before issue; and

(iii)   fixed success fees in RTA, ELA and ELD cases, also set out in CPR Part 45.

Although it was not possible to obtain "industry agreement" on the figures and models presented by Professor Fenn, the contributions made by the parties at the facilitation meetings have given me considerable assistance in reaching my conclusions on fixed costs in the fast track.

4.3   Agreement that Professor Fenn's analysis of the data is statistically reliable. At the first facilitation meeting in relation to RTA claims, and in the absence of industry-agreed figures, an important and helpful written agreement was reached by

---

litigation on the issue of costs; (iv) predictability, if not certainty, of the amount of the costs; and (v) proportionality.

the parties that "*the analysis by Fenn of the data provided to him is statistically reliable*". This agreement was also a feature of the ELA and PLA facilitations. In the ELD facilitation the wording of the agreement was amended to include the words "*subject to the reservations expressed by Professor Fenn himself*" (see section 5 below). I have carefully considered Professor Fenn's statistically reliable data.

4.4   Agreement for additional written submissions.   At the RTA and ELA facilitations it was also agreed that the parties could make additional written submissions on five areas, namely (i) the effect of inflation; (ii) efficiency savings/cash flow benefits; (iii) the effect of referral fees; (iv) escape criteria; and (v) future review of fixed costs/a Costs Council. At the PLA facilitation three further areas for additional submissions were included, namely (i) the definition and scope of public liability; (ii) success fees; and (iii) the effect on the public purse. All the additional submissions, and the submissions received in Phase 2, have been carefully considered by me in arriving at my conclusions as set out in this chapter and resulting in my final proposed charts of recommended fixed costs in the fast track at appendix 5 to this report.

4.5   The positions of the parties in relation to personal injury claims.   The claimant representatives are opposed in principle to further extension of fixed costs in the fast track. However, if costs are to be fixed, they have helpfully set out their submissions as to what those fixed costs should be. The defendant representatives support the principle of fixed costs and they too have set out their submissions as to what those costs should be. I shall refer further to the arguments of both sides in section 5 below.

4.6   Need for Costs Council.   It was agreed that there needed to be a clearly defined and regular review process for all fixed costs. It was also agreed that a Costs Council should be established for this purpose.

4.7   The positions of the parties in relation to housing disrepair.   Both landlord and tenant groups support fixed success fees, but are opposed to fixed costs. They accept that there is poor behaviour in a number of claims. They believe that the Pre-Action Protocol for Housing Disrepair Cases should be tightened considerably to correct such behaviour. Both groups believe that there is an insufficient number of HD cases to warrant fixed costs. They comment that the majority of HD cases are brought on legal aid. Virtually no HD cases are brought on CFAs in the south of England, but a considerable percentage of HD cases are brought on CFAs in the north.

4.8   The Bar.   Representatives of the Bar maintain that if fixed costs are introduced for the fast track, then counsel's fees in respect of all work done before trial should be treated as disbursements. The Bar Council and PIBA lodged written submissions during the course of the facilitative meetings to the following effect. There are 1,300 practising barrister members of PIBA, many of whom are under 10 years call and do work in fast track cases. In fast track cases the Bar is presently instructed to:

- Advise on evidence and/or liability (on paper or in conference).

- Draft pleadings, sometimes to prepare schedules.

- Advise on offers.

- Provide advocacy at trials, case management conferences ("CMCs") and applications.

Usually between 20% and 33% of a barrister's fee income goes in chambers expenses. Thus when counsel conducts a fast track trial for the fees specified in CPR Part 46, that represents good value for money. Any future fixed costs regime for fast track personal injury cases must allow for counsel to do the pre-trial work mentioned above on a disbursement basis. Counsel have a high level of expertise to offer. This is particularly important in respect of fast track cases, which may be handled by more junior employees of insurance companies or solicitors firms. Accordingly PIBA proposes a matrix of fixed fees for "Bar style" work.[9] Also, there should be a provision for costs to be in the discretion of the trial judge when particularly novel, unreasonable or complex issues arise.

5. PERSONAL INJURY CLAIMS

(i) Road traffic accident, employers' liability accident and public liability accident cases

5.1 Separate consideration of RTA, ELA and PLA cases. The facilitative meetings examined each of these three topics separately and in detail. The claimant representatives and the defendant representatives have each put in separate written submissions concerning RTA personal injury claims, ELA personal injury claims and PLA personal injury claims. APIL has provided a separate and composite submission about all three categories. I have considered each of the written submissions individually. However, since I have come to essentially the same conclusion in respect of all three categories of personal injury cases, it would make this chapter excessively long if I dealt with each of the three categories in a separate section.

5.2 In the case of PLA, there was some debate as to what was included under this rubric. Most PLA cases are slips and trips or similar accidents. However, there will be some more complex PL cases involving personal injury,[10] which may (a) be allocated to the multi-track (despite having a value less than £25,000) or (b) fall within the escape clause discussed below.

5.3 The starting point. The starting point for any consideration of fixed costs in the fast track is Professor Fenn's analysis of the actual costs currently being incurred in relation to fast track personal injury cases. Those figures, described as the "base" model or "Fenn 1", were presented to the facilitative meetings in a series of tables. The meetings proceeded on the basis of two fee stages post-issue and pre-trial. However, at a late stage in the meetings all parties stated that there should be three fee stages post-issue.[11] Accordingly, Professor Fenn has subsequently re-analysed the data in order to present the Fenn 1 figures on the basis of three fee stages post-issue.

5.4 Fenn 2. Professor Fenn derived from the base model a set of costs figures which, in his view (after hearing the oral arguments and considering the written submissions), it would be reasonable to incorporate into any fixed costs regime. This second set of figures was described as the "mid" model or "Fenn 2". Professor Fenn derived the Fenn 2 figures by a process which he summarises as follows:

---

[9] A matrix of suggested counsel fees in RTA cases was produced during the facilitative meetings. This is divided into three columns for simple, moderate and complex cases.

[10] For example, child abuse, PL disease, false arrest or imprisonment, stress, failure by social services to remove children, social services removing children inappropriately, single incident mass pollution. Such claims may involve psychiatric harm, if not physical injury.

[11] The option of three stages post-issue was canvassed in chapter 22 of the Preliminary Report.

"Because the base model figures were derived from agreed profit cost data on claims settled across the period 2006 to 2009, it was necessary to adjust these for inflation, in order that the recommended fixed costs are in 'current price' terms. The agreed profit costs at the culmination of each claim are in the nature of agreed prices, and the most appropriate inflation index to apply is therefore a suitable consumer price index (CPI). In the absence of a specific CPI index for legal services, the ONS CPI index for miscellaneous services (DKB9) was used in producing the Fenn 2 figures. It was also important to recognise that there are likely to be some cost savings in the form of reduced overheads resulting from the introduction of fixed costs. The precise level of these savings is difficult to estimate, but defendant sources put forward a reasoned justification for the 'costs of costs' amounting to approximately £400 per claim. However, this ignores the need for some continuing overhead required to provide information on inputs/costs in order that the fixed cost regime can be properly reviewed and regulated. On this basis the Fenn 2 figures were subject to a reduction of £200 per claim to take account of the likely cost savings from the fixed cost regime."

5.5   The claimants' contentions. The claimant representatives argue that, if costs are going to be fixed, the levels of fixed costs should be approximately £400 higher than Fenn 2. The gist of the claimants' arguments is as follows. The data analysed by Professor Fenn are historic, having been based on cases concluded between 2006 and 2009 (and for which work was probably done between 2003 and 2009). The cost of undertaking the work has increased during this period and this should be reflected in the figures. The claimants suggest that this is most accurately and readily achieved by reference to the increases in guideline hourly rates for solicitors ("GHRs"). They suggest an uplift of 15%. A further allowance should be made for inflation, including future inflation until the proposed fixed costs rules are applied. Account should also be taken of the fact that the figures forming the basis of the Models are those in the current FRC based on an agreement seven years ago. Any savings to claimants as a consequence of fixed costs are minimal and the amount speculative. They would be more than offset by the additional non-recoverable costs claimants will incur due to fixed costs weakening the incentives on insurers under the current system to minimise the costs claimants incur. Both amounts are speculative and either cancel each other out or warrant an additional sum, not a deduction. Claimants argue that no reduction should be made to take account of referral fees. Banning or limiting the level of referral fees is a separate professional conduct issue and should be considered separately from fixed costs. The claimants make a number of points on the data, which are specific to ELA and PLA claims.

5.6   The defendants' contentions. The defendant representatives argue that the levels of fixed costs should be approximately £400 lower than Fenn 2 and there should be a further reduction to take account of general efficiency savings. The gist of the defendants' arguments is as follows. The Fenn data must be viewed and adjustments made in light of the new process. No increase is necessary to account for inflation as this is already reflected in GHRs and the current FRC linked to damages levels. Account should be taken of savings to claimant solicitors by a reduction in costs on costs, less management time and better cash flow. Defendants argue that costs should be set to drive an increase in efficiency. A reduction should be applied to reflect the disproportionate referral fee element of current base fees. In the future, when other measures are introduced to improve efficiency (e.g. a damages assessment tool), costs should further reduce to reflect the reduced work needed and to share the benefits of efficient improvements between lawyers and the public.

5.7   APIL's contentions. APIL opposes fixed costs in principle. It argues that extending fixed costs throughout the fast track whilst the process remains unpredictable will cause the injured person to suffer. The inequality of arms which already exists between the corporate insurer and the individual injured person will only deepen. APIL expresses disappointment that discussions at the facilitative meetings remained focused entirely on claimant data and questions why similar consideration was not given to defendant costs. It argues that the proper interpretation of the CPR and the intention behind Lord Woolf's reforms is that proportionality must go to the issues in the individual's case and not simply to the value of the claim. In particular, APIL does not believe that ELA and ELD claims are suitable for a fixed costs regime. Although APIL does not support the proposals for a fixed costs regime, it does also make submissions in respect of the data analysed by Professor Fenn. Many of the points it makes mirror those contended by the claimants and summarised in paragraph 5.5 above.

5.8   Decision in principle. I have carefully considered the competing arguments. My conclusion is that all costs for personal injuries litigation in the fast track should be fixed. I am not persuaded by the arguments of APIL and others that this fundamental element of Lord Woolf's recommendations should be abandoned. Furthermore, in my view, it is possible to arrive at reasonable fixed costs for RTA, ELA and PLA cases on the basis of (a) the data available and (b) the detailed analyses and submissions which have emerged from the CJC's series of facilitative meetings. I do not accept the Law Society's argument that the introduction of fixed costs is a reform *"weighted towards savings for defendants and insurers."* In my view, there is a high public interest in making litigation costs in the fast track both proportionate and certain. Since personal injury claims constitute a substantial part of contested fast track cases,[12] there is an obvious public interest in tackling these cases first. I accept APIL's argument that I must also consider the costs incurred by defendants. I shall address the defendant's recoverable costs later in this chapter. However, since in personal injuries litigation defendant costs are significantly lower than claimant costs,[13] it would be disadvantageous to claimant lawyers if fixed costs are set by reference to defendant costs as opposed to the Fenn data.

5.9   Levels of fixed costs. On the basis of the present data, I consider that the Fenn 2 figures are the correct starting point. Many of the arguments advanced on the claimant and defendant side cancel each other out. However, two important points stand out:

(i)   Claimant solicitors will no longer have to maintain documentation required for costs assessment or spend time arguing about costs. Thus the hitherto substantial "costs of costs" will be saved.

(ii)   A fixed costs regime is bound to generate business process efficiencies in the form of reduced management costs or overheads.[14]

I expect that these two factors will lead to substantially greater savings than the figure of £400 per case, which is allowed in Fenn 2. Nevertheless, these are matters which can be reviewed in due course by the Costs Council. For the time being, I recommend that the Fenn 2 figures are used as the basis for fixed costs, subject to one

---

[12] See PR chapter 5 section 2 and appendices 1, 2 and 8.

[13] This is plain from the tariffs of fixed fees agreed between liability insurers and their solicitors.

[14] This is illustrated by the recent experience of the FRC scheme, which was introduced in October 2003. Referral fees have risen since then from about £350 per case to about £750 per case. Nevertheless, the fixed costs figures which I propose in this chapter do not take into account the savings which will accrue to claimant solicitors if and when referral fees are banned or limited, as recommended in chapter 20 below.

qualification. I have set out below a separate provision for the collection of costs information for review purposes. Professor Fenn has allowed £200 per case for this purpose. After reviewing the evidence and discussion with my assessors of the work which would be involved, I have concluded that the allowance for providing information required for review purposes should be reduced from £200 to £100 per case.

5.10 <u>The Bar.</u> I accept that the Bar has a valuable role to play in fast track personal injury cases, both in the pre-trial work mentioned in paragraph 4.8 above and also at trial. Professor Fenn's data indicate that the costs of instructing counsel are on average as follows: post-issue RTA claims - £100; post-issue ELA claims - £225; post-issue PLA claims - £300. Obviously, the precise figure varies from case to case, because some cases require counsel input post-issue, whereas others do not. However, on a "swings and roundabouts" basis, if these figures are added to the fixed costs of every case, that will be sufficient to cover the current level of usage of counsel in RTA, ELA and PLA cases.

5.11 The next question arising is whether the allowance for counsel should be by way of fixed disbursements, ring fenced for counsel. Alternatively, should it be by way of a general increase to the Fenn 2 figures? Lord Woolf confronted a similar issue in his *Access to Justice* inquiry in relation to the trial advocacy fee. Lord Woolf decided to recommend a single figure for trial advocacy, to cover the immediate preparation (including a conference) and the trial itself. The same fee would be payable, irrespective of whether the advocate was a solicitor or barrister: see Lord Woolf's Final Report,[15] chapter 4, paragraphs 37 and 38. This recommendation has been adopted in CPR Part 46. In practice the trial advocacy is sometimes done by the claimant's solicitor (who then receives the trial advocacy fee) and is sometimes entrusted to counsel (who is then paid a brief fee). The total amount of costs recoverable from the opponent remains the same, irrespective of whether the work is done by solicitor or counsel. In my view a similar approach should be adopted in respect of work before trial. The sums which I have specified in the previous paragraph should be added to the figures for fixed costs, rather than specified as disbursements. The fixed costs will then be sufficient to permit the instruction of counsel to undertake appropriate work pre-trial. The claimant's solicitor will have a choice. He or she may (a) carry out all pre-trial work in-house or (b) instruct counsel to carry out part of that work. In the latter event, the fixed costs will be shared between solicitors and counsel in such manner as may be negotiated between the solicitors and counsel's clerk. Junior counsel represent good value for money in respect of "Bar style" work. My expectation in adopting this approach is that junior counsel will continue to be used, where appropriate, for pre-trial work in respect of fast track personal injury cases.

5.12 I have carefully considered the proposals put forward by the Bar Council and PIBA for fixed counsel fees in respect of different elements of work, with gradations according to the complexity of the case. In my view, this would introduce an unacceptable degree of complexity into the fast track fixed costs rules. If I were to go down this route, it would be necessary to specify the circumstances in which solicitors are entitled to incur the various barristers' fees set out in the Bar's proposed matrix. This matrix has 48 different boxes for RTA cases alone. So presumably there would be 144 different boxes for RTA, ELA and PLA cases collectively. Having dealt with that issue, I would then have to specify what sums the solicitors could recover in respect doing the work referred to in each of those 144 boxes, if the solicitors chose to undertake that work in-house. Any set of rules which gives effect to the Bar's

---

[15] HMSO, July 1996.

proposals would ultimately become an impenetrable jungle. Such rules would generate endless opportunities for satellite litigation. In my view, the only realistic approach to fixed costs in respect of legal work on personal injury cases is to have a simple matrix of global sums, which (taking one case with another) will provide proper remuneration for all the lawyers involved, including barristers, solicitors and other fee earners.

5.13   In relation to this issue, there are also two points of principle to bear in mind:

(i)   The primary aim of fixed costs is to ensure that the total costs reflect the complexity of the case as a whole, not the decisions made as to what type of lawyer should do the work.

(ii)   Any system of bolt-ons tends to incentivise the activity which triggers the additional payment. Solicitors will always be better off claiming the Bar fee as an additional item from the opponent rather than having to do that work and pay for it out of their fixed fee.

5.14   <u>The proposed matrices.</u> Taking into account all of the above matters, I have prepared two alternative matrices of fixed costs for adoption in RTA, ELA and PLA cases. These matrices are attached as appendix 5 to this report. The difference between the two matrices is that the second (table B) incorporates an allowance for early admission of liability. If table B is adopted, where the defendant admits liability within the protocol period, discounts of £250 pre-issue or £500 post-issue (i.e. where quantum only proceedings are issued) will apply at each stage. As a consequence of this discount being available, the fixed costs in table B have been inflated by £50, to take into account the fact that in a proportion of these claims the discounted figure will be paid. The logic behind this version of the matrix is that it has the potential to influence behaviour, such that defendants are incentivised to admit liability at an early stage, thereby increasing the chance of early settlement.

5.15   The figures shown in the matrices include (i) the fixed costs which I propose should be adopted for RTA, ELA and PLA cases and (ii) the existing levels of fixed recoverable costs and advocacy fees already provided for in CPR Parts 45 and 46. I include these latter figures for information purposes only, as I have not conducted a review of the existing fixed costs figures. If my recommendations in this chapter and in chapter 6 above are accepted, then the Costs Council should conduct a regular review of all fixed costs across the fast track.[16]

5.16   <u>Children and protected persons.</u> In cases where the claimant is a child or protected person, any settlement requires court approval. In such cases I propose that the following be added to the fixed recoverable costs in respect of the pre-issue period: (a) a fixed fee of £500 for the solicitors, (b) £150 for counsel (as a disbursement) to advise on quantum and (c) court fee for approval application.

5.17   <u>Additional factors.</u> I have considered whether special provision should be made for the additional factors[17] referred to in PR paragraph 22.2.3 (ii) and paragraph (vi) of the Law Society's submission quoted in section 3 above. Professor Fenn advises me that his data include cases with all these factors. Therefore allowance has already been made for all these factors in the figures now proposed.

---

[16] See paragraphs 2.8 to 2.10 of chapter 6 above.
[17] Other than children and protected persons, as discussed in the previous paragraph.

5.18   Escape clause. The escape clause in the existing FRC scheme[18] is contained in CPR rules 45.12 and 45.13. It applies where (a) the court considers that there are exceptional circumstances and (b) upon assessment the costs turn out to be at least 20% higher than the fixed costs. This escape clause[19] has proved satisfactory and has not led to any mass escapes from the FRC regime. I am advised that the escape clause is seldom used; it does not in practice undermine the principle of the FRC regime.[20] I recommend that an escape clause in similar terms be incorporated in the new comprehensive fixed costs regime for personal injury cases.

5.19   In my view, there should be no further escape clauses. If a case is of particular complexity, it may be allocated or re-allocated to the multi-track. If a party acts unreasonably (as opposed to presenting its case in the normal way and losing) the court can override the fixed costs regime by making an order for indemnity costs.

5.20   Interim hearings or case management conferences. In the great majority of fast track cases there are no CMCs or interim hearings. Either the case proceeds to trial on the basis of written directions[21] or (far more often) the case settles without coming to a hearing. Paragraph 2.2 of the practice direction supplementing CPR Part 28 provides that whenever possible the court will give directions in writing and it will expect the co-operation of the parties in this regard. Paragraph 2.3 provides:

> "The court will however hold a hearing to give directions whenever it appears necessary or desirable to do so, and where this happens because of the default of a party or his legal representative it will usually impose a sanction."

5.21   The normal approach should be that any CMC or interim hearing falls within the fixed costs. However, the court should have discretion to order that the costs of a CMC or other interim hearing (as summarily assessed) should be paid by a party and should not form part of the fixed recoverable costs. Clearly it must be a matter for the court how it exercises that discretion in any individual case. However, I envisage that the discretion may be exercised against a party whose unreasonable conduct has made the hearing necessary.

5.22   Medical reports. In my view the sums recoverable for obtaining medical reports and medical records should be capped at the levels currently specified in the MRO Agreement. The claimants should be entitled to recover those sums for procuring medical reports and medical records, irrespective of whether they do so directly or through the agency of an MRO. The fixed maximum costs for obtaining medical reports and medical records should be regularly reviewed by the Costs Council.[22]

5.23   Other disbursements. The new fixed costs rules should contain a provision akin to CPR rule 45.10[23] in respect of other disbursements. Also prompt steps should be taken to secure the fixing of other disbursements in the same way that (if my recommendation is accepted) the costs of medical reports will be fixed.

5.24   Defendants' costs. In the great majority of personal injury cases either costs are payable by the defendant to the claimant or there is no order for costs.[24]

---

[18] CPR Part 45, section II.
[19] Which is substantially more generous than the escape clauses in legal aid fee schemes.
[20] See the Law Society's submissions summarised in section 3 above.
[21] Generally following the standard directions appended to the Part 28 practice direction.
[22] If the recommendation in chapter 6 above is accepted.
[23] Which provides that the court may allow a claim for certain types of disbursements.
[24] See e.g. PR paragraph 25.2.6.

Nevertheless, provision must be made for those cases where the claimant is ordered to pay the defendant's costs. I recommend that the same fixed costs regime should apply when costs are recoverable by defendants as when costs are recoverable by claimants. It should be noted, however, that in practice defendants never have CFAs with their solicitors. Therefore the references in the matrix to success fees will not apply when defendants recover costs.[25]

5.25   Where the defendant wins on liability. In cases where the claimant loses on liability, the damages which were in issue must be assessed for the purpose of ascertaining the fixed costs to which the defendant is entitled. This figure should be the pleaded value of the claim, alternatively its apparent value on the basis of the facts pleaded. In the absence of agreement between the parties, the court when making an order for costs against the claimant should state what damages were in issue.

5.26   Where the defendant wins on quantum. In cases where the claimant fails to beat a defendant's offer, the amount of damages will, of course, be known. The court is likely to order (a) the defendant to pay the claimant's costs up to the date when the offer should have been accepted and (b) the claimant to pay the defendant's costs thereafter. The claimant will then recover his fixed costs up to the relevant date. The defendant will recover his fixed costs (as derived from the matrix) for the period between the date when his offer should have been accepted and the date of judgment. There can then be a set off between the two sums of fixed costs which each party is entitled to recover.

5.27   Response to Professor Zuckerman's comments. I have taken into account Professor Zuckerman's concerns, as expressed in his article in Civil Justice Quarterly.[26] I am satisfied that the fixed costs system proposed above will not be "self-defeating". It will achieve a genuine reduction in the costs of fast track litigation and it will ensure that costs are more proportionate to the sums at stake.[27] At the same time it will be fair to the lawyers involved on both sides.

(ii) Employers' liability disease cases

5.28   Fixed costs. I do not accept the argument advanced by some speakers at the fixed costs seminar that ELD cases are a special category, which should be excluded from the fixed costs regime. I do accept, however, that some ELD cases have complicating features, which necessitate allocation to the multi-track despite that fact that the damages claimed fall within fast track limits.

5.29   ELD data. The participants in the CJC's facilitative meetings reached the following agreement about Professor Fenn's data on ELD cases:

> "It is agreed that the Fenn figures i.e. the analysis by Fenn of the data provided to him is statistically reliable, subject to the reservations expressed by Professor Fenn himself."

At the time of the facilitative meetings the only data available to Professor Fenn had come from the claimant side. These data did not separate out multi-defendant cases

---

[25] This paragraph will only be applicable in exceptional cases, if and when my recommendation to introduce qualified one way costs shifting for personal injuries litigation (see chapter 19 below) is accepted.

[26] Cited in paragraph 3.10 above.

[27] Costs will become truly proportionate if and when the reforms recommended in chapters 9, 10 and 17 of this report are implemented.

or take account of apportionment. Professor Fenn stated that he would obtain supplementary data from insurers on ELD cases.

5.30   I propose that Professor Fenn continues his collection and analysis of ELD data and provides that material both to myself and to the claimant and defendant representatives from the CJC facilitative meetings by 31st March 2010. Those representatives can then have a period of six weeks to submit their written observations on that material. I will consider those written observations and then recommend a matrix of fixed costs for fast track ELD cases, drawing on the advice of the Senior Costs Judge and the CJC.

(iii) Need for regular reviews

5.31   <u>Role of Costs Council.</u> I have recommended in chapter 6 above that a Costs Council should be established. If this recommendation is accepted, the Costs Council would set GHRs and would review the levels of all fixed costs. The Costs Council should review the fixed costs for personal injury cases every year and set revised figures if appropriate.

5.32   In order to provide data which will inform the annual reviews, the Costs Council will need to obtain hard data about the costs being incurred by claimant solicitors and to analyse such data. The Law Society, as approved regulator, has the statutory power to make rules prescribing the requirements which must be satisfied by solicitors in order to be recognised as being suitable to undertake the provision of legal services.[28] In practice, the Law Society delegates this power to the Solicitors Regulation Authority (the "SRA"). The SRA has already made rules whereby it requires solicitors to provide certain information every year for this purpose.[29] I propose that the SRA, with the support of the Legal Services Board as oversight regulator, should be given wider powers so as to make rules requiring solicitors to provide such further information as the Costs Council requires for the purpose of performing its functions. The fixed costs figures which I recommend contain an allowance of £100 per case for the collection and provision of data required by the Costs Council: see paragraph 5.9 above.

(iv) Need to avoid satellite litigation

5.33   If the above recommendations are accepted, rules to implement them will need to be drawn with care, in order to prevent opportunities for satellite litigation. It will also be necessary to watch closely how those rules operate in practice. If claimant or defendant solicitors embark upon satellite litigation, in order to exploit the new fixed costs regime, the rules must be amended to remove the temptation for such satellite litigation.

6. NON-PERSONAL INJURY CASES

6.1   I propose that there should be a dual approach to non-personal injury fast track cases. First, there should be an overall limit on recoverable costs in all cases. Secondly, so far as the subject matter allows, there should be matrices of fixed costs for specific categories of fast track cases.

---

[28] Section 9(1)(b) and (c) of the Administration of Justice Act 1985, as amended by the Legal Services Act 2007.
[29] Rule 20.05(2)(a) of the Solicitors' Code of Conduct 2007.

6.2   Upper limit of £12,000 up to trial. I propose that there be a limit of £12,000 upon the pre-trial costs that can be recovered for any non-personal injury fast track case, unless an order for indemnity costs is made. Court fees (which are set by the MoJ) and the trial advocacy fee (which is fixed under CPR Part 46) should be separate. That figure of £12,000 is inclusive of counsel fees, expert fees, other disbursements, and all other pre-trial outlays. The only exceptions which I would make are success fees and ATE insurance premiums. For the reasons set out in chapters 9 and 10 above, I recommend that these should cease to be recoverable, since they have the effect of rendering costs disproportionate in every case. However, unless and until that recommendation is accepted, I must accept (out of deference to existing legislation) that success fees and ATE insurance premiums should fall outside the proposed cap. There should be a 12.5% increase in respect of the upper limit for pre-trial costs, when the solicitors are a London firm.

6.3   Reasons for choosing £12,000. I arrive at the figure of £12,000[30] for three reasons:

(i)   The fast track is designed for relatively straightforward cases with a maximum value of £25,000, where the trial can be concluded within one day: see CPR rule 26.6. In chapter 3 above I have argued that recoverable costs, assessed on the standard basis, should never exceed a proportionate sum. If the analysis in that chapter is accepted, there must be some sensible limit upon the recoverable costs which any party can incur in bringing or defending a fast track claim. An upper limit of £12,000[31] for pre-trial costs, in my view, accords with the principles set out in chapter 3 above. Any litigant in the fast track should have the comfort of knowing that his pre-trial costs exposure cannot exceed £12,000.[32]

(ii)   In practice it is rare for pre-trial base costs plus disbursements in any fast track case to be assessed in a sum larger than £12,000 (or £13,500 in London): see table 15.1 below. Therefore the cap which I propose would only bite upon a small proportion of cases where base costs and disbursements would otherwise be disproportionate.

(iii)   The Senior Costs Judge, having taken into account the results of the judicial survey appended to the Preliminary Report,[33] shares my view that £12,000 (or £13,500 in London) is a reasonable upper limit for recoverable costs in the fast track.[34]

6.4   The judicial survey conducted earlier this year encompassed a total of 970 county court cases dealt with by circuit judges, recorders, district judges and deputy district judges, during the course of which costs were assessed. Within these 970 cases there were 56 cases which met the following criteria: (i) they were not personal injury claims; (ii) they were not non-personal injury RTA claims;[35] and (iii) they fell

---

[30] Or £13,500 in London.
[31] Or £13,500 in London.
[32] Or £13,500 in London; also success fees and ATE insurance premiums must be added if, contrary to my advice, these remain recoverable.
[33] See PR appendices 1, 2 and 8.
[34] The Senior Costs Judge accepts that if (contrary to my recommendation) success fees and ATE insurance premiums remain recoverable, then these would fall outside the upper limit of £12,000.
[35] I exclude these cases because specific matrices of fixed costs are proposed for these categories.

within the present fast track limits.[36] These cases are summarised in table 15.1 below. It can be seen that these cases generally fell within the limit which I am proposing. This analysis confirms my view that £12,000 (or £13,500 in London) is a reasonable upper limit for pre-trial costs in respect of cases assigned to the fast track.

Table 15.1: Table summarising non-PI and non-RTA fast track cases from the judicial surveys[1]

REF[2]	PR APP	CASE NUMBER	TYPE OF CASE	PLEADED VALUE /RELIEF SOUGHT	SUM AWARDED /RELIEF GRANTED	TOTAL COSTS ALLOWED[3]
1	PR APP1	12	Contract	£5,593	£5,593	£4,095
2	PR APP1	117	Debt	£6200 + interest	£6200+ interest of £2430.68	£4,475
3	PR APP1	118	Contract	£9,500	Dismissed	£2,022
4	PR APP1	135	Building dispute	£7,467	£6,619	£5,798
5	PR APP1	153	Credit hire	£9,081	Adjourned	£1,345
6	PR APP1	192	Contract	£8,305	Struck out	£776
7	PR APP1	209	Contract	Enforce Tomlin order	Granted	£320
8L	PR APP1	214	Contract	£15,000	Claim against d3 dismissed	£1,735
9	PR APP1	219	Contract	£12,000	Summary judgment	£2,400
10L	PR APP1	232	Landlord/tenant	Amended directions	Granted	£777
11L	PR APP1	244	Contract	Summary judgment for £20000	Dismissed	£2,578
12	PR APP1	250	Landlord/tenant	Possession	Possession + £1964	£4,671
13	PR APP1	255	Contract	£11,000	Security for costs	£2,359
14	PR APP1	274	Cohabitee dispute	£15,410	Return of goods	£4,963
15	PR APP1	328	Possession			£11,688
16	PR APP1	337	Possession			£3,144
17	PR APP1	364	Costs only	£23,947	£12425 (costs of main case)	£1,832
18	PR APP1	412	Contract	£9,435	£9,135	£3,282
19	PR APP1	452	Contract	£9,400	Summary judgment	£1,550
20	PR APP1	470	Rent arrears	£3480 (counterclaim £6000)	£3,480	£3,633
21	PR APP1	515	Mortgage shortfall	£67,292	£33,133	£4,863
22	PR APP1	528	Not stated	Relief from sanctions	Granted	£1,075
23	PR APP1	529	Not stated	Unless order	Granted	£591
24	PR APP1	576	Contract	£5,000	Strike out refused	£1,765
25	PR APP1	588	Land dispute	To call second expert	Granted	£1,325
26	PR APP1	638	Contract	£11,500	£11,900	£4,000
27	PR APP1	639	Land dispute	Adjournment	Refused	£709
28	PR APP1	651	Contract	£8,200	£8,050	£5,910
29L	PR APP1	657	Contract	Interlocutory application	Unless order	£645
30	PR APP1	662	Animals act	£6,750	£7,156	£2,720
31L	PR APP1	668	Building dispute	£6000 (counterclaim £25000)	Part 18 order	£750
32	PR APP2	1	Overcharging works/defects	Application specific disclosure etc	Application granted	£4,000
33	PR APP2	2	Contract	£22,000	£21,000	£8,000
34	PR APP2	3	Contract	£16,000	£15,807	£6,000
35	PR APP2	5	Appeal in debt case £15.7k	Re-hearing	Appeal allowed	£3,643
36L	PR APP2	6	Debt	£21,500	£5,000	£3,750
37	PR APP2	20	Contract	£25,000	£25,000	£15,652
38	PR APP2	57	Credit Hire quantum	£12,000	£0	£2,640
39	PR APP2	59	Application for wasted costs	costs in issue £1,990	Order for £1,250	£1,996
40	PR APP2	77	Contract	App under CPR 47.10		£1,075
41	PR APP2	95	Contract	App to set aside jdg't of £7,625	?	£757
42L	PR APP2	125	Return of money, gift or loan	£11,000	£11,000	£9,607
43L	PR APP2	127	Commercial contract (£15k)	Interim Application		£548
44	PR APP8	16	Credit hire	£6,000	£4,500	£3,970
45	PR APP8	22	Insurance contract	£16,200	£12,900	£7,573
46	PR APP8	28	Unlawful arrest	<£5,000	Claim struck out	£1,548
47	PR APP8	53	Repayment of loan	£ 7,000 + interest	£8,686	£9,012
48	PR APP8	58	App. For relief from sanction	£5,000 +	Relief granted	£175

---

[36] At the time of the judicial survey, the fast track limit the upper limit for the fast track was £15,000. It has subsequently been raised to £25,000. So I include on the present table multi-track cases up to £25,000.

REF[2]	PR APP	CASE NUMBER	TYPE OF CASE	PLEADED VALUE /RELIEF SOUGHT	SUM AWARDED /RELIEF GRANTED	TOTAL COSTS ALLOWED[3]
49	PR APP8	75	Breach of contract	£5,720	£4,900	£4,715
50	PR APP8	82	ASBI s.153A-C Act	injunction	Injunction granted	£4,602
51	PR APP8	95	App. For summary judgment	?	Application refused ?	£1,499
52	PR APP8	104	?	<£5,000	£4,369	£4,178
53	PR APP8	112	Contract	£3,300	Summary judgment £3,300	£1,138
54	PR APP8	122	Poss. Of business premises	£1,500	Poss given + £1,500	£2,742
55	PR APP8	124	Contract	£5,635	£5,635	£1,929
56	PR APP8	137	Contract £5154	App. to set aside judgment	Agreed £2,560 owed	£953

Notes

1. Data taken from PR Appendices 1, 2 & 8. All cases which are not personal injury or non-personal injury RTA claims and fall within the present fast track limits (excludes claims which were not allocated to either track).

2. Cases heard in London denoted by L suffix.

3. Total costs allowed to trial include court fees, other disbursements and (where applicable) trial advocacy fees.

6.5 <u>Need for review by Costs Council.</u> The figure of £12,000[37] proposed above needs to be kept under regular review. If my recommendation for the establishment of a Costs Council is accepted, I recommend that the Costs Council should review that figure every year.

6.6 <u>Effect of upper limit on lower value claims.</u> If £12,000[38] is accepted as being the upper limit for pre-trial costs in the heaviest cases (measured by complexity and/or value) falling within the fast track which are fully contested, that should be a yardstick which would assist judges in determining what pre-trial costs are reasonable and proportionate in fast track cases[39] which are of lower value or lesser complexity or which are settled before trial. In the case of litigation which proves more complex, the judge retains the power to re-allocate to the multi-track under CPR rule 26.10.

6.7 <u>Controlling the costs of expert evidence in the fast track.</u> If my recommendation for an overall cap on recoverable costs in the fast track is accepted, it will be important to control the costs of expert evidence. The fast track is specifically designed for cases where the expert evidence (if any) will be limited: see CPR rule 26.6(5)(b). The court's power to control the recoverable costs of expert evidence is derived from CPR rule 35.4(4). This provision (as amended with effect from 1st October 2009) provides:

> "The court may limit the amount of a party's expert's fees and expenses that may be recovered from any other party."

Although it must be a matter for the judge in any individual case, I suggest that consideration should always be given to making use of this provision when the court gives permission for expert evidence[40] in fast track cases.[41] The application for permission to adduce expert evidence will usually be dealt with on paper. The applicant should furnish an estimate of the cost of the proposed expert evidence together with his application.[42]

---

[37] Or £13,500 in London.

[38] Or £13,500 in London.

[39] I.e. cases for which no matrix of fixed costs has been created.

[40] Other than medical evidence which is dealt with in paragraph 5.22 above.

[41] The standard fast track directions envisage that a limit will be placed upon the recoverable fees and expenses of the expert: see the fifth paragraph of the standard directions appended to the practice direction supplementing CPR Part 28.

[42] As to which, see chapter 38 below.

(ii) Specific categories of fast track cases

(a) Road traffic accident cases not involving personal injury

6.8   The costs of fast track RTA cases not involving personal injury should be fixed. The main heads of claim are usually vehicle damage and cost of hire. For a non-personal injuries case to be in the fast track, the measure of damages will be between £5,000 and £25,000.

6.9   <u>Fixed costs proposed.</u> I propose fixed costs for cases in this category as follows. For claims resolved pre-issue, the fixed costs should be £626 plus 4% of damages. For claims resolved post-issue the fixed costs should be £1,583 plus 9% of damages. If the case goes to trial, the trial advocacy fee specified in CPR Part 46 should be added to those fixed costs.

6.10   <u>Same rules for claimants and defendants.</u> The same fixed costs rules should apply, whether it is the claimant or the defendant who obtains an order for costs. If the claimant is victorious, fixed costs should be ascertained by reference to the amount of damages awarded. If the defendant is victorious, fixed costs should be ascertained by reference to the amount of damages claimed.

6.11   The fixed costs which I propose for non-personal injury fast track cases are based upon the data obtained and analysed during Phase 1 of the Costs Review. These proposed fixed costs were set out in chapter 22 of the Preliminary Report.[43] None of the submissions received during Phase 2 of the Costs Review has persuaded me that these figures should be changed.

(b) Housing cases

6.12   <u>The position at the facilitative meetings.</u> The data available at the facilitative meetings were insufficient for the purpose of producing any matrix of fixed costs in respect of possession claims or HD claims. Concern was expressed by the participants that there were so many variables that fixing costs was impossible.

6.13   <u>Housing disrepair cases.</u> HD cases are a matter of particular concern, because claims with a value between £1,000 and £5,000 fall within the fast track. This is the only area of litigation (apart from personal injury) where, for policy reasons, such low value claims are included within the fast track.

6.14   <u>Possession claims.</u> In possession claims it is normally the landlord who obtains an order for costs. In my view, there would be benefits for both parties if the costs of such proceedings (where they fall outside the regime of CPR rule 45.1)[44] were fixed. It should also be noted that in their recent report *"Turning the Tide"* AdviceUK, Citizens Advice[45] and Shelter recommend that: *"The Ministry of Justice should consider introducing a fixed fee regime for mortgage possession claims".*[46]

6.15   Professor Fenn is currently exploring the possibility of obtaining further data on housing cases. He anticipates completing this exercise and providing an analysis of any such data by 31st March 2010. Subject to what the data may reveal, it is my intention to invite the submissions of both landlord and tenant organisations upon that data before recommending any matrix of fixed costs for fast track housing cases.

---

[43] See table 22.2 on page 205.
[44] As to which, see PR paragraphs 31.2.9 to 31.2.11.
[45] The National Association of Citizens Advice Bureaux.
[46] *"Turning the Tide"*, 15th December 2009, page 17.

I hope then to be in a position to recommend a matrix of fixed costs for possession claims and HD claims, drawing on the advice of the Senior Costs Judge and the CJC.

6.16   In recommending any matrix of fixed costs for housing cases, there are two matters which I shall take into account. First, lawyers who specialise in housing depend upon recovered costs in cases which they win, in order to cross-subsidise their other activities. This is because much of the work of those solicitors comprises providing advice and assistance to clients on legal aid. Legal aid rates for advice and assistance have fallen far behind inflation in recent years, although the move to standard fees may have allowed for some efficiency savings. The second matter is the availability of solicitors firms and law centres which are willing and able to undertake housing work in areas where tenants need their services: see PR paragraphs 31.2.6 and 31.5.1. It is important not to set fixed fees at a level which exacerbates that problem.

6.17   <u>An alternative approach to low value housing disrepair claims.</u> An alternative approach to low value HD claims might be to set up an ombudsman scheme to deal with such claims. This is the sort of area where, traditionally, ombudsman schemes have proved highly effective: see *"Civil Justice in England and Wales – beyond the courts. Mapping out non-judicial civil justice mechanisms"* by Dr Magdalena Tulibacka.[47] If such a scheme is introduced and proves successful, it might then be possible to make £5,000 (rather than £1,000) the boundary between the small claims track and the fast track. This would bring HD claims into line with all other litigation apart from personal injury claims. This is not a recommendation which I make, because the proposal was not canvassed in the Preliminary Report. It is simply a matter which I raise for possible future consideration.

(c) Other areas of litigation

6.18   The cases discussed above (RTA, personal injury and housing cases) account, in volume terms, for a large part of contested litigation in the fast track: see PR chapter 5 and appendices 1 and 2. Nevertheless, there remain many other categories of fast track litigation which I have not so far addressed, save by the proposal for an overall cap. If my recommendations for a totally fixed costs regime in the fast track are accepted in principle, I propose (i) to seek data in respect of those other categories of cases during 2010 and (ii) to propose matrices of fixed costs, drawing on the advice of the Senior Costs Judge and the CJC.

7. RECOMMENDATION

7.1   I recommend that the recoverable costs of cases in the fast track be fixed.

7.2   The details of my proposals for fast track fixed costs are set out in this chapter, but do not need to be re-iterated in the list of recommendations.

---

[47] Centre for Socio-Legal Studies, Oxford University, available at:
http://www.csls.ox.ac.uk/european_civil_justice_systems.php.

CHAPTER 16. FIXED COSTS OUTSIDE THE FAST TRACK

INDEX

1. INTRODUCTION

1.1   The primary focus of this chapter is whether any categories of multi-track litigation should be subject to fixed costs. A separate issue to consider is whether any other categories of litigation (excluding fast track claims) should be subject to fixed costs. The only category of litigation which has so far been suggested is routine insolvency litigation, but other categories may emerge in the future.

2. MULTI-TRACK CLAIMS

(i) Policy considerations and competing views

2.1   Policy considerations. The relevant policy considerations are set out in PR chapter 23.

2.2   Phase 2 submissions. Respondents during Phase 2 were divided on the question whether (a) all costs should be at large in the multi-track or (b) there should be some fixing of, or restriction upon, recoverable costs in the lower regions of the multi-track. Lord Justice Dyson has proposed that there should be fixed costs or scale costs for multi-track claims up to at least £100,000. One substantial City firm of solicitors supports the proposal for fixing costs in the lower multi-track claims with the following arguments:

> "We can see the merit in introducing a fixed costs regime to certain categories of litigation above the fast track. We agree with the policy arguments identified in the Preliminary Report in favour of this approach. Whilst it is true that from a purist perspective it is unjust that a vindicated party should bear part of its own costs, in practice we believe this is a pragmatic way in which to control the costs of litigation and increase certainty. It is our view that in matters other than major high value litigation, commercial litigants will particularly welcome the certainty that such a regime could bring and, as the Preliminary Report points out, many will also regard the risk of failing to recover part of their costs if they win as better than the risk of incurring an indeterminate costs liability to the other side if they lose. We anticipate that most categories of litigation could be subjected to a fixed costs regime, although all such rules should be subject to the discretion of the court to adapt, amend or ignore them as appropriate. However, we are firmly of the view that this approach would not be appropriate for heavy litigation as it would simply be insufficiently flexible to cater for such matters."

2.3   Another firm of solicitors sees the issue as more finely balanced. It argues:

> "We recognise that there are advantages to fixed costs above the fast track. In particular:
>
> (a)   they ensure that costs liability is proportionate to the financial amount at stake;
>
> (b)   they provide certainty as to the level of costs recovery, enabling a claimant to take an informed view as to whether, in the light of its lawyer's estimate of actual costs and the likely level of recovery, it is economically worthwhile pursuing the claim; and
>
> (c)   assessing costs is quick and easy.
>
> There are, however, also disadvantages in a system of fixed costs. These include:
>
> (a)   the cost of pursuing some claims is inevitably disproportionate to the amount that might be recovered, but that does not necessarily mean that the claim should not be brought or that a party doing so should be penalised by a low costs' recovery;
>
> (b)   some claims, eg for an injunction, have no obvious financial value against which to assess financial proportionality or costs;
>
> (c)   the claimant has a choice as to whether it wishes to pursue a claim given the level of costs recovery, but the defendant has no such choice;
>
> (d)   to a defendant who is successful, any irrecoverable costs represent a disproportionate expenditure; and
>
> (d)   one of the attractions of the English system on the international stage is the ability to recover a sum that at least bears a relationship to the actual costs a party may have incurred.
>
> The central problem in any system of fixed costs is the wide range of different types of case to which the system must apply. This wide range will inevitably lead to some parties receiving an arbitrary windfall in costs (or, at least, full recovery) and some suffering a shortfall. On balance, therefore, we consider that costs should continue to be assessed retrospectively..."

2.4   The majority of respondents oppose any fixing of costs in the multi-track. Both the Law Society and the Bar Council oppose any extension of the fixed costs regime above the fast track. The Bar Council writes:

> "Save in relation to the Patents Court, we cannot see any justification for the implementation of a fixed costs regime in cases in the Chancery Division, Commercial Court or TCC[48] depending on the value of the claim or the size or turnover of one or both claimants."

2.5   In relation to intellectual property ("IP") litigation, it is generally recognised that there is a case for limiting or fixing recoverable costs in respect of claims up to about £500,000. There is a groundswell of support amongst IP practitioners and court users for reforms along these lines: see chapter 24 below.

---

[48] The Technology and Construction Court.

2.6   Survey by Federation of Small Businesses.   The Federation of Small Businesses (the "FSB") recently, at my request, conducted a survey of a pool of FSB members. It asked the following question:

"Which would you prefer?

(i)   A regime in which (a) if you win you recover all the legal costs which you have reasonably incurred in pursuing your claim or defence; BUT (b) if you lose you pay all the legal costs which the other side has reasonably incurred; OR

(ii)   A regime in which (a) if you win, you recover a fixed sum in respect of legal costs; BUT (b) if you lose, you only pay a fixed sum to the other side in respect of legal costs.

In regime (ii) the fixed sum would be set out in the rules of court and would probably represent about half of the actual costs (more than half in a simple case, less than half in a complex case)."

2.7   The FSB summarises the survey responses as follows:

"Although neither of these options is ideal from a small business perspective, the view from small businesses seems to be that a fixed costs regime for lower value business disputes (paragraphs 4.26/28)[49] and especially small building disputes (Part 7 chapter 30) would be beneficial."

The FSB then quotes one of its respondents, who said this:

"We would be reluctant to commence legal action, even if we felt it just, if we faced the risk that we might have to bear not only our own costs but those of the other party in the event of failing to convince the judge. This would be particularly the case if the action was against a larger or better funded organisation and the magnitude of the costs was not capped."

2.8   Fixed costs seminar.   At the fixed costs seminar on 22nd July 2009 two partners of CMS Cameron McKenna LLP made a short presentation on the possibility of fixing costs in lower value multi-track cases. They made the point that lawyers are generally happy with the present regime of costs being at large, but clients are not.[50] The principal concerns are lack of proportionality of costs compared to the sums in dispute and predictability of the adverse costs liability if the case is lost. They proposed the following scheme for fixed recoverable costs in cases within the range £25,000 to £250,000: if the case settles pre-issue, recoverable costs would be 10% of the settlement sum.   If the case settles post-issue but pre-allocation, then the percentage goes up to 15%. The percentage[51] goes up in stages. If the action proceeds to trial recoverable costs are 40% of the judgment sum (or of the sum claimed, if the defendant is victor).[52] The scheme must include safeguards so that in exceptional

---

[49] This is a reference to PR paragraphs 29.4.26 to 29.4.28.
[50] This observation is consistent with the FSB survey results, which came in a week after the seminar.
[51] The percentages put forward in the presentation were illustrative. Whether those percentages should go up or down and whether they should be treated as inclusive or exclusive of disbursements are major questions for debate, if the principle is accepted.
[52] This scheme was developed in a paper sent in after the seminar, with some worked examples based upon applying the scheme percentages to actual figures from past cases to illustrate the likely effect on future cases. In these worked examples the winning party typically recovers between about 25% and 60% of the level of actual costs in past cases, depending upon the circumstances. The scheme was

cases or where a party behaves unreasonably there can be full costs recovery.[53] During the discussion which followed this presentation, there was some support for a scheme along the lines proposed. I took a straw poll at the end of this discussion. Of the 45 or so persons present, 13 voted in favour of a fixed costs scheme, nine voted against and the remainder abstained. I shall refer to the scheme debated on this occasion as the "CMS scheme".

(ii) My opinion

2.9 Having considered the competing arguments advanced during Phase 2, I think that it would be premature to embark upon any scheme of fixed costs or scale costs in respect of lower value multi-track cases for the time being. The top priority at the moment must be (a) to achieve a comprehensive scheme of fixed or predictable costs in the fast track and (b) to introduce a scheme of capped scale costs for lower value multi-track IP cases. These proposals are set out in chapters 15 and 24 respectively.

2.10 Once the necessary reforms have been implemented in the fast track and in multi-track cases in the Patents County Court (the "PCC"), there must be a period of evaluation. Following that period of evaluation, I recommend that further consideration should be given to the possibility of introducing a scheme of fixed costs or scale costs into the lower reaches of the multi-track. When that consideration takes place, the views of court users should be elicited by surveys of the kind that the FSB kindly undertook during Phase 2. Such surveys should be undertaken on a more extensive basis amongst a variety of categories of court users.

2.11 If, following that future consultation process, any scheme of fixed costs or scale costs is to be adopted, there will be a variety of models for consideration. One model would be a system of scale costs subject to an overall cap, such as that which is planned for the PCC. Another model would be the CMS scheme. A third model would be a scheme of fixed costs of the kind operated in Germany. The German costs regime is described in PR chapter 55. Since the German civil justice system is structured differently from our own, the German costs rules could be a general guide but not, of course, a template. These are all questions for the future but not, I suggest, the remote future.

3. INSOLVENCY LITIGATION

3.1 There are certain routine procedures in insolvency proceedings which would be amenable to fixed costs. I therefore set up a working group to look into this issue, as set out in chapter 1 above[54] and chapter 28 below.

3.2 On the basis of the working group's recommendations (which I accept), I recommend a scheme of benchmark costs for bankruptcy petitions and winding up petitions. These recommendations are set out in chapter 28 below.

---

proposed as a way of encouraging parties to change their approach to budgeting for lower value disputes and thus bring about greater proportionality through direct interest in the financial outcome.
[53] I.e. actual costs assessed on the standard or indemnity basis, as appropriate.
[54] See chapter 1 above, paragraph 3.11.

4. CONCLUSION

4.1 I do not recommend that any general scheme of fixed costs be introduced into the multi-track at the present time. However, this question should be reconsidered after experience has accumulated of fixed costs in the fast track and capped scale costs in the PCC.

CHAPTER 17. INTEGRATION OF RECOMMENDATIONS FOR FIXED COSTS WITH RECOMMENDATIONS IN RESPECT OF ADDITIONAL LIABILITIES

INDEX

1. INTRODUCTION

1.1   <u>Recommendations in respect of additional liabilities.</u> In chapter 9 above and chapter 19 below I recommend that after-the-event ("ATE") insurance premiums should cease to be recoverable and that instead there should be qualified one way costs shifting in personal injury cases. In chapter 10 above and chapter 41 below I recommend that success fees should cease to be recoverable and that three measures should be taken to assist personal injury claimants in paying success fees: (i) success fees should be capped at 25% of damages, excluding damages referable to future loss; (ii) general damages should be increased by 10%; and (iii) unbeaten claimant offers under Part 36 should attract an additional reward, namely a 10% enhancement of damages.

1.2   <u>Recommendations for fixed costs.</u> In chapter 15 above I recommend a regime of fixed costs, which assumes (i) that ATE insurance premiums are recoverable; (ii) that there is two way costs shifting; and (iii) that success fees are recoverable. The question therefore arises as to how these apparently inconsistent recommendations should be reconciled.

1.3   <u>Reconciliation.</u> My recommendations for fixed costs in respect of fast track personal injury claims are capable of implementation in the near future, in the event that those recommendations find favour with the Lord Chancellor, the Master of the Rolls and the Civil Procedure Rule Committee.   The subject matter of those recommendations has already been the subject of detailed discussion with interested parties at a series of facilitative meetings hosted by the Civil Justice Council. Furthermore those recommendations are based upon data which all parties accept to be statistically reliable.

1.4   In order to assist speedy implementation (if that course is regarded as appropriate), my recommendations for fixed costs in respect of fast track personal injury claims are based upon the statutory regime that now exists. That statutory regime provides for recoverable ATE insurance premiums and recoverable success fees.

1.5   In the event that at a later date my recommendations are accepted that ATE insurance premiums and CFA success fees should cease to be recoverable, a separate question will arise: how should those reforms be integrated with the regime of fixed recoverable costs? I shall address this question in section 2.

2. PROPOSED INTEGRATION

2.1   Assumptions.   For the purposes of this section, I shall make three assumptions:

(i)   A regime of fixed costs for road traffic accident claims and personal injury claims, (as proposed in chapter 15 above) is put in place by October 2010.

(ii)   At a later date, as a result of primary legislation, success fees and ATE insurance premiums become irrecoverable (as proposed in chapters 9 and 10 above).

(iii)   The payment of referral fees for personal injury cases is banned or capped (as proposed in chapter 20 below).

2.2   On the date when success fees and ATE insurance premiums become irrecoverable (the "relevant date"), claimants will in most cases cease to be liable for adverse costs if they lose. General damages for personal injuries will rise by 10%. In those rare cases which go to trial, claimants will be able to secure a further 10% increase of all their damages (not just general damages) by making an unbeaten Part 36 offer.

2.3   With effect from the relevant date all provisions in the rules entitling parties to recover success fees will be repealed. That repeal will include the provisions regarding recoverable success fees in the rules and matrices concerning recovery of fixed costs. Solicitors will be free to charge whatever success fees they may negotiate with their clients, subject to the proviso that the success fee can never exceed 25% of damages (excluding damages referable to future loss). Subject to that proviso, the solicitor will be free to charge as a success fee whatever percentage (up to 100%) of base costs may be agreed between solicitor and client.

2.4   Personal injury solicitors will be free to advertise on the internet and elsewhere the levels of success fees which they will charge. Thus under the new regime solicitors will compete upon the basis of which solicitors are charging the lowest success fees to clients, rather than which solicitors can pay the highest referral fees to claims management companies or before-the-event ("BTE") insurers. Thus the beneficiaries of competition will be the consumers, not claims management companies, BTE insurers or similar bodies.

2.5   Clients will no doubt find it easier to grasp the concept of a deduction of a percentage of their damages and solicitors will find it easier to advertise on that basis. Rule 7.02 of the Solicitors' Code of Conduct requires any advertisements to be clear as to the basis of charging and is sufficient to cover percentage deductions from damages, but those deductions must of course still be reasonable when calculated as a proportion of the costs incurred. Practitioner bodies such as the Association of Personal Injury Lawyers ("APIL") will no doubt wish to keep under review any difficulties that their members encounter when advertising such concepts.   I recommend that they work closely with the Law Society and the Solicitors Regulation Authority in this area.

2.6   There should be an easy mechanism available for clients to resolve any disputes or complaints over deductions from damages. To some extent the Legal Services Ombudsman and the Legal Complaints Service will already cover this, but the experience with the Miners' Compensation Scheme cases has demonstrated that these may be rather unwieldy. Consideration should be given to establishing a simple arbitration service, binding on the lawyer but not on the client, by which such disputes are resolved. This could probably be established through a mediation organisation such as CEDR[55] or perhaps Trust Mediation Ltd, which specialises in personal injury cases.[56]

2.7   <u>The overall result.</u> If the entire package of proposed reforms is introduced, there will be five consequences:

(i)   Most personal injury claimants will recover more damages than they do at present, although some will recover less.

(ii)   Claimants will have a financial interest in the level of costs which are being incurred on their behalf.

(iii)   Claimant solicitors will still be able to make a reasonable profit.

(iv)   Costs payable to claimant solicitors by liability insurers will be significantly reduced.

(v)   Costs will also become more proportionate, because defendants will no longer have to pay success fees and ATE insurance premiums.

2.8   <u>Consequence (i).</u> Professor Paul Fenn, my economist assessor, has calculated that the majority of claimants will be better off if general damages are increased by 10% and success fees (at present levels) cease to be recoverable under costs orders. Claimants will receive additional damages and will pay success fees out of those damages at the rates set out in appendix 5 to this report.

2.9   If (as recommended in chapter 20 below) referral fees are banned or capped, the success fees which solicitors charge will become substantially lower. This will happen naturally as a result of competition. The funds which are currently being channelled into referral fees will be re-directed towards the lowering of success fees. This will further increase the amount of damages received by claimants.

2.10   <u>Consequence (ii).</u> Consequence (ii) is self-evident, but is nonetheless important. One of the reasons for escalating costs has been the fact that claimants are indifferent to the costs being incurred in their name. However, if claimants have to pay a proportion of base costs (viz the success fee) out of damages, they will be concerned to ensure that unnecessary expenditure is avoided.

2.11   <u>Consequence (iii).</u> Solicitors will still be able to make a reasonable living under the new costs regime. Solicitors will only charge lower success fees if they can still operate profitably. In the event that referral fees are capped or banned, solicitors will be able to operate profitably on substantially lower success fees than are currently charged.

2.12   <u>Consequence (iv).</u> Costs payable to claimant solicitors by liability insurers will be significantly reduced, because those costs will no longer include success fees or ATE insurance premiums. This will inure to the benefit of motorists and all others who pay premiums to liability insurers.

2.13   <u>Consequence (v).</u> I have previously expressed the view that a regime of recoverable success fees and recoverable ATE insurance premiums makes costs disproportionate in every case. That is because base costs reflect the expenditure which it was reasonable and proportionate for the receiving party to incur. Any sums

---

[55] The Centre for Effective Dispute Resolution.
[56] See chapter 36 below.

added to base costs (to reflect assumed losses by the claimant's solicitors on other cases) makes the total figure disproportionate. Thus it will only be when success fees and ATE insurance premiums cease to be recoverable that the fixed costs which I am recommending will become truly proportionate.

2.14   Overall result. The overall result of the reforms which I am recommending is that substantial costs will be saved, because of (i) efficiencies generated by the fixed costs regime; (ii) the banning of referral fees; and (iii) CFA success fees and ATE insurance premiums becoming irrecoverable. The benefits of these savings will be shared between (a) personal injury claimants; (b) motorists and others who pay liability insurance premiums; and (c) government and non-government bodies and taxpayers generally.

3. CONCLUSION

3.1   This chapter does not make any freestanding recommendations. Instead it sets out a roadmap which (if my various recommendations are accepted) both rule makers and the legislature might consider following.

3.2   If all of the above recommendations are accepted and implemented in the manner suggested, it is my opinion that the fast track will have a regime of fixed costs which are both reasonable and proportionate.

REVIEW OF
CIVIL LITIGATION COSTS

PART 4. PERSONAL INJURIES LITIGATION

CHAPTER 18. UPPER LIMIT FOR PERSONAL INJURY CASES ON THE SMALL CLAIMS TRACK

INDEX

1. INTRODUCTION

1.1   The upper limit. The upper limit for personal injury claims on the small claims track in respect of general damages (the "PI small claims limit") is currently set at £1,000. There has been no increase to the PI small claims limit[1] since 1999.

1.2   Preliminary Report. Chapter 24 of the Preliminary Report sets out the arguments for and against raising the PI small claims limit.[2] It puts forward the following four options for consideration:

• An increase to the PI small claims limit from £1,000 to £5,000 ("option 1").

• A lesser increase to the limit (e.g. an increase to £2,500) ("option 2").

• An increase in line with inflation ("option 3").

• No increase to the limit ("option 4").[3]

It also suggests, at PR paragraph 24.4.2, some safeguards which would need to be introduced for unrepresented claimants if the PI small claims limit were increased.

2. DEBATE DURING PHASE 2

2.1   Birmingham seminar. A number of speakers at the Birmingham seminar, held on 26th June 2009, argued in favour of option 4. Anthony Hughes, the President

---

[1] Or to the general small claims limit of £5,000.
[2] See PR chapter 24 section 2.
[3] See PR paragraph 24.4.1.

of the Forum of Insurance Lawyers ("FOIL"), said that FOIL had previously favoured an increase of the PI small claims limit to £2,500, as stated in PR paragraph 10.10.11. However, in view of the new process which is being established for personal injury claims, an increase is not now necessary. The limit should remain at £1,000.

2.2   Trade unions. A number of trade unions oppose any increase to the PI small claims limit. The Trades Union Congress (the "TUC") argues that option 1, an increase to £5,000, would have a *"devastating effect on access to justice"* and estimates that around 75% of all union cases would be removed from the fast track system where costs are recoverable. The TUC states that if the limit were raised in accordance with option 2 to £2,500, the legal support which unions give to their members would be unsustainable because of the no-costs regime in the small claims track. Approximately 50% of the claims which unions support fall within this limit. The TUC also opposes any inflationary increase to the PI small claims limit on the following basis:

> "Taking into account damages have failed to increase as recommended by the Law Commission 11 years ago, and a substantial increase in the limit occurred in 1999 when £1,000 related to general damages alone, we believe the limit does not need any further change – to do so would limit justice, denying claimants rights."

The TUC argues that the issues in personal injury cases are often complex and many of these claims simply could not be brought by members as litigants in person. The TUC considers that the safeguards proposed in PR paragraph 24.4.2 would not be effective. The views of the TUC are echoed by GMB[4] and Usdaw,[5] both of which argue strongly that there should be no increase in the PI small claims limit.

2.3   Claimant personal injury lawyers. Claimant law firms have also expressed strong opposition to any increase in the PI small claims limit. They repeat the argument put forward by the trade unions that, unlike many other types of small claims, personal injury cases often involve complex issues of liability and quantum. One firm notes that personal injury claims in practice always involve an individual taking on a multi-national insurance company. The starting point is therefore an inequality of arms. This is to be contrasted with non-personal injury cases falling within the small claims track. Another firm agrees that there is clearly inequality of arms in these types of cases, and argues that the increase of the PI small claims limit of £1,000 would effectively remove access to justice for those claimants who are unable to recover legal fees and will be left to conduct their claim alone. It expresses the view that the new claims process presented by the Ministry of Justice (the "MoJ"), following its review into case track limits and claims process for personal injury claims,[6] should be given time to be piloted and viewed in practice.

2.4   Another firm of claimant personal injury lawyers would support option 3, an inflationary increase in the PI small claims limit, but only if there were a corresponding increase in damages:

> "The underlying problem is that general damages have hardly risen at all during the last decade, certainly not in line with inflation. If damages were increased in line with inflation since, let us say a point 15 years ago and then

---

[4] A general trade union.
[5] Union of Shop, Distributive and Allied Workers.
[6] See PR paragraphs 24.3.1 to 24.3.3. The MoJ's post-consultation report is available at http://www.justice.gov.uk/consultations/docs/case-track-limits-response.pdf.

the small claims court limit were increased by the same percentage, then I would have no problem. This would be proportionate and fair."

2.5   Association of Personal Injury Lawyers. The Association of Personal Injury Lawyers ("APIL") refers to the MoJ's recent review in this area, which concluded that the PI small claims limit should remain at £1,000, and does not think that the issue should be revisited at this stage. In any event, APIL believes that the small claims procedure is not appropriate for personal injury claims. The small claims procedure is designed to resolve disputes concerning issues such as "*a faulty fridge or other consumer matters*", not one aimed at compensating a person for bodily injury. APIL makes the point raised by claimant lawyers that the process of proving even a relatively low value personal injury claim is complex. If the small claims limit is raised, more claimants will have to try and settle their claims without legal advice and this will result in a significant number of claimants not receiving "*proper*" levels of compensation.

2.6   Motor Accident Solicitors Society. The Motor Accident Solicitors Society ("MASS") agrees with the claimant law firms and with APIL that option 4 is the most appropriate. An increase in the PI small claims limit would deny access to justice because claimants would be deprived of advice, assistance and representation unless they paid for this from their own pockets. That would result in claimants accepting far less than their claim is worth or perhaps being deterred from claiming at all. MASS argues that whilst it is quite easy for lawyers and politicians to describe sums of £1,000 or £2,000 as "*low values*", to many claimants this is a large sum of money and represents real redress. MASS submits that the PI small claims limit should remain unchanged and instead the proportionality of legal costs should be tackled.

2.7   Personal Injuries Bar Association. The Personal Injuries Bar Association ("PIBA") believes that personal injury claims should not be subject to any increase at all in the small claims limit, save possibly in accordance with inflation. Liability issues in personal injury cases are "*wholly unsuited*" to the small claims regime. PIBA reiterates the concern expressed by claimant lawyers that an increase in the PI small claims limit would lead to inequality of arms. PIBA also considers it to be in the public interest that junior counsel should gain experience in the fast track litigation, which is possible under the current limit, before conducting more serious cases. Although PIBA does not support any increase in the PI small claims limit, it recognises that an uplift equal to inflation (i.e. to no more than £1,300) has something to commend it. However, no change should be introduced in cases where liability or causation is in issue.

2.8   Peter Thompson QC. Peter Thompson QC, general editor of *Civil Court Practice*, wrote an article in the New Law Journal on 24th July 2009 commenting on personal injury issues in the present Costs Review arising from the Preliminary Report. Mr Thompson favours raising the PI small claims limit. He argues that lower value personal injury claims are not complex and that district judges are well able to decide such claims fairly without legal representation on either side. Furthermore medical reports are now easier to obtain, since general practitioners have a duty to provide copies of a patient's notes and records at cost. Mr Thompson concludes:

> "So, sad as it may be for those whose practice revolves around small personal injury claims, I foresee the personal injury small claims limit going up to £2,500 if not £5,000."

2.9   North Eastern Circuit. Members of the personal injury bar on the North Eastern Circuit express *"grave reservations"* about the extension of the PI small claims limit in personal injury cases. They are concerned that an extension of the limit would deny effective representation to many on modest incomes.

2.10   Liability insurers. One liability insurer favours an increase in the PI small claims limit to £5,000. It argues that unless the limit is increased, there will soon be almost no personal injury claims that fall within it:

> "It is [our] view that it is the maintenance of the Small Claims Track limit at £1,000 which has defeated the purpose of the small claims track and allowed far too many very simple PI claims to end up in the fast track causing an overall disproportionate costs outcome."

The Association of British Insurers (the "ABI") emphasises, in its Phase 2 submission, the advantages to the claimant of using the small claims track: it is quick, cost-effective, accessible and efficient and achieves high levels of consumer satisfaction.[7] However, since the PI small claims limit was introduced in 1991, progressively less claims have been eligible for allocation to the small claims track, forcing claimants to use the *"less-friendly, more complex, slower and less efficient full-court system"*. The ABI summarises its position on the PI small claims limit as follows:

> "The ABI supports raising the small claims limit in personal injury claims to £5,000, once the MOJ reforms[8] have been implemented and bedded in, and a suitable damages assessment tool is developed to allow claimants and defendants to transparently assess claims. Raising the limit to £5,000 will allow straightforward claims to be dealt with in the most appropriate track. However, the ABI does not support raising the limit to a mid-point."

2.11   Defendant personal injury lawyers. Law firms which predominantly act for insurers and defendants in personal injury cases generally support an increase in the PI small claims limit. One such firm considers that, although increasing the limit to £5,000 would be *"a step too far"* and include too many cases where a litigant might benefit from legal assistance, the limit should be increased to £2,500. This would bring minor injury road traffic accident claims into the small claims track with significant costs savings. This firm states that use of Colossus type software[9] to assist in the assessment of damages at this level would address any concerns of under-settlement if a litigant chooses not to take legal advice. Another defendant firm expresses support in its submission for an increase in the PI small claims limit to £2,500 or preferably to £5,000. If there was a genuine risk that claimant practices would be decimated by the loss of business if the limit were increased to £5,000,[10] an interim increase might be justified to assess the impact.

2.12   Forum of Insurance Lawyers. The Forum of Insurance Lawyers ("FOIL"), on the other hand, is now of the view that the small claims limit should remain at £1,000. On the basis that the Costs Review will address unjustifiable costs on the fast track regime, the current figure represents a reasonable balance between the need for claimants to be legally represented when appropriate, and the concern that legal costs should not be incurred and recovered needlessly. FOIL continues:

---

[7] In this regard the ABI refers to a survey undertaken by Which?, referred to in PR paragraph 10.12.4.
[8] In the area of low value personal injury claims arising out of road traffic accidents.
[9] See PR paragraphs 10.8.8 and 10.8.9.
[10] A concern expressed by APIL.

"In reality, when looking at the personal injuries dispute resolution landscape overall, in many ways a focus on the small claims limit misses the point. It is more sensible to focus on the benefits which the new MoJ claims process reform will introduce – a quick and efficient service for claims up to £10,000 at a reasonable cost."

2.13   Law Society. The Law Society, in its Phase 2 submission, considers that the proposal to increase the PI small claims limit should be abandoned. Raising the PI small claims limit would deprive many injured people of legal advice. It would also lead to more litigants in person representing themselves, which would overload the already under-resourced civil courts. The Law Society states that the results of a survey on small claims undertaken in 2006 showed that 99% of solicitors said that their clients would not have pursued the claim without the help of a solicitor.

2.14   In 2006, the Law Society's Strategic Research Unit carried out a study of claimants who had recently brought a lower value[11] personal injury claim in the fast track with the aid of a solicitor.[12] According to the results of that survey, 83.2% of respondents felt that having a solicitor's advice on the value of their claim had been "*very important*". Over three quarters of respondents (79.3%) claimed to be "*not very confident*" or "*not at all confident*" at the thought of bringing the case themselves.

2.15   Bar Council. The Bar Council is also opposed to any substantive extension of the small claims track regime.[13] It argues that many cases which fall within even the current small claims track limit are complex (despite their relatively low value) and therefore require the involvement of lawyers. The small claims track was not intended to be for cases where one side is represented and the other was not – this is likely to the result in personal injury cases if the PI small claims limit is raised.

2.16   Judiciary. One experienced circuit judge is of the view that the PI small claims limit should be raised. Account has to be taken of inflation. Furthermore, awards of between £1,000 and £2,000 are "*commonplace*" and it is almost impossible to keep costs within reasonable bounds in comparison with the sum recovered. He proposes that the small claims limit be raised to £2,000 or £2,500. However, the judge recognises the legitimate concern that claimants without the benefit of legal help will "*fall prey to insurers making unscrupulously low offers*". Appropriate consumer protection could be provided by amending CPR 27.14(2)(b)[14] to enable a claimant to recover a sum for professional advice in personal injury claims. A district judge, with long experience of personal injuries litigation, considers that the costs provision under CPR Part 27 should remain as currently drafted but that the PI small claims limit should be raised in line with inflation. There is no logical reason for the limit staying at the current level and none of the arguments advanced in favour of retaining the £1,000 merit close scrutiny. Lord Justice May called for the PI small claims limit to be raised in his judgment in *Crane v Canons Leisure* [2007] EWCA Civ 1352 at [1]; [2008] 1 WLR 2549.

---

[11] I.e. between £1,000 and £5,000.

[12] There had been 119 respondents to the survey at the time of the Law Society's interim report dated 30th November 2006.

[13] The Bar Council does, however, record some support for an inflationary increase to the limit.

[14] Which deals with costs on the small claims track.

3. ASSESSMENT AND CONCLUSIONS

3.1   I can see considerable force in the arguments for raising the small claims limit for PI cases. On the other hand I acknowledge the strength of feeling about this issue on all sides. I do not think that now is the right time to review that limit.

3.2   In my view, the top priority at the moment should be (a) to fix all costs on the fast track and (b) to establish an efficient and fair process for handling personal injury claims (which constitute a major part of fast track work). I therefore propose that in the first phase of reforms which will follow publication of this report (if my recommendations are accepted), there should be no change to the PI small claims limit.

3.3   If a satisfactory scheme of fixed costs is established for fast track personal injury cases (both contested and uncontested) and if the process reforms bed in satisfactorily, then all that will be required in due course will be an increase in the PI small claims limit to reflect inflation since 1999. A series of small rises in the limit would be confusing for practitioners and judges alike. I therefore propose that the present limit stays at £1,000 until such time as inflation warrants an increase to £1,500.

3.4   If a satisfactory scheme of fixed costs is not established or if the process reforms prove unsatisfactory, then the question of raising the PI small claims limit will have to be revisited at the end of 2010. I would be willing to undertake that task, if so requested.

3.5   For the reasons set out above, I do not currently make any recommendation for raising the PI small claims limit.

CHAPTER 19. ONE WAY COSTS SHIFTING

INDEX

1. INTRODUCTION

1.1 <u>Scope of this chapter.</u> In this chapter I discuss the possible adoption of one way costs shifting in personal injuries litigation in the event that after-the-event ("ATE") insurance premiums cease to be recoverable. This option was identified in chapter 25 of the Preliminary Report as one possible way forward. For the purpose of this chapter, I am treating personal injuries litigation as a broad concept, including claims where the claimant's injuries were caused by clinical negligence.

1.2 <u>Important features of personal injuries litigation.</u> There are two important features of personal injuries litigation. First and self-evidently, the claimant is an individual. For the vast majority of individuals it would be prohibitively expensive to meet an adverse costs order in fully-contested litigation. The most recent Social Trends report[15] shows that 73% of all households have savings (made up of securities, shares, currency and deposits) of less than £10,000. Defence costs can easily be many times higher than £10,000 in fully-contested litigation. This would mean that for three quarters of households their other financial assets (their own home in most cases) would be at risk from an adverse costs order. Secondly, the defendant is almost invariably either insured or self insured. By "self insured", I mean that the defendant is a large organisation which has adopted the policy of paying out on personal injury claims as and when they arise, rather than paying substantial liability insurance premiums every year.

1.3 <u>Factors pointing towards one way costs shifting.</u> The factors which make one way costs shifting a serious candidate for consideration in relation to personal injuries litigation are the following:

(i) Claimants are successful in the majority of personal injury claims. Defendants seldom recover costs, so they derive little benefit from two way costs shifting.

(ii) Personal injuries litigation is the paradigm instance of litigation in which the parties are in an asymmetric relationship, as discussed in chapter 9 above.

(iii) The principal objective of recoverable ATE insurance premiums is to protect claimants against adverse costs orders. One way costs shifting would be a less expensive method of achieving the same objective.

(iv) One way costs shifting is not a novel concept in personal injuries litigation. Between 1949 and 2000, the vast majority of personal injury claims

---

[15] See Social Trends 39, Chapter 5 Table 5.21 available at www.statistics.gov.uk/socialtrends39.

proceeded under a one way costs shifting regime, namely the legal aid shield.[16]

In the case of clinical negligence cases, I accept that the success rate of claimants is lower. But the other factors set out above are present. Furthermore, the level of ATE insurance premiums is significantly higher in clinical negligence cases than in ordinary personal injury cases, so that factor (iii) above gains greater force.

1.4   Definitions. In this chapter I shall refer to the Community Legal Service (Costs) Regulations 2000 (SI 2000/441) as the "Costs Regulations". I shall refer to the Community Legal Service (Cost Protection) Regulations 2000 (SI 2000/824) as the "Cost Protection Regulations".

2. FINANCIAL CONSEQUENCES

2.1   The experience of insurer X. In chapter 25 of the Preliminary Report, I set out the most recent year's figures of insurer X, a liability insurer. These figures demonstrate that one way costs shifting would be cheaper for insurer X than the present regime of recoverable ATE insurance premiums.

2.2   Other liability insurers. During Phase 2 some insurers stated that their experience differed from insurer X. For example, one major insurer, whose figures are different from X's, writes:

> "[We] can see the attraction in a proposal which would remove the need for ATE Insurance to cover the risk of having to pay defendant's costs, and we concur with the view that removing this layer of activity from the process could serve the public interest. However, we are sceptical that this proposed process would in fact benefit defendants to the extent claimed in the Report."

2.3   On the other hand some insurers report a similar pattern in their figures to that of insurer X. The Association of British Insurers (the "ABI") states:

> "The general consensus from relevant ABI members is that their experience is not dissimilar to that outlined at para 2.6, Chapter 25, of Review of Civil Litigation Costs Preliminary Report: Volume One, i.e. there is very limited costs recovery."

2.4   Comment. Although the figures of individual liability insurers will differ, the overall effect of substituting one way costs shifting for recoverability of ATE insurance premiums is bound to be one of costs saving. This is because the ATE insurers (a) pay out adverse costs in unsuccessful cases (except where they repudiate),[17] (b) cover their own administration costs and (c) make a profit. For the breakdown of ATE insurance premiums into risk premium, brokerage and administration costs see chapter 9, section 3 above.

2.5   The Legal Expenses Insurance Group. The Legal Expenses Insurance Group (the "LEIG"), which comprises twelve leading legal expenses insurers and their intermediaries, strongly disagrees with my proposal for one way costs shifting and strongly disputes the data provided to the Costs Review by insurer X. Nevertheless

---

[16] See section 17(1) of the Legal Aid Act 1988 and earlier legislation to the same effect.
[17] See chapter 9 above, section 3.

the LEIG accepts that ATE insurance is now a profitable business. In its Phase 2 submission LEIG states:

> "Over the last few years ATE insurers have been able to improve their underwriting models in order to achieve adequate rewards and ensure the business can generate a profit and be in existence in years to come."

It follows from this statement that the premium income received by ATE insurers comfortably exceeds the sums which ATE insurers pay out in respect of adverse costs orders and disbursements.

2.6   Data from Medical Protection Society. The Medical Protection Society (the "MPS") has provided data in respect of 3,504 claims and pre-claims[18] which it closed during the 18 month period 1st January 2008 to 30th June 2009. The MPS estimates that it was entitled to recover costs of £906,000 from claimants on 61 of 2,516 claims in that period. The MPS actually recovered costs (either fully or in part) in only 29 cases, the remaining 32 cases having a nil recovery. The total defence costs recovered amounted to £368,000, with unrecovered costs amounting to £538,000.

2.7   The MPS does not keep comprehensive data on ATE insurance premiums paid as part of claimant costs on cases which it settles. However, it has used available data from one ATE insurer to calculate a theoretical cost that claimants would have incurred (but the MPS would have paid) if ATE insurance cover had been taken out on all the claims which the MPS settled between 1st January 2008 and 30th June 2009. There were 1,127 cases settled between 1st January 2008 and 30th June 2009 in which the MPS paid damages to the claimant. These are therefore the cases on which the MPS would have been liable to meet the costs of the claimants' ATE insurance cover, if any was taken out. The MPS incurred defence costs of £9,069,000 on those 1,127 claims. The MPS estimates that, on this basis, if all those cases had ATE insurance, it would have paid claimants nearly £7 million in respect of ATE insurance premiums. If one assumes that 40% of those cases had ATE insurance, then the MPS would have paid out approximately £2.8 million in ATE insurance premiums. In return for this assumed outlay, MPS recovered just £368,000 as costs in cases where the insured health care professionals were vindicated.

2.8   Data from a liability insurer. One liability insurer took data from two of its panel solicitors, who handled over 1,600 litigated cases on the insurer's behalf from 2006 to summer 2008. Of these, 11 cases were won by defendants at trial and 159 were discontinued by claimants, making a total of 170 "defeated" claims. Costs were recovered on eight occasions in respect of defeated claims.

2.9   The insurer also provided data showing the yearly change in average ATE insurance premiums paid between 2002 or 2003[19] and 2009. The position is as follows:

(i)   In respect of motor claims under the fixed recoverable costs ("FRC") scheme,[20] there was a 9.3% drop in average premiums between 2004 (with an average premium paid of £408) and 2005 (with an average premium paid of £370), when the effects of the FRC scheme were felt. Thereafter, average ATE

---

[18] Pre-claims were cases opened following an intimation of an intention to claim, but in which no claim was made. The figure of 3,504 comprises 2,516 claims and 988 pre-claims.

[19] Depending on when ATE insurance policies became available in respect of that particular category of claim.

[20] See CPR Part 45.

insurance premiums in this category have been rising, albeit at a lower rate than other categories. The average premium for 2009 is £391.

(ii) In all other categories of case (employers' liability, public liability and motor; litigated and non-litigated; fast track and multi-track) the average premium increased. In 2002, the average premium ranged between £285 and £458 depending on the type of claim. By 2009, the lowest average premium paid was £413 (non-litigated motor claims in the multi-track). The highest was £1,994 (litigated public liability claims in the multi-track). The percentage increase in ATE insurance premiums between 2002 or 2003 and 2009 in each category of case ranged between 9.11% and 412.6%.[21]

Although the precise total of ATE insurance premiums paid out by the insurer is not available, it can be seen that the ATE insurance premiums paid out in respect of successful claims far exceeded the costs received on defeated claims.

2.10 This liability insurer states that the sharpest increases in ATE insurance premiums were largely due to the uptake of staged premiums, which are increasingly prevalent. One example given is in respect of a road traffic accident ("RTA") claim. Where there is a full admission of liability after the letter of claim but within the protocol period, the ATE insurance premium is £225. This rises to £350 where there is no admission but the matter settles pre-issue. If a claim is issued, then the ATE insurance premium increases to £750. The level of indemnity provided is also likely to be staged.

2.11 <u>Conclusion.</u> On the basis of the material provided during the Costs Review, it seems to me inevitable that, provided the costs rules are drafted so as (a) to deter frivolous or fraudulent claims[22] and (b) to encourage acceptance of reasonable offers, the introduction of one way costs shifting will materially reduce the costs of personal injuries litigation. One layer of activity, namely ATE insurance against adverse costs liability, will have been removed from the personal injuries process.

3. THE DEBATE DURING PHASE 2

3.1 In chapter 9 above, I have summarised a number of contributions made at meetings or in submissions concerning the question whether one way costs shifting should be substituted for recoverability of ATE insurance premiums. I shall not repeat that summary in this chapter.

3.2 <u>The Association of Her Majesty's District Judges.</u> The Association of Her Majesty's District Judges states:

"While we are not convinced that there should be a departure from the general rule that costs follow the event, we can see the attraction of one way costs shifting in personal injury litigation. It has the huge advantage of certainty as to the costs position of the Claimant and such a system would eliminate the need for ATE insurance in personal injury litigation."

3.3 The Association of Her Majesty's District Judges also sees attraction in the incentive scheme proposed by the Forum of Insurance Lawyers ("FOIL"), set out in PR paragraph 10.10.8. It then comments:

---

[21] The average premiums paid in some categories of case fluctuated between years but, with the exception of motor claims under the FRC scheme, are higher in 2009 than in 2002/2003.
[22] As to which see paragraphs 4.5 to 4.8 below.

"By analogy with a penalty of 10% where the claimant recovers damages equal to or lower than the Defendant's offer, the uplift percentage where the Claimant recovers damages equal to or greater than the Claimant's offer should also be 10%."

3.4   Amongst court users and practitioners there is a wide spread of views on the question of one way costs shifting. Some respondents support the proposal with a variety of qualifications. Others oppose the proposal in principle. Some respondents suggest that there should only be one way costs shifting in certain categories of case, for example only in CFA cases (suggested by the Medical Defence Union – the "MDU") or only in claims under £25,000 (suggested by the ABI).

3.5   Some respondents, for example the MPS, acknowledge that one way costs shifting would be cheaper than the present regime, but nevertheless oppose it on grounds of principle or pragmatism. The MPS points out that not all defendants are insured and that it is harsh for a healthcare professional facing a weak claim to have no prospect of recovering costs. Some respondents fear that one way costs shifting will encourage unmeritorious claims.

3.6   FOIL points out that the data analysed in chapter 25 of the Preliminary Report comes from only one insurer, probably a motor insurer. FOIL comments that evidence from companies covering disease and other longer cases may disclose more costs orders in favour of the defendant, but adds *"it still seems likely that the figures would show that one way costs shifting would reduce costs"*.

3.7   FOIL then refers to the incentive scheme which it previously proposed, now set out at paragraph 10.8 of the Preliminary Report. FOIL states:

"FOIL believes that the 'incentive regime' it has put forward would encourage sensible decision-making and remove the tactical gamesmanship that is sometimes seen in the rejection of reasonable offers. Too often disproportionate costs are incurred to recover a very small sum over and above a sum that is broadly reasonable. The incentive scheme would discourage such tactics and in putting a small percentage of damages at risk would introduce something akin to market forces, giving a claimant a financial interest in the litigation being conducted sensibly and proportionately."

4. MY VIEW

4.1   In my view, the regime of recoverable ATE insurance premiums is indefensible for the reasons set out in chapters 9 and 10 above. On the other hand, most claimants in personal injury cases have for many years enjoyed qualified protection against liability for adverse costs and there are sound policy reasons to continue such protection. The only practicable way that I can see to achieve this result is by qualified one way costs shifting.

4.2   Despite the arguments of the MDU, the ABI and others, I do not regard it as practicable to introduce one way costs shifting for limited categories of personal injury cases, such as low value cases or CFA cases. Either one way costs shifting is introduced across the board for personal injury cases or, alternatively, two way costs shifting remains the rule, except for those protected by the legal aid "shield". Given that stark choice, I favour introducing qualified one way costs shifting for all personal injury cases.

4.3   The legal aid shield. Section 11(1) of the Access to Justice Act 1999 (the "1999 Act") provides:

> "Except in prescribed circumstances, costs ordered against an individual in relation to any proceedings or part of proceedings funded for him shall not exceed the amount (if any) which is a reasonable one for him to pay having regard to all the circumstances including:
>
> (a)   the financial resources of all the parties to the proceedings, and
>
> (b)   their conduct in connection with the dispute to which the proceedings relate..."

It can be seen that this protection against costs liability is qualified protection, rather than total protection.

4.4   How the legal aid shield works in practice. Section 11 of the 1999 Act is supplemented by the Costs Regulations, the Cost Protection Regulations and sections 21 to 23 of the Costs Practice Direction. The effect of these provisions is that the judge making a costs order against a legally aided party may specify the amount to be paid or may direct that the amount be determined at a separate assessment. Before that separate assessment, the legally aided party files and serves a statement of resources. Whilst on its face section 11 of the 1999 Act appears to give the court a wide discretion to order costs to be paid, in practice the section operates as something very close to complete immunity from costs liability. It is not hard to see why this is the case. Pursuing an order will involve the receiving party in significant costs and the prospects of making any significant recovery, when the paying party is by definition of very limited means, are low. Although no official figures exist my understanding, confirmed by discussion with my assessors, is that it is rare indeed for a successful opponent even to attempt recovery against a legally aided party.

4.5   The necessary elements of a one way costs shifting regime. A one way costs shifting regime for personal injuries litigation (including clinical negligence) needs to have the following elements:

(i)   Deterrence against bringing frivolous claims or applications.

(ii)   Incentives for claimants to accept reasonable offers.

4.6   Deterrence against frivolous claims or applications. The claimant must be at risk of some adverse costs, in order to deter (a) frivolous claims and (b) frivolous applications in the course of otherwise reasonable litigation. In my view, the best formula is that contained in section 11(1) of the 1999 Act. This provides a proper degree of protection against adverse costs without eliminating all personal risk. It is a formula which is tried and tested, having been included in all legal aid legislation since the original Legal Aid and Advice Act 1949.[23]

4.7   Proposed rule. I therefore propose that all claimants in personal injury cases, whether or not legally aided, be given a broadly similar degree of protection against adverse costs. In order to achieve this result I propose that a provision along the following lines be added to the CPR:

---

[23] See section 2(2)(e).

"Costs ordered against the claimant in any claim for personal injuries or clinical negligence shall not exceed the amount (if any) which is a reasonable one for him to pay having regard to all the circumstances including:

(a)   the financial resources of all the parties to the proceedings, and

(b)   their conduct in connection with the dispute to which the proceedings relate."

If this proposal is adopted, there will have to be consequential provisions of the kind that currently exist to enable section 11(1) of the 1999 Act to be operated. The details of these consequential provisions will be a matter for the Civil Procedure Rule Committee.

4.8   I do not think it should be necessary in most cases to require a detailed enforcement procedure to determine liability under this provision. In the great majority of cases it should be determined at the conclusion of the case whether an order should be made and, if so, the amount should be determined summarily. Furthermore the making of a costs order will be the exception, rather than the rule. Nevertheless, the formula suggested above will enable the court to make a costs order in three specific situations where such an order would be appropriate: (a) where the claimant has behaved unreasonably (e.g. bringing a frivolous or fraudulent claim); (b) where the defendant is neither insured nor a large organisation which is self-insured; or (c) where the claimant is conspicuously wealthy.

4.9   Consistency with overriding objective. The new rule suggested above would be consistent with the overriding objective. CPR rule 1.1(2) provides:

"Dealing with a case justly includes, so far as is practicable –

(a)   ensuring that the parties are on an equal footing...

(c)   dealing with the case in ways which are proportionate...

    (iv)   to the financial position of each party..."

The proposed new rule has the effect of putting parties who are in an asymmetric relationship onto a more equal footing. It ensures that a party is not denied access to justice because of the prospect of incurring liability for adverse costs beyond its means.

4.10   Incentives to accept reasonable offers.   Having regard to the various submissions and arguments advanced in the course of Phase 2, I propose the following scheme:

(i)   If defendant fails to beat claimant's Part 36 offer, then, in addition to the current consequences,[24] damages will generally be increased by 10%.

(ii)   If the claimant fails to beat the defendant's offer, then the existing consequences as set out in CPR rule 36.14(2) will generally apply.

My proposal in relation to the first scenario (defendant fails to beat claimant's offer) will be developed in chapter 41 below. As to the second scenario (claimant fails to beat defendant's offer), the defendant will have adequate protection: the court will be likely to make a costs order against the claimant in respect of the post-offer period in circumstances where (a) the claimant was acting unreasonably in rejecting a proper

_____

[24] See CPR rule 36.14(3).

offer and (b) the costs in respect of the pre-offer period plus the damages recovered by the claimant provide sufficient funds out of which the claimant can reasonably be expected to pay at least some costs.[25]

4.11   A further advantage of this reform is that all personal injury claimants and clinical negligence claimants, whether legally aided or not, will come under a similar costs shifting regime. This will contribute towards the simplification of the rules which I have advocated in chapter 4 above.

4.12   <u>Comparison with overseas.</u> A one way costs shifting regime (qualified so far as necessary to incentivise reasonable litigation conduct) would be very much better for claimants than (a) the no costs shifting regime in the USA and (b) the two way costs shifting regime in every other overseas jurisdiction which I have studied. Thus, if qualified one way costs shifting is introduced, the position of personal injury claimants in England and Wales will still compare favourably with that of their counterparts in overseas jurisdictions.

5. DISBURSEMENTS

5.1   Claimants' disbursements are currently insured under ATE insurance policies, whereby (a) if the claim succeeds the defendant pays the premium; (b) if the claim fails the ATE insurer pays the disbursements.

5.2   I have previously recommended that ATE insurance premiums should cease to be recoverable. Although it will still be open to claimants to insure in respect of disbursements in unsuccessful cases, this may be thought a somewhat expensive method of meeting such disbursements.

5.3   <u>Level of disbursements in personal injury cases.</u> One costs negotiator provided data on claims settled between July 2006 and January 2009, covering a range of claim types, including the amount of claimant disbursements agreed.[26] The level of claimant disbursements by claim type was as follows:

(i)   For employers' liability accident (7,747 claims) claimant disbursements, the median cost was £588. Disbursements were less than £1,000 in 74% of cases (with 91% of cases incurring disbursements less than £2,000).

(ii)   For public liability (4,954 claims) claimant disbursements, the median cost was £532. Disbursements were less than £1,000 in 79% of cases (with 94% of cases incurring disbursements less than £2,000).

(iii)   For employers' liability disease (384 claims) claimant disbursements, the median cost was £590. Disbursements were less than £1,000 in 77% of cases (with 91% of cases incurring disbursements less than £2,000).

(iv)   For RTA (35,680 claims) claimant disbursements, the median cost was £441. Disbursements were less than £1,000 in 81% of cases (with 93% of cases incurring disbursements less than £2,000).

---

[25] It has been suggested to me that such a regime is open to abuse by defendants, in that they could make an offer of £10 in every case. In my view, a stratagem like this would be doomed to fail. A miniscule offer is in effect no offer. Furthermore if the claimant loses on liability (as opposed to recovering damages lower than the amount of a Part 36 offer), he or she does not acquire any funds out of which to meet an order for costs.

[26] In claims where a global settlement was offered, an allocation as to the amount related to disbursements has been made by the costs negotiator.

5.4 <u>Level of disbursements in clinical negligence cases.</u> During Phase 2 I did not receive any submissions with detailed data on the level of claimant disbursements incurred in clinical negligence claims. I subsequently requested information on disbursements in clinical negligence cases from a number of organisations.

5.5 The Legal Services Commission (the "LSC"), in its Statistical Information 2008/09 pack,[27] shows the total amount paid out for costs, including disbursements, across a number of different claim types. Included in the data are clinical negligence claims. The LSC data show that on unsuccessful clinical negligence claims the average cost met from public funds for disbursements is approximately £2,600 per case. On successful clinical negligence cases the average cost agreed with and met by opponents for disbursements is approximately £8,200 per case.

5.6 One claimant firm of solicitors which deals with clinical negligence claims provided information on the level of disbursements incurred. The data show that on unsuccessful clinical negligence claims the average cost for disbursements is approximately £2,250[28] per case. On successful clinical negligence cases the average cost for disbursements is approximately £4,250 per case for claims settled pre-issue and £14,000 per case for cases settled post-issue.

5.7 One clinical negligence defence organisation has subsequently provided me with data on 638 claims settled pre-issue. The average claimant disbursements paid amount to £1,400 per case. Disbursements were less than £1,000 in 70% of cases (with 90% of cases incurring disbursements less than £2,000). These cases were all settled pre-issue.

5.8 <u>Conclusion.</u> In my view, the claimants' disbursements in unsuccessful cases must be borne either by the claimants[29] or by their solicitors, depending upon what may be agreed between them. At the moment, the defendants pay those disbursements, albeit indirectly, through the mechanism of ATE insurance premiums in cases which defendants lose. There is no justification for requiring defendants, either collectively or individually, to pay claimants' disbursements in cases which claimants lose. Defendants will be making a more than sufficient contribution in such cases by bearing their own costs.

5.9 I recommend in chapter 20 below that the payment of referral fees for personal injury cases (currently running at a remarkably high level) be either banned or subjected to a cap. Claimant solicitors may see fit to re-allocate some part of the referral fees thus saved towards paying disbursements in unsuccessful cases.

5.10 If (a) contrary to my recommendation in paragraph 5.5 above, it is decided as a matter of policy that someone other than the claimants or the claimants' solicitors should pay the claimants' disbursements in cases which claimants lose and (b) no private funding solutions are available, then I would suggest that this burden falls upon the Legal Aid Fund, if the claimants' means fall within legal aid limits.[30] To suggest that the defendants, who have been vindicated in those cases, should still be liable to pay the claimants' disbursements is perverse.

---

[27] Available online at http://www.legalservices.gov.uk/aboutus/how/strategic_publications.asp.

[28] Although no split is available the majority of these claims would presumably have been dropped pre-issue.

[29] Alternatively their insurers, if cover has been taken out.

[30] In the case of clinical negligence, legal aid is still available. In the case of ordinary personal injuries litigation, legal aid could not be provided to cover disbursements without statutory amendment.

6. RECOMMENDATION

6.1   I recommend that a regime of qualified one way costs shifting be introduced for personal injury cases.

CHAPTER 20. REFERRAL FEES

INDEX

1. INTRODUCTION

1.1   In this chapter I discuss the question whether referral fees for personal injury cases should be banned, alternatively capped or otherwise regulated. Referral fees constitute a major head of expenditure in personal injuries litigation, which claimant solicitors have to recover from defendants if they are to operate profitably. Accordingly referral fees, although not recoverable as a discrete item of costs, have a substantial impact upon the costs of personal injuries litigation.

1.2   The wider question. There is a wider question than that addressed in the present chapter, namely whether referral fees should be banned or capped in respect of all litigation, not just personal injury cases. Because the most worrying impact of referral fees is felt in the area of personal injuries litigation,[31] that has been the focus of debate and investigation during the Costs Review. Nevertheless if my recommendations concerning personal injury referral fees are accepted, serious consideration should be given to banning, alternatively capping, referral fees in other areas of litigation.

1.3   Historical background. The historical background is as follows. Advertising or touting for business by solicitors was prohibited until 1987, when the ban was lifted. Solicitors were prohibited from having arrangements with third parties for the introduction or referral of business until 1988, when that ban was also lifted. However, the Law Society retained a ban on "rewarding introducers". In 1991 the Solicitors Conduct Rules were amended in relation to conveyancing, to permit contractual referrals between lenders and solicitors.

1.4   OFT report. In March 2001 the Office of Fair Trading (the "OFT") published the report by the Director General of Fair Trading *Competition in professions*. The Director General set out his approach on page 3 as follows:

> "Indeed, the professions are run by producers largely on behalf of producers. In the economy generally it is competition that impels producers to act in the interests of consumers. Restrictions on competition – on the freedom of suppliers of services to compete with one other – imposed by professions should therefore be subject to close and careful scrutiny.

---

[31] The submissions relating to referral fees which I received during Phases 1 and 2 of the Costs Review were directed to personal injury cases.

The aim of the Office of Fair Trading (OFT) is to make sure that markets work well – for the ultimate benefit of consumers. To that end, we have examined restrictions on competition in the professions selected. The aim has been to identify significant adverse effects on competition. We have not examined in detail whether or not every particular adverse effect on competition is justified by countervailing consumer benefits that could not otherwise be achieved. But where restrictions are causing significant adverse effects on competition, from a policy perspective, they should be removed unless their proponents can demonstrate strong justifications for them in terms of consumer benefit. In any event, the professions should not be shielded from the competition laws that apply elsewhere in the economy."

1.5   In relation to referral fees paid by solicitors, the Director General stated as follows on page 14 of the OFT report:

"Restrictions on receiving a payment for referring a client (Solicitors' Practice Rule 3).

The current regime also prevents solicitors from making payments for work that is referred to them by a third party. This may be hampering inter alia the development of an online marketplace that could bring clients and solicitors together. As with advertising restrictions, there are welcome indications that this restriction may be abolished."

1.6   In March 2004 the Solicitors Conduct Rules were amended to allow solicitors to pay referral fees, subject to certain conditions and safeguards.

1.7   <u>Current rules.</u> Rule 9 of the Solicitors Code of Conduct 2007 governs the referrals of business to and from solicitors. Rule 9.01 provides that, when making or receiving referrals of clients to or from third parties, a solicitor must do nothing which would compromise their independence or ability to act and advise in the best interests of their clients. Rule 9.02 includes additional requirements where a solicitor enters into a financial arrangement with an introducer. The agreement between the solicitor and the introducer must be in writing. Before accepting instructions to act for a client referred in these circumstances, the solicitor must give to the client in writing all relevant information concerning the fact that they have a financial arrangement with the introducer and the amount of any payment to the introducer which is calculated by reference to that referral.

1.8   One issue which has repeatedly arisen during the Costs Review is whether the payment of referral fees should be banned, alternatively capped or otherwise regulated.

2. VIEWS EXPRESSED AT MEETINGS AND SEMINARS

2.1   It is fair to say that at the various meetings and seminars which I have attended there has been considerable hostility to the concept of solicitors paying fees for the referral of personal injury clients.

2.2   <u>Association of Personal Injury Lawyers debate.</u> On 23rd April 2009 the Association of Personal Injury Lawyers ("APIL") held a debate during its annual conference on the question *"Referral fees and advertising – is it too late to put the genie back in the bottle?*"[32]   About 280 people were present, the vast majority of whom were claimant personal injury solicitors. The panel comprised the head of claims management regulation at the Ministry of Justice, the President of APIL and representatives from the Solicitors Regulation Authority (the "SRA") and the Insurance Fraud Bureau (the "IFB"). There were lively speeches from the floor, evincing serious concern about referral fees. A solicitor from a smaller firm protested about clients being shunted to firms who paid bigger referral fees, some of whom (he said) under-settled cases in order to get a quick result.[33] A senior QC argued that it was wrong in principle to buy and sell the claims of injured persons; such a practice was offensive. Another speaker pointed out that any injured person could easily find out through the internet the identity of local solicitors doing personal injury work; referral fees were unnecessary. Those in favour of referral fees pointed to the need for competition and to the increased access to justice which referral fees facilitated. It was suggested that the referral fee system enhances the client's choice and enables unsophisticated persons to be referred to good solicitors. The President of APIL argued that referral fees were inevitable, once advertising was permitted. He had originally opposed advertising by solicitors, but considered that it was not now possible to put the clock back. The representative of the IFB said that the Bureau saw tens of thousands of pounds paid by solicitors to claims management companies for claims, many of which turned out to be manufactured. At the end of the debate a show of hands was taken. Although the votes were not counted, I could see that a very substantial majority voted in favour of banning referral fees.

2.3   <u>Birmingham seminar.</u> The Birmingham seminar on 26th June 2009 was focused upon personal injuries litigation, with both claimant and defendant practitioners present. During the floor discussion (following the presentations by the Lord Chief Justice and Professor Dame Hazel Genn) one speaker raised the issue of referral fees, stating that they were "*the elephant in the room*". He said that referral fees were one way of achieving access to justice, but at huge cost. The next speaker stated that their effect was to drive up the general level of costs, because solicitors had to compete with colleagues who were paying ever higher referral fees. Speakers stated that they paid referral fees to before-the-event ("BTE") insurers, claims management companies and trade unions. A number of claimant solicitors kindly filled in slips of paper during the seminar indicating the levels of referral fees paid. These ranged between £250 and £900, excluding VAT.

2.4   <u>Oxford seminar on costs.</u> At an Oxford University seminar on costs chaired by Professor Zuckerman on 16th June 2009, one of the issues debated was the difference between claimant solicitor hourly rates and defendant solicitor hourly rates. Professor Stephen Nickell[34] stated that he had done some rough calculations which indicated that referral fees could explain the difference between those two rates.

2.5   <u>Claims Standards Council Conference.</u> The Claims Standards Council (the "CS Council") is the trade association which represents claims management companies. I attended their annual conference in Manchester on 2nd July 2009 (chaired by Neil Rose, freelance legal journalist) and engaged in a dialogue with them on the question whether claims management companies added value to the personal injuries compensation process and whether the payment of referral fees by solicitors to claims management companies was beneficial. Essentially three arguments were

---

[32] The debate was chaired by John Stapleton of GMTV, who commented "My overall impression was that the majority would like to get rid of referral fees, but realise the moment for that has probably passed".
[33] He furnished details to me of example cases, on a confidential basis, after the debate.
[34] Warden of Nuffield College Oxford and chairman of the Advisory Committee on Civil Costs since its establishment in 2007: see PR paragraph 52.2.6.

put forward by representatives of the claims management companies: (i) Referral fees paid to claims management companies are a form of marketing costs. It is cheaper and more effective for solicitors to pay referral fees to claims management companies than to engage in direct marketing to the public. (ii) The average person does not have confidence to approach a solicitor. Such persons feel more comfortable talking to representatives of claims management companies. (iii) Claims management companies require high standards of service from the solicitors to whom they refer cases. This is for the benefit of claimants.

2.6   <u>London seminar.</u> At the London seminar on 10th July 2009 the Chairman of the Bar said this:

> "Finally, a word about referral fees. There is no concealing the fact that in the field of publicly funded criminal work, the ability to pay solicitors referral fees, when such behaviour would be treated by the Bar Standards Board as serious misconduct is a cause of serious resentment towards HCAs.[35]   I therefore welcome the discovery by Sir Rupert that there appears to be a general view amongst solicitors on both sides of the fence that these are an unwelcome addition to personal injury costs which bring little benefit to either lawyers or clients. I trust that the Solicitors Regulation Authority will now take note. In the past the Chairman, Peter Williamson, has said the Authority was determined to stamp the practice out, but earlier this year they changed tack and adopted the defeatist view that the practice is too endemic to be banned."

2.7   In the debate following that address one solicitor[36] expressed the view that referral fees were unwelcome and that they may have pushed up ordinary marketing costs. Another solicitor[37] stated that referral fees were a necessary evil. Another solicitor pointed out that many organisations received referral fees, including insurance brokers, credit hire companies and motoring organisations. A member of the Bar said that it was the overwhelming view of barristers in the Personal Injuries Bar Association ("PIBA") that referral fees should be abolished. Cases were badly prepared because the solicitors concerned had to pay referral fees out of the costs which they recovered. Another barrister[38] argued that competition is generally desirable, but that the competition which referral fees generate does not raise the quality of service; if claims management companies went out of business, then (a) the costs of advertising would go down and (b) the Law Society could advertise its Accident Line Scheme.[39] The President of the Law Society, expressing his personal view, said that he had always been opposed to referral fees; the key was to demonstrate quality and competence; the Law Society could become active in advertising the services offered by solicitors. A very experienced claimant personal injuries solicitor expressed the view that referral fees are distasteful, but we have them and they serve a purpose. He doubted that any advertising scheme by the Law Society would be sufficient. He added that it was very much rarer for referral fees to be paid in clinical negligence cases.

---

[35] Higher court advocates.

[36] A member of the Law Society's Civil Litigation Committee, but expressing his personal opinion.

[37] A former chairman of the Motor Accident Solicitors Society, but expressing a personal view.

[38] An assessor to the Costs Review.

[39] Accident Line is a personal injury insurance and referral scheme, endorsed by the Law Society and managed by Abbey Legal Protection. According to its website at http://www.accidentlinedirect.co.uk/background.php, Accident Line is a freephone service which puts individuals seeking to make a personal injury compensation claim in contact with a specialist personal injury solicitor who can give them expert advice.

2.8   Meeting with Legal Expenses Insurance Group.   The Legal Expenses Insurance Group (the "LEIG") comprises a number of leading BTE insurers. On 23rd July 2009 I had a meeting with representatives of the LEIG. They informed me that they charged referral fees when they referred the claims of their insureds to solicitors. If referral fees were banned, they would still refer such claims to solicitors, but the premiums for BTE policies would rise.

3. VIEWS EXPRESSED IN WRITTEN SUBMISSIONS

3.1   Claims Standards Council.   The CS Council in its submission helpfully outlines the historical background and sets out the arguments for permitting referral fees to be paid. The CS Council summarised its principal arguments as follows:

> "Claims management companies promote access to justice by increasing awareness of the right of those who have suffered accidents to claim compensation and by facilitating the claims process. They provide the marketing and case management skills that are essential in any consumer facing service industry where the product is opaque and most people use the service only once.

> Solicitors can obtain personal injury claims only if their service is marketed, directly, by a marketing agency acting on their behalf or by a claims management company. Referral fees are a marketing cost in the same way as direct advertising or the costs of employing business development managers. Abolishing referral fees would have no effect on marketing costs; it would merely change their composition. In practice referral fees, in a disguised form, would continue to be paid – as they were before they were formally permitted."

3.2   The CS Council argues that claims management companies have particular skill at matching claimants with solicitors who are appropriate, either by reason of geography or by reason of the type of claim. The CS Council dismisses the trade unions' concerns about claims management companies[40] as a *"rather hysterical view"*, based on factual errors. The CS Council maintains that past malpractices have been dealt with by regulation under the Compensation Act 2006. The CS Council maintains that it is *"naïve and mischievous to single out referral fees as some sort of 'problem' and even to talk about abolishing them in isolation"*.

3.3   Other claims management companies in their written submissions have supported the comments of the CS Council and expressed broadly similar views.

3.4   BTE insurers.   BTE insurers, who are also major recipients of referral fees, have put up a less united front. One major motor insurer wrote as follows:

> "With regard to referral fees, in keeping with both, the insurance market and solicitors, we receive income from referral fees. In round numbers, in respect of credit hire claims we receive £250 and for PI £750. We consider that referral fees should be abolished although in making this proposal we must then highlight the need to make a corresponding reduction in the fees that Claimant's Solicitors charge. If referral fees of this type can be paid within the Predictive Fees scale,[41] that then suggests that the scale is too high."

---

[40] Recorded in PR paragraph 10.15.5.
[41] This is a reference to the fixed recoverable costs scheme in CPR Part 45.

3.5 Another insurer, part of a group which receives premiums on the BTE side and pays out on the liability side, writes as follows:

> "[We] are a very strong advocate of outlawing referral fees. They create a feeding frenzy at the point of accident and a downstream level of activity which does not serve the claimant, increases costs unnecessarily and delivers no discernible value. We believe there is opportunity here to take out a layer of costs without detriment and will have the added benefit of avoiding behaviour which seek to bypass predictable fees in order to fund the referral fee."

Similar views were expressed orally to me by a very substantial insurer, which receives large referral fee income.

3.6 Other insurers favour the status quo. One major insurer points out in its submissions that referral fees "*constitute an important revenue stream*" and that this has been built into that insurer's business model.

3.7 <u>Trade unions.</u> Trade unions refer the personal injury claims of their members to solicitors on union panels. Trade unions may charge referral fees, albeit at a lower level than BTE insurers or claims management companies. For example, one union informs me that it receives a referral fee of £200 for every case which proves to be "*worthy of investigation*". Other trade unions do not charge referral fees as such, but instead receive certain free legal services from the solicitors for their members.

3.8 <u>Personal Injuries Bar Association.</u> The PIBA carried out a survey of its members. 255 members favoured abolition of referral fees for personal injury cases; 39 opposed abolition; five favoured regulation or capping. In its submission the PIBA wrote as follows:

> "So far as the Bar is concerned, they are not allowed by the Code of Conduct. We can see no benefit in permitting referral fees for solicitors either. In many cases the referral fee is a substantial proportion of the costs required to conduct a case and it has led to cost cutting by solicitors and cases being insufficiently prepared to the detriment of Claimants. Referral fees mean that the solicitor who conducts the case is the highest payer but not necessarily the best solicitor for the Claimant. The market is driven by who pays the most, not who provides the best or most efficient or cheapest service. There is no doubt that referral fees have fuelled the costs war...
>
> We can see no public interest in retaining referral fees on competition or economic grounds. They often result, in our view, in poorer quality service at a greater price and they do nothing to enhance competence or quality. There are undoubtedly some firms who pay referral fees and maintain high standards, but this is in spite of not because of referral fees. There was competition between solicitors prior to the introduction of referral fees. We do not advocate banning of advertising by solicitors and we encourage the Law Society to advertise a provision of easily accessible information to the public about services solicitors can provide in every locality."

3.9 <u>Bar Council.</u> The Bar Council argues for abolition of referral fees, adopting similar arguments to those of PIBA.

3.10 <u>Solicitors.</u> Individual firms of solicitors take different views on this issue. Some argue strongly for retention of referral fees. One major firm argues that referral fees are now both necessary and entrenched. Some solicitors liken those who oppose referral fees to King Canute (in relation to the tide) or to Luddites (who could not uninvent the knowledge of how to make textile machines). The views of many solicitors are encapsulated in the claimant solicitor submissions of Manchester Law Society, which can be summarised as follows.

- Fees paid to claims management companies for referrals of business are no more than a business cost of the solicitor. Although claimant lawyers would obviously prefer not to pay referral fees, they would equally like their other overheads (such as rent and salaries) to be lower. There is a *"fundamental lack of understanding"* as to how much solicitors must inevitably pay by way of marketing costs. Advertising by claims management companies increases awareness of the product and informs the potential claimant of the ability to bring a claim. A good claims referrer can market on a much bigger scale and achieve certain economies that an individual law firm cannot.

- The payment of referral fees does not harm the client's position so long as there remains an effective level of regulation and monitoring, and the client does not lose any of their compensation. Without the free market created by referral fees, consumer choice would be restricted with only a few large law firms remaining in the market. In addition, many liability insurers are reliant on referral fees to maintain their service levels. Without the referral income, the cost of the BTE premium would *"increase significantly and probably price it out of the reach of most"* since BTE premiums can only be priced as competitively as they are because the BTE insurer does not rely on the premium to fund its costs.

- Aside from the perceived merits of referral fees, the Manchester Law Society submits that their continued existence is inevitable. It points out that the development of claims management companies and insurers charging referral fees was not the choice of claimant lawyers; rather it was the result of the removal of legal aid. Consequently:

  > "...it is now neither practical or possible to return to a system where the payment of referral fees are banned. We see it as inevitable that there will be abuse of the system. The benefit of the system as it is now is one of transparency."

3.11 Other solicitor firms take the opposite view. One major firm with an extensive personal injuries practice in the north of England writes:

> "With regard to claims management companies, we see no merit in them. In the modern communication age, there should be sufficient information available for claimants to identify solicitors in the right speciality to assist them or if they contact a firm who cannot assist, for that firm to refer on. If necessary, the Law Society, LSC and groups such as APIL and AVMA should do more.
>
> Claims management companies add a cost to the process as middle men, but not value. They actually take away the freedom of people to freely choose solicitors. If claims management companies were prevented from being involved, we do not believe that this would impair the services that solicitors can provide to claimants.
>
> From a PI / CN perspective, therefore, we would have no objection to a ban on claims management / referral fees. Approximately 50% of CN work is carried

out by way of Public Funding, and referral fees do not significantly affect our business model as there is a prohibition on paying referral fees in publicly funded cases. From a CN perspective, we have no objection to a general ban on claims management / referral fees."

3.12   Accident Compensation Solicitors Group.   The Accident Compensation Solicitors Group ("ACSG") writes as follows:

"Since the introduction of referral fees, the whole scope of the claims process in road traffic accident claims has shifted from independent and impartial advice from qualified and experienced staff, to low quality advice by inexperienced staff: leading to what ACSG believe, regular and significant under settling of claims.

In a road traffic claim, very few claims are handled outside the following business model. Within an hour of the insured reporting a road traffic accident to their insurer, all injured persons are contacted by a firm of solicitors, stating they have been appointed to act on behalf of the Claimant. Very rarely is the Claimant informed that a referral arrangement is in place, nor that the referral fee is typically up to £900, which is in breach of the Solicitors' Referral Code. The Claimant is not told that the referral fee is not recouped from the party at fault, so that economies have to be taken in running the claim, either by reducing the amount of time spent running the claim, or reducing the level of fee earner to the minimum level. This is usually young, inexperienced, unqualified staff, poorly trained and equally poorly supervised, if at all."

3.13   Association of Personal Injury Lawyers.   APIL states in its written submissions that it never wanted to remove the ban on referral fees. APIL members are concerned about the high level of referral fees, which may affect the way a case is handled. APIL is concerned that the bidding process operated by the BTE insurers tends to force up referral fees. APIL believes that there should be full transparency of referral fees and that the possibility of capping referral fees should be explored.

3.14   Law Society.   The Law Society in its submissions acknowledges that referral fees are a difficult and contentious issue. The Law Society supports referrers paying referral fees while other providers are permitted to do so, but would support a review to see whether it would be practicable to prohibit payment of such fees altogether. The Law Society continues:

"Solicitors pay referral fees to claims handlers because it provides them with access to work. They cannot compete with the large marketing budgets of these firms.[42] Some argue that paying a referral fee is the most cost-effective way of obtaining work and, if they were unable to have relationships with claims handlers, their overheads would be increased considerably, although no research has been conducted on this.

It is also strongly arguable that claims management companies are highly successful in enabling those who have suffered injury to gain redress. They have played a strong role in educating the public about their remedies.

Against this, it is arguable that the payment of such fees may affect client choice of solicitor and may well put pressure on the solicitor's duties to the

---

[42] Claims management firms.

client. Some of the fees are so high that it is difficult to understand how solicitors can make a profit and maintain standards, particularly in a fixed fee regime.

The Law Society lifted the ban reluctantly because of these concerns. However, since the ban has been lifted, the Law Society considers that solicitors should be able to pay referral fees if they wish and if it suits their business model. Solicitors are highly regulated professionals and the overwhelming majority will be able to take the business decision as to how much they are prepared to pay for work without compromising their duties to the client."

3.15   Lloyd's Market Association.   The Lloyd's Market Association (the "LMA") represents all businesses which underwrite insurance at Lloyd's. The LMA argues that referral fees are an unnecessary addition to litigation costs and that they should be either banned or capped. The existence of such fees indicates that the current costs recovery regime is over-generous. The LMA acknowledges that insurers have partly created the present situation by selling claims, but adds that the insurance industry *"cannot now undo this situation"*.

3.16   District judges.   A number of district judges have expressed concerns about the effects of referral fees. Their concerns are twofold. First, the solicitors who get the work through referral fees are far removed from their clients geographically. Secondly, the quality of work done by solicitors (who have paid substantial referral fees) is diminished. These concerns are echoed by District Judge Oldham (President of the Association of Her Majesty's District Judges) in his article in the Law Society Gazette *"Getting Back on Track"*.[43]

3.17   A specialist personal injury firm has expressed support for the views of district judges, as follows:

"We agree with the observation of District Judges that the lack of client contact impairs the levels of representation performed by BTE panel solicitors. We are frequently asked to takeover the conduct of serious injury claims that have initially started off in the hands of BTE panel solicitors and on virtually every occasion files come to us demonstrating a surprising low level of activity or planning of what are significant claims for life changing injuries. In a surprisingly high percentage there have been no visits to the client, who at the early stages will often be a hospital in-patient. From our perspective this makes it near impossible for clients with serious injuries to be properly represented, for instance in relation to their immediate rehabilitation needs."

3.18   Supplementary information.   I detected a certain reticence among respondents to reveal the full amount of referral fees which they were receiving or paying (as the case may be). I therefore made inquiries through my judicial assistant of one major BTE insurer as to what referral fees it received. The response was to the following effect. The going rate for a fast track personal injury claim[44] is between £600 and £900. The bulk of such referral fees are towards the top of the bracket, i.e. £800 to £880. Where the volume of cases being referred is low, the referral fees are lower. For claims above the fast track, referral fees are more bespoke and are often linked to profit costs.

---

[43] Law Society Gazette, 9th April 2009.
[44] RTA, employers' liability or public liability.

4. ANALYSIS

(i) Competition issues

4.1   Office of Fair Trading's position. The OFT set out its current view on the competition issues in an email to my judicial assistant dated 6th August 2009.

> "In order to assess the quality of legal services, a significant degree of judgement is required, which may be beyond a lay consumer's experience. One of our major concerns in the market for legal services is the asymmetry of information between providers and consumers who are not always able to judge the quality of the service provided. Consumers generally find it difficult to access information about professional services.
>
> By contrast, referrers may develop a good understanding about the services on offer and the service providers. They are therefore in a better position than some clients to identify high quality services providers for relative good value and to use their bargaining power in order to negotiate better services and better value. On that basis a referral fee arrangement is likely to minimise the effects of information asymmetry in the legal services market between lawyers and clients, and a prohibition on referral fees would prevent such benefit. We therefore consider that referral arrangements can enhance competition as solicitors will have to compete with each other in order to obtain referral work. Solicitors who are involved in referral fee schemes also have an incentive to maintain a high standard of service so as to get repeat custom from referred clients as well as the referrer. Referral fee arrangements can also act as a competitive tool for new firms entering the market, where such arrangements are not common practice in the market. For these reasons we consider that a total prohibition on solicitors from entering into referral fee arrangements with non-lawyers can unnecessarily impede competition."

4.2   My view. I can fully see how the OFT arrived at its conclusion in March 2001 and why the OFT still adheres to essentially the same conclusion. However, the evidence which I have received points strongly to the opposite conclusion. In very many cases, though not of course all cases, referrers simply refer cases to the highest bidder. That is in no sense matching case to solicitor or remedying the information asymmetry. On occasions it leads to clients being sent to the wrong solicitors with potentially damaging results: see the comments of the solicitors firm quoted in paragraph 3.17 above. The effect of allowing referral fees is that clients now have less choice than they would if referral fees were prohibited.

4.3   The normal effects of competition are distorted in the context of personal injuries litigation, because the clients generally do not pay the costs. Those costs may be paid by the other side or they may be borne by the client's own solicitor (if the case is on a CFA and is lost). Under the present regime, solicitors are not competing to get business on price. Nor are they competing on quality of service. They are usually competing to see who can pay the highest referral fee. Such competition is not beneficial to claimants or indeed to anybody else, apart from the referrers. Where cases fall under the fast track fixed recoverable costs scheme in CPR Part 45, the amount of costs available is a fixed sum. The more of that sum is paid to the referrer, the less are the resources available to devote to the handling of the case. In the context of fixed costs the effect of referral fees is either to drive up the level of fixed costs or to drive down the quality of service or both.

4.4   In my view there is no benefit in competition terms to be gained from allowing referral fees.

4.5   I have also considered European competition law, in particular the impact of Articles 49, 56 and 101 of the Treaty on the Functioning of the European Union.[45] I have considered the effect of *Wouters et al v Algemene Raad van de Nederlandse Orde van Advocaate*[46] and *Cipolla v Fazari and Macrino*.[47] The purpose of a ban on referral fees would be to further the public interest, namely by controlling the costs of civil litigation. I do not consider that such a ban would be disproportionate to the objective. In my view, a ban upon referral fees would not be inconsistent with European competition law.

(ii) General

4.6   The practice of referring clients to distant firms of solicitors is a cause of resentment. BTE insurers have the right to determine which solicitors shall represent the client right up to the moment of commencing proceedings. At that point, although the claimant could insist upon solicitors of his choice acting, by then it is usually impracticable to change solicitors. See chapter 8 above in respect of BTE insurance.

4.7   On the basis of all the evidence that I have read and heard during the Costs Review, I consider that BTE insurers and claims management companies charge referral fees without adding any commensurate value to the litigation process. On the contrary, referral fees have now escalated to such a level that some solicitors cut corners in order to (a) cover the referral fee and (b) make a profit on the case. In straightforward road traffic accident ("RTA") cases often more than half the fees paid to the solicitors are paid out in referral fees.[48] This is to the detriment of the client, the solicitors and the public interest.

4.8   I accept that solicitors would still pay marketing costs if referral fees were banned, but those marketing costs would no longer be driven upwards by the ratcheting effect of referral fees. I see considerable force in the arguments advanced during Phase 2 that referral fees have driven up normal marketing costs.

4.9   I do not accept that referral fees are necessary for access to justice. Claimants with personal injury claims would be well aware of their right to claim damages, even if claims management companies did not exist. I do not accept that access to justice was denied or restricted prior to 2004, when the ban on referral fees was lifted.

4.10   The availability and identity of solicitors conducting personal injuries work could be publicised perfectly satisfactorily through the internet, through Law Society advertising, through the APIL website and similar means. BTE insurers could perfectly well refer their insured to appropriate solicitors (local to the insured and possessing relevant expertise) without receiving a referral fee for every case. Indeed they have confirmed to me that this is what they would do, if referral fees were banned. If they receive a premium for BTE insurance, surely the insurers could

---

[45] Formerly articles 43, 49 and 81 of the Treaty Establishishing the European Community. The Treaty Establishing the European Community became the Treaty on the Functioning of the European Union on 1st December 2009.

[46] Case C-309/99, [2002] ECR I-1577.

[47] Joined Cases C-94/04 and 202/04, [2006] ECR I-11421.

[48] Members of the Motor Accident Solicitors Society may pay referral fees of £700 per case: see chapter 21 below at paragraph 2.4.

perform that modest service for their insured without expecting to receive several hundred pounds through the back door.

4.11   There is also a wider point. In my view, it is offensive and wrong in principle for personal injury claimants to be treated as a commodity. BTE insurers should not be in the position of auctioning off the personal injury claims of those whom they insure. It is equally unacceptable for claims management companies to buy in personal injury claims from other referrers and then sell them on at a profit. Indeed the very language of the claims management industry characterises personal injury claims as a commodity. Strong cases ready to be pursued are described as "*oven ready*".[49]

4.12   The practice is, in my view, even more abhorrent when the referrer not only demands a referral fee from the solicitor but also takes a slice of the claimant's damages (without having added any value to the case). I am aware of one claims management company which charges its clients a fee of £379 out of damages received.

4.13   It is argued by some that a prohibition on payment of referral fees could not be enforced. I am not persuaded by this argument. In my view, the vast majority of solicitors are honourable professionals and would respect such a prohibition, whether imposed by legislation or by rules of conduct.

4.14   I have discussed the enforcement issue with the SRA which has considerable experience of enforcing the ban on "rewarding introducers" up until 2004. The SRA makes the point that defining what a referral fee is requires some care, in order to catch disguised referral fees but to permit legitimate marketing. I accept this advice and have requested the SRA to assist in formulating an appropriate definition of "referral fee" and in keeping that definition under review. The Legal Services Board (the "LSB") will also have a role in this regard. The definition which I propose, subject to review by the SRA and LSB, is "any form of payment or other consideration to a party for introducing clients to a solicitor".

4.15   The point has been made with some force that the landscape will change dramatically in or after 2011 when Alternative Business Structures ("ABSs") come into being. I accept that the landscape will change. The LSB (with whom I discussed this issue at a full board meeting on 28th September 2009) has not yet reached any position on the question whether referral fees should be banned. The LSB makes the point that it is not possible to predict how people will behave once the market has been freed up to allow the operation of ABSs. I accept this point. ABSs may or may not desire (absent any ban) to pay referral fees. However, I do not believe that the existence of a ban upon referral fees could be a serious fetter upon their operations. ABSs will incur such marketing costs as they see fit in relation to personal injury claims. There will be no benefit to consumers in allowing ABSs to trade in personal injury claims either between themselves or with third parties. Both before and after 2011 the effect of referral fees can only be to drive up legal costs (since the referee must recoup its outlay) and/or to depress quality of service. In my view essentially the same arguments will make it appropriate to ban, alternatively cap, referral fees after 2011 as apply now.

4.16   In my view the fact that referral fees are paid as a matter of routine is one of the factors which contributes to the high costs of personal injuries litigation. The lifting of the ban on referral fees in 2004 has not proved to be of benefit either to

---

[49] This is a term which I have often heard and which is used in the CSC's submission.

claimants or to the providers of legal services. The only winners are the recipients of referral fees.

5. RECOMMENDATION

5.1   Recommendation.   I recommend that the payment of referral fees for personal injury claims be banned.

5.2   Implementation.   If this recommendation is accepted, it could be implemented in one of two ways. There could be primary legislation, which would prohibit anyone from buying or selling personal injury claims. Alternatively, the Solicitors' Code of Conduct could be amended, so that solicitors are prohibited from paying referral fees. In the latter event, the codes of conduct binding upon other legal representatives would have to be similarly amended.

5.3   Fallback position.   If my primary recommendation is rejected, then I recommend that referral fees be capped at a modest figure, which I suggest should be £200.

5.4   The wider question.   If either of the above recommendations is accepted, serious consideration will have to be given to the question[50] whether referral fees should be banned or capped in other areas of litigation.

---

[50] See paragraph 1.2 above.

CHAPTER 21. ASSESSMENT OF GENERAL DAMAGES FOR PAIN, SUFFERING AND LOSS OF AMENITY

INDEX

1. INTRODUCTION

1.1   <u>Preliminary Report.</u> In chapter 27 of the Preliminary Report I described the points-based systems for assessing personal injury damages, which are used in Italy, France and Spain. In chapter 28 I reviewed the software systems currently used by insurers in England and Wales for assessing general damages for pain, suffering and loss of amenity. The two main software systems are Colossus and Claims Outcome Advisor ("COA"). In PR paragraph 28.6.3 I invited comments on three issues, namely:

(i)   Whether a judicially approved points-based software system might be developed and, in due course, brought into general use.

(ii)   Whether under-settlement is currently perceived as being a significant problem and, if so, whether the use of such a system might benefit claimants by reducing the risks of under-settlement.

(iii)   Whether the use of such a system might assist in reducing the costs of handling lower value personal injuries claims.

1.2   <u>Abbreviations.</u> In this chapter I shall use the abbreviation "PSLA" for pain, suffering and loss of amenity, consequential upon personal injury. I shall, as before, refer to the provider of Colossus as "CSC" and the provider of COA as "ISO". I shall refer to the Association of Personal Injury Lawyers as "APIL", the Motor Accident Solicitors Society as "MASS", and the Forum of Insurance Lawyers as "FOIL". I shall refer to the Judicial Studies Board as the "JSB". I shall refer to the Civil Justice Council as the "CJC".

1.3   <u>SMART Evaluate.</u> During Phase 2 I received a submission from Doctors Chambers Ltd ("DCL") and Smart Report Ltd ("SRL") concerning an online quantum assessment tool called "SMART Evaluate". SRL and DCL state that SMART Evaluate has recently been launched and is currently being piloted by a number of law firms.

2. MEETINGS AND SEMINARS DURING PHASE 2

2.1   <u>Birmingham seminar.</u> The Birmingham seminar on 26th June 2009 was focused upon personal injuries litigation. The ex-President of APIL in her address said that individual insurers calibrate their software systems differently. APIL members have never failed to beat an offer generated by such systems. In the ensuing discussion an insurer representative said that he used to share those concerns, but many APIL members accept the insurers' first offer, as do trade unions. A number of speakers then indicated that, in cases which go to trial, the damages awarded always exceed the sums which insurers have previously offered on the basis of their software systems. The insurer representative said that he would welcome the establishment of a judicially approved software system, based on negotiated settlements rather than court awards. The APIL ex-President said that APIL would support the investigation of such a venture. The President of FOIL argued that lawyers are not currently selling their clients short. He did not accept that current software systems are significantly inaccurate. However, he would not dismiss the suggestion for a standardised software system.

2.2   Croydon meeting. On 29th June 2009 I attended a meeting in Croydon (the "Croydon meeting") with representatives of Royal & Sun Alliance Insurance plc, AXA Insurance, Premier Medical Group, Parabis Law LLP, APIL, MASS, FOIL, IBM, CSC and ISO. The two software providers, CSC and ISO, gave a demonstration of their respective software systems. One of the matters which emerged from these demonstrations was the large difference in levels at which different insurers settle low value personal injury claims. At the end of this meeting a working group was set up (see below).

2.3   Manchester seminar. At the Manchester seminar on 3rd July 2009 there was some discussion about personal injury cases which settled soon after issue (thus escaping the fixed recoverable costs scheme under CPR Part 45). It emerged that one reason for this was the making of offers by insurers pre-issue on the basis of their software systems. The solicitors subsequently instructed by insurers may make higher offers, but by then proceedings have been issued.

2.4   Meeting with MASS. On 23rd July 2009 I had a meeting with representatives of MASS. They expressed support for the proposal to establish an authoritative software system for assessing damages for PSLA. Such software would set the parameters within which claims should be settled. The MASS representatives stated that at the moment claims handlers employed by insurers are given a very narrow range within which they can offer. This range is derived from current software systems and tends to be too low. Any common software system would require regular review and should be subject to judicial oversight. Judicial decisions rather than settlement data should be used as the benchmark for levels of damages. In relation to referral fees, the MASS representatives stated that some of their members pay £700 per case. In MASS' view, the payment of referral fees for personal injury claims yields no obvious benefit and a ban should be considered.

3. WRITTEN SUBMISSIONS DURING PHASE 2

3.1   Claimant solicitors. The views of claimant solicitors range from (a) opposition to the use of software tools for assessment of general damages for PSLA to (b) cautious support for the concept. One firm emphasises the subjective and objective elements which are involved in assessing general damages. The firm points out that one must look not only at the nature and severity of the injury, but also at its impact upon the particular claimant. Factors which influence such assessment include:

- The age of the claimant.

- The sex of the claimant.

- The nature of the claimant's pre-accident life.

- The nature of the injuries, both physical and mental.

- The effect on the claimant's life in the period of recovery.

- The nature and extent of medical investigation and treatment.

- The extent of any residual symptoms, their duration and the effect on the claimant's life post-accident.

- The influence of the claimant's previous medical history on the extent and duration of those symptoms.

- The claimant's marital and child status.

3.2   Another, very substantial, claimant firm takes a more positive view. It believes that a judicially approved software system for assessing damages could facilitate quicker and easier assessment. However, to do so, it would need a number of components. Unlike Colossus, which is a tool of the defendant, the system would need to have the confidence of both claimants and defendants. It would need to have detailed criteria so as to produce a flexible tool which fairly discriminated between various claims to arrive at an assessment which was individually tailored to the claim. The system would need to be transparent. There would need to be a mechanism to update and modify the software on a regular basis. It would need to have considerable resource both in terms of the IT process and the review and ongoing updating of the software. The system would be suitable only for a certain level of claim, fundamentally a claim where the only issue is quantum, there is one medical report, and the claimant suffered relatively minor injuries. Certain types of claim would have to be automatically taken out of the process. This firm notes that the current online bid system[51] provides a good way of circumventing the normal delays in dealing with the insurance companies' claims handlers.

3.3   APIL. APIL does not object to the use of technology where practitioners find this helpful. However, it points out that there is a risk of databases becoming swamped with decisions with either a claimant or defendant bias. APIL believes that the proposal to introduce a new and compulsory computerised assessment tool is a defendant driven attempt to save costs, rather than to ensure that injured people receive appropriate damages. APIL goes on to set out a number of detailed reservations, supported by reference to litigation in the USA. APIL believes that where software systems are used there is a serious risk of under-settlement. It does not believe that the development of such systems might benefit claimants by reducing the risk of under-settlement.

3.4   MASS. MASS takes an intermediate view. MASS supports the creation of a judicially approved database, based on recent court decisions and closely aligned to an expansion of the JSB Guidelines. However, MASS counsels extreme caution in moving towards either a points system or a software system. After a detailed review MASS concludes that the assessment of general damages for PSLA could be made simpler and more predictable in lower value cases. MASS proposes that Colossus and COA could be used to produce a matrix of damages using recent judicial decisions. This could supplement the JSB Guidelines. It could be available both on paper and electronically. Embryonic products, such as PICAS,[52] could continue to be trialled on a voluntary basis until such time as they have been properly tried and tested.

---

[51] Described in PR chapter 28, section 5.
[52] The Personal Injury Claims Assessment Service, developed by ISO.

3.5   Defendant solicitors. Defendant solicitors are supportive of the proposals in the Preliminary Report. FOIL states:

> "Although the assessment of general damages can never be an exact science FOIL believes that the use of Colossus or COA provides consistency. It does not believe there is any evidence (other than the inevitable occasional anecdote) to suggest that use of the tools results in widespread under-settlement.

> FOIL welcomes the work being undertaken currently to look further at a general damages assessment tool.

> FOIL believes that the use of such a tool would reduce costs by taking out some of the fee earner work spent on research and valuation."

3.6   Trade unions. Trade unions are generally opposed to the use of software systems in this context. The Trades Union Congress (the "TUC") maintains that an adaptation of the current software systems in place will not ensure that claimants receive full compensation. On the contrary, computer-based systems tend to depress the level of settlements and indeed were designed for this purpose. The National Union of Teachers (the "NUT") expresses similar concerns. Both the TUC and the NUT foresee considerable difficulties in developing a software tool, which would be fair to claimants.

3.7   A firm of solicitors which does a great deal of trade union work expresses similar views. That firm sees IT based systems as part of the problem, not part of the solution. The firm maintains that mere re-calibration of the systems will not solve the problem. It states:

> "[T]he calibration or input of data is simply the top level input. The system itself, the programme, is the base level, what it does with what it is fed is crucial. But the insurers and those who own the rights to the system won't say how it works. Only a system that is wholly transparent and made available to all parties for detailed analysis and critique would be acceptable to play any part in the assessment of damages...

> Given that the machine has been designed for insurers, and used by insurers, it is wholly unsatisfactory that Claimants would be expected to simply accept the programme as it is, without any opportunity to inspect or challenge it. This would effectively amount to a transfer of control of adjudication from the judiciary in a transparent process as at present, to a private contractor in a process cloaked in secrecy and confidentiality."

The firm regards as dangerous anything which suggests that computers can replace competent lawyers or an independent judiciary.

3.8   Action against Medical Accidents. Action against Medical Accidents ("AvMA") can see the value of an authoritative software system for assessing general damages for PSLA in low value clinical negligence claims. Claimant solicitors must have access to the whole system, not just extracts from it. However, AvMA does not think that such a software tool would be useful in complex clinical negligence cases, where a large element of the claim relates to permanent disability.

3.9   Liability insurers. Liability insurers are strongly supportive of the proposal to develop an authoritative software system for assessing general damages for PSLA.

They dispute that the current software leads to under-settlements. One insurer comments that the introduction of a judicially approved quantum assessment tool would reduce the extent of negotiation between the parties and reduce costs. It adds that the activity that goes into assessing and negotiating the value of PSLA is one of the great contributors to costs in lower value injury claims. The insurer backs up this comment with print outs showing the breakdown of costs in a number of files relating to low value personal injury claims. The time spent on assessing and negotiating damages ranges between 30 minutes and 6.8 hours. Another insurer argues that at present the calculation of general damages is both overly complicated and too time consuming. It does not accept that the present software systems generate under-valuations, but adds that the software tools can in any event be "tuned" to deliver different outcomes. This insurer proposes that there should be a single authoritative software system, which is available to all parties and which is moderated from time to time (say every two years) by the Ministry of Justice. Another insurer states that it would welcome the introduction of a standardised assessment tool for all fast track claims, in order to overcome the uncertainty which attaches to the otherwise subjective assessment of damages.

3.10   The Bar.   The Bar is generally opposed to the use of software tools for assessing general damages for PSLA. A set of chambers in Liverpool points out that a software system cannot cope with individual nuances of each claimant's injuries; adopting such software would be tantamount to introducing a CICA[53] tariff into this area. The North Eastern Circuit opposes any attempt to "computerise" the assessment of damages in fast track cases, which it believes will have harmful unintended consequences. The assessment of damages should remain a judicial task. The North Eastern Circuit proposes that the JSB Guidelines should give clearer guidance in respect of low value cases.

3.11   The Personal Injuries Bar Association ("PIBA") is concerned that current software systems used by insurers are under-calibrated by about 20%. It states that very few claimants have lost a quantum only case, where insurers were relying on a computer assessment of damages. PIBA's survey of members revealed that this only happened in 1% of cases.[54] PIBA considers that no computer programme could be calibrated to deliver justice in this regard. PIBA maintains that a computer programme could not produce any meaningful figure for the following:

- Scars which can only be assessed on sight of the scar itself and the effect of it on a particular claimant.

- Multiple injuries.

- Pre-existing conditions e.g. aggravation of a previous injury or acceleration of symptoms from an underlying condition.

- Unusual subjective responses by claimants to their injury.

3.12   District judges.   The Association of Her Majesty's District Judges does not support points based or software based assessment of general damages in personal injury clams. The Association believes that much more work would need to be done to justify introducing a system that would effectively abolish the jurisdiction of the courts in such assessments. The Liverpool District Judges, in their joint submission, doubt that a computer or "points" system would achieve justice. They acknowledge, however, that no two judges will necessarily produce the same figure for a particular

---

[53] Criminal Injuries Compensation Authority.
[54] The claimant failed to beat the Part 36 offer in only 19 out of 1,349 cases.

case. They add the comment that greater precision by reporting doctors would assist in the assessment of general damages. They state:

> "We do, however, see advantages in requiring the reporting doctor to ascribe 'points' to relevant injuries on an established and medically recognised scale to assist the court making the final determination. At present the District Judges in Liverpool are aware of a certain lack of precision in the prognoses given by experts, particularly when the examination is very soon after the accident. Often a GP or orthopaedic surgeon examining a claimant at one to two months post accident will describe soft tissue injuries ('a classic whiplash') and opine that the claimant should recover 'within 12 months'. Experience has shown that a number of claimants recover well inside this period – yet the Court is expected to deal with it as a 12 month recovery."

3.13 <u>Software companies.</u> CSC and ISO have each sent in helpful submissions, describing their respective software systems. Both companies maintain that their software systems promote consistency, as well as fair and speedy settlements. Both companies support the concept of achieving judicially approved calibration of their software systems. SRL and DCL in their submission state that SMART Evaluate is a new software system, which is targeted at claimant solicitors, rather than being an insurer tool. SRL and DCL explain the particular benefits of SMART Evaluate and the respects in which SMART Evaluate differs from Colossus and COA. Beyond stating that a third software system (not mentioned in the Preliminary Report) has now come onto the market, I cannot undertake any comparative review of the three different commercial products.

4. WORKING GROUP REPORT

4.1 <u>Working group set up.</u> At the end of the Croydon meeting I set up a working group. The remit of the working group was to endeavour to agree calibration instructions, which could be adopted by all existing software systems for the valuation of general damages in respect of PSLA up to £10,000. The calibration should reflect the levels of general damages currently awarded by the courts for personal injuries. The working group comprised representatives from APIL, MASS, insurers, ISO and CSC. It was agreed that the working group would report by 6th November 2009 their agreed calibration instructions or, in the event of disagreement, the areas of disagreement. Subsequently a representative from SRL and DCL joined the working group.

4.2 <u>Working group report.</u> The working group, in its report dated 5th November 2009, identifies one key issue[55] between claimant and defendant representatives, namely whether and to what extent data from settlements, as opposed to judicial decisions, could be used for calibrating the software systems. On the one hand, there is a paucity of judicial decisions. On the other hand, the data available from the far more numerous settlements may well not reflect what courts would have awarded if all those cases had been litigated. The working group concluded that a pilot scheme may possibly be appropriate in order to provide (a) methodology on gaining unbiased data and (b) on the basis of these data, proof that a system can work. Claimant representatives would speak with their respective organisations about possible involvement in a pilot when details were available.[56]

---

[55] In commenting on this paragraph in draft, APIL states that another issue is the inability to produce calibration instructions which could cater for every injury and the effects on different claimants.
[56] MASS has subsequently sent me a statement to the effect that quantum assessment tools currently produce figures which are too low. MASS has an open mind about the pilot, which will need to

4.3 <u>Joint statement from ISO and CSC.</u> The working group report includes a joint statement from CSC and ISO, the first part of which reads as follows:

"Both the Colossus and COA systems work on a severity points basis. Held within each system is intelligence around the relevant severity of injuries, treatments, complications, outcomes along with other medical information and facts pertinent to PSLA evaluation. Further system intelligence applies algorithms (calculations) on an individual case basis, such as in a multiple injury cases, to derive the correct end severity. Each system has its own unique severity points scale and algorithms for determining the end result but the systems are broadly similar in terms of order of severity ranking and manner of end calculation.

Calibration is the method by which each system's end severity points, which will always remain the same within each system for a given case, are converted into a monetary amount. Whilst the severity remains static the monetary assessment can be altered by way of nodes set in the calibration. These nodes specify that for a particular severity level the monetary assessment will equal £x. There are a number of calibration nodes typically, with each system applying an algorithm to calculate the correct assessment for cases that do not fall directly on a node point but fall in-between two nodes.

Each system's ability to consistently rank severity without human intervention and any ensuing subjectivity flowing from that, along with a similar method of calibration, provided the basis for this proof of concept investigation."

4.4 <u>Comparison exercise.</u> The working party report also includes the results of an exercise to compare how the three software systems each assessed a series of hypothetical, low value cases. COA and Colossus achieved broadly similar results, although in some instances there were differences ranging between 5% and 13%. The same hypothetical cases were assessed by SMART Evaluate. In some instances SMART Evaluate's valuation was the same. In other instances there were discrepancies, somewhat larger than those between Colossus and COA. I express no view as to which system achieves the closest approximation to what a court would award.

5. ANALYSIS

5.1 It is necessary to approach the issues concerning quantum assessment tools with a measure of realism. The software already exists. It is used and will continue to be used by insurers for settling a large number of cases every year.

5.2 <u>Proposal for new working group.</u> In my view, work needs to be put in hand in order to ensure that all software systems in general use for assessing damages for PSLA are calibrated in a manner which approximates as closely as possible to the damages which the courts would award in those cases. The exercise recently undertaken by the working group shows that different software systems are capable of producing broadly consistent assessments. What now needs to be done is to set up a new working group comprising (a) two district judges with personal injury and IT

---

demonstrate correct and consistent compensation figures. Flexibility to make awards appropriate to individual claimants' injuries is essential.

expertise, (b) representatives of each software provider, (c) two claimant representatives (one from APIL and one from MASS), and (d) two representatives of liability insurers. Possibly the working group should also include a trade union representative and a consumer representative. The function of this new working group should be to establish a consistent calibration for all software systems. The calibration should accord as nearly as possible with the awards of general damages for PSLA up to £10,000, which would be made by the courts if cases were litigated. I accept that in some areas there are insufficient data to arrive at a reasonable calibration. However, the presence of two district judges on the working group should enable a reasonable view to be taken of the data derived from settled cases. I propose that this working group should be set up by the CJC and should operate under the auspices of the CJC.

5.3   I request that the working group should also consider the format of medical reports. If a particular format of medical report would assist in the effective use of properly calibrated software tools, please would the working group give appropriate guidance on how medical reports should be prepared? If the working group decides to give such guidance, I suggest that it should co-opt a medical representative.

5.4   <u>How should the recommendations of the new working group be used?</u> No software provider can be compelled to calibrate its software in a particular way. However, software systems which have been calibrated in accordance with the recommendations of the new working group are likely to be more widely used and to carry greater weight in negotiations. Those software tools should be made available to both claimant and defendant representatives.[57] Likewise medical practitioners and medical reporting organisations cannot be compelled to follow whatever guidelines the working group may give in respect of medical reports. On the other hand, solicitors may see fit to include those guidelines in any contracts which they make with medical practitioners. Furthermore, solicitors may decide only to deal with medical reporting organisations which follow those guidelines.

5.5   <u>How should the software tools be used in contested cases?</u> I quite accept that computers cannot replace judges. In any case which comes to a hearing the judge should assess general damages for PSLA by reference to the current tariff, reported judicial decisions and the circumstances of the particular case. The judge will consult text books and law reports, as now. The judge will also be free to have regard to the computer generated figure, if he or she sees fit. However, any figure for general damages derived from text books, law reports or software systems can only be a starting point. The judge will then adjust that figure as necessary, in order to take account of the particular features of the case before him or her.

5.6   <u>How should the software systems be used in settled cases?</u> The representatives on both sides negotiating a settlement will be able to derive a figure from their software systems, calibrated in accordance with the recommendations of the proposed working group. Hopefully this will assist the representatives in arriving at an appropriate settlement in the individual case. No computer generated figure will be the complete answer, since regard must be had to the particular circumstances of the claimant and the effect of the injuries upon him or her. Nevertheless, it is a fact of life that software systems already have a substantial influence over settlements. It is desirable that they should be calibrated as accurately and fairly as possible.

---

[57] Some software systems are already available to both parties: see PR paragraph 28.5.5.

5.7   <u>What benefits will the proposed calibration exercise achieve?</u> I foresee three benefits of the proposed calibration exercise. First, the software systems are likely to generate figures which are closer to the "correct" figures. This will reduce the risks of under-settlement which currently exist. Secondly, the settlement figures offered will be less dependent upon which insurer is involved or which software system is being used. Thirdly, settlement of quantum issues is likely to be achieved more rapidly and in a higher proportion of cases. Accordingly, costs will be saved.

5.8   <u>The longer term.</u> If this project is successful, some mechanism must be put in place for maintaining an appropriate calibration for all software systems which assess general damages for PSLA. Possibly the working group should remain in existence for a period in order to perform this function. Alternatively, it may be appropriate for some independent body, judicially chaired and including appropriate industry representatives, to perform this function. This body could be a committee of either the CJC or the JSB. In order to avoid any proliferation of quangos, it is important to work within existing structures.

6. RECOMMENDATION

6.1   I recommend that a working group be set up to establish a uniform calibration for all software systems used in assessment of damages for PSLA up to £10,000. That calibration should accord as nearly as possible with the awards of general damages that would be made by the courts.

CHAPTER 22. PERSONAL INJURIES LITIGATION: PROCESS AND PROCEDURE

INDEX

1. INTRODUCTION

1.1   Preliminary Report. Personal injuries litigation is discussed in Part 6 of the Preliminary Report. The process for personal injuries litigation and the costs of such litigation are reviewed in PR chapter 26. The new process being developed by the Ministry of Justice (the "MoJ") for handling personal injury claims arising out of road traffic accidents ("RTA claims") up to £10,000 where liability is admitted (the "new process") is also discussed in PR chapter 26.

1.2   Other abbreviations. In this chapter I shall refer to the Pre-Action Protocol for Personal Injury Claims as the "personal injury protocol" or the "protocol". I shall refer to the Civil Justice Council as the "CJC".

2. MEETINGS AND SEMINARS DURING PHASE 2

2.1   Forum of Insurance Lawyers Annual Seminar. On 10th June 2009 I attended the annual seminar of the Forum of Insurance Lawyers ("FOIL"). Concern was expressed by some speakers that personal injuries litigation was being conducted in a manner which was disproportionate to the issues and the amount at stake. It was suggested that judges should enforce orders more effectively and take more interest in costs issues. One insurer advocated more use of mediation in larger cases.

2.2   Manchester Law Society Civil Costs Conference. On 15th June 2009 I attended the Manchester Law Society's 8th Annual Civil Costs Conference. There was discussion about the new process and how this might dovetail in with any scheme for fixed costs emerging from the Costs Review. A wide range of views were expressed about the reforms canvassed in the Preliminary Report. One speaker warned against the danger of unintended consequences and a return to the costs war. Judge Richard Holman, Designated Civil Judge at Manchester, spoke in favour of fixing costs across the whole of the fast track, whereas others feared that such a scheme would lead to satellite litigation, for example over what "stage" had been reached when a case was concluded. Professor John Peysner spoke in favour of fixing fast track costs and commended the system of scale costs which formerly prevailed in the county court. He argued that in the multi-track there should be a regime of costs budgeting and costs capping. A number of practitioners spoke in favour of costs management. Judge Holman supported costs management (not least because it would reduce the number of detailed assessments) but warned that this would lead to longer case management conferences.

2.3   Cardiff seminar. At the Cardiff seminar on 19th June 2009 Mr David Fisher of AXA Insurance gave a presentation on costs issues.[58] In the course of his talk he said:

> "Coinciding with the withdrawal of legal aid and the introduction of CFAs[59] there has been an increase in the number of anonymous stakeholders involved in the injury claims process such as claims management companies, medical reporting agencies and the like. Many of these organisations layer costs into the process and cause inflationary pressures as the lawyer looks to recoup the referral fee paid. This is an example of the 'upward pressure on costs' that Hoffmann spoke of.[60] Is it more than a coincidence that the increase in fraud, particularly motor fraud, corresponds with the introduction of CFAs, additional liabilities and the layering of the process by these anonymous stakeholders?"

2.4   In the discussion which followed this presentation Mr Fisher said that the fee paid to a medical reporting organisation (an "MRO") for a medical report is normally £195. Typically, out of that £195 the sum of £50 is paid to the doctor, a referral fee of £50 is paid to the solicitors and about £100 is retained by the MRO. Other speakers challenged the split suggested by Mr Fisher. One speaker stated that MROs had streamlined the process of obtaining medical reports. A solicitor from a large personal injuries firm said that his firm had no "cash back" arrangements with MROs and he believed that they were cost effective.

2.5   Birmingham seminar. The Birmingham seminar on 26th June 2009 was primarily focused upon personal injuries litigation. Both Amanda Stevens[61] of the Association of Personal Injury Lawyers ("APIL") and Anthony Hughes[62] of FOIL presented papers, which can be seen on the Costs Review website.[63] Ms Stevens stressed that claimants must retain 100% of the damages awarded by the court, as full damages are necessary to achieve restoration. She stated that there were about 500,000 RTA claims per year under £10,000 and these would fall within the new process. That would leave about 250,000 claims per year which would fall outside the new process, which are less susceptible to standardisation. She argued that there should be effective sanctions against defendants who did not comply with the

---

[58] The presentation is available on the Costs Review website, at http://www.judiciary.gov.uk/docs/costs-review/costs-rules-influence-behaviour-liability-insurers.pdf.
[59] Conditional fee agreements.
[60] This is a reference to the speech of Lord Hoffmann in *Callery v Gray* [2002] UKHL 28.
[61] President of APIL until 23rd April 2009
[62] The then President of FOIL.
[63] At http://www.judiciary.gov.uk/docs/costs-review/costs-pi-litigation.pdf and
http://www.judiciary.gov.uk/docs/costs-review/costs-personal-injury-litigation.ppt respectively.

protocol (and thus failed to identify the issues) and that all personal injury cases should be managed by specialist district judges. In relation to quantum, she stated that APIL members have never failed to beat an offer based on "Colossus" or "Claims Outcome Advisor".[64] Mr Hughes argued that all costs in the fast track should be fixed. He accepted that there is a minimum amount of work to be done on all personal injury cases, but maintained that costs are at the moment disproportionate to the sums at stake and the nature of the cases. Something is going wrong with the majority of cases, not just the tip of the iceberg. The present conditional fee agreement regime tends to drive up costs.

2.6 In the discussion which followed those two presentations concern was expressed about both claimant and defendant behaviour. On the defendant side it was said that claimant solicitors issue applications for pre-action disclosure at the first opportunity, thus unnecessarily increasing costs. On the claimant side it was said that a number of insurers routinely do not comply with the protocol, so that an application to the court is the only way forward. One defence solicitor very fairly accepted that this does sometimes happen. There was then a discussion as to whether the protocol should be amended, either to permit pre-action applications or to impose a "show cause" procedure when defendants are in default. A district judge suggested that the procedure be amended so that a pre-action disclosure application could include an application for the defendant to send a proper response to the letter of claim. Possibly this should be dealt with on paper. The alternative view was that if the defendant did not comply with the protocol, the claimant should simply issue proceedings. However, the difficulty with this course was that the claimant would be issuing proceedings without knowing what the defendant's case was. There was a debate about the information provided by claimants. On one view they should provide more disclosure about quantum, even in cases where liability was denied. The Vice-President of APIL argued that there should be a procedure for paper applications to deal with non-compliance with the protocol and promised to provide a suggested draft. There was discussion whether the costs of such applications could be accommodated within a fast track fixed costs regime. There was a general view that docketing was desirable and discussion followed concerning the practicalities of docketing. A number of practitioners called for more effective case management of personal injury cases. In the panel session at the end of the day Professor Ian Scott, general editor of the White Book, argued that procedural reforms have always been driven by personal injuries litigation. It would be better to treat personal injuries litigation separately and make special provision for it in a specialist list within the CPR. The Vice-President of APIL expressed misgivings about this approach, but accepted that the new process was a move in that direction.

2.7 <u>Manchester seminar.</u>[65] Following a presentation by Judge Stephen Stewart, Designated Civil Judge for Merseyside, on the costs wars,[66] there was a debate about personal injuries litigation costs. One defendant solicitor explained that in the pre-issue period many insurers handle the negotiations themselves and only make "Colossus" offers which are too low; the insurers then instruct solicitors when proceedings are issued (or are about to be issued) with the result that the case comes out of the fixed recoverable costs regime.[67] He also expressed strong criticisms of claimant solicitors for costs building. A claimant solicitor stated that in his experience about 60% of insurers responded to a claimant's Part 36 offer within three weeks. In relation to the other insurers it was immensely difficult to talk to the

---

[64] As to which, see PR chapter 28, section 3.
[65] Held on 3rd July 2009.
[66] The presentation is available on the Costs Review website at http://www.judiciary.gov.uk/docs/costs-review/costs-wars.pdf.
[67] See CPR Part 45.

relevant people on the telephone or to discover what their position was. He accepted, however, that some claimant firms did engage in costs building. A district judge said that in his experience litigation solicitors always round up six minute units in their bills. If they spend seven minutes on a task, they will put that down as two six minute units. However, solicitors should round down as well as up. As at Birmingham, there was extensive discussion about docketing. Judge Stewart explained that docketing was achieved to some extent in Merseyside. Judge Holman said that there was a degree of docketing at Manchester. At Manchester there are three clinical negligence district judges, two industrial disease district judges and one district judge who deals with sexual abuse cases. This provides a degree of consistency. There was also discussion about the need for specialism. The view was expressed that there should be specialist judges for personal injuries and clinical negligence work.

2.8   Meeting with APIL. On 23ʳᵈ July 2009 representatives of APIL came to see me. They produced a proposal for pre-action applications to "show cause", as foreshadowed at the Birmingham seminar. They argued that there should be stricter enforcement of protocols and orders than happens at present, but there should not be the degree of rigour advocated by Professor Adrian Zuckerman at the Manchester seminar.[68] They urged that effective sanctions for non-compliance will be particularly important if fixed costs are introduced across the fast track.

3. WRITTEN SUBMISSIONS DURING PHASE 2

(i) Concerning process and procedure generally

3.1   Association of Personal Injury Lawyers. APIL maintains that there should be specialist judges to deal with personal injury cases. It believes that a good knowledge of personal injury law is more pertinent at case management stage than at trial. APIL states:

> "At case management stage, however, only a personal injury specialist may properly be able to quickly identify the relevant issues in a case and make directions as to the evidence to be produced accordingly.
>
> Specialist judges would be able to efficiently manage cases back to the protocol, by imposing sanctions where necessary, and forward to settlement or trial, by ensuring that the issues are narrowed and necessary evidence will be adduced.
>
> At the moment, however, it is possible to come before a judge who has never conducted a personal injury case while practising law, having spent all their career specialising in, for example, family law."

APIL also supports docketing for personal injury cases.[69]

3.2   Claimant criticisms of defendant conduct. Claimant criticisms of the conduct of liability insurers and their solicitors are recorded in PR paragraphs 10.13.4, 10.15.7, 10.17.13, 10.18.6 and 26.2.5. Similar criticisms have been voiced during Phase 2 of the Costs Review. The National Accident Helpline (the "NAH") believes that defendant insurer behaviour is one of the two most important factors that

---

[68] As to which see chapter 39 below, section 2.
[69] The question of specialist judges and docketing will be discussed in chapter 39 below.

determine the costs in a personal injury case.[70] Defendant insurers dedicate insufficient resources to early investigation. They do not use effective systems or promote a culture of sensible risk assessment. This leads to inordinate delay in the settlement of cases, even when it is clear that liability rests with the defendant. The NAH identifies a number of respects in which defendants (or their insurers) fail to comply with pre-action protocols, including: failing to respond properly (if at all) to claimants within the protocol period; using delay and obfuscation as a tactic; delaying admissions of liability; failing to provide pre-action disclosure; and making unreasonably low settlement offers. From the NAH's experience, costs significantly rise when defendants fail to admit liability or provide an early realistic settlement offer.

3.3   A personal injuries barrister states that it is defendant conduct more often than claimant conduct which leads to racking up of costs. He cites four alarming examples of cases where incompetence on the defence side (during the protocol period and during the proceedings) led to inflated costs before a sensible resolution was reached. He states that he encountered these four cases within the space of ten days. His analysis of the cause of this problem is as follows:

> "The reason that these unnecessary costs are incurred (and these matters are repeating many hundreds of times throughout the year) is not because too much is being spent on lawyers but because insurers are under investing in litigation. When representatives of the insurance industry are allowed to speak with candour, and asked why matters are defended so badly (a point readily conceded) , they reply that the wrong things are measured. There is a drive to keep overheads down, to delay payments (in some cases) and hope that cases will go away. It is often readily conceded that this is a false economy. Insurers have under-resourced their staff and driven down the costs of defending. This has led to junior staff handling cases (who have no real experience of the court and litigation process) and who are extremely overworked. I suspect that they are undervalued and underpaid."

3.4   Interestingly the same barrister also describes his experience of acting for defendants:

> "I have direct experience (on many occasions) of being instructed by defendants to attend trials and assessments of damages. The offers made by the defendant are clearly inadequate and yet my instructions are that I have no instructions or authority to negotiate because the figure has been calculated by 'computer'. I could (for usually a fairly nominal figure) negotiate a settlement prior to the hearing which would mean that the additional liability of 100% would not be incurred and there would be a saving in costs far higher than the additional sum in damages. However I am not allowed to do so. It is made clear that there is no point seeking instructions because those instructing me have no power in the matter. On any proper commercial basis this is nonsensical."

The author adds that his comments are not an attack on the insurance industry as a whole. In major personal injury and clinical negligence cases the defendants' lawyers appear to be properly resourced and are of considerable experience.

3.5   <u>Defendant criticisms of claimant conduct.</u> Liability insurers and their solicitors maintain that it is abuses by claimant lawyers, rather than defendant

---

[70] The second important factor is the nature and complexity of a case.

conduct, which drive up the costs of personal injuries litigation. See PR paragraphs 10.10.3 and 26.2.8 to 26.2.13. The Liverpool district judges made similar comments: see PR paragraphs 10.17.3 to 10.17.9. FOIL rejects the assertion that there is any systemic failure by insurers to comply with the protocol. On the contrary, many of its members take the view that the pre-action protocol regime has been abused by claimants. In some cases the process has become a "*profit centre*" in its own right, for example, through applications for pre-action disclosure. FOIL members have their own experience of claimants failing to produce information as required, or treating the pre-action stage as a "*hoop to jump through to enable proceedings to be commenced and costs increased*". A major concern of FOIL is claimant behaviour which is led by the desire to increase profitability or reach the next costs stage in a fixed costs situation rather than by a wish to resolve the case proportionately. The incentives for such behaviour will increase if fixed costs are introduced across the fast track. FOIL believes that the courts must adopt a tough approach to deter such behaviour.

3.6   Individual firms of defendant solicitors make similar criticisms of claimant conduct. One firm states that the abuses which it sees most often in the fast track are:

- Failure to disclose the medical evidence until after proceedings are issued.

- Failure to disclose a full and final detailed schedule of loss until after proceedings are issued.

- Failure to disclose documentary evidence in support of losses until after proceedings are issued.

- Failure to negotiate and/or make any offer of settlement until after proceedings are issued.

- Failure to respond to an offer of settlement until after proceedings are issued.

3.7   The middle view. The Institute of Legal Executives believes that there is force in the criticisms made by both sides. It states:

> "However, there is no escaping the fact that there appears to be fault on both sides of the fence, in particular in relation to personal injuries (PI) litigation. Some Claimant solicitors will tend to cost build, others not; some Defendant insurers (and claim handlers) will review cases sensibly, making admissions of liability where appropriate within the protocol periods and/or narrowing the issues between the parties and in personal injury cases co-operate with the Claimant's lawyer to ensure that the Claimant's rehabilitation needs are assessed and met as soon as possible; others simply maintain unreasonable denials of liability, particularly in PI and insurance backed work."

3.8   A firm of solicitors which acts for both claimants and defendants states that some claimant lawyers generate unnecessary costs by investigating liability, when that is not required. It also states that over the years the insurance industry has been losing skilled claims managers and negotiators; they are replaced by young and inexperienced staff, who are unable or unauthorised to take the decisions necessary to achieve prompt and efficacious settlements.

(ii) Concerning the new process

3.9   The view that the new process should be extended. One liability insurer states that it supports the new process. However, its objectives could be taken to a far more satisfactory conclusion with the successful delivery of the key aims of the Costs Review. It does not feel that the costs proposals of the new process are radical enough and it states that no costs sanctions are proposed for claimants. The Manchester Law Society is concerned that the proposals from the present Costs Review will overlap with the new process; therefore the new process is likely to be a short lived affair. The Manchester Law Society suggests a total suspension of one or the other or a road map for dovetailing the two. A firm of defence solicitors believes that the new process should be extended to employers' liability (excluding disease) and public liability cases.

3.10   The Lloyd's Market Association (the "LMA") represents all businesses which underwrite insurance at Lloyd's of London. It writes:

> "We were very disappointed with several aspects of the MoJ reforms to date, not least the abject failure to introduce measures to reduce unnecessary costs such as referral fees and ATE[71] premiums, and the complete absence of any retained risk for claimant representatives."

The LMA considers that any successful proposals arising from the present Costs Review should dovetail in with the MoJ's new process.

3.11   <u>The opposite view.</u> APIL points out that stakeholders have devoted an enormous amount of time to developing the new process, which is specifically designed for RTA claims under £10,000 where liability is conceded. APIL believes that the new process (due for implementation in April 2010) should be allowed to bed in and that it should not be extended to other forms of personal injury claims. The Law Society expresses similar views. The Law Society is critical of the Preliminary Report for venturing to suggest that the MoJ's new process might possibly be dovetailed with any reforms from this review which are adopted.[72]

3.12   <u>Risks of abuse.</u> A firm of defence solicitors identifies numerous methods by which astute claimant solicitors could exploit the new process in order to increase their costs recovery. It states that the Civil Procedure Rule Committee must take such matters into account when formulating the new rules.

(iii) The Pre-Action Protocol for Personal Injury Claims

3.13   A firm of solicitors with long experience of both claimant and defendant work recommends the following reforms to the protocol in respect of fast track personal injury claims:

- In all fast track claims (i.e. up to £25,000) the defendant cannot obtain its own medical report unless there are truly exceptional circumstances.

- If the defendant wishes to raise questions of the medical expert, it must do so within 28 days of receiving the expert's report. In the absence of any objections being made or questions being asked by the defendant within 28 days of service, the defendant should be taken to agree to the medical report (save in truly exceptional circumstances).

---

[71] After-the-event insurance.

[72] See PR paragraph 26.3.8 and the Law Society's Response paragraph 6.3, available online at http://www.lawsociety.org.uk/secure/file/181240/e:/teamsite-deployed/documents/templatedata/Internet%20Documents/Non-government%20proposals/Documents/response-review-civil-litigation-costs-jul09.pdf.

- The claimant should serve a schedule of losses pre-action which cannot subsequently be varied (except for the addition of new items of loss incurred since the schedule) save in truly exceptional circumstances. The defendant must respond to the schedule within 28 days, stating which items are agreed, which disputed and why and where further proof is required. To the extent the defendant fails to respond, it will be deemed to admit that part of the claim.

- Before issuing proceedings the parties should prepare a joint statement of the issues between them that are preventing a settlement. The statement will be binding on the parties in relation to issues.

- Claimant solicitors should propose informal mediation to attempt to settle the claim pre-action, with the defendants to be given a limited period in which to agree to the proposal. If this is agreed, then the parties would be referred to a new national mediation service with facilities for cost effective medication.

(iv) The Personal Injury Multi-Track Code

3.14 The Personal Injury Multi-Track Code (the "Multi-Track Code") for handling personal injury claims above £250,000 was agreed between APIL, FOIL and a number of insurers. This has been piloted since July 2008: see PR paragraph 10.9.21. This Code contains important provisions concerning early notification, collaboration between the parties, rehabilitation and similar matters.

3.15 One defence solicitor states:

"This initiative between APIL, FOIL, several major insurers and the MIB[73] is still in its infancy but it has demonstrated the benefits that can be derived by early and effective engagement, as opposed to a relationship that hides behind correspondence that might comply with the letter of the protocol but still fails to advance the case effectively or in a cost effective manner."

3.16 APIL informs me[74] that the Multi-Track Code has been working well. The claims handlers involved for insurers in these cases are of a higher standard than those dealing with lower value cases. The pilot has recently been extended, so that it will run for a period of between 18 months and two years. According to an interim report on the pilot dated 24th November 2009, the feedback from all parties is positive. The process is becoming less adversarial; there is earlier access to rehabilitation and greater structure is being achieved in cases from an earlier stage.

(v) Medical reporting organisations

3.17 _Emergence of medical reporting organisations._ MROs are a relatively recent arrival on the personal injuries litigation scene. Their use is sanctioned by paragraph 2.15 of the protocol: _"Some solicitors choose to obtain medical reports through medical agencies, rather than directly from a specific doctor or hospital."_ The use of MROs has expanded since the decision in _Woollard v Fowler._[75]

3.18 _Circuit judge._ A circuit judge with long experience of personal injuries litigation writes:

---

[73] The Motor Insurers' Bureau.

[74] At a meeting on 26th January 2009.

[75] A decision of Senior Costs Judge Peter Hurst, sitting as a recorder in the Weston-super-Mare County Court, dated 24th May 2006. The Senior Costs Judge held that fees paid to an MRO were recoverable as a disbursement under the fixed recoverable costs scheme set out in section II of CPR Part 45.

"There is no doubt that [medical agencies] add to the cost of personal injury litigation. In my experience they do not add value to the process and their use leads to delay and unnecessary expense. When I was in practice I never used one and I am not sure that they even existed. You went straight to the doctor for a medical report. The rationale most commonly advanced to me by practitioners for using them is that their clients are not necessarily based locally and they do not know of suitable experts in the area where the client lives. However, it is not as though this never happened years ago (although it was rarer) and the solution was simple. You rang up a leading firm in the locality, spoke to someone in the litigation department and found out who they used. 5 minutes work!

As to delay, everything has to go through the agency. Generally the solicitor is barred from direct contact with the expert. Thus another link into the chain is introduced...

As to cost, there is no transparency about charges. An invoice is presented as the fee for the report, but no breakdown is provided between the fee received by the doctor and the fee charged by the agency."

3.19   MROs. A number of MROs have sent in helpful and detailed submissions concerning the services which they render. These include providing a "one stop shop" for obtaining medical evidence all around the UK by creating expert panels; arranging medical appointments; undertaking all the work associated with obtaining medical evidence; obtaining medial records; negotiating fixed rates with general practitioners ("GPs") and consultants for medical reports; developing report writing software.

3.20   Letter from the Association of Medical Reporting Organisations. The Association of Medical Reporting Organisations ("AMRO") has a membership which provides over 85% of all medico-legal reports required per year. It has sent in a very full account of its history and its activities. During Phase 2 of the Costs Review I enquired of the chairman of AMRO whether it was the case that less than half the fees charged by MROs were paid to the doctors who wrote the reports. The chairman sent a letter in response outlining the negotiations leading up to the agreement reached between the MROs and numerous liability insurers in April 2009. He then stated:

"As a consequence of these process changes, terms have been renegotiated with some experts resulting in a lower report price to the MRO, who in return could offer shorter payment terms, often 30 to 90 days from completion of the report and guaranteed volumes of work for the expert.

The agreement has therefore, in a significant number of cases, resulted in expert's fees becoming a smaller proportion of the whole fee than that of the MRO but only ever in the case of GP reports. The differential for other expert specialties, predominantly Consultant Orthopaedic Surgeons and Consultants in Accident and Emergency Medicine remains in favour of the expert."

A large number of medical reports are now written by GPs. AMRO points out that many of the overheads[76] which would normally be reflected in the GPs' fees have effectively been outsourced to the MROs.

---

[76] For example, secretarial and administration, access to report writing and case management software, in many cases provision of consulting rooms and funding arrangements.

3.21   General practitioners.   Some GPs are concerned that MROs have too much power.   AMRO states that it has "*some sympathy*" with this general assertion. However, AMRO points out that some medical experts have become dependent on instructions from MROs, because those experts cannot provide, for an acceptable fee, the services which MROs collectively provide.[77]   One GP has written to the Costs Review, expressing concern that such a low proportion of MROs' fees is paid to the doctor. He states:

> "The commercial firms [i.e. MROs] have large staff and overheads and offer the benefit to solicitors that they usually have databases of doctors throughout the country and can assist when clients are widespread. On the other hand, they introduce a third party into the relationship so that authority (for example to obtain authority for additional investigations such as X ray reports) has to be passed through the agency who will then communicate with the solicitor; this frequently generates delay to such extent that the patient has to return on a second occasion rather than undertake the test on the same day.

> Commercial operations will usually have arrangements to pay a referral fee to the supplier of the work...

> Those firms that are members of AMRO appear to be paying the least to the Doctor.   Often they will only pay 35-50% of the agreed rate for early payment."

4. FAST TRACK CASES

(i) The MoJ's new process

4.1   Preliminary Report.   In the Preliminary Report I expressed the view that a process along the lines set out by the Department of Constitutional Affairs in its consultation paper dated April 2007 made good sense.[78]   The original proposal would have encompassed all personal injury claims in the fast track where liability was admitted.

4.2   The MoJ's current proposals.   The MoJ's current proposals are the product of lengthy negotiations between claimant representatives and the representatives of liability insurers, which have been hosted and mediated by the CJC.   The MoJ proposes a new process for handling RTA claims up to £10,000 where liability is admitted.   At the time of drafting this chapter the proposed new process is set out in drafts of a new protocol, new rules, new practice direction provisions and new forms. These documents are still evolving.

4.3   Concerns.   I have two concerns about the new process in its present form.   My first concern is the sheer complexity of the process.   Over 80 pages of new material will be added to the rule book, in order to deal with the simplest category of litigation which exists, namely low value RTA claims where liability is admitted.   I fear that collectively these procedures might possibly open up a new theatre for the costs war. As stated in chapter 1 of this report, one reason for high costs is the complexity and length of the rules.   We should now be looking for ways to simplify the rules, rather

---

[77] Also AMRO states that it is easier for a doctor to deal with five or six MROs than a large number of solicitors' firms.
[78] See PR paragraphs 26.3.1 to 26.3.8.

than add to their volume. My second concern is that the new process, contrary to the original intention, does not embrace all categories of personal injury claims, in particular employers' liability and public liability claims, nor does it apply to the whole of the fast track.

4.4   <u>The way forward.</u> Having expressed my two concerns, I recognise that a huge amount of work has gone into the new process and that, if it works smoothly, it will achieve significant costs savings in relation to low value RTA claims. The MoJ plans to implement the new process during 2010 and all stakeholder groups have been gearing up for that event. In my view, the right course now is for the new process to be implemented in the form that is emerging. However, it will be necessary to keep the operation of the new process under review, in order to ensure that the costs savings which it achieves are not negated by satellite litigation and avoidance behaviour.

4.5   Amendments will have to be made to that new process subsequently if my recommendations for abolishing recoverability of success fees and ATE insurance premiums are accepted.

(ii) Fast track personal injury cases outside the MoJ's new process

4.6   In chapter 15 above I recommend that there should be fixed costs for all personal injury cases in the fast track. I also recommend a matrix of fixed costs for such cases. If these recommendations are accepted, both claimant lawyers and defendant lawyers will wish to co-operate in order to ensure that all fast track personal injury cases are progressed both efficiently and fairly within the expanded fixed costs regime.

4.7   I recommend that there be discussions between claimant and defendant representatives, under the aegis of the CJC, in order to develop a streamlined process for all fast track personal injury cases which fall outside the MoJ's new process. I recommend that the parties should aim for a procedure which is much simpler and much shorter than that devised for the new process. It is neither practical nor necessary to spell out every little detail of what must be done in every situation.

5. MULTI-TRACK CASES

5.1   <u>Multi-Track Code.</u> By all accounts the Multi-Track Code, which has been piloted since July 2008, is proving successful.[79] It promotes speedier resolution of cases at lower overall costs.

5.2   The Multi-Track Code applies to cases valued over £250,000 where solicitors were instructed after 1st June 2008. Pilot testing of the Code has involved 25 claimant firms, six major insurers and the MIB. Although to date the number of cases in the pilot is less than 30, I understand that the firms and insurers involved are positive about the benefits of using the Code. I also understand that some firms that are not within the pilot are also adopting the spirit of the Code. One of the underlying aims of the Code is to focus on rehabilitation of the injured claimant, agreed timetables and case planning that promotes resolution by negotiation rather than trial.

---

[79] The pilot will run until early or mid 2010: see paragraph 3.16 above.

5.3   The Multi-Track Code will no doubt be finalised after the results of the pilot have been collated and analysed. I support the aims of the Code and welcome the progress that has been made in that regard. It is, however, debatable, whether that Code should be embodied in the CPR or practice directions. Those documents have already attained considerable length. The Code has been drawn up jointly by APIL and FOIL. I see no reason why it should not remain a voluntary code drawn up by those two bodies. No doubt APIL and FOIL will encourage all their members to subscribe to that Code. Having attended conferences and meetings with the members of both those bodies, I have no doubt that the members will be quite willing to subscribe to the Code, which is in the best interests of their respective clients. In the unlikely event that the Code is not generally accepted, then this issue can be re-visited.

5.4   Costs management. Costs management is discussed in chapter 40 below. I recommend that the judge should decide in any individual case whether to adopt costs management as an adjunct to case management. This course would be appropriate in any case where there appears to be a risk of costs becoming disproportionate either to the sum at stake or to the complexity of the case.

5.5   In chapter 23 below I make proposals for costs management of clinical negligence claims, including costs management pre-issue. Clinical negligence litigation is a subset of personal injuries litigation, where the risk of disproportionate costs is particularly significant. In chapter 23 I propose a pilot of costs management in respect of clinical negligence litigation. When the results of any such pilot exercise are known, consideration should be given to drawing up a scheme for costs management of all "heavy" personal injury cases, both pre-issue and post-issue.

6. REHABILITATION

6.1   Good progress has been made in recent years in recognising that the physical and mental rehabilitation from injury is a central part of post-accident recovery alongside the monetary compensation needs of a claimant. The personal injury protocol makes reference to rehabilitation and the Rehabilitation Code.[80] The protocol is currently under review to reflect the new process.

6.2   Organisations that have played their part in raising awareness of the importance of rehabilitation include:

(i)   The Ministry of Justice. The Claims Notification Form in the new process includes a short rehabilitation section asking whether the claimant has been medically advised to undergo treatment and, if so, requesting details of the provider. If no treatment has been undertaken the claimant's solicitor can raise the question of rehabilitation with the insurer.

(ii)   The UK Rehabilitation Council. This body, comprised mainly of health care providers, is supported by the MoJ and the National Health Service as well as the Department of Work and Pensions (the "DWP"). The DWP has provided funding for the production of quality standards for rehabilitation to satisfy PAS150 (British Standards Institute) by Spring 2010. The Council is not

---

[80] At paragraph 4. The Rehabilitation Code is a code of best practice, endorsed by both claimant and insurer organisations, whose aim is *"to promote the use of rehabilitation and early intervention in the compensation process so that the injured person makes the best and quickest possible medical, social and psychological recovery"*. The Rehabilitation Code is attached to the personal injury protocol at Annex D.

currently involved in rehabilitation issues relating to the process of compensation for injury.

(iii)   The International Underwriting Association of London and the Association of British Insurers. These bodies were responsible for the Rehabilitation Code.

(iv)   The British Association of Rehabilitation Companies. This body represents approximately 20 commercial intermediaries who source rehabilitation service providers in personal injury claims.

(v)   The Case Management Society of the UK. This is a non-profit association of case managers who assist in addressing the rehabilitation needs of an injured claimant who is seeking compensation.

(vi)   The Bodily Injury Claims Management Association. This body comprises approximately 20 individuals from claimant and defendant solicitors firms, insurers, the Bar and the judiciary. It was closely involved in development of the Rehabilitation Code. It promotes early post-accident intervention and awareness of the benefits of rehabilitation. In 2008 it established a telephone mediation scheme to resolve within seven days of referral any issues arising from the "Initial Needs Assessment". It has also produced a set of quality standards that have been subscribed to by over 100 rehabilitation providers.

(vi)   The Civil Justice Council. The CJC has played a part in liaising with rehabilitation organisations including those listed here through its rehabilitation sub committee.

6.3   The above list clearly demonstrates that a great deal of attention is rightly being given to the importance of helping an injured person to recover and (where appropriate) return to work as soon as reasonably possible. To be rehabilitated, so that he or she can do so, is plainly in the health and welfare interests of the injured person. It is also in the interests of the wider economy (hence the support of Government departments). Rehabilitation is an essential part of the overall cost of the compensation process.

6.4   Substantial benefit could be gained by encouraging co-ordination of effort between the public and private sector rehabilitation organisations referred to above. I would also urge all stakeholders involved in personal injury claims to support the Rehabilitation Code and to take rehabilitation seriously, as an essential ingredient of the proper conduct of personal injury claims within the civil justice system. No doubt the CJC will continue to take the lead in encouraging this approach. I do not therefore make any recommendation in respect of rehabilitation.

7. OTHER ISSUES

(i) Protocol issues

7.1   <u>Medical evidence in fast track personal injury cases.</u> Paragraph 2.14 of the protocol is intended to promote the use of one medical expert only in lower value personal injury cases. Concerns have been expressed that this is not working effectively: see paragraph 3.13 above and chapter 38 below at paragraph 3.10. In my view there is force in the proposal that the defendant should have a limited period in which to put questions to the claimant's expert. There is also force in the proposal that the defendant, having approved the claimant's choice of medical expert, should not then instruct a separate expert without good reason. The CJC is about to embark upon a review of protocols. No doubt the CJC will take these matters into account in the course of its review. Therefore I do not make this issue the subject of any separate recommendation.

7.2   The protocol generally. It is clear from all the submissions which I have received that the personal injury protocol has been a success. The front loading of costs which it has generated is more than offset by the number of early settlements (and better informed settlements) which it promotes. Indeed the drop off in contested personal injuries litigation since April 1999, when the protocol came into force, bears witness to this fact. Nevertheless, there are concerns about compliance with the protocol. I address these concerns in chapter 39 below.

(ii) Medical reporting organisations

7.3   Yet another group of middlemen? MROs are yet another group of middlemen who have recently arrived upon the scene and draw remuneration from the personal injuries process. They are enabled to do so because the rules permit their fees to be recoverable as a disbursement.

7.4   Rule change not recommended at the moment. My initial inclination was that the rules should be changed, so that fees paid to medical practitioners should be recoverable as a disbursement, but fees paid to MROs should not be so recoverable. However, having considered the evidence with the assistance of my assessors, I am persuaded that the intervention of MROs has had the overall effect of controlling the costs of obtaining medical evidence in personal injury cases. Therefore I do not, at the moment, recommend any change in the rules so as to reverse the effect of *Woollard v Fowler*.[81]

7.5   Need for continuing scrutiny. The effect of MROs upon the costs of personal injuries litigation is a matter which must be kept under close scrutiny. I would suggest that such scrutiny is carried out by the Costs Council, if one is established.[82] If ever it appears that the involvement of MROs is increasing the costs of the personal injuries process, then serious consideration should be given to rule change. In that event, the appropriate course might be for the rules to provide that the only fees recoverable for an expert report are the fees properly charged by the expert, as evidenced by an invoice from the expert.

7.6   Contact between solicitor and medical practitioner. The comment has been made from a number of sources that sometimes MROs do not permit direct contact between solicitors and the medical practitioners whom MROs instruct on behalf of those solicitors. In my view, such a restriction is contrary to the public interest. It is liable to cause delay and increased costs. I therefore recommend that direct communication should always be permitted between a solicitor and any medical expert whom the MRO instructs on behalf of that solicitor. This matter should be dealt with in the MRO Agreement,[83] when that agreement comes to be renegotiated in March 2010.

8. RECOMMENDATIONS AND CONCLUSION

8.1   Recommendations. I make the following recommendations:

---

[81] See paragraph 3.17 above.
[82] As recommended in chapter 6 above.
[83] Defined in paragraph 1.3 of chapter 15 above.

(i)   The new process for low value RTA claims should be monitored to ensure that the costs savings achieved are not negated by satellite litigation and avoidance behaviour.

(ii)   There should be discussions between claimant and defendant representatives, under the aegis of the CJC, in order to develop a streamlined process for all fast track personal injury cases which fall outside the MoJ's new process.

(iii)   The effect of MROs upon the costs of personal injuries litigation should be kept under close scrutiny.

(iv)   Direct communication should always be permitted between a solicitor and any medical expert whom an MRO instructs on behalf of that solicitor.

8.2   <u>Recommendations made elsewhere.</u> A number of the concerns which have been identified in this chapter will be dealt with by recommendations in later chapters. In particular, I shall make proposals for the use of specialist judges and docketing in chapter 39 below. I shall also make proposals in that chapter to deal with non-compliance with protocols.

8.3   <u>Support for recent initiatives.</u> In the course of this chapter I have expressed support for a number of recent initiatives, in particular in respect of the Multi-Track Code and rehabilitation. Whilst placing my opinion on record, I do not make any specific recommendations in respect of those matters.

CHAPTER 23. CLINICAL NEGLIGENCE

INDEX

1. INTRODUCTION

1.1   <u>Preliminary Report.</u> Data provided by the Legal Services Commission (the "LSC") and the Compensation Recovery Unit (the "CRU") concerning success rates and costs in clinical negligence cases are reviewed in chapter 6 of the Preliminary Report. Data provided by the National Health Service Litigation Authority (the "NHSLA"), the Medical Protection Society (the "MPS") and the Association of Personal Injury Lawyers ("APIL") concerning clinical negligence cases are reviewed in chapter 11 of the Preliminary Report.

1.2   <u>Definitions.</u> In this chapter I refer to the Pre-Action Protocol for the Resolution of Clinical Disputes as the "clinical disputes protocol" or the "protocol". Annex B to the protocol is entitled "A Protocol for Obtaining Hospital Medical Records". The purpose of this annex is to standardise and streamline the procedure for obtaining medical records. It sets out helpful information about forms to be used, charges to be made, quality of copying and so forth.

1.3   <u>The costs of clinical negligence litigation which are borne by the general public.</u> According to the NHSLA's most recent annual report,[84] the total sums paid out by the NHSLA in clinical negligence cases in the last three years are as follows:

2006/07	£579,391,000
2007/08	£633,325,000
2008/09	£769,225,000

These figures include both damages and costs. I am told that, on the present figures, there will be a further increase in respect of the year 2009/2010. The level of damages and costs paid out is analysed in the NHSLA accounts by cases settled in the year as this provides a more meaningful comparison on the ratio of costs to damages (as all the costs of a case are captured and timing differences are excluded). Taking

---

[84]NHSLA Annual Report and Accounts 2009, available online at http://www.nhsla.com/Publications/.

the data for cases settled in the financial year 2008/09 (rather than the total sums paid out), the breakdown is as follows:

Damages paid to claimants	£312,454,000
Costs paid to claimant solicitors	£103,632,000
Costs paid to own solicitors	£39,638,000
Total	£455,744,000

It should be noted that these figures relate to the NHSLA alone. These figures do not take account of the damages and costs paid out by other medical defence organisations. It should also be noted that a significant part of the costs paid out by the NHSLA to claimant solicitors relates to success fees and after-the-event ("ATE") insurance premiums: see section 9 of chapter 2 above.

1.4   Two objectives. There are two objectives which have to be borne in mind in relation to this area of litigation. First, patients who have been injured as a result of clinical negligence must have access to justice, so that they can receive proper compensation. Secondly, this huge area of public expenditure must be kept under proper control, so that the resources of the health service are not being squandered unnecessarily on litigation costs.

1.5   Achieving the two objectives. The general reforms proposed in Part 2 of this report will assist in achieving those objectives. In this chapter I shall concentrate on issues specific to clinical negligence litigation, with the same two objectives in mind.

2. MEETINGS AND SEMINARS DURING PHASE 2

2.1   Meeting with defendant lawyers. On 22nd May 2009 I attended a meeting with clinical negligence defence lawyers. They made the following points. Claimant lawyers run up huge costs pre-issue, often unnecessarily. There should be some mechanism to control these costs. The protocol currently gives claimant lawyers a mandate to front load. The defendant seldom has any advance notice of a claim before the letter of claim arrives. Claimant hourly rates are excessive and substantially above defendant hourly rates. The delay in paying claimant solicitors for their work justifies some differential, but nothing remotely like the present differential. The Advisory Committee on Civil Costs sets rates which are too high, both because they are substantially above the rates set by the market for this sector and because they produce bills disproportionate to the sums at stake. Claimant solicitors enter into conditional fee agreements ("CFAs") on day one, before investigating, and justify 100% success fees on this basis. The solicitors then inflate base costs by costs building. The court should undertake costs management and limit the recoverable costs of both sides. Clinical negligence cases must be managed and tried by specialist judges. There must be docketing, as currently happens in London and Manchester. There should be standard directions for clinical negligence cases, which are used nationally.

2.2   Meeting with claimant lawyers. On 12th June 2009 I attended a meeting with claimant clinical negligence lawyers. The claimant lawyers made the following points during the meeting. There are about one million adverse incidents in healthcare per year, of which less than 1% result in claims. So there is an access to justice gap, in that many people with good claims do not pursue them. It is feared that any reforms resulting from the Costs Review will further erode the number of claimants. The comparison drawn between the charges of claimant lawyers and defendant lawyers in clinical negligence is unfair for a number of reasons. It should also be noted, however, that rates paid by the NHSLA, the Medical Defence Union (the "MDU") and the MPS are so low that many good firms are refusing to do clinical negligence defence work. Costs are run up because the NHSLA does not investigate early. The NHSLA and other defendant organisations often refuse to admit liability in respect of strong claims until late in the day. Indeed many cases settle at roundtable conferences shortly before trial, because that is when the defence team (possibly with leading counsel recently instructed) has fully considered the issues. When claimants' offers are successful (i.e. they are in line with the final judgment, despite having been rejected by the defendant), claimants do not get adequate or consistent support from the courts, e.g. indemnity costs.[85] Defendants often fail to comply with the protocol. This causes real problems for claimants. A claimant needs to know what the defendant's case is before issuing proceedings. There should be stronger penalties for non-compliance with the protocol. Two particular problems at the moment are that (i) records are often not provided within 40 days as required by the protocol; and (ii) defendants often delay in sending their letters of response beyond the three month period allowed by the protocol.

2.3   I enquired of the claimant lawyers whether some firms "cherry picked", so that in effect they made a handsome profit from doing cases on CFAs. One lawyer said yes, this did happen. Others said no, it did not. They advised me that no firm would be likely to open up its accounts, so as to enable this to be investigated. This was because (a) there would be significant difficulties about client confidentiality and (b) merely opening accounts would not give a proper analysis of the issues within this area. In relation to case management, the point was made that it is now harder to get trial dates at the start of a case. The claimant lawyers would welcome the harmonisation of case management directions for clinical negligence claims. They commented that at the moment Master Ungley's directions are used in London, but not at all court centres around the country. They also stated that the trial date should be fixed at the start of a case, since this would drive the process to a conclusion.

2.4   Meeting with APIL. On 23rd July 2009 representatives of APIL came to see me. They expressed particular concern about the clinical disputes protocol. They stated that this protocol is honoured far more in the breach than in the observance.

3. WRITTEN SUBMISSIONS DURING PHASE 2

3.1   Papers on costs budgeting. The senior partner of a firm specialising in clinical negligence defence work has submitted two papers entitled "Costs Budgets – A Call for Action". The thesis of these two papers is that high litigation costs are deterring parties from proceeding to trial. Claimant hourly rates are grossly distorted and then multiplied by two as a result of success fees. The effect of the protocol is that work is done twice over. Courts must control costs in the manner proposed by Professor John Peysner.[86] Sometimes recoverable costs are capped in order to promote access to justice: see R (on the application of Campaign for Nuclear Disarmament) v Prime Minister [2002] EWHC 2712 and the Corner House line of cases.[87] The same principles should be applied to clinical negligence. The author then sets out detailed proposals for costs budgeting in clinical negligence cases, both before and after issue.

3.2   Medical Defence Union. The MDU supports the proposals for costs budgeting referred to in the previous paragraph. The MDU is also concerned that case

---

[85] I shall take this point up in chapter 41 below.
[86] In his article entitled "Predictability and Budgeting", [2004] 23 CJQ 15; see PR paragraphs 48.3.13 and 48.3.14.
[87] See PR paragraphs 35.3.4 to 35.3.7.

management should be more effective than it currently is. Therefore the MDU presses for docketing and for specialist judges to manage and try clinical negligence cases. The MDU also proposes that there should be standardised case management directions for clinical negligence cases, to be applied nationally. The MDU does not support increased sanctions for breaches of orders, because very often such breaches are due to difficulty in getting information or reports from practising clinicians. It believes that the best course is to provide for ready access to the courts for dealing with such matters. The MDU encourages the use of telephone hearings.

3.3   In relation to protocols, the MDU states:

> "Overall, the clinical disputes pre-action protocol has been beneficial but it has undoubtedly become very costly, with disproportionate frontloading of costs. In clinical negligence actions claimants' pre-action costs can be considerable: examples of costs we have seen fall between £50,000 - £100,000. Work undertaken pre-action bears no scrutiny by the court until the conclusion of the action. Parties cannot access the court if a matter is not being progressed."

The MDU maintains that if costs budgeting were introduced pre-action, most clinical negligence cases could be investigated on a budget of £5,000 to £7,500. It adds that in only 20% of cases does it know that a claim is on the way before actually receiving a letter of claim.

3.4   In relation to settlement, the MDU states that it is sometimes instructed to settle a claim, but not to make any formal admission of liability. It therefore proposes that a provision be added to the protocol to the following effect. If during the pre-action phase a defendant indicates a firm desire to settle with no admissions, there should be a three month moratorium on the issue of proceedings with costs penalties if the claimant is in breach.

3.5   <u>Medical Protection Society.</u> The MPS makes a number of points which are similar to those of the MDU. In addition the MPS proposes that the protocol should allow six months for the defendant's letter of response, instead of three months. Defendants cannot prepare for clinical negligence claims before claimants articulate them. The MPS also discusses a number of wider issues. It states:

> "It is also important to consider that in personal injury and clinical negligence cases justice, for both claimants and defendants, may also include outcomes often not delivered by the adversarial system within the civil courts. Outcomes such as being heard, acknowledged, understood, reconciled, receiving non-financial redress or ensuring that risks are identified, addressed and better managed in future. MPS believes that any system of civil justice needs to promote and protect the possibility of such outcomes. They can be achieved by redress or Ombudsman schemes wholly outside the civil courts or by processes linked to the civil courts, such as pre-action dialogue or mid-litigation ADR.[88]"

3.6   The MPS does not regard damages as inviolable and believes that claimants should have a stake in the costs of the litigation. The MPS emphasises the importance of early resolution of clinical negligence claims, not only for the sake of the claimants but also for the sake of the clinicians, who may be greatly affected by the incident in question.

---

[88] Alternative dispute resolution.

3.7　Action against Medical Accidents.　Action against Medical Accidents ("AvMA") is a charity which provides advice and support for patients and their families who have been affected by medical accidents. They make the point that they need skilled solicitors, who can run their practices and survive in the commercial world. AvMA recognises the need to review the system to reduce unnecessary costs. AvMA supports the continuance of legal aid for clinical negligence cases and believes that financial eligibility limits should be raised, so that fewer clinical negligence cases are conducted on CFAs. AvMA accepts that some legally aided claimants suffer deductions from their damages. AvMA recommends that consideration be given to implementing the NHS Redress Act 2006 (the "2006 Act"). AvMA is concerned about global settlements, which may put solicitors in conflict with their clients. There is an irreducible minimum of work that must be done, which includes getting at least two expert reports in order to cover liability and causation. Disclosure takes longer than it should, with repeated requests for copies of documents, the originals of which are held by defendants. In relation to costs management, AvMA states:

> "Provided the budget was set by experienced judges at the CMC[89] on an individual case basis, the addition of certainty may be of advantage to a claimant."

3.8　In relation to the protocol, AvMA's members report considerable variations in compliance. They report problems of incomplete disclosure and sometimes outright refusal when documents concerning an untoward incident are requested. There are often delays in responding to the letter of claim. Frequently claimant solicitors are contacted three months after the letter of claim by defendant solicitors, who say that they have only just been instructed. Defendant lawyers then seek extensions of three or even six months before sending letters of response. These delays increase costs and may damage the relationship between the claimant and his or her solicitors.

3.9　NHSLA.　The NHSLA argues that case management should be conducted in conjunction with costs management. It states:

> "It is entirely proper that claimant lawyers should investigate before proceeding. We have no doubt they will say that by doing so they can and do reject many claims without merit. They should not, however, be able to accumulate bills of high five or six figures before even issuing a protocol compliant letter of claim. A defendant might have been happy to make early admissions a year or more earlier, and in some clinical cases even five years or more beforehand.

> We therefore advocate a system of prospective budgeting, even at the pre-proceedings stage of the case. Details of what such a system might entail are outlined in the Beachcroft paper to which we have also subscribed, so it would be superfluous to repeat them here."

3.10　The paper by Beachcroft LLP, which the NHSLA adopts, states that in claims where less than £50,000 are awarded, the total of claimant and defendant costs usually exceeds damages. Costs incurred on the claimant side are always three to four times higher than defence costs and sometimes the differential is much greater. Claimant solicitors will often spend £100,000 pre-action. Success fees are invariably claimed at 100%, regardless of when the defendant made admissions. Claimant firms in the City of London charge City rates (i.e. £420 per hour before success fee) without achieving better outcomes for their clients. The court should undertake both effective

---

[89] Case management conference.

case management and effective costs management. The costs incurred by claimants pre-action should also be subject to budgetary control. Budgets should be set for both parties at the first CMC. There should be early disclosure of evidence, with claimants serving their expert evidence together with the letter of claim. Case management directions in clinical negligence cases should be standardised nationally following wide consultation.

3.11 <u>Forum of Complex Injury Solicitors.</u> The Forum of Complex Injury Solicitors ("FOCIS") addresses clinical negligence in an appendix to its Phase 2 submission. FOCIS opposes sequential exchange of expert evidence, not least because clinical negligence is an area where the defendant has far more knowledge of the relevant facts than the claimant. FOCIS opposes further court control of costs, beyond the controls which already exist. Defendants should state at the first CMC how many professional witnesses of fact they will call. Expert discussions must be managed properly, if they are going to save costs rather than increase costs.

3.12 <u>Claimant solicitors.</u> A number of claimant solicitors have sent in submissions. One firm identifies the following problems in relation to compliance with the protocol:

- The failure by the defendants to respond at all to the letter of claim. This happens on countless occasions with the NHSLA in particular.

- The unreasonable refusal by the defendants to respond in accordance with the protocol. For example, in cases requiring significant quantum investigation, defendants often advance technical arguments to the effect that the claimants have not provided sufficient quantum evidence and have not, therefore, complied with the protocol. Identifying heads of loss is sufficient but some defendants will simply not agree and refuse to respond until they receive a schedule, thus causing delay and increased cost.

- The failure by defendants properly to respond to the letter of claim. NHS defendants often respond only with clinician comments, not having obtained expert opinion. The result is that proceedings have to be commenced and the pre action protocol has simply caused delay and increased cost.

This firm would welcome a uniform approach by the courts to dealing with non-compliance.

3.13 Other claimant solicitors emphasise the complexity of clinical negligence litigation. If defendants operated proper risk assessment they should be able to identify which cases are likely to proceed. Claimants do not rack up costs, once defendants have indicated an intention to settle. There is a massive imbalance of power between the parties, in favour of defendants. Also defendants have extensive networks of "hidden" resources. In relation to the alleged differential between claimant and defendant rates, one claimant firm writes:

> "Comparisons of Defence and Claimant costs put out by the NHSLA and Defence organisations are bogus. For a start the work they are required to do is very different. Secondly, Defendant solicitors get paid an agreed hourly rate for every single item of work they do. They are able to deliver bills to their institutional clients at agreed regular intervals and be paid in full within 30 days. Most of the Defendant firms who do clinical negligence litigation also have substantial property, commercial and employment healthcare practices for the same clients. The uncomfortable reality is that the lawyers

who do well out of the health service are those who act for it, not those who sue it."

3.14   Another firm emphasises that clinical negligence cases are high risk and strongly disputed. A firm which specialises in high value cases comments on the NHSLA graphs at PR appendix 21.   Graph A3 shows that both claimant and defendant legal costs have risen, but damages have risen even more sharply.   In relation to graph A7, the firm states that it uses a split success fee approach, unlike many other claimant firms. It states that the data in graph A16 are contrary to all the previous figures provided by the NHSLA. Moving away from the graphs, the firm comments that it is very rare indeed for the NHSLA to send a response letter under the protocol within three months. The NHSLA is usually aware that a claim will be coming, but does nothing. The firm adds:

> "The NHSLA chooses to only investigate claims once the Protocol Letter of Claim is received. Even then, the Trust in question generally waits until the 3 month period is due to expire before passing the letter on to panel solicitors. This combined with the practice of sending the letter to the treating clinician for comment before considering whether it is necessary to obtain expert evidence leads to significant delays in responding under the Protocol. As the only effective sanction available to a claimant under the Protocol is to issue proceedings this is often what claimants are forced to do faced with no response from the defendant or repeated requests for extensions of the time to respond under the Protocol. For a seriously injured claimant in real need of rehabilitation, accommodation, care and so on, delay of this magnitude is not an option."

3.15   One claimant clinical negligence firm argues that defendant conduct is the cause of high costs.   It states that the NHSLA does not commission its own independent expert report, as it should, before responding to a letter of claim. Nor does the NHSLA pro-actively investigate or manage cases. Furthermore, the NHSLA claims managers with whom this firm liaises are overburdened with cases and de-motivated.   There are incentives on the claimant side to improve efficiency and effectiveness, but no such incentives on the defendant side. This firm urges that the way forward is to reform the structure and operating methods of the NHSLA and, in particular, to reduce the current caseload of 300 cases per case manager which, it says, is now routine.

3.16   Defence solicitors. One firm of solicitors, which has acted for the NHS and NHSLA for many years, begins by emphasising that every penny spent on legal costs comes out of patient care. It then states:

> "We have been driven to complete this submission after having seen at first hand the way in which the unjust and excessive enrichment of legal advisers (predominantly on the Claimant's side) has increased dramatically over recent years to the detriment of the NHS and the reputation of our profession."

The firm mounts a strong attack on the CFA and ATE insurance regime, which have been discussed in earlier chapters of this report. It is strongly critical of the hourly rates charged by claimant firms. It supports costs management in conjunction with case management and states that costs judges must be involved in this process. Another firm draws attention to the lengthy time[90] which claimant solicitors take to

---

[90] See paragraph 4.2 below.

prepare letters of claim, in contrast to the short period allowed to defendants for response letters.

3.17   Another firm deplores the wide gulf between claimant and defendant costs. It states that hourly rates for its partners are £175, or £185 in respect of two nominated partners; however, a claimant firm in the same street of the same London suburb is charging £315 per hour for partners (before success fee). The rate rises to £402 per hour (before success fee) for partners in the City of London without any change in the quality of service. The firm states that (like claimant firms) it does a large amount of non-chargeable work: it has to prepare tenders, to ensure appropriate quality standards are met and so forth. The firm deplores the lack of control over costs either before proceedings are issued or afterwards. It states:

> "The first opportunity for scrutiny of costs by the Court comes with the costs estimate which must be filed with the Allocation Questionnaire. It would be a relatively simple extension of the Case Management role of the District Judge or Queen's Bench Master to manage the costs as well as the directions for the future conduct of the case, but this is not done. Instead, there is no judicial control of the costs before they are spent in all but the most exceptional of cases."

This firm maintains that detailed assessment is ineffective to control costs for a number of reasons, including (a) the fact that the money has already been spent and (b) the substantial costs of assessment proceedings.

3.18   Defendant solicitors also express concern about the failures by claimant solicitors to provide proper quantum information in their letter of claim or in response to subsequent requests. Indeed often schedules of special damages and future loss served with particulars of claim are uninformative, because they include entries such as "TBA". One defendant firm acknowledges that many cases are resolved before issue, so the protocol has achieved its aim to a large extent. However, excessive costs are often incurred before the letter of claim, even in cases which defendants would be willing to settle. It states:

> "Our impression is that preparing the letter of claim is often the final step taken by claimants' solicitors before they issue proceedings, after they have carried out a detailed investigation and obtained expert evidence, and often it is done very close to that deadline. Claimants' solicitors are rarely willing to divulge the basis of the claim or its value prior to service of the letter of claim and therefore in practice there is little opportunity to halt the burgeoning pre action costs. The letter of claim simply duplicates the particulars of claim or vice versa."

This firm urges that the protocol should either be strengthened or abandoned.

4. CONTROL OF COSTS PRE-ACTION

(i) The problems and the competing arguments

4.1   Requirements of the protocol. The protocol provides that health records should be provided within 40 days of a request. If the claimant decides to pursue a claim, his letter of claim should set out the relevant facts, the main allegations of negligence, a description of his injuries and an outline of any financial losses. The defendant should acknowledge the letter of claim within 14 days and send a reasoned response within three months. If the claim is denied, the letter of response should include specific comments on the allegations of negligence and the defendant's version of any facts which are disputed.

4.2   Time for defendants to investigate. Defendant organisations have drawn my attention forcefully to the disparity between the time taken by claimants to investigate their claims and the time allowed to defendants. One defendant firm has analysed a block of recent cases and ascertained that the time lag between the claimant requesting medical records and sending a letter of claim is, on average, 22 months. Another firm says that the time lag is 26 months. I am told that in the great majority of cases, the defendant does not realise that a claim is coming until the letter of claim (or claim form, if the protocol is not followed) arrives. Copies of medical records are frequently requested nowadays, therefore such a request is neither (a) a warning of a possible claim[91] or (b) a matter which comes to the attention of defence organisations. Defence solicitors maintain that they need more than the three month period allowed by the protocol in order to respond.

4.3   Delay in provision of health records. Complaint is made by claimants that some health trusts are unduly slow in providing health records. I do not know how widespread this problem is, but (absent special circumstances) such delay is unacceptable. I recommend that if a health authority fails to provide copy records within the 40 day time limit, then it should not be entitled to payment for the provision of records.[92] If the delay continues beyond 60 days, then there should be some financial penalty for the health authority, unless there is a reasonable explanation for the delay.

4.4   Failure by the NHSLA to instruct solicitors promptly. Claimant solicitors complain that claims against health trusts often are not acted upon until the end of the three month period allowed by the protocol. At that point, defence solicitors get in touch and say that they have just been instructed. I have recently put this allegation to senior representatives of the NHSLA and they admit that there is some truth in it. They state that sometimes NHS Trusts and similar bodies fail to pass on letters of claim to the NHSLA.

4.5   Failure by defendants to get to grips with the issues. Claimant solicitors complain that in many cases the defence team (once instructed) simply does not get to grips with the issues. The defence team seeks comments from the healthcare professional concerned, but does not take independent advice. The defendants advance untenable arguments which are not abandoned until late in the day. And so forth. The claimant solicitors support these complaints by citing cases in which they have acted for claimants with strong claims, where no settlement was offered until a late stage.

4.6   Escalation of claimant costs before and during the protocol period. Defence organisations are concerned that sometimes huge costs are run up during the period before the letter of claim. They may (a) know nothing about the claim and (b) upon notification be willing to make a rapid admission of liability. Thus, it is said, substantial costs are racked up to no useful purpose.

---

[91] The application form contains a box upon which the applicant may indicate an intention to pursue a claim. However, I understand that such an intention is not often stated. Moreover, any indication given by the applicant at the time of requesting records and before receiving expert advice may be of limited assistance.

[92] The payment provisions are set out in Annex B to the protocol.

(ii) My conclusions

4.7   Settlement is not usually achieved during the protocol period. The evidence summarised in PR chapters 6 and 11 shows that only a minority of meritorious clinical negligence claims are settled before issue of proceedings. In the majority of such cases the claimant issues proceedings before settlement is achieved. This factor generates unnecessarily high costs. It is therefore necessary to analyse the causes of these high costs and how they may be tackled.

4.8   Causes of excessive costs in relation to claims which ought to settle before issue.   Having considered the evidence and discussed the problems with the protagonists on both sides, I conclude that excessive costs are being incurred in relation to meritorious clinical negligence cases which ought to (but do not) settle early, for seven reasons:

(i)   There is no effective control over the costs which claimant lawyers may incur before sending a letter of claim or between the date of the letter of claim and the date when proceedings are issued.

(ii)   When NHS Trusts and similar bodies receive letters of claim, they sometimes fail to notify the NHSLA.

(iii)   In a number of cases it is not possible for the defendant's advisers to investigate the claim "from scratch" within three months, starting on the date when the letter of claim is received. Thus the limited period allowed to defendants by the protocol can lead to proceedings being issued unnecessarily.

(iv)   Although the MDU and MPS normally obtain independent expert evidence upon receipt of a letter of claim, the NHSLA seldom does so. Instead, the NHSLA usually relies upon comments obtained from the clinicians involved or others at the relevant NHS Trust.

(v)   In some cases the defence team fails to come to grips with the issues until too late.

(vi)   In some cases either the claimant's advisers or the defendant's advisers send protocol letters which do not comply with either the letter or the spirit of paragraphs 3.14 to 3.25 of the protocol. For example, the claimant may not provide quantum information or the defendant may not give proper reasons for denying liability.

(vii)   On some occasions the defendant is willing to settle without admitting liability, but the protocol makes no provision for this.

4.9   How to tackle those causes of high costs. In section 6 of this chapter I make proposals for controlling the level of recoverable costs which claimants are permitted to incur before sending a letter of claim or before issue of proceedings. In this section I propose a series of practical measures in order to tackle the other causes identified.

4.10   Time for response letter. I have considered whether the protocol should provide a requirement for early notification of claims in advance of the protocol letter of claim. Indeed I have tried to draft such a provision. However, this proposal would add an unwelcome layer of complexity and so I have rejected the idea. Instead I recommend that the time allowed for the response letter under the protocol be increased from three months to four months. I also recommend that any letter of claim, which is sent to (a) an NHS Trust or (b) an Independent Sector Treatment

Centre (an "ISTC"), should be copied to the NHSLA. This would remove the potential for delay in the NHSLA being notified by the NHS Trust or ISTC.

4.11   Defence expert evidence. I recommend that the NHSLA should change its practice in relation to independent expert evidence. In respect of any claim (other than a frivolous claim) where the NHSLA is proposing to deny liability, the NHSLA should obtain independent expert evidence on liability and causation during the four month period allowed for the response letter.

4.12   Incentivising defendants to get to grips with the issues during the protocol period. I have considered whether any amendments are required in order to deal with the problem identified in paragraph 4.8(v) above. It seems to me that economic incentives[93] already exist for the defendant (a) to admit liability early in clear cases and (b) to adopt a realistic approach to quantum before costs escalate. The best way to tackle this problem is not by rule changes but by better liaison between (a) claimant solicitors and (b) the defence organisations. The NHSLA, the MDU, the MPS and similar bodies should each nominate an experienced and senior officer to whom claimant solicitors should report egregious cases **after** the final resolution of such cases. It is clearly in the interests of defence organisations to investigate egregious cases and prevent repetition by means of (a) advice and training or (b) in extreme cases removal of solicitors from the panel. Furthermore, if there is any systemic problem within the NHSLA (as some claimant solicitors allege, but it is not practical for me to investigate), this procedure should bring such systemic problem to light.

4.13   Procedure for cases where the defendant is willing to settle without a formal admission of liability. I am satisfied that there are some cases where (a) the defendant's insurers desire to settle, (b) the defendant is willing for them to settle although he is not willing to make any formal admission and (c) the claimant is desirous of a financial settlement regardless of whether or not the defendant makes any formal admission. How frequently such cases arise is a matter of controversy. Nevertheless such cases do exist and it is in the interests of all parties to provide for them. I propose that the protocol should permit the following:

(i)   The defendant's solicitor states that, whilst the defendant does not admit liability, its insurers (or the NHSLA) are prepared to pay a reasonable sum in settlement of the claim.

(ii)   There is then a three month moratorium on the issue of proceedings, during which the parties endeavour to agree settlement. If the claimant commences proceedings during that three month period without good reason (e.g. expiry of the limitation period) then he or she is not entitled to recover the costs referable to those proceedings during the three month period.

4.14   Penalties for non-compliance with the protocol. Both claimant and defendant solicitors have expressed concern that the courts do not police the protocol properly. They do not impose sanctions for non-compliance and this allows lax practices to flourish: inadequate letters of claim, inadequate response letters, delays and so forth. These concerns echo what many practitioners submitted during Phase 1 and I accept that they are well founded. I therefore make recommendations for ensuring that there is compliance with protocols in chapter 39 below.

---

[93] These incentives will be strengthened if the proposals in chapter 41 below for enhancing the effect of claimant offers are accepted.

4.15   Screening costs. Claimant solicitors make the point that they incur screening costs in respect of cases which they decide not to take on. These costs must somehow be met in any future regime, in which success fees and ATE insurance premiums cease to be recoverable. I accept the general proposition that these costs must somehow be met. However, I firmly reject the proposition that such costs should fall upon the NHSLA or the medical defence organisations, as happens at the moment in CFA cases.[94] I do not see why either the NHS or medical practitioners should bear the costs of investigating allegations against themselves, which are unfounded. That is neither right in principle nor a wise use of NHS resources.

4.16   The question arises, therefore, as to how the screening costs should be met. It must obviously be a matter for individual solicitors how they manage their practices. However, I suggest the following as one viable means of dealing with screening costs: claimant solicitors charge all new clients a fee for screening their cases. If the case is subsequently pursued and won, the solicitors will recover the screening costs as part of recoverable costs (as now). If not, then the client bears the screening costs. There will be some clients who cannot afford the initial screening costs. Those clients will be eligible for legal aid. They can obtain legal aid to cover the initial screening costs. Thereafter the clients can proceed with any litigation either as legally aided claimants or on CFAs, as may be appropriate. I understand from Colin Stutt (who is one of my assessors and also Head of Funding at the LSC) that this already happens in practice in some cases. There are already some clinical negligence claimants who proceed on CFAs, after having obtained legal aid for the purpose of the initial investigation.

5. CASE MANAGEMENT OF CLINICAL NEGLIGENCE LITIGATION

5.1   Harmonisation of case management directions. Concern has been expressed by both claimant and defendant solicitors that different approaches to case management are adopted at different court centres. By way of example, the standard directions given in clinical negligence cases are not the same in Newcastle as in London. It is entirely understandable that such a situation has arisen, but it needs to be addressed. I recommend that a Queen's Bench ("QB") judge[95] be given the task of harmonising case management directions for clinical negligence cases across England and Wales. This exercise will involve attending meetings of court user committees and district judges at the major court centres and, in London, with Masters Yoxall and Roberts together with representatives of claimant and defendant practitioners. The object of this consultation exercise would be to identify the best practices which have been developed in different court centres and to codify these into a standard format which will be used at all court centres.

5.2   Docketing. I use the term "docketing" as defined in PR paragraph 43.5.9. In the context of clinical negligence litigation, docketing means that a case is assigned to the same judge or pair of judges throughout its life. Out of London each clinical negligence case should be assigned to a specific district judge and a specific circuit judge.[96] At some court centres docketing already exists for clinical negligence cases. In London clinical negligence cases are assigned to Master Yoxall or Master Roberts for case management and then to a QB judge for trial. In Manchester there are two district judges, who specifically do clinical negligence work. Every clinical negligence case in Manchester is assigned to one of those two district judges for case

---

[94] Through the mechanism of recoverable success fees and ATE insurance premiums in completely different cases where claimants succeed.
[95] If no QB judge is available, I am perfectly prepared to do this myself during 2010. I undertook a similar exercise in order to harmonise case management of construction litigation during 2005.
[96] Or QB judge if the case is to be tried by a QB judge.

management and then to a circuit judge or High Court judge for trial. In some court centres, however, no district judge is specifically assigned to clinical negligence work. Such cases are liable to pass from one district judge to another and then, of course, move to a new judge for trial.

5.3   In my view, docketing of clinical negligence cases is essential. What is already achieved in some court centres ought to be achievable in other court centres, even the smaller ones. Views to this effect have been expressed by many respondents during Phase 2, both at meetings and in written submissions. This is one of the relatively few matters upon which claimant and defendant practitioners are agreed. In chapter 39 below, I make recommendations both for docketing and for the use of specialist judges in clinical negligence litigation.

5.4   Resources for management of clinical negligence cases in London. During 2007 there were 578 new clinical negligence claims issued at the Royal Courts of Justice (the "RCJ") in London.[97] In 2008 the figure was 545. I understand from a recent meeting with the Senior Master, Master Yoxall and Master Roberts, that the number of clinical negligence claims issued in London will rise this year. Sufficient time for case management and (if my recommendations are accepted) sufficient time for costs management of clinical negligence litigation are essential in order (a) to promote access to justice for claimants and (b) to control costs.

5.5   I understand that one QB master will retire in January 2010 and that there is a prospect of two new QB masters being appointed in April 2010, one of whom will have specialist clinical negligence expertise. If this happens, the complement of QB masters dealing specifically with clinical negligence claims will rise to three. Although the next round of judicial appointments is entirely a matter for the Judicial Appointments Commission (the "JAC"), I wish to place on record that if the JAC sees fit to take that course, I would welcome it. I believe that the appointment of a third clinical negligence master will (a) be of benefit to claimants and (b) lead to savings to the public purse. The costs of appointing a third QB master for clinical negligence need to be weighed against the huge costs of clinical negligence litigation, which currently fall upon the taxpayer.[98]

6. COSTS MANAGEMENT OF CLINICAL NEGLIGENCE CASES

6.1   Costs management generally. Costs management generally is discussed in chapter 40 below.

6.2   Clinical negligence cases. In the context of clinical negligence litigation, a powerful case has been made out for the use of costs management both before and after the issue of proceedings. This is because of (a) the high costs of clinical negligence litigation and (b) the substantial costs which are sometimes run up before the defendant is first notified of a claim. According to the MDU, pre-action costs incurred by claimants sometimes range between £50,000 and £100,000.

(i) Costs management after issue of proceedings

6.3   Master Yoxall's proposal. Master Yoxall proposes that as soon as possible after the issue of proceedings the claimant's solicitors should complete a costs budget questionnaire in the form set out in appendix 6 to this report. Master Yoxall then

---

[97] See PR paragraph 5.3.4 and table 5.1.
[98] See section 1 above.

proposes that the budget should be set on paper, unless it his necessary to hold a budget hearing. Any budget hearing will not last more than 10 minutes. It will usually take place by telephone. The defendant will not be notified of the hearing or permitted to make representations. The defendant will be permitted to apply to vary a costs budget order, but such applications will be discouraged.

6.4   In my view, Master Yoxall's approach is an extremely sensible one. Any QB master or district judge with specialist experience of clinical negligence litigation should be able to set a reasonable budget on the basis of key facts elicited in response to that sort of questionnaire. If the case has special features which require a higher or lower budget figure, then those matters can be dealt with at a budget hearing. The budget set in response to the questionnaire will not be the last word. There will be opportunity for that budget to be revised upwards or downwards at later case management conferences, as the case develops.

6.5   I recommend that costs management of clinical negligence cases in accordance with Master Yoxall's proposal be piloted for two years.[99] That proposal has been discussed at a recent meeting of the Clinical Negligence Court Users Group. The details of the proposal should now be the subject of wider consultation. A practice direction authorising the pilot should be made under CPR Part 51. The pilot could either be confined to London or, alternatively, extended to other court centres. That is a matter which might usefully be decided after consultation.

6.6   Timetable.   If my proposal for piloting costs management of clinical negligence cases is accepted by the Secretary of State and the Civil Procedure Rule Committee, I would respectfully suggest that such a pilot should begin on Tuesday 1st June 2010, provided that a third clinical negligence master is in place at the RCJ by then. There are three reasons for suggesting that particular date:

(i)   A start date of 1st June 2010 allows sufficient time for consultation on the details of the proposal.

(ii)   The two existing costs management pilots are each running for one year and are due to conclude on 31st May 2010[100] and 30th September 2010[101] respectively. The feedback from those two pilots will be assessed during 2010. It will be highly advantageous to start receiving feedback from the clinical negligence costs management pilot as soon as possible.

(iii)   At my recent meeting with the Senior Master, Master Yoxall and Master Roberts a start date of 1st June was regarded as feasible.[102]

(ii) Costs management before issue of proceedings

6.7   I accept that there is a strong case for costs management before issue of proceedings in those clinical negligence cases where pre-issue costs become, or are likely to become, particularly high. The correct approach is to identify a threshold figure; then to provide that the claimant must apply to the court for authority to

---

[99] I propose two years, rather than one year for the pilot, because that would allow for some clinical negligence cases under the pilot to proceed from issue to judgment. Two years was the period proposed at my recent meeting with the QB Masters. If a general costs management rule comes into force during the two year period, it would be possible to end the pilot and to bring all clinical negligence cases under the rubric of the general rule.

[100] The Birmingham pilot discussed in chapter 40 below is due to end on 31st May 2010.

[101] The defamation costs management pilot discussed in chapters 32 and 40 below is due to end on 30th September 2010.

[102] Subject to the appointment of a third clinical negligence master.

exceed that figure. The prospective defendant should not be given notice of that application, unless the court specifically directs.

6.8   I propose a threshold figure of £15,000 for expenditure up to the date of the letter of claim and a further £15,000 (i.e. £30,000 in all) as the threshold figure up to the start of proceedings. This proposal does not mean that it will always be reasonable for claimants to incur costs of £30,000 before issue of proceedings. Indeed, such expenditure will usually be unreasonable, although that will depend upon the circumstances of the case. The proposal simply is that the costs budgeting mechanism will not come into operation unless (a) the claimant incurs £15,000 costs before sending a letter of claim or (b) the claimant incurs a total of £30,000 costs before issuing proceedings.

6.9   The form of questionnaire to be used pre-issue will be simpler that that proposed for the post issue period. The form which I propose is set out at appendix 7 to this report. I recommend that the costs management of clinical negligence cases which is to be piloted should include the management of pre-issue costs by this means.

6.10   It must be accepted that in the absence of primary legislation, no pilot practice direction under CPR Part 51 can empower masters to make binding orders pre-issue which will limit recoverable costs post-issue. Therefore, unless and until such legislation is passed, any pilot in respect of pre-issue costs management will be informal. The master will simply be giving an indication of what costs he would be likely to approve or disapprove post-issue.

6.11   The future. If the pilots proposed above are successful, I recommend that costs management, both pre-issue and post-issue, should become a permanent feature of clinical negligence litigation. Primary legislation will be required, in order to enable masters and district judges to make binding orders pre-issue limiting future recoverable costs.

(iii) Hourly rates

6.12   The hourly rates being claimed on the claimant side are a matter of concern. For example, the current guideline hourly rate specified for solicitors in the City of London with eight years' qualified experience is £402.[103] It is open to question whether that is an appropriate guideline rate for claimant clinical negligence solicitors who choose to be located in the City of London. However, these are issues for the Costs Council, if my recommendation to establish such a body is accepted.

6.13   I am aware of a number of recent cases in which hourly rates are being claimed at between £400 and £450 per hour for partners plus, of course, success fees at 100%. This means that legal fees up to £900 per hour are being claimed. It is necessary to look at the rates claimed rather than rates allowed, because in the vast majority of cases costs are resolved by negotiation of an overall settlement. (Detailed assessment proceedings before a costs judge would generate yet further substantial expense.) Even allowing for a modest discount on settlement, I do question whether the payment of legal fees at the rates currently claimed is a wise use of NHS resources.

6.14   General issues concerning hourly rates are discussed in chapters 44 and 45 below. The relevant recommendations are made in those chapters.

---

[103] See PR paragraph 52.2.11.

7. NHS REDRESS ACT 2006

7.1   The 2006 Act. The 2006 Act[104] provides for a scheme to be administered by the NHSLA for the resolution of lower value claims for clinical negligence in respect of hospital treatment. The scheme provides for a variety of forms of redress. These include payment of compensation; provision of treatment; giving an apology or explanation; taking risk management activity following investigation: see section 3 of the 2006 Act. Fixed fees are to be paid by the NHSLA to claimant lawyers. Claimants are not at risk of adverse costs liability in respect of unsuccessful claims.

7.2   Previous pilot. The 2006 Act was drawn up following a successful pilot exercise carried out between December 2001 and July 2002. During the pilot exercise 258 cases were referred to the scheme and evaluated by an independent expert. Compensation or other redress was provided in those cases where the claim was found to be valid.

7.3   Present position. The 2006 Act cannot be implemented until the Department of Health draws up regulations and the draft regulations have been laid before Parliament: see section 16 of the 2006 Act. No regulations have yet been drawn up. The House of Commons Select Committee on Health has expressed concern about the delay in this regard.[105]

7.4   My view. The scheme envisaged by the 2006 Act is a sensible one, which will facilitate the early and economic resolution of lower value clinical negligence claims in respect of hospital treatment. An important factor is that, within the court system, clinical negligence claims of whatever value are assigned to the multi-track. This increases litigation costs. In my view, it would now be appropriate to draw up regulations in order to implement the 2006 Act. The proposed redress scheme is one which will promote access to justice at proportionate cost.

7.5   The detailed content of any regulations made under the 2006 Act will require consultation. The regulations will cover matters such as the upper limit for financial compensation, what legal costs should be paid in respect of successful claims under the scheme, what legal work those costs should cover and so forth. I appreciate that drawing up draft regulations and then consulting AvMA, claimant solicitors, defendant solicitors, the NHSLA and others will take a little time. Nevertheless the Government has now had three years since the 2006 Act was drawn up. This matter should now be taken forward both in the interests of patients and (no less important) in the interests of saving the NHS from paying out unnecessary litigation costs.

8. RECOMMENDATIONS

8.1   I make the following recommendations:

(i)   There should be financial penalties for any health authority which, without good reason, fails to provide copies of medical records requested in accordance with the protocol.

---

[104] The origins of this Act are to be found in the Government Chief Medical Officer's report "*Making Amends*" (2003), available online at
http://www.dh.gov.uk/en/Publicationsandstatistics/Publications/PublicationsPolicyAndGuidance/DH_4010641.
[105] In its report entitled "*Patient Safety*", dated 3rd July 2009 at paragraphs 85 to 89 and 97. The report is available online at
http://www.publications.parliament.uk/pa/cm200809/cmselect/cmhealth/151/151i.pdf.

(ii)   The time for the defendant to respond to a letter of claim should be increased from three months to four months. Any letter of claim sent to an NHS Trust or ISTC should be copied to the NHSLA.

(iii)   In respect of any claim (other than a frivolous claim) where the NHSLA is proposing to deny liability, the NHSLA should obtain independent expert evidence on liability and causation during the four month period allowed for the response letter.

(iv)   The NHSLA, the MDU, the MPS and similar bodies should each nominate an experienced and senior officer to whom claimant solicitors should, after the event, report egregious cases of defendant lawyers failing to address the issues.

(v)   The protocol should provide a limited period for settlement negotiations where the defendant offers to settle without formal admission of liability.

(vi)   Case management directions for clinical negligence cases should be harmonised across England and Wales.

(vii)   Costs management for clinical negligence cases should be piloted.

(viii)   Regulations should be drawn up in order to implement the 2006 Act.

REVIEW OF
CIVIL LITIGATION COSTS

PART 5. SOME SPECIFIC TYPES OF LITIGATION

CHAPTER 24. INTELLECTUAL PROPERTY LITIGATION

INDEX

1. INTRODUCTION

1.1   Preliminary Report. Intellectual property ("IP") litigation was dealt with quite briefly in the Preliminary Report: see PR chapter 29 section 5. More attention has been focused on IP litigation during Phase 2 of the Costs Review than during Phase 1.

1.2   Role of IP. The creation and use of IP plays a crucial role in economic activity and in the achievement of many social goals, such as effective health care or renewable energy. The background to any IP regime must be a civil justice system which enables parties to assert or defend their IP rights ("IPR"). Such a civil justice system must deliver correct judgments at affordable cost in the complex field of IP. This is no easy task.

1.3   Organisations which have made submissions to the Costs Review. Of the organisations which have made submissions in respect of IP litigation, three merit brief explanation. The Intellectual Property Lawyers Association (the "IPLA") is a representative body for law firms in England and Wales who do IP work. Some 66 firms are members of the IPLA and they state that between them they conduct the vast majority of all IP litigation and transactional work. The Strategic Advisory Board for Intellectual Property Policy ("SABIP") is a non-departmental public body, which reports to the Intellectual Property Office (the "IPO") and to the Minister of State for Intellectual Property. It is the function of SABIP to provide long term, strategic, evidence-based policy recommendations. SABIP has commissioned and submitted a report by Dr Sivaramjani Thambisetty of the London School of Economics as its contribution to Phase 2 of the Costs Review. The Intellectual Property Court Users'

Committee (the "IPCUC") is a body which represents users of the High Court in the field of IP. On 28th April 2009 the IPCUC set up a working group (the "IPCUC Working Group") to formulate proposals for the reform of the Patents County Court (the "PCC"). The IPCUC Working Group included representation from the PCC Users Committee. The IPCUC Working Group produced a consultation paper dated 15th June 2009 and a final report dated 31st July 2009. This final report constituted the Phase 2 submission by the IPCUC to the Costs Review.

1.4   On 10th June 2009 the Minister of State for Intellectual Property hosted a forum, which was organised by the IPO and SABIP, on the theme: "*The economic value of intellectual property: an agenda for policy – relevant research*". I shall refer to this forum as the "IP forum". An interim report of the proceedings of the IP forum is available on the internet at http://www.sabip.org.uk/forum-report.pdf.

1.5   The Law Society's comments on IP issues were provided by the Intellectual Property Working Party (the "IPWP"), which consists of solicitors who specialise in such matters.

1.6   <u>Abbreviations used in this chapter.</u> In this chapter I shall refer to the practice direction supplementing CPR Part 63 as the "Practice Direction". I shall refer to the Patents Court and Patents County Court Guide as the "Guide".

1.7   <u>The surveys by SABIP.</u> At my request, SABIP kindly commissioned three internet surveys between August and October 2009, namely (i) copyright and design rights survey, (ii) patent survey and (iii) trade marks survey. In the first survey over 7,000 freelancers and small and medium enterprises ("SMEs") were sampled. In the second survey 500 patentee firms and 500 non-patentee firms in patent-intensive industries were sampled. In the third survey 500 firms with registered trademarks were sampled. The response was sufficient in the first survey to allow inferences to be drawn,[1] but very poor in the second[2] and third[3] surveys. The surveys addressed two issues: first, whether there was an unmet need for a small claims track and a fast track for IP cases; secondly, whether the proposed caps upon damages of £500,000 and recoverable costs of £25,000 and £50,000[4] would make the PCC more attractive to SMEs. SABIP will shortly be publishing a full report on its surveys and conclusions to be drawn. For present purposes, I shall concentrate on the first survey, which was the only one to yield a suitable number of responses. SABIP advises me that the second and third surveys did not generate robust statistical datasets.

1.8   <u>Conclusions from the first survey.</u> SABIP sets out its preliminary conclusions from the first survey as follows:

> "With regard to proposed caps on damages or recoverable costs, though many firms were neutral (just under 50% of respondents), no clear picture emerges, with some firms opposing the proposals and others supporting it. Further analysis of the data will determine whether there are patterns in the data – the spread of results may indicate differences in opinion and experience across different industries.

---

[1] In the first survey over 600 businesses and freelancers accessed the survey and over 300 completed all relevant questions.

[2] In the second survey only 49 businesses accessed the survey and only 25 completed all relevant questions.

[3] In the third survey on 33 businesses accessed the survey and only 11 completed all relevant questions.

[4] Discussed in paragraphs 3.2 and 3.3 below.

There was overwhelming support for both a fast track (72.2%) and a small claims forum (78.7%). Furthermore, the survey indicates high levels of potential usage for both these options: respondents indicated their assessment that they would be likely to bring 81 cases in the next year and 287 cases over the next five years to a fast track (cases between £5,000 and £25,000), and 197 cases in the next year and 883 cases over the next five years to a small claims venue (cases of under £5,000).

Given these results, it seems highly likely that high levels of demand exist for both a fast track and a small claims court for copyright and design rights cases. Although it is likely that the survey respondents may have overstated their potential usage of these mechanisms, any proposal to implement these tracks should take into consideration the need to quickly build capacity. Indeed, if the demand implied by our survey were to materialise, there is a risk of the procedures being swamped."

2. MAJOR IP LITIGATION

2.1 <u>The Patents Court.</u> The Patents Court is a specialist court within the Chancery Division. The Patents Court deals primarily with patents, designs (including semiconductor topography rights) and plant varieties. The general Chancery Division deals with other IPR cases, although chancery judges assigned to the Patents Court frequently hear such cases. Eight of the Chancery Division judges are assigned patent judges and thus sit in the Patents Court. Of those eight assigned judges, three are patent specialists and five are general chancery judges[5] with some patent experience.

2.2 <u>Level of costs.</u> Litigation in the Patents Court requires specialist solicitors, specialist counsel and appropriate experts. Therefore a significant level of costs is unavoidable. I have set out in chapter 2 above a summary of the costs involved in 15 recent High Court patent cases: see chapter 2 above paragraphs 8.1 to 8.6 and appendix 3 to this report.

2.3 <u>High quality, high cost.</u> The Law Society points out that the UK courts, with the benefit of specialist judges, offer a high quality forum for dispute resolution in IP cases; however, the costs are such that parties frequently perceive London as too expensive and therefore take cases to other jurisdictions. Others point out that the Rolls Royce system offered by the Patents Court in London tends to attract particularly complex, high value patent litigation in which legal costs are not the prime concern. In a paper presented to the IP forum, reviewing costs across different EU states, Dietmar Harhoff[6] stated:

> "The **UK system** is the most costly one, and this aspect is generally noted as negative. Costs are also considered to be a decisive factor in generating a large number of settlements in the UK system. The rarity of preliminary injunctions is also noted as a drawback by practitioners. On the positive side, the UK courts are considered highly competent and experienced, proceedings are very fast, the timetable is organized very strictly, there are satisfactory means of cost recovery and adequate damage awards. To some parties, the availability of a coercive method of securing evidence ('disclosure') had been attractive (prior to the harmonization of enforcement)."

---

[5] Not all of these five general chancery judges sit regularly in the Patents Court.
[6] Ludwig-Maximilians-Universität, Munich.

Dr Thambisetty in her report comments on the high volume of patent litigation in Germany. She then adds:

> "In fact there appears to be a natural separation of cases between the UK and Germany with highly technical and complicated litigation involving both infringement and counterclaims of invalidity finding a natural home within English procedure, with firms attracted by some of the most highly regarded patent judges in the world."

Dr Thambisetty adds later in her report that the UK (in contrast to many overseas jurisdictions) seems to attract a smaller number of more substantial patent battles.

2.4   <u>Calls to further strengthen the Patents Court.</u> Despite the general comments in the previous paragraph, practitioners have made a number of recommendations for the improvement of the Patents Court. The IPLA proposes that there should be greater independence of the Patents Court from the general Chancery Division. The Bar Council points out that IP litigation now occupies a "*sizeable chunk*" of Chancery Division business. According to the Bar Council, there is concern that most of the judges who sit in the Patents Court are not patent specialists at all. I understand that the specialist patent judges take a different view. They see advantages in non-specialist judges sitting in the Patents Court (for example so that they may take such experience upwards to the Supreme Court). They also see advantages in a flexible listing system which may use specialist patent judges for general chancery work. Judicial appointments do not fall within my terms of reference and I therefore make no recommendations in this regard. However, I draw attention to the competing views expressed, so that others might take them into account when considering whether a greater number of patent specialists should be appointed within the Chancery Division.

2.5   <u>Case management in the Patents Court.</u> The Patents Court is already a court which has active case management, as set out in CPR Part 63, the Practice Direction and the Guide. Despite these strengths, there are calls for more robust case management. The IPLA proposes that greater consideration should be given to the adequacy of statements of case; parties should not be allowed to get away with non-admissions; where an allegation is denied, a short explanation should be given as to the basis of the denial; the parties should set out their case on common knowledge at an earlier stage than exchange of expert evidence.[7] The IPLA also proposes that issues be narrowed at an earlier stage with active involvement of the future trial judge. The Law Society also calls for more active case management, although not at too early a stage of litigation. The Law Society comments:

> "More active judge-led case management in which preliminary indications on strengths and weaknesses of particular issues may be expressed will encourage the parties to identify and narrow their issues."

The Law Society also notes that there is little comment in the Guide about narrowing of issues. Some members of the Law Society's IPWP have had experience of *Markman* hearings[8] in the USA and consider that some similar procedure might be adapted for use in the Patents Court.

---

[7] This was also proposed by Floyd J in *Ratiopharm GmbH v Napp Pharmaceutical Holdings Ltd* [2008] EWHC 3070 (Pat) at [154].
[8] A *Markman* hearing, also known as a "claim construction hearing", is a pre-trial hearing in a US district court during which a judge considers the meanings and scope of a patent claim.

2.6   I see some force in the proposals made by the IPLA and the Law Society, although I understand that the patent judges take a less optimistic view. Implementation of those proposals might promote effective case management and reduction of costs. On the other hand, the details of these proposals must be for the IP specialists. I therefore recommend that consideration be given by the Patents Court judges and the IPCUC together to the question whether the Guide should be amended to include any of the proposals set out in paragraph 2.5 above.

2.7   <u>Costs management.</u>   In chapter 40 below I discuss the use of costs management in appropriate cases. Whether this would be beneficial in IP litigation must be for IP court users, practitioners and judges to consider.[9]   I draw their attention to the contents of that chapter, but make no specific recommendation in this regard.

2.8   <u>Counsel's fees.</u>   Concern has recently been expressed to my assessors about the high level of counsel's fees in substantial IP cases.   In chapter 6 above I recommend that the Costs Council should give guidance in respect of the extent to which counsel's fees should be recoverable *inter partes*.   No doubt that guidance will include appropriate (recoverable) fee levels in substantial IP and similar cases. Furthermore, if costs management is adopted in any IP case, then a budget for counsel's recoverable fees will be set in advance. It will always be the case, however, that some members of the Bar (like some solicitors) are able to command significantly higher fees than would be recoverable upon any assessment of costs. If litigants wish to instruct such counsel, at their own expense, there can be no objection to them doing so.

3. LOWER VALUE IP LITIGATION

3.1   <u>The Patents County Court.</u> The history of the PCC has been outlined in PR paragraph 29.5.2. The PCC exists in order to resolve lower value IP disputes and IP disputes between SMEs.   There is concern that at the moment many SMEs do not have access to justice in respect of IP disputes, because of the prohibitively high costs of litigating in the PCC.[10] As set out in PR paragraphs 29.5.2 to 29.5.11, there have recently been calls for the reformation of the PCC and its procedures.

3.2   <u>Consultation paper published by the Intellectual Property Court Users Committee.</u> On 15th June 2009 the IPCUC published a consultation paper prepared by its Working Group, setting out proposals for reform of the PCC. In essence the Working Group proposed as follows:

(i)   The PCC should be re-named the "Intellectual Property County Court", in order to make clear the breadth of that court's work.

(ii)   The procedures of the PCC should be reformed, so that parties set out their respective cases fully at the outset. The initial pleadings would contain the evidence and the arguments relied upon. After completion of pleadings there would be a main case management conference, at which the judge (applying a cost-benefit test) would decide whether to order or permit further evidence, further written argument or specific disclosure. Any other hearings would be dealt with by telephone. The trial would be limited to one to two days.

---

[9] The IPLA suggests that Patent Judges might make more use of costs estimates in managing litigation and limiting costs recovery at the end.
[10] The importance of SMEs having the ability to enforce or defend their patents and other IP rights was stressed by a number of speakers at the IP forum.

(iii)   The recovery of costs should be governed by scale fees.[11] Total recoverable costs would be capped at £50,000 in contested actions for patent infringement and validity, and at £25,000 in all other cases.

(iv)   There should be a limit of £250,000 on the financial remedies available in the PCC.

3.3   <u>Final report published by the Intellectual Property Court Users Committee.</u> On 31st July 2009 the IPCUC published the final report prepared by its Working Group, following consultation on the proposals set out in the consultation paper. The Working Group reported that it had consulted a broad spectrum of court users, including professional and trade representative bodies, lawyers, patent and trade mark attorneys and academics. The respondents were almost universally supportive of the proposals. The Working Group therefore adhered to its original proposals, subject to certain modifications. The principal modification was that the financial limit for remedies available in the PCC should be £500,000, not £250,000. The Working Group made a number of detailed recommendations, including that the Guide should contain guidelines to assist in determining transfer applications as between the PCC and the Patents Court.[12]

3.4   <u>Comments of others on the IPCUC's proposals.</u> The Bar Council is supportive of the proposals for limiting costs recovery in the PCC. However, the Bar Council emphasises that it regards IP as a special case.[13] The Law Society in its Phase 2 submission notes, apparently with approval, the proposals of the IPCUC. The IPLA notes that the role of the PCC is to provide access to justice in respect of low value IP disputes. The IPLA suggests that the model proposed by the IPCUC might be extended, or alternatively some of its features might be adapted, for use more generally after there has been some experience of it in practice. The IP Committee of the City of London Law Society supports the general thrust of the reforms proposed. The IP Committee points out that the PCC, however reformed, needs to be properly resourced both with judges and administrators to deal with an increasing caseload. The Federation of Small Businesses (the "FSB") supports the proposal to develop a streamlined and simplified PCC, building on the litigation procedures of continental Europe.

3.5   A note of caution about the proposed reforms of the PCC is sounded by Dr Thambisetty. She points out that there is *"very little comprehensive empirical evidence for the 'unmet demand' for litigation faced by SMEs"*.

3.6   <u>My view.</u> I accept that there is very little comprehensive empirical evidence, of the kind mentioned by Dr Thambisetty. I also note that *"no clear picture emerges"* from the SABIP survey in this regard. However, the fact that almost universal support for the IPCUC's proposals was expressed during the consultation exercise is compelling. My own experience this year suggests that it is rare for court users or lawyers to agree about anything which is on the reform agenda. It should also be noted that Arnold J cited some powerful evidence in support of his thesis that court users are more fearful about indeterminate costs liability if they lose than about shortfall in costs recovery if they win: see PR paragraph 29.5.8. A further pointer in

---

[11] Modelled on the IPO's scale fee system.
[12] This paragraph and the preceding paragraph summarise the Working Group's proposals with extreme brevity. I do not attempt to reproduce the Working Group's consultation paper or final report in full. They are available on http://www.judiciary.gov.uk/docs/pub_media/pcc-report.pdf.
[13] The Bar Council makes it clear that its support for limiting costs recovery in lower value IP litigation is not to be taken as support for the heretical suggestion in my Preliminary Report that costs recovery might be limited in any other categories of lower value business disputes.

the same direction is the fact that few SMEs are litigating IPR in England and Wales at present. This is in marked contrast to the position in some other EU territories.

3.7   I find the reasoning in the IPCUC Working Group's consultation paper and final report to be powerful and I am persuaded by it. I believe that if the proposed package of reforms is adopted, this will promote access to justice at proportionate cost for SMEs and other parties involved in lower value IP disputes. I therefore recommend that the proposals of the final report be implemented.

3.8   The PCC judge. The identity and case management skills of the PCC judge who is appointed after the reformation will be crucial to the success of the venture. Dr Thambisetty recommends that the PCC judge *"should be given the opportunity to be promoted to the High Court"*. SABIP states that it endorses this recommendation without reservation. I would comment that every circuit judge has *"the opportunity to be promoted to the High Court"*, although purely as a matter of arithmetic only a small proportion of circuit judges can achieve such promotion. The sentiment underlying Dr Thambisetty's recommendation and SABIP's firm endorsement is that the appointee should be a patent specialist of outstanding ability who is likely to merit such promotion. Although judicial appointments are outside my terms of reference, I strongly agree with that sentiment. It is entirely a matter for the Judicial Appointments Commission whether or not it sees fit to take notice of the views expressed in this paragraph.

3.9   Length of tenure at the PCC. The PCC judge should always be a senior circuit judge. As a practical matter, it may be sensible for the PCC judge to be appointed for a five year term. The demands of this post will be heavy. If the appointee is reasonably youthful and if he/she demonstrates conspicuous ability whilst at the PCC, then after five years he/she might be promoted to the High Court with full promotion prospects thereafter.[14] Alternatively, in order to avoid any judge getting "stale" in the post, after five years the PCC judge could either (a) be transferred to another senior circuit judge post, thus making way for a new appointee, or (b) have his/her appointment renewed, if that course is appropriate. I therefore suggest that, after reformation of the PCC, appointment to the post of PCC judge should be for a five year term, after which the incumbent may either have his/ her appointment renewed or alternatively be transferred to some other judicial post of equivalent or higher status. Since judicial appointments do not fall within my terms of reference, I put this forward as a suggestion, rather than a formal recommendation.

3.10   Form of pleadings in the reformed PCC. This is discussed in some detail by the IPCUC Working Group both in its consultation paper and in its final report. The Working Group suggests that pleadings might follow the format which is envisaged for the proposed European Patents Court. I do not venture into the detail of this debate. However, I note that both the Working Group and Dr Thambisetty advocate the use of model pleadings. I agree with this proposal. Such guidance will be particularly important in the early days immediately after introduction of the new procedure. I therefore recommend that, after reformation of the PCC, the Guide be amended to give clear guidance on the requirements for statements of case, illustrated by model pleadings annexed to the Guide.

---

[14] In the same way that a young practitioner appointed to be a senior circuit judge in the TCC may, if successful, be promoted to the High Court bench at about the age of 50.

4. VERY LOW VALUE IP DISPUTES

4.1 <u>Comments of the Federation of Small Businesses.</u> The FSB in its Phase 2 submission states:

> "Businesses have also suggested to us that reform of intellectual property litigation should embrace wider difficulties that they are experiencing in resolving relatively straightforward copyright issues (especially in relation to the music business) at a reasonable cost and within a sensible timescale. For example, many small music businesses such as independent record companies, publishers, composers and performers are vulnerable to their intellectual property rights being infringed, but at present only have the option and risk of getting involved in expensive lengthy and complex chancery litigation procedures. It is suggested that what is required (which is understood to exist in other European jurisdictions) is a simply and cost effective procedure for resolving conflicts or establishing rights, especially in cases where the issues are clear but the value of the outcome of the dispute is not large. This type of IP right is the bread and butter of many of those types of business (and generates a considerable amount of foreign earnings for UK PLC) and yet those businesses are effectively barred from access to justice by the factors mentioned above. See Part 7 Chapter 33 on Chancery Litigation which has no pre-action protocols applicable.
>
> What is required is a small claims procedure to enable those cases to gain access to justice."

4.2 This part of the FSB submission touches upon an important point. At the moment all IP litigation is assigned to the multi-track: see CPR rule 63.1 (3). There is no small claims track and no fast track for litigation in the PCC. Nor is there any district judge attached to the PCC. The Law Society is also concerned about this lacuna.

4.3 <u>Unmet need for justice.</u> In my view there is an unmet need for justice in this regard. One can cite many other examples beyond those mentioned by the FSB. For example, a journalist whose articles have been reprinted without permission might have a claim for a few hundred pounds. A photographer whose photographs have been downloaded from the internet and reproduced without permission might have a claim for a few hundred pounds. It may be difficult for such claims be pursued at the moment. There is no small claims track in the PCC and there is little IP expertise in most other county courts.

4.4 <u>Confirmation from SABIP survey.</u> Having formed the preliminary view set out in the previous paragraph, I asked SABIP to investigate whether there was an unmet need for justice in this regard. The results of SABIP's survey, which are summarised in paragraphs 1.7 and 1.8 above, confirm that there is such an unmet need.

4.5 <u>Remedy.</u> In my view, there ought to be a small claims track in the PCC for IP claims with a monetary value of less than £5,000 and a fast track for IP claims with a monetary value of between £5,000 and £25,000. I accept that when declarations or other non-monetary remedies are claimed, there is room for argument about how a claim should be valued, but this problem is not insuperable, as demonstrated by the IPCUC Working Group's final report and by the experience of the German courts. If a small claims track is created for IP claims below £5,000, there will effectively be no costs shifting for such claims and small businesses will be able to represent themselves: see chapter 49 of the Preliminary Report. If a fast track is created for IP claims valued between £5,000 and £25,000, the parties will get the benefits of the fixed costs regime proposed in chapter 15 above.

4.6   I recommend that the district bench should be able to deal with small claims and fast track IP cases. I leave others to decide whether that is best achieved by (a) the appointment of a district judge with specialist patent experience specifically to a newly created post within the PCC; (b) the creation of a cadre of existing district judges with the knowledge, training and experience necessary to decide such cases; or (c) making greater use of IP solicitors and counsel sitting in the PCC as recorders, as suggested by the Law Society. A further alternative which merits consideration is the possibility that IPO hearing officers (with appropriate qualifications) could serve as deputy district judges in the PCC, if necessary by video link from their Newport office.[15]

5. PRE-ACTION PROCEDURES

5.1   There is concern amongst practitioners that a legitimate letter before action in respect of infringement may result in a claim for "groundless threats" by the recipient under section 26 of the Registered Designs Act 1949 (the "1949 Act"), section 70 of the Patents Act 1977 (the "1977 Act"), section 253 of the Copyright Designs and Patents Act 1988 (the "1988 Act") or section 21 of the Trade Marks Act 1994 (the "1994 Act"). The Law Society recommends the abolition of "groundless threats". This would be a change to substantive law, which lies outside my terms of reference. In any event such a change would not be made without a careful re-evaluation of the policy which underlies section 26 of the 1949 Act, section 70 of the 1977 Act, section 253 of the 1988 Act and section 21 of the 1994 Act.

5.2   At the moment there is no pre-action protocol for IP claims. The IPLA suggests that such a protocol might assist. In my view, there are two possible ways forward. First, IP practitioners and judges could consider whether a pre-action protocol geared to the specific needs of IP litigation would be beneficial. If so, such a protocol could be drafted after consultation with all stakeholders. I am conscious, however, from submissions received during Phases 1 and 2, that protocols are viewed with disfavour by many chancery practitioners.[16] An alternative course might be that the Guide be amended to include some simple guidance concerning what pre-action conduct is required, similar to that given in the Admiralty and Commercial Courts Guide.[17] It may be thought desirable on policy grounds that if a party complies with approved pre-action guidance as a precursor to *bona fide* litigation or ADR,[18] it should not incur liability for groundless threats. However, the statutes referred to above create torts of strict liability. Whether any amendment should be made to section 26 of the 1949 Act, section 70 of the 1977 Act, section 253 of the 1988 Act or section 21 of the 1994 Act in order to give additional comfort to such a party lies outside my terms of reference.

5.3   I recommend that there be consultation with court users, practitioners and judges, in order to ascertain whether there is support either for (a) an IP pre-action protocol[19] or (b) the Guide to give guidance regarding pre-action conduct.

---

[15] This final alternative may require statutory amendment.

[16] Some years ago an attempt was made to produce a pre-action protocol for IP claims, but this ended in failure for a number of reasons, including the wide differences between different types of IP claims.

[17] See paragraphs B3.1 to B3.4.

[18] Whether or not successful in obtaining a remedy.

[19] Despite the earlier failed attempt to create one.

6. RECOMMENDATIONS

6.1   I make the following recommendations:

(i)   Consideration should be given by the Patents Court judges and the IPCUC to the question whether the Guide should be amended to include any of the proposals set out in paragraph 2.5 above.

(ii)   The proposals in the IPCUC Working Group's final report for reforming the PCC should be implemented.

(iii)   After reformation of the PCC, the Guide should be amended to give clear guidance on the requirements for statements of case, illustrated by model pleadings annexed to the Guide.

(iv)   There should be a small claims track in the PCC for IP claims with a monetary value of less than £5,000 and a fast track for IP claims with a monetary value of between £5,000 and £25,000.

(v)   One or more district judges, deputy district judges or recorders with specialist patent experience should be available to sit in the PCC, in order to deal with small claims and fast track cases.

(vi)   There should be consultation with court users, practitioners and judges, in order to ascertain whether there is support either for (a) an IP pre-action protocol or (b) the Guide to give guidance regarding pre-action conduct.

CHAPTER 25. SMALL BUSINESS DISPUTES

INDEX

1. INTRODUCTION

1.1   Preliminary Report. In chapter 29 of the Preliminary Report I reviewed the work of the Mercantile Courts and discussed issues surrounding small business disputes. I used the term "small business disputes" loosely to embrace two concepts: first disputes between small and medium enterprises ("SMEs"); secondly lower value disputes between businesses of any size.

1.2   I shall continue to use the term "small business disputes" in the same sense as was used in the Preliminary Report. For the reasons set out in the Preliminary Report small businesses make a massive contribution to Gross Domestic Product. It is of critical importance to the UK economy that small business disputes are resolved efficiently and at proportionate cost.

2. DISCUSSIONS AND SUBMISSIONS DURING PHASE 2

(i) Meetings

2.1   Meeting with Federation of Small Businesses. On 20th May 2009 I met with representatives of the Federation of Small Businesses (the "FSB"). They made the point that their members avoid litigation *like the plague* because of the costs involved. They also urged that, in relation to disputes between businesses, claims up to £15,000 should proceed on the small claims track. Any competent business person should be able to represent his firm in disputes up to that level. They also pointed out that many small businesses are like individuals and should be treated as such. The level of costs recoverable by litigants in person should be reviewed. The FSB representatives stated that some sectors of industry have their own arbitration schemes, which small businesses use. Some small businesses use the services of the CEDR.[20] However, mediation is not adopted as widely as it should be. In relation to fixed costs for lower value business cases, the FSB kindly agreed to survey its members.

2.2   Commercial Litigation Association conference. On 9th June 2009 I attended a conference of the Commercial Litigation Association ("CLAN"). In relation to business disputes generally, there was support for costs budgeting, which merited further consultation and debate. The point was made that commercial clients

---

[20] The Centre for Effective Dispute Resolution.

increasingly request fixed budgets for cases. However, judges must be properly trained for the exercise and each case requires continuity of judge.

2.3   SMEs seminar. On 28th July 2009 I attended a seminar hosted by Holman Fenwick Willan LLP on business disputes involving SMEs (the "SMEs seminar"). At this seminar there was some criticism of the role of before-the-event ("BTE") insurers in relation to small business disputes. The focus of most complaints was upon the insistence of BTE insurers in using their own solicitors rather than the insured's regular solicitors.[21] The point was also made that BTE insurers sometimes reject claims which are notified late, because the insured was unaware of the existence of cover. There was general, but not universal, support for costs management. The point was made that, at the start of the case, properly detailed budgets should be produced but not in Form H format. It was suggested that it should be produced in similar detail to that which is provided to the client. Budgets should be lodged at court and exchanged with the other side. The court should take case management decisions with an eye on the budget. There was general, but not universal, opposition to fixed costs for small business disputes. The point was also made that smaller businesses, unlike large companies, are often unaware of the benefits of mediation.

(ii) Written submissions

2.4   Data from Mercantile Courts. The judges and users of the Mercantile Courts in Bristol and Manchester submitted some helpful data concerning recent cases in those courts. The sums in issue ranged between £30,000 and £7 million, with over half being between £100,000 and £600,000. Of those cases which were concluded at the date of the submission of the data, 83% were settled before trial. The data were provided by a number of different sources. In a number of cases separate figures for costs were not available. It is not therefore possible to discern any relationship between costs and sums at stake.

2.5   The Bristol Mercantile Court users committee proposes a procedural and costs regime for the management of small business disputes, which it calls the "SBD regime". This entails a streamlined procedure, coupled with tight control of recoverable costs. The Manchester mercantile judges, after consultation with their users committee, propose a regime of active case management for business cases and describe a number of innovations which have been made in the Manchester / Liverpool Mercantile Court. One innovation is that a judge looks at the file as soon as a defence is served and issues "pre-CMC directions". As the mercantile judges rightly observe, they have in effect a docket system, which is a huge advantage.

2.6   The Birmingham Mercantile Court has been piloting costs management during Phases 2 and 3 of the Costs Review (the "Birmingham pilot scheme").[22] Also, since 1st June 2009, the court has been sending in reports of cases proceeding in its list, whether or not they are under the pilot scheme. The picture which emerges of Mercantile Court business in Birmingham is similar to that in other Mercantile Courts.

2.7   Practitioners. The commercial practitioners in the Manchester Law Society stress the importance of active case management, although they have reservations about costs management. Many other practitioners and practitioner associations express support for pro-active case management, the use of specialist judges and

---

[21] This criticism will be met if the first of my recommendations in chapter 8 concerning BTE insurance is accepted.
[22] As to which, see chapter 40 section 2 below.

docketing. A number of respondents say that I should not look at the Mercantile Courts in isolation. They are part of a group of courts which handle business disputes. That group also includes the Chancery Division, the Chancery Courts at regional centres, the Queen's Bench Division, the Technology and Construction Court (the "TCC") and the county courts. The Commercial Bar Association points out that the definition of "SME" is wide and includes many companies which would be likely to litigate in the Commercial Court.

2.8   Federation of Small Businesses. The FSB kindly conducted a survey of members. This revealed a low awareness of the existence of Mercantile Courts and a preference for fixed costs in business disputes up to £500,000. The FSB states that most of its members are "*micro businesses*", for whom the loss of relatively small sums of money can have devastating effects. The FSB proposes that there should be a special streamlined procedure for "*resolving smaller scale business versus business disputes at a reasonable cost and within a shorter times*cale". The FSB supports the use of BTE insurance. The FSB urges that the small claims limit be raised to at least £15,000 for claims involving businesses ("*not just business v business claims*"). The FSB states that many businessmen conduct their own cases and that for them the litigant in person rate of £9.25 per hour is absurdly low. The FSB is concerned about the increasing charge rates of lawyers ("*the elephant in the room*") and urges the reversal of *Agassi v Robinson* [2005] EWCA Civ 1507.

2.9   In relation to the special procedure for smaller scale business disputes above the small claims limit, the FSB states:

> "In particular, where new small claims procedures for business litigation are being considered lodging of a core bundle of key documents early in the litigation process may assist court management. Usually, business litigants will know the key evidence from the outset and early disclosure of the key elements of it to the court may assist settlement or reduce areas for dispute. Having such a bundle of both sides key documents available at the first case management conference could be useful and save time and expense for the court and litigants."

3. THE MERCANTILE COURTS

3.1   It is accepted that the Mercantile Courts are not the only courts which deal with small (and indeed large) business disputes. However, the Mercantile Courts have an advantage over the Chancery Courts, the Queen's Bench Division and the county courts in that they can offer a docketing system. In the Mercantile Courts the same judge usually manages a case throughout its life and finally (if the case does not settle) conducts the trial. The TCC also offers a docketing system and there is, of course, some overlap between TCC business and Mercantile Court business. However, that area of overlap is limited. The vast majority of TCC cases relate to buildings or information technology.

3.2   There are Mercantile Courts at ten court centres. At most court centres the Mercantile Court has its own court guide. These guides can be found in the "Publications" section of the HMCS[23] website.[24] There is also a "Mercantile Court"

---

[23] Her Majesty's Courts Service.
[24] http://www.hmcourts-service.gov.uk/publications/guidance/admiralcomm/index.htm. At the time of writing (December 2009) I am told that these individual guides will soon become redundant and that litigants will be advised to consult the Admiralty and Commercial Courts Guide. Although the Admiralty

section of the HMCS website, which gives much helpful information about the Mercantile Courts and their procedures. As can be seen from section 2 above, the Mercantile Courts are, collectively, a powerhouse of ideas. New procedures are regularly being developed and tested: for example, those operated at Manchester, those proposed at Bristol and the costs management pilot at Birmingham. I thus adhere to the view expressed in my Preliminary Report that the Mercantile Courts play a vital role in the civil justice system. They are the natural forum for business disputes which require specialist judicial management but fall outside the narrow purview of the Commercial Court.[25]

3.3 Despite all the foregoing advantages, in my view the Mercantile Courts lack two crucial features. First, there is no judge in charge of the Mercantile Courts. Secondly, there is no uniform Mercantile Courts guide. As to the first point, all other specialist courts have a judge in charge. The Chancellor is in charge of the regional Chancery Courts. The judge in charge of the TCC, currently Ramsey J, is in charge of all regional TCC courts. The Mercantile Court judges do not have any single judge who may be regarded as their "line manager" or co-ordinator. If there were such a judge, he or she could co-ordinate their procedures and give overall leadership. This leads on to the second point. If there were a judge in charge, one of his or her first tasks would be to produce a single Mercantile Courts Guide (the "Guide"). This would draw upon the individual guides which currently exist. The Guide would also gather up the best practices developed by different Mercantile Courts. No doubt the judge in charge would be assisted in this process by attending Mercantile Court user committee meetings around the various court centres as and when he was sitting in the various Mercantile Courts. In my view, this reform would make a significant contribution to promoting access to justice for the parties to small (and large) business disputes. I therefore recommend that:

(i)   A High Court judge should be appointed as judge in charge of the Mercantile Courts.

(ii)   A single court guide should be drawn up for all Mercantile Courts.

3.4 In the course of drawing up the Guide, I recommend that consideration be given to devising a special streamlined procedure for business disputes of lower value. The precise definition of "lower value" must be a matter for the authors of the Guide. The Bristol Mercantile Court Users Committee suggests that the financial upper limit for its SBD regime should not be less than £100,000 although there is a case for putting the figure as high as £150,000. As to the content of this special streamlined procedure, that too must be a matter for the authors of the Guide after wide consultation. No doubt regard will be paid to the Bristol scheme summarised above as well as to the proposals of the FSB.

4. OTHER MATTERS

4.1   Fixed costs for small business disputes.   In the Preliminary Report I canvassed the possibility of introducing a scheme of fixed costs for lower value business disputes in the multi-track. It is clear from the consultation responses during Phase 2 that there is not sufficient support to implement such a proposal at the present time. In chapter 16 above I have concluded that it would be premature to

---

and Commercial Courts Guide is excellent for the Admiralty and Commercial Courts, it is not targeted upon the specific needs of Mercantile Court users.

[25] There is a regular interchange of cases between the London Mercantile Court and the Commercial Court.

embark upon any scheme of fixed costs in respect of lower value multi-track cases for the time being. Nevertheless, I believe that this issue should be revisited after the other recommendations in this report (in so far as accepted) have been implemented and allowed to bed down. It is an uncomfortable fact that the vast majority of respondents during Phase 2 were lawyers. The views of lawyers may not be identical in every respect to the views of those who employ them. The FSB (one of the few non-legal bodies to respond) specifically recommended:

> "The introduction of a fixed costs scheme in fast track and multi-track cases would give businesses a chance at recovering some costs without risking their entire business."

I do not make a formal recommendation about the more future distant future, but I express the hope that this matter will be revisited in due course.

4.2   BTE insurance. I discussed BTE insurance in chapter 8 above and there expressed the view that an expansion of BTE insurance would be beneficial for small businesses. I note the concerns about BTE insurance which were expressed at the SMEs seminar. However, the principal concern would be addressed if my earlier recommendation for amendment of regulation 6 of the Insurance Companies (Legal Expenses Insurance) Regulations 1990 is accepted. The other problem highlighted at the SMEs seminar was that the insured is unaware of cover until too late with the result that its late notification is rejected. The answer to this point must be the promotion of better awareness of BTE insurance, again as recommended in chapter 8 above. Finally, the complaint is sometimes made that BTE insurance cover may prove to be inadequate. As to this complaint, of course the insured only receives the level of cover for which it pays. Nevertheless, even £50,000 or £100,000 legal expenses cover is better than none. Also it is to be hoped that the procedural reforms under consideration will bring down the costs of litigating lower value business disputes.

4.3   Mediation. Mediation is discussed in chapter 36 below. It was stated both at my meeting with the FSB and at the SMEs seminar that smaller businesses (unlike large companies) are often unaware of the benefits of mediation. This is unfortunate. Most lawyers and judges already make strenuous efforts to commend mediation. Perhaps business organisations and trade associations could also assist in this regard. I accept, of course, that no-one should be forced to mediate,[26] not least because mediation can be an expensive process. However, before small businesses opt to incur the even more substantial costs of litigation, their decision not to mediate must, at the very least, be properly informed.

4.4   Costs management. Costs management is discussed in chapter 40 below. Having regard to the comments made at the CLAN conference and the recent experience of the Birmingham pilot scheme, I believe that costs management will make a significant contribution to controlling costs in small business disputes.

4.5   Small claims track. I accept the point made by the FSB that businessmen are usually well able to represent themselves in disputes above the present small claims limit of £5,000. However, I do not accept that when such a businessman is appearing against an individual (often a customer), he should have the benefit of an expanded small claims track. The individual on the other side is likely to need representation.

---

[26] See PR chapter 4.

4.6   When two businesses are involved in a dispute valued between £5,000 and £15,000, I do accept that such a matter may be suited to the small claims track, so that each side can appear in person. The best way to achieve this would be for both parties to consent at the outset to allocation to the small claims track. Indeed, in such a case the court may well encourage such a course at the first opportunity, if the parties have not thought of it for themselves. Once the claim is allocated (or transferred) to the small claims track the district judge will be more interventionist and thus can promote efficient resolution of the dispute without the assistance of lawyers. No rule change is required to facilitate such consensual allocation to the small claims track: see CPR rules 26.7(3) and 26.8(1)(h).

4.7   <u>Guidance.</u> The county court already provides a leaflet for the assistance of litigants who conduct their own cases on the small claims track and I understand that this is helpful. This leaflet is not really suited, however, to the needs of businessmen who are conducting "business" disputes up to £15,000 on the small claims track. It would be of considerable assistance to such litigants if a separate, and rather fuller, guide were prepared for "small business disputes". Such a guide would explain (i) the options for mediation and (ii) the procedures on the small claims track, what needs to be done in preparation for the hearing and what will happen at the hearing. It should be written for the intelligent layman, who is well accustomed to expressing himself or herself at meetings and who now needs to resolve a small business dispute efficiently and effectively without the expense of employing lawyers.

5. RECOMMENDATIONS

5.1   I make the following recommendations:

(i)   A High Court judge should be appointed as judge in charge of the Mercantile Courts.

(ii)   A single court guide should be drawn up for all Mercantile Courts.

(iii)   Consideration should be given to devising a special streamlined procedure for business disputes of lower value.

(iv)   HMCS should prepare a guide in respect of "small business disputes" for the assistance of business people who wish to deal with such disputes themselves without the assistance of lawyers, either by mediation or on the small claims track.

CHAPTER 26. HOUSING CLAIMS

INDEX

1. INTRODUCTION

1.1   Preliminary Report. I outlined issues concerning the costs of housing claims in chapter 31 of the Preliminary Report.

2. COMPLEXITY OF THE SUBSTANTIVE LAW

2.1   Opinion expressed in Preliminary Report. In PR paragraphs 31.1.3 to 31.1.5, I suggested that the complexity of substantive law in relation to housing was a cause of increased costs. I therefore echoed the call made by Lord Woolf thirteen years ago for a review of the law in this field, with the aim of consolidation and simplification.

2.2   Comments during Phase 2. Most respondents[27] during Phase 2 agreed with those paragraphs of the Preliminary Report. The Law Society states:

> "The Society agrees with Jackson LJ's view (paragraph 1.5) that, to a great extent, the principle of simplification of the rental market across the social housing sector by adoption of a limited number of different types of tenancy agreements, as recommended by the Law Commission several years ago, would assist tenants and landlords alike, as well as the judiciary. Any decrease in the different types of statutory regimes would also have a positive impact on the efficiency and speed with which cases are dealt with by the courts once issued, as well as an impact on costs."

2.3   Current proposals for reform. The proposals of the Law Commission in its report "Renting Homes"[28] are discussed in PR paragraphs 31.1.4 to 31.1.5. In May 2006 the Law Commission published "Renting Homes: The Final Report". Volume 1 explains the recommendations and contains an illustrative model secure contract and standard periodic contract.[29] Volume 2 comprises a draft Rented Homes Bill.[30]

2.4   Shortly after the publication of the Costs Review Preliminary Report, in May 2009, the Government issued a paper entitled "The private rented sector:

---

[27] However, the London Solicitors Litigation Association disagrees.
[28] Law Com No 284, November 2003, which can be found at http://www.lawcom.gov.uk/docs/lc284.pdf.
[29] http://www.lawcom.gov.uk/docs/lc297_vol1.pdf.
[30] http://www.lawcom.gov.uk/docs/lc297_vol2.pdf.

professionalism and quality".[31] This was in response to the "Rugg Review", an independent review of the private rented sector which was commissioned in January 2008. In that paper, at section 1 paragraph 17, the Government expresses the view that "*the time is not right for the upheaval for tenants and landlords which [the type of fundamental change in tenure that is proposed in Renting Homes] would entail.*"

2.5   The other current proposals for reform in the area of housing claims are summarised in the following paragraphs.

2.6   The Law Commission's report "*Housing: Proportionate Dispute Resolution*"[32] considers how housing problems and disputes may be solved and resolved proportionately. Although that report addresses problems with the housing system rather than focusing on reform of substantive law, the Law Commission believes that a system developed along the lines proposed could prevent many housing problems from arising in the first place. The report reaches the following three broad conclusions:

- An enhanced scheme for the provision of advice and assistance, known as "triage plus", should be adopted in relation to housing problems and disputes.

- Other means of resolving disputes, outside of formal adjudication, should be more actively encouraged and promoted.

- There should be some rebalancing of the jurisdictions as between the courts and the First-tier and Upper Tribunals in the new Tribunals Service,[33] combined with modernisation of procedural rules which affect the ability of the courts to act as efficiently as possible.

2.7   The Law Commission published a third report on housing matters in August 2008 entitled "*Housing: Encouraging Responsible Letting*".[34] This report deals with issues arising from the first two reports, focusing on the private rented sector. Before setting out detailed conclusions, the Law Commission identifies two "fundamental issues" underpinning its recommendations. First, implementation of the recommendations in *Renting Homes* would make a significant contribution to encouraging responsible renting. Secondly, there should be a new approach to the private rented sector, grounded in principles of smart regulation. The report then sets out the following principal conclusions:

- Meeting the regulatory challenges of the private rented sector demands a new comprehensive approach.

- The costs of compliance with this regulatory approach must be reasonable and proportionate.

- Bringing about effective change of culture in the residential lettings market may ultimately require the introduction of a compulsory system of self-regulation.

- Moving directly to a scheme of enforced self-regulation would not be practicable and there should instead be a staged programme of reforms.

---

[31] http://www.communities.gov.uk/documents/housing/pdf/1229922.pdf.
[32] Law Com No 309, May 2008, which can be found at http://www.lawcom.gov.uk/docs/lc309.pdf.
[33] Any proposed reform of tribunals falls outside my terms of reference.
[34] Law Com No 312, August 2008, which can be found at http://www.lawcom.gov.uk/docs/lc312.pdf.

2.8   In June 2009 the new regulator for social housing in England, the Tenant Services Authority (the "TSA")[35] set out its proposals for a new regulatory regime in its discussion paper *"Building a New Regulatory Framework"*.[36]   The TSA's proposals are based on the principle of "co-regulation" which aims to strike a balance between (i) direct regulation (where national standards are developed and evaluation of performance is assessed directly by the regulator) and (ii) self-regulation (where local standards are developed with tenants by landlords themselves).   As the Property Bar Association notes in its Phase 2 submission, the TSA's paper makes no reference to the draft Rented Homes Bill.

2.9   I remain of the view, expressed in PR paragraph 31.1.5, that simplifying substantive housing law would considerably reduce the costs of litigation in that area and improve access to justice.   I recommend that the Government should reconsider undertaking such a process of simplification, as proposed by the Law Commission in its papers of November 2003, May 2006 and August 2008.

3. POSSESSION CLAIMS BY LANDLORDS

3.1   Issues concerning possession claims are discussed in PR paragraphs 31.2.1 to 31.2.30.

3.2   Fixed costs. The extent to which costs of possession proceedings are currently fixed is set out in PR paragraphs 31.2.9 to 31.2.10.   I now propose that all possession proceedings which are brought in the fast track should be the subject of fixed costs, as set out in chapter 15 above.   This will be beneficial to tenants, who are frequently ordered to pay the costs of such proceedings.

3.3   Costs of issue. As set out in PR paragraph 31.2.13, the costs of issuing possession proceedings manually at a county court are 50% higher than the costs of issuing such proceedings online under PCOL.[37]   The Civil Legal Aid Sub-Committee of the Bar Council ("CLASC") proposes that where the landlord could use PCOL but chooses to issue manually, he should only be able to recover an amount equivalent to the PCOL issue fee.   This is a sensible proposal, which will (a) encourage use of the online facility, thus reducing the burden on court staff, and (b) reduce the costs burden on tenants.   I therefore recommend adoption of this proposal.

3.4   Pre-action protocols. There are two relevant pre-action protocols, namely the Pre-Action Protocol for Possession Claims based on Rent Arrears (the "Rent Arrears Protocol") and the Pre-Action Protocol for Possession Claims based on Mortgage or Home Purchase Plan Arrears in respect of Residential Property (the "Mortgage Protocol").   There is a general perception that pre-action protocols are working well in this field.   The Association of Her Majesty's District Judges states in its submission:

> "The development of various pre-action protocols has contributed significantly to the management of Housing claims. The real issues are identified early so that unnecessary costs do not accumulate."

---

[35] The TSA is responsible, under the Housing and Regeneration Act 2008, for regulating housing associations and the housing activities of local authorities who own their own stock.

[36] http://www.tenantservicesauthority.org/upload/pdf/Building_a_new_reg_framework_disc_paper.pdf.

[37] Possession Claims Online, as to which, see chapter 43 below.

3.5   Compliance and enforcement. Despite the general support for the protocols, a note of caution has been sounded. CLASC suggests that the effect of the Rent Arrears Protocol may be "wearing off". The Housing Law Practitioners Association ("HLPA") reports problems of non-compliance with that protocol.[38] I do not recommend any rule change in order to deal with this. The court's existing powers under paragraph 4.6 of section II of the Practice Direction – Pre-Action Conduct (the "PDPAC") are quite sufficient in this regard.[39] I draw the attention of practitioners and judges to that provision. Courts should impose effective sanctions under paragraph 4.6 upon landlords who disregard the provisions of the Rent Arrears Protocol.

3.6   Proposed amendment of the Rent Arrears Protocol. In PR paragraphs 31.2.21 to 31.2.22 I expressed support for amendments to the Rent Arrears Protocol, which are currently proposed by the Civil Justice Council Housing and Land Committee. The purpose of these amendments is (a) to achieve compliance with the developing Strasbourg jurisprudence concerning ECHR[40] article 8 and (b) to avoid lengthy and costly battles about the effect of article 8 in possession proceedings.

3.7   There was general support for these proposals in the Phase 2 responses. However, HLPA comments:

> "In the meantime HLPA gives a cautious welcome to the HLC-CJC proposal. The caution is because we are concerned that it be made clear to the occupants that the information is being sought to enable the public authority to decide whether to issue proceedings or not. Otherwise there is likely to be an understandable reluctance to answer inquiries about personal circumstances. In addition allowance needs to be made for the inarticulate, illiterate, or non English speaking occupant if a genuine attempt to obtain relevant information is to be made.
>
> The opportunity could be taken to make it clear that the Protocol applies to all social landlord possession cases where the reason for seeking possession is rent arrears even those where the tenant had no security of tenure (eg because the tenancy was granted pursuant to the local authority's powers and duties under the homelessness legislation – Schedule 1 para 4 Housing Act 1985)."

3.8   As the proposed protocol amendments set out in PR paragraph 31.2.21 are already under consideration by the Civil Justice Council, I do not make any recommendation as to the detailed drafting of the protocol amendments. I do, however, recommend that the Rent Arrears Protocol be amended, in order to set out what steps should be taken by landlords so as to comply with their obligations under ECHR article 8. I see force in the comments of HLPA quoted in the preceding paragraph and hope that those comments will be taken into account in the drafting of the protocol amendments.

3.9   Mortgage Protocol. The Mortgage Protocol has only recently come into force. As respondents point out in their Phase 2 submissions, it is too early to say how effective that protocol is. However, the same observations concerning compliance and enforcement apply to the Mortgage Protocol as apply to the Rent Arrears

---

[38] Similar concerns have been expressed by the National Association of Citizens Advice Bureaux ("Citizens Advice"): see paragraph 4.4 of chapter 1 above.
[39] Elsewhere in this report I recommend that paragraph 4.6 of the PDPAC be strengthened, in order to deal with non-compliance with protocols in other areas of civil litigation. Those recommendations, if implemented, will not detract from the existing powers under paragraph 4.6.
[40] The European Convention on Human Rights.

Protocol.[41] In their recent report *"Turning the Tide"*[42] Advice UK, Citizens Advice and Shelter report non-compliance with the Mortgage Protocol in a significant number of cases. They call upon the Judicial Studies Board *"to introduce training to ensure judges are informed of the sanctions already available to them if lenders have not complied with the pre-action protocol"*. In my view, the courts already have sufficient powers to deal with non-compliance and I repeat my comments in paragraph 3.5 above.

3.10   Having considered the representations received during Phase 2, I do not recommend any change to the costs rules in respect of costs recoverable by mortgagees, as set out in section 50 of the Costs Practice Direction, save that I propose fixed costs in fast track cases.[43]

3.11   <u>Lack of public funding for representation for tenants.</u> The restrictions upon legal aid and the low hourly rates paid by the Legal Services Commission (the "LSC") have led to a decline in the number of solicitors willing, or indeed able, to act for tenants. This is discussed in PR paragraphs 31.2.6 and 31.5.1. The Legal Aid Practitioners Group in its Phase 2 submission helpfully sets out how the current legal aid regime operates:

> "First, individuals are provided with advice and assistance (short of representation in the court) under the Controlled Work scheme. Such work is currently paid under a national fixed fee scheme. The fixed fee is £174. This represents 3.4 hours work at an hourly rate of £51.05 per hour (£54.15 in London). Suppliers are required to provide unlimited work for clients at this rate. Only if the work exceeds 10.2 hours will the supplier actually be paid at £51.05 per hour. In all other cases, they get just £174 per case. Because of the high proportion of cases where the work exceeds the fixed fee but falls below the 10.2 hour threshold, in practice the actual hourly rate at which work is done under this fixed fee scheme is commonly as low as £20 to £25 per hour. The work is nonetheless of great importance: it is here that legal work is undertaken to resolve disputes without the need to resort to the courts.

> Second, where it is necessary for the individual to be represented in the county court, funding is provided under the scheme for Licensed (or certificated) work. For this the rate is £66 per hour (£70.00 per hour in London). This rate is paid regardless of the degree of experience of the solicitor concerned."

3.12   <u>The LSC's view.</u> The LSC has published a report[44] on the initial impact of fixed fees which paints a rather different picture to that set out above. Fixed fees for housing and all other areas of civil advice were introduced in October 2007 on a cost neutral basis i.e. if behaviour did not change average earnings of practitioners would be unchanged on the "swings and roundabouts" approach which is central to any fixed fee system. In fact the average time spent on cases has fallen in response to fixed fees (by approximately 6% in housing) and profitability of the work has risen (by 19% in housing but that may in part be because complex cases have not fully

---

[41] Concerns were expressed by Citizens Advice at the meeting with me on 25th November 2009: see paragraph 4.4 of chapter 1 above.
[42] Published by AdviceUK, Citizens Advice and Shelter on 15th December 2009.
[43] See chapter 15 above. It should be noted that AdviceUK, Citizens Advice and Shelter recommend that the Ministry of Justice should consider introducing a fixed fee regime for mortgage possession claims: see *"Turning the Tide*, 15th December 2009, page 17.
[44] LSC Phase 1 Fee Schemes Review Final Report, March 2009.

worked through the system). In chapter 7 above I set out the further views of the LSC in relation to housing.

3.13   Comment. I remain of the view, as expressed in chapter 7 above, that legal aid rates should be set at a level which allows properly organised solicitors to operate viably, taking into account the role played by *inter partes* costs in legal aid cases. However, *inter partes* rates should be set at a level which is fair for both publicly and privately funded housing cases – legal aid rates can then be reviewed in that context. As to whether legal aid rates currently are at too low a level to be economic, that is not an issue which can be resolved within the scope of this review for the reasons given in chapter 7 above.

4. DISREPAIR CLAIMS BY TENANTS

4.1   Housing disrepair claims are discussed in PR paragraphs 31.3.1 to 31.3.4. The factual summary in those paragraphs has not been challenged, save for the statement that "*CFAs*[45] *now provide an alternative method of funding such litigation*". In relation to that sentence HLPA comments:

> "The observation in the report that 'CFAs now provide an alternative method of funding such litigation' (para 3.3) is correct in the sense that it is an alternative method in certain circumstances and not the alternative method. In our experience disrepair cases supported by CFAs are outside the norm. There are a number of reasons why that should be so. The main purpose of most disrepair cases is to obtain an order for works rather than damages. If clients qualify for public funding (which, in most cases, social housing tenants will) then it would be professionally suspect to advise them to conduct the case under a CFA. Nor is the insurance industry geared to deal with disrepair cases in the same way as it is with personal injury- a factor not unrelated to the potential complexity of housing cases (as referred to above)."

4.2   I agree that, in the client's interest, housing disrepair cases should generally be brought on legal aid where that is available, rather than under CFAs. This is because legally aided claimants have the protection of section 11 of the Access to Justice Act 1999 (the "1999 Act"). I am told that after-the-event insurance is seldom available for housing disrepair cases. Furthermore, from the point of view of landlords (as well as tenants) disrepair claims brought on CFAs generate substantial problems, as set out in Birmingham City Council's Phase 2 submission.

4.3   If a housing disrepair claim is successful, the claimant's lawyers will recover their costs from the defendant landlord.[46] If the claim is unsuccessful, the lawyers will be remunerated by the LSC at the rates mentioned above. My earlier comments about legal aid rates are equally applicable in this context.

4.4   One way costs shifting. Most claimants in housing disrepair claims already benefit from one way costs shifting, because they are legally aided. There is, however, a strong case for saying that non-legally aided claimants in housing disrepair cases should benefit from qualified one way costs shifting, for broadly similar reasons to those set out in chapters 9 and 19 above. I am told by the Lambeth Law Centre that a number of clients with housing disrepair claims fall just above the legal aid limit.

---

[45] Conditional fee agreements.
[46] My proposals for fixed costs in respect of such cases are discussed in chapter 15 above.

Some of these clients are currently deterred from proceeding due to the adverse costs risk.

4.5   The parties to housing disrepair cases are in an asymmetric relationship. If all claimants have protection equivalent to that provided by section 11 of the 1999 Act, those claimants whose means are above the legal aid threshold will have a degree of protection which is proportionate to their means and resources. This matter is dealt with in chapter 9 above. I do not therefore make any recommendation in relation to one way costs shifting in this chapter.

4.6   <u>Fixed costs.</u> My proposals for fixed costs in respect of fast track housing disrepair cases are set out in chapter 15 above.

4.7   <u>Pre-action protocol.</u> The Pre-Action Protocol for Housing Disrepair Cases (the "Disrepair Protocol") has been in force since December 2003. No problems with this protocol were identified in the Preliminary Report. Nor were any such problems identified in the Phase 2 submissions. HLPA states: *"it is our experience that the protocol has worked well leading to the settlement of most cases at an early stage"*. I do not recommend any amendments to this protocol.

5. HOMELESSNESS APPEALS

5.1   The regime for homelessness appeals is described in PR paragraphs 31.4.1 and 31.4.2. Such proceedings are brought under section 204 or 204A of the Housing Act 1996 (the "1996 Act"). The proceedings, although brought in the county court, are akin to judicial review in the Queen's Bench Division. The court is being asked to review administrative decisions made by housing authorities in response to applications from homeless persons.

5.2   The procedure for such appeals is governed by CPR Part 52. Both HLPA and CLASC point out that the use of Part 52 for such proceedings gives rise to anomalies. Part 52 is designed primarily to provide for appeals from one court (which has made relevant findings of fact) to a higher court. There is no provision in Part 52 requiring disclosure of the housing authority's file, although this evidence will be crucial to the court's decision. CLASC states that different county courts adopt widely varying approaches to this problem and use different standard directions. A number of suggestions have been made for dealing with this problem, ranging from creating a protocol for homelessness appeals to amending CPR Part 52 or its accompanying practice direction so as to make specific provision for homelessness appeals.

5.3   Although sensible pre-action correspondence is necessary (in so far as time allows) I do not recommend the creation of yet another protocol. In my view the best way to deal with this problem is to amend paragraph 24.2 of the Part 52 practice direction,[47] in order to set out what categories of documents the respondent should lodge and when. Such clarification would be beneficial for both appellants and housing authorities, as well as for the county courts dealing with such appeals. This should lead to a saving of costs.

---

[47] Paragraph 24.2 deals with homelessness appeals under sections 204 and 204A of the 1996 Act.

6. LANDLORDS' OFFERS TO SETTLE WITH NO ORDER AS TO COSTS

6.1   CLASC points out that where the tenant is legally aided, there is a conflict of interest between the tenant and his solicitor, which the landlord may exploit. CLASC cites two examples:

> "(a)   A social landlord offers to compromise a possession action by inviting the court to only make a conditional postponed possession order, on terms that there is no order as to costs. The landlord had not made such an offer in its Rent Arrears protocol letter or earlier in the possession claim.
>
> (b)   A LHA[48] offers to compromise a Homelessness Appeal in the county court on condition that there is no order as to costs.
>
> In each case, the legally aided client has secured an effective outcome. In a monetary claim, such a compromise would not be possible because of the impact of the statutory charge; costs would inevitably follow the event. But in these two non-monetary claims, it is in the interests of the individual to take the offered compromise even if this will see their lawyers remunerated at less than half of what would be paid if the matters were pressed to successful outcomes."

6.2   I accept that this state of affairs creates difficulties for solicitors, who are already operating in a harsh environment. CLASC suggests that where a housing claim is settled in favour of a legally aided party, that party should have the right to ask the court to determine which party should pay the costs of the proceedings. That right should not be capable of being overridden by the terms of settlement. The chairman of HLPA points out that the county court could deal with the issue of costs on paper (in the same way that the Administrative Court does). In my view, this is a sensible proposal which merits consultation. It was not an idea canvassed in the Preliminary Report. I therefore recommend that this proposed reform be the subject of early consultation. I say early consultation, because the low level of remuneration for legal aid solicitors has already led to a dearth of legal advice for tenants, as set out in the Preliminary Report. It is not right that the difficulties of solicitors who practise in this area should be compounded.

7. RECOMMENDATIONS

7.1   I make the following recommendations:

(i)   The Government should reconsider undertaking a simplification of substantive housing law, as proposed by the Law Commission in 2003, 2006 and 2008.

(ii)   Where a landlord could use PCOL to issue possession proceedings but chooses to issue manually, he should only be able to recover an amount equivalent to the PCOL issue fee.

(iii)   The Rent Arrears Protocol should be amended in order to set out what steps should be taken by landlords, so as to comply with their obligations under ECHR article 8.

---

[48] A Local Housing Authority.

(iv)   Paragraph 24.2 of the Part 52 practice direction should be amended in order to set out what categories of documents should be lodged by the respondent in homelessness appeals and when these should be lodged.

(v)   Consultation should be carried out on the proposal that where a housing claim is settled in favour of a legally aided party, that party should have the right to ask the court to determine which party should pay the costs of the proceedings.

CHAPTER 27. LARGE COMMERCIAL CLAIMS

INDEX

1. INTRODUCTION

(i) General

1.1   Preliminary Report. In chapter 10 of the Preliminary Report I set out the views and concerns of a number of users of the Commercial Court at section 2 (GC100 Group), section 7 (Commercial Court Users) and section 11 (commercial litigators). In chapter 32 of the Preliminary Report I outlined a number of issues concerning large commercial claims and summarised the proposals of the Commercial Court Long Trials Working Party (the "LTWP"). Those proposals were the subject of a pilot during 2008.

1.2   Most large commercial claims are brought in the Commercial Court and the business of that court will be the principal focus of this chapter. However, as stated in PR paragraph 32.1.4 some large commercial claims are brought in other courts, pre-eminently the Technology and Construction Court (the "TCC") and the Chancery Division. So reference should also be made to the chapters discussing those courts.

1.3   Consultation during Phase 2. During Phase 2 I have received written submissions from various users of the Commercial Court. I have discussed the issues with three Commercial Court judges. I also attended four important meetings at which relevant issues were discussed with court users, namely:

(i)   A meeting held at the Royal Courts of Justice on 18th June 2009 with senior practitioners (one silk and a number litigation partners in City firms) to discuss disclosure in heavy commercial cases (the "senior practitioners meeting").

(ii)   A lunch time meeting on 13th July 2009 with practitioners and clients who regularly use the Commercial Court, hosted by Norton Rose LLP (the "Norton Rose meeting").

(iii)   A seminar of the Commercial Litigators Forum and the City of London Law Society, hosted by Freshfields Bruckhaus Deringer on the evening of 13th July 2009 (the "commercial litigators seminar").

(iv)   A meeting of the Costs Sub-Committee of the Commercial Court Users Committee on the 16th July 2009 (the "users meeting").

1.4   <u>Abbreviations.</u> In this chapter I shall refer to the Costs Sub-Committee of the Commercial Court Users Committee as the "Costs Sub-Committee". I shall refer to the Admiralty & Commercial Courts Guide as the "Guide".

<u>(ii) Level of satisfaction with the Commercial Court</u>

1.5   <u>General tenor of responses during the Costs Review.</u> It is not the function of this Costs Review to tinker with parts of the civil justice system which are thought to be working well and where costs are usually proportionate. I should, therefore, record that respondents during Phase 2 expressed a high degree of satisfaction with the service provided by the Commercial Court to court users. The Bar Council states that in the Commercial Court case management *"is thought to be satisfactory"*. The Law Society commends the excellent work done by the LTWP and believes that the LTWP proposals (after piloting in the Commercial Court) might possibly be applied to other types of claims.

1.6   One international law firm, whose English litigation is principally conducted in the Commercial Court, states:

> "The English Commercial Court is widely recognised as one of the best centres for dispute resolution in the world and many international parties, including many of our clients, choose to resolve their disputes before the English courts notwithstanding the costs involved in doing so. Whilst we recognise that litigating in England can be costly (particularly at the disclosure stage), therefore, we would caution against radical reform to a system which clearly works well and is popular.
>
> ...
>
> [Since Lord Woolf's reforms] there has certainly been more (and better) judicial case management of cases. Lead times in the Commercial Court are impressive and many of our international clients are delighted to be told, for example, that they might get a two hour interim application before a Commercial Court Judge in 6-8 weeks. Further, we also note in this context that the availability of this information on the internet is very helpful and much appreciated by clients."

At the Norton Rose meeting both practitioners and clients told me of international cases which were attracted to London precisely because of the "Rolls Royce" service offered and the extensive disclosure regime.

1.7   <u>Cases concluded at proportionate cost.</u> The data supplied by users during Phase 1 indicated that most (but not all) cases in the Commercial Court are resolved at proportionate cost: see PR paragraph 10.2.6, paragraph 10.7.14, appendix 9 and appendix 11. During Phase 2 an international law firm commenting on the data stated:

> "...in large commercial cases, costs are by and large proportionate. This should not be forgotten, and nor should the fact that the Commercial Court has already (through the Long Trials Working Party), following extensive consultation with those who actually use the Court, taken a number of steps to make its procedures more efficient and cost-efficient."

1.8   Reputation. The Costs Sub-Committee states (quite correctly) in its Phase 2 submission:

> "The Commercial Court enjoys a formidable reputation for commercial dispute resolution. It has many competitors overseas, yet research by survey has shown that in 80% of cases in the Commercial Court, one of the parties carried on business outside this jurisdiction and in 52% of cases both parties did. Thus a great many of the disputes handled by the Commercial Court involve overseas commercial parties who have chosen London as their forum, and specifically the Commercial Court.
>
> This is of importance to the UK economy as a whole. If English commercial law maintains its position as the world's commercial law of choice, that helps sustain the direction of international business choice towards the UK - and not just for law."

1.9   Comment. Complacency is dangerous for obvious reasons. On the other hand, given the tenor of responses received during Phase 2, I should be extremely cautious before recommending major changes to the existing procedures of the Commercial Court. The Commercial Court is named as the dispute resolution forum in very many overseas contracts. Indeed the majority of the Commercial Court's work consists of litigation which overseas parties have chosen to bring to London. The importance of the international work dealt with by the Commercial Court is discussed in section 1 of chapter 32 of the Preliminary Report. Those paragraphs remain valid. It is important not to make procedural changes which will render London unattractive to commercial litigants from overseas.

1.10   A further reason for caution is that a new edition of the Guide was published shortly after my Preliminary Report in May 2009. The new edition of the Guide gives effect to many, but not all, of the recommendations made in the LTWP report, following completion of the pilot exercise. There has so far been only limited experience of litigation under the new provisions of the Guide.

1.11   Bearing the above factors in mind, I shall now discuss a small number of issues which have emerged during the Costs Review concerning the management and the costs of commercial litigation.

2. CASE MANAGEMENT

(i) Disclosure

2.1   Disclosure is recognised as a major source of costs in commercial litigation. One City firm states in its Phase 2 submission:

> "...in 'heavy' commercial litigation, by far the largest costs driver is disclosure. The costs incurred in the disclosure process have significantly increased over recent years, principally because litigants, their advisers and the courts have struggled to grapple with the practical and logistical difficulties involved with e-disclosure."

2.2 The rules and the Guide. As the rules now stand, standard disclosure under CPR rules 31.5 and 31.6 is the default position, unless the court orders some different extent of disclosure. In the Commercial Court, the Guide (following recent amendments) encourages the court to consider a number of alternative orders, namely:

- dispensing with or limiting standard disclosure: rule 31.5(2);

- ordering sample disclosure;

- ordering disclosure in stages;

- ordering disclosure otherwise than by service of a list of documents, for example, by service of copy documents; and

- ordering specific disclosure: rule 31.12.[49]

2.3   The menu option.   One issue which I have canvassed during Phase 2 is whether, in respect of heavy commercial cases, the rules should be amended so that standard disclosure ceases to be the default position. Eight possible approaches are canvassed in chapter 41 of the Preliminary Report, of which option 5 reads as follows:

> "No default position.   Another possibility is that the various breadths of disclosure could be set out in the relevant practice direction. With no default position, at the first CMC[50] the parties and the court would be forced to turn their mind to what would be the most appropriate process to adopt in those proceedings."

This approach became known during Phase 2 as the "menu option", because the court would be choosing from a range of possible disclosure orders, with no steer from the rules towards a particular outcome.

2.4   Views expressed during Phase 2.   In respect of personal injuries litigation and most general litigation, there was no appetite for any departure from standard disclosure. However, in respect of major commercial litigation a groundswell of support emerged for the menu option. After some debate, the menu option became the favoured approach at the senior practitioners meeting. Indeed at the end of that meeting a working group was set up to produce a draft rule encapsulating the menu option. That draft went through a number of amendments over the next six weeks, as it was debated with others.

2.5   At the Norton Rose meeting, a number of speakers supported the menu option. At the commercial litigators seminar there was a full debate about disclosure and copies of the working group's draft rule were tabled. At the end of that debate I took a vote. There were 45 votes in support of the menu option, 16 votes in favour of the International Bar Association (the "IBA") approach, three votes in favour of standard disclosure and eight abstentions. At the users meeting there was general support for the menu option and a number of suggestions were made for improvement of the draft. The Commercial Bar Association ("COMBAR") also expresses support for the menu option. COMBAR adds that for this to work there must be proper exchange of information and consideration of the practicalities of disclosure before the first case management conference ("CMC").

2.6   Costs Sub-Committee.   In its Phase 2 submissions the Costs Sub-Committee states:

---

[49] Paragraph E2.1 of the Guide.
[50] Case management conference.

"The Sub Committee would support the introduction of a new rule (CPR 31.5A), in the form discussed with the Review, that would offer a menu of disclosure orders and directions to allow a tailored approach in substantial cases (defined to include any case before the Commercial Court). This is very much in the spirit of the Aikens Report."[51]

2.7   Rider re judicial training.   One rider which was expressed by some respondents in relation to the menu option was that it was important that judges should receive more training in relation to e-disclosure. This is a matter to which I shall revert in chapter 37 below.

2.8   Conclusion.   I agree with the majority view referred to above. In relation to large commercial claims (but certainly not in relation to all claims), the rules ought to provide for the menu option. I shall take this matter forward in chapter 37 below, when formulating my recommendations in respect of disclosure.

(ii) Lists of issues

2.9   LTWP recommendation.   One of the recommendations of the LTWP was that a list of issues should be judicially settled at the first CMC and that this should become the keystone to the proper management of the case; thereafter the pleadings would have only secondary importance. There were some concerns during the piloting of the LTWP proposals that this procedure may not be beneficial. The LTWP proposals were modified to some degree in the light of those concerns. The revised edition of the Guide now provides:

> "D6.1   After service of the defence (and any reply), the solicitors and counsel for each party shall produce a list of the key issues in the case. The list should include both issues of fact and issue of law. A separate section of the document should list what is common ground between the parties (or any of them, specifying which).
>
> D6.2   (a)   The list of issues is intended to be a neutral document for use as a case management tool at all stages of the case by the parties and the court. Neither party should attempt to draft the list in terms which advance one party's case over that of another.
>
> (b)   It is unnecessary, therefore, for parties to be unduly concerned about the precise terms in which the list of issues is drafted, provided it presents the structure of the case in a reasonably fair and balanced way. Above all the parties must do their best to spend as little time as practicable in drafting and negotiating the wording of the list of issues and keep clearly in mind the need to limit costs.
>
> (c)   Accordingly, in most cases it should be possible for the parties to draft an agreed list of issues. However, if it proves impossible to do so, the claimant must draft the list and send a copy to the defendant. The defendant may provide its comments or alternative suggested list to the court (with a copy to the claimant) separately."

---

[51] The LTWP report.

Section D6 of the Guide goes on to provide that the list of issues shall be updated from time to time and shall be used for case management purposes; however, it shall not supersede the pleadings, which remain the primary source for each party's case.

2.10   Division of opinion. A division of opinion about the utility of these provisions was apparent during Phase 2. Some practitioners believe that section D6 of the Guide provides an extremely effective tool for case management. The London Solicitors Litigation Association (the "LSLA") supports the use in case management of a list of judicially settled issues. Others are more sceptical. One major City firm writes:

> "On the usefulness of lists of issues, we agree with the TCC's experience (Chapter 34, paragraph 5.5),[52] and, in particular, we remain concerned as to whether it is realistic for the Guide to comment that the list of issues should be a 'neutral document for use as a case management tool at all stages of the case by the parties and the court. Neither party should attempt to draft the list in terms which advance one party's case over that of another...It is unnecessary, therefore, for parties to be unduly concerned about the precise terms in which the list of issues is drafted' (paragraph D6.2). Pleadings are rightly intended to advance each party's case, and in many cases it is difficult to see how any document derived from them at an early stage can genuinely be neutral or how the parties could be unconcerned by the terms of a document that the court will use to manage the case. The parties will often have different issues upon which they wish to focus, and the phrasing of an issue can have a significant impact."

2.11   A division of opinion as to whether the list of issues is (a) an invaluable tool for case management or (b) expensive to prepare and a waste of money, was apparent at the users meeting. It is, of course, early days. The current Guide provisions concerning lists of issues have only recently come into force. I suspect that the differing views expressed during Phase 2 reflect the differing experience of practitioners in individual cases.

2.12   Recommendation. The question whether section D6 of the Guide promotes saving of costs (through better case management) or causes wastage of costs (because lists of issues are expensive to prepare and of little utility) is a question of obvious importance to the present Costs Review.

2.13   Having considered all material and arguments advanced during Phase 2, I do not recommend that the "list of issues" procedure be adopted in relation to large commercial claims outside the Commercial Court. In relation to the Commercial Court, I recommend that section D6 of the Guide be reconsidered afresh after 18 months experience of litigating under the new provisions has accumulated.

(iii) Docketing

2.14   Discussion in Preliminary Report. The question of docketing or not docketing was discussed in the Preliminary Report at paragraphs 10.11.11, 32.2.13 and 43.5.9 to 43.5.14.

2.15   Debate during Phase 2. This issue has generated much discussion during Phase 2. Many practitioners and court users have urged upon me the great benefits of assigning every case to a single judge. It is said that this is particularly important

---

[52] This is a reference to PR paragraph 34.5.5.

in relation to large commercial cases, which by definition require much reading-in time. For example, the Litigation Committee of the City of London Law Society states:

> "If one judge runs a case from start to finish under a 'docket' system, he / she will be much better placed than judges are under the present system (where they dip in and out of cases) to exercise the case management powers which already exist – in other words, they would be better placed to exercise informed case management. He or she would be much better placed to impose sanctions for non-compliance, deal with interim applications, encourage the use of ADR and require costs estimates as appropriate for various stages of the proceedings. Docketing could therefore be a key element of cost reduction in commercial litigation.

> The Commercial Court has declined to introduce a docket system, apparently on the basis that its judges prefer not to be confined to commercial cases...and wish to be able to continue to turn their hand to criminal cases in particular. In a world where clients increasingly expect specialisation in the resolution of their problems, this approach is, in our view, not the right one. It would be better for efficient case management, and for promoting the English courts internationally, if a case within a broad category (e.g. commercial / business) were to be handled by a judge habitually engaged in cases in that category."

2.16 On the other hand there is a tradition, going back almost 900 years, of the King's or Queen's justices going out on circuit for a substantial part of each year and this has become a cornerstone of the administration of justice. There are strong policy arguments for retaining that system, at least in relation to the majority of Queen's Bench judges.

2.17 <u>Issue for future consideration.</u> It is not within my terms of reference to recommend any substantial change to the circuit system and I do not do so. However, I put on record that the question may need to be considered on a future occasion whether those specialist High Court judges to whom is entrusted the management of major commercial or construction litigation should continue to undertake lengthy criminal trials on circuit or whether (like the majority of Chancery Division judges) they should be permanently based in London (or in some other major centre of commercial litigation).[53] If that question does come to be considered in the future, regard might possibly be paid to Professor Dame Hazel Genn's report "*The Attractiveness of Senior Judicial Appointment to Highly Qualified Practitioners*".[54] In paragraph 54 she states that about half of the practitioner respondents mentioned the requirement to go on circuit as a major disincentive to applying for the High Court bench. She adds that the circuit requirement was mentioned even more frequently than salary as the principal reason why a respondent would not consider applying for appointment.

2.18 <u>Recent improvements.</u> Both Commercial Court judges and the Costs Sub-Committee tell me that substantial improvements have been made in relation to docketing within the existing structure. It is now possible to ensure that any case which has particular need for docketing is duly assigned to a single judge. When that judge is on circuit, he or she can maintain involvement with the case by telephone or email or by holding case management hearings on circuit. I am told that if a request is made (for good reason) for assignment to a single judge at the first CMC, it is

---

[53] For example, the new Civil Justice Centre at Manchester.
[54] Which can be found online at http://www.judiciary.gov.uk/docs/report-sen-jud-appt.pdf.

generally possible to comply with such request. I am also told that such requests are not frequently made.

2.19   Section D4 of the Guide provides:

> "D4.1   Cases which are exceptional in size or complexity or in having a propensity to give rise to numerous pre-trial applications may be allocated to a designated judge.
>
> D4.2   An application for the appointment of a designated judge should be made in writing to the Judge in Charge of the List at the time of fixing the case management conference.
>
> D4.3   If an order is made for allocation to a designated judge, the designated judge will preside at all subsequent pre-trial case management conferences and other hearings. Normally all applications in the case, other than applications for an interim payment, will be determined by the designated judge and he will be the trial judge."

2.20   <u>Comment.</u> In my view, the provisions of section D4 of the Guide should no longer be restricted to cases which are exceptional in size or complexity or in having a propensity to give rise to numerous pre-trial applications. Having regard to the matters set out in paragraph 2.18 above, I recommend that the category of cases which may be assigned to a designated judge be broadened, so that paragraph D4.1 is no longer confined to "exceptional" cases. If this recommendation is accepted, the revised wording of that paragraph must be a matter for the Commercial Court judges. I also recommend that section D8 of the Guide be amended to provide that the question whether a case warrants assignment to a single judge should be specifically considered at the first CMC.

(iv) General case management points

2.21   A number of practitioners, whilst acknowledging the proactive case management of the Commercial Court, argue that it should be more robust. One City firm comments that "*one of the main ways to reduce and limit costs is for the courts to use their case management powers more robustly*". The LSLA states:

> "We firmly support the views of the Long Trials Working Party that a prime way to reduce costs is for the Court to use its case management powers to promote the more efficient and costs-effective resolution of disputes. If we have a difference of emphasis, it is that we believe that those powers should be used more robustly and more consistently, including through the use of docketing especially for the heavy and complex cases that require that level of judicial attention.
>
> There is something in the fact that these powers have not been used effectively to date. Judges have for a long time been armed with all the powers they need to ensure parties stick to timetables, control any delays that might arise, reduce unnecessary documentation and penalise uncooperative or even obstructive behaviour."

2.22   The point is made by some practitioners that Commercial Court judges should take a firmer line in enforcing their orders and dealing with instances of non-compliance. However, there is no support for the hard line approach canvassed in PR paragraph 43.4.21 and eloquently urged by Professor Adrian Zuckerman at the Costs Review seminar in Manchester on 3rd July 2009.

2.23   Issues such as how robust or firm case management should be are not easy to decide in the abstract. I do not make any specific recommendation for reform in this regard. However, since similar points have been made by a number of practitioners, I draw them to the attention of the Commercial Court and its Users Committee for consideration.

(v) Costs management

2.24   In chapter 40 below I advocate the use of costs management for certain categories of litigation. The general view (even amongst those who support the concept of costs management) is that this would not be appropriate for the high value cases which generally pass through the Commercial Court.

2.25   I do, however, see force in the suggestion made by one Commercial Court judge that the Commercial Court should have a discretion to adopt costs management in an individual case if, after hearing submissions, the judge deems that course appropriate. I also note the support expressed by the Costs Sub-Committee for *"sensible and proportionate arrangements to ensure an exchange of information on incurred costs and projected costs"*. The LSLA believes that the court should be able to ask the parties at any stage how much has been spent and how much is likely to be spent. However, the LSLA doubts the benefit of requiring the parties to produce budget estimates.

2.26   In my view, the question whether costs management should be adopted in Commercial Court litigation should be left to the discretion of judges in individual cases. However, I would encourage judges actively to adopt costs management in any lower value cases[55] which are brought in the Commercial Court.

3. RECOMMENDATIONS

3.1   I make the following recommendations:

(i)   After 18 months, the question whether section D6 of the Guide ought to be repealed or amended should be reconsidered in the light of experience.

(ii)   Sections D4 and D8 of the Guide should be amended to permit more frequent allocation of appropriate cases to designated judges.

3.2   In respect of disclosure, my recommendations are set out in chapter 37 below. In respect of costs management, my recommendations are set out in chapter 40 below. I therefore make no recommendations about those matters in the present chapter.

---

[55] By this I mean "lower value" when compared with the general run of Commercial Court cases.

CHAPTER 28. CHANCERY LITIGATION

INDEX

1. INTRODUCTION

1.1   The costs of chancery litigation are discussed in chapter 33 of the Preliminary Report. As set out in PR paragraph 33.1.1, chancery litigation covers a multiplicity of different types of claims and applications. The costs principles governing different types of chancery litigation vary substantially. I attempted to summarise these principles in the Preliminary Report. I also invited comment on aspects of chancery litigation where costs might be excessive or where reforms might promote access to justice at proportionate costs.

2. COMMENTS RECEIVED DURING PHASE 2.

(i) Seminars

2.1   Cardiff seminar. At the Cardiff seminar on 19th June 2009 the President of the Insolvency Lawyers' Association (the "ILA") made a presentation at the chancery session. He argued that an important feature of many chancery actions was their "class" character. The rights of third parties are affected and the court has a supervisory jurisdiction. The issues in such cases can only be resolved judicially (not by alternative dispute resolution ("ADR")). In such litigation there is scope for costs management, because the court's responsibility includes controlling expenditure of costs. He argued that, in relation to chancery litigation, more attention should be paid to class proceedings during Phase 2 of the Costs Review. Following the Cardiff seminar, at my request, the President of the ILA amplified his proposals in a paper written jointly with the Chief Bankruptcy Registrar. In this joint paper it was proposed that there should be fixed costs in straightforward insolvency matters and costs management in more complex insolvency proceedings.

2.2   Chancery seminar. The chancery seminar on 24th July 2009 had the lowest attendance of all seminars during Phase 2. The issues discussed on this occasion were protocols, fixed costs in insolvency and other chancery proceedings, conditional fee agreements and costs management. In relation to insolvency proceedings the view was expressed that routine matters would be amenable to fixed costs, but that an application to restrain the presentation of a winding up petition or bankruptcy petition would not be amenable to fixed costs. In relation to fixed costs generally, some support was expressed for the CMS scheme[56] outlined in chapter 16 above.

2.3   In relation to costs management (as proposed in chapter 48 of the Preliminary Report), there was general support for the development of this in chancery proceedings, provided that judges had sufficient time and sufficient expertise for the exercise. The point was made that it would promote good case management if judges understood the costs consequences of what they were ordering. By way of example, an action was cited where case management directions (formulated in the quest for perfection) had resulted in grossly disproportionate costs. One practitioner made the point that in Part 8 proceedings (e.g. contentious probate proceedings or claims under the Inheritance (Provision for Family and Dependants) Act 1975) there is no allocation questionnaire and so no opportunity to lodge an estimate of costs at the outset. If both parties were to lodge their costs budgets at the outset, this would promote settlement. Another practitioner said that in lease renewals (whether contested or uncontested) both the lodging of proper budgets by the parties and subsequent costs management by the court would be beneficial. At the moment, sometimes costs estimates are lodged together with the allocation questionnaires in lease renewal proceedings and sometimes not.

(ii) Written submissions

2.4   Chancery Bar Association. The Chancery Bar Association (the "ChBA") makes detailed submissions about the use of fixed costs in the fast track and opposes any extension of fixed costs above the fast track. The ChBA advocates more effective and pro-active case management as the key to controlling costs. The ChBA reports the result of a survey of its members upon the issues raised in PR chapter 33. The ChBA helpfully sets out its views on a number of issues which are not specific to chancery litigation; these views are taken into account in other chapters of this report.

2.5   Property Bar Association. The Property Bar Association (the "PBA") asserts that the present system is basically sound:

> "The initial question which the PBA poses is: what is wrong with the current system? The basic principles are that: (subject to a wide judicial discretion) the successful party will obtain his costs from the unsuccessful party; the costs recoverable are however only those which are reasonably incurred, reasonable in amount and proportionate to the issues involved; if those costs cannot be agreed then there is a system for their assessment. As a matter of principle, the PBA does not think that there is anything wrong with this system."

The PBA analyses the pros and cons of fixed recoverable costs. It also comments on a number of specific issues raised in PR chapter 33.

2.6   The PBA expresses similar views to the ChBA concerning case management. At paragraph 26 of its submission the PBA states:

> "Further, the PBA recalls that one of the central tenets of the CPR was that judges would take much greater control of cases procedurally. Members' experience is, however, that judges (particularly at County Court level) do not have the time the inclination or the material properly to get to grips with a

---

[56] A scheme proposed by two partners of CMS Cameron McKenna LLP at the fixed costs seminar on 22nd July 2009.

case at an interim stage. Many of the supposed benefits of the CPR have been missed because of the failure (perhaps through not much fault of their own) of judges adequately to acquaint themselves with cases before hearings: documents don't reach court files; skeleton arguments do not reach the judge; files are lost completely; lists are too crowded to allow proper reading time. The PBA believes that in those specialist courts (such as the TCC,[57] the Commercial Court or the Chancery List at the Central London Trial Centre) where interim or directions hearings are held before Judges, the situation is much less unsatisfactory."

2.7   The Law Society. The Law Society comments in some detail on the issues raised in PR chapter 33. Those comments have been provided by the Law Society's Wills and Equity Committee. The Law Society also makes detailed comments on case management and costs management, but for obvious reasons those comments are not specifically focused upon chancery litigation.

2.8   City of London Law Society. The City of London Law Society's Litigation Committee (the "CLLSLC") has furnished detailed comments on the chancery issues raised in PR chapter 33. Like the Law Society, the CLLSLC addresses case management issues in general terms, rather than with specific reference to chancery litigation.

2.9   Solicitors and counsel. A number of solicitors firms and counsel have commented on the specific chancery issues raised in PR chapter 33. I take these comments into account in section 4 below.

2.10   Get your tanks off our lawn. At one of the Phase 2 seminars, a chancery barrister stated that the ChBA would be submitting that Jackson should *get his tanks off our lawn*". A very experienced, and rather more senior, chancery counsel puts the matter more diplomatically in his written submission. He suggests that as I am not a chancery specialist I should be identifying problems and suggesting possible solutions; but that I should leave the task of working out the details and suggesting specific reforms to others. He writes:

> "10.   What a single individual, helped by assessors, can do is what the Report does very well (to judge by Chapter 33), that is identify problems and suggest solutions. I think, however, that the task of considering the suggested solutions, and deciding what the solutions ought to be, can best be carried out in a different way.
>
> 11.   The way I favour is the appointment of committees to examine specific areas, the members of the committees being people with knowledge and experience of those areas (and they should include, if possible, people who are not lawyers but who have that knowledge and experience). The committees can then recommend specific changes, in the light (in the present case) of the contents of the Report."

---

[57] The Technology and Construction Court.

3. CHANCERY FAST TRACK CASES

(i) Which chancery cases are fast track?

3.1   Part 7 proceedings. There is not a specific "chancery fast track" as such. However, chancery cases begun under CPR Part 7 will be classified as fast track if they meet the criteria set out in rule 26.6(4).

3.2   Part 8 proceedings. Chancery actions are often commenced under CPR Part 8. Such claims are treated as allocated to the multi-track: see rule 8.9(c). I understand that a number of chancery actions begun under Part 8 are of a character which suits them for the fast track. For example, a boundary dispute where the issue turns upon the interpretation of a small number of documents may be suitable for the fast track. Likewise Land Registry Adjudicators sometimes refer to the county court disputes about beneficial interests[58] and these disputes may be amenable to resolution on the fast track. Not every litigant with a property dispute welcomes the full panoply and costs of multi-track proceedings. However, in determining whether a Part 8 case merits allocation to the fast track, regard must be had to complexity and all the circumstances, not simply to the monetary value of the claim.[59] As the rules now stand, the court cannot allocate a Part 8 case to the multi-track until the first hearing: see paragraph 8.2 of the Part 8 practice direction.

3.3   I recommend that CPR Part 8 be amended to enable the court to assign a case to the fast track at any time. This would enable the court to assign appropriate cases to the fast track by a direction in writing at an early stage. The parties would then gain the full benefit of the fixed costs regime which is proposed in chapter 15 above. I agree with the observation of the Law Society that the fast track could only be used "*for those disputes which are of lower value and where the legal and evidential issues are also reasonably straightforward*".

3.4   Possession proceedings. The allocation rules in respect of possession claims are satisfactory. The court has discretion under CPR rules 55.8 and 55.9 to allocate possession actions to the fast track, when appropriate.

(ii) Fixed costs for chancery fast track cases

3.5   Trial costs. Trial costs in the fast track are already fixed under CPR rule 46.2. However, the ChBA has concerns about friction between rules 46.1 and 46.2(2). The ChBA states that solicitors sometimes instruct counsel at a fee below the specified fixed costs,[60] but then recover the full amount of the specified fixed costs upon summary assessment. I have considered whether the rules should be amended as proposed by the ChBA. I have concluded that such amendment would not be appropriate, given my recommendation in chapter 5 above that the indemnity principle be abolished. I would suggest that the remedy lies in the hands of counsel's clerks, who should insist that brief fees accord with the table set out in CPR rule 46.2(1).

3.6   Costs between issue and trial. The ChBA in its submission rightly emphasises the variety of chancery cases which may proceed in the fast track. It proposes that

---

[58] Section 110(1) of the Land Registration Act 2002 provides that "*the adjudicator may, instead of deciding a matter himself, direct a party to the proceedings to commence proceedings within a specified time in the court for the purpose of obtaining the court's decision on the matter*".
[59] This point is emphasised both by the Law Society and others who have commented on the "chancery fast track" issue.
[60] In rule 46.2(1).

any scale fees must be realistic. I agree. However, scale fees or fixed costs must also be proportionate to the sums in issue or the value of the rights in issue. Litigation is inherently uncertain and in most contested cases both parties are at risk of an adverse costs order. Where parties are litigating about the construction of a right of way worth, say, £10,000 it is unacceptable for them both to be exposed to an adverse costs risk of many times that amount. I have studied the pros and cons of fast track fixed recoverable costs set out by the PBA. In my view, at the very least there must be an overall limit upon the costs recoverable in chancery fast track cases. If possible, there should be a matrix of fixed costs for chancery fast track cases, similar to that proposed for other areas of fast track litigation.

3.7   My general proposals in respect of fixed costs in the fast track are set out in chapter 15 above.

4. SPECIFIC CHANCERY ISSUES

4.1   <u>Contested probate claims.</u> Having read the detailed submissions received during Phase 2, I do not recommend any change to the rules governing probate claims. There is, however, an acknowledged problem in achieving settlement of such claims. As previously noted, because of the "all or nothing" approach to such claims, it is difficult for any party to secure protection by a Part 36 offer. A number of respondents (on the basis of experience) have stressed the benefits of mediation in such cases. It has also been pointed out that formal pre-action letters tend to drive parties into entrenched positions. Although I make no specific recommendation for amending CPR Part 57 and the accompanying practice direction, I would respectfully draw the attention of all practitioners to the especial importance of commending ADR at an early stage in this category of dispute.

4.2   The Law Society advocates that the parties should be made aware of the costs risk at an early stage, rather than work upon the assumption that costs will be met out of a central pot. The Law Society also considers that judges could pay greater attention to the costs impact of litigation on the estate or fund. I agree with these observations. In my view both objectives will be fulfilled if proper costs management is introduced into chancery litigation.

4.3   <u>Costs out of trust fund or estate.</u> The circumstances in which costs are taken out of a trust fund or estate are discussed in PR chapter 33 at paragraphs 3.4, 5.8, 5.9 and 6.5. I raised the question whether there should be any restriction upon the amount of costs so recovered. In a survey of members recently conducted by the ChBA (the "ChBA survey") seven members expressed the view that only proportionate costs should come out of the estate with all costs above the proportionate limit being borne by the party incurring them (or by the losing party). Ten members expressed the opposite view. Those who favoured such a restriction expressed certain qualifications. In particular, proportionality should be assessed by reference to the complexity of the issues as well as the value of the estate. Those who opposed such a restriction pointed out that the importance of the issue often exceeds the money value. One commented: "*it is unnecessary to change anything – if the estate is exhausted, it is usually because one party has behaved unreasonably; have the usual rules in hostile litigation; in non-hostile litigation it can be difficult to say one or other is the winner or loser*".

4.4   I venture with some diffidence into an area where expert chancery opinion is almost evenly divided. However, I would suggest that we ought not to view with equanimity a procedural regime which allows the entire estate to be exhausted, however intricate the legal issues may be. If the entire estate is exhausted in the resolution of those issues, there is no difficulty about the question who is the winner or loser. Everyone is a loser (except for the lawyers). I am reinforced in this view by the comments of the Law Society, which believes that there should be a limitation (appropriate to each case) on the amount of costs that can come out of the trust fund or estate.

4.5   In my view, the amount of costs deductible from the trust fund or estate ought to be set at a proportionate level at an early stage of the litigation. That proportionate level should be determined by reference to the value of the trust fund or estate and the complexity of the issues. Whether the balance of costs should be paid by the party who incurred them or by some other party should be determined by the judge. With this framework in place, it is likely that the parties and the court will co-operate in managing the litigation in a proportionate manner.

4.6   I leave the drafting of appropriate rules to chancery specialists, in the event that my recommendation is accepted. However, the general approach which I recommend in the preceding paragraph is in line with the overall principles of this report.

4.7   _Beddoe_ applications. _Beddoe_ applications are discussed in PR chapter 33, paragraphs 3.7, 3.8, 4.4 and 6.3. I raised two questions for consideration during Phase 2: first, whether _Beddoe_ applications are being made too often out of abundance of caution; secondly whether more _Beddoe_ applications could be dealt with on paper. In relation to the first question, in the ChBA members were almost evenly divided. Ten said yes and twelve said no. In relation to the second question, the outcome was much more definitive. Seventeen members said yes and one said no.

4.8   Having considered not only the voting but also the comments made by ChBA members, I do not advocate any rule change in order to discourage inappropriate _Beddoe_ applications. I agree with the observation of the Law Society that it is difficult to see how the rules themselves could be amended to address the problem. This is a matter for guidance by textbooks, the profession and, possibly, the Chancery Guide.

4.9   In relation to the second matter, I see considerable force in the almost unanimous view expressed by ChBA members and in their supporting comments. The CLLSLC also suggests that it might be helpful to encourage more _Beddoe_ applications to be dealt with on paper. CPR Part 64 and Practice Direction B give only a mild steer towards dealing with _Beddoe_ applications on paper: see section 6 of the practice direction. In my view, these provisions need to be firmed up. The rules or practice direction should provide that, save in exceptional cases, all _Beddoe_ applications will be dealt with on paper.

4.10   Neighbour disputes. In Preliminary Report chapter 33 paragraphs 5.10 and 6.6 I discussed disputes between neighbours concerning boundaries, rights of way and so forth; in particular, what measures should be taken to prevent the costs of such litigation getting out of hand. In relation to this issue, a number of respondents stressed the importance of boundary disputes to the parties. The PBA in an eloquent passage urged upon me that such disputes are frequently complex and a person's home is of paramount importance to him. The PBA concluded:

> "Although judges dislike this type of dispute, they should recognise that they are there to resolve them...If apparently (or perhaps 'otherwise') rational

adults wish to spend their money on this type of litigation, then the state cannot and should not try to stop them."

4.11 The Civil Mediation Council (the "CM Council") takes a less purist view. The CM Council urges upon me the wisdom of the approach adopted by His Honour Judge Oliver-Jones QC in the West Midlands. In any domestic boundary dispute he orders an allocation hearing, which the parties and their lawyers are required to attend in person. The judge requires realistic estimates of past and future costs to be produced. The judge draws the parties' attention to the levels of costs involved, the nature of the issues at stake and the merits of mediation. In his experience such cases almost invariably settle thereafter through mediation or otherwise.

4.12 Having considered the range of submissions made on this issue from a number of sources, I do not advocate any rule change in relation to neighbour disputes. Nor do I make any formal recommendation in relation to such disputes. I do, however, commend to both practitioners and judges the practice set out in the previous paragraph. Domestic boundary disputes and similar property disputes between neighbours are particularly well suited to mediation. Judicial encouragement[61] in this regard at an early stage is highly beneficial for the parties. For those cases which, despite such exhortations, proceed to trial I agree with the observation of the ChBA that case management by a judge with conveyancing expertise would be beneficial.

4.13 _Agassi._ In chapter 33 of the Preliminary Report at paragraphs 3.18 and 6.2 I summarised the Court of Appeal's decision in _Agassi v Robinson_[62] and raised the question whether the effect of that decision should be reversed. At first sight the suggestion that _Agassi_ should be reversed is attractive. However, as pointed out by the CLLSLC and by the Law Society, any authorised litigator has responsibilities and must be familiar with the rules relating to privilege and so forth. In my view, the better solution is not to reverse _Agassi_, but for a suitable body of tax experts to become an "approved regulator" within section 20 of the Legal Services Act 2007 (the "2007 Act").[63]

4.14 Other specific chancery issues. A number of other specific chancery issues were raised in my Preliminary Report and have given rise to conflicting responses by chancery practitioners. No clear picture has emerged in respect of those matters and I do not make any specific recommendations for reform. Instead I shall adopt the course urged upon me by chancery counsel, as set out in paragraph 2.10 above. I recommend that the Law Society (perhaps through its Wills and Equity Committee) and the ChBA should set up a working group of the kind described in paragraph 2.10 above and that that working group should consider the other issues raised in my Preliminary Report and debated in the responses to that report. The outcome of that working group's deliberations will hopefully be available by the summer of 2010, so that any proposed reforms can be included in any implementation programme following this report.

4.15 Costs management. Costs management is discussed in chapter 40 below. A number of chancery actions of the kind discussed above would, in my view, benefit particularly from costs management. The point has been made by solicitors, both at the chancery seminar and in written submissions, that there is a need for the early

---

[61] In addition to whatever private advice may have been given to the parties by their lawyers.
[62] [2005] EWCA Civ 1507.
[63] This comes into force on 1st January 2010. It replaces section 28(5) of the Courts and Legal Services Act 1990.

lodging of costs estimates in Part 8 proceedings.[64] Currently the rules do not require this, because there is no allocation questionnaire in Part 8 proceedings. I see considerable force in this point. I recommend that Part 6 of the Costs Practice Direction (the "Costs PD") be amended to require parties in Part 8 proceedings to lodge costs estimates 14 days after the acknowledgment of service (if any) has been filed. If there is no acknowledgement of service, I doubt that the costs of lodging a costs estimate would be justified.

5. INSOLVENCY PROCEEDINGS

5.1   The two general issues concerning insolvency proceedings that arose from the Cardiff seminar were whether it is desirable (i) that recoverable costs in insolvency proceedings be fixed (or benchmarked), and if so in what circumstances; and (ii) to introduce costs management into insolvency proceedings. Two working parties were subsequently set up to consider those issues:

- Fixed costs working group.[65] The terms of reference for the fixed costs working group were to recommend (a) categories of insolvency proceedings for which fixed costs would be appropriate; and (b) figures or bases for fixed costs in respect of each of those categories of proceedings.

- Costs management working group.[66] The terms of reference for the costs management working group were to consider, in relation to insolvency proceedings, and in particular insolvency proceedings in which an office-holder is a party, whether and how it would be beneficial and cost effective for the court to manage (a) the recoverable costs as between the parties and (b) the costs and remuneration of the office-holder as between the office-holder and the insolvent estate.

5.2   The two working parties reported back in October 2009. I am most grateful for their assistance.

(i) Fixed costs

5.3   The current system.   There is currently a system of benchmark costs in bankruptcy proceedings under which HM Revenue & Customs' ("HMRC") costs are summarily assessed in the Royal Courts of Justice. The fixed costs working group considered (a) whether the scheme currently in operation could be extended and (b) the categories of work to which it could be extended.

5.4   Expansion of the HMRC scheme.   The unanimous view of the fixed costs working group was that the scheme currently in operation for HMRC could and should be extended (in the manner discussed below) to "routine" bankruptcy and winding up petitions, whether they result in the making of a bankruptcy or winding up order or dismissal of the petition. The merits of using a fixed costs regime for certain types of litigation were discussed in the Preliminary Report,[67] and there are likely to be benefits to court users in having a regime of fixed or benchmark costs in insolvency cases, at least for "routine" matters. The question then arises as to which

---

[64] Part 8 applies to many chancery actions.
[65] The members of this working party were Mr Registrar Baister, District Judge Robert Jordan, Costs Judge Colin Campbell, Stephen Davies QC and Chris Berry of Edwin Coe.
[66] The members of this working party were Sir Gavin Lightman, Stephen Davies QC and Mr Registrar Baister.
[67] See in particular chapter 23.

matters are "routine" (and should be subject to a fixed or benchmark costs regime), and which are not. The working group concluded that most bankruptcy and winding up petitions fall into this category, irrespective of whether they result in the making of a bankruptcy or winding up order or, alternatively, are dismissed.

5.5   Recovering costs on a fixed or benchmarked basis.   The working group recommended a procedure for recovering costs for "routine" matters on a fixed costs or benchmarked basis as an option for a party who obtains a costs order in his or her favour, without requiring that costs be assessed.[68] If a party exercised its option of seeking to recover costs by application of the fixed or benchmarked amount for the particular step in the proceedings, such an amount would be awarded to that party, usually without further inquiry. This should lead to cost assessments being dealt with swiftly and ideally by the agreement of the parties. Nevertheless, a party could seek to recover its costs without reference to the fixed or benchmarked amount, but if it failed to recover significantly more than the fixed or benchmarked amount, appropriate cost sanctions could be applied against that party due to it having caused a greater amount of party and court time to be consumed to no useful purpose.

5.6   In my view, this is a sensible procedure and I adopt the recommendations of the working group. The figures which the working group recommends are set out in four sample petitioners' statements of costs, which are at appendix 8 to this report. The figures used in the statements of cost were arrived at by the working group by, among other things, having regard to sample bills of assessed costs and the experience of court users as to appropriate levels of cost. It has been assumed that as the work is routine it has been undertaken by a grade C fee earner. Again I accept the working group's advice and recommend that these figures be adopted. These figures should be treated as benchmark costs, rather than fixed costs. For a description of benchmark costs and the respects in which they differ from fixed costs, see PR chapter 23, section 4.

(ii) Costs management

5.7   In respect of more complex insolvency proceedings, the question arises whether the court should exercise any prospective control over (a) costs between the parties or (b) the costs and remuneration of office-holders. During the course of Phase 2, concerns have been expressed about (a) the level of charges paid by office-holders to the lawyers whom they instruct and (b) the level of remuneration charged by office-holders for their work in connection with litigation. Such concerns have been expressed to me by judges. Also I note that three respondents to the survey conducted by the ChBA expressed concerns, which the ChBA summarises as follows in its submission:

> "(i)   There is a perception that these officials milk each case e.g. attendances by more than one partner and several juniors.
>
> (ii)   Lawyers acting for trustees in bankruptcy charge excessive hourly rates; the courts and creditors have little opportunity to monitor these costs; the court should set much lower hourly rates.
>
> (iii)   Trustees in bankruptcy, liquidators, receivers and administrators, the official receiver do not always act reasonably; courts should be more willing to apply the costs follow the event rule so that office holders act

---

[68] It may, as a matter of terminology, be preferable to refer to such an approach as one involving benchmark costs rather than fixed costs, given that recoverable costs are not fixed at an immutable amount or rate. The possibility of introducing benchmark costs was raised by Lord Woolf in his Final Report: see Preliminary Report, chapter 23, paragraph 4.2.

with the same discipline as others. Costs orders made against these officials will not deter people acting as these office holders."

5.8   Costs management[69] may make a useful contribution in this field. The insolvency proceedings costs management working group has helpfully examined my general proposal for costs management in the context of this specialist area.

5.9   The working group considers that flexibility in any cost management measures is essential; the court should only order the parties to file and exchange budget statements in proceedings which are of sufficient complexity to warrant the expense of undertaking costs management procedures. Subject to that *caveat*, the working group proposes the following procedure:

(i)   At the first effective hearing of any application or petition for relief under the Insolvency Act 1986 or in any proceedings to which an office-holder is a party (including any proceedings where the office-holder acts as the agent of a party), and at any subsequent hearing, the court may order/direct the parties to file and exchange budgets of their estimated costs in an appropriate form.

(ii)   In considering whether to exercise its discretion the court will have regard to:

    (a)   the nature of the application;

    (b)   its complexity;

    (c)   the likely length and number of any interim applications and the time estimate of the final application; and

    (d)   the value of any sum in issue.

(iii)   At the first effective and any subsequent hearing the court may also require the solicitors acting for any office-holder to file evidence that:

    (a)   (where appropriate) the office-holder has sanction to bring or defend the proceedings;

    (b)   the office-holder's solicitors have provided him with a budget in accordance with paragraph 2.03 of the Solicitors Code of Conduct; and

    (c)   the creditors' committee (including any informal creditors' committee), the general body of creditors or (where appropriate) the principle creditors have been provided with the information in paragraph (iii)(b) above and any estimate of the non-recoverable remuneration of the office-holder expected to be incurred in connection with the proceedings.

(iv)   At each subsequent hearing and at trial the court may:

    (a)   receive updated figures in order to ascertain what departures have occurred from each party's budget and why; and/or

    (b)   either by agreement between the parties or after hearing argument, approve or disapprove such departures from the previous budget as has occurred.

(v)   If any party exceeds the costs previously estimated for any activity, it shall notify all other parties and the court of the amount of the excess.

---

[69] Discussed in chapter 40 below.

(vi)   Any order for directions will be given to the parties on each side by their respective lawyers, together with copies of the budgets which the court has approved or disapproved.

(vii)   At any time in the course of insolvency proceedings, whether or not the court has ordered/directed the parties to exchange costs budgets, the court may, either of its own motion or on the application of any person affected by the proceedings, apply for the costs of any party to be capped.

(viii)   At the end of the proceedings the court conducting a detailed or summary assessment will have regard to the budget estimates of the receiving party and will generally, save for good reason, approve as reasonable and proportionate any costs claimed which fall within any previously approved total.

5.10   In my view these are extremely sensible proposals, which should be considered by the Insolvency Rule Committee (the "Committee"). If the Committee accepts the proposals, no doubt it will draw up a suitable budget form for use in insolvency proceedings. If my recommendations in chapter 40 below are accepted, a budgeting form for general litigation will be developed in the light of experience from the current pilot exercises. The Committee may care to take that material into account when drawing up any budget form for use in insolvency proceedings.

5.11   Having considered the views of the working group, I do not propose that the rules should provide for any further prospective intervention by the court in respect of (a) costs to be incurred by office-holders in relation to litigation or (b) office-holders' remuneration in respect of work connected with litigation. Ferris J gave helpful guidance on the principles concerning office-holders' remuneration in *Mirror Group Newspapers plc v Maxwell (No. 1)* [1998] BCC 324; [1998] 1 BCLC 638, Ch D. These principles were subsequently developed in the report of the working group which Ferris J chaired.[70] Those principles have now been distilled in the practice statement entitled *"The Fixing and Approval of the Remuneration of Appointees"*.[71] This practice statement was approved by the Insolvency Court Users' Committee in 2004. I note that three respondents to the ChBA's survey expressed satisfaction with the approach set out in the practice statement. If further measures (going beyond my costs management proposals) are required in order to control the costs incurred or charges levied by office-holders, this must be a matter for lawyers and judges who specialise in insolvency to take forward. It is beyond the capacity of this Costs Review to delve into the detail of specialist areas of litigation.

6. RECOMMENDATIONS

6.1   I make the following recommendations:

(i)   CPR Part 8 should be amended to enable the court to assign a case to the fast track at any time.

(ii)   The amount of costs deductible from a trust fund or estate should be set at a proportionate level at an early stage of litigation. Whether the balance of costs should be paid by the party who incurred them or by some other party should be determined by the judge.

---

[70] Report of Mr Justice Ferris' Working Party on the remuneration of office-holders and certain related matters, July 1998.
[71] Available online at http://www.hmcourts-service.gov.uk/cms/files/bankruptcy-practice-statement.doc.

(iii) Practice Direction B supplementing CPR Part 64 should be amended to provide that, save in exceptional cases, all *Beddoe* applications will be dealt with on paper.

(iv)   A suitable body of tax experts should become an "approved regulator" within section 20 of the 2007 Act.

(v)   Part 6 of the Costs PD should be amended to require parties in Part 8 proceedings to lodge costs estimates 14 days after the acknowledgment of service (if any) has been filed.

(vi)   A scheme of benchmark costs should be implemented for bankruptcy petitions and winding up petitions.

(vii) Costs management procedures should be developed in order to control the costs of more complex insolvency proceedings.

(viii) The Law Society and the ChBA should set up a working group in order to consider the remaining chancery issues raised by the Preliminary Report.

CHAPTER 29. TECHNOLOGY AND CONSTRUCTION COURT LITIGATION

INDEX

1. INTRODUCTION

(i) General

1.1   The nature of litigation in the Technology and Construction Court (the "TCC") and the issues arising in respect of that litigation are set out in chapter 34 of the Preliminary Report.

1.2   <u>King's College survey.</u> The results of the King's College survey of TCC cases are set out in PR chapter 34, section 2. The overall conclusions which I draw from those survey results are set out in PR paragraph 34.2.17. Respondents during Phase 2 appeared to be in general agreement with those conclusions.

(ii) Level of satisfaction with the TCC

1.3   <u>General tenor of responses during Phase 2.</u> It is not the function of this Costs Review to tinker with parts of the civil justice system which are thought to be working well and where costs are usually proportionate. I should, therefore, record that respondents during Phase 2 expressed a high degree of satisfaction with the service provided by the TCC to court users. The Bar Council states that in the TCC case management *"is thought to be satisfactory"*. The Law Society *"supports the use of specialist judges and docketing in the TCC"* and believes that this approach should be followed in other courts.

1.4   <u>Cases concluded at proportionate cost.</u> The data supplied by the Technology and Construction Solicitors Association ("TeCSA") during Phase 1 indicated that most cases[72] in the TCC are resolved at proportionate cost: see PR paragraphs 34.3.1 to 34.3.4. The Technology and Construction Bar Association ("TECBAR") expresses agreement with those paragraphs in its Phase 2 submission. TECBAR then states:

> "Accordingly, although it may be that in relation to certain types of litigation there are significant concerns as to the proportionality of the costs which it involves, litigation in the TCC is not (on the whole) one of them."

---

[72] But certainly not all cases: see PR paragraph 34.3.3.

1.5   Case management. In relation to case management TECBAR writes:

> "The TCC benefits very considerably from what is in effect the system of docketing which it operates, as a consequence of which the same Judge deals with a case from start to finish.
>
> It is understood that a serious concern of other areas of the Bar (but not of TECBAR) is that too often the Judge who is assigned to hear a Case Management Conference has been given too little time to familiarise himself or herself with the detail of the case. Accordingly, it is understood that, for example, the Chancery Bar Association intends to put forward a strongly argued case in favour of a system of case management which (in broad terms) reflects the current practice of the TCC.
>
> As a result of the docketing system, it is TECBAR's view that the current approach to case management in the TCC is working well, and does not require substantial reform."

1.6   Submission of TCC High Court judges. The TCC High Court judges in a joint submission state:

> "The TCC has operated successfully and efficiently for many years now. Its Judges are experienced at case managing trials which are complex as well as those which require speedy justice (such as adjudication enforcements)."

1.7   Regional TCC. Similar comments have been made about the TCC courts at regional court centres outside London. The Manchester Law Society states that the TCC is working well in that region. Similar comments are made by a major commercial firm of solicitors practising in the north of England.

1.8   Small construction disputes. In relation to small construction cases (concerning domestic extensions etc) there are specific concerns about disproportionate costs. These will be discussed in section 4 below.

1.9   Conclusion. Complacency is dangerous for obvious reasons. On the other hand, given the tenor of responses received during Phase 2, I should be extremely cautious before recommending any significant changes to the existing procedures of the TCC. The TCC is now named as the dispute resolution forum in a number of overseas contracts. Therefore, in respect of the TCC (as in respect of the Commercial Court) it is important not to make procedural changes which will be unacceptable to overseas litigants, who choose London as their forum.

2. CASE MANAGEMENT IN THE TCC

2.1   Rules and Guide. Case management[73] procedures for the TCC are set out in CPR Part 60 and its accompanying practice direction. The details of how case management is conducted are set out in the TCC Guide.[74]

2.2   Prolix pleadings. The tendency of some parties to serve overlong and discursive statements of case was identified in PR paragraph 34.5.8. This gives rise to additional costs, both for the offending party and for all other parties. During

---

[73] Case management generally is discussed in chapter 39 below.
[74] Second edition, first revision, 2007.

Phase 2 differing views were expressed as to how this problem should be addressed. Some favour an order that the offending party do re-plead; some favour disallowance of costs at the end of the case.

2.3 Having considered the various submissions my conclusion is that where shortcomings in statements of case can be clearly identified at the outset, the court should direct the offending party to re-plead. In other instances, where the deficiencies or irrelevancies in a party's statement of case only become apparent later (for example, because at trial that party has made clear how it puts its case), the proper course should be for the trial judge to give a direction to the costs judge as to what costs should be disallowed in respect of that matter. The court already has the power to give such directions. However, if it is proposed to use this power more frequently, that should be clearly signposted to practitioners. I therefore recommend that section 5 of the TCC Guide be amended to include such a provision.

2.4 <u>Prolix witness statements.</u>[75] Prolix witness statements are a particular problem in construction litigation. Every construction project generates a mass of contemporaneous documents, evidencing every stage and nuance of the project: site meeting minutes, variation orders, interim applications for payment, site instructions and so forth. Some witnesses find irresistible the temptation to go through the bundle commenting upon each recorded event. TECBAR states in its Phase 2 submission:

> "TECBAR shares the concern that witness statements have become unnecessarily long, and too often provide a narrative account of events by detailed reference to and/or repetition of documents in respect of which the witness in question is not able to give direct evidence (being neither the creator nor the contemporaneous recipient of the documents in question) and/or the contents of which can be read by everyone for themselves in any event. The costs of those parts of witness statements which are unnecessary or irrelevant should be disallowed."

2.5 TeCSA accepts that witness statements tend to be over-long and discursive. TeCSA believes that *"the problem is, in large measure, borne out of a concern on the part of those responsible for advising on their content about the loss of the right to comment on material facts, the significance of which might not have been fully appreciated at the time of drafting the statement"*. I am not wholly convinced by this argument. I do not see how any party's position is improved or protected by inclusion in witness statements of material of the kind described in the previous paragraph. I do, however, accept TeCSA's contention that the court should be more flexible about allowing supplementary evidence-in-chief. This is dealt with in chapter 38 below regarding witness statements.

2.6 In my view, once it is established that the court will adopt a more flexible approach to supplementary evidence-in-chief, TeCSA's concerns will have been met. If witness statements containing much irrelevant or unnecessary material continue to be lodged, then a costs sanction should be imposed. At the end of the proceedings, the trial judge could deal with the matter directly, for example by saying that the successful party shall only recover, say, 90% of its costs. Alternatively, the trial judge could give an indication to the costs judge as to what costs should be disallowed in respect of the offending witness statements. Any indication which the trial judge gives in relation to disallowance of costs should be expressed clearly. The indication should be in a form which can readily be applied by the costs judge, who will be

---

[75] This issue is discussed more generally in chapter 38 below.

carrying out a detailed assessment of costs without any prior involvement in the litigation.[76]

2.7   Lists of issues. In the Preliminary Report I expressed the view that in TCC litigation it was seldom worthwhile to put the parties to the expense of agreeing a list of issues. The majority of respondents agreed with that view. The Bar Council comments:

> "Amongst TCC practitioners, there is a widespread view that lists of issues yield little or no benefit and only increase costs."

TECBAR expresses a similar view in trenchant terms. TeCSA points out that pleadings should identify the issues, so that there should be no need for an additional obligation to produce lists of issues with consequential costs.

2.8   The TCC High Court judges state in their joint submission:

> "The Judges are not in favour of rules which <u>require</u> List of Issues to be prepared by the parties. If the pleadings are managed properly, they will identify what the material issues are. The experience in the TCC broadly has been that unnecessary time and cost are expended on the parties seeking to agree issues, largely because one side wants a list of generic issues whilst the other wants a micro list of every conceivable issue which can run to scores of pages. The Rules as they stand permit the Court to order lists when appropriate and there is no need to change that."

2.9   A number of firms of solicitors expressed similar views. One firm of solicitors acknowledged that lists of issues can be problematic, but went on to make the following suggestion:

> "We would support the introduction of a process whereby the parties are invited to describe, in a fairly general way (and perhaps subject to a limit on the number of words used) what they consider the key issues to be, with a view to the Judge deciding upon and formulating the precise wording of any issues that might be dealt with as discrete exercises either before or during the main trial."

2.10   I agree with the general view expressed by practitioners in relation to lists of issues.   The only recommendation which I make in this regard is that the requirements in paragraphs 14.4.1 and 14.4.2 of the TCC Guide be simplified, so that those paragraphs are focused upon the key issues, rather than upon all issues in the case.

2.11   Disclosure. The majority of respondents during Phase 2 believe that standard disclosure is the proper approach in most TCC cases. A similar view was expressed by the great majority of those who attended the conference on construction law at King's College on 9th July 2009. TeCSA, however, takes a different line on this point, arguing that the approach of the International Bar Association (the "IBA") should be the default position in typical TCC cases.

2.12   In chapter 37 below I conclude that the menu option is the best approach to disclosure issues in relation to substantial cases. If a new CPR rule 31.5A is adopted along the lines proposed in chapter 37, this rule will apply to substantial cases in the

---

[76] See *Richardson Roofing Company Ltd v The Colman Partnership Ltd* [2009] EWCA Civ 839.

TCC as in all other courts. I accept that, when such a rule comes to be applied, standard disclosure may well be ordered more often in the TCC than in the Commercial Court. There cannot, however, be any different or special rule for disclosure in TCC cases.

3. DOCUMENT MANAGEMENT

3.1   Volume of documents. In construction projects many contractors, sub-contractors, trade contractors, professional firms and others interact. Such projects generate inordinate quantities of letters, reports, meeting minutes, emails, electronic records and so forth. During my four years as a TCC judge I experienced some trial bundles of daunting proportions, on one occasion exceeding 500 ring files. The effective management of documents by the parties and by the court is of cardinal importance in controlling the costs of TCC litigation.

3.2   Proposal in Preliminary Report. In PR paragraph 34.5.3 I made some proposals for document management in relation to TCC cases. The essence of those proposals was that the trial bundle should be created progressively during the pre-trial process. Some solicitors express support for this proposal, although they point out that proper IT will be necessary.

3.3   Development of e-working.[77] E-working, which was introduced into the TCC under the pilot scheme from 20th July 2009, may provide the solution to the problem. On 23rd September 2009 I attended a demonstration of e-working, as currently installed in the London TCC. I understand from the developers of the software that it may be possible to develop a facility for documents lodged at different stages of the proceedings to be added to a chronological bundle. In other words the documents will be re-ordered into date order, regardless of when they were lodged. Other means of re-organising the electronic file should also be available. I make no specific recommendation in this regard. However, I express the hope that relatively soon IT may provide the solution to the problem identified in PR paragraph 34.5.3.

4. LOW VALUE CONSTRUCTION DISPUTES

4.1   Discussion in Preliminary Report. In PR paragraphs 30.3.4 and 30.3.5 I discussed the particular problem posed by small building disputes, which can generate disproportionate (and on occasion horrific) costs. I suggested that the problem be tackled in three ways, namely introducing a fixed costs regime where possible; ensuring that such cases were managed and tried by judges with specialist expertise; and greater use of alternative dispute resolution ("ADR").

4.2   Fast track cases. Some small building disputes satisfy the criteria set out in CPR rule 26.6(4) and (5). The sum in issue is no more than £25,000; the trial can be concluded within a day[78] and there is one expert on each side.[79] The best way to deal

---

[77] E-working is discussed in chapter 43 below.
[78] Some low value building disputes can be tried out within a day at the county court. I have conducted such cases as counsel.
[79] I have recently discussed with construction lawyers how many TCC cases would, in practice, satisfy the fast track criteria. Different views have been expressed. However, there can be no doubt that at least some small building disputes would satisfy those criteria. I recall when at the Bar conducting county court building cases, with one expert on each side, where the trial was completed within a day.

with such cases is to assign them to the fast track, so that the parties will gain the benefit of the fixed costs regime which is proposed in chapter 15 above.[80]

4.3   At the moment there is no fast track in the TCC: see CPR rule 60.6(1). I recommend that CPR Part 60 or its accompanying practice direction be amended to permit TCC cases to be allocated to the fast track, when appropriate.   I also recommend that a small number of district judges, with suitable construction experience,[81] be authorised to try fast track TCC cases. This recommendation will require some statutory amendment, so as to permit district judges to exercise this jurisdiction.   At the moment TCC judges derive their jurisdiction by a somewhat arcane route, namely by way of "official referees' business" under section 68(1)(a) of the Senior Courts Act 1981 (the "1981 Act").   If this recommendation is adopted, it will then be possible for TCC fast track trials to be conducted by authorised circuit judges, recorders or district judges, depending upon availability.

4.4   <u>Lower value cases above the fast track limit.</u> Low value building disputes may fall outside the scope of the fast track, for example because the trial cannot be completed within a day or because the expert evidence is more extensive than envisaged by rule 26.6(5). Such cases must be assigned to the multi-track, but they can still be dealt with as county court cases. The Manchester Law Society states in its submission:

> "Our only other comment in relation specifically to TCC work is to suggest that greater publicity be given to the fact that there is County Court jurisdiction for TCC work, to support the concept of having TCC liaison District Judges (who would work closely with the TCC Judges) and to make as a general point that Judges could and should generally be more alert to the possibility of transferring suitable cases to the TCC."[82]

4.5   I agree with that observation. Lower value construction disputes which are outside the scope of the fast track should be assigned to the county court TCC at the earliest possible time, so that such cases can be managed and tried by judges or recorders with specialist expertise. Indeed it is one of the functions of a TCC liaison district judge (a position formally established in October 2005) to draw the attention of his or her colleagues to the need to transfer such cases at an early stage to the TCC. I do not make this the subject of any recommendation, because it is fully dealt with in the TCC Guide and the TCC's annual reports: see, for example, page 12 of the Annual Report of the TCC for the year ended 30th September 2008.[83]

4.6   <u>Encouraging ADR.</u> Mediation is dealt with in chapter 36 below. The two principal forms of ADR are conventional negotiation and mediation. ADR has proved effective in resolving construction disputes of all sizes.[84] In relation to small building disputes, however, it is particularly important to pursue mediation, in the event that conventional negotiation fails.

---

[80] This proposal is supported by a firm of solicitors, which acts for house builders and has experience of defending claims for alleged defects in new homes.   The firm states that some of these cases are sufficiently straightforward for allocation to the fast track and that a fixed costs regime would be for the benefit of all parties.

[81] Some TCC liaison district judges might be well suited to this role. Also district judges who dealt with construction disputes in their former practices would also be suited to the role.

[82] The Commercial Litigation Association in its Phase 2 submission makes similar comments.

[83] By Ramsey J, judge in charge of the TCC; dated January 2009.

[84] See the results of the King's College survey, set out PR chapter 34.

5. COSTS MANAGEMENT

5.1   Costs management is discussed in chapter 40 below. One form of costs management has been piloted in the Birmingham TCC since 1st June 2009. The results so far are encouraging.

5.2   I do not believe that costs management should be made compulsory in the TCC. The process brings its own costs. A decision must be made in every case whether costs management will be beneficial. If the CPR are amended in the manner proposed in chapter 40 below, it will be a matter for the discretion of the TCC judge in every case whether or not to adopt costs management.

6. RECOMMENDATIONS

6.1   I make the following recommendations:

(i)   Section 5 of the TCC Guide should be amended to draw attention to the power of the court to disallow costs in respect of pleadings or witness statements which contain extensive irrelevant or peripheral material.

(ii)   Paragraphs 14.4.1 and 14.4.2 of the TCC Guide should be amended, so that they are focused upon key issues rather than all issues in the case.

(iii)   The CPR should be amended so that appropriate TCC cases can be allocated to the fast track. The 1981 Act should be amended, so that district judges of appropriate experience may be authorised to manage and try fast track TCC cases.

(iv)   Mediation should be promoted with particular vigour for those low value construction cases in which conventional negotiation is unsuccessful.

CHAPTER 30. JUDICIAL REVIEW

INDEX

1. INTRODUCTION

1.1 <u>Preliminary Report.</u> Chapter 35 of the Preliminary Report contains a discussion of judicial review proceedings, protective costs orders and the various options for reform, including one way costs shifting. Chapter 36 includes a discussion of environmental judicial review claims, the Aarhus Convention[85] and options for reform of the costs rules in this area.

1.2 <u>Abbreviations.</u> In this chapter I use the abbreviation "PCO" for protective costs order; "C" for claimant; "D" for defendant. I use the following abbreviations for well known cases in the judicial review field:

"*Bolton*" means *Bolton Metropolitan District Council v Secretary of State for the Environment* [1996] 1 All ER 184, [1995] 1 WLR 1176, HL.

"*Boxall*" means *R (on the application of Boxall) v Waltham Forest LBC* (2001) 4 CCLR 258.

"*Buglife*" means *R (on the application of Buglife, The Invertebrate Conservation Trust) v Thurrock Thames Gateway Development Corporation* [2008] EWCA Civ 1209, [2008] All ER (D) 30 (Nov).

"*Corner House*" means *R (on the application of Corner House Research) v Secretary of State for Trade and Industry* [2005] EWCA Civ 192; [2005] 1 WLR 2600.

I refer to the Convention on Access to Information, Public Participation in Decision-Making and Access to Justice in Environmental Matters, signed in Aarhus, Denmark, on 25th June 1998, as the "Aarhus Convention". I refer to the Pre-Action Protocol for Judicial Review as the "protocol". As in chapter 1 above, I refer to the seminar on judicial review and environmental claims as the "judicial review seminar", since environmental judicial review and general judicial review were the main focus of that seminar.

---

[85] See paragraph 1.2 below.

1.3   *Boxall.* In *Boxall*, the claimants (who were legally aided) brought a claim for judicial review against a local authority. In the event, the proceedings were resolved without a full hearing. Scott Baker J nevertheless had to address the question of what costs order should be made. He gave the following guidance:

(i)   The court has power to make a costs order when the substantive proceedings have been resolved without a trial but the parties have not agreed about costs.

(ii)   It will ordinarily be irrelevant that the claimant is legally aided.

(iii) The overriding objective is to do justice between the parties without incurring unnecessary court time and consequently additional cost.

(iv)   At each end of the spectrum there will be cases where it is obvious which side would have won had the substantive issues been fought to a conclusion. In between, the position will, in differing degrees, be less clear. How far the court will be prepared to look into the previously unresolved substantive issues will depend on the circumstances of the particular case, not least the amount of costs at stake and the conduct of the parties.

(v)   In the absence of a good reason to make any other order the fall back is to make no order as to costs.

(vi)   The court should take care to ensure that it does not discourage parties from settling judicial review proceedings for example by a local authority making a concession at an early stage.

1.4   Article 9 of the Aarhus Convention provides:

"2. Each Party shall, within the framework of its national legislation, ensure that members of the public concerned

(a)   having a sufficient interest

or, alternatively,

(b)   maintaining impairment of a right, where the administrative procedural law of a Party requires this as a precondition,

have access to a review procedure before a court of law and/or another independent and impartial body established by law, to challenge the substantive and procedural legality of any decision, act or omission subject to the provisions of article 6[86] and, where so provided for under national law and without prejudice to paragraph 3 below, of other relevant provisions of this Convention...

3. In addition and without prejudice to the review procedures referred to in paragraphs 1 and 2 above, each Party shall ensure that, where they meet the criteria, if any, laid down in its national law, members of the public have access to administrative or judicial procedures to challenge acts and omissions by private persons and public authorities which contravene provisions of its national law relating to the environment.

4. In addition and without prejudice to paragraph 1 above, the procedures referred to in paragraphs 1, 2 and 3 above shall provide adequate and effective remedies, including injunctive relief as appropriate, and be fair, equitable, timely and not prohibitively expensive."

---

[86] Article 6 provides for public participation in decisions on specific activities affecting the environment.

1.5   In *Commission of the European Communities v Ireland*, Case C-427 07 (16th July 2009), the European Court of Justice considered the effect of directives implementing the Aarhus Convention. The Court held that procedural rules must be sufficiently certain in their operation, in order to avoid prohibitive expense. The fact that the Irish courts had discretion not to order the unsuccessful party to pay the other party's costs was not sufficient to achieve compliance: see paragraphs 92 to 94.

2. MEETINGS DURING PHASE 2

(i) Judicial review seminar

2.1   The seminar. The judicial review seminar was held on 27th July 2009 and hosted by Herbert Smith LLP. About 30 people attended, including one lord justice of appeal (Sullivan LJ) and a reasonable spread of practitioners (both solicitors and counsel) who act for both claimants and defendants in judicial review cases.

2.2   The FB paper. The judicial review seminar began with the presentation (in their absence) of a paper by Michael Fordham QC and Jessica Boyd, to which I shall refer as the "FB paper". The FB paper argues that judicial review is special and that it is wrong to carry over into judicial review the costs practices and presumptions which apply in private law cases. The FB paper states:

> "A public law costs regime should promote access to justice. It should be workable and straightforward. It should facilitate the operation of public law scrutiny on the executive, in the public interest. This is the key point. For judicial review is a constitutional protection, which operates in the public interest, to hold public authorities to the rule of law. It is well-established that judicial review principles 'give effect to the rule of law'...The facilitation of judicial review is a constitutional imperative."

2.3   The FB paper proposes that one way costs shifting should be the default position in judicial review, subject to any different order which might be made at the permission stage. The paper points out that there is no need for costs rules to deter frivolous claims, because the permission requirement achieves this. It is argued that one way costs shifting would be fair:

> "Take the fairness rationale. It must be remembered that public authorities have at the heart of their function and being the duty to act in the public interest...The facilitation of judicial review scrutiny is itself in the public interest. There is no 'unfairness' in the State absorbing the cost of this vital public law audit. The State readily absorbs the costs of an ombudsman investigation, an inquest, a public inquiry. Viewed in this light, there is nothing 'unfair' in the State being expected to absorb the cost where the Court has 'called in' a public law matter, having identified viable grounds of challenge at the permission stage. The threat of a costs order will never prevent the authorities of the State from defending themselves on judicial review. There is nothing 'unfair' in removing the costs-risk bar which would serve to exclude judicial review claimants."

2.4   The FB paper is critical of the PCO regime. It draws attention to the fact that Canada applies one way costs shifting in judicial review cases without difficulty. So also does the European Court of Human Rights in Strasbourg.

2.5   <u>Use of conditional fees agreements and after-the-event insurance.</u>   The practitioners present stated that conditional fee agreements ("CFAs") are quite often used in judicial review, but mainly in environmental cases. They stated that after-the-event ("ATE") insurance is rare, but is occasionally obtained. Apparently ATE insurers are generally reluctant to cover judicial review cases. An in-house lawyer at the Civil Aviation Authority (the "CAA") stated that international finance companies sometimes litigate against the CAA with the benefit of CFAs. In his view, it is absurd that CFAs can be used in this context.

2.6   <u>Legal aid.</u> Legal aid is still available for judicial review. It was stated that many immigration cases are done on legal aid. The fact of legal aid, of course, brings with it one way costs shifting, as speakers pointed out.

2.7   <u>One way costs shifting.</u> There was a lively debate about the merits of one way costs shifting in judicial review. The practitioners expressed a range of views. Sullivan LJ argued that one way costs shifting should be the default position. A solicitor with long experience of environmental judicial review cases said that his firm's main concern was adverse costs. If one way costs shifting were introduced, he and his colleagues would be prepared to forego success fees and to act on CFAs with recovery of base costs only in successful cases. Other practitioners disagreed and said that even with one way costs shifting, they must still have success fees in cases which they win.

2.8   One practitioner argued that any one way costs shifting regime should be qualified, so that claimants were always at some risk as to costs. Possibly there should be a benchmark figure for the costs liability of individuals. A solicitor from Liberty spoke in favour of the proposal in the FB paper. He argued that when the court is considering the appropriate costs regime, it should focus on the means of the claimant, rather than the merits of the dispute (since the merits are dealt with by the grant or refusal of permission).

2.9   The solicitor from the CAA argued that in judicial review cases brought by airlines against the CAA, there should be no question of one way costs shifting. If the CAA wins, it should get its costs.

2.10   <u>Protective costs orders.</u> Concern was expressed by practitioners that PCOs are complex and expensive to obtain. Any mechanism to protect claimants against adverse costs should be simple.

2.11   <u>Permission stage.</u> Bearing in mind the costs consequences of granting permission, one practitioner argued that judges should be more robust about refusing permission in weak cases. The fact of litigation has a chilling effect on projects. In planning and environmental matters, a weak claim, for which permission has been granted, may put a project on ice. Another practitioner argued that the permission hearing is not the right occasion to deal with costs.

2.12   <u>Possible middle way.</u> After listening to the argument, I suggested a possible middle way as follows: the default position is that C's liability for adverse costs is £3,000 up to permission and (if permission is granted) £5,000 up to the end of the proceedings. Sullivan LJ supported this proposal. One practitioner commented that this would satisfy the requirement in the Aarhus Convention to protect claimants against "prohibitive expense". In his view if claimants are protected against prohibitive expense in environmental cases, as required by the Aarhus Convention, then "prohibitive expense" should not be allowed in other areas. There should be a uniform regime for all judicial review cases.

2.13   No bifurcation. A member of the Planning Bar supported the view that there should not be any bifurcation between environmental cases and other judicial review cases. He pointed out that it is sometimes difficult to tell whether a case should be classified as "environmental". No-one at the seminar spoke in favour of the proposition that there should be one costs regime for "environmental" judicial review and a different costs regime for other judicial review cases.

2.14   *Boxall.* A number of practitioners expressed concern about *Boxall*. It was pointed out that quite often defendants, after receiving the claim form, agree to re-take the impugned decision. The case settles on that basis and the court, following *Boxall*, makes no order for costs. I suggested that the *Boxall* test is beneficial, because it encourages settlement. Most practitioners present disagreed. They said that *Boxall* was reasonable in cases where C does not follow the protocol; but in cases where C follows the protocol D should settle after receiving the letter of claim and, if D does not settle until after issue, then D should pay the costs. However, some practitioners considered that this was a bit harsh on public authorities. Sullivan LJ suggested that the "trigger point" should be the grant of permission. A member of the Bar suggested a trigger point of three or four weeks after grant of permission.

2.15   Statutory review. Some practitioners expressed regret that there is no permission requirement for statutory reviews under section 288 of the Town and Country Planning Act 1990. They said that a permission hearing would provide a natural opportunity to deal with one way costs shifting. Sullivan LJ said that on an earlier occasion he has put forward a proposal to amend section 288 in order to include a permission requirement, but this proposal has not been pursued.

2.16   Voting. At the end of the meeting I took a vote on whether there should be one way costs shifting in environmental judicial review. The votes were "yes" 14; "no" six; the remainder abstained. I also took a vote on whether there should be one way costs shifting in judicial review generally. The voters were "yes" 15; "no" seven; the remainder abstained.

(ii) Meeting with Coalition for Access to Justice for the Environment

2.17   Coalition for Access to Justice for the Environment. Four members of the Coalition for Access to Justice for the Environment ("CAJE") came to see me on 23rd July 2009. The meeting included in-house lawyers for the Environmental Law Foundation ("ELF"), WWF-UK and Friends of the Earth ("FoE") and the legal representative for Greenpeace. WWF-UK informed me about complaints CAJE is pursuing against the UK with the European Commission and the Aarhus Convention Compliance Committee of the United Nations Economic Commission for Europe (the "Compliance Committee") on the grounds that the costs of environmental litigation are excessive.

2.18   In relation to judicial review, they said that many of their claims involved multiple defendants and thus carried the risk of liability in costs to more than one party. They stated that in practice they rarely pursue ATE insurance for judicial review claims. Insurers usually refuse to offer it and where cover is offered the premiums are extremely high.

2.19   The in-house solicitor for FoE said that its Rights and Justice Centre ("RJC") runs public interest environmental cases for individuals and groups on CFAs. It does not charge success fees. If a case is won, FoE simply recovers base costs. The Greenpeace representative confirmed that it relies on solicitors using CFAs for its cases. They do not charge success fees because this would be inconsistent with achieving affordable environmental justice.   ELF provided a list of recent environmental cases with good prospects of success that were unable to proceed for costs reasons.

3. WRITTEN SUBMISSIONS DURING PHASE 2

(i) Environmental judicial review cases

3.1   Firm of solicitors. A firm of solicitors specialising in environmental judicial review urges that there must be one way costs shifting in order to comply with the UK's obligations under the Aarhus Convention.   It states that PCOs are "*very troublesome creatures*". The *Corner House* conditions are very difficult to comply with in practice.   Furthermore solicitors are in the considerable difficulty of embarking upon litigation without knowing whether or not a PCO will be granted. By the time the PCO decision is made, substantial costs may have been incurred, not least because PCO applications are always opposed and require lengthy and expensive hearings. In *Buglife* the PCO problem accounted for about a quarter of the costs of the entire case.

3.2   The solicitors argue that one way costs shifting would not lead to frivolous claims in the field of environmental judicial review: "*people do not bring frivolous claims, because they usually have to pay their own lawyers*". They point out that if the case is done on a "partial CFA" (i.e. no win, low fee) the client will still have to pay something if the case is lost.   As to interested parties, they are usually substantial corporations which can bear their own costs. Anyway, due to the *Bolton* rules they do not expect to get costs.

3.3   In relation to foregoing success fees in return for one way costs shifting, the solicitors state:

> "You picked up on our suggestion of a quid pro quo of no success fees in return for this.[87] It will be interesting to see how others react to the idea. Of course, we like success fees too, but (albeit to simplify the issue somewhat) we would be sceptical of solicitors claiming 100% success fees and only winning half of the cases. One suspects that success fees are not critical to whether or not the solicitors want to do the work. (In this connection your 16.5.6[88] raises a similar query.)"

The solicitors add the qualification that, if they are to forego success fees, they would expect to be paid their full base costs.

3.4   The solicitors acknowledge that a few defendants, such as parish councils, would be seriously prejudiced by one way costs shifting. Such defendants should be permitted to apply for a variation of that regime.

3.5   CAJE. CAJE in its submission sets out details of adverse costs orders made against its members in a number of recent unsuccessful cases. Such adverse costs orders range up to £50,000. However, members of CAJE have conducted a number of recent judicial review challenges where their potential costs risk was substantially higher than that. CAJE states that, because of the high costs involved, its members

---

[87] This is a reference to PR paragraph 36.4.5.
[88] PR paragraph 16.5.6.

only pursue a small proportion of the cases which those members identify as meriting pursuit.

3.6   Two members of CAJE, namely Greenpeace and WWF-UK, state that they never apply for PCOs. This is because they cannot satisfy the last of the five conditions[89] set out in *Corner House*, which requires that they would drop the case if the PCO is refused. Another member of CAJE, namely FoE, states that when it brings cases in its own right, it does not apply for PCOs. However, when FoE acts for individuals or community groups through its RJC, then it usually applies for a PCO unless legal aid has been obtained. CAJE members find it very difficult to obtain ATE insurance.

3.7   CAJE endorses the recommendations of the Sullivan Report.[90] CAJE also draws my attention to the current state of the proceedings against the UK before the Compliance Committee.

3.8   <u>United Kingdom Environmental Lawyers Association.</u> The United Kingdom Environmental Lawyers Association ("UKELA") argues that the current judge-made rules governing PCOs are unsatisfactory. UKELA has drafted, and helpfully annexes to its Phase 2 submission, a suggested new rule to govern the making of PCOs. This draft rule would permit PCOs to be made in any proceedings, subject to criteria derived from recent case law, but would make PCOs the norm in environmental judicial review cases.

3.9   <u>ClientEarth.</u> ClientEarth in its submission to the Costs Review adopts many of the submissions which it has previously made to the Compliance Committee. ClientEarth states that ATE insurance is difficult to obtain and places a prohibitive costs burden on the claimant or defendant, depending upon which party pays for it. ClientEarth adds:

> "Therefore, it is our view that ATE insurance simply provides yet another obstacle to access to justice in environmental cases through its additional lawyers of complexity and uncertainty."

3.10   ClientEarth advocates one way costs shifting in environmental cases. It also believes that the present CFA regime should be maintained as a means of financing environmental cases in the public interest.

3.11   <u>Proceedings against the UK.</u> At the time of writing this chapter (December 2009) three complaints against the UK are proceeding in Geneva before the Compliance Committee. There has been a hearing on 24th September 2009, but no decision has yet been given by the Compliance Committee. One of the matters complained of in those proceedings is that environmental judicial review proceedings are prohibitively expensive, taking into account the claimant's own costs and in particular the claimant's potential liability for adverse costs. The complainants contend that the present PCO regime, though well-intentioned, does not address the problem of prohibitive costs, and can generate yet further costs through satellite litigation.

3.12   A complaint raising similar issues has been made against the UK to the European Commission, alleging failure to comply with article 3(7) of Directive

---

[89] All five conditions are set out in paragraph 74 of *Corner House*, which is quoted at PR paragraph 35.3.4.
[90] See PR paragraph 36.4.3.

2003/35/EC of the European Parliament and Council (known as the Public Participation Directive). This amended Council Directive 85/337/EEC (known as the Environmental Impact Assessment Directive) by inserting article 10A. This article makes provision in similar terms to article 9 of the Aarhus Convention, namely that a review procedure which is *"fair, equitable, timely and not prohibitively expensive"* must be available to challenge the legality of decisions, acts or omissions subject to the public participation provisions of the Directive. The Commission is investigating the complaint against the UK, although the procedure was previously put on hold pending the outcome of infraction proceedings against Ireland (*Commission v Ireland*, case C-427/07).

(ii) General judicial review

3.13   <u>Comments of US lawyer.</u> An American lawyer of long experience sent in a response to the Preliminary Report, urging the merits of the US no costs rule. He points out that *Brown v Board of Education of Topeka*, 347 US 483 (1954) (the seminal decision which ended racial segregation in schools) could not have been pursued if there had been a costs shifting rule. The plaintiff's backers put up enough funds to support the case, but not enough to meet any adverse costs. The plaintiff, who had well paid employment and owned his house, could not have proceeded if he was putting all his assets at risk. The American lawyer adds that this is true of the other great civil rights cases in the USA. Those cases could not have been brought under the English costs shifting rule.

3.14   <u>Comments of City solicitors.</u> Views differ. One firm supports the present PCO regime, but with a slight widening of the "no private interest" test. This firm also states:

> "We note the desirability of a claimant of modest means not being discouraged from bringing a meritorious claim by the threat of crushing costs liability. Where the claimant has modest means, therefore, we consider that the level of costs liability could properly be capped to reflect the means of the claimant. This would be a discretionary matter, and should bear in mind the important balance between enabling meritorious claims to be brought, and fixing the unsuccessful party with an appropriate contribution to the costs of the successful party, who has been required to incur substantial time and expense in fighting (generally defending) the claim."

3.15   Another firm regards the present PCO regime as unsatisfactory, but believes that PCOs must be restricted to cases which involve a public interest. This firm can see some merit in one way costs shifting, where judicial review claims concern matters of public interest, but argues that care must be taken to protect defendants against unmeritorious claims. The point is made that judicial review proceedings are increasingly used as a commercial tool. This firm also argues that *Bolton* should be applied more flexibly, so that costs are more often awarded to interested parties.

3.16   <u>Liberty.</u> Liberty has sent in a submission, picking up a number of themes from the judicial review seminar and arguing in support of one way costs shifting, subject to any different costs regime which the court may direct at the permission hearing. Liberty accepts that commercial organisations which bring judicial review claims should be exposed to the full risk of adverse costs. In relation to CFA success fees, Liberty adopts a realistic stance:

"...we would only say that, were a scheme of one way costs shifting to be introduced for judicial review cases, we would find it hard to justify ever claiming a success fee ourselves."

3.17   Public Law Project. The Public Law Project ("PLP") is a national charity, whose central aim is to improve access to public law remedies for those who are poor or otherwise disadvantaged. PLP considers that the present test for PCOs is too wide. PLP proposes that in judicial review claims concerning matters of public interest there should be one way costs shifting. In return, the claimants' solicitors should forego recovery of success fees.

3.18   Set of chambers. A set of chambers specialising in public law work has sent in submissions on two issues. First, chambers considers that the PCO criteria should be widened, so that the claimant's private interest is not a bar, provided that the case raises large public interest issues. Secondly, chambers makes submissions about *Boxall*, as noted in paragraph 3.22 below.

3.19   Claimant solicitors. A firm of solicitors with extensive experience of acting for claimants in major public law cases states that it agrees with my provisional view (expressed in PR paragraph 35.4.7) that no reforms are needed to the judicial review process in order to bring down costs. The crucial question concerns the allocation of those costs between the parties. Of the options canvassed in PR chapter 35, this firm strongly supports one way costs shifting. However, *"the usual rule should be rebuttable where a claimant's motives are primarily financial or commercial"*. The firm does not agree that recoverable success fees should end as a quid pro quo.

3.20   Civil Legal Aid Sub-Committee of the Bar Council. The Civil Legal Aid Sub-Committee of the Bar Council ("CLASC") states:

"We take the view that it is inappropriate to award costs against claimants in public interest cases, for much the same reasons those which commend themselves to Canada: see Chap 35 [3.9]."[91]

CLASC adds that it believes that these proposals have a much wider application than judicial review cases and will be relevant to many appeals.

(iii) Concerns about *Boxall*

3.21   A number of respondents have expressed concern about *Boxall*. PLP points out that *Boxall* was decided before the protocol came into effect. PLP states that research shows that approximately 60% of judicial review cases are now settled following the letter of claim. Nevertheless some authorities wait to see whether proceedings will in fact be issued and whether permission will be granted before settling. Furthermore, many judicial review claims settle following the grant of interim relief, such as interim accommodation or an order for community care assessment. Yet the effect of *Boxall* is that claimants seldom recover costs in these cases. PLP propose that, if C has followed the protocol but D has not, there should be a presumption that D should pay C's costs. This would encourage reasonable litigation behaviour on the part of defendants. Also it would transfer the costs burden in many cases from the legal aid fund to the defendant authorities. Similar arguments are advanced by the firm of claimant solicitors mentioned above.

---

[91] This is a reference to PR paragraph 35.3.9.

3.22   The set of chambers mentioned in paragraph 3.18 above notes that legal aid rates are far lower than the normal hourly rates for lawyers. Yet the effect of *Boxall* is that there is no order for costs in many cases which settle after issue, thus leaving the claimant's lawyers to receive payment at legal aid rates only. Public authorities which settle after issue, having ignored an earlier protocol letter of claim, often take this approach for tactical reasons. Chambers maintains that costs orders ought more often to be made in favour of claimants in such cases.

3.23   CLASC considers that the *Boxall* approach is unsatisfactory for similar reasons to those set out above. CLASC is also concerned about cases in which claimants are successful on some issues only and then only recover part of their costs. The reason for this concern is that legal aid hourly rates are far below the proper rates which solicitors need in order to operate successfully. Therefore CLASC makes two proposals, namely:

(i)   Where, in a public interest case, the claimant obtains a successful outcome, he shall be entitled to all of his costs, irrespective of whether he succeeds on every issue in dispute in the case.

(ii)   Where a claim is settled shortly after the service of proceedings, and the claimant had sent a letter of claim in compliance with the pre-action protocol, there shall be a presumption that the defendant is liable for the claimant's costs.

I shall refer to these two proposals as "CLASC's first proposal" and "CLASC's second proposal" respectively. CLASC states that both proposals have been put to the Civil Justice Council and are under consideration.

4. ASSESSMENT

(i) One way costs shifting

4.1   <u>In principle.</u> Having considered the competing arguments advanced during Phase 2 as well as the factors set out in PR chapters 35 and 36, I am quite satisfied that qualified[92] one way costs shifting is the right way forward. There are six principal reasons for this conclusion:

(i)   This is the simplest and most obvious way to comply with the UK's obligations under the Aarhus Convention in respect of environmental judicial review cases.

(ii)   For the reasons stated by the Court of Appeal on several occasions,[93] it is undesirable to have different costs rules for (a) environmental judicial review and (b) other judicial review cases.

(iii)   The permission requirement is an effective filter to weed out unmeritorious cases. Therefore two way costs shifting is not generally necessary to deter frivolous claims.

(iv)   As stated in the FB paper, it is not in the public interest that potential claimants should be deterred from bringing properly arguable judicial review proceedings by the very considerable financial risks involved.

---

[92] I say "qualified" one way costs shifting, because only some categories of claimants merit protection against liability for adverse costs.
[93] See PR paragraph 36.4.9.

(v) One way costs shifting in judicial review cases has proved satisfactory in Canada: see PR paragraphs 35.3.8 and 35.3.9.

(vi) The PCO regime is not effective to protect claimants against excessive costs liability. It is expensive to operate and uncertain in its outcome. In many instances the PCO decision comes too late in the proceedings to be of value.

4.2 <u>In practice.</u> A more difficult question is how a one way costs shifting rule should be formulated, in order to sift out cases where claimants do not merit costs protection. Should one way costs shifting be restricted to claimants who are human, rather than corporate? Should there be a default position from which the court may depart? Or would this be a recipe for satellite litigation?

4.3 <u>Legally aided claimants.</u> Judicial review is one of the areas of civil litigation where legal aid is still available. A substantial number of judicial review claims are brought on legal aid every year: see PR paragraphs 6.2.1 to 6.2.9. A claimant who is legally aided is protected by section 11(1) of the Access to Justice Act 1999 (the "1999 Act"). I have set that provision out in chapter 19 above and explained how it operates in practice. The practical effect is that legally aided claimants in judicial review cases have the benefit of one way costs shifting.

4.4 <u>The best approach for non-legally aided claimants.</u> I have explored all manner of approaches to one way costs shifting in judicial review and debated the options with my assessors. In the end (having torn up many earlier drafts of this chapter) I conclude that the best approach is that advocated in chapter 19 above. The same "shield" should be given to all claimants in judicial review cases, whether legally aided or not. The legal aid costs shield was skilfully designed, some sixty years ago,[94] so that it only avails claimants of modest means. Wealthy claimants or commercial claimants will inevitably, and quite rightly, be exposed to the full rigour of two way costs shifting.

4.5 <u>Proposed rule.</u> If this recommendation is accepted, the proposed rule set out in chapter 19 should be adapted so as to include judicial review cases. The rule will then read as follows:

"Costs ordered against the claimant in any claim for personal injuries, clinical negligence or judicial review shall not exceed the amount (if any) which is a reasonable one for him to pay having regard to all the circumstances including:

(a) the financial resources of all the parties to the proceedings, and

(b) their conduct in connection with the dispute to which the proceedings relate."

As stated in chapter 19 above, if this proposal is adopted, there will have to be consequential provisions of the kind that currently exist to enable section 11(1) of the 1999 Act to be operated. The details of these consequential provisions will be a matter for the Civil Procedure Rule Committee.

4.6 The language of the proposed rule, being copied from section 11(1) of the 1999 Act, effectively includes an "unreasonable conduct" exception. This is because the court takes account of conduct when deciding what amount of costs to order.

---

[94] See section 2(2)(e) of the Legal Aid and Advice Act 1949. A similar provision has been included in all subsequent legal aid legislation up to and including section 11(1) Access to Justice Act 1999.

4.7   Should there be a default position? One issue which has been much debated during the Costs Review is whether there should be a default position. One possible default position, which was canvassed at the judicial review seminar, is that the claimant's liability for adverse costs should be up to £3,000 up to the grant of permission and (if permission is granted) up to £5,000 up to the end of the case. If there is to be a default position, what degree of weight should attach to it and should it feature in the rule or in a practice direction?

4.8   My view. Having reflected on the arguments and the various views of my assessors, I have come to the conclusion that there should be no default position. Precisely the same rule should apply both to legally aided claimants and to non-legally aided claimants. The application of that rule, however, will be very different. For persons of modest means, the effect will be precisely the same whether they are legally aided or not. Other claimants will face potential liability for adverse costs, proportionate to their means. As previously mentioned, commercial and similar claimants will automatically be exposed to the full risk of adverse costs, as they are now. Bearing in mind the huge range of circumstances of different cases and different claimants, I doubt that a default position would assist. A further attraction of this approach is that precisely the same costs rule will apply for all judicial review claimants (whether legally aided or not) and for all personal injury claimants (whether legally aided or not). The rule will be one which is familiar to both the courts and the profession, having been in use for half a century. Such an approach conforms to the requirement of simplicity, which is one of the goals stated in chapter 1 above.

4.9   Alternative approach. If the view expressed in the previous paragraph is rejected and it is decided to have a default position, I propose that this should be set out in a practice direction, not the rule. A practice direction can be more easily amended, if the figures need adjusting. The practice direction should provide that, save in exceptional circumstances, (i) the cap on the claimant's liability for adverse costs up to the grant of permission should be no less than £3,000; and (ii) if permission is granted, the cap on the claimant's liability for adverse costs (in respect of the whole case) should be no less than £5,000.

4.10   No recoverable success fee. If qualified one way costs shifting is introduced, in my view that will strike the right balance as between claimant and defendant in judicial review proceedings. There is no justification for imposing upon defendants the additional burden of paying, potentially huge, success fees. Significantly, a number of respondents from both sides of the fence have recognised this principle during Phase 2. The success fee payable, if any, must be a matter between the claimant and the claimant's solicitor.

4.11   It should also be remembered that claimants can substantially improve their position financially by making a well judged Part 36 offer. See further chapter 41 below.

(ii) *Boxall*

4.12   Need for modification. The *Boxall* approach made eminently good sense at the time that case was decided. However, now that there is an extremely sensible protocol in place for judicial review claims, I consider the *Boxall* approach needs modification, essentially for the reasons which have been urged upon me during Phase 2.

4.13   Recommendation. I recommend that in any judicial review case where the claimant has complied with the protocol, if the defendant settles the claim after (rather than before) issue by conceding any material part of the relief sought, then the normal order should be that the defendant pays the claimant's costs. A rule along these lines would not prevent the court from making a different order in those cases where particular circumstances[95] warranted a different costs order. Accordingly, I substantially accept CLASC's second proposal.

4.14   CLASC's first proposal. I disagree with CLASC's first proposal. In my view it is wrong in principle for the court to make a more favourable costs order than the circumstances of the case warrant, simply because the Legal Services Commission pays rates which are perceived as too low. Such an approach is unprincipled. The rates recovered *inter partes* and the principles under which costs are awarded must be set to achieve a fair and proportionate system regardless of whether a case is funded publicly or privately. I accept that legal aid solicitors and barristers have to operate on a combination of *inter partes* costs in successful cases and lower legal aid "risk rates" in unsuccessful ones, but whether legal aid rates are currently set at the right level is not a issue which can be resolved within this review for the reasons given in chapter 7 above.

5. RECOMMENDATIONS

5.1   I make the following recommendations:

(i)   That qualified one way costs shifting should be introduced for judicial review claims.

(ii)   That if the defendant settles a judicial review claim after issue and the claimant has complied with the protocol, the normal order should be that the defendant do pay the claimant's costs.

---

[95] For example, the defendant has settled for pragmatic reasons, despite having a strong defence to the claim.

CHAPTER 31. NUISANCE CASES

INDEX

1. INTRODUCTION

1.1   <u>Preliminary Report.</u>   Statutory nuisance proceedings in the magistrates' courts are discussed in chapter 36 of the Preliminary Report at section 2.   Private nuisance actions in the civil courts are discussed in PR chapter 36 at section 3.

1.2   <u>Aarhus Convention.</u>   Articles 9.3 and 9.4 of the Aarhus Convention[96] are set out in paragraph 1.4 of the previous chapter.   Article 9.3 requires that the UK shall ensure that *"members of the public have access to administrative or judicial procedures to challenge acts and omissions by private persons...which contravene provisions of its national law relating to the environment"*.   Article 9.4 requires that those judicial procedures *"shall provide adequate and effective remedies, including injunctive relief as appropriate, and be...not prohibitively expensive"*.

1.3   <u>The Aarhus Convention applies to some private nuisance actions.</u>   The law of nuisance, which is essentially a creature of the common law,[97] encompasses a variety of anti-social acts.   Some of those anti-social acts may be damaging to the environment, in particular toxic torts such as pollution of watercourses.   I therefore conclude that the Aarhus Convention is capable of applying to private nuisance actions in the civil courts.   This interpretation of the Aarhus Convention is supported by Professor Gerrit Betlem in his article for the Cambridge Law Journal *"Torts, a European ius commune and the private enforcement of Community law"*.[98]   This interpretation is also supported *obiter* by the Court of Appeal in *Morgan v Hinton Organics Wessex Ltd* [2009] EWCA Civ 107 at [42]-[44].   In *Morgan* the claimants alleged that smells from a composting site near their homes constituted a private nuisance.   The Court of Appeal at an interlocutory appeal observed that if the nuisance existed, it affected the whole locality.   Article 9.4 of the Aarhus Convention requires that the procedures for dealing with those particular civil actions shall be "not prohibitively expensive".

1.4   Having considered the material cited in the previous paragraph as well as the UNECE[99] Implementation Guide,[100] I conclude that articles 9.3 and 9.4 of the Aarhus Convention apply to those private nuisance actions in which the alleged nuisance is

---

[96] The Convention on Access to Information, Public Participation in Decision-Making and Access to Justice in Environmental Matters, signed in Aarhus, Denmark, on 25th June 1998.

[97] See *Clerk & Lindsell on Torts*, 19th edition (2006), chapter 22.

[98] [2005] CLJ 126 at pages 132-133.

[99] The United Nations Economic Commission for Europe.

[100] Available online at http://www.unece.org/env/pp/acig.pdf.

an activity (a) damaging the environment and (b) adversely affecting the wider public, rather than the claimants alone.

2. DEBATE DURING PHASE 2

2.1   Judicial review seminar. Towards the end of the judicial review seminar held on 27th July 2009 discussion turned to private nuisance actions. One speaker said that 60% prospects of success were required to get after-the-event ("ATE") insurance in private nuisance cases. However, in many cases the claimant has before-the-event ("BTE") insurance and so there is no need for ATE insurance. Some speakers expressed the view that the present regime of recoverable success fees and ATE insurance premiums was a satisfactory regime for private nuisance claims. Others disagreed, pointing out that the claimant in private nuisance actions was not always David and the defendant was not always Goliath. One speaker urged me to go for the "*simple solution*" and recommend one way costs shifting for all private nuisance claims.

2.2   Written submissions. A number of claimant solicitors argue that the present regime of recoverable success fees and recoverable ATE insurance premiums is the appropriate means of funding private nuisance actions: see chapter 10 above, paragraph 3.23.

2.3   One firm of solicitors, realistically recognising that ATE insurance premiums and success fees may not continue to be recoverable in perpetuity, argues for one way costs shifting in place of recoverable ATE insurance premiums. It states:

> "In relation to proceedings (eg. environmental nuisance) for which ATE is obtainable, one way fee shifting would in fact primarily benefit defendants by their not having to pay large insurance premiums. You cite *Bontoft*. There the premium was in the region of 60% of defendant's costs. We have experience of it going nearer to 95%, including IPT. The ATE premium can be in excess of our and counsel's fees, including success fees, put together.

> As you recognise, one-way cost shifting would at a stroke cut out a huge cost in litigation where ATE is involved. It would also reduce costs in many other ways, such as the time spent drafting proposal forms, paying fees associated therewith, doing risk assessments and negotiating with insurers."

2.4   That firm of solicitors adds that it would be prepared to forego success fees under conditional fee agreements ("CFAs") in return for one way costs shifting. However, if solicitors are foregoing success fees, it is argued that they should recover full base costs. The firm points out that in statutory nuisance proceedings in the magistrates' court,[101] where CFAs are permitted, no success fees can be charged by solicitors acting on CFAs.[102]

2.5   The Coalition for Access to Justice for the Environment ("CAJE") points out that the Aarhus Convention applies to private nuisance actions and, therefore, that the costs rules for such actions must comply with Article 9.4. CAJE also draws attention to the proceedings against the UK for non-compliance.

---

[101] Discussed in PR paragraphs 36.2.1 to 36.2.5.
[102] See sections 58 and 58A of the Courts and Legal Services Act 1990, paragraph 3 of the Conditional Fee Agreements Order 2000/823 and section 82 of the Environmental Protection Act 1990.

2.6   Proceedings against the UK. At the time of writing, three complaints against the UK are proceeding in Geneva before the Aarhus Convention Compliance Committee of the United Nations Economic Commission for Europe (the "Compliance Committee"). There has been a hearing on 24th September 2009, but no decision has yet been given by the Compliance Committee. One of the matters complained of in those proceedings is that private nuisance actions are prohibitively expensive, when one takes into account both the claimant's own costs and the claimant's potential liability for adverse costs.

3. ASSESSMENT

3.1   No recoverability of additional liabilities. For the reasons set out in chapters 9 and 10 above, I have concluded that the current regime of recoverable success fees and ATE insurance premiums is no longer sustainable. That regime generates disproportionate costs and is grossly unfair upon defendants. It is by no means always the case that the claimant is the impecunious party and the defendant is the wealthy party.

3.2   The question. The question therefore arises as to how nuisance proceedings between private parties should be funded and how adverse costs orders should be met.

(i) Statutory nuisance proceedings

3.3   In relation to statutory nuisance proceedings in the magistrates' court, I have come to the conclusion that the present costs rules are satisfactory. The claimant can engage solicitors on a CFA without success fee: see sections 58 and 58A of the Courts and Legal Services Act 1990, paragraph 3 of the Conditional Fee Agreements Order 2000/823 and section 82 of the Environmental Protection Act 1990 (the "EPA 1990").

3.4   The complainant's entitlement to costs, if the case is successful, is set out as follows in section 82(12) of the EPA 1990:

> "Where on the hearing of proceedings for an order under subsection (2)[103] above it is proved that the alleged nuisance existed at the date of the making of the complaint…, then, whether or not at the date of the hearing it still exists or is likely to recur, the court…shall order the defendant…(or defendants…in such proportions as appears fair and reasonable) to pay to the person bringing the proceedings such amount as the court…considers reasonably sufficient to compensate him for any expenses properly incurred by him in the proceedings."

3.5   Costs recovery under section 82(12) in the magistrates' court is somewhat more generous than costs recovery on the standard basis in the civil courts. However, as previously mentioned there is no success fee. Furthermore, the complainant is not usually at risk of an adverse costs order in the magistrates' court: see PR paragraph 36.2.4.

---

[103] An order (a) requiring the defendant to abate the nuisance and to execute any works necessary for that purpose and/or (b) prohibiting a recurrence of the nuisance and requiring the defendant to execute any works necessary to prevent the recurrence.

3.6   Costs in the magistrates' court are generally lower than in the civil courts. It seems to me that, collectively, the above provisions strike the right balance in relation to the costs of statutory nuisance proceedings. No serious complaint about those costs rules has been made during Phase 2. I make no recommendation for reform in relation to statutory nuisance proceedings in the magistrates' court.

(ii) Private nuisance proceedings in the civil courts

3.7   <u>One way costs shifting?</u> I have considered whether one way costs shifting should be introduced to protect claimants in private nuisance actions. The difficulty with this approach is that by no means all private nuisance actions fit into the paradigm of claimant with modest means claiming against well resourced defendant. Sometimes the claimant has larger resources than the defendant. This point has been made by practitioners during Phase 2. It is also confirmed by my own experience at the Bar. Therefore I do not positively advocate this course.

3.8   Despite the comments made in the previous paragraph, qualified one way costs shifting could be introduced for private nuisance claims, if this reform were deemed desirable on policy grounds. The regime would be based on the same model as is set out in chapters 9 and 19 above. Qualified one way cost shifting would be cheaper for defendants than a regime of recoverable ATE insurance premiums. Such a regime has the added benefits of (a) affording no protection to a claimant who is well resourced and (b) enabling the court to take conduct into account when deciding the extent to which a costs order should be enforced.

3.9   <u>Before-the-event insurance.</u> The point was made at the judicial review seminar that many property owners have BTE insurance, which covers them for bringing private nuisance claims. This, I would suggest, is the best way forward. The vast majority of claimants are property owners. A substantial number of property owners already have BTE insurance as an add-on to their household insurance policies. Most such policies will cover the bringing of claims for private nuisance: see section 5 of chapter 8 above. Only a minute proportion of property owners ever need to make a claim for private nuisance. Encouragement of further take up of BTE insurance is, in my view, the best means of promoting access to justice in respect of private nuisance claims. It would also be highly beneficial if household insurers were to increase their normal level of cover to £100,000. (At the moment in many cases the limit is £50,000.) A fund of £100,000 should be sufficient to cover the vast majority of private nuisance claims brought by individuals. Indeed, a fund of £100,000 would have been just about sufficient to cover the claimants' costs in *Bontoft v East Lindsey DC*,[104] if there had been no CFA.

3.10   If my earlier recommendation to ban recoverability of success fees and ATE insurance premiums is implemented, this event will attract widespread public attention. That event would provide a golden opportunity to alert all property owners to the fact that, as from the appointed date, they should all have cover in respect of private nuisance and similar litigation, in the same way that they have cover against subsidence, burglary and so forth.

3.11   I appreciate the difficulties of making BTE insurance compulsory. I also appreciate the difficulties of persuading the whole population to take out BTE insurance against litigation costs generally. However, I believe that with proper marketing it should be feasible to bring about widespread BTE insurance cover as an add-on to household insurance.

---

[104] [2008] EWHC 2923 (QB); discussed in PR paragraphs 36.3.3 to 36.3.6.

3.12   Use of CFAs.   If the claimant does not have BTE insurance, he can still proceed on a CFA.   However, the claimant will have to pay the success fee (at whatever level may be agreed with his solicitor) out of damages.   I have recommended in chapter 10 above that the level of general damages for torts of this nature should be increased by 10%.[105]   This modest increase should assist in meeting the success fee.   If the case settles early (as most civil claims do), the success fee will be low.   If the case proceeds to trial, then the success fee will be substantially higher.   However, in that circumstance, the claimant can substantially improve his position by making an effective claimant's offer.   This is dealt with in the next paragraph.

3.13   Effect of claimant's offer.   If the reforms proposed in chapter 41 below are implemented, then claimants in nuisance actions will be able to substantially improve their position by making realistic Part 36 offers.   If the claimant's offer is vindicated, then the court will award an additional sum representing 10% of (a) the damages awarded and (b) the value (as summarily assessed by the judge) of any non-financial relief, such as an injunction.

4. CONCLUSION

4.1   Compliance with Aarhus Convention.   Only a small proportion of private nuisance claims will engage the UK's obligations under the Aarhus Convention, essentially for the reasons spelt out by the Court of Appeal in *Morgan* at paragraphs 42 to 44.   The claimants in such cases can usually enforce their rights by one of two routes.   First, they can bring proceedings for statutory nuisance in the magistrates' court.   Secondly, if the claimants have BTE insurance cover as part of their household insurance, they can bring an action for private nuisance in the civil courts, usually the county court.   I appreciate that neither of these circumstances availed the claimants in *Morgan*.   However, at least in relation to private nuisance claims, I am not at all sure that the problem is so widespread as to put the UK in breach of its obligations under the Aarhus Convention.[106]   Furthermore, if the other recommendations in this report are implemented, claimants will be able to engage solicitors on style 1 CFAs, even if they do not have BTE insurance.[107]   The matters referred to in paragraphs 3.12 and 3.13 above will improve claimants' ability to meet the (irrecoverable) success fees.

4.2   Fallback position.   If, in the consultation exercise following publication of this report, a strong view emerges that the abolition of recoverable ATE insurance premiums gives rise to a breach of the Aarhus Convention or an obstacle to access to justice for claimants in private nuisance, then a remedy is at hand.   Qualified one way costs shifting could be introduced for private nuisance claims, as set out in paragraph 3.8 above.

4.3   Recommendation already made.   In chapter 8 above I have recommended that positive efforts be made to encourage the take up of BTE insurance as an add-on to household insurance policies.   Therefore there is no need to repeat that recommendation in this chapter.

---

[105] See chapter 10 above at paragraph 5.6.
[106] Different considerations arise in relation to environmental judicial review claims.   These are discussed in the previous chapter.
[107] As defined in PR chapter 16, section 3.

CHAPTER 32. DEFAMATION AND RELATED CLAIMS

INDEX

1. INTRODUCTION

(i) Preliminary Report

1.1   Preliminary Report.   I discussed costs issues relating to defamation and related claims in chapter 37 of the Preliminary Report.

1.2   PR appendix 17. Appendix 17 to the Preliminary Report sets out details of 154 libel and privacy claims which were brought against the media in 2008 and which resulted in payments to the claimants. These actions comprised 137 claims for libel, 15 claims for breach of privacy and two combined claims for both libel and breach of privacy. Appendix 17 enables a broad comparison to be made between damages and costs in cases where claimants were successful. I have set out an analysis of the appendix 17 data in section 7 of chapter 2 above, together with the accompanying tables.

(ii) The wider debate

1.3   The debate. There is currently much debate in progress about the substantive law of libel and whether the law strikes the right balance between free speech and reputation.

1.4   The defendant perspective. Many articles have recently appeared in the press concerning libel tourism and the effects of current libel law and the costs regime. A report entitled *Free Speech is not for Sale* by English PEN and Index on Censorship ("EPIC") was published in November 2009 and gained wide publicity. The report argues that English libel law imposes excessive restrictions on free speech and has a chilling effect upon journalism and publishing. EPIC makes a number of recommendations for reform, one of which is:

"Cap base costs and make success fees and 'After the Event' (ATE) insurance premiums non-recoverable."

The other recommendations made by EPIC relate to the scope of the law of libel, available defences and other matters of substantive law or procedure.

1.5   The claimant perspective. Unsurprisingly, most of the recent papers and articles on this issue have come from pro-media organisations or individuals who are actively seeking a change in the law. I am not aware of any comparable papers in defence of the status quo by those who act for claimants. However, from informal discussions I am aware that those who act for claimants (and some who act both for claimants and defendants) are quick to point out that (a) if defendants publish what is true (or more accurately what they can show to be true), then they have a defence; (b) there is no public interest in misinformation; (c) the current debate gives too little attention to those two simple and related matters; and (d) publishers, in certain circumstances, have a defence to libel actions even when what they have published is false (or deemed to be false), despite the damage to a claimant's reputation.

1.6   My position. These wider issues concerning libel law are not within my terms of reference. I am solely concerned with the costs of litigating defamation and related cases.

1.7   In relation to costs, I am in agreement with certain of EPIC's conclusions. In particular, for the reasons set out in chapters 9 and 10 above, I consider that success fees and after-the-event ("ATE") insurance premiums should cease to be recoverable. However, contrary to EPIC's view, I consider that if this step is taken, other measures must be put in place in order to ensure that claimants have access to justice.

2. COMMENTS RECEIVED DURING PHASE 2

(i) Written submissions

2.1   Media Lawyers Association submission. The Media Lawyers Association (the "MLA") in a detailed submission argues that success fees and ATE insurance premiums should cease to be recoverable; that there should be more proactive early costs management; that costs which are disproportionate to the amount involved and the nature of the claim should be irrecoverable; that there should be procedural changes to facilitate early resolution of preliminary matters.

2.2   Counsel's opinion obtained by MLA. The MLA appends to its submission an opinion by counsel, Lord Pannick QC and Anthony Hudson, concerning costs and ECHR article 10.[108] Counsel state in their opinion:

> "Recovery of success fees from the paying party results in a manifestly and inherently disproportionate sum of costs when added to the base costs in a freedom of expression case. It is inherently disproportionate to require an unsuccessful defendant in a case involving freedom of expression to pay success fees to the lawyers of the successful claimant on the spurious basis that it will enable those lawyers to take on other cases which might not be successful, particularly when there is no mechanism to ensure that the success fee will be used in this way. The disproportionality is compounded by the

_____

[108] Article 10 of the European Convention on Human Rights, concerning the right to freedom of expression.

relevant costs rules which require the judge assessing costs to ignore the disproportionality of the entire sum: Costs Practice Direction 11.9.

> The consequences of the current CFA[109] system produce a gross and serious interference with freedom of expression. It cannot be convincingly established (as it must be to be compatible with Article 10 of the ECHR) that the availability of CFAs with a success fee which is recoverable from the paying party is necessary and proportionate to the legitimate aim pursued."

2.3   Comments of claimant solicitors. One firm of claimant solicitors has put in detailed submissions in response to the Preliminary Report. The claimant solicitors point out that the article 8 rights[110] of claimants are no less important than the media's article 10 rights;[111] defendants only face adverse costs orders (including success fees and ATE insurance premiums) in cases where they have been held liable; it is inappropriate to contrast levels of damages with costs, because the claimant's primary aim in such proceedings is to restore reputation or protect privacy. The claimant solicitors make a number of points about the tactics of defendants. They point out that there is often a huge inequality of arms between media defendants and individual claimants. Media defendants may have an in-house team working on a case in addition to external solicitors. The claimant solicitors point out that there are reasons for the disparity between claimant lawyers' fees and defendant lawyers' fees. In particular, defendant defamation lawyers can expect repeat business and therefore discount their rates substantially, whereas claimant defamation lawyers have no such expectation of repeat business from their clients. The claimant solicitors oppose any extension of costs capping, because of the unpredictable nature of defamation litigation and the high costs of the costs capping process. The claimant lawyers propose that there should be a change in the substantive law in order to determine the legality of articles or statements before they are published. They point out that at the moment the media are not obliged to give notice to a person prior to a publication which might infringe his article 8 rights. Thus the opportunity to seek an injunction (to protect privacy) may be lost and injunctions are not currently available in libel where the defendant avers that the allegation is true.

2.4   A substantial City firm of solicitors which (in the defamation field) I believe does mainly claimant work has put in helpful submissions on many issues. In relation to defamation, it echoes many of the points above. It notes that trials are increasingly before judge alone, rather than a jury. It makes the point that media defendants often instruct external lawyers at the last possible moment. It defends the way CFAs are used and the CFA/ATE insurance regime generally. It opposes the proposals for controlling costs in the Ministry of Justice ("MoJ") consultation paper.[112] It fears that court involvement in approving costs budgets would simply increase costs.

2.5   Submission from Irish Solicitors. A firm of solicitors practising in Dublin have sent in a helpful account of defamation litigation in Ireland. They state:

> "In my experience more than 90% of libel and privacy plaintiffs (perhaps more than 95%) are represented on a 'no foal, no fee' basis. The vast majority of civil litigation in Ireland proceeds on this basis because plaintiffs do not

---

[109] Conditional fee agreement.
[110] Article 8 of the ECHR, concerning the right to respect for private and family life, home and correspondence.
[111] In relation to this point the MLA observes that some proceedings engage article 10, but not article 8.
[112] See PR paragraph 37.1.3.

have access to civil legal aid.[113] As you say, this means that legal advisers will only seek to recover costs from the client in the event that the claim is successful and will generally not look for costs cover over and above the level recovered from the losing party. As a result lack of funds is not a barrier to litigating and access to justice is maintained, save that litigants remain at risk of the winning side's costs if they lose.

In general costs follow the event and a party that obtains an order for costs on an interlocutory application can proceed to have those costs assessed, which can assist with cash flow where lawyers are acting on a 'no foal, no fee' basis. It is also correct to say that success fees are not a feature of the Irish costs regime, and contingency fees are not permitted."

2.6   Law Society. The Law Society in its submission states that it is important not to attach unnecessary emphasis to the arguments of the media defendants, given their *"disproportionate voice"*. Many of the costs issues concerning defamation proceedings equally concern other civil proceedings. The Law Society questions the value of the data provided the MLA, appearing in PR appendix 17. The Law Society is critical of the Oxford Study, cited in PR chapter 37, section 5. It does not believe that media and non-media defamation proceedings should be treated differently or that cases involving ECHR article 10 should have a different costs regime. The Law Society supports staged success fees under CFAs. It sees significant difficulties in capping recoverability of ATE insurance premiums *"in circumstances where the premiums are determined on the open market by providers of ATE insurance"*. The Law Society sees difficulties with costs capping, but supports active case management and costs management for defamation proceedings.

2.7   London Solicitors Litigation Association. The London Solicitors Litigation Association (the "LSLA") believes that the costs regime for defamation proceedings should be the same as that for other civil proceedings. It opposes the proposals in the MoJ consultation paper[114] for specific measures to control the costs of defamation proceedings alone. The LSLA regards costs capping as inappropriate in most cases. It supports early notification of ATE insurance in all cases, not just defamation. The LSLA believes that ATE insurance premiums should be recoverable, unless the defendant makes an admission or offer of amends within 21 days.

(ii) Meeting on 21st July 2009

2.8   Meeting at Farrer & Co. On 21st July 2009 I attended a meeting at the offices of Farrer & Co ("Farrers") with a number of defamation practitioners. Those present generally acted for defendants although some had experience of claimant work. It was urged upon me that in publication proceedings the defendants had the burden of proving justification; therefore it was anomalous for claimant costs to be so much higher than defendant costs. Alastair Brett of The Times explained the arbitration scheme offered by The Times for the resolution of meaning, alternatively quantum at an early stage. Concern was expressed about the level of success fees and ATE insurance premiums. It was suggested that the Pre-Action Protocol for Defamation (the "defamation protocol") ought to require the claimant to state the meaning for which he or she contended in the letter of claim. Some of those present thought that a contingent legal aid fund (a "CLAF")[115] might be viable for the support of

---

[113] Save in family law disputes.
[114] See PR paragraph 37.1.3.
[115] Also known as a Contingency Legal Aid Fund or a Civil Legal Aid Fund. See chapter 13 above.

defamation claims, in the event that success fees and ATE insurance premiums ceased to be recoverable.

2.9   Setting up of working group. At the end of the meeting on 21st July 2009 I set up a working group, chaired by Alastair Brett, to consider the viability of a CLAF for defamation claims (the "Libel CLAF Working Group"), as set out in chapter 1 above. That working group included equal representation of claimant and defendant defamation lawyers.

(iii) Working group report

2.10   The report. The Libel CLAF Working Group delivered its report on 5th October 2009. The report is lengthy and detailed. I only offer a brief summary in this chapter, although I have given careful consideration to the whole report.

2.11   Conclusions on the main issue. The group concluded that a special CLAF for libel cases, alternatively libel and privacy cases, would not be viable. It gave a number of reasons for this conclusion, including the low number of such cases (approximately 200 to 250 libel cases issued in the High Court each year), the likelihood of adverse selection in favour of CFAs, the difficulty of obtaining seed corn funding and the lack of any viable financial model, having regard to current levels of costs and damages. Damages in most cases are unlikely to average even £40,000, whereas costs may be very much higher. So a CLAF could not function on the basis of taking a share of damages in won cases and paying out costs in lost cases. The group concluded that a privately run CLAF could not survive. This was confirmed when two members of the working group met a commercial litigation funder, who indicated that he would be looking for a return equivalent to an interest rate of 18-20% per annum. The group could not see any way of "*internalising*" the cost of libel cases, like road traffic accident cases, within the insurance industry. Legal expenses insurance usually excluded defamation.

2.12   The CFA regime. It was accepted that the present CFA regime helped many claimants gain access to justice, but it imposed heavy costs burdens upon defendants. The media members of the group felt that success fees should come out of damages and should not be recoverable from defendants. They argued that defamation differed from clinical negligence, since libel claimants did not need their damages to pay for future care. The claimant practitioners disagreed, since "*success fees enabled them to consider a raft of potential claims without charging*". However, some concessions were made on the claimant side in this regard:

> "There was little or no support for 100% success fees continuing to be recoverable. While the private practitioners were against the abolition of success fees, they did accept that (a) they had to be staged and (b) base costs had to be within reasonable margins."

2.13   Costs shifting and ATE insurance. Most members of the group considered that one way costs shifting would be unfair. However, they agreed that if a defendant agreed to accept one way costs shifting, then there would be no need for ATE insurance or for ATE insurance premiums to be recoverable. One small area of common ground emerged, viz: "*It was generally agreed that many middle class claimants would feel deeply uneasy about taking on the national press or a television company without some kind of BTE*[116] *or ATE insurance and possibly risking the roof over their head*". The benefits of ATE insurance for claimants who

---

[116] Before-the-event.

would not otherwise be in a position to litigate were acknowledged by defendant representatives. On the other hand, concern was expressed about the expense of obtaining ATE insurance. ATE insurance cover of £100,000 could cost up to £65,000 as a premium.

2.14   Staging. The question of staging success fees and/or ATE insurance premiums was discussed. Success fees and ATE insurance premiums might be kept at a low level if cases were settled early.

2.15   Proposal for early resolution procedure. The working group put forward an interesting proposal for an *"early resolution"* procedure in order (i) to determine meaning and (ii) to give the parties an early opportunity to test a *"fair comment"* defence.[117]   The working group also canvassed a form of limited one way costs shifting, namely that only defendants should be at risk as to costs during the early resolution procedure.   However, if this course was adopted, the media representatives argued that all ATE insurance premiums and success fees should be made irrecoverable.

2.16   Case management. The working group members believed that good case management reduced costs. The group was divided on the issue of costs capping. It was agreed that there needed to be more certainty surrounding CFAs, in order to avoid satellite litigation.   The working group report concluded on a matter of common ground:

> "The Group felt that case management had a vital role to play in reducing the cost of libel proceedings and the Group looked forward to the results of the pilot scheme coming into effect on 1st October 2009."

3. THE CFA REGIME

3.1   Cases brought under CFAs invariably involve a success fee if the claimant wins and, usually, ATE insurance as well. My discussion in this section is focused upon cases where, currently, the claimant has both a CFA and ATE insurance. In chapters 9 and 10 above I have discussed the issues concerning recoverability of success fees and ATE insurance premiums. I have there expressed the view that these additional liabilities should be borne by the party who incurs them and should not be recoverable from the opposing party.[118] Instead, special measures should be put in place for those categories of litigation where, for reasons of social policy, claimants require (a) assistance in paying the success fee or (b) protection against adverse costs. If my primary recommendations in those two chapters are accepted, then the question will arise what special measures should be taken in respect of defamation.

3.2   In this section I shall discuss what measures should be put in place, in order to facilitate access to justice for claimants when success fees and ATE insurance premiums cease to be recoverable.

(i) CFA success fees

3.3   Level of damages. There is a loose relationship between levels of defamation damages and levels of personal injury damages. This is because of the policy that compensation for injury to feelings should not become disproportionate to

---

[117] This proposal is discussed further in section 5 below.
[118] See in particular the reasoning in section 4 of chapter 9 and section 4 of chapter 10.

compensation for bodily injury.[119] It is abhorrent if a claimant with serious personal injuries is treated less generously by the courts than a defamation claimant, who (although distressed) remains fit and well. In chapter 9 above I have recommended that general damages for personal injuries should be increased by 10%. Defamation and breach of privacy damages are less precisely calibrated than personal injury damages. I recommend that the ceiling for damages in this area be increased and that courts should have regard to this higher ceiling in the case of serious libel or slander. The general level of damages for defamation and breach of privacy should be increased by 10% as from the date when CFA success fees cease to be recoverable.

3.4   Level of success fees. Success fees will continue to be a proportion of base costs, but will now have to be borne by the claimant. The level of success fee will be a matter for negotiation between the claimant and his lawyers at the start of the case. I anticipate that in future CFAs will provide that the success fee is to be x% of base costs subject to a cap, the cap being y% of damages. The claimants in these cases (unlike personal injury claimants) do not need to devote any part of their damages to future care. Their main remedy (as claimant lawyers have stressed in the Phase 2 submissions) is vindication by the judgment of the court or the statement in court after settlement. I see no reason why such claimants should not be prepared to pay a substantial proportion of the damages to their lawyers as success fees.[120]

3.5   I do not accept that such a regime would amount to a denial of justice. In overseas jurisdictions the fact that success fees cannot be recovered from defendants is not perceived as constituting a barrier to access to justice. Indeed, under the overall package that I propose for defamation and privacy cases, claimants will be much more generously treated in England and Wales than in they are in any other jurisdiction which I have researched. Nor do I accept that solicitors and counsel would be unwilling to act on CFAs under the proposed new regime. On the basis of information which I have received from a number of sources, it appears that claimants are successful in the vast majority of CFA cases.

3.6   It should be noted that if the recommendations in chapter 41 below are accepted, the claimant can substantially enhance his or her financial recovery by making a realistic claimant's offer. If such offer is not accepted, but subsequently proves sufficient, then the judge will, unless he considers it unjust to do so (which is unlikely) award indemnity costs and additional damages.

(ii) ATE insurance premiums and adverse costs

3.7   In many, but not all, cases there are strong policy reasons why the claimant should be protected against liability for adverse costs. This is because in the paradigm libel case the claimant is an individual of modest means and the defendant is a well resourced media organisation.

3.8   The present system for achieving costs protection for claimants is, in my view, the most bizarre and expensive system that it is possible to devise. I reach this conclusion for three reasons:

(i)   Defendants pay a heavy price in order to ensure (a) that claimants within the CFA regime are protected against adverse costs liability and (b) that defendants can still recover costs if they win.

---

[119] *John v MGN Ltd* [1997] QB 586 at 613-614.
[120] In chapter 10 above it is recommended for policy reasons that there be a cap upon the level of success fee deductible from damages in personal injury cases. I do not recommend any similar cap in defamation cases.

(ii)   Despite paying out large ATE insurance premiums in cases which they lose, the defendants' costs recovery in cases which they win may be only partial. This is because the defendants' costs recovery will be subject to the policy limits agreed by claimants in those cases.

(iii)   The present regime of recoverable ATE insurance premiums is indiscriminating. A wealthy celebrity suing a hard pressed regional newspaper publisher is fully entitled to take out ATE insurance, effectively at the expense of the defendant. The present regime provides protection against adverse costs, but it is in no way targeted upon those claimants who need such protection.

3.9   In my view, a regime of qualified one way costs shifting would be a better and less expensive means of achieving the intended social objective. I propose the same regime for defamation and breach of privacy cases as I have proposed for personal injury and judicial review cases, namely one that is modelled upon section 11(1) of the Access to Justice Act 1999 (the "1999 Act").[121]

3.10   If this recommendation is accepted, a new provision of the CPR would provide:

> "Costs ordered against the claimant in any claim for defamation or breach of privacy shall not exceed the amount (if any) which is a reasonable one for him to pay having regard to all the circumstances including:
>
> (a)   the financial resources of all the parties to the proceedings, and
>
> (b)   their conduct in connection with the dispute to which the proceedings relate."

If this proposal is adopted, there will have to be consequential provisions of the kind that currently exist to enable section 11(1) of the 1999 Act to be operated. The details of these consequential provisions will be a matter for the Civil Procedure Rule Committee.

3.11   The form of words proposed in the previous paragraph is one that has been tried and tested over half a century, albeit in the context of legal aid legislation. It affords protection to a claimant of modest means who is litigating against a well resourced defendant. However, it would provide little protection to those wealthy claimants who can currently take advantage of CFAs and ATE insurance, in order to litigate at the expense of the other side. The other advantage of the formula suggested above is that it enables the court to take account of (a) the means of the defendant (as well as the means of the claimant) and (b) the conduct of both parties when assessing what level of costs should be paid by the unsuccessful claimant.

3.12   One important issue in defamation and breach of privacy claims is the seriousness of the subject matter. Some libellous statements (e.g. a false allegation of paedophilia) are more serious than others. Some invasions of privacy (e.g. as in the *Mosley* case[122]) are more distressing than others. These matters fall within the phrase "*all the circumstances*". However, it may possibly be worth spelling this out in the accompanying practice direction. That must be a matter for the Civil Procedure Rule Committee, in the event that my primary recommendation is accepted.

---

[121] See chapters 9, 19 and 30 above.
[122] *Mosley v News Group Newspapers Limited* [2008] EWHC 1777 (QB); [2008] E.M.L.R. 20.

3.13   For the reasons set out above I recommend that, if recoverability of additional liabilities is abolished, the claimant's position should be protected by (a) raising the general level of damages in defamation and breach of privacy proceedings by 10% and (b) introducing a regime of qualified one way costs shifting.

3.14   If, contrary to my recommendations, additional liabilities continue to be recoverable and the costs shifting regime remains as now, then my fallback recommendations are as in chapters 9 and 10 above. In other words there should be fixed and staged success fees, staged ATE insurance premiums and so forth.

4. PRE-ACTION PROTOCOL

4.1   On the evidence which I have received during the Costs Review, the defamation protocol is generally beneficial and tends to produce early settlements.

4.2   The one criticism which has been voiced on several occasions concerns paragraph 3.3. That paragraph currently reads:

> "It is desirable for the Claimant to identify in the Letter of Claim the meaning(s) he/she attributes to the words complained of."

4.3   It has been suggested that the language should be strengthened to require the claimant to state the meaning which is alleged. I see considerable force in this criticism. In cases where only one meaning is possible, such an obligation would be no hardship upon the claimant. In cases where there is doubt about meaning, it is highly desirable that the claimant should make his case clear at the start. If the claimant is not required to do this, much of the benefit of the (expensive) protocol procedures is lost.

4.4   I therefore recommend that paragraph 3.3 of the defamation protocol be amended to read:

> "The Claimant should identify in the Letter of Claim the meaning(s) he/she attributes to the words complained of."

I use "should" in this context, because that is the word used elsewhere in the defamation protocol to indicate what the parties are required to do.

5. CASE MANAGEMENT AND COSTS MANAGEMENT

5.1   <u>Pro-active case management.</u>   Many of the submissions in respect of defamation and related claims have stressed the importance of pro-active case management. The parties to these cases generally have the benefit of specialist judges. Usually such cases are dealt with by one master and one judge, so that in effect there is a docketing system. Case management is already carried out to a high standard and, therefore, I make no recommendations in this regard.

5.2   <u>Early resolution procedure.</u> The Libel CLAF Working Group has put forward an interesting proposal for an early resolution procedure. In my view, the working group's proposal and the issue of early resolution generally merit consideration by specialist practitioners and judges. I commend these matters to them for further analysis. One particular question for consideration is how any early resolution procedure before a judge could be linked to the final trial before a jury, if there is a jury. For example, would the jury be directed to impute a particular meaning to the relevant words, even if the jury interpreted them differently? It is not the function of this Costs Review to become involved in the procedures for defamation litigation at that level of detail. Therefore, beyond observing that the working group's proposal merits serious consideration (not least because it has the support of experienced claimant and defendant practitioners), I do not make any formal recommendation in this regard.

5.3   Costs management. Costs management is dealt with in chapter 40 below. One form of costs management has been piloted in defamation cases proceeding in London and Manchester since 1st October 2009, pursuant to Practice Direction 51D – Defamation Proceedings Costs Management Scheme ("PD51D"). I understand from discussion with an experienced[123] libel solicitor that it takes him approximately one hour to prepare estimates of costs for his clients, using bespoke costs budgeting software. It is his practice to prepare such estimates anyway. It takes him a further half hour (approximately) to set that information out in Form HA, as required by PD51D. A costs draftsman tells me that he expects firms of solicitors to instruct him to fill in Form HA on their behalf. Provided that he receives proper information from the solicitors, he expects that the task will take him about one hour for non-exceptional cases.

5.4   At the time of writing this chapter there has been insufficient experience of the defamation proceedings costs management pilot. I therefore propose that this pilot should be monitored during 2010 until its conclusion. My general recommendations in respect of costs management are set out in chapter 40 below.

6. JURY TRIALS

6.1   Section 69 of the Senior Courts Act 1981 provides as follows:

"Where, on the application of any party to an action to be tried in the Queen's Bench Division, the court is satisfied that there is in issue...

(b)   a claim in respect of libel, slander, malicious prosecution or false imprisonment...

the action shall be tried with a jury, unless the court is of opinion that the trial requires any prolonged examination of documents or accounts or any scientific or local investigation which cannot conveniently be made with a jury."

6.2   In recent years there has been an increasing tendency towards trial by judge alone in defamation cases. In 2008 at the Royal Courts of Justice in London there were four jury libel trials and four libel trials by judge alone. At the time of writing,[124] in 2009 there have so far been four jury trials and nine trials by judge alone. The question must now be asked whether the use of juries in such cases is still appropriate.

6.3   The principal argument in favour of juries, at least in publication cases, is that twelve citizens chosen at random are likely to be representative of the general public

---

[123] Experienced in both defamation litigation and costs estimating.
[124] 1st December 2009.

who will have read or heard the allegedly defamatory comments. The principal arguments against juries are (a) in cases that go to trial juries increase trial costs by 20 to 30%; (b) judges are well able to decide the issues; (c) if there is any error at first instance, it is much easier to appeal a reasoned judgment than a jury verdict.

6.4   If costs are now regarded as a serious impediment to access to justice in the field of defamation, then there is an argument for saying that all trials should be by judge alone. At this stage I do not go that far. Instead, I recommend that, after proper consultation, the question whether to retain trial by jury in defamation cases be reconsidered.

7. RECOMMENDATIONS

7.1   I make the following recommendations:

(i)   If recoverability of success fees and ATE insurance premiums is abolished:

    (a)   The general level of damages for defamation and breach of privacy claims should be increased by 10%.

    (b)   A regime of qualified one way costs shifting should be introduced.

(ii)   Paragraph 3.3 of the defamation protocol should be amended to read as follows:

    "The Claimant should identify in the Letter of Claim the meaning(s) he/she attributes to the words complained of."

(iii)   The question whether to retain trial by jury in defamation cases should be reconsidered.

CHAPTER 33. COLLECTIVE ACTIONS

INDEX

1. INTRODUCTION

1.1 <u>Preliminary Report.</u> The rules governing costs and costs shifting in collective actions are set out in chapter 38 of the Preliminary Report. That chapter outlines a number of possible reforms to the costs rules for collective actions. These include a no-costs rule[125] (discussed in PR paragraph 38.5.11) and one way costs shifting. Chapter 38 of the Preliminary Report also discusses existing mechanisms for funding collective actions, as well possible new mechanisms which merit consideration.

1.2 <u>Civil Justice Council's proposals for reform.</u> The proposals of the Civil Justice Council (the "CJC") for the reform of collective actions were published in the CJC's report "*Improving Access to Justice through Collective Actions*".[126] The CJC's proposals are summarised in PR chapter 38.

1.3 <u>Representative actions.</u> Representative proceedings are not usually a satisfactory vehicle for pursuing claims on behalf of a group, essentially because of the technical requirements of CPR rule 19.6. This is illustrated by the recent decision of Sir Andrew Morritt C in *Emerald Supplies Ltd v British Airways plc* [2009] EWHC 741 (Ch); [2009] 3 WLR 1200.[127]

2. DEBATE DURING PHASE 2

2.1 <u>Herbert Smith LLP conference on 14th May 2009.</u> On 14th May I attended a conference held by Herbert Smith LLP, entitled "*Class action reform: a business perspective*". Herbert Smith partners stated that they had done a survey of 15 major businesses and institutions. Most respondents did not think that there was an unmet need for reform of collective actions. Concern was expressed that we should not create a regime for collective actions in England and Wales resembling class actions in the USA. Respondents differed on the issue of opt-out. Respondents in favour of opt-out argued that this should achieve finality, greater administrative efficiency and

---

[125] I.e. A rule that each side bears its own costs, save in exceptional circumstances.

[126] London, 2008.

[127] Discussed by Professor Rachel Mulheron in "*Emerald Supplies v British Airways plc; a century later the ghost of Markt lives on*" [2009] Comp Law 159. At the time of writing (December 2009) this decision is under appeal, but no decision is expected before the end of term.

lower overall costs. Respondents against opt-out argued that it created a divergence of interests between those driving the litigation and those who had suffered the loss. The general view was that a consumer group or, better, a regulator should bring the action as representative claimant on behalf of the group. All respondents agreed that collective actions should be certified by High Court judges against strict criteria. Another speaker pointed out that 13 of the 24 EU states have collective action regimes. They are all different, some being opt-in and some opt-out. She stated that almost all respondents to the Herbert Smith survey opposed the CJC's proposals for cy-près.[128] Views were split about the use of third party funding for collective actions. All respondents were opposed to the use of contingency fees. All respondents supported the retention of costs shifting in collective actions, in order to deter weak claims.

2.2   In the discussion which followed these presentations a broad range of views was expressed, regarding whether there was a need for reform of collective redress, the sort of "design features" which any reform should include, and how costs and funding could be handled. Most speakers were opposed to a no-costs regime. However, Professor Rachael Mulheron argued that there were times when costs shifting should be departed from in group actions, and that the strict certification and preliminary merits criteria proposed by the CJC for an opt-out collective action would amply do the work of deterring frivolous or weak claims. She added that if we retain costs shifting for any opt-out collective redress regime that may be introduced, then there will need to be a fund similar to the Ontario Class Proceedings Fund,[129] both to protect a losing representative claimant from an adverse costs award and to provide a winning defendant with a realistic, as opposed to a theoretical, prospect of recovering its costs. It will be recalled from PR paragraphs 18.2.6 to 18.2.8 and 38.7.12 that this fund has operated since 1993 to support class actions; for those actions which the Class Proceedings Committee decides to fund, it takes 10% of the proceeds of successful actions and pays adverse costs plus disbursements in unsuccessful actions.

2.3   <u>Consumer Focus.</u> Consumer Focus is not opposed in principle to a no-costs regime, but would prefer this to apply only to collective actions brought by recognised consumer organisations, such as itself. Consumer Focus points out that it is a public body, with a remit to campaign for the consumer interest and subject to Parliamentary scrutiny; these features are a sufficient safeguard against the bringing of frivolous claims. Consumer Focus also notes the advantages of one way costs shifting, but states that this regime would require appropriate checks and balances to safeguard against abuse.

2.4   <u>Association of Personal Injury Lawyers.</u> The Association of Personal Injury Lawyers ("APIL") does not support a general no-costs regime for collective actions, stating that under such a regime many low value actions would cease to be viable. APIL considers that one way costs shifting in group actions might have merit. However, APIL's view is that the third option canvassed in the Preliminary Report is the best way forward, namely that there be no rigid costs rule for all collective actions. Instead in each individual case, at an early stage, the court should consider how to deal with costs: in particular the court should consider whether full costs shifting is appropriate or whether there should be a protective costs order or costs

---

[128] Cy-près was originally an equitable doctrine which provided the court with a method for fairly distributing a charitable trust fund, remaining as close as possible to the intention of the testator or settlor, in order to prevent the trust from failing. The doctrine has subsequently been applied in the context of damages distributions in collective actions in the United States, Canada and (far more rarely) in England, in order to distribute proceeds from class actions where it is not feasible or practicable to distribute to the class members technically entitled to the funds.
[129] As to which, see PR paragraphs 18.2.6 to 18.2.8.

capping order. APIL commends the set of rules for collective actions proposed by the CJC, including a certification process during which the claimants must establish that they have a proper case to pursue. APIL adds that claimants need protection against any "harsh" adverse costs order up to the certification stage. This scheme is, essentially, a development of the proposal made by APIL during Phase 1: see PR paragraphs 10.9.22 to 10.9.24 and 38.5.14.

2.5   Forum of Complex Injury Solicitors. The Forum of Complex Injury Solicitors ("FOCIS") agrees with the proposal in the Preliminary Report that the removal of costs shifting should be an option in suitable cases. FOCIS also agrees with the tentative view in the Preliminary Report that costs capping should be the exception rather than the norm in collective actions. FOCIS believes that conventional case management should usually be sufficient to control costs to proportionate levels and, by way of example, cites the Seroxat litigation in which the Senior Master adopted a form of costs management. FOCIS is critical of the decision in *Eli Lilly & Co Ltd v James* [2009] EWHC 198 (QB) and maintains that a costs cap should be used to protect claimants against excessive exposure to costs, when the defendant is a wealthy corporation.

2.6   Confederation of British Industry. The Confederation of British Industry (the "CBI") expresses the grave concerns of business about opt-out. The CBI maintains that retention of costs shifting is particularly important in the context of collective actions. It states:

> "Collective actions present problems of funding but we would be opposed in principle to this funding being provided by defendants, which would be the effect of a 'no costs' regime. Access to justice should not in our view be paid for by defendants."

2.7   GC100 Group. The GC100 Group[130] believes that costs shifting is an important safeguard against unmeritorious collective actions. It recognises, however, that in particular cases the costs shifting rule might inhibit access to justice. The GC100 Group therefore makes the following proposal:

> "A better solution would be to keep the costs shifting rule as the norm in group actions but to allow a reasonable amount of judicial discretion to order that costs should lie where they fall, or be capped, in appropriate, exceptional circumstances. Examples would include where there is a genuine concern as to access to justice, unconscionable behaviour by the defendant, or overwhelming merits."

2.8   Liability insurers. Liability insurers generally support opt-in, rather than opt-out, and strongly oppose any reforms which might encourage US style class actions in this jurisdiction. They support costs shifting in collective actions. The Association of British Insurers (the "ABI") states that alternative dispute resolution ("ADR") should be promoted, because this can resolve collective claims before the issue of proceedings. The ABI stresses the importance of proper judicial scrutiny before a collective action is allowed to go forward. This should include questions such as whether the claimants should provide a costs deposit. Although the ABI opposes a no-costs regime, it does offer a partial concession in this regard:

---

[130] The GC100 Group comprises the general counsel and company secretaries of the FTSE 100 companies; see PR paragraph 10.2.1.

"In principle, the ABI would support using a lower costs scale, provided this is set at a proportionate level, which allows genuine claims to be brought forward."

2.9 <u>Professional bodies.</u> The Law Society offers a balanced view of the difficult issues surrounding collective actions. It states that any collective redress procedure should include provision for ADR, subject to court approval. It considers that the judiciary should adopt the role of gatekeeper. In relation to costs, the Law Society states:

"The costs rules should be reviewed, in so far as they are applicable to collective redress actions, for the mutual protection of both claimants and defendants but without stifling access to justice."

2.10 The City of London Law Society's Litigation Committee (the "CLLSLC") is in favour of retaining costs shifting for collective actions. The CLLSLC believes that third party funding will become the usual way of funding group actions. In those circumstances, the CLLSLC proposes that successful defendants should recover their costs from the litigation funders.[131]

2.11 <u>The Government's Response to the CJC's Report.</u> On 20th July 2009 the Ministry of Justice published *"The Government's Response to the Civil Justice Council's Report: 'Improving Access to Justice through Collective Actions"* (the "Government's Response"). This states that the Government does not support the CJC's proposal for a generic collective action procedure. The Government believes that a sector-based approach to the introduction of collective action rights would be better and more achievable. The Government states that ADR should be explored before the parties resort to litigation. The Government believes that in some sectors suitable representative bodies should be authorised to bring collective actions on behalf of the individuals affected. In relation to the opt-in or opt-out issue, the Government generally favours a hybrid model. The Government agrees with the CJC's recommendation for a strict certification procedure for group actions. The Government believes that the costs shifting rule should be maintained in collective actions, in order to deter unmeritorious claims.

2.12 At the time of writing (December 2009) the Financial Services Bill 2009 (the "2009 Bill") is being debated in Parliament. Sections 18 to 25 give effect to the Government's proposal mentioned in the previous paragraph. A sector-based approach is being adopted. Section 18 of the 2009 Bill enables the court to permit collective proceedings to be brought in respect of financial services claims. Section 19 requires the court to direct whether such proceedings shall be brought on an opt-in or an opt-out basis. Sections 22 and 23 permit the Treasury to make regulations about such collective proceedings, including regulations concerning the assessment and distribution of damages.

3. ANALYSIS RE COSTS SHIFTING

3.1 <u>Personal injury claims.</u> If my recommendations in chapter 19 above are accepted, qualified one way costs shifting will be the norm for personal injury claims. This regime would therefore be imported into group personal injury actions.

---

[131] This last observation coincides with the views which I have expressed concerning the costs liability of third party funders in chapter 11 above.

3.2   The competing arguments. The arguments advanced during Phase 2 range between two principal positions: (i) there should be no costs shifting or one way costs shifting; and (ii) there should be full costs shifting. Justification for the first position is that this is necessary to promote access to justice; otherwise the collective claimants would be deterred by fear of adverse costs liability. Justification for the second position is that full exposure to adverse costs is necessary to deter frivolous claims.

3.3   The middle way. As recognised by many of the submissions, there is a possible middle way. Whilst two way costs shifting provides a necessary discipline in many (perhaps most) collective actions, there are cases where claimants simply cannot accept the risk of unlimited liability for adverse costs.

3.4   Having weighed up the submissions and the arguments in Phase 2, I propose the following costs regime for collective actions:

(i)   The starting point or default position in personal injury actions is qualified one way costs shifting[132] and, in all other cases, is two way costs shifting.

(ii)   At the certification stage the court, after considering the nature of the case, the funding arrangements and the resources of the parties, may direct that a different costs regime shall operate.

Whatever costs regime operates, however, the general rule in CPR rule 48.6A should apply: the individual litigant is only liable for his proportion of the common costs.[133]

3.5   The advantage of this regime is that it contains the necessary flexibility that many respondents have suggested is necessary. Furthermore, where a claim is weak or lacking in merit, the court will no doubt insist that two way costs shifting should prevail.

4. ANALYSIS RE FUNDING

4.1   In principle, claimants with a viable collective action should have as many means of funding available to them as possible.

(i) Conditional fee agreements

4.2   If the recommendations set out in chapter 10 above are accepted, success fees will cease to be recoverable. This abolition of recoverability will apply equally in collective actions. Conditional fee agreements will nevertheless continue to be one possible method of funding group litigation, with any uplift on lawyers' fees to be paid by the claimants. Economies of scale may mean that success fees in collective actions represent a lower proportion of any damages awarded than in single claimant litigation.

(ii) Third party funding

4.3   As the CLLSLC points out, third party funding may be suitable for many group actions. If the claimants are advised that the proposed funding agreement is

---

[132] As explained in chapter 19 above. The mechanism proposed enables costs orders to be enforced against wealthy unsuccessful claimants. It also enables costs orders to be enforced against claimants who conduct litigation unreasonably.
[133] This rule applies unless the court orders otherwise. See further PR paragraphs 38.2.1 to 38.2.5.

appropriate and if the funders subscribe to the voluntary code referred to in chapter 11 above, this would be a proper means of funding many collective actions.

4.4   In my view, there is no objection in principle to third party funders supporting collective personal injury actions. This may be the most effective means of promoting access to justice for a claim against, say, a multi-national pharmaceutical company. I recommend that rule 9.01(4) of the Solicitors' Code of Conduct 2007 should be amended, so as to permit at least the third party funding of collective personal injury claims.

(iii) Contingency fees

4.5   If the recommendations set out in chapter 12 above are accepted, it will be legitimate for both solicitors and counsel to conduct litigation on a contingent fees basis. This method of funding may be appropriate for group actions where (a) the lawyers have sufficient confidence in success and (b) the claimants receive independent advice that the terms of the proposed contingency fee agreement are reasonable. The CJC has suggested on two occasions that contingency fees might be suitable for use in collective actions: see recommendation 10 in the CJC's August 2005 paper *"Improved Access to Justice – Funding Options and Proportionate Costs"* and recommendation 4 in its June 2007 report *"Improved Access to Justice – Funding Options and Proportionate Costs; The Future Funding of Litigation – Alternative Funding Structure"*.

(iv) Supplementary Legal Aid Scheme

4.6   In chapter 13 above, I have identified the practical difficulties which stand in the way of creating a viable large scale Supplementary Legal Aid Scheme ("SLAS"). Nevertheless, as the CJC has pointed out, a SLAS may be viable for collective actions: see PR paragraph 38.7.10. I recommend that, after decisions have been made about the wider costs and funding regime, serious consideration be given by the Legal Services Commission (the "LSC") to the establishment of a SLAS specifically dedicated to collective actions.[134]

4.7   Experience of the Ontario Class Proceedings Fund shows that the Contingency Legal Aid Fund structure is peculiarly well-suited to collective litigation: see PR paragraphs 18.2.6 to 18.2.8 and 38.7.12. The Ontario fund makes provision for own disbursements and adverse costs. Nevertheless I do not see why a SLAS set up on similar principles in this jurisdiction should not provide funding for claimant costs, even though it may need to deduct more than 10% from damages.

(v) Distribution of damages

4.8   CJC recommendations. Recommendation 7 of the CJC proposals[135] for the reform of group actions stated: *"Where a case is brought on an opt out basis the court should have the power to aggregate damages in an appropriate case."* In recommendation 10 of the same proposals the CJC proposed: "*Unallocated damages from an aggregate award should be distributed by a trustee of the award according to general trust law principles. In appropriate cases such a cy près distribution could be made to a Foundation or Trust.*"

---

[134] For the reasons set out in section 3 of chapter 13 above, the SLAS option cannot usefully be pursued until it is known which recommendations of this report are accepted and will be implemented.
[135] See paragraph 1.2 above and PR paragraph 38.4.1.

4.9   The question which may arise. Whether or not those recommendations of the CJC either will or should be accepted is a matter which lies outside my terms of reference. My concern is with the costs consequences. Here, I am bound to say, I see an opportunity. If, following the Government's response to the CJC's Report, legislation is introduced to permit the court to order an opt-out collective action in an appropriate case and to permit the aggregation of damages, the question will arise as to where any surplus damages should be distributed. Indeed this question will arise, in respect of damages awarded in "collective proceedings"[136] if section 23 of the 2009 Bill is enacted in its current form.

4.10   A modest proposal. In October 2009 the Access to Justice Foundation (the "AJF") was established as the charitable body to receive monies recovered pursuant to an order made under section 194 of the Legal Services Act 2007 (the "2007 Act"). That section enables a *pro bono* assisted litigant to recover costs from the losing party, such costs to be paid to the AJF.[137] The purpose of the AJF is to make grants by way of distributing its funds in promotion of access to justice.[138] The effect of this arrangement is that costs recovered in a *pro bono* case under section 194 of the 2007 Act and paid over to the AJF amount to new money to promote access to justice. The same approach could be adopted by using the AJF as the destination for any surplus damages arising from an opt-out collective action. Since this proposal is contingent upon decisions about matters outside my terms of reference, I do not make this matter the subject of a specific proposal. However, I draw attention to the opportunity which may possibly arise to promote access to justice in the future.

5. RECOMMENDATIONS

5.1   I make the following recommendations:

(i)   The starting point or default position in collective actions should be (a) in personal injury actions, qualified one way costs shifting and (b) in all other actions, two way costs shifting. At the certification stage, the judge may direct that a different costs regime shall operate.

(ii)   Rule 9.01(4) of the Solicitors' Code of Conduct 2007 should be amended, so as to permit the third party funding of collective personal injury claims.

5.2   My recommendation in respect of financial modelling for a SLAS is set out in chapter 13 above and will not be repeated here.

---

[136] As defined in section 18(2) of the 2009 Bill.
[137] The AJF's website is at www.accesstojusticefoundation.org.uk.
[138] It should be noted that this is yet another exception to the indemnity principle.

CHAPTER 34. APPEALS

INDEX

1. INTRODUCTION

1.1   Preliminary Report. Appeals to the Court of Appeal are discussed in chapter 39 of the Preliminary Report. The factual background and general comments in that chapter remain valid. The impact which recoverable success fees and after-the-event insurance premiums may have upon costs in the Court of Appeal is illustrated by the cases summarised in PR appendix 14.

1.2   New Part 52 practice direction. The new practice direction supplementing CPR Part 52 did not enter the public domain during Phase 2, as had been hoped. Therefore it has not been the subject of debate during the Costs Review. Indeed, although I have seen the new practice direction in draft, I understand that a final version of the practice direction will not enter the public domain until after this report has gone for printing.

1.3   CPR and case management appeals. There are specific issues concerning appeals from case management decisions and consistency of Court of Appeal decisions concerning the interpretation and application of the CPR. These issues are addressed in chapter 39 below.

2. COMMENTS DURING PHASE 2

2.1   During Phase 2 (as during Phase 1) relatively little attention was paid to appeals both by the authors of written submissions and by those who invited me to meetings. Nevertheless, I should draw attention to the submissions mentioned below.

2.2   Civil Legal Aid Sub-Committee of the Bar Council. The Civil Legal Aid Sub-Committee of the Bar Council raises three important points concerning appeals:

(i)   The appeal rules should be looked at more generally, not only with regard to appeals to the Court of Appeal.

(ii)   Consideration should be given to creating a no-costs rule for appeals from jurisdictions which have no costs shifting.

(iii)   Consideration should be given to making greater use of issue-related costs orders on appeals, since appellate judgments usually identify individual grounds of appeal as "successful" or "unsuccessful".

2.3   Chancery Bar Association. CPR rule 44.3(3)(b) provides that the general rule about costs (that the unsuccessful party should be ordered to pay the successful party's costs) does not apply to appeals to the Court of Appeal in probate proceedings. The Chancery Bar Association in a survey of its members asked whether this departure from the general costs rule should be maintained in probate appeals. Of those that responded to this question, seven voted "yes" and nine voted "no".

2.4   City of London Law Society Litigation Committee. In PR paragraph 39.2.6, I raised the question whether we should adopt any of the case management procedures developed by the Court of Appeal in Victoria. The City of London Law Society's Litigation Committee (the "CLLSLC") made helpful submissions on this issue, extracts of which I set out below:

> "The question is raised as to whether additional case management might reduce the costs of appeals, following the example of the Court of Appeal in Victoria. In that example, an Associate Justice controls the volume of documents included in the appeal bundles, the length of skeleton arguments to be submitted and the length of hearings. We do not regard any of these points to be of major concern, each of which is considered in turn.
>
> (A)   Hearing
>
> The anticipated length of an appeal to the Court of Appeal has to be certified by the advocates appearing on the appeal. In our experience, such estimates are generally both relatively modest and reasonably accurate.
>
> (B)   Bundles
>
> Appeal bundles are invariably prepared on a conservative basis, including all documents that may possibly be relevant to the appeal. This seems to us inevitable. The danger of omitting something of relevance is considered a greater danger than including documents in the bundles that are not, in the event, required. It must be doubtful if a lengthy discussion at a case management conference as to what should, or should not, be included in appeal bundles would be productive. The contents of the bundles should be left to the good sense of those preparing the appeal.
>
> (C)   Skeleton arguments
>
> The Court of Appeal is free to limit the length of skeleton arguments, if thought desirable, through the CPR. Our experience in commercial cases is that it is rare for skeletons, prepared by experienced advocates, to be substantially longer than is required.
>
> ...our overall view is that the current mechanisms are working reasonably well and that the introduction of more formal case management will inevitably serve to increase costs, while an appeal is pending. It seems to us improbable that these additional costs will be offset by a reduction in the length of the appeal (which is managed by the Court in any event) or any saving in preparatory work. Further, if additional case management were to be considered, we would need to be convinced that it would engender a real costs saving; in our experience an increase in case management is often accompanied by a commensurate increase in costs".

2.5   Intellectual Property Court Users Committee. As set out in chapter 24 above, the Intellectual Property Court Users' Committee (the "IPCUC") in its final report dated 31st July 2009 has proposed making radical reforms to the Patents County Court (the "PCC"). These reforms include imposing a cap upon recoverable costs, in order that SMEs should not be deterred from litigating by the fear of indeterminate liability for adverse costs. In relation to costs on appeal the IPCUC states:

> "...we are confident that the Court of Appeal would be sensitive to the question of costs on appeal from the reformed PCC, and would be unlikely to award more by way of appeal costs than the first instance costs."

There is an important issue here as to whether (a) this is a matter which should be left to the general discretion of the Court of Appeal or (b) the rules should make special provision for costs on appeals from the (reformed) PCC.

2.6   Firm of solicitors specialising in environmental claims. A firm of solicitors specialising in environmental claims comments on the risk of adverse costs orders on applications for permission to appeal, as follows:

> "Our experience of the Court of Appeal on permission applications is usually satisfactory, i.e. that there will be no costs exposure until a PTA[139] is granted. However, we have had situations where, without explanation, this rule has been departed from. You will appreciate that this causes severe fright and means that one can never advise prospective appellants confidently that there will be no costs liability. This is particularly relevant in cases where one has lost a legal aid matter at first instance, and needs to get PTA before re-approaching the LSC,[140] confident that it is worth continuing applying for funding. Similarly, of course, if one way fee shifting were introduced, that problem would also evaporate. This is a yet further example of the difficulty we have in confidently advising our clients of the risk of adverse costs under the current regime."

2.7   Association of Personal Injury Lawyers. The Association of Personal Injury Lawyers ("APIL") states that, because of lack of funding, claimants are seldom the appellants in personal injury cases. The insurance industry is *the effective driver* of appeals to the Court of Appeal. Insurers bring such appeals, because they are concerned to obtain decisions which will *ensure future profit*. APIL believes that this imbalance could be addressed by introducing one way costs shifting, as canvassed in chapter 25 of the Preliminary Report.

3. ANALYSIS

3.1   I adhere to the view expressed in PR paragraph 39.2.2 that the control of costs on appeal to the Court of Appeal, although an important topic in its own right, must be addressed after decisions have been made about what steps, if any, should be taken to control costs at first instance. Any process reforms made in respect of first instance litigation will impact upon appeals. Likewise any changes to the costs rules at first instance will impact upon the costs of appeals. There is a precedent for this approach. It will be recalled that the reform of appeal procedures was the subject of a separate review under Sir Jeffrey Bowman,[141] which commenced some time after

---

[139] Permission to appeal.
[140] Legal Services Commission.
[141] A summary of the Report to the Lord Chancellor by the Review of the Court of Appeal (Civil Division), dated 6th November 1997, can be found at http://www.dca.gov.uk/civil/bowman/bowfr.htm.

Lord Woolf's Final Report on Access to Justice. It will also be much easier to debate the issues concerning appeals when the new practice direction supplementing Part 52 has been published, which is not the case at the time of writing.

3.2   Although I am recommending that there be a separate review of appeal procedures and costs rules on appeals, in this chapter I shall offer preliminary observations on the issues that have arisen and make one interim recommendation.

(i) Appeals from a no-costs regime to a court with costs shifting

3.3   Examples of such cases. In this chapter I use the phrase "no-costs regime" to mean a regime in which (absent special circumstances) each side bears its own costs. The small claims track is virtually a no-costs regime: see PR chapter 49. Appeals in small claims to a circuit judge are subject to restrictions on recoverable costs.[142] However, appeals on small claims which reach the Court of Appeal (as second appeals) are subject to full costs shifting. Also appeals from tribunals to the courts commonly move from a no-costs regime to a costs shifting regime.

3.4   The two cultures. In chapter 46 of the Preliminary Report I discussed the conflicting traditions of tribunals and the courts in relation to costs. The culture of the courts is that costs shifting promotes access to justice; therefore costs shifting is the norm or the default rule in most forms of litigation. The culture of tribunals is that costs shifting inhibits access to justice; therefore no costs shifting is the norm or the default rule in most tribunal proceedings.[143] This conflict of approaches gives rise to tensions and sometimes to intractable problems at the interface between courts and tribunals: for example, when functions of the courts are transferred to tribunals (as is now happening under the Tribunals Courts and Enforcement Act 2007) or when cases pass upwards from tribunals to courts.

3.5   Recent illustration. These problems have recently been illustrated by the Court of Appeal's decision in *Eweida v British Airways plc*.[144] That case concerned a claim by Miss Eweida that her employer, British Airways plc ("BA"), had unlawfully discriminated against her on the grounds of her religious belief. The Employment Tribunal (the "ET") dismissed the claimant's claim. The Employment Appeal Tribunal (the "EAT") dismissed her appeal. Both the ET and the EAT are no-costs regimes, so the claimant was at no risk as to BA's costs in those proceedings. The claimant then appealed to the Court of Appeal. She applied for an order that she should have no liability, alternatively a limited liability, for adverse costs in the event of losing the appeal. The Court of Appeal dismissed her application on the grounds that in the circumstances it did not have power to make either a protective costs order[145] or a costs capping order.[146]

3.6   Short term measure. As a short term measure, I propose that appellate courts should have a discretionary power, upon granting permission to appeal or receiving an appeal[147] from a no-costs jurisdiction, to order (a) that each side should bear its own costs of the appeal or (b) that the recoverable costs should be capped at a

---

[142] See CPR rule 27.14(2).
[143] See PR paragraph 46.3.6.
[144] [2009] EWCA Civ 1025.
[145] A protective costs order is available in public law litigation, where a liability for the other side's costs would be likely to prevent, in effect, a claimant from bringing or continuing proceedings, and thereby prevent a matter of public interest and importance being considered by the court.
[146] A costs capping order is made on the basis that the litigant is at risk as to the other side's costs, in the ordinary way, but seeks to prevent that liability from being inflated by the incurring of disproportionate amounts in respect of costs; see CPR rule 44.18 to 44.20.
[147] If permission is not required.

specified sum. In exercising that discretion the court should have regard to (a) the means of both parties, (b) all the circumstances of the case and (c) the need to facilitate access to justice for any party which has good grounds to challenge or to support the decision under appeal.

(ii) Other matters

3.7   <u>Case management and the reforms made by the Victoria Court of Appeal.</u> I can see the force of the points made by the CLLSLC, and generally agree with them. It seems to me that, if anything, creating a new position in the Court of Appeal to manage cases coming to the Court has the potential to add to the costs of litigation. If parties are required to make representations to any such court officer over, for example, what hearing length is appropriate, or the appropriate size and content of bundles or skeleton arguments, this exercise could itself generate significant expense. Given that the current system generally works satisfactorily, the cost of implementing the reform canvassed in PR paragraph 39.2.6 is likely to outweigh any benefit.

3.8   <u>Appeals from the Patents County Court.</u> If the reforms to the PCC proposed in chapter 24 above are implemented, costs at first instance will be capped at £50,000 in patent infringement and validity cases and at £25,000 in other cases. In my view, in order to give effect to the policy underlying those reforms there ought to be commensurate caps upon recoverable costs in appeals from the PCC. However, this is a question which cannot sensibly be addressed until (a) it is known whether the proposed reforms to the PCC will be implemented and (b) an outline of the required legislation and rules for the PCC have been drawn up.

3.9   <u>Costs on permission to appeal applications.</u> The point identified by the environmental solicitors is one of general application. Unsuccessful applicants for PTA generally do not incur liability for adverse costs. However, if the respondent at the court's request (a) provides written submissions or (b) attends an oral hearing of the permission application, then normally the court will award costs to the respondent if permission is refused. As the solicitors point out, if one way costs shifting is introduced for environmental judicial review claims,[148] then the problem should evaporate, at least for the clients of those solicitors.

3.10   <u>Effect of one way costs shifting at first instance.</u> This is another issue which cannot be taken forward until decisions have been reached about the primary recommendations in this report. My present view is that any litigation which is subject to one way costs shifting at first instance should also be subject to one way costs shifting on appeal. I reach this view for three principal reasons:

(i)   If a category of litigation[149] at first instance merits one way costs shifting for policy reasons, then those same policy considerations should apply on appeal.

(ii)   Most appeals are subject to a permission application, so that frivolous appeals are rarer than frivolous actions.

(iii)   If a party not at risk of adverse costs is successful below, it is harsh to expose that party to the risk of adverse costs on an appeal brought by his opponent.

3.11   <u>APIL's concerns about the imbalance in personal injury appeals.</u> APIL acknowledges that its concerns about the imbalance in personal injury appeals will be

---

[148] As is proposed in chapter 30 above, having regard to the UK's obligations under *Aarhus* and other policy considerations.
[149] E.g. environmental judicial review claims or personal injury claims.

addressed if one way costs shifting is introduced for personal injuries litigation. I agree with that analysis.

3.12 <u>Possibility of a suitors' fund.</u> Where a litigant wins at first instance, but loses on appeal, he is likely to be ordered to pay the costs of the other party. It may be thought unjust that a litigant should be saddled with a huge costs bill because of errors made by the judge below. In New South Wales a "suitors' fund" has been established to provide for this contingency.[150] Money for the fund comes out of court fees. Section 5 of the Suitors' Fund Act 1951 provides that money paid into the fund is not to exceed 10% of court fees collected. A party who wins below but loses on appeal may apply for a "suitors' fund certificate". If granted, such a certificate entitles that party to recover part of his costs from the fund.

3.13 If and when a full review of the Court of Appeal procedures and costs rules is undertaken, consideration should be given to the possibility of establishing a suitors' fund in England and Wales. The size and purpose of such a fund would be a matter for future debate. One possibility is that the fund could provide support for litigants who succeed in a no costs shifting regime and then lose in the Court of Appeal. As the law now stands, parties who start to litigate in a forum with no risk of adverse costs may end up facing a huge costs bill as a result of somebody else's mistake. In my view, this state of affairs is unsatisfactory and inhibits access to justice.

3.14 <u>Costs management.</u> Costs management is discussed in chapter 40 below. If the proposals for costs management of first instance proceedings are introduced and are successful, consideration will have to be given to costs management of appeals. Appeal proceedings can be expensive, as is shown by PR appendix 14. There may well be appeals where at least some of the parties would welcome judicial control of recoverable costs in advance. This is a matter which will have to be looked at in the context of a general review of Court of Appeal procedures and costs rules.

4. RECOMMENDATIONS

4.1 I make the following recommendations:

(i) There should be a separate review of the procedures and costs rules for appeals, after decisions have been reached in relation to the recommendations in this report concerning first instance litigation.

(ii) Pending that review, appellate courts should have a discretionary power, upon granting permission to appeal or receiving an appeal from a no-costs jurisdiction, to order (a) that each side should bear its own costs of the appeal or (b) that the recoverable costs should be capped at a specified sum.

---

[150] See http://www.lawlink.nsw.gov.au/Lawlink/lsb/ll_lsb.nsf/pages/lsb_suitors_fund.

REVIEW OF
CIVIL LITIGATION COSTS

PART 6. CONTROLLING THE COSTS OF LITIGATION

CHAPTER 35. PRE-ACTION PROTOCOLS

INDEX

1. INTRODUCTION

(i) Background

1.1   Preliminary Report. The relevant facts and issues for consideration are set out in PR chapter 43, section 3.

1.2   Approach in this chapter. In this chapter I treat chancery, commercial and construction litigation as separate topics, even though there is an overlap between them. In 2011 these three jurisdictions[1] will move from the Royal Courts of Justice and St Dunstan's House to the Rolls Building.

1.3   The protocols. There are ten pre-action protocols dealing with specific areas of civil litigation ("specific protocols"), namely:

(i)   Pre-Action Protocol for Personal Injury Claims.

(ii)   Pre-Action Protocol for the Resolution of Clinical Disputes.[2]

(iii)   Pre-Action Protocol for the Construction and Engineering Disputes.

(iv)   Pre-Action Protocol for Defamation.

(v)   Professional Negligence Pre-Action Protocol.

(vi)   Pre-Action Protocol for Judicial Review.

(vii)   Pre-Action Protocol for Disease and Illness Claims.

(viii)   Pre-Action Protocol for Housing Disrepair Cases.

(ix)   Pre-Action Protocol for Possession Claims based on Rent Arrears.

(x)   Pre-Action Protocol for Possession Claims based on Mortgage or Home Purchase Plan Arrears in respect of Residential Property.

1.4   There is also the Practice Direction – Pre-Action Conduct (the "PDPAC"), which came into effect on 6th April 2009 (towards the end of Phase 1 of the Costs Review): see PR paragraph 43.3.4. This practice direction has several different functions. Section II of the PDPAC sets out how the courts will secure compliance with the specific protocols. Section III of the PDPAC operates as a general protocol for all civil litigation[3] which is not the subject of specific protocols. Section IV of the PDPAC imposes additional pre-action obligations in respect of all civil litigation,[4] whether or not subject to a specific protocol.

1.5   In effect, therefore, there are eleven pre-action protocols. These comprise (a) ten specific protocols and (b) one general protocol which is contained in sections III and IV of the PDPAC. I shall refer to sections III and IV of the PDPAC as the "general protocol".

(ii) Costs of compliance

1.6   I have not received any data, during either Phase 1 or Phase 2, which quantify the costs of complying with pre-action protocols specifically. Nor have I seen any comparison of the costs incurred before and after the introduction of pre-action protocols, other than the research set out in PR paragraph 9.5.2. Such a comparison would be difficult to obtain now. Nevertheless, data have been supplied concerning pre-action costs, as set out in the following paragraphs. However, it is not possible to attribute specific sums to compliance with the protocols.

1.7   Personal injury. In appendix 1 to this report, I set out two tables summarising PR appendix 18: CFA cases won by claimant, total costs and damages paid. Table 10 contains data for the CFA cases and shows that 415 of the cases analysed settled pre-issue with total damages of £2,111,739.30 and total claimant costs of £1,078,194.72.

---

[1] In so far as they are based in London.
[2] A Protocol for Obtaining Hospital Medical Records is annexed to this pre-action protocol.
[3] Subject to the limited exceptions set out in PDPAC, paragraph 2.2.
[4] Subject to the limited exceptions set out in PDPAC, paragraph 2.2.

The total claimant costs as a percentage of damages were 51%. Table 11 shows that, in the non-CFA, no ATE insurance premium cases which settled pre-issue, the ratio of claimant costs to damages was 41% (with total damages of £1,596,364.21 and total claimant costs of £647,113.28).

1.8   Clinical negligence. One set of data provided to me by the Medical Defence Union towards the end of Phase 1 showed that, amongst a sample of CFA funded medical claims settled pre-issue during the first half of 2008, the average claimant base costs to damages ratio (i.e. not taking into account the success fee) was 76%. Once success fees are taken into account, this ratio increased to 123% and the claimant's average costs exceeded damages in 74% of cases. Similar data in respect of dental claims settled pre-issue showed an average base costs to damages ratio of 87% excluding the success fee and 122% once the success fee is taken into account.

(iii) The general picture which has now emerged

1.9   During Phase 1 of the Costs Review I encountered a formidable battery of conflicting arguments concerning the merits and demerits of protocols. Indeed I confessed to finding the issues surrounding pre-action protocols to be some of the most intractable questions in the Costs Review: see PR paragraph 43.3.23.

1.10   During Phase 2 the comments made at meetings and in written submissions were, quite understandably, more detailed and more focused upon individual protocols. During the course of Phase 2 the fog gradually lifted. Except in respect of the Pre-Action Protocol for Construction and Engineering Disputes,[5] there was a high degree of unanimity that the specific protocols serve a useful purpose. In certain instances amendments would be beneficial, as discussed below. In general terms, however, I was surprised by the degree of enthusiasm and support for the specific protocols.

1.11   There is also a high degree of unanimity concerning the general protocol. One size does not fit all and that protocol serves no useful purpose. Court users do not want it. In respect of large commercial and chancery claims, the general protocol has the potential to cause substantial delays and wastage of costs.

2. COMMERCIAL LITIGATION

(i) Views expressed during Phase 2

2.1   There is a clear majority view amongst commercial solicitors and counsel, shared by Commercial Court judges, that pre-action protocols are unwelcome in commercial litigation. They generate additional costs and delay to no useful purpose. I understand that clients, especially overseas clients, share this view.

2.2   Commercial Court Users Committee. The Costs Sub-Committee of the Commercial Court Users Committee proposes in its final paper to the Costs Review that the PDPAC should be disapplied in the Commercial Court and for large commercial claims generally, for example large commercial claims in the Chancery Division.

2.3   Manchester Law Society. The commercial litigation practitioners of the Manchester Law Society comment as follows in their submission:

---

[5] The subject of substantial dispute, discussed in section 4 below.

"We adopt entirely the concerns expressed in the Preliminary Report with regard to the 'frontloading' of costs. Whilst we accept that, in principle, constructive pre-action conduct is a commendable objective and to be encouraged, our experience is that the reality is that (because of the need to 'frontload' costs) the effect of the general pre-action protocol ('the protocol') is often to stand in the way of a settlement (rather than to facilitate it). In particular, where there is a large amount of evidence on which a claim will depend, the costs of simply getting a claim ready, even at the pre-claim stage, become a major stumbling-block to settlement. There will often be a large amount of evidence that will need to be marshalled, and this has to be exchanged at a very early stage of the claim…

In our view, in large commercial cases, with substantial sums at stake and complex issues, it is very unlikely that settlement at a very early stage will be achieved as a result of the protocol. If parties are able to resolve their dispute, our experience is that the chances are that they will have done so before they come to instruct solicitors; by that stage, in our experience, they have already exhausted all 'amicable' solutions and have reached the point where they are ready (and needing) to litigate in order to make progress. Our experience is that clients are both hostile and unwilling to the idea of delaying further action unduly by the operation of lengthy and substantial pre-action letters, and our experience is that litigants' faith in the legal system is thereby lessened. The fact that so few pre-action protocol letters actually result in pre-action settlement rather vindicates the litigants' concerns in this regard."

2.4   Commercial Litigation Association. The Commercial Litigation Association, whose members include solicitors, barristers, third party funders and underwriters, comments:

"The existing system of PAP and pleadings result in a duplication of efforts, resources and costs. We suggest that there is no need for both and our opinion is that pleadings are preferred with the importance of PAP downgraded or eliminated."

2.5   Northern Circuit Commercial Bar Association. The Northern Circuit Commercial Bar Association, an association of commercial and chancery barristers practising principally on the Northern Circuit, states:

"We consider that there is a strong case for dis-applying the PD on Pre-action Conduct in respect of high value, heavy and complex business disputes. We consider that in these types of case an involved pre-action process is unlikely to be able to do more than scratch the surface of the dispute, and consequently that it is unlikely to save costs by promoting an early resolution if the parties have been unable to achieve that themselves."

2.6   Individual firms of solicitors. A number of individual firms of solicitors have expressed similar views. One major firm, with an extensive personal injuries practice, comments upon the usefulness of protocols in relation to personal injury and clinical negligence claims. The firm (which also has a substantial commercial practice) goes on to contrast that state of affairs with commercial litigation, where protocol letters are *very time consuming and expensive* but yield little benefit. Similar views were expressed at many of the seminars and meetings in Phase 2.

2.7   Admiralty & Commercial Courts Guide. The new edition of the Admiralty & Commercial Courts Guide (published after the publication of my Preliminary Report) records that the parties must comply with the PDPAC, but discourages elaborate or expensive pre-action procedures. It provides that the letter of claim and letter of response should both be concise and that only essential documents should be supplied. A number of respondents in Phase 2 commended that approach.

(ii) My conclusion

2.8   I agree with the majority view which has been expressed that there is no need for a commercial pre-action protocol. Furthermore the general protocol should no longer be applied to commercial litigation. Whether this result should be achieved by (a) repealing the general protocol or (b) disapplying it to commercial claims will be discussed below. The Admiralty & Commercial Courts Guide (after references to the PDPAC have been deleted) will contain quite sufficient guidance in relation to pre-action conduct.

3. CHANCERY LITIGATION

(i) Views expressed during Phase 2

3.1   Chancery practitioners. There is general hostility to pre-action protocols amongst chancery practitioners. For example, in its submission the Chancery Bar Association wrote:

> "Protocols increase costs. We suggest that a culture of sensible correspondence (on all sides) should be promoted before litigating rather than a formal protocol. A general principle applicable to all cases requiring a fair statement of the case in a letter before action and a responding fair statement of any defence, with all such letters automatically being 'without prejudice save as to costs', might be a better way to approach matters and reduce costs. There is no need for further rules providing for specific costs consequences; it should be sufficient to rely on the general discretion to have regard to *Calderbank* letters when dealing with costs, so that if a party can be seen with hindsight to have behaved unreasonably and thereby increased costs, this can be taken into account."

3.2   Similar views were expressed at the chancery seminar on 24th July 2009. The point was also made, however, that focused protocols prepared by practitioner associations for specialised areas of chancery litigation can be helpful. For example, the Association of Contentious Trust and Probate Specialists ("ACTAPS") has prepared a protocol for contentious probate disputes. ACTAPS members generally follow this protocol and find it to be effective.

3.3   Chancery judges. The chancery judges expressed strong opposition to the PDPAC before it was introduced. They pointed out that the (then draft) PDPAC contained principles which were inconsistent with the principles of much chancery litigation. In many instances chancery proceedings are not "*a step of last resort*", as asserted in PDPAC, paragraph 8.1; on the contrary, the policy in such proceedings may be that the court should take immediate control because the rights of persons who are not parties may be affected. The Chief Chancery Master in his submission to the Costs Review has commended that approach.

3.4 Having considered the written submissions and the debates at the seminars, I am satisfied that there is no need to introduce any new pre-action protocols for chancery litigation. Furthermore I consider that the existing general protocol is not helpful. Because of the multifarious forms that chancery litigation may take, no single protocol could possibly achieve the objective of providing useful pre-action guidance for such cases. In my view, the general protocol should no longer be applied to chancery litigation. Whether this result should be achieved by (a) repealing the general protocol or (b) disapplying it to chancery litigation will be discussed below.

3.5 Where litigation in the Chancery Division or the Chancery Courts falls within the ambit of a specific protocol, such as the Professional Negligence Pre-Action Protocol, the terms of that protocol will continue to govern pre-action conduct. In addition, practitioners will serve the best interests of their clients if, in appropriate cases, they follow the informal protocols developed by professional associations, such as ACTAPS. However, in my view no formal protocol should be binding upon chancery litigation as such. It will be sufficient if the Chancery Guide gives general guidance about pre-action correspondence along the lines set out in paragraph 3.1 above.

4. CONSTRUCTION LITIGATION

(i) The relevant protocol

4.1 Construction litigation is subject to one of the specific protocols, namely the Pre-Action Protocol for Construction and Engineering Disputes (referred to in this section as the "protocol"). The protocol came into force in October 2000. It was revised with effect from April 2007 in accordance with the recommendations of a working party. That working party was chaired by Mr Justice Ramsey, who is now the judge in charge of the Technology and Construction Court (the "TCC").

(ii) Views expressed during Phase 2

4.2 TCC judges. The TCC High Court judges (the "TCC judges") state in their submission:

> "There is a widespread view that the Pre-Action Protocol can often be a waste of time and costs. Those costs can often be substantial, running into many and sometimes hundreds of thousands of pounds. The steps taken during that process can often be duplicative; for instance, the letter of claim will mirror (but in less detail) the Particulars of Claim."

The TCC judges go on to suggest that, if the protocol is to be retained, the steps required by the protocol should be taken after issue of proceedings, during a period when the action is stayed. This would have the advantage that the assigned judge could oversee the process and give any necessary directions. This proposal was first raised during Phase 1 and is referred to in PR paragraph 34.4.3.

4.3 TECBAR. The Technology and Construction Bar Association ("TECBAR") states as follows in its Phase 2 submission:

> "The unanimous view of the TECBAR committee and the respondents to the survey referred to above was that PAP substantially and unnecessarily

increases costs. It is now commonplace to see very detailed letters of claim supported by voluminous appendices, and equally detailed letters of response, which, in the event that the meeting between the parties does not result in a settlement, are then reproduced and often elaborated as pleadings.

It was also the unanimous view of the committee and respondents that the formal PAP should be abolished, and replaced with a more informal process which is limited to a summary letter of claim, a summary letter of response and a meeting."

4.4   Construction solicitors. The views of construction solicitors have been made clear during the Phase 2 meetings and seminars, and also in the written submissions of the Technology and Construction Solicitors Association ("TeCSA"). Construction solicitors take a different view from their colleagues at the Bar. They believe that the protocol procedures, when followed sensibly, promote early settlements and lead to saving of costs. TeCSA states in its written submissions:

"Although opinion is divided on the most effective means of dealing with these issues, the majority view is that the Protocol procedure should remain pre-action. It has been suggested that issues of non-compliance could be eliminated by clear judicial guidance, as and when the opportunity arises, as to what constitutes proper compliance, although it is recognised that much will depend on the facts of individual cases; but guidelines would emerge from a body of case law. An alternative suggestion which attracts general approval is that there might be a change of the rules in order to confer jurisdiction on the TCC to deal with applications in respect of compliance with the Protocol prior to the issue of the claim form."

4.5   King's College conference. On 9th July 2009 I attended a conference of construction experts and solicitors, where the protocol was one of the issues debated. There was strong opposition to the idea that the protocol processes should be carried out post-issue. The majority of delegates favoured a reform whereby applications could be made to the court for directions during the protocol process, if matters were going awry. In other words these would be pre-action applications similar to the pre-action applications for disclosure which already exist.

4.6   The threshold question. The threshold question, which emerges from the debates during Phase 2, is whether the protocol procedure should be (a) abolished, (b) converted into a post-action process or (c) retained as a pre-action process.

(iii) My conclusion on the threshold question

4.7   Having considered the submissions and arguments advanced during Phase 2 (and also drawing upon my own experience as a former TCC judge) I conclude that for the time being the protocol procedure should be retained as a pre-action process. However, a number of steps should be taken in order to address the concerns which have been raised.

(iv) Steps necessary to address concerns

(a) Controlling undue front loading of costs

4.8   The proportionality provision. Paragraph 1.5 of the protocol provides:

> "In all cases the costs incurred at the Protocol stage should be proportionate to the complexity of the case and the amount of money which is at stake. The Protocol does not impose a requirement on the parties to marshal and disclose all the supporting details and evidence that may ultimately be required if the case proceeds to litigation."

This provision is repeated in paragraph 2.1.3 of the TCC Guide.[6]

4.9   Non-compliance. It is clear from the submissions of TECBAR and from other submissions received that the proportionality provision is often honoured in the breach.

4.10   Remedy. Consideration should be given to strengthening the wording of the proportionality provision. Consideration should also be given to making paragraph 3 (re letter of claim) and paragraph 4 (re letter of response) of the protocol less prescriptive. It should be made clear in the protocol that the claim letter should not annex or reproduce a draft pleading and that expert reports should not normally be served at the protocol stage.[7] Documents should not be annexed to the claim letter or the response letter, unless there is good reason to do so. Documents in the possession of both sides should not be supplied.

4.11   Costs penalty. As the law now stands, the costs incurred by each party during the protocol process[8] may, in principle, be recovered as costs incidental to the litigation: see *Roundstone Nurseries Ltd v Stephenson Holdings Ltd* [2009] EWHC 1431 (TCC) at [45] – [47]. I recommend that it should be provided[9] that, in so far as a party has gone beyond the requirements of the protocol, the costs of those excessive labours shall not be recoverable.[10] The costs estimates lodged by both parties before the first case management conference ("CMC") should expressly state what costs have been incurred in complying with the protocol. If it is found that either party has gone substantially beyond the requirements of the protocol, the judge should so certify at the first CMC and should decide the amount of costs to be disallowed.

4.12   I appreciate that this recommendation, if accepted, will impose a substantial additional burden upon TCC judges. On the other hand, it is to be hoped that a few robust judicial decisions will rapidly have the desired effect upon pre-action behaviour, thus reducing the need for cost disallowance applications. Furthermore where one or both parties run up excessive costs in the pre-action period, it must be

---

[6] Second edition, first revision, October 2007.
[7] Unless these reports have necessarily been obtained as part of the investigation of the claim and it would promote the chances of settlement for them to be disclosed.
[8] But not the costs of a separate stand-alone ADR process, which is separate from the pre-action meeting required by paragraph 5.1 of the protocol.
[9] Either in the protocol or in the TCC Guide, as appropriate.
[10] This disallowance should apply even if those excessive labours were subsequently of benefit in the litigation. The objective of my proposal is to stamp out excessive front loading: see *The Cost of Civil Justice: Time for Review or Revolution*, Lexis Nexis White Paper by Elsa Booth, which can be found at http://www.lnbconnect.co.uk/images/the%20cost%20of%20civil%20justice.pdf, at pages 4-7.

hoped that the solicitors[11] will be able to agree what costs should be disallowed. At the moment, I can see no other way of controlling the excesses of which complaint is made.

(b) Provision for protocol applications

4.13 Court users from a number of disciplines have suggested that the court should have the power to give directions pre-action, where there is a serious problem in relation to the protocol process. I see force in this proposal, having seen extensive evidence during the Costs Review of non-compliance causing serious problems. I therefore recommend that such a power should be added by way of amendment to CPR rule 25.1. This recommendation is dealt with in chapter 39 below.

4.14 In chapter 39 below I set out a number of orders which the court should be permitted to make where there is non-compliance with a protocol. These include:

(i)   That the parties are relieved from the obligation to comply or further comply with the protocol.

(ii)   That a party do take any step which might be required in order to comply with the protocol.

4.15 It is possible to think of many situations in which the court might make an order under (i) above: for example, a substantial case where there is no real prospect of pre-trial settlement and compliance with the protocol would simply involve duplication of costs; or a case where D has failed to send a proper letter of response in time and C wishes to get on with the litigation. It is also possible to think of many situations in which the court might make an order under (ii) above. In a case where C fails to comply with the (attenuated) protocol requirements for the letter of claim, the court may have a choice between making an order under (i) or (ii). The court may say that since C has failed to send a proper letter of claim, it is not entitled to a response letter; or the court may direct C to send a proper letter. The appropriate order in any instance will depend upon the circumstances of the case.

(v) Need for further review

4.16 I am conscious that the decision whether to retain a pre-action protocol for construction and engineering disputes is finely balanced. There is a strong body of opinion to the effect that the protocol serves to increase, rather than reduce, costs. When the TCC moves into the Rolls Building in 2011 the anomalous situation will arise that the TCC has a pre-action protocol applicable to most of its cases, but the other two jurisdictions within that building (Commercial Court and Chancery Division) have not.

4.17 I recommend that after the TCC has moved into the Rolls Building in 2011, the whole question of the protocol should be reviewed. The three jurisdictions in that building will all deal with business disputes. There will be benefit in the TCC taking account of the position in the Commercial Court and Chancery Division, when the different specialist jurisdictions have come together under one roof. The users of the TCC, both litigants and lawyers, may possibly conclude at that stage that their pre-action procedures should be aligned with those prevailing in those other

---

[11] In my experience, the solicitors who regularly practise in the TCC are for the most part specialists, who are well able to reach sensible agreements on matters of this sort thus saving their clients unnecessary hearing costs.

jurisdictions. However, the outcome of that review must be a matter for the TCC judges and practitioners after 2011.

5. OTHER SPECIFIC PROTOCOLS

5.1   Judicial review. Judicial review claims are subject to the Pre-Action Protocol for Judicial Review. I have received no complaints about this protocol.

5.2   Research has shown that in approximately 60% of cases in which a letter before claim was sent, the dispute was resolved before issue of proceedings.[12] Furthermore, *"solicitors generally value the [Pre-Action Protocol] and believe that it plays a positive role in enabling early settlement by improving channels of communication between the parties and helping to clarify issues".*[13]

5.3   Concern has been expressed by the Public Law Project that some judicial review claims are settled too late, despite the protocol. But this is not the fault of the protocol. The suggested remedy is to revise the *Boxall* principles. This topic is addressed in chapter 30 above, concerning judicial review.

5.4   Professional negligence. Professional negligence claims[14] are subject to the Professional Negligence Pre-Action Protocol.

5.5   Comments made in written submissions and at meetings during Phase 2 indicate general satisfaction with this protocol. This view was supported by straw polls which I took during (a) the IBC Professional Negligence and Liability Forum and (b) a meeting with Barlow Lyde & Gilbert LLP practitioners and clients.[15]

5.6   I understand that approximately 90 to 95% of professional negligence claims are resolved during the protocol period.[16] I am told that many of these claims are resolved by the professional indemnity insurers direct without involving solicitors. Indeed quite often neither party instructs solicitors.

5.7   Personal injury and clinical negligence. Personal injuries litigation is subject to the Pre-Action Protocol for Personal Injury Claims and the Pre-Action Protocol for Disease and Illness Claims. Clinical negligence litigation is subject to the Pre-Action Protocol for the Resolution of Clinical Disputes. The procedure for obtaining medical records from hospitals is regulated by the Protocol for Obtaining Hospital Medical Records.[17]

5.8   It is clear from the extensive comments received during Phase 2 that these protocols are regarded as making a valuable contribution. The majority of personal injury claims and a substantial minority of clinical negligence claims are resolved during the protocol period.

---

[12] Varda Bondy and Maurice Sunkin, *"Dynamics of Judicial Review Litigation"* report page 31 (see http://www.publiclawproject.org.uk/documents/TheDynamicsofJudicialReviewLitigation.pdf).
[13] Ibid page 31.
[14] Other than claims against health care providers and construction professionals, because these are covered by other specific protocols.
[15] Both events were held on 11th June 2009.
[16] This percentage is derived from the written submissions made on behalf of Claims Against Professionals ("CAP"), an informal body of professional indemnity insurers from both the Lloyd's and Companies markets.
[17] Annexed to the Pre-Action Protocol for the Resolution of Clinical Disputes.

5.9   It is also clear from the extensive comments received that (a) a number of amendments to these protocols merit consideration and (b) there are significant problems of non-compliance.   These matters are closely bound up with case management issues and are therefore dealt with in chapters 22 and 23 above, concerning personal injuries and clinical negligence litigation.

5.10   Housing litigation.   Three specific protocols deal with housing litigation, namely the Pre-Action Protocol for Housing Disrepair Cases, the Pre-Action Protocol for Possession Claims based on Rent Arrears and the Pre-Action Protocol for Possession Claims based on Mortgage or Home Purchase Plan Arrears in respect of Residential Property.   I shall refer to these three protocols collectively as the "housing protocols".

5.11   It is clear from the comments received during Phase 2 that the housing protocols are regarded as making a valuable contribution, but that certain amendments merit consideration.   These matters are bound up with issues of substantive law and case management.   They are therefore dealt with in chapter 26 above, concerning housing claims.

5.12   Defamation.   Defamation claims are subject to the Pre-Action Protocol for Defamation.   It is, I understand, widely acknowledged that the protocol makes a valuable contribution to the early resolution of defamation claims.   Indeed it is a reasonable inference from the figures quoted in PR appendix 17 that a significant number of all defamation claims against the media resolved during 2008 were settled either pre-issue or at an early stage in proceedings.

5.13   Suggestions have been made for the improvement of the Pre-Action Protocol for Defamation in one respect.   I address that issue in chapter 32 above, concerning defamation and related claims.

5.14   Conclusion.   In my view, all of the specific protocols should be retained.   Some amendments to the protocols concerning personal injury, clinical negligence and housing, merit consideration as discussed above.   The Civil Justice Council (the "CJC") is intending to conduct a review of pre-action protocols during 2010.   It may therefore be appropriate for the CJC to consider in the course of that review the amendments to specific protocols which are recommended in this report.   No doubt the CJC will do so in close consultation with the various stakeholder groups which are affected.

6. THE PRACTICE DIRECTION - PRE-ACTION CONDUCT

6.1   The general protocol should be repealed.   The majority of the PDPAC comprises the general protocol.   That general protocol serves no useful purpose, because one size does not fit all.   Furthermore, in many instances the general protocol is productive of substantial delay and extra cost.   I recommend that the general protocol (sections III and IV of the PDPAC) be repealed.   I am reinforced in this conclusion by the fact that during the consultation exercise before the general protocol was introduced, the majority of consultees were opposed to it.[18]

6.2   The repeal of the general protocol will not absolve parties from the obligation to conduct sensible pre-action correspondence.   It has always been the case (both

---

[18] See the CJC's Phase 2 submission, page 2: "*A sizeable minority of consultees supported the idea of the General Pre-Action Protocol, but the majority of respondents were opposed.*"

before and after the introduction of the CPR) that a claimant who begins contentious proceedings without giving appropriate notice to other parties, and appropriate opportunity to respond, is at risk as to costs. This will remain the position. For the avoidance of doubt, however, I propose that the PDPAC should contain a simple provision along the following lines:

> "In all areas of litigation to which no specific protocol applies there shall be appropriate pre-action correspondence and exchange of information."

6.3　Need for a debt protocol. Annex B to the PDPAC sets out certain information which should be given in debt claims where the claimant is a business and the defendant is an individual. These provisions do not belong in a general protocol or in a general practice direction about protocols. These provisions should be salvaged and put in a more natural home, ideally a short protocol specifically dealing with debt claims where the claimant is a business and the defendant is an individual. Since claims of this nature constitute a huge swathe of the business of the courts,[19] it would seem reasonable for them to have their own specific protocol. Experience has shown that specific protocols tailored to the needs of narrowly defined categories of litigation are beneficial.

6.4　Sections I and II. If the general protocol is repealed, what will remain will be sections I and II of the PDPAC. Section I is an introduction, most but (not all) of which will become redundant. Section II sets out how the courts will assess compliance and punish non-compliance with the protocols. It is clear from the Phase 2 submissions that there are serious problems in relation to compliance. In section 4 of this chapter and (more fully) in chapter 39 below, I make suggestions as to how non-compliance with protocols might more effectively be dealt with. If the recommendations are accepted, then it will be necessary to amend section II of the PDPAC, in order to mesh in with those reforms.

7. RECOMMENDATIONS

7.1　I make the following recommendations:

(i)　The Pre-Action Protocol for Construction and Engineering Disputes should be amended, so that (a) it is less prescriptive and (b) the costs (or at least the recoverable costs) of complying with that protocol are reduced. The need for that protocol should be reviewed by TCC judges, practitioners and court users after 2011.

(ii)　The general protocol, contained in Sections III and IV of the PDPAC, should be repealed.

(iii)　Annex B to the PDPAC should be incorporated into a new specific protocol for debt claims.

7.2　My recommendations in relation to the other pre-action protocols and in relation to securing compliance with protocols are set out in other chapters of this report.[20]

---

[19] See PR para 5.2.2.
[20] Chapters 22, 23, 26, 32 and 39.

CHAPTER 36. ALTERNATIVE DISPUTE RESOLUTION

INDEX

1. INTRODUCTION

1.1　_Preliminary Report._ A general account of alternative dispute resolution ("ADR") is given in the Preliminary Report at chapter 4, section 2 and chapter 43, section 6. I shall take these sections of the Preliminary Report as read and will not repeat their contents.

1.2　_Mediation._ For cases which do not settle early through bilateral negotiation, the most important form of ADR (and the form upon which most respondents have concentrated during Phase 2) is mediation. The reason for the emphasis upon mediation is twofold. First, properly conducted mediation enables many (but certainly not all) civil disputes to be resolved at less cost and greater satisfaction to the parties than litigation. Secondly, many disputing parties are not aware of the full benefits to be gained from mediation and may, therefore, dismiss this option too readily.

1.3　_Joint settlement meetings._ Another form of ADR which can be highly effective is to hold a joint settlement meeting. A scheme for joint settlement meetings in personal injury cases has been piloted in Manchester. The results show that such meetings can be effective in promoting settlements. His Honour Judge Richard Holman (Designated Civil Judge in Manchester) has concluded that, because of the expense involved, joint settlement meetings are better suited to the larger multi-track claims, possibly from £500,000 upwards.

1.4　_Other forms of ADR._ For a comprehensive definition of ADR, see PR paragraph 43.6.3. One other form of ADR which should be noted is early neutral evaluation. This is carried out by someone who commands the parties' respect, possibly a judge. In 2008 the Association of Her Majesty's District Judges put forward to the Civil Justice Council (the "CJC") a proposal for judicial neutral evaluation. I understand that this will be the subject of a pilot in Cardiff. If the results of the pilot are favourable, then judicial neutral evaluation may pass into more general use and become an effective means of promoting early, merits-based settlements.

1.5　_Relevance of ADR to the Costs Review._ ADR is relevant to the present Costs Review in two ways. First, ADR (and in particular mediation) is a tool which can be used to reduce costs. At the present time disputing parties do not always make sufficient use of that tool. Secondly, an appropriately structured costs regime will encourage the use of ADR. It is a sad fact at the moment that many cases settle at a late stage, when substantial costs have been run up. Indeed some cases which ought to settle (because sufficient common ground exists between the parties) become incapable of settlement as a result of the high costs incurred.[21] One important aim of the present Costs Review is to encourage parties to resolve such disputes at the earliest opportunity, whether by negotiation or by any available form of ADR.

2. SUBMISSIONS DURING PHASE 2

(i) Mediation generally

2.1   Confederation of British Industry. The Confederation of British Industry (the "CBI") emphasises the strong business interest in avoiding litigation and settling disputes through ADR. The CBI sees this as having the greatest potential for savings in litigation costs.

2.2   Centre for Effective Dispute Resolution. The Centre for Effective Dispute Resolution ("CEDR") states that there are something like 4,000 mediations per year, excluding small claims mediations, which number about 2,000.[22] CEDR is concerned that too few cases settle during the pre-action protocol period. Procedural judges need to raise questions of their own motion about whether mediation has been tried before issue and where dissatisfied with the replies *"impose a sanction on either or both parties"*. Even if there is a good reason why mediation cannot take place pre-issue, judges are entitled to ensure that a provision for mediation is inserted into the case management timetable at the appropriate stage. CEDR adds:

> "A degree of oversight and if need be compulsion may even be needed to be exercised over procedural judges in terms of implementing such a policy."

CEDR considers that mediation should be built into the case management timetable in all cases except where good reason is given for excusing it. CEDR notes that at the moment some district judges and masters are enthusiasts for mediation, but others are not. Therefore more training is needed for judges in this regard. CEDR provides examples of instances where high litigation costs already incurred proved to be an insurmountable obstacle to settlements which may otherwise have flowed from mediation.

2.3   Civil Mediation Council. The Civil Mediation Council (the "CM Council") promotes mediation in all areas of dispute resolution. In its submission dated 21st July 2009 the CM Council states that returns from 52 of its provider members report 6,473 mediations so far this year,[23] which is an increase of 181% over the 2007 baseline.[24] There were 8,204 mediations conducted in 2008 by members. In its submission the CM Council outlines the benefits of mediation in a number of discrete areas, such as Mercantile Court cases, neighbour disputes, chancery litigation etc. The CM Council states that it is currently holding discussions with the Ministry of Justice (the "MoJ") about the future organisation of the National Mediation Helpline ("NMH") scheme. The CM Council commends the excellent work done by the Small Claims Mediation Service, which last year won a CEDR award and an EU award for excellence. It states that personal injury and clinical negligence practitioners have been particularly resistant to mediation, but even they are now becoming less resistant. The CM Council refers to specific mediation schemes, in particular:

---

[21] I have seen such cases.
[22] But see also paragraph 2.3 below.
[23] This figure presumably includes the CEDR mediations referred to in paragraph 2.2 above. CEDR is represented on the CM Council.
[24] This was based on returns from fewer information sources.

- Law Works provides *pro bono* mediation. It has 150 trained mediators on its panel. This is a resource which is very seriously under-used.

- Inter-Resolve is a company which provides a low cost telephone mediation service.

The CM Council believes that public awareness of mediation needs to be increased, especially among small and medium sized businesses, insurers, central and local government bodies. The courts should have in place effective procedures to refer to Law Works litigants who qualify for *pro bono* assistance.

2.4 Representatives of the CM Council came to see me on 23rd July 2009. At that meeting they reinforced the points made in their paper. They expressed the view that more lawyers would be willing to provide *pro bono* mediation services through Law Works. This is a project which should be encouraged, although commercial mediation should not thereby be downgraded. One of the representatives at that meeting subsequently sent in helpful supplementary submissions.

2.5 <u>Lloyd's underwriters.</u> The Lloyd's Market Association (the "LMA") represents all businesses which underwrite insurance at Lloyd's of London. The LMA states that ADR is used only in a very small percentage of cases. The LMA believes that a cultural change is necessary, so that lawyers will embrace ADR more readily. Claims Against Professionals ("CAP") is a body comprising some of the leading professional indemnity insurers from the Lloyd's and Companies' markets. In a survey of CAP members 65% agreed with the proposition that a party should be required to participate in ADR even when it is unwilling to do so.

2.6 <u>Association of Her Majesty's District Judges.</u> The Association of Her Majesty's District Judges states:

> "The Small Claims Track Mediation Service provided by HMCS[25] has assisted in resolving claims in advance of the final hearing listed before the District Judge. We take the view that consideration should be given to a system of compulsory referral to the HMCS mediation service where all the parties in a Small Claims Track case are unrepresented. There is a high settlement rate. Where claims do not settle by such mediation, the parties can have their day in court. Perhaps the cost to HMCS of this service could be met at least in part by a partial (as opposed to a complete) refund of the hearing fee that the Claimant will in any event have paid. More referrals to this mediation service will free up more District Judge time."

2.7 <u>Association of Northern Mediators.</u> The Association of Northern Mediators (the "ANM") identifies the key benefits of ADR[26] as follows: saving time, saving direct and indirect costs, preventing damage to business relationships and reputation, alleviation of stress, achieving remedies beyond the powers of the court and (if no settlement is achieved) narrowing issues for trial. The ANM points to the rising number of mediations and concludes that there should be greater encouragement for parties to enter into ADR before issue of proceedings. The ANM suggests that the rules should give greater prominence to ADR at the pre-action protocol stage, especially towards the end of that stage. The ANM believes that some members of the judiciary have not fully appreciated or embraced ADR. The ANM agrees that ADR should not be made compulsory, but would welcome universal adoption of

---

[25] Her Majesty's Courts Service.
[26] Which includes principally mediation, but also structured negotiations and other settlement techniques

Master Ungley's direction on ADR (the "Ungley order"). It maintains that not all businesses involved in lower value disputes are aware of what ADR has to offer.

2.8   Individual mediators. Two experienced mediators, one a member of the CJC and one a member of the Civil Procedure Rule Committee, sent in a joint submission on mediation issues. They state that the majority of businesses are not regular court users and not generally aware of what ADR has to offer. The problem is compounded because many lawyers have no experience of ADR. They urge that ADR should be brought into the mainstream of case management and should become an integral part of our litigation culture. They comment that there are many cases where case management ought to involve ADR, but apparently does not: for example *Peakman v Linbrooke Services Ltd* [2008] EWCA Civ 1239.[27] They state that the NMH is probably on the way to being a satisfactory substitute for the various court-based mediation schemes which it replaced.

2.9   Law Society. The Law Society states:

> "The Law Society continues to support the use of all forms of ADR in circumstances where it may be assist the parties to come to terms and they are willing to do so. We also support the principle of 'legal proceedings as a last resort only'. However, mediation is not the panacea which some consider it to be and is not appropriate in all cases. Neither should it be made mandatory. Indeed, there are views among practitioners that there is no consistency about which cases are suitable for mediation – some may well be mediated which are more suitable for trial, and vice versa. We consider that firmer guidelines are needed on what is and is not suitable for mediation."

The Law Society points out that all solicitors engage in negotiations, which are the simplest form of ADR. Many civil litigation solicitors are also mediators, but they frequently report that mediation can increase the costs of a case. Therefore the Law Society considers that more research is required.

2.10   Bar Associations. The Commercial Bar Association ("COMBAR") agrees with the observation in the Preliminary Report that in the context of business disputes parties and their advisers are well aware of what ADR has to offer. A number of respondents to the COMBAR questionnaire expressed that view. COMBAR considers that mediation should be de-formalised; however, this is a matter for parties and mediators to attend to, not for rules or legislation. The Bar Council expresses very similar views to COMBAR on these issues.

(ii) Mediation for personal injury claims

2.11   Trust Mediation Ltd. Trust Mediation Ltd ("TML") is a specialist provider of fixed costs mediations in personal injury cases. All of its mediators are not only experienced in mediation, but also have long experience of personal injuries litigation. TML estimates that in 95% of personal injury cases mediation will never be necessary. Compulsory mediation is therefore inappropriate. However, TML does recommend that in the remaining 5% of cases where the resolution of disputes is delayed and costs escalate, mediation should become the "*natural tool to draw from the litigator's toolkit*". TML's experience shows that mediation almost always succeeds, even in apparently entrenched cases where there are enormous differences, if skilled and fluent mediators apply effective "*reality testing*" techniques against objective criteria. In addition, the cost of the mediation process is a small fraction of

---

[27] Discussed at PR paragraph 30.3.4.

the cost of a trial and the solutions derived from mediations are often much more satisfactory than those which a court could impose. Mediation also provides an opportunity for the costs of proceedings to be agreed. TML states that it has obtained successful results through mediation: between January 2008 and June 2009 it conducted mediations in 53 cases with an 88.7% success rate.[28] Users have ascribed this success rate to the fact that the mediators are skilled and deeply experienced personal injury practitioners.

2.12   Representatives of TML came to see me on 23rd July 2009. I suggested to them that mediation is a facilitative process, designed to arrive at a mutually acceptable outcome rather than the legally correct result; accordingly mediation in this particular area carried with it the risk that claimants would be under-compensated, for example in respect of future care costs. The representatives essentially had two answers to this challenge. First, in practice the results of such mediations always did reflect fair compensation for the claimant. Secondly, closure was in itself extremely important for the claimant. The representatives also expressed concern that when one party refuses to mediate, the district judge does not encourage mediation.

2.13   Sir Henry Brooke reinforces the submissions of TML by furnishing an account of a recent mediation which he conducted in a fatal accident case. Both the process and the outcome brought considerable satisfaction to all parties involved.

2.14   CEDR. CEDR has provided a separate paper on mediating personal injury and clinical negligence claims, making the following points. Mediating personal injury and clinical negligence claims is the norm in many overseas jurisdictions. The outcomes which claimants typically seek in personal injury cases are: full or partial vindication in respect of the accident; damages constituting proper compensation; a chance to say what impact the accident has had on them; a response from the defendant delivering some acknowledgement; and a reasonably swift and risk-free outcome. The outcomes which claimants typically seek in clinical negligence cases are: an apology; an explanation as to what happened; reassurance of reform to ensure that there is a reduced or eradicated chance of the same thing happening again; and (occasionally) revenge in the form of regulatory intervention. The objectives which defendants seek may vary depending on the nature of the litigation. Insurers seek a commercial solution and minimal expenditure. Employers sued by employees may have different objectives: to protect the business by keeping their workforce stable and satisfied; to avoid floodgate claims; to be seen as a caring employer; not to lose the services of valuable employees; and to learn from mistakes and be seen to be sensitive to health and safety matters. These objectives are best achieved by mediation. All types of personal injury cases are suitable for mediation, from small claims to substantial group actions. The mediator adds value at all stages of the process. There are specialist mediators for clinical negligence claims. The utility of mediation in clinical negligence has been demonstrated by a pilot. Nevertheless, mediation is insufficiently used in clinical negligence.

2.15   Solicitors. A firm of solicitors with offices across the south of England, which acts for both claimants and defendants in personal injuries litigation, states that mediation is particularly efficacious in that field but is grossly under-used. The firm does not favour compulsory mediation, but does favour orders requiring the parties to discuss the case with a view to mediation. Mediation should not be a routine stage in every case, but the courts should be more pro-active in directing the parties to

---

[28] I.e. Of those 53 cases, 47 settled on the date or shortly thereafter as a result of the mediation and six did not settle.

discuss mediation in appropriate cases. The firm believes that a major cause of the slow adoption of mediation is the innate conservatism of the solicitors' profession. The firm states:

> "Our own experience is that mediation is very popular with individuals who have benefited from its cathartic process in personal injury claims."

The firm endorses the submissions of CEDR about the great benefits which mediation can bring to those involved in personal injuries litigation. The firm hopes that further provision will be made for mediation in the rules, in particular in a fixed fee regime within the fast track.

2.16 <u>Liability insurers.</u> One major liability insurer writes:

> "We agree that in the context of personal injury cases there remains a need for better education and information about ADR and mediation in particular. In the context of PI claims, mediation is an under utilised tool. Feedback from claimant solicitors who mediate regularly say that:
>
> a.   claimants like it as it is not as daunting as a trial and they can have their say in a less threatening environment;
>
> b.   it improves cash flow by bringing about early resolution.
>
> From an insurer's perspective mediation is a constructive way of seeking to bring about resolution of a case. It provides an opportunity to risk assess the merits of a particular claim and make decisions based on that assessment. Mediation can be carried out earlier in the process; one does not need to have all the evidence completely together in order to form a view that may lead to settlement.
>
> The consensual approach to mediation also means that both parties come out of mediation with a resolution that is satisfactory to them."

This insurer would like to see court ordered mediation. It believes that, in respect of mediation, the present approach of the judiciary is not sufficiently robust.

2.17 <u>Defendant solicitors.</u> A firm of defendant solicitors states that ADR might be mediation or, alternatively, a joint settlement conference. Unfortunately many claimant solicitors are simply "*preparing for trial*". The firm believes that this mentality is encouraged by the Civil Procedure Rules, which should be re-focused towards resolution with trial as a last resort. In the firm's experience 90% of cases settle within a short time of a joint settlement meeting. Another firm of defendant solicitors writes:

> "[We] welcome any encouragement to litigants to undertake ADR during the litigation process in appropriate cases. Part of the reason for the poor take up is insufficient knowledge of the process and the perceived cost. Further education is needed rather than rule changes.
>
> [We] do not support compulsory ADR as not all cases are suitable."

2.18 The Forum of Insurance Lawyers ("FOIL") takes a positive view of both mediation and joint settlement meetings. FOIL believes that in order to encourage greater use of mediation, it is not rule change that is needed but culture change. FOIL does not believe that compulsory mediation would be a satisfactory way forward.

2.19   Clinical negligence. The Medical Defence Union (the "MDU") states in its submission that ADR works best in cases where quantum is the only issue between the parties.   The MDU believes that mediation should take place early in the proceedings, but once expert evidence is in the arena. It proposes that standardised directions should be rolled out across the courts, including the Ungley order.

3. ASSESSMENT

3.1   Benefits of ADR not fully appreciated. Having considered the feedback and evidence received during Phase 2, I accept the following propositions:

(i)   Both mediation and joint settlement meetings are highly efficacious means of achieving a satisfactory resolution of many disputes, including personal injury claims.

(ii)   The benefits of mediation are not appreciated by many smaller businesses. Nor are they appreciated by the general public.

(iii)   There is a widespread belief[29] that mediation is not suitable for personal injury cases. This belief is incorrect. Mediation is capable of arriving at a reasonable outcome in many personal injury cases, and bringing satisfaction to the parties in the process. However, it is essential that such mediations are carried out by mediators with specialist experience of personal injuries litigation.

(iv)   Although many judges, solicitors and counsel are well aware of the benefits of mediation, some are not.

3.2   Not a universal panacea. Mediation is not, of course, a universal panacea. The process can be expensive and can on occasions result in failure. I adhere to the general views expressed in the Preliminary Report at paragraphs 4.2.1 to 4.2.6. The thesis of this chapter is not that mediation should be undertaken in every case, but that mediation has a significantly greater role to play in the civil justice system than is currently recognised.

3.3   Timing of mediation. It is important that mediation is undertaken at the right time. If mediation is undertaken too early, it may be thwarted because the parties do not know enough about each other's cases. If mediation is undertaken too late, substantial costs may already have been incurred. Identifying the best stage at which to mediate is a matter upon which experienced practitioners should advise by reference to the circumstances of the individual case.

3.4   Judicial encouragement of mediation. In spite of the considerable benefits which mediation brings in appropriate cases, I do not believe that parties should ever be compelled to mediate. What the court can and should do (in appropriate cases) is (a) to encourage mediation and point out its considerable benefits; (b) to direct the parties to meet and/or to discuss mediation; (c) to require an explanation from the party which declines to mediate, such explanation not to be revealed to the court until the conclusion of the case;[30] and (d) to penalise in costs parties which have unreasonably refused to mediate. The form of any costs penalty must be in the discretion of the court. However, such penalties might include (a) reduced costs

---

[29] Which was shared by myself until Phase 2 of the Costs Review.
[30] This is the essence of the Ungley order. The point has been made by some commentators that most cases ultimately settle and therefore this provision seldom bites. Whilst I see the force of this, the provision nevertheless has value. At the stage of refusing to mediate a party does not know whether the case will ultimately settle.

recovery for a winning party; (b) indemnity costs against a losing party, alternatively reduced costs protection for a losing party which has the benefit of qualified one way costs shifting.

3.5   Need for culture change, not rule change.   I agree with the view expressed by FOIL and others that what is needed is not rule change, but culture change. I do not agree with the proposals made by CEDR for sanctions, including sanctions against all parties. Nor do I agree with the CEDR's proposal for "compulsion" to be exercised over judges. Judges must have discretion to give such case management directions as they deem appropriate in the circumstances of the individual case.

3.6   The pre-action protocols draw attention appropriately to ADR. The rules enable judges to build mediation windows into case management timetables and some court guides draw attention to this facility. Many practitioners and judges make full use of these provisions. What is now needed is a serious campaign (a) to ensure that all litigation lawyers and judges (not just some litigation lawyers and judges) are properly informed about the benefits which ADR can bring and (b) to alert the public and small businesses to the benefits of ADR.

3.7   Fragmentation of information.   One of the problems at the moment is that information about ADR is fragmented. In the course of the Costs Review I have received details about a number of providers of mediation from different sources. By way of example, Law Works Mediation Service sent me details of the excellent *pro bono* mediation service which it runs. TML provided similar details to me of its own services. Details of the NMH are available on the HMCS website.[31] CEDR has sent to me a brochure about the excellent mediation services which CEDR offers. Wandsworth Mediation Service has sent to me details of the valuable mediation services which it provides to the community in Wandsworth, either *pro bono* or on a heavily discounted basis. And so forth.[32]

3.8   Need for a single authoritative handbook.   There already exist MoJ leaflets and material about ADR. There is also a helpful HMCS mediation "toolkit" in the form of the Civil Court Mediation Service Manual on the Judicial Studies Board ("JSB") website.[33] In my view there now needs to be a single authoritative handbook, explaining clearly and concisely what ADR is (without either "hype" or jargon) and giving details of all reputable providers of mediation. Because of the competing commercial interests in play, it would be helpful if such a handbook were published by a neutral body. Ideally, this should be done under the aegis of the CJC, if it felt able to accept that role. If possible, the handbook should be an annual publication. The obvious utility of such a work means that it would be self-financing. It needs to have a highly respected editor, perhaps a recently retired senior judge. It needs to become the *vade mecum* of every judge or lawyer dealing with mediation issues. It should be the textbook used in every JSB seminar or Continuing Professional Development ("CPD") training session. I am not proposing any formal system of accreditation, although that would be an option. However, inclusion of any mediation scheme or organisation in this handbook will be a mark of respectability. The sort of handbook which I have in mind will be a work of equivalent status to the annual publications about civil procedure. Most judges and litigators would have the current edition of the proposed handbook on their bookshelves.

---

[31] At http://www.hmcourts-service.gov.uk/cms/14160.htm.
[32] For example, a telephone mediation scheme established by the Bodily Injuries Claims Management Association in 2008. See chapter 22 above, paragraph 6.2(vi).
[33] At http://www.jsboard.co.uk/publications.htm.

3.9   <u>Training of judges and lawyers.</u> The education of judges and lawyers in the merits of mediation is a gradual process, which has been occurring over the last 20 years and which will continue. Both the JSB and the various CPD providers have an important role to play in this regard. In my view, it is important that in delivering training to judges and lawyers who lack first hand experience of mediation, experienced mediators (such as those who have contributed to Phase 2 of the Costs Review) should play an active part.

3.10   <u>Public education.</u> So far as the general public and small businesses are concerned, the problem is of a different order. It is very difficult to raise public awareness of what mediation has to offer. I fear that no television company would be persuaded to include a mediation scene in any courtroom drama or soap opera (helpful though that would be). The best and most realistic approach would be to devise a simple, clear brochure outlining what ADR has to offer and for that brochure to be supplied as a matter of course by every court to every litigant in every case.[34]

4. RECOMMENDATIONS

4.1   For the reasons set out above, I do not recommend any rule changes in order to promote ADR. I do, however, accept that ADR brings considerable benefits in many cases and that this facility is currently under-used, especially in personal injury and clinical negligence cases.

4.2   I recommend that:

(i)   There should be a serious campaign (a) to ensure that all litigation lawyers and judges are properly informed about the benefits which ADR can bring and (b) to alert the public and small businesses to the benefits of ADR.

(ii)   An authoritative handbook should be prepared, explaining clearly and concisely what ADR is and giving details of all reputable providers of mediation. This should be the standard handbook for use at all JSB seminars and CPD training sessions concerning mediation.

---

[34] It could be included with the allocation questionnaire.

CHAPTER 37. DISCLOSURE

INDEX

1. INTRODUCTION

1.1   <u>Preliminary Report.</u> In chapter 40 of the Preliminary Report I set out in some detail what is involved in e-disclosure, how it is carried out in practice, what the pitfalls are and how they should be avoided. I also set out the costs involved in a number of illustrative cases. Finally, I reviewed the approach to e-disclosure in the USA and Australia.

1.2   In chapter 41 of the Preliminary Report I reviewed the current disclosure rules and how those rules operate in practice. I expressed the view that the operation of the disclosure rules gives rise to problems and generates excessive costs in relation to larger multi-track cases. I outlined ten possible options for reform. These are:

(i)   Maintain the current position with standard disclosure remaining the default disclosure order.

(ii)   Abolish standard disclosure and limit disclosure to documents relied upon, with the ability to seek specific disclosure.

(iii)   Introduce "issues based" disclosure akin to the approach being trialled by the Commercial Court.

(iv)   Revert to the old system of discovery with the "trail of enquiry" test.

(v)   No default position with the parties and court being required to consider the most appropriate process for disclosure at the first case management conference ("CMC"). This option has generally been referred to as the "menu" option.

(vi)   More rigorous case management by the court, including greater use of sanctions against parties who provide disclosure in a haphazard manner, or late, or ordering the parties to agree a constructive process and scope.

(vii)   Use of experienced lawyers as disclosure assessors in "heavy" cases to identify which categories of documents merit disclosure.

(viii) Restrict the number of specific disclosure applications and/or raise the standard to be met.

(ix)   Reverse the burden of proof in specific disclosure applications, with the costs of the disclosure exercise being met by the requesting party unless documents of real value emerge.

(x)   Allocate a single judge at the outset of substantial cases to enable him or her to become more familiar with the facts and procedural history.

2. E-DISCLOSURE

2.1   <u>E-disclosure is inevitable in many cases.</u> The first point which needs to be made about e-disclosure is that it is inevitable in cases where the parties hold the relevant material electronically. For the parties to print all the material out and then exchange it in hard copy would often be impracticable. With all but the smallest volumes of material, that course would not be cost effective. Thus in cases where e-disclosure is a consideration, it is often a practical necessity rather than an optional course.

2.2   <u>E-disclosure demonstration.</u> On 22nd June 2009 I attended an e-disclosure demonstration at 4 Pump Court chambers. Three different specialist providers each took data from the *Enron* case and demonstrated how their respective software systems could search, sample, categorise and organise the data. The object of each of these systems is (i) to whittle down as far as possible the potentially relevant documents which will be passed to the lawyers for review and (ii) to enable the lawyers to search and organise documents passed to them. I am bound to say that the systems developed by each of those specialist providers are extremely impressive. I am sure that it would assist other members of the judiciary to know what technological help is available to the parties, to enable them to manage the disclosure process.

2.3   <u>The Senior Master's working party.</u> In July 2009 the e-disclosure working party chaired by Senior Master Whitaker[35] completed its deliberations and submitted a draft practice direction to the Civil Procedure Rule Committee (the "Rule Committee") for consideration. At the time of writing (December 2009) the Rule Committee is considering and refining the draft. The intention is that the practice direction will be finalised soon and will be brought into effect in April 2010.

2.4   <u>Draft practice direction.</u> The draft "Practice Direction Governing Disclosure of Electronically Stored Information"[36] provides, in essence, as follows.

•   Parties and their legal representatives should consider, at an early stage, the use of technology in order to identify potentially relevant material, to collect, analyse and review it. Subsequently this will assist with the creation of lists of documents to be disclosed and giving disclosure by providing documents in electronic format.

•   Unless a party intends to request that the action be allocated to the small claims track or the fast track, that party must exchange with the other party or parties and file with the court Answers to the ESI Questionnaire attached to the Practice Direction.

•   The ESI Questionnaire requires the parties to provide information about any documents which they hold in electronic form and which are to be disclosed in the proceedings, along with details of their electronic storage systems. They are also asked to detail any issues that may arise about the accessibility of such documents. The Answers to the ESI Questionnaire must be supported by a statement of truth.

---

[35] As to which see PR paragraph 40.2.10.
[36] Electronically Stored Information is abbreviated in the practice direction to "ESI".

- After exchange of Answers to the ESI Questionnaire and before the first CMC, the parties must discuss the disclosure of ESI, including the scope of the reasonable search for ESI and any tools and techniques which might reduce the burden and cost of disclosure of ESI.

- If the parties encounter difficulties or cannot reach agreement, issues arising in relation to the disclosure and inspection of ESI should be referred to a judge for directions, if possible at the first CMC.

- The extent of the reasonable search will depend upon the circumstances of the case. The parties should bear in mind the overriding principle of proportionality. Many of the factors that may be relevant in deciding the reasonableness of a search for ESI are listed in paragraph 2A.4 of the current practice direction supplementing CPR Part 31.

- Where a party is giving disclosure of ESI, a List of Documents may by agreement between the parties be an electronic file in a defined and agreed format.

- Unless the parties agree otherwise or the court directs otherwise, where electronic copies of disclosed documents are provided to another party, the electronic copies should, unless this is not reasonably practicable, be provided in their native format.

2.5   In my view, the substance of this practice direction is excellent and it makes appropriate provision for e-disclosure. On the assumption that this practice direction will be approved in substantially its present form by the Rule Committee, I do not make any recommendation for procedural reform in relation to e-disclosure.

2.6   <u>Submissions during Phase 2.</u> The Law Society expresses concern about the impact of e-disclosure upon the litigation process. Referring to the cases cited in PR chapter 40, the Law Society states:

> "What these cases appear to show is that commercial practice and the memory and storage capacity of day-to-day IT equipment is such that the amount of information potentially available in respect of any transaction is now so enormous as to be practically unmanageable.
>
> If the litigation process is to remain cost-effective, there must be improved ways of dealing with the exponential growth in the availability of information."

2.7   The Bar Council states:

> "The disclosure of emails and other electronic documents throws up a number of problems.
>
> A particular concern which has been expressed was the tendency of the disclosing party to provide material indiscriminately and without regard to its relevance to the issues in dispute, with consequent wastage of costs.
>
> We suggest that such problems can be avoided or reduced by appropriate case management, at a case management conference at which the extent and purpose of the <u>proposed</u> e-disclosure is actively considered (that is before, not after, such disclosure has commenced).

That will, of necessity, involve an understanding on the part of both counsel and judges of the workings of document management systems and the practicalities of performing electronic searches for documents. It will also require early and clear articulation of the specific issues that are likely to affect the disclosure process in any given case."

2.8 A number of specialist providers and other experts in e-disclosure have sent in submissions on the technical details of e-disclosure, such as how relevant material should be located, searched and so forth. I will not embark upon a paraphrase of those submissions, since I have attempted to outline the general principles of e-disclosure in the Preliminary Report. The important point which has been stressed by many respondents is that judges, solicitors and counsel need to acquire (or have access to someone who has) a much more detailed understanding of the technology available and how it functions. Both practitioners and judges need such an understanding, so that the court can manage the litigation properly and keep the costs of e-disclosure within sensible bounds.[37] As is pointed out in one of the Phase 2 submissions, lawyers need both education and training in respect of e-disclosure. They need education in the broad capabilities of the ever developing software systems and in the variables which make one software system different from another. They also need training in how to make the best use of whatever software systems are adopted.

2.9 Recommendation. I recommend that e-disclosure as a topic should form a substantial part of (a) Continuing Professional Development ("CPD") for solicitors and barristers who will have to deal with e-disclosure in practice and (b) the training of judges who will have to deal with e-disclosure on the bench. Service providers will have a part to play in such CPD or training. Indeed they will have a commercial interest in contributing to the process. However, they should do so within the context of a well structured programme, which is provided or approved by the relevant professional bodies.

2.10 Meeting with the Judicial Studies Board. On 30th September 2009 I attended a meeting with the chairman and the course directors of the Judicial Studies Board (the "JSB") responsible for civil education of the judiciary in order to outline my proposed recommendation. I understand that the JSB will be able to offer a basic, half day course on e-disclosure for judges at all civil seminars. The JSB will also be able to offer a further, and more advanced, half day course on e-disclosure for those judges who wish or need to study the subject in greater depth.

2.11 Law Society. I have recently raised this matter with the Law Society. The Law Society makes the point that there are many post qualifying education providers, including the Law Society itself. However, I understand that the Law Society shares my view that better training in e-disclosure for both solicitors and barristers will reduce the costs of higher value complex cases. I make the following recommendation to the Law Society and other post qualifying education providers: e-disclosure should form a substantial part of CPD which is offered to solicitors who will have to deal with e-disclosure in practice.

2.12 Bar Standards Board. I have also raised this matter with the Bar Standards Board. I understand that a working group will be established in January 2010, under the chairmanship of Derek Wood QC, to undertake a complete review of the CPD which is offered to barristers. I make the following recommendation to that working

---

[37] See *Earles v Barclays Bank PLC* [2009] EWHC 2500 (Mercantile).

group: e-disclosure should be a substantial part of CPD which is offered to barristers who will have to deal with e-disclosure in practice.

3. DISCLOSURE GENERALLY

(i) Standard disclosure

3.1   The rules. CPR Part 31 provides a strong steer towards standard disclosure in every case. Rule 31.5 provides that standard disclosure is the default position. Rule 31.6 defines what documents must be disclosed under standard disclosure. Rule 31.7 explains what constitutes a reasonable search for the purpose of standard disclosure. Rule 31.10 sets out the procedure for standard disclosure. If parties comply strictly with the rules, there are often two consequences:

(i)   each party discloses fewer documents than it would have disclosed under the pre-April 1999 Rules of the Supreme Court (the "RSC"); and

(ii)   each party incurs higher costs than it would have incurred under the RSC.

These two consequences occur because it is now necessary for a lawyer to review all documents gathered in the "reasonable search"[38] individually and to consider whether each document (a) adversely affects his own case, (b) adversely affects another party's case or (c) supports another party's case. In carrying out this exercise the lawyer must have in mind all the issues arising from the pleadings. Indeed, because of the continuing obligation imposed by rule 31.11, the exercise may have to be repeated if the pleadings are amended.

3.2   What happens in practice. I am told that, following an order for standard disclosure, quite often solicitors simply disclose everything that might be relevant. In other words, they continue to follow the old rules, thus saving costs (on their own side) but disclosing a greater quantity of documents than should be disclosed.

(ii) Views expressed during Phase 2

3.3   The two camps. Views expressed during Phase 2, both at meetings and in written submissions, covered a wide range. Essentially there are two schools of thought.

3.4   On one view, disclosure (whether "standard" under the CPR or old style under the RSC) is fundamental to our civil justice system and must be preserved, save in those cases where there is good reason to dispense with it. The Professional Negligence Bar Association (the "PNBA") advances this view with some force in its written submissions:

> "The rule at the heart of the process (and principle) of disclosure – that opposing litigants must reveal documents to their opponents which are adverse to their own case – has a reach which far exceeds the disclosure process itself. It is fundamental to the way in which litigation in our common law jurisdiction is conducted. There can be legitimate debate as to how that principle is best captured (for example whether by the standard disclosure test provided for by the CPR or by the *Peruvian Guano* test of relevance under the old RSC), but the importance of having a generally applicable test should not be under-estimated (a) because of the need to preserve the essential

---

[38] Required by CPR rule 31.7.

underlying principle and (b) because a generally applicable test provides a tangible and clear reference point against which the duty of disclosure can be measured. It is true that one size does not fit all, but the fitting should involve tailoring the same cloth, not many different types of cloth. The fact that the standard disclosure test is the normal starting point and known to all practitioners leads to it having a generally beneficial effect on the conduct of litigation."

3.5 The alternative view is that the disclosure process has become prohibitively expensive, so that the rules must be changed to reduce the extent of the process. Absent some radical rule change, the costs of disclosure are such as to deny access to justice altogether to some litigants.[39] This alternative view is argued by the Commercial Litigation Association ("CLAN"). CLAN states in its Phase 2 submission:

"The IBA[40] system offers a clear means to lower cost. By ensuring only core, crucial documents are collected costs are reduced in all areas. The clear caveat that would need to be placed with this is that the possibility of interlocutory relief from the rigours of the new system could be obtained...

A comparison with other countries only illuminates the fact that our system is failing and the suggestion that there should be a reduction in the amount of disclosure is welcomed. Their systems should be used as a basis to explore how the reduction can be formulated, with alterations that take into account our adversarial system. This is an issue for further, discrete consultation...

Our responses to the specific points made are:

1) We do not agree that the current scope of disclosure is correct.

2) We do not believe when factoring in commercial realities that an appropriate balance can be obtained in all circumstances. Indeed the realisation must be if the situation is distilled in to the simple question 'justice or costs?' costs, commercially, must prevail."

3.6 <u>Disclosure assessors.</u> Likewise there are strongly opposing views about the suggestion in my Preliminary Report that disclosure assessors might be used in document heavy cases. Some respondents consider that this is a very bad idea, which will add another layer of costs to no useful purpose. They argue that controlling disclosure is a judicial function, no part of which could be sub-contracted. Others take a more sanguine view. The London Common Law and Commercial Bar Association considers that this is "a very good idea and could be enormously helpful in substantial cases". In a client survey carried out by Herbert Smith LLP, 34 respondents (59%) supported the use of disclosure assessors for "heavy" cases. The Law Society takes an intermediate view on this issue:

"The use of disclosure assessors would be likely to increase costs considerably – though it might also result in significant savings in trial costs. It could usefully be piloted before a view was taken."

---

[39] This view was put to me with some force by a US federal judge, when I visited Washington this year for the purposes of the Costs Review. She believes that the civil courts are pricing themselves out of the market because of the costs of discovery, especially e-discovery. Such costs are driving parties to mediation and to other procedures outside the court system, which lack transparency.
[40] International Bar Association.

3.7   <u>The areas in which the disclosure rules require amendment.</u> Once again, there are sharp differences of perception. The Council of Her Majesty's Circuit Judges states:

> "While clearly a problem in large commercial cases, and sometimes in clinical negligence and the more complex type of employers liability litigation, we do not feel that in run of the mill county court litigation this aspect of case preparation too often gets out of hand."

3.8   On the other hand, CLAN is scathing in its rejection of the suggestion that disclosure is satisfactory in medium sized cases:

> "Lord Justice Jackson appears to consider that the current disclosure rules work well in all significant areas of litigation apart from large multi-track cases. We challenge this analysis and question the evidence upon which it has been based. Practitioners who deal with non-City litigation other than personal injuries have a great deal of concern over the costs of litigation and in particular over the expenditure incurred in disclosure and the preparation of witness statements."

3.9   After referring to the limited disclosure regime in patent cases, CLAN looks at disclosure more widely. It states:

> "However, perhaps the default position should be that parties would disclose only those documents upon which a party wished to rely, but that it was open to either party to seek more general disclosure if appropriate. This was the approach adopted when the modern form of the county courts was being introduced in the 19th century."

3.10   The Northern Circuit Commercial Bar Association (the "NCCBA") believes that standard disclosure is one of the less beneficial aspects of the Woolf Reforms. The NCCBA states:

> "We consider that the correct answer to the disclosure question is ultimately that it is a matter to be looked at on a case by case basis with the aim of limiting disclosure to that reasonably necessary to achieve justice in the particular circumstances of the case."

3.11   <u>Large commercial cases.</u> This is the one area of litigation in which a clear majority view emerged during Phase 2 of the Costs Review. The general view amongst commercial practitioners and judges[41] is that the menu option is the best way forward. A draft rule 31.5A, encapsulating the menu option, was initially prepared by the disclosure working group.[42] That draft underwent a number of revisions following various consultation meetings. The final version, which emerged following my meeting with the Commercial Court Users, reads as follows:

> **"Draft New Rule 31.5A: Disclosure in a substantial case**
>
> (1)   In a substantial case this rule replaces rule 31.5.
>
> (2)   A "substantial case" in this rule is:
>
>> (a)   a case before the Commercial Court or the Admiralty Court; or

---

[41] Those who contributed during Phase 2.
[42] See chapter 1 above, paragraph 3.13.

(b) a case in which the total of the sums in issue exceeds £1 million; or

(c) a case in which the total value of any assets in issue exceeds £1 million; or

(d) a case agreed by the parties to be a substantial case; or

(e) a case marked, whether because of the nature or extent of the disclosure the case is likely to involve or otherwise, as a substantial case by the court at the point of allocation to the multi-track or at any other point.

(3) If –

(a) the parties agree proposals for the scope of disclosure; and

(b) the court consider that the proposals are suitable;

the court may approve them without a hearing and give directions in the terms proposed.

(4) Not less than 14 days before the first case management conference each party must file and serve a report, verified by a statement of truth by the solicitor or other person who will have the conduct of giving disclosure for that party, which:

(a) describes in broad terms what documents exist or may exist that are or may be relevant to the matters in issue in the case;

(b) describes where and with whom those documents are or may be located (and in the case of electronic documents and metadata how the same are stored);

(c) estimates the broad range of costs that could be involved in giving standard disclosure in the case;

(d) states whether any and, if so which, of the directions under (7) below are to be sought.

The solicitor or other person who will have conduct of giving disclosure for a party should be present at the first case management conference.

(5) Not less than 7 days before the first case management conference, and on any other occasion as the court may direct, the parties must, at a meeting or by telephone, discuss and seek to agree a proposal in relation to disclosure that meets the overriding objective.

(6) At the first or any subsequent case management conference the court shall decide which of the following orders to make in relation to disclosure:

(a) an order dispensing with disclosure; or

(b) an order that a party disclose the documents on which it relies, and at the same time requests any specific disclosure it requires from any other party; or

(c) an order that (where practical) directs, on an issue by issue basis, the disclosure to be given by a party on the material issues in the case; or

(d) an order that a party give standard disclosure;

(e) an order that a party disclose any documents which it is reasonable to suppose may contain information which may (i) enable the party applying for disclosure either to advance his own case or to damage that of the party giving disclosure, or (ii) lead to a train of enquiry which has either of those consequences; or

(f) any other order in relation to disclosure that, having regard to the overriding objective, the court considers appropriate.

(7) The court may at any point give directions as to how the disclosure ordered is to be given, and in particular:

(a) what searches are to be undertaken, of where, for what, in respect of which time periods and by whom;

(b) whether lists of documents are required;

(c) how and when the disclosure statement is to be given;

(d) in what format documents are to be disclosed (and whether any identification is required);

(e) what is required in relation to documents that once existed but no longer exist;

(f) whether (under rule 31.13) disclosure shall take place in stages.

(8) In exercising its discretion under paragraphs (6) and (7) the court will consider what disclosure would be proportionate to the circumstances of the case."

3.12 <u>The draft rule will require revision.</u> It has now become clear that there are inconsistencies between (a) the above draft rule and (b) the draft practice direction subsequently produced by Senior Master Whitaker's working party, which is currently being revised by the Rule Committee. I should therefore emphasise that I am not recommending that the above draft rule be adopted in its present form. I have, however, set out full draft rule, in order to make plain what was being discussed during Phase 2 under the rubric "menu option". I do not believe that it is feasible to finalise any draft rule in respect of the menu option until the e-disclosure practice direction has reached its final form.[43]

(iii) My conclusions

3.13 <u>Large commercial and similar claims.</u> In relation to large commercial and similar claims, for the reasons set out in chapter 27 above, I recommend that the menu option be adopted. In order to implement this recommendation, I propose that a new CPR rule 31.5A be drafted and that the draftsmen take as their starting point the draft set out in paragraph 3.11 above. A number of amendments will have to be made, in order to achieve consistency with the practice direction on e-disclosure (which will have come into force before the Rule Committee can consider rule 31.5A). It should be noted that GC100 (the Association of General Counsel and Company Secretaries of FTSE 100 companies) in its Phase 2 submissions supports the menu option "*very much as proposed in the current draft rule*". In my view, it is important that full scale *Peruvian Guano*[44] disclosure be included as one of the options in the menu. This level of disclosure is sometimes appropriate in fraud cases.

---

[43] That will be after I have finished drafting this chapter, but probably before the publication date for this report.
[44] See PR paragraph 41.2.12.

3.14   Other actions. I have carefully considered all of the representations made and all of the comments received concerning the ten options canvassed in the Preliminary Report. I have come to the conclusion that the menu option ought not to be confined to large commercial cases. It ought to be extended to any case where the costs of standard disclosure are likely to be disproportionate. This could be achieved by adding to paragraph (2) of the draft rule 31.5A "(f) any case in which the costs of standard disclosure are likely to be disproportionate to the sums in issue or the value of the rights in issue". I also recommend that personal injury claims and clinical negligence be excluded from the provisions of rule 31.5A. Disclosure does not give rise to such serious and frequent problems in those categories of case as to warrant displacing standard disclosure as the normal order.[45]

3.15   I regret that the principal recommendation made in this chapter involves adding yet another provision to CPR Part 31. However, as the Bar Council and many others are at pains to emphasise, one size does not fit all. Whereas standard disclosure is satisfactory as a starting point for personal injury actions and for many other actions, there is a swathe of litigation where standard disclosure ought not to be the starting point. Instead, without any steer towards a particular outcome, the court should apply itself to a suite of possible orders and select the order which is most appropriate to the instant case. This new provision will also encourage more rigorous case management in relation to disclosure. Option 6 in the disclosure chapter of the Preliminary Report is "more rigorous case management" and this option has attracted a fair amount of support in the Phase 2 submissions.

3.16   Disclosure assessors. As mentioned above, this proposal generated mixed responses during Phase 2. I do not recommend any formal rule change to provide for disclosure assessors. However, it would be possible for parties to agree in any given case, subject to the approval of the court, to engage a disclosure assessor in the manner suggested in PR paragraphs 41.6.8 and 41.6.9. Presumably this would only occur in cases where all parties and the judge happen to be supporters of option 7 in the Preliminary Report. If the device of disclosure assessor is tried out on a voluntary basis and proves to be effective in saving costs in "heavy" cases, then consideration could be given to providing for this as an option in the rules. Before making any such reform to the CPR on a future occasion, it would be necessary to gather up to date information about the US experience of magistrate judges and special masters supervising discovery. As to this see chapter 60 of the Preliminary Report concerning the USA.[46] At the present time, however, I do not make any recommendation in respect of disclosure assessors.

3.17   Reversing the costs burden. The use of specific disclosure applications for tactical purposes is not unknown. A judge who does not see the content of the documents sought may not always be sufficiently confident to dismiss the applications. Mr Justice David Steel, commenting on the Preliminary Report, writes:

"Lack of cooperation is a blight on our procedures as any reading of a file of solicitors' correspondence will reveal. But it should not be assumed that the problem is confined to only one side (or even one side's lawyers) or that the court is in a position to undertake effective sanctions against parties for want of cooperation or even to intervene at a useful stage. In any event, the only sanction is by way of costs but, in my experience, the process merely adds to them. Nonetheless it may well be that it is desirable to require parties to pay

---

[45] From which, of course, exceptions can be made in appropriate cases.
[46] Paragraphs 1.8 and 1.9 discuss the problems of discovery in the US federal courts and the use of magistrate judges and special masters to supervise that process.

up front for the expenses incurred by their opponents in providing discovery which is of more marginal value."

3.18   Other commentators also point out the utility of ordering the party which seeks disclosure to pay the costs. I am told by US judges that such a reverse costs order is effective in controlling demands for excessive discovery.[47] Again, however, there are strong opposing views. The Law Society believes that this proposal might cause significant disadvantages to the party seeking disclosure or generate further hearings to determine the value of the documents sought. The PNBA considers that there is already sufficient flexibility in the rules for the court to order that the party seeking disclosure should pay the costs in the first instance.

3.19   It seems to me that the court's case management powers under CPR Part 3 are wide enough to embrace (a) an order that the party seeking disclosure do pay the other side's costs of giving disclosure or (b) an order that those costs shall be treated as part of the costs of the action. Thus if the party seeking disclosure is ultimately vindicated, it may recover the costs which it has paid out. I draw attention to this power, but I do not consider that it merits any further exegesis in the rules.

3.20   Option 10. So far as option 10 is concerned, as indicated in other chapters I favour the allocation of all complex cases to specific judges, so far as practicalities and the existing circuit system allow. This approach should help to promote good case management in relation to disclosure issues.

4. RECOMMENDATIONS

4.1   I make the following recommendations:

(i)   E-disclosure as a topic should form a substantial part of (a) CPD for solicitors and barristers who will have to deal with e-disclosure in practice and (b) the training of judges who will have to deal with e-disclosure on the bench.

(ii)   A new CPR rule 31.5A should be drafted to adopt the menu option in relation to (a) large commercial and similar claims and (b) any case where the costs of standard disclosure are likely to be disproportionate. Personal injury claims and clinical negligence claims should be excluded from the provisions of rule 31.5A.

---

[47] See PR paragraph 40.7.3.

CHAPTER 38. WITNESS STATEMENTS AND EXPERT EVIDENCE

INDEX

1. INTRODUCTION

1.1   <u>The principal complaint.</u> The principal complaint that was made in Phase 2 about witness statements and (to a lesser extent) expert evidence was prolixity. If witness statements and expert reports are longer than they need to be, or address (at length) matters that are irrelevant or at best peripheral, or which ought not be covered in a witness statement or expert report at all, it is self-evident that the costs will increase to no useful purpose. This is due to (i) the costs incurred in their preparation; and (ii) the time spent by opponents and the court in reading those documents and considering their effect.

1.2   <u>The extent of the problem.</u> It is difficult to gauge the extent to which prolixity in witness statements and expert reports is causing the unnecessary expenditure of time and money in civil litigation. The evidence I have received has largely been general and anecdotal (e.g. of witness statements that repeat or simply refer to documents, without adding anything to what the documents say).

1.3   What is apparent, however, from the feedback received in Phase 2 is that although there are many practitioners who have encountered prolixity in witness statements and expert reports, this is not a universal problem. In many cases prolixity is not an issue at all. Indeed, my own experience as trial judge includes both cases where costs have been materially increased by unnecessary prolixity and cases where this has not been a problem at all.

1.4   <u>Recent amendments to CPR Part 35.</u> I mentioned at PR paragraph 42.1.6 that both the Civil Justice Council (the "CJC") and the Civil Procedure Rule Committee (the "Rule Committee") were reviewing CPR Part 35 with a view to making amendments, effective from 1st October 2009. The CJC and the Rule Committee have now completed that review and have made substantive amendments to CPR Part 35 and to the practice direction on experts and assessors supplementing Part 35 (now to be called "practice direction 35"). The wording has been improved and in places made more concise. More importantly, there are changes of substance. In particular, there is a requirement that questions put under rule 35.6 must be proportionate. Clear and sensible guidance has been given as to when it is appropriate to instruct a single joint expert. Useful ground rules for expert meetings have been set. Cross-examination of experts on their instructions has been restricted. These reforms, which I welcome, meet some of the concerns which have been raised during Phase 2 of the Costs Review (which concluded two months before the Part 35 amendments were made).

2. WITNESS STATEMENTS

(i) Prolixity

2.1   The role of witness statements. As was explained in chapter 42 of the Preliminary Report, witness statements serve a number of purposes, including (a) reducing the length of the trial (by largely doing away with the need for anything more than short examination-in-chief); (b) enabling the parties to know in advance of the trial what the factual issues are; (c) enabling opposing parties to prepare in advance for cross-examination; and (d) encouraging the early settlement of actions.[48] To this I would add the objective of providing useful and relevant information to the court to enable it to adjudicate upon the case in an efficient manner.

2.2   Having considered the extensive submissions on this issue, I conclude that witness statements can and do fulfil the important objectives identified in the previous paragraph. I do not consider that the fact that some witness statements are too long means that they should be done away with as a tool of civil litigation. The problem is primarily one of unnecessary length, rather than whether witness statements should be used at all in civil litigation. One reason for unnecessary length is that many witness statements contain extensive argument. Such evidence is inadmissible and adds to the costs.

2.3   Measures to control prolixity. There are two primary measures that should be deployed to try to ensure that witness statements are not unnecessarily lengthy. The first is case management, and the second is imposition of costs sanctions.

2.4   Case management. Under our current system, there are few restrictions in practice on a party's ability to produce and rely upon witness statements in civil proceedings. The courts do not, in general, inquire as to how many witnesses a party proposes to call, upon what matters they will give evidence (and whether those matters are relevant to the real issues in dispute) and how long their witness statements will be. Nevertheless CPR Part 32 gives the court power to do all of this. The Commercial Court is now exercising these powers, as part of that court's commitment to more active case management: see section H1 of the Commercial Court Guide, as revised in May 2009. In my view the best way to avoid wastage of costs occurring as a result of lengthy and irrelevant witness statements is for the court, in appropriate cases, to hear argument at an early case management conference (a "CMC") about what matters need to be proved and then to give specific directions relating to witness statements. The directions may (a) identify the issues to which factual evidence should be directed, (b) identify the witnesses to be called, (c) limit the length of witness statements or (d) require that any statement over a specified length do contain a one page summary at the start with cross-references to relevant pages/paragraphs. Any CMC which goes into a case in this level of detail will be an expensive event, requiring proper preparation by the parties and proper pre-reading by the judge. I certainly do not recommend this approach as a matter of routine. It should, however, be adopted in those cases where such an exercise would

---

[48] PR paragraph 42.3.1

be cost effective, in particular in cases where the parties are proposing to spend excessive and disproportionate sums on the preparation of witness statements.[49]

2.5   German procedure. A not dissimilar approach is the "Relationsmethode" of German civil procedure, which is mentioned in chapter 55 of the Preliminary Report.[50] As I understand it, the procedural rules in German civil proceedings require each party to identify the witnesses whom they intend to rely upon to prove the factual matters contained in the pleadings. After the pleadings are in, the presiding judge will review them and identify which factual matters are in dispute and (in consequence) which witnesses the judge will receive evidence from on particular matters.

2.6   Possible adoption in England and Wales. The aspect of the "Relationsmethode" which I believe can and should be adopted in civil litigation in England and Wales is the identification of proposed witnesses by reference to the pleadings. If in any given case the court so directs, each party should identify the factual witnesses whom it intends to call and which of the pleaded facts the various witnesses will prove. This is a task which the parties will be doing internally anyway, so hopefully it will not add unduly to costs. The filing of such a document (which might possibly be a copy of the pleadings with annotations or footnotes or an extra column) will be necessary groundwork for any case management conference at which the judge is going to give effective case management directions, for the purpose of limiting and focusing factual evidence, in order to save costs.

2.7   Costs sanctions. To the extent that case management does not prevent parties from producing prolix witness statements, costs sanctions should be applied against the party responsible for adducing the prolix or irrelevant statements. A simple example (which involves the use of case management) is where a court has ordered at a CMC that witness statements are not to exceed 10 pages. If a party serves a witness statement that is, say, 30 pages in length, there should be a presumption that the party is to face an adverse costs order in relation to the witness statement, unless there are good reasons for the court not to make such an order. An adverse costs order could (in the case of an otherwise successful party) be that the party is not to receive its costs of preparing the statement, or (in the case of an otherwise unsuccessful party) that the party is to pay its opponent's costs on an increased basis. The court would retain a discretion not to make an adverse costs order, which could be exercised if a witness statement is only slightly over the ordered limit or if there is good reason for the excess.

2.8   Even in cases where the court has given no detailed directions about factual evidence (i.e. the majority of cases), the judge can still impose costs sanctions for prolix or irrelevant evidence. The judge can either give an indication about costs to be disallowed or allowed on detailed assessment or, alternatively, take those matters into account immediately upon summary assessment.

2.9   Views expressed in Phase 2. In making the proposals set out above, I am drawing on many of the submissions made during Phase 2, without identifying them individually. It should, however, be noted that in a survey of clients carried out by one major City firm 84% of respondents (i.e. 49 out of 58) considered that the courts should be readier to impose costs sanctions for irrelevant evidence. Furthermore at the Professional Negligence Lawyers Association Conference in Birmingham on 25th June 2009 I specifically invited debate about witness statements. None of the

---

[49] If my recommendations in chapter 40 below are accepted, it will be apparent from costs estimates lodged by parties what sums they propose to spend on preparing witness statements.
[50] PR paragraph 55.4.5.

options set out in PR paragraph 42.6.3 found favour. A number of experienced solicitors and counsel contributed to the debate. The general view was that more effective case management was the way forward. The judge at the first CMC should identify the key issues to be addressed by witnesses. Witness statements should then be focused on those key issues and deal with any other matters more briefly and summarily.

(ii) Other matters

2.10 <u>Exhibits to witness statements.</u> One of the proposals canvassed in the Preliminary Report, as a way of reducing the duplication of documents in court bundles, and minimising the amount of cross-referencing of documents exhibited to witness statements, was (ideally) for the parties to collaborate and agree on a paginated bundle of documents, to which witness statements could be cross-referenced.[51] I caveated this suggestion with the comment that it might be unacceptable to litigation solicitors. The feedback during Phase 2 indicated that this was indeed the case. As one international law firm wrote, "*it is simply not practicable to expect litigation solicitors who are busy finalising (often very many) witness statements to liaise with their opposite numbers attempting to agree a bundle at the same time*". I accept that, in the short term, we must live with the present system. This sometimes results in multiple copies of the same documents being bound up as exhibits to different witness statements, which are then exchanged and inflicted upon the court.[52] In the longer term, however, technology may provide the solution.

2.11 <u>Use of computer technology.</u> The practical difficulties associated with solicitors attempting to agree on a bundle of exhibited documents may be overcome with an increased use of technology. If e-working is rolled out across the court system,[53] it will become possible for the parties to lodge electronic bundles in all civil courts. Witness statements and other documents used in the proceedings could be hyperlinked to the documents in an electronic bundle, thus reducing the amount of work required by the parties (and the overall costs of the proceedings). This would do away with the need for each party to prepare bundles of its own exhibits for witness statements (with references), and then for those same witness statements to be cross-referred to a differently-paginated trial bundle that is produced subsequently. Instead the witness statements would be hyperlinked once to the relevant document. This process allows cross references to trial bundles to be added to electronic versions of the witness statements more easily at a later stage when trial bundles are produced. I understand from Mr Justice Ramsey that this is already being done in large trials at courts where e-working is available.

2.12 <u>Supplementary oral evidence.</u> It is sometimes said that exhaustive witness statements are required because a party is concerned that the evidence of the witness will not be capable of being amplified at trial.[54] The court already has discretion to allow supplementary evidence-in-chief under CPR rule 32.5(3). In the experience of many judges[55] (and also my own experience) it is usually helpful to hear short supplementary evidence-in-chief, especially if that oral evidence goes to the central

---

[51] PR paragraphs 42.6.4 and 42.6.5.

[52] One incidental advantage for the judge is that if important documents in the trial bundle are illegible (as required by Sedley's Laws of Documents [1996] JR 37), pristine legible copies may well be found in the witness exhibits. Whilst at the TCC I used to keep witness exhibits stacked up in a corner for this purpose.

[53] As recommended in chapter 43 below.

[54] See PR paragraph 42.4.3. Similar points were made during Phase 2.

[55] As confirmed by the submission of the Council of Her Majesty's Circuit Judges.

issues in the case. I am told by the Bar that judges differ in their approach to supplementary oral evidence: some judges are receptive to such evidence, whereas others will not allow it save for good reason (e.g. a new development in the trial). Total consistency is unachievable, but a broadly similar approach is desirable. In my view, judges should generally be willing to allow a modest amount of supplementary oral evidence (a) because this approach is generally helpful to the court and (b) because this approach reduces pressure on solicitors to cover every conceivable point in witness statements.[56]

2.13   No rule change is required in order to implement the various proposals set out above. All that is required is effective use of the existing rules, as set out in paragraphs 2.4, 2.6, 2.7, 2.8 and 2.12 above. Nevertheless, courts which give detailed guidance in their court guides may care to indicate in those guides an intention to use the existing powers in respect of witness statements more actively.

3. EXPERT EVIDENCE

(i) Submissions during Phase 2

3.1   <u>Concerns about prolixity.</u> During Phase 2, as during Phase 1, concerns were expressed about the length of expert reports. For example, one experienced circuit judge writes:

> "Certain disciplines show a marked tendency towards prolixity – in particular, accident reconstruction experts, psychiatrists and pain management clinicians. Notwithstanding the comments of the Court of Appeal in *Liddell v Middleton*[57] there continues to be regular use in serious injury RTAs of accident reconstruction experts. Their reports are long, show a distinct tendency to go outside their remit and are often speculative. All these disciplines display an inclination to analyse witness statements (despite, again, the clear statement in *Liddell* that this is impermissible). Another contributor to lengthy reports is over analysis of medical records."

3.2   <u>Law Society.</u> The Law Society acknowledges that experts' fees significantly increase the costs of litigation and proposes that the whole topic of expert evidence should be reviewed by the CJC together with relevant stakeholders.

3.3   <u>Bar Council and a set of chambers.</u> The Bar Council comments that experts' fees can be a "*sizeable costs centre*" and proposes that, in appropriate cases, the court should determine the scope of expert evidence at the first CMC. One set of chambers (whose members have done many cases in front of me involving expert evidence) writes:

> "Chambers suggests that in TCC cases, especially heavy TCC cases, it would be advantageous to have a separate CMC to deal with expert evidence in which the Court identifies the names of the experts, the subject matter of their reports and the length of those reports in more detail than is currently possible. Additional control over expert evidence would help to keep costs down."

---

[56] This approach is urged by, amongst others, the Manchester Law Society.
[57] (1996) PIQR, P36.

3.4   <u>Professional Negligence Bar Association.</u> The Professional Negligence Bar Association (the "PNBA") states that there is a conundrum concerning expert evidence. On the one hand the expert owes a duty to the court and is obliged to give a balanced opinion and to state the facts upon which he relies. The expert is liable to be criticised by the court if he fails in that duty.[58] On the other hand, the court is anxious to restrict the length and the costs of expert evidence so that they are proportionate to the issues in the litigation and the sums at stake. The PNBA argues that different approaches are required to expert evidence, depending upon the type of litigation (commercial, clinical negligence, personal injury, construction etc) and the size of claim (fast track, low value multi-track, high value, etc). The PNBA argues that no single approach to expert evidence is a panacea; instead the approach to using expert evidence and the content of the report should be tailor–made to suit the requirements of the particular dispute.

3.5   <u>General approval of the present system for expert evidence.</u> Overall, a greater level of satisfaction with the present arrangements was expressed during Phase 2 than during Phase 1 of the Costs Review. Many of the proposals for reform which were suggested by respondents during Phase 1 and which are recorded in chapter 42 of the Preliminary Report received general rejection during Phase 2. A number of practitioners comment that expert evidence, if it is going to be of value to the court, is bound to be expensive; furthermore the present rules generally work well.[59] The Council of Her Majesty's Circuit Judges comments about experts:

> "Either they are necessary or they are not. If they are, then they have to be paid their market price, which, in the case of eminent people, may be considerable. As has now been recognised, is not fair to the parties to try to force them to a single expert in many situations, and this tendency in fast track cases can in effect lead to trial by expert, not by Judge. However, it is frequently the case that parties are often anxious to assemble a larger range of experts than may actually be needed for fair determination of the issues, and this can be dealt with by judicial case management. Sensible trial management, encouraging agreement for example that experts be heard back to back as early in the trial as possible can also save significant sums in attendance fees."

3.6   <u>When experts should be instructed.</u> In relation to the question when experts should be instructed (in so far as the costs of the experts are to be recoverable) widely differing views have been expressed. Some practitioners urge that experts must be instructed at an early stage in order to ascertain whether the claimant has a case fit to advance in a letter of claim. Others take the opposite view. For example, the Commercial Litigation Association states:

> "We do not see how an expert's report can be obtained before the documents upon which the report will be based are disclosed. We contend there is little benefit in defining issues on which experts will be asked to comment when disclosure and a significant number of documents have yet to be seen. Identification of the need for an expert may come before disclosure (i.e. due to the obvious complexity of the case that may present itself), with issues to be decided later. We therefore support the current position where the expert report is obtained post disclosure but before service of witness statements. In this way witness evidence can be prepared in the light of expert evidence and this sequence can clarify factors possibly leading to encouragement to settle."

---

[58] See e.g. *Great Eastern Hotel Company Ltd v John Laing Construction Ltd* [2005] EWHC 181 (TCC).
[59] Indeed I would add in this regard that I have conducted many trials with the benefit of expert reports which were excellent and concise.

3.7   Single joint experts. In relation to the general use of single joint experts for quantum issues, there was a similar spread of views during Phase 2 as there was in Phase 1.[60] The general view of practitioners is that single joint experts are beneficial for less important and less controversial quantum issues. The City of London Law Society's Litigation Committee commends this approach in commercial litigation. The PNBA commends this approach for professional negligence cases. It states:

> "...in all cases relating to costings simpliciter, there should be a jointly instructed expert report. To take an obvious example, in an acquired brain injury claim, whilst each party will usually be permitted to instruct its own medically qualified experts in the relevant fields of expertise, those experts whose reports will be dependent on the views reached by the medically qualified experts (e.g. an accommodation expert, a physiotherapist, an occupational expert and/or an employment expert) will often be ordered to be produced by a jointly instructed expert."

3.8   Sequential or simultaneous exchange? At the case management seminar on 29th July 2009 a number of speakers favoured sequential exchange of expert reports. It was suggested that the problem with simultaneous exchange is that the reports may be *"like ships passing in the night"*. A number of commercial practitioners have commended sequential exchange. Indeed this approach gains some support from the Commercial Court Guide, which provides at paragraph H2.11:

> "In appropriate cases the court will direct that the reports of expert witnesses be exchanged sequentially rather than simultaneously. The sequential exchange of expert reports may in many cases save time and costs by helping to focus the contents of responsive reports upon true rather than assumed issues of expert evidence and by avoiding repetition of detailed factual material as to which there is no real issue. Sequential exchange is likely to be particularly effective where experts are giving evidence of foreign law or are forensic accountants. This is an issue that the court will normally wish to consider at the case management conference."

3.9   On the other hand a number of respondents were strongly opposed to sequential exchange. For example a group of claimant clinical negligence solicitors writes:

> "The almost inevitable consequence of sequential exchange of expert evidence is that it encourages expert evidence which is tailored to meet the opposing expert report (as opposed to the factual and expert issues) and thus Trial by expert report. Such a system risks the re-emergence of the partisan expert."

The PNBA believes that simultaneous exchange should be retained in professional negligence cases, despite the additional expenditure involved. This is to ensure that both experts provide opinions independently.

3.10   Personal injuries litigation. The Forum of Insurance Lawyers ("FOIL") believes that the system of selecting medical experts in personal injury cases is working well and dismisses suggestions to the contrary which were made during Phase 1. The Association of Personal Injury Lawyers ("APIL") takes a more gloomy view. APIL states:

---

[60] See PR paragraph 42.14.1

"There are disagreements in many personal injury cases about the selection of experts. It is common for claimant solicitors to write to defendants/their insurers with a list of three suggested experts, and an invitation to object to the instruction of these. A common response (if one is received at all) is: this is not a joint instruction, so we are not objecting to your proposed experts, but we reserve the right to instruct our own expert. The defendants then receive a report they don't like from the expert instructed by the claimants, and apply to the court to obtain their own. We do not believe however, that such applications should be routinely allowed."

3.11   This last issue between APIL and FOIL is more related to personal injuries litigation procedure than to the rules governing expert evidence. In my view that is best dealt with by the procedural reforms proposed in chapter 22 above.

3.12   <u>Concurrent evidence.</u> I have received a large number of comments on the issue of "hot tubbing", as canvassed in PR paragraph 42.14.2. Broadly speaking respondents fall into three camps, namely (a) outright opposition, (b) general support and (c) cautious support subject to a pilot. In addition, an Australian judge has written to say that, although "hot tubbing" is a term used by many practitioners,[61] the correct name for the procedure is "concurrent evidence".

(ii) Analysis

3.13   There is now a wealth of guidance on the use of expert evidence: CPR Part 35 (as recently amended); practice direction 35; the Protocol for the Instruction of Experts to give evidence in Civil Claims; the Model Form of Expert's Report published by the Academy of Experts; and also a wealth of judicial decisions on what experts should or should not do, when single joint experts might be appropriate, and so forth. It is doubtful whether either lawyers or litigants or experts will welcome yet another raft of rules about expert evidence emerging from this review. Instead, I shall concentrate on four key issues which emerge from the mass of arguments and submissions about this topic which I have received over the last year.

<u>(a) Case management</u>

3.14   <u>The benefits of good case management.</u> On those occasions when a proper CMC take place (i.e. the judge actually gets to grips with the issues and debates with counsel what needs to be proved, how and why – rather than making formulaic comments about costs, length of trial etc), huge costs savings can be achieved in relation to the future conduct of the case. This is clear to me both from talking to practitioners and court users and from comments made in written submissions. These comments are confirmed by my own experience as counsel and as judge.

3.15   <u>The only effective way to control expert costs is by good case management.</u> The suggestion made by the Bar Council and by a set of chambers set out in paragraph 3.3 above is a sensible one, but is only appropriate for cases where the sums at stake and the potential costs make the exercise worthwhile. If (a) the parties are prepared to spend money on a CMC, a large part of which will be devoted to determining the scope of expert evidence, (b) trial counsel attend that CMC well prepared and (c) the judge reads into the case properly first, then such an exercise will yield huge dividends. The judge will be able to make a focused order stating what expert evidence each party can call and upon what issues. The judge can also identify with precision any topics which require a single joint expert. If the judge makes a

---

[61] Including all practitioners whom I met during the Costs Review visit to Australia.

focused order of this nature, it will be much easier to resolve the conundrum identified by the PNBA in its submissions. It will be clear to the experts how far they must go and what ground they must cover.

3.16   Caveat.   I advise against incurring the expense of a full scale CMC to determine the scope of expert evidence unless (a) there is a commitment by all parties to prepare for it properly and (b) listing arrangements are such that the judge has time to read into the case properly. The degree of preparation required clearly depends upon the nature of the case. A multi-track personal injury case may require less preparation time (for specialist counsel and judges) than say a complex accountants' negligence case. Nevertheless the requisite preparation must be done by all involved. To incur substantial expense and then achieve nothing of value from the CMC is the worst of all worlds and, incidentally, brings case management into disrepute.

3.17   Even in more routine cases, where expert evidence forms one item amongst many on the agenda for a CMC, good case management can focus the expert evidence. A well drawn order for expert evidence will not only identify the expert or the expert discipline, but also identify the issues which the expert will address.

3.18   Orders limiting recoverable expert fees and expenses.   The court has power under CPR rule 35.4(4) to make an order limiting the fees and expenses of expert witnesses recoverable from the opposing party. The wording of that rule has been tightened, as part of the batch of amendments made to Part 35 on 1st October 2009. That power is seldom exercised in practice. I suggest that, whether or not the proposals for costs management made in chapter 40 below are accepted, judges might in future make greater use of their powers under rule 35.4(4) to restrict recoverable costs in respect of expert evidence. To that end, I recommend that Part 35 or its accompanying practice direction be amended in order to require that a party seeking permission to adduce expert evidence do furnish an estimate of the costs of that evidence to the court. This should not involve extra work or expense, since any solicitor instructing an expert is bound to obtain an estimate of the expert's likely fees and expenses. The solicitor would obtain such an estimate (a) as a matter of good sense and (b) so that he would be able to comply with paragraph 7.2 of the Protocol for the Instruction of Experts annexed to practice direction 35.

3.19   When single joint experts should be instructed.   In the small claims track or the fast track there is a presumption that there will only one expert witness (who may or may not be a single joint expert) on any particular issue: see CPR rule 35.4(3A), as recently amended. In relation to multi-track cases the debate about when single joint experts should be instructed has now been overtaken by the new section 7 of practice direction 35. That section gives admirable and clear guidance as to the factors which the court should take into account, when deciding whether to make an order for a single joint expert.

(b) One size does not fit all

3.20   The present rules are broad enough to provide for all sizes.   Many of the submissions during Phase 2 are themselves "*like ships passing in the night*", to echo comments made at the case management seminar. This is because the requirements for effective expert evidence in personal injury cases, commercial cases, construction cases, clinical negligence cases, valuation disputes, insurance disputes, tree root claims and so forth are all totally different. A web of differing practices in relation to expert evidence has been created by practitioners and judges in different specialities.

The rules in Part 35, practice direction 35 and the Protocol[62] are wide enough to embrace those different practices. But they do not spell out what forms of order are conventional in all the myriad types of litigation, nor realistically could they do so.

3.21 Annex C to the Practice Direction – Pre-Action Conduct. Annex C to the Practice Direction – Pre-Action Conduct ("Annex C") provides guidance on instructing experts applicable to all cases, except those where a specific pre-action protocol contains provisions about instructing experts. Annex C contains a number of well intentioned provisions, which are undoubtedly helpful in some cases. For example, the provision requiring parties to agree upon the selection of an expert before proceedings may make sense in some cases. However, in many construction cases[63] or commercial cases[64] a party may need an expert report in order to decide which party to sue, or indeed whether to sue at all. In cases such as these it may be impracticable and a waste of costs for the party to comply with the elaborate requirements of Annex C. In my view, there is a flaw at the heart of Annex C, namely that one size does not fit all. It is quite impossible to have any useful set of guidance rules applicable to instructing experts in a vast mass of different types of case. I therefore recommend that Annex C should be repealed.

(c) Costs sanctions

3.22 Where, as sometimes happens, expert evidence strays materially beyond the issues in the case (whether or not the court has given focused directions for expert evidence), the judge already has power to impose costs sanctions, for example by disallowing half the costs of the expert report. The judge could do this either (a) in the course of summary assessment or (b) by giving an indication to the costs judge who will do the detailed assessment. Of course, the vast majority of detailed assessments settle before coming to a hearing, but any direction by the trial judge will impact upon the settlement reached. Having considered the submissions made during the Costs Review, I recommend that judges be more willing to exercise this power in cases where prolix or irrelevant expert evidence has led to wastage of costs.[65]

(d) Concurrent evidence

3.23 Proposal for a pilot. A number of experts, practitioners and judges have expressed support for the use of concurrent evidence (known colloquially as "hot tubbing") in appropriate cases. It is said to be particularly effective in valuation and similar disputes. I recommend that concurrent evidence be piloted, but only in cases where the parties, the experts, the lawyers and the judge all consent to this procedure.

3.24 Possible future rule change. The results of any pilot study must be evaluated with care, in order to ascertain (a) the types of case in which concurrent evidence is successful, (b) what costs are saved and (c) whether the parties and their advisers perceive the process as enabling each side's case to be properly considered. If the results of this assessment are positive, then consideration should be given to amending Part 35, so that it expressly enables the judge to direct that the concurrent evidence procedure be used in appropriate cases.

---

[62] Referred to above.

[63] The protocol for which gives no guidance on instructing experts, with the result that Annex C applies to all construction cases.

[64] For which there is no protocol, with the result that Annex C applies to all commercial cases.

[65] For a reported example of case where expert evidence led to wastage of costs, see *Liddell v Middleton* (1996) PIQR, P36.

4. CONCLUSION AND RECOMMENDATIONS

4.1 <u>Conclusion.</u> In the course of this chapter, and in the light of debate during the Costs Review, I have suggested a number of areas where judges and practitioners might make more effective use of powers conferred by the existing rules, in order to reduce the costs of witness statements and expert evidence.

4.2 I make no separate recommendation in respect of Annex C. If my recommendations in chapter 35 above are accepted, the entire general protocol (including Annex C) will be repealed. Therefore the comments in paragraph 3.21 above should be read as additional support for the recommendations made in chapter 35 above.

4.3 <u>Recommendations.</u> I make two recommendations:

(i) CPR Part 35 or its accompanying practice direction should be amended in order to require that a party seeking permission to adduce expert evidence do furnish an estimate of the costs of that evidence to the court.

(ii) The procedure developed in Australia, known as "concurrent evidence" should be piloted in cases where all parties consent. If the results of the pilot are positive, consideration should be given to amending CPR Part 35 to provide for use of that procedure in appropriate cases.

CHAPTER 39. CASE MANAGEMENT

INDEX

1. INTRODUCTION

1.1   <u>Focus of this chapter.</u> In this chapter I shall concentrate principally upon multi-track cases proceeding (a) in the county courts and district registries around the country and (b) in the general Queen's Bench ("QB") Division in London. Although there will be some reference to other courts, I shall avoid repeating what is set out in other chapters specifically devoted to those other courts. Some of the comments in this chapter, especially in sections 5 and 6, are equally applicable to both fast track and multi-track cases. It must be accepted, however, that the cases with greatest need for "hands on" case management are multi-track cases. The fast track is designed to enable cases to progress from issue to trial without interim hearings and with the minimum of expense: see paragraphs 2.1 and 2.2 of the practice direction supplementing CPR Part 28.

1.2   <u>Definitions.</u> In this chapter I use the term "docketing" in the same sense as in PR chapter 43, section 5. I use the abbreviation "CMC" for case management conference and "PTR" for pre-trial review. I use the term "interim hearing" to mean any hearing before the trial, including a CMC or PTR.

2. MEETINGS AND SEMINARS DURING PHASE 2

2.1   <u>Manchester seminar.</u> At the Manchester seminar on 3rd July 2009 Professor Adrian Zuckerman presented a paper[66] on litigation management. Professor Zuckerman argued that the courts must deliver judgments within a reasonable time and at reasonable cost. The courts, like the National Health Service, are a public service. Their function is to adjudicate disputes with available resources. Court users are only entitled to their fair share of court resources. At the moment judges, following the precept of CPR rules 3.8, 3.9 and 3.10 are far too indulgent to litigants in default. This causes not only delay but also unproductive waste of court resources in dealing with the effects of litigant failure to meet deadlines. It is only in truly extreme circumstances that the courts will strike out a party which is in default. Such extreme circumstances are exemplified by *Marine Rescue Technologies Ltd v Burchill* [2007] EWHC 1976 (Ch). After reviewing the tortuous history of that case Professor Zuckerman stated:

---

[66] On the Costs Review website at http://www.judiciary.gov.uk/docs/costs-review/lit-managment-under-cpr.pdf.

"By no stretch of the imagination can this be considered an efficient use of court resources, nor was it fair to other litigants waiting in the queue, nor did it provide effective protection to the defendant from being unnecessarily subjected to 6 years of futile litigation...

The main responsibility for this state of affairs must be accepted by the Court of Appeal. The Court of Appeal has steadfastly declined to develop a coherent policy for enforcing compliance with rules and case management directions. Its refusal to provide leadership in this regard is nowhere more apparent than in relation to its interpretation of CPR 3.9."

2.2   A little later Professor Zuckerman stated:

"Even more corrosive of good management practice is the Court of Appeal inability to speak with one voice. The understanding of the overriding objective varies greatly amongst its judges, with some judges still holding the view that their only duty is to decide cases according to the facts and the law, no matter how long it takes and how much it costs.

Management standards will not improve unless the Court of Appeal is willing to provide leadership. To do so it would have to revise its approach to the enforcement of compliance with case management directions and therefore to the operation of CPR 3.9. It would have to adopt a policy that gives practical expression to the need to ensure that court resources are properly utilised. This means, amongst others, that a litigant who has failed to take advantage of the opportunity of prosecuting his case will not get another opportunity, unless he has been prevented from doing so by circumstances beyond his control."

2.3   Professor Zuckerman in his oral address (though he did not touch on this in his paper) commended the approach which is canvassed as one possible way forward in PR paragraph 43.4.21. He concluded by arguing that the civil justice system like all other public services must be adequately managed, so as to deliver a satisfactory service. He added:

"The management task that the court is expected to discharge is relatively uncomplicated: to ensure that case management directions are implemented as laid down, unless a change of circumstances demands otherwise. But this simple task requires the court to abandon its almost religious attachment to the one dimensional understanding of justice and accept that doing justice means more than delivering a judgment on the merits; that time and the use of resources are just as significant imperatives of justice."

2.4   Unsurprisingly Professor Zuckerman's presentation provoked a measure of disagreement and lively discussion. One speaker made the point that if the court sets an unrealistic timetable, as sometimes happens, that encourages a culture of non-compliance. In a vote at the end of this discussion 32 people agreed with Professor Zuckerman's thesis, 14 disagreed and there were 22 abstentions.

2.5   <u>London seminar.</u> At the London seminar on 10th July 2009 Paul Marsh, then President of the Law Society, stated that judges (most of whom come from the Bar) need to have a better understanding of *"the reality of a solicitor's work and responsibilities"*.[67]   In the discussion following this address there was much

---

[67] Mr Marsh's speaking notes are on the Costs Review website at

discussion of case management. A course director at the Judicial Studies Board (the "JSB") stated that all civil judges are trained in case management. A solicitor stated that CMCs were meant to be occasions when cases were grabbed by the scruff of the neck. However, in practice, many CMCs resulted in directions which were close to formulaic. A practitioner stated that CMCs were most effective in ancillary relief proceedings in family cases. This was because the judges had read the papers and were able to narrow issues. One district judge stated that in the county courts district judges were hampered by lack of IT. Very often the first he knows of a problem in a case is when he sees the pre-trial checklist. District Judge Cawood (who sits in Portsmouth) stated that all bigger cases should be docketed to specific judges, in order to achieve consistent case management. Other speakers, both practitioners and judges, spoke in favour of docketing. District Judge Cawood said that docketing was perfectly possible in care cases and it ought to be achieved more successfully in larger civil cases. For example, a clinical negligence case should be allocated to a single district judge for management and then to the Designated Civil Judge for trial. I took a vote at the end of this section of the discussion. There were 67 votes in agreement with the views of District Judge Cawood and two votes in disagreement.

2.6   At the same seminar Desmond Browne QC, Chairman of the Bar, called for more effective case management. In his written paper[68] he stated:

> "Costs could undoubtedly be saved by more active judicial case management throughout the life of the case. Perhaps we should even consider something like the docket system. Many barristers find that often the Court lets things drift between the case management conference and the pre-trial review, and that by the time that the PTR takes place, it is too late for the Court to exert any beneficial effect. In this way the Court too often misses the opportunity to define the issues rigorously, and then limit disclosure accordingly."

In his oral presentation, building on the observations of District Judge Cawood and the vote just taken, Mr Browne declared that the message should go out from the District Registry in Portsmouth that England expects all courts to adopt docketing for cases of substance.

3. SUBMISSIONS DURING PHASE 2

3.1   <u>The Law Society.</u>   The Law Society maintains that pro-active case management is the key to achieving proportionate costs. It supports the increased use of specialist judges and docketing. The Law Society is concerned that rules to control the progress of cases are not applied fully or at all. There therefore needs to be a change in the attitudes of judges and court users. The Law Society supports the possibility of sanctions to bolster effective case management and compliance with the rules, but does not believe that sanctions should be used as a standard response.

3.2   <u>The Chester and North Wales Law Society.</u> The Chester and North Wales Law Society (adopting the submissions of one of its member firms) also supports a more robust use of sanctions, in order to back up case management. In addition it proposes that each party should be required to prepare a case plan at the outset, together with a summary of the issues involved, the evidence required to deal with those issues and the likely costs.

---

http://www.judiciary.gov.uk/docs/costs-review/paul-marsh-notes.pdf.
[68] Available on the Costs Review website at http://www.judiciary.gov.uk/docs/costs-review/bar-council-perspective.pdf.

3.3   The Bar Council. The Bar Council, like the Law Society, believes that the best way to control costs is by the court engaging in more effective case management. The Bar Council considers that case management is satisfactory in the Commercial Court, the Technology and Construction Court (the "TCC") and some patent cases, but that it is inadequate in other areas of practice. The Bar Council states that, in some areas, courts are rarely "up to speed" at CMCs and so cannot manage cases effectively; that time is wasted when specialist cases are dealt with by non-specialist judges. The Bar Council believes that docketing of some (but not all) cases would lead to substantial savings of costs. It also supports the use of lists of issues, except in the TCC. The Bar Council does not support the imposition of tougher sanctions (other than costs orders) upon defaulting parties. Steps should be taken to make skeleton arguments shorter and truly "skeletal". If the court requires written submissions, as opposed to skeleton arguments, it should so direct.

3.4   Individual firms of solicitors. Many firms of solicitors have written in with helpful comments on case management, based upon their own experience. The general view expressed is that more active case management by the court will save costs. Allied to this is the need for docketing and the assigning of more complex cases to specialist judges. The Association of Personal Injury Lawyers ("APIL") supports this approach.[69]

3.5   Views differ as to whether courts should be more robust in imposing sanctions upon defaulting parties. One solicitor, who does a great deal of trade union work, writes:

> "I am in favour of stricter management of the cases by the District Judges. I would also be in favour of docketing, if it was possible. There is a limited amount of this that occurs in Liverpool County Court, and it works very well. One of the reasons I would welcome stricter management by the District Judges is because of the behaviour of the Solicitors based at the [...], as previously mentioned. Once proceedings are issued we find that they constantly fail to comply with Directions but there are very few penalties imposed. One of the problems may be of course that they do not have to account to any client for any adverse Costs Orders. I think that if it is the fault of the legal representative that the Direction has not been complied with, for example they have failed to prepare a list of documents or a statement, then the penalties should be quite severe, however if it is the fault of a third party, such as a delay by a medical expert, the Courts should be more lenient."

The Forum of Insurance Lawyers ("FOIL") views the imposition of sanctions as a matter of balance, although a tough approach is required to deal with certain tactics adopted by claimant lawyers to inflate costs.

3.6   One firm of clinical negligence defence solicitors deplores the failure of the courts (a) to exercise their case management powers with sufficient vigour or (b) to impose sanctions for delay. It states:

> "We suggest that greater attention needs to be paid to the prejudice to the judicial system as a whole as a consequence of widespread delays and disregard for procedural deadlines and the resulting inflation of costs as well as the impact on judicial resources."

---

[69] See chapter 22 above.

3.7   Bar associations. The London Common Law and Commercial Bar Association (the "LCLCBA") points out that costs have increased as changes in the division of labour between the Bar and solicitors have occurred. It maintains that the Bar is able to provide skilled advice and advocacy at lower cost than a firm of solicitors. The LCLCBA is also concerned that the system should be reformed to ensure that judges have sufficient pre-reading time before CMCs. The Commercial Bar Association is opposed to any general policy of imposing sanctions for non-compliance with orders, beyond adverse judicial comment and possibly costs orders.

3.8   The Property Bar Association (the "PBA") states:

> "Further, the PBA recalls that one of the central tenets of the CPR was that judges would take much greater control of cases procedurally. Members' experience is, however, that judges (particularly at County Court level) do not have the time, the inclination or the material properly to get to grips with a case at an interim stage. Many of the supposed benefits of the CPR have been missed because of the failure (perhaps through not much fault of their own) of judges adequately to acquaint themselves with cases before hearings: documents don't reach court files; skeleton arguments do not reach the judge; files are lost completely; lists are too crowded to allow proper reading time. The PBA believes that in those specialist courts (such as the TCC, the Commercial Court or the Chancery List at the Central London Trial Centre) where interim or directions hearings are held before Judges, the situation is much less unsatisfactory."

3.9   Association of Her Majesty's District Judges. The Association of Her Majesty's District Judges believes that PTRs should be used to compel parties to narrow issues and to explore options for settlement. In relation to case management and sanctions, the Association states:

> "...District Judges who are prepared to make the unpalatable decisions and to use available sanctions robustly must be supported by the appellate courts when discretion is exercised appropriately in imposing sanctions."

3.10   In relation to docketing, the Association says:

> "One way of managing a case, small or large, would be to develop a docket system (Chapter 43, 5.9).[70] We respectfully agree with the opinion of the author of the Preliminary Report at Chapter 43, 5.11[71] and would support a docket system which is likely in the early period of its development to be easier to manage in the larger value, multi-track, cases. Changes in 'boxwork' procedures would be needed."

3.11   Support for docketing was also expressed by a designated civil judge, subject to the limits of practicality.

3.12   Council of Her Majesty's Circuit Judges. The Council of Her Majesty's Circuit Judges states that judges must not over-manage, because this generates unnecessary expense. A light touch is particularly appropriate when litigation is being conducted by experienced solicitors and counsel.

---

[70] This is a reference to PR paragraph 43.5.9.
[71] This is a reference to PR paragraph 43.5.11.

3.13   Comments on interventionist case management.   One firm of solicitors comments that a phone call or email from the judge is particularly effective in galvanising lawyers into action.   I understand that this approach is adopted by the Senior Master and has been taken one step further by the regular use of email for "problem solving" in the case management process, in order to ensure that directions in mesothelioma cases (where the claimant may not have long to live) are effective and are complied with.   A number of respondents during Phase 2 have told me that American judges may schedule conference calls, attended by attorneys for each side, in order to enquire what progress has been made in complying with procedural directions.   This is said to be highly effective.

3.14   Professor Michael Zander.   On the issue of sanctions for non-compliance, Professor Zander adopts the opposite position to that argued by Professor Zuckerman at the Manchester seminar.   Professor Zander has "*the strongest criticism*" of the approach signalled as a possibility in PR paragraph 43.4.21.   He counsels against a policy of tough enforcement and regular use of sanctions.   Instead Professor Zander commends the view of Sir Jack Jacob in his Note of Reservation to the Report of the Winn Committee:

> "The admonition by Lord Justice Bowen that 'courts do not exist for the sake of discipline' should be reflected in the principle that rules of court should not be framed on the basis of imposing penalties or producing automatic consequences for non-compliance with the rules or orders of the court. The function of rules of court is to provide guidelines not trip wires and they fulfil their function most when they intrude least in the course of litigation."[72]

4. DOCKETING AND SPECIALISATION OF JUDGES

4.1   Specialisation of district judges.   In recent years a number of the larger court centres (starting with Birmingham) have been developing specialisation of judges. District judges indicate to court managers their areas of existing expertise or interest.[73]   So far as possible multi-track cases are assigned to judges who have indicated interest in the relevant area.   Thereafter, so far as possible, cases are managed by the same district judge.   I understand from District Judge Michael Walker[74] that this system works well and there is scope for its expansion.   Likewise, in London the QB masters specialise so far as is practicable.[75]

4.2   Concerns of court users and practitioners.   During the recent consultation period (Phase 2 of the Costs Review) I have received a clear message from court users and practitioners that (a) specialisation by judges and (b) docketing of cases to specific judges are welcomed.   This promotes better and more consistent case management.   It leads to savings of costs.   The point has been made on several occasions that there is scope for considerably more docketing of cases to district judges and circuit judges than is currently achieved.[76]   It has also been urged upon me that costs are increased if (a) cases are passed between district judges during case management or (b) cases are managed by district judges who lack relevant

---

[72] Winn, "*Report of the Committee on Personal Injuries Litigation*" Cmnd.3691 (1968) 151-52, [2].
[73] By "areas of interest" I mean areas of law in which the judge would like to develop expertise, even if outside his or her existing experience.
[74] Secretary of the Association of Her Majesty's District Judges.
[75] For example, Senior Master Whitaker deals with all mesothelioma cases.
[76] For example, the observations of District Judge Cawood to this effect at the London seminar on 10th July 2009 were supported by the Chairman of the Bar and by very many others present.   Similar points were made at the Manchester seminar on 3rd July 2009.

expertise.[77] I accept that sometimes these situations are unavoidable, but they should be minimised. The docketing of multi-track cases will be assisted if those cases, when commenced in outlying courts, are transferred in at an early stage to the court centre where the trial will take place.

4.3   Circuit judges. There are fewer circuit judges dealing with civil business than district judges dealing with civil business. So the opportunities for specialisation are more limited. Nevertheless, so far as practicable, cases should be allocated to circuit judges in accordance with their specialist skill and experience. Likewise, so far as practicable, once a circuit judge has dealt with one hearing in a case (e.g. an appeal from a district judge) the same circuit judge should deal with subsequent hearings in that case and also the trial.[78] The extent to which this is practicable will depend upon the size of each court centre and the exigencies of administration and listing.

4.4   Specialisation by judges. The specialist skills of judges cannot be solely defined by their historic areas of practice as solicitors or counsel. All judges develop new areas of skill and expertise upon the bench. They do this by means of attendance at JSB training courses, study of textbooks, seeking guidance from colleagues and also practical experience on the bench. Nothing in this chapter is intended to discourage judges from extending their range of skills, which is to the benefit of court users as well as the judges themselves. The thrust of this chapter is that, so far as possible, judges should not undertake work in fields in which they neither possess expertise nor are developing expertise.

4.5   Queen's Bench judges. Concern has been expressed that occasionally QB judges are asked to try cases in respect of which they have no existing expertise (despite their excellence in other areas). For example, on occasions at the start of a clinical negligence action brought on behalf of a child with serious brain injury the judge has had to request some basic assistance because this type of litigation is outside his or her experience.[79] Costs are liable to increase when a judge is trying a case in an area with which he is unfamiliar. On occasions this is inevitable and it must, of course, be accepted. On the other hand, such a situation should be avoided where practicable. In my view High Court judges, like other judges, ought to record their areas of expertise and interest.[80] So far as practicable, complex cases requiring trial by QB judges should be allocated to judges in accordance with their specialist skill and experience. However, save in respect of a small number of especially complex cases (where assignment to a named judge is already the practice), no system of docketing to individual QB judges is either feasible or compatible with the circuit system. If the docketing of cases to individual QB judges is going to be achieved on any extensive scale, there will have to be a review of the circuit system on some future occasion.[81]

4.6   Recommendations. I recommend that:

(i)   All High Court judges, circuit judges and district judges should complete questionnaires indicating their areas of existing expertise and their areas of interest.   The information contained in such questionnaires should be

---

[77] The example cited at one of the seminars was that of a district judge, with a background as family law solicitor, managing a clinical negligence case.

[78] The majority of cases, of course, will settle before further hearings are required.

[79] This example was cited at the Manchester seminar on 3rd July 2009. The speaker said that he had seen such cases more than once.

[80] I do not imagine that any judge would object to this. Every lord justice is required to fill in such a questionnaire upon joining the Court of Appeal.

[81] As to which, see chapter 27 above at paragraph 2.17.

digested in a convenient form and made available to listing officers at the relevant court centres.

(ii) So far as possible, at every court centre each multi-track case should be assigned for case management purposes (a) to a district judge[82] who specialises in that type of case and (b) to the same district judge throughout the life of the case.

(iii) So far as possible, each multi-track case which requires a hearing before a circuit judge should be assigned (a) to a circuit judge who specialises in that type of case and (b) to the same circuit judge throughout the life of the case.

(iv) So far as possible, complex cases requiring trial by QB judges should be allocated to judges in accordance with their specialist skill and experience.

5. CASE MANAGEMENT HEARINGS AND DIRECTIONS

5.1 <u>Problems identified.</u> Two matters have been identified in the consultation period, which tend to generate unnecessary costs:

(i) Individual district judges have their own preferred standard directions for different types of case (personal injury, clinical negligence, housing disrepair etc). These standard directions, which are often to similar effect, vary from one district judge to another and from one court centre to another. Some district judges use the civil templates which are available online, whereas others do not.

(ii) In some instances CMCs (especially initial CMCs) are not used as occasions when the court gets to grips with the case and narrows the issues, but rather as ritualistic occasions when the district judge issues standard directions in his or her standard form.[83] CMCs, even when conducted by telephone, are expensive events. When nothing substantial is achieved, those costs are wasted.

5.2 <u>Solutions.</u> In my view, steps must be taken to deal with both these matters. In relation to the first matter, the solution is to develop a more extensive menu of standard directions than currently exists. I deal with this in paragraph 5.3 below. In relation to the second matter, the solution is to dispense with formulaic CMCs altogether. Either a CMC should achieve some useful purpose and should involve serious discussion about the issues in the case or it should not happen at all. I deal with this in paragraphs 5.4 to 5.7 below.

5.3 <u>Standard case management directions.</u> In my view, a menu of standard paragraphs for case management directions should be prepared for each type of case of common occurrence and made available to all district judges both in hard copy and online.[84] These standard directions should then be used by district judges as their starting point in formulating initial case management directions. This practice has been adopted in relation to construction cases since 2005 (following consultation with TCC judges and court users at all main court centres around the country) and, I

---

[82] I.e. one of the district judges who is a "district judge of the High Court" pursuant to section 100(4) of the Senior Courts Act 1981.
[83] This point was made, for example, in the discussion following the President of the Law Society's presentation at the London seminar on 10th July 2009.
[84] The standard directions should be available online in amendable form.

understand, has proved satisfactory.[85] The directions should ideally set out a timetable for the entire action, including PTR and trial date or trial window.[86] Such paragraphs can of course be deleted in those cases where it would be premature to lay down the entire timetable for the action at the outset. The use of standard directions in the fast track, following the model set out in the appendix to CPR Part 28, has proved successful. In my view the time has now come to extend this approach.

5.4   Initial directions. In my view, a CMC should only be convened at the start of a multi-track case if some useful purpose is likely to be achieved, e.g. narrowing issues, focusing or limiting factual or expert evidence (as discussed in chapter 38 above),[87] deciding contested applications etc. Absent any order to the contrary, the procedure for securing case management directions at the start of a multi-track case should be that each party submits its proposed case management directions[88] to the court, together with any comments; the district judge then issues case management directions in writing, giving both parties permission to apply to vary within seven days. If any party or the court believes that some useful purpose will be achieved by holding a CMC at the outset, then that party may apply for such a hearing or the court may order such a hearing of its own motion before the "paper" procedure is followed. The objectives of this reform are (i) to save those costs which are sometimes incurred in purely formulaic CMCs and (ii) to ensure that when CMCs take place at an early stage in multi-track litigation, they serve some useful purpose.

5.5   Effective CMCs. Whenever a CMC does take place, it will be taking place for a serious purpose. Accordingly, the judge will have an active role and will be interventionist when required. All the feedback which I have received during the Costs Review indicates that (despite academic scepticism) both costs and time are saved by good case management. By good case management, I mean that a judge of relevant expertise takes a grip on the case, identifies the issues and gives directions which are focused upon the early resolution of those issues. I accept that this evidence is anecdotal, although it is supported by my own experience both as a barrister and as a judge.

5.6   Case management after initial directions. The majority of multi-track cases for which initial directions are given will settle before there is need for any case management hearing or further hearing. The case management hearings which may be required after the initial directions have been given will vary from case to case. There may need to be one or more CMCs. Alternatively, the case may proceed directly to the PTR. The initial case management directions should stipulate (a) if required, the dates for future CMCs and (b) in any event, the date for the PTR. Dates for future CMCs could be (a) vacated if not required or (b) changed by agreement between the parties and the court or by order of the court. The guiding principle in setting or vacating dates for CMCs should be that the purpose of case management by the court is to progress cases justly and expeditiously and to save costs (not to incur costs needlessly).

---

[85] See the case management and directions form at appendix B to the second edition of the Technology and Construction Court Guide which is available online at http://www.hmcourts-service.gov.uk/docs/tcc_guide.htm. These cases are managed by TCC judges, rather than district judges.

[86] See paragraph 5.7 below.

[87] For example, in some personal injury cases a CMC is required at the outset in order to define the scope of expert evidence. In chapter 38 above I propose that the court should, in appropriate cases, give directions which will limit and focus the factual and/or expert evidence to be called.

[88] These will usually take the form of the standard directions for that type of case, with suggested amendments.

5.7   Pre-trial review. PTRs in multi-track cases are held pursuant to CPR rule 29.7. The purpose of the PTR is (a) to ensure that all existing orders have been complied with and that the case is ready for trial; and (b) to give such directions as are appropriate in respect of the conduct of the trial. It may also be an occasion for settlement negotiations, which would otherwise be postponed to the eve of trial. The PTR should, so far as practicable, be conducted by the trial judge. It should only be dispensed with if all parties and the court agree that no useful purpose would be served by the PTR. In that event, any pre-trial directions should be given on paper.

5.8   Fixing the trial date. The point has frequently been urged in consultation that early fixing of the trial date concentrates minds and promotes settlement. The court can fix trial dates early in the knowledge that the great majority of cases will settle. The benefits of such early listing, in my view, outweigh the drawback that occasionally clashes of trials will occur. Experience shows that skilled listing officers can make optimal use of judicial resources with a very low rate of mishaps. I therefore propose that trial dates or trial windows should be fixed at an early stage of every multi-track case and, so far as possible, in the initial case management directions. If this recommendation is accepted, CPR rule 29.8 (which provides for the fixing of trial dates at a late stage) will require amendment.

5.9   Pre-reading. It is vital that the judge is given, and also makes use of, sufficient time for pre-reading. At the moment there is considerable concern amongst practitioners that many interim hearings are undermined because judges have not had proper opportunity to pre-read.

5.10   Summary. The reforms which I advocate in this section have two crucial elements: (i) streamlining the process and dispensing with unnecessary interim hearings; and (ii) ensuring that any interim hearing which does take place will promote expeditious disposal of the case and saving of costs.

5.11   Need for research. Professor Zander has pointed out that there needs to be more research on the effects of case management. The RAND Study in the USA found that case management by US federal courts[89] tended to increase costs rather than reduce them.[90] A research study on the effects of case management in England and Wales, conducted on a similar scale to the RAND Study, would be of considerable benefit. If any university proposes to carry out such research, it may be sensible to start after any reforms consequential upon this report have been implemented. I do not make this matter the subject of a specific recommendation. However, I draw the attention of the academic community to the need for such research.

5.12   Recommendations. I recommend that:

(i)   A menu of standard paragraphs for case management directions for each type of multi-track case of common occurrence should be prepared and made available to all district judges both in hard copy and online in amendable form.

(ii)   A CMC should only be convened at the outset of a multi-track case if some useful purpose is likely to be achieved (for example, defining the scope of

---

[89] For a summary of the US costs rules, see PR chapter 60. The role of the federal courts is discussed in paragraph 60.1.4.
[90] *"An Evaluation of Judicial Case Management Under the Civil Justice Reform Act"* (1996) by RAND Corporation's Institute For Civil Justice, discussed by Professor Zander in two articles both entitled *"How does judicial case management work?"* (1997) 147 NLJ 353 and (1997) 147 NLJ 539.

factual or expert evidence). Otherwise the initial case management directions should be dealt with on paper.

(iii)   Subsequent CMCs should be held if they are needed to progress the case justly and expeditiously or to save costs.

(iv)   The PTR should, so far as practicable, be conducted by the trial judge. The PTR should be dispensed with if it is agreed that it would serve no useful purpose, in which case any pre-trial directions should be given on paper.

(v)   In multi-track cases the entire timetable for the action, including trial date or trial window, should be drawn up at as early a stage as is practicable. If possible, the trial date or trial window should be included in the initial case management directions. CPR rule 29.8 should be amended accordingly.

(vi)   Every interim hearing which is held should be an occasion for effective case management. Before every interim hearing the judge should be given, and should make use of, sufficient time for pre-reading.

6. ENFORCEMENT OF PROTOCOLS, RULES AND DIRECTIONS

6.1   <u>Pre-action protocols.</u> I am satisfied on the basis of all the evidence which has come in during Phase 2 that there are serious problems of non-compliance with pre-action protocols. These problems arise in many areas of litigation. Both claimants and defendants (or their insurers) are culpable. See, for example, chapters 22 and 23 above in respect of personal injuries litigation and clinical negligence litigation. The remedy, in my view, is to permit applications to the court in order to deal with serious instances of abuse or non-compliance. There is legislative precedent for pre-claim intervention by the court. Section 33 of the Senior Courts Act 1981 and section 52 of the County Courts Act 1984 permit applications for disclosure of documents before a claim has been made. I recommend that primary legislation should permit applications to be made before proceedings have been commenced, in respect of breaches of pre-action protocols.

6.2   I recommend that CPR rule 25.1 should be amended so as to permit any party to apply to the court if another party is failing to comply with a pre-action protocol and thereby causing serious prejudice to the applicant. The remedies which should be available upon such application should be any of the following directions:

(i)   That the parties are relieved from the obligation to comply or further comply with the protocol.

(ii)   That a party do take any step which might be required in order to comply with the protocol.

(iii)   That the party in default do pay such costs as may be summarily assessed by the court as compensation for losses caused by that default.

(iv)   That the party in default do forego such costs as may be specified in the event that it subsequently secures a favourable costs order.

(v)   If the case is in the fast track, that the fixed costs regime do cease to apply to that case.

I am not persuaded that it would be appropriate to include the "show cause" order suggested by APIL.[91] I accept that such an order is appropriate in the mesothelioma

---

[91] As to which see paragraph 2.8 of chapter 22 above.

cases, because of the special circumstances of those cases. However, such an order is not appropriate in the general run of personal injury cases where there is non-compliance with the protocol.

6.3   The proposed new provision has the potential to generate costs and satellite litigation unless closely controlled. I recommend that applications under this provision be dealt with either on paper or orally, as the court may direct. Sometimes a paper application may be quicker and cheaper. On other occasions, when the parties are minded to create a snowstorm of written submissions, responses, counter-arguments and so forth, the simplest course is for the judge to hold a short hearing, at which he or she will deal firmly with (a) any material breaches of the protocol or (b) any abuses of the application procedure.

6.4   The new procedure which I am proposing must not be allowed to get out of hand. I recommend that the Court of Appeal should take an early opportunity to give firm and consistent guidance to the profession in order to stamp out (a) frivolous applications under the new provision and (b) pre-action conduct which makes a mockery of the protocols.

6.5   <u>Enforcement of rules and directions generally.</u> There is a wide spread of views about this issue, amongst both practitioners and distinguished academic commentators. The conclusions to which I have come are as follows. First, the courts should set realistic timetables for cases and not impossibly tough timetables in order to give an impression of firmness. Secondly, courts at all levels have become too tolerant of delays and non-compliance with orders. In so doing they have lost sight of the damage which the culture of delay and non-compliance is inflicting upon the civil justice system. The balance therefore needs to be redressed. However, I do not advocate the extreme course which was canvassed as one possibility in PR paragraph 43.4.21 or any approach of that nature.

6.6   <u>Comparison with overseas.</u> The shift in balance which I am advocating for England and Wales has echoes elsewhere across the common law world. See, for example, the civil procedure reforms which are to be introduced in Ontario in January 2010;[92] the massive procedural reforms introduced in Hong Kong on 2nd April 2009; and the strict approach to case management adopted by the Australian Federal Court in respect of those cases which can be tried within eight days.[93] The decision of the High Court of Australia in *Aon Risk Services Australia Ltd v Australia National University* [2009] HCA 27 marks a much tougher attitude by that court to delays by parties. The decision also signals a clear shift in the balance which is struck between case management considerations and pure justice.

6.7   <u>Proposed rule change.</u> I recommend that sub-paragraphs (a) to (i) of CPR rule 3.9 be repealed and replaced by:

"(a)   the requirement that litigation should be conducted efficiently and at proportionate cost; and

(b)   the interests of justice in the particular case."

This form of words does not preclude the court taking into account all of the matters listed in the current paragraphs (a) to (i). However, it simplifies the rule and avoids

---

[92] Outlined in chapter 61 of the Preliminary Report.
[93] Described in PR paragraphs 58.4.15 and 58.4.16. Since the publication of the Preliminary Report the fast track procedure has been extended from the Federal Court in Melbourne to the Federal Court across the whole of Australia. I am informed by the Chief Justice that it is working effectively.

the need for judges to embark upon a lengthy recitation of factors. It also signals the change of balance which I am advocating.

6.8   Judicial monitoring. Securing compliance with case management directions is far preferable to punishing non-compliance. I therefore recommend that, if and in so far as time allows, judges or clerks on their behalf should contact parties at appropriate stages in order to enquire what progress has been made in complying with orders and directions. I am told by practitioners who have litigated in the USA that nothing galvanises lawyers into action more effectively than an enquiry from the judge as to how they are getting on.

7. LEADERSHIP FROM THE COURT OF APPEAL

7.1   Consistent guidance re interpretation of the CPR. The criticisms of the Court of Appeal for giving inconsistent guidance are not accepted. Until July 2006 Lord Justice Brooke was usually a member of the Court in any case where interpretation of the Civil Procedure Rules arose. This led to a high degree of consistency amongst those judgments. I do accept, however, that no lord justice has fulfilled this role since 2006. I recommend that the Master of the Rolls should designate two lords justices, at least one of whom will so far as possible be a member of any constitution of the civil division of the Court of Appeal, which is called upon to consider issues concerning the interpretation or application of the CPR. In this way consistency of guidance concerning the interpretation of the CPR will be promoted. Consistency of guidance will be particularly important in relation to appeals concerning sanctions for non-compliance with orders and relief from sanctions.

7.2   Upholding case management decisions. It is a well-established principle that the Court of Appeal will be reluctant to interfere with case management decisions made by a first instance judge who has applied the correct principles, unless the decision is "*so plainly wrong that it must be regarded as outside the generous ambit of discretion entrusted to the judge*".[94] Concern has recently been expressed that, despite this principle, the Court of Appeal is on occasions too ready to substitute its own views on case management issues.[95] It would not be right for me to comment on the merits of individual decisions. Nevertheless, going forward, I do regard it as vital that the Court of Appeal supports first instance judges who make robust but fair case management decisions. If the costs of litigation generally are driven up by the Court of Appeal's efforts to protect a party against the consequences of his lawyers' mistakes in an individual case, many other litigants will be denied access to justice altogether. Furthermore, whenever permission is granted to appeal against a case management decision, the timetable for the litigation in question is thrown into disarray.

7.3   The comments made in paragraph 7.2 above are of a general nature. If the recommendation in paragraph 7.1 above is accepted, the two nominated lords justices will have a significant influence in determining where the balance should be struck in relation to case management appeals.

7.4   District judges sitting as assessors. When costs issues arise, the Court of Appeal sometimes sits with a costs judge as assessor. Consideration should also be given to the possibility of the Court of Appeal sitting with an experienced district

---

[94] See *Royal & Sun Alliance Insurance Plc v T & N Ltd* [2002] EWCA Civ 1964 at [38] and *Walbrook Trustee (Jersey) Ltd v Fattal* [2008] EWCA Civ 427 at [33].
[95] See Stephanie Wilkins, "*Collins v Gordon: Is postponing trial a measure of last resort?*" (2009) 28 CJQ 306.

judge as assessor when case management issues arise. This could be particularly important in relation to fast track cases, which may be outside the recent experience of lords justices. Any guidance given by the Court of Appeal in relation to fast track cases has far-reaching effects.

8. RECOMMENDATIONS

8.1   I make the following recommendations:

(i)   Measures should be taken to promote the assignment of cases to designated judges with relevant expertise.

(ii)   A menu of standard paragraphs for case management directions for each type of case of common occurrence should be prepared and made available to all district judges both in hard copy and online in amendable form.

(iii)   CMCs and PTRs should either (a) be used as occasions for effective case management or (b) be dispensed with and replaced by directions on paper. Where such interim hearings are held, the judge should have proper time for pre-reading.

(iv)   In multi-track cases the entire timetable for the action, including trial date or trial window, should be drawn up at as early a stage as is practicable.

(v)   Pre-action applications should be permitted in respect of breaches of pre-action protocols.

(vi)   The courts should be less tolerant than hitherto of unjustified delays and breaches of orders. This change of emphasis should be signalled by amendment of CPR rule 3.9. If and in so far as it is possible, courts should monitor the progress of the parties in order to secure compliance with orders and pre-empt the need for sanctions.

(vii)   The Master of the Rolls should designate two lords justices, at least one of whom will so far as possible be a member of any constitution of the civil division of the Court of Appeal, which is called upon to consider issues concerning the interpretation or application of the CPR.

(viii)   Consideration should be given to the possibility of the Court of Appeal sitting with an experienced district judge as assessor when case management issues arise.

CHAPTER 40. COSTS MANAGEMENT

INDEX

1. INTRODUCTION

1.1   **Preliminary Report.** Costs management is discussed in chapter 48 of the Preliminary Report. That chapter canvasses, as one method of controlling costs, that the court should undertake costs management in conjunction with case management. A number of possible approaches to costs management are considered in that chapter.

1.2   **Definitions.** In this chapter I refer to the Technology and Construction Court as the "TCC". I shall refer to Precedent H, which is annexed to the Costs Practice Direction (the "Costs PD") as "Form H".

1.3   **Form H and Form HA.** Form H is the form in which parties are currently required to lodge estimates of costs: see paragraph 6.5 of the Costs PD. Throughout the Costs Review there has been widespread criticism of Form H. Also I am told that many litigants ignore the requirement to lodge estimates and that, when they do lodge estimates, they seldom use Form H. Form HA is the precedent which parties are required to use if they are subject to the Practice Direction – Defamation Proceedings Costs Management Scheme. Form HA is in a completely different format from Form H and represents an attempt to meet some of the criticisms of Form H. It is anticipated that further improvements can be made to the forms in the light of experience during the pilot exercises.

1.4   **The essence of costs management.** The essential elements of costs management are the following:

(i)   The parties prepare and exchange litigation budgets or (as the case proceeds) amended budgets.

(ii)   The court states the extent to which those budgets are approved.

(iii)   So far as possible, the court manages the case so that it proceeds within the approved budgets.

(iv)   At the end of the litigation, the recoverable costs of the winning party are assessed in accordance with the approved budget.

1.5   Issues for consideration.   If costs management becomes a feature of civil litigation in the future, many issues will have to be considered before any set of costs management rules is drawn up. In particular:

(i)   What form should the litigation budgets for exchange take?

(ii)   What procedure should be adopted for securing court approval of budgets or amended budgets?

(iii)   To what extent should the last approved budget be binding, alternatively influential, upon the final assessment of costs?

(iv)   In so far as the last approved budget is binding, should it operate as an upper limit upon recoverable costs or should it operate as a form of assessment in advance?

(v)   What form of training should lawyers and judges receive in order to perform the above tasks?

(vi)   What steps should be taken to ensure that the process is cost-effective, i.e. that the litigation costs saved exceed the costs of the process?

1.6   Recent developments in Australia.   In chapter 58 of the Preliminary Report I outlined the civil justice reforms which are being implemented in Australia, in order to control costs and promote access to justice.   Since the publication of the Preliminary Report, the Access to Justice (Civil Litigation Reforms) Amendment Bill 2009 (Cth) has been brought before the Commonwealth Parliament.   This bill contains provisions which allow the court to direct lawyers to submit estimates of costs, including *"(i) the costs that the lawyer will charge to the party; and (ii) any other costs that the party will have to pay in the event that the party is unsuccessful in the proceeding or part of the proceeding"*.[96]

1.7   The Attorney-General's Department of the Australian Government published a report by its Access to Justice Taskforce in September 2009, entitled *"A Strategic framework for Access to Justice in the Federal Civil Justice System"*.[97]   The authors argue that lack of information about costs restricts the ability of people to make decisions about dispute resolution. Greater transparency about costs would improve access to justice. The authors propose that, in the Federal Court,[98] lawyers should be required to provide their clients with a litigation budget and to provide copies of that budget both to the court and to opposing parties.[99]   Recommendation 9.3 of the Access to Justice Taskforce is as follows:

"The Attorney General's Department should work with the Federal Court to develop options to require parties to litigation in the Federal Court to exchange with each other and the court a litigation budget which includes an

---

[96] Section 37N(3)(b).
[97] Available online at
http://www.ag.gov.au/www/agd/agd.nsf/Page/Publications_AStrategicFrameworkforAccesstoJusticein theFederalCivilJusticeSystem.
[98] As to which, see PR paragraphs 58.2.15 to 58.2.19.
[99] See the passage entitled *"Exchange of litigation budgets"* on pages 125 and 126.

estimate of the costs identified by reference to the stages and activities the party proposes are necessary to progress to resolution.

As an initial step this Recommendation could be implemented as a pilot, with a judicial discretion to order the preparation of such a budget."

2. THE BIRMINGHAM COSTS MANAGEMENT PILOT

(i) Nature of the pilot

2.1   Setting up of pilot.   In order to test some of the reforms canvassed in the Preliminary Report, I set up a pilot exercise in the Birmingham Mercantile Court and TCC (the "Birmingham pilot").   This was a voluntary pilot, the nature of which I explained at a joint meeting of the Birmingham Mercantile Court Users Committee and the Birmingham TCC Users Committee, held on 26th May 2009.[100]   The pilot commenced on 1st June 2009 and will conclude on 31st May 2010.

2.2   Guidelines.   The Guidelines for the Birmingham pilot read as follows:

"1   The parties will submit detailed budgets of their 'estimates of costs' as attachments to their Case Management Information Sheets and Pre-trial Check Lists (or at such other time as ordered by the court).

2   At the CMC[101] and PTR,[102] the judge will have before him/her these detailed budgets of both parties for the litigation.   He/she will take into account the costs involved in each proposed procedural step when giving case management directions.   The judge:

(i)   Will, either by agreement between the parties or after hearing argument, record approval or disapproval of each side's budget for each step in the action.

(ii)   May order attendance at regular hearings (by telephone if appropriate), the purpose of which is to monitor expenditure. Parties will be expected to provide to the judge any budget revisions in good time before such hearings to enable the judge to prepare for the hearing.

(iii)   May include provision in the directions for any party to apply to the court for assistance if it considers that another party is behaving oppressively in seeking to cause that party to spend money unnecessarily.

3   The budgets will be in a standard Excel template form, as per the attached example.   Each side will include separately in its budget:

(i)   reasonable allowances for intended activities: e.g. disclosure (if appropriate, showing comparative electronic and paper methodology), preparation of witness statements, obtaining expert reports, mediation or any other steps which are deemed necessary for the particular case;

(ii)   reasonable allowances for specified contingencies e.g. specific disclosure application (if an opponent fails to give proper

---

[100] See paragraph 2.2 below.
[101] Case management conference.
[102] Pre-trial review.

disclosure); resisting applications (if made inappropriately by opponent).

4   The budget must include reasonable allowances for disbursements, in particular, court fees, counsel's fees and any mediator or expert fees.

5   It is intended that a party's budget will be no more detailed than that which the solicitor provides to his client for the purposes of paragraph 2.03 of the Solicitors' Code of Conduct 2007. Accordingly, no costs should be involved on either side in the preparation of such estimate. A budget provided to the court will not (without consent) be released to any other party, until that party is ready to exchange but it is expected that the parties should discuss their budgets during the budget building process and before CMC, as they should do in the instance of electronic disclosure (CPR 31PD2A.2).

6   At each subsequent CMC, PTR and at trial the judge will receive updated figures, in order to ascertain what departures have occurred from each side's budget and why. A judge will, either by agreement between the parties or after hearing argument, approve or disapprove such departures from the previous budget as have occurred.

7   If any party exceeds the costs previously estimated for any activity, it shall notify all other parties and the court of the amount of the excess.

8   Directions orders produced at the end of CMCs will be given to the parties on each side by their respective lawyers, together with copies of the budgets which the court has approved or disapproved.

9   Bearing in mind that in the majority of TCC and Mercantile cases costs are the most important single issue, the judge will seek to manage the costs of the litigation as well as the case itself. When the court or a party relies upon one party's estimate of costs, the judge will record the fact of such reliance in the case management directions (for the purpose of any future argument concerning paragraph 6.5A of the Costs Practice Direction).

10   The objective of costs management is to control the litigation in such manner that the costs of each party are proportionate to the amount at stake and to ensure that the parties are on an equal footing.

11   At the end of the litigation the judge conducting a detailed or summary assessment will have regard to the budget estimates of the receiving party and will generally approve as reasonable and proportionate any costs claimed which fall within the previously approved total.

12   Where all parties to an action agree that costs management as described above should be undertaken by the court, the claimant's solicitor should notify the court manager of such agreement on behalf of all parties."

2.3   <u>Template form for budget.</u> The template form for the budget referred to in paragraph 3 of the Birmingham Guidelines is at appendix 9 to this report. It is in excel format, so that many of the calculations are done automatically. The form has been made as user friendly as possible, in an attempt to overcome some of the criticisms of Form H. I shall refer to this document as the "Birmingham form".

(ii) Monitoring the pilot

2.4   Monitoring. One of my judicial assistants has made two visits to Birmingham to attend case management conferences ("CMCs"). She has talked to the judges and also to solicitors and counsel in a number of the cases. She has also received and collated written reports from the Birmingham courts about cases proceeding under the pilot. For the purposes of this report I have looked at the experience of the pilot over the first five months, namely June to October 2009. As previously mentioned, the pilot is running for a year. A full assessment will not be possible until after the pilot has concluded on 31st May 2010.

2.5   Reports from the Birmingham Mercantile Court and the Birmingham TCC. The Birmingham Mercantile Court and the Birmingham TCC have been sending in reports of cases proceeding in their lists since 1st June 2009. The picture which emerges is as follows. The rate of take up of the pilot was initially (and unsurprisingly) slow with the majority of cases heard by the court choosing not to adopt the pilot. The sums in issue in the cases adopting the pilot ranged between £50,000 and £450,000 and the costs budgets prepared by the claimant solicitors on those cases ranged between £20,000 and £158,000. The defendant solicitor costs budgets ranged between £18,000 and £121,000.

2.6   Extent of participation by users of both courts. As at 31st October 2009, the parties in eleven cases in the Mercantile Court or TCC have voluntarily participated in the pilot. In a number of other cases the parties have lodged or agreed to lodge budgets in the standard form, even though not submitting to the provisions of the pilot.

(iii) Experience of solicitors

2.7   Feedback gathered by my judicial assistant. Completing the budget form is a new and unwelcome exercise for many solicitors. Some solicitors find the task easier than others. Apparently the exercise, if done efficiently, takes about two and a half hours. One solicitor commented that completing the budget form is a useful exercise, because it forces the solicitor to focus on the issues and on what needs to be done to build his case. It is reported that the parties often find it helpful to see what the other side's costs are likely to be. Commercial parties find the quantum of their potential adverse costs risk to be useful information in evaluating whether to continue pursuing or defending the claim. Indeed the Birmingham form has also assisted some solicitors in fulfilling their obligations under rule 2.03(1) of the Solicitors' Code of Conduct 2007.[103] I should add that, although completing the Birmingham form takes time, no-one has yet suggested that this exercise takes longer than completing Form H.

2.8   Direct feedback from one lawyer. I have recently had a meeting with a lawyer, in order to receive some direct feedback. The personal view was that the Birmingham form was a useful document, which this lawyer used as a template for giving estimates to clients. In the event that a matter is litigated, the form can then be updated for use at the first CMC. It took this lawyer about two hours to complete the form properly. Some practitioners may however under-estimate in their budgets. Therefore it would help if the costs management rules had more "teeth". Also, the lawyer was concerned that practitioners may unnecessarily "tweak" the form, which extends the costs discussion at the CMC. This lawyer has noticed that the Birmingham judges are now "comfortable" with costs management. That aspect is

---

[103] Which requires them to provide certain information about costs to their clients.

dealt with at the hearing in about five or so minutes. Even if there are serious objections by one party to an opponent's budget, the matter can usually be dealt with quite swiftly. In this lawyer's view, the Birmingham costs management system is beneficial. It prevents over-resourcing of cases.

(iv) Experience of judges

2.9 <u>Usefulness of budget estimates lodged.</u> Judges report that they find the parties' budget estimates (set out in the new standard form) to be an extremely useful adjunct to case management.[104] They sometimes approve the budget as lodged and sometimes approve a different figure.[105] Judge Simon Brown states that CMCs take longer, if costs management is included. Thus greater demands are made upon the resources of the court. On the other hand, he adds:

> "The Costs Schedules are wonderful tools for both Costs and Case proper management – indeed essential. They are most effective when the cost paying customers are present at CMCs. Perhaps most importantly, it ensures that clients (they are the court consumers, customers and users not the lawyers) know how much they are at risk for if they are 'unsuccessful' (and in some quite astonishing cases I have had even what their <u>own</u> lawyers bills are as they do not appear to have been told!). I believe that most appearing in front of me at CMCs have better been able to make a Cost benefit analysis of their litigation due to the exchange of cost schedules and the court giving some guidance at that stage. I have had two cases settle within the week of a CMC. In another case, the barrister said the parties were now equipped for mediation without further expenditure in preparing the case towards trial – he said that as a mediator himself the exchange of such costs schedules was the first thing he suggested before any mediation."

2.10 <u>Preparation time.</u> Judge Brown reports that reading and considering the costs budget forms takes about 15 minutes. Judge David Grant reports that it takes about 15 to 30 minutes. I suspect that the slight difference is due to the divergence between mercantile and TCC cases. Some TCC cases involve a large amount of technical detail, which will be the subject of factual and expert evidence (as well as generating disclosure issues).

2.11 <u>Hearing time.</u> I have asked the Birmingham judges how much time at hearings is spent dealing with costs management issues. Judge Brown's response is as follows:

> "This does not take much extra time in court. It all becomes part of the case management process, which is more thorough than it was before we had the costs management pilot tool to help us come to grips with proportionality. I now rarely just sign off agreed consent orders for directions as I used to. I am able to ask what the preparation plans for the litigation are by each party and how much they really plan to spend in fulfilling them. It does take some extra time but it makes case management much more realistic e.g. I ask about disclosure and how much they really want bearing in mind the costs of doing it e.g. electronic disclosure which may require an expert at some cost. I have increasingly used the cost benefit analysis here to order iterative specific disclosure rather than blanket standard disclosure. I am also much better

---

[104] See also *Earles v Barclays Bank PLC* [2009] EWHC 2500 (Mercantile) at [85].
[105] Which may be lower or higher.

able to control experts costs, and increasingly use a single joint expert if I feel the court will need expertise it does not have e.g. tax or investments experts."

Judge Grant's response to the same question is as follows:

"An additional 15 to 30 minutes to hear submissions and make the appropriate order. This element can vary significantly, depending on the circumstances of the case and my experience here is thus rather different to that of HHJ Brown QC. Sometimes I have had really quite detailed submissions on what the proper order should be; perhaps this is not surprising as costs are an important aspect of the case, and the order made per the Costs Pilot Scheme will have a significant impact on the way the case is conducted thereafter."

2.12 <u>Pilot cases which have concluded.</u> No case subject to the Birmingham pilot has yet proceeded to trial, nor is likely to for some time, given the time lag between first CMC and trial. Some of the pilot cases have now settled. It appears from the comments of Judge Brown that the costs management process (a) assists the parties in making informed settlement decisions and (b) may help to accelerate the settlement process.

3. DEFAMATION COSTS MANAGEMENT PILOT

3.1 <u>The pilot.</u> A different form of costs management, which has more teeth, is being piloted in defamation cases proceeding in London and Manchester for the 12 month period commencing 1st October 2009. This pilot, unlike the Birmingham pilot, is mandatory. The rules for the pilot are set out in the Practice Direction – Defamation Proceedings Costs Management Scheme, which supplements CPR Part 51.[106] I shall refer to this as the "defamation pilot". The budget form which the parties are required to complete (adapted as necessary to the circumstances of the case) is Form HA, annexed to the Practice Direction.

3.2 <u>The practice direction.</u> The practice direction requires the parties to lodge budgets, or revised budgets, as a case proceeds setting out the assumptions on which they are based. The court will approve or disapprove the budgets or revised budgets. It will manage the costs of the litigation as well as the case itself in a manner which is proportionate to the value of the claim and the reputational issues at stake. Paragraph 5.6 of the practice direction provides:

"The judge conducting a detailed or summary assessment will have regard to the budget estimates of the receiving party and to any view previously expressed by the court pursuant to paragraph 5.3.[107] Unless there has been a significant change in circumstances the judge will approve as reasonable and proportionate any costs claimed which fall within the last previously approved budget. Save in exceptional circumstances the judge will not approve as reasonable and proportionate any costs claimed which do not fall within the last previously approved budget."

---

[106] Set out in the second supplement to the 2009 White Book at pages 69-71.
[107] Paragraph 5.3 provides as follows: "*At any case management conference, costs management conference or pre-trial review, the court will, either by agreement between the parties or after hearing argument, record approval or disapproval of each side's budget and, in the event of disapproval, will record the court's view.*"

3.3   No feedback available yet. At the time of writing no feedback is available from the defamation pilot. However, it is anticipated that data from the pilot will become available during 2010. I am told by a defamation solicitor, who happens to be experienced in costs budgeting, that it takes him about an hour to prepare an estimate of costs for his clients and a further half hour to set that information out in Form HA, as required by the practice direction.[108] However, it is hoped that some solicitors will avoid duplication of effort by using Form HA to prepare an estimate both for their client and for the court.

4. MEETINGS AND SEMINARS DURING PHASE 2

4.1   Meeting with Pinsent Masons LLP. On 18th May 2009 I attended a meeting with Pinsent Masons LLP, at which the firm demonstrated its proprietary costs budgeting software. The software ("Smartplan") generates budget costs for each stage of an action, on the basis of the assumptions which are keyed in. As the assumptions change (for example, there is an unexpected order for expert evidence or a postponement of the trial date), the assumptions can be revised and new budget figures are automatically generated. Smartplan can aide project management in that it generates, on a daily basis if needed, comparisons between (a) actual costs and disbursements and (b) estimated costs and disbursements.

4.2   Meeting with the Users Committees of the Birmingham Mercantile Court and the Birmingham TCC. On 26th May 2009 I attended a joint meeting of the Users Committees of the Birmingham Mercantile Court and the Birmingham TCC in order to discuss costs management. A range of views were expressed concerning the potential problems of costs management and the potential benefits. Some speakers were sceptical about the court becoming involved in costs issues. A number of speakers considered that the existing Form H was unsatisfactory and that the form proposed for the Birmingham pilot looked more promising. It was pointed out that budgets can change as the case proceeds. On the other hand, it was pointed out that solicitors have been producing costs budgets for arbitrations (where the arbitrator has power to cap recoverable costs)[109] for many years. It was also suggested that an exchange of costs budgets would assist parties who were going to mediation. At the end of the meeting I took a vote. The majority of solicitors present were willing to participate in a voluntary costs management pilot subject, of course, to the approval of their clients in any individual case.

4.3   Commercial Litigation Association annual conference. The annual conference of the Commercial Litigation Association included a session on costs. Most speakers were supportive of the proposals for costs management. However, one speaker criticised the Birmingham form for setting out the "*bricks*" (witness statements, expert reports, CMCs etc) but not allowing for the "*cement*" which holds litigation together. By "*cement*" he meant emails to the client, reviews, strategy meetings and so forth.[110] Other speakers stated that openness about costs was necessary, in the same way that the CPR required openness about other aspects of litigation. The point was made that judges must take more interest in costs than hitherto, and that for costs management to work cases must be assigned to specific judges. Costs Judge Haworth expressed the view that the Birmingham pilot showed the way forward. A

---

[108] See chapter 32 above, paragraph 5.3.
[109] See section 65 (1) of the Arbitration Act 1996.
[110] This criticism has been heeded. In the defamation costs management pilot a note under the various stages states: "*Assumed into the costs of each stage should be the time costs for (a) attendance on own client, (b) correspondence with the other party and (c) the general project and strategy management of each stage*".

costs draftsman stressed that all budgets must set out the assumptions on which they are based. It was suggested that costs judges could sit with other judges at costs management hearings. Indeed there would be fewer detailed assessments to be done by costs judges, if costs management were successful. The general view was that costs management was different from costs capping and that costs management was the way forward.

4.4   Commercial Litigation Funding Conference. At the Commercial Litigation Funding Conference on 23rd June 2009, organised by No5 Chambers, there was some discussion about costs management. Funders made the point that they require their solicitors to produce a realistic litigation budget and to stick to it. One speaker said that she allowed solicitors a 10% to 15% leeway from their budget. The general view of speakers from funding organisations was that budgets prepared for the client should be disclosed to the court; and that the court should manage both the timetable and the budget for the litigation. There was criticism of Form H. It was said that Form H was routinely ignored by litigants, without any demur from the court. In view of the interest in costs management expressed at this meeting, I set up a working group of representatives of third party funders to consider the issues in greater depth.[111] I shall summarise the working group's report in the next section.

4.5   CMS Cameron McKenna LLP meeting. On 30th June 2009 I attended a meeting with practitioners and clients of CMS Cameron McKenna LLP ("Camerons"). A number of speakers strongly supported the use of costs budgeting. One in-house counsel of a construction company stated that her company did not want to spend millions of pounds on litigation. Costs management by the court would assist both parties and would provide discipline for lawyers and clients. Even very large cases are projects and must be managed accordingly. Other in-house lawyers expressed similar views. I took a vote at the end of this discussion. There was a large number[112] of votes in favour of the court adopting costs management and seven votes against. Following the meeting Camerons conducted a survey of attendees and others. Of those who responded 73% agreed or strongly agreed with the proposition: *"Costs budgets should be used in most types of court proceedings (other than those involving fixed costs or no costs shifting) as a matter of course."*

4.6   Commercial litigators seminar. At the commercial litigators seminar on 13th July 2009,[113] hosted by Freshfields Bruckhaus Deringer LLP, there was some discussion about costs management towards the end. Speakers feared that that this would become another recipe for satellite litigation or that judges would not be able to perform the task properly. However, one speaker expressed support and anticipated that, with practice, courts would get better at costs management.

4.7   SMEs[114] seminar. At the SMEs seminar on 28th July 2009, hosted by Holman Fenwick Willan LLP, most speakers were strongly supportive of costs management. One speaker said that some companies would only litigate if the court undertook costs management. A recent survey of FTSE 100 and FTSE 250 companies showed that many would no longer accept hourly rates. One costs draftsman described his firm's costs budgeting software, which was similar to that referred to in paragraph 4.1 above. However, he had reservations about judges doing costs management, because they were not good at summary assessment. The general view was that certainty about costs was desirable and that costs management along the lines of the Birmingham pilot would promote this. Costs management would be important for

---

[111] See chapter 1 above, paragraph 3.16.
[112] A forest of raised arms, not counted.
[113] This seminar is discussed more fully in chapter 27 above.
[114] Small and medium enterprises.

SMEs. At the end of this discussion there were 16 votes in favour of costs management, four votes against and four abstentions.

4.8 <u>Case management seminar.</u> At the case management seminar on 29th July 2009, hosted by Mayer Brown International LLP, the merits of costs management were debated. One speaker stressed the difficulty of producing accurate budgets for big cases. Other speakers stressed the importance of transparency in respect of costs and the benefits of filing estimates in the Birmingham form. One speaker suggested that a dummy set of facts should be compiled and different firms should be asked to estimate the future litigation costs.[115] There were differing views as to whether costs budgeting would be easier than costs capping.

5. REPORT OF THE COSTS MANAGEMENT WORKING GROUP

5.1 <u>The working group.</u> As stated above, the working group was set up at the Commercial Litigation Funding Conference. The members were representatives of third party funders. Their report reflects the views of such funders.

5.2 <u>Gist of the report.</u> The gist of the working group's report is as follows. A realistic litigation budget is crucial for the funder. It forms a major part of the funder's decision whether to proceed. Thereafter it is an integral part of the funding agreement which governs the relationship between the claimant and the funder. The working group states:

> "It is certainly our experience that solicitors often fall into the trap of not subjecting the claim to a detailed enough costs and project management analysis at the outset.
>
> The common theme we detect is that lawyers simply do not explore cases in sufficient detail upfront in the way that funders do - it is a case of the client turning up, starting to tell the story and then receiving a letter of engagement setting out hourly rates and little more about the process. The client is then off and running, often with little notion of what the ultimate costs will or should be. No other commercial relationship is based on such high levels of uncertainty.
>
> If a sensible period of time is spent with the client at the outset, the client and the lawyer should be able together to figure out, at that point in time, what is likely to be involved in the case.
>
> Despite the perceived difficulty in predicting how a defendant might run a case, we feel that it is distinctly possible to assess what a case should cost at the outset by understanding what is going to be involved in the dispute, how long it is going to take, the number of documents and witnesses involved, whether an expert will be required and so on. Equally, it is simple to ascertain whether certain disbursements are likely to increase in amount over the life of an action e.g. Counsel's fees upon taking Silk etc.
>
> A common issue which we have experienced in varying degrees is that few lawyers explain to the client what the litigation process involves and therefore what they will be charging them. Lawyers tend to be over optimistic about

---

[115] This sensible suggestion might be taken up if my recommendations below in respect of Continuing Professional Development for solicitors and barristers are accepted.

how long a case will last, how much it will costs and how soon it will settle. This can reflect itself in the budget suggested by the lawyers. Certainly some funders sense that lawyers are afraid to tell their clients the full story of the costs implications for fear they might not appoint them. The funders' view is that it is far better that all concerned know what the journey looks like upfront rather than being disappointed almost immediately it is commenced.

Clearly any estimate/budget may be subject to '(un)known unknowns' in the course of the litigation and thus it is important that the new costs/case management culture allows costs budgets to be 'organic', living documents. But we feel that an experienced solicitor ought to be able to provide a working estimate, with contingencies factored in, such that in all the actual costs expended as against the predicted costs should not deviate by more than 20-25%."

5.3   The working group is not impressed by the current skills of judges, solicitors or barristers in relation to costs budgeting. It states:

"Our overarching concern is that from our experience few solicitors (and fewer barristers or their clerks) are equipped or really motivated to adequately manage litigation costs and litigation 'projects' in the most costs efficient manner. Certainly we are not aware of any professional training that the profession is provided at Law/Bar School as to costs or to management of claims. Moreover, we are bound to say that that lack of expertise/training is evident on the Bench too."

5.4   In relation to the judiciary the working group adds:

"We consider that more costs education for the Bench is required. Enormous variations have been seen in what Judges think elements of litigation should costs (which will depend on the nature of their erstwhile practice) and this is unhelpful. Somehow some sort of consistency needs to be achieved."

5.5   The working group maintains that the above deficiencies must be addressed if courts are to undertake costs management. Subject to that, the working group favours clear rules (not practice directions) allowing the court to control the parties' costs budgets and the costs of the proceedings generally. The working group then states:

"It seems to us that a key issue is for procedures to exist whereby at the outset the parties provide a detailed budget in respect of the action which they file at Court and spend some time with the Judge understanding what a given case involves in order that he/she is able to test the parties' lawyers' assumptions underpinning their respective budgets. If the Judge can sit down with the parties and test their assumptions he/she can better understand their predictions."

5.6   The working group regards Form H as a failure. It maintains that parties should provide regular updates of costs, which the court should assess. The working group considers that for costs management to work, each case must be assigned to a specific judge. In relation to the form in which budgets should be lodged the working group regards the Birmingham form as a great improvement of Form H. However, it proposes that provision for mediation should be added.[116]   The working group also

---

[116] This advice has been heeded in drafting Form HA for the defamation pilot.

proposes some more specific amendments, the relevance of which will depend upon other issues in the Costs Review (e.g. the future of conditional fee agreements).

6. WRITTEN SUBMISSIONS DURING PHASE 2

6.1 A huge volume of written submissions have come in addressing the merits and demerits of costs management. Since many of those submissions cover similar ground (and this is no fault of the contributors) I shall not embark upon the daunting task of producing a précis of all relevant submissions. Instead I shall highlight a small number of submissions, which neatly encapsulate the differing views and the issues.

6.2 <u>Council of Her Majesty's Circuit Judges.</u> The most elegant and forceful attack upon the whole concept of costs management was delivered by Her Majesty's Council of Circuit Judges. The Council states in its written submissions:

> "Judicial cost management. We view with trepidation and antipathy yet another area of out of court invigilation which it might be suggested the judiciary should take on. Consideration of parties' budgets would be a very significant and difficult exercise. It would also be very time consuming. If a Judge is worrying his way through two rival litigation budgets, assuming he had somehow acquired the expertise to do so, he will not be trying cases. Judicial productivity would be likely to fall as fast as morale if we are required to do this work. It is work at which (whatever training may be provided) a judge is likely to be far less competent than the solicitors whose budgets are being managed. If the budget management was badly done it could cripple the proper preparation of a case. It would be likely to result in much ancillary litigation. We are not in favour of moving down this road, however beguilingly professors may argue for a quasi business approach to litigation 'projects'. The best way to minimise costs is for skilled people to work briskly and economically because they want to, not because somebody is trying to control them."

6.3 <u>Association of Her Majesty's District Judges.</u> The Association of Her Majesty's District Judges commends the approach of District Judge Lethem, as set out in section 5 of PR chapter 45. This approach involves both costs capping and costs management. However, the Association acknowledges that to some extent a party can choose how much to spend on a piece of litigation and that the court should not devote too much time and money on costs control. The Association then states:

> "There is surely scope for tightening the rules that require solicitors to keep their client/the funder informed about the amount of costs incurred to a certain point in the litigation and provide an estimate of future costs and so we agree the approach suggested at Chapter 48, 3.15,[117] namely that costs statements and estimates should be provided to the client, and filed at court, at regular intervals and that the costs capping facility (see 8.7 above)[118] should be available."

6.4 One regional costs judge in his Phase 2 submission takes the proposal one stage further. He proposes costs budgeting for higher value personal injury and clinical negligence cases. He then states:

---

[117] This is a reference to PR paragraph 48.3.15.
[118] This is a reference back to the paragraph commending the approach of District Judge Lethem.

"My main concern arising out of a system of prospective cost capping after the issue of proceedings is that by the time the court intervenes, significant costs have already been incurred, negating the ability of the court to control all costs adequately. To try to address this concern the proposal advanced sees court intervention on costs pre-issue with cost control dating back to the outset of the claim. Whilst I accept that this inevitably will result in an increase in court intervention at an early stage, I hope that there will be a reduction of court involvement at a later stage."

6.5　Bar Council. The Bar Council is critical of the proposals for costs management set out in chapter 48 of the Preliminary Report, in particular at PR paragraph 48.3.21. The Bar Council states:

"We can understand the initial attraction of these sorts of orders in certain cases (principally those rare cases in which costs capping orders are made now). However, such an approach is neither necessary, nor appropriate across all civil litigation:

a.　Firstly, there is already considerable scope within the existing rules to control the unnecessary proliferation of costs, both on summary assessments made during the course of the proceedings, and at the conclusion of the proceedings, when costs unreasonably incurred at a particular stage of the proceedings can be challenged on assessment.

b.　Secondly, we suspect that such orders are likely in many cases to be highly controversial. One can well imagine, for example, a defendant with a weak case seeking to press the Court to limit the costs that might be incurred by the claimant to a level beneath that which the claimant might reasonably need to incur to establish its case. Not only is this likely to lead to a proliferation of arguments, essentially about costs, but the result is unlikely to satisfy either party.

c.　Thirdly, and as we have said more generally in relation to active case management, at the early stages of proceedings, the Court can, and should, use its case management powers to limit or simplify the evidence that it receives and the extent of disclosure, thereby effectively 'capping costs'.

d.　Fourthly, unless this is carried out by a judge wholly familiar with the detail of the cases, including the legal and factual complexities, costs management by the Court may well prove to be ineffective and unfair."

The Commercial Bar Association expresses similar views to those of the Bar Council.

6.6　Law Society. The Law Society takes a different view. It supports the proposals for costs management and sees the Birmingham pilot as a good starting point.[119] The Law Society sets out a helpful summary of what costs management entails:

---

[119] The Law Society criticises the short period of the Birmingham pilot and adds: "*To make matters worse, it takes place over the summer months further compounding this flaw.*" (Quite how the pilot could have begun before 1st June, given that the Preliminary Report proposing costs management was not published until May 2009, is not explained.)

"i)   Costs budgeting

This is a term which describes the association of a budget with specific steps in the course of civil litigation and has been extensively used by some firms of solicitors as part of the management of their retainer with their client. Some firms use computer programs which they have developed in house but others use an Excel spreadsheet which works effectively. The crucial characteristic is that budgeting takes place prospectively whereas other forms of costs management are reactive.

Budgeting is not costs capping although the terms have been used interchangeably by the profession and the judiciary for some years as this section of the Report makes clear.

ii)   Costs management – a form of project management

The Law Society's Civil Justice Committee supports Professor Peysner's approach to the project management of litigation and some of its members have worked with him in developing those ideas.[120] Support was also shown for the concept at the Law Society's Multi Track event in February 2009 which Jackson LJ attended.

In commercial litigation a database of hours per task is more elusive as the cases vary so much. However, this does not mean an allocation of time cannot be made. The database reposes within the collective experience of practitioners who apply their professional experience.

The Law Society agrees with the points made about a possible approach in Chapter 48 paragraphs 3.15-3.20 inclusive of the preliminary report. However, such project management will come at a price as budgets/estimates take time to prepare and authorise which will add to the costs of a case...

iii)   Taking costs management one stage further

If the cost of litigation is to be controlled then the 'price tags' referred to in paragraph of chapter 48 must be appended to stages and further restrictions must be placed on the steps parties may pursue taking into account the value and complexity of the case in question. Otherwise the realisation of proportionate litigation and effective case/costs management will not be achieved."

6.7   The Law Society states that costs will increase as a result of costs management. However, this is not a reason for not undertaking the exercise. In the Law Society's view, the additional costs generated *are likely to be offset by real savings if the budgeting regime is applied effectively*".

6.8   The Law Society states that judges should receive proper training in costs management. The Law Society agrees in principle[121] with the following six propositions set out in PR paragraph 48.3.28:

---

[120] Professor Peysner's views are summarised at PR paras 48.3.13-48.3.14.
[121] However, the Law Society adds, it should not be forgotten that restricting recoverable costs can lead to inequality of arms, as the court cannot restrict the amount that a party wishes to spend.

(i)   Litigation is in many instances a "project", which both parties are pursuing for purely commercial ends.

(ii)   Any normal project costing thousands (or indeed millions) of pounds would be run on a budget. Litigation should be no different.

(iii)   The peculiarity of litigation is that at the time when costs are being run up, no-one knows who will be paying the bill. There is sometimes the feeling that the more one spends, the more likely it is that the other side will end up paying the bill. This gives rise to a sort of "arms race".

(iv)   Under the present regime, neither party has any effective control over the (potentially recoverable) costs which the other side is running up.

(v)   In truth both parties have an interest in controlling total costs within a sensible original budget, because at least one of them will be footing the bill.

(vi)   The parties' interests may, in truth, be best served if the court (a) controls the level of recoverable costs at each stage of the action, or alternatively (b) makes less prescriptive orders (e.g. requiring notification when the budget for any stage is being overshot by, say, 20% or more).

6.9   Other submissions. For the reasons mentioned above, I do not attempt to summarise all the submissions on this topic individually. However, the majority of submissions are supportive of costs management, albeit with greater or lesser degrees of enthusiasm. Some respondents call for costs management to be carried out pre-issue.

6.10   Clients are somewhat keener on costs management than solicitors. Occasionally solicitors record, somewhat ruefully, that their clients are keener on costs management than they are. The Technology and Construction Solicitors Association ("TeCSA") argues that costs management would increase costs; that judges are not keen to do it; and that there are risks of judicial inconsistency. TeCSA then adds very fairly:

> "It is also necessary to record comments made by in-house representatives, which are strongly supportive of the costs management proposal, as a necessary step to encourage a cultural shift in the focus of practitioners."

6.11   One firm of City solicitors sets out the usual arguments against costs management: producing budgets is expensive; the court does not have resources to do costs management; and so forth. It welcomes the indication in the Preliminary Report that costs management would be inappropriate in most commercial cases. The firm also, however, helpfully sets out the results of a survey of its own clients. Under the heading "costs management" clients were asked: "do you believe the court should be given greater power to manage and control costs?" In answer to this question, 75% of respondents said yes, 20% said no and the rest abstained.

7. ANALYSIS

(i) Is the game worth the candle?

7.1   It must be accepted that costs management is an exercise which generates additional costs and which makes additional demands upon the limited resources of the court. These are two powerful negative factors. On the other hand, there are two powerful factors in support of costs management. First, case management and costs management go hand in hand. It does not make sense for the court to manage a case without regard to the costs which it is ordering the parties to incur. The Rubicon was crossed on 26th April 1999, when the court assumed under the CPR wide powers and responsibilities for case management. Very few respondents (although there are some) suggest that we should return to the north bank of the Rubicon. Secondly, I am in full agreement with the Law Society's view that costs management, if done properly, will save substantially more costs than it generates.

7.2   The balance of costs versus benefits. Any measures to control the costs of a project are themselves a source of some expense. Quantity surveyors have to be paid professional fees for their services in monitoring the costs of a construction project and determining what amounts are payable at each stage or what sums are due in respect of variations. But no-one suggests that quantity surveyors should be dispensed with, in order to "save" the costs of employing them. The costs of any multi-track case can be substantial, ranging from tens of thousands of pounds to tens of millions of pounds. In other words, the costs of every multi-track case, unless it settles early, are comparable to at least the costs of a small building project and sometimes they are comparable to the costs of a major building project. There is precisely the same need to control the costs of litigation as there is need to control the costs of any other project.

7.3   Effective costs management is in the interests of clients. As previously noted,[122] lawyers are human. Those who are spending other people's money sometimes have a tendency to be over-generous, particularly when they are paying that money to themselves and expect the costs to be borne by their opponents.[123] There therefore needs to be some effective control over the costs which are expended on litigation. Non-commercial, first time litigants often are in no position to know what work needs to be done or to control expenditure. I accept that business litigants are better placed to control what their lawyers spend on litigation. But these are the very clients[124] who seem most keen on costs management being undertaken by the court: see the earlier sections of this chapter.

7.4   I readily accept that no case has been yet made out for introducing costs management into the Commercial Court. However, in my view, a powerful case has been made out for introducing costs management in those rather more modest multi-track cases, where the level of costs is a matter of concern to the parties or at least to the paying party.

(ii) Is it possible for lawyers and judges to do costs management?

7.5   Current level of skills. All the evidence suggests that a modest number of solicitors,[125] a far smaller number of barristers and an even smaller number of judges currently possess the requisite skills to carry out costs management. In my view (which is shared by many respondents during Phase 2) the solution is not to abandon the enterprise as hopeless, but to insist that proper training is delivered. I am fortified in my view that judges can develop the requisite skills by the experience of the Birmingham pilot: see paragraph 2.8 above. It should also be noted that Coulson J made a form of costs management order in *Barr v Biffa Waste Services Ltd* [2009] EWHC 2444 (TCC) at paragraphs 53 to 60.

---

[122] See chapter 10 above.

[123] This comment is directed to litigation conducted under conditional fee agreements.

[124] Except for those very large enterprises which litigate in the Commercial Court and tell me they are unconcerned about the level of costs: see PR paragraphs 10.2.6 and 10.7.10 to 10.7.14.

[125] All solicitors know about time recording and billing. Only a minority appeared to be skilled in costs budgeting for litigation. However, the number of solicitors who possess this skill is steadily growing. Many law firms have now acquired costs budgeting software.

7.6 <u>The mindset of lawyers.</u> Like many other judges, in the past I have not been hugely interested in the subject of costs. Nor, during the current review, can I claim to have encountered a groundswell of enthusiasm amongst either judges or practitioners for learning all about costs.[126] The burgeoning jurisprudence about costs and the interstices of the Costs PD may be an acquired taste. Nevertheless, facts must be faced. Costs are an important facet of every contested action. In a large number of cases they are the most important single issue, sometimes towering above all else.[127] I have regretfully come to the conclusion that it is simply unacceptable for judges or practitioners to regard "costs" as an alien discipline, which need only be understood by costs judges, costs draftsmen and solicitors who specialise in that kind of thing.

7.7 <u>Need for training and form of training.</u> In my view judges, barristers and litigation solicitors need to be trained not only in the assessment of costs, but also in costs budgeting and costs management. The form of training must be a matter for those who deliver it. However, I suggest that such training should include practical exercises.

7.8 <u>Training in costs assessment.</u> Greater skill in the assessment of past costs is an important first step to understanding costs budgeting. Mock summary assessments, based on the facts of real cases, would be helpful. Such exercises could be done on paper, with the benefit of the actual written submissions of both parties (suitably anonymised). The results could then be discussed in a group session, in the same format as is used in criminal sentencing seminars.

7.9 <u>Training in costs budgeting.</u> Training in costs budgeting could be done in a similar manner. It would be possible for participants to take the facts of a case as known at the outset and to use those facts as the basis for producing an estimate of future costs. Then there could be a discussion of the various estimates in a group session. At the same time the actual history of the case and the actual amount of costs allowed on assessment could be revealed. I have recently attempted such an exercise myself at the offices of Olswang LLP, using their software. Olswang gave me the facts of a recent case, the initial expert report and a copy of the letter before action. They then invited me to estimate the "future" costs, without revealing what those costs actually were. The exercise took two hours and was an invaluable learning experience.

7.10 Those solicitors who have developed expertise in costs budgeting would be well placed to assist in the development of training programmes for judges, barristers and solicitors. Costs judges would also be well placed to assist in the development of those training programmes.

7.11 <u>Training in costs management.</u> Costs management is really an adjunct to case management. It is best carried out by judges who have developed skills in costs budgeting, so that they can make realistic assessments of what each task in a case should cost. Training in costs management is best combined with training in case management, which is already provided by the Judicial Studies Board (the "JSB").

7.12 <u>Ability to deliver training.</u> From such informal contact as I have had, I see no reason to doubt that both the Bar and the solicitors' profession would be able to

---

[126] Some people have candidly indicated to me their dismay at the direction in which the Costs Review is heading. They believe that a case costs what it costs and any attempt to control costs in advance is (a) doomed and (b) not something which they feel able to undertake.
[127] See e.g. *Multiplex Constructions (UK) Ltd v Cleveland Bridge UK Ltd* (No. 6) [2008] EWHC 2220 (TCC) at [1671].

include effective costs budgeting and costs management training within the Continuing Professional Development ("CPD") training which is approved and delivered to practitioners. Likewise, I believe that the JSB would be able to include costs budgeting and costs management in the civil training for judges which would be provided as from October 2010.

7.13 I recommend that the linked disciplines of costs budgeting and costs management be included in CPD training for those solicitors and barristers who undertake civil litigation. I also recommend that costs budgeting and costs management be included in the training offered by the JSB to judges who sit in the civil courts.

7.14 <u>Judicial time.</u> I accept that CMCs which include costs management take more time than traditional CMCs. The experience of the Birmingham judges in that regard is set out in paragraph 2.11 above.

7.15 There will, however, be a saving of judicial time in two respects. First, some cases will settle earlier as a result of litigants gaining a fuller understanding of their costs exposure. Secondly, effective costs management as an adjunct to case management will control some of the present excesses of litigation. Thus trial lengths may be reduced to a degree. I am in no position to quantify these savings, but draw attention to the fact that costs management involves not only expenditure of time, but also saving of time.

7.16 <u>Conclusion.</u> On the basis of all that I have learnt during the Costs Review I conclude that effective costs budgeting is a skill which all lawyers could acquire, if they are prepared to give up time to being trained; effective costs management is well within the abilities of all civil judges, if properly trained; effective costs management has the potential to control the recoverable costs, and sometimes the actual costs, of litigation to more acceptable levels.

(iii) The way forward

7.17 <u>A gradualist approach.</u> In my view, the correct way forward is to adopt a gradualist approach. First there needs to be an effective training programme, as discussed above. At the same time rules should be drafted, setting out a standard costs management procedure, which judges would have a discretion to adopt if and when they see fit, either of their own motion or upon application by one of the parties. At least in the early stages, I think it would be wrong to make costs management a compulsory procedure.

7.18 <u>Drafting costs management rules.</u> I suggest that the rules for costs management should be drafted in the summer of 2010, once feedback from the present pilot exercises has been gathered and analysed. Allowance must be made for the fact that the participants in the present pilot exercises have not yet received the training which is advocated in this chapter. Those who draft the new costs management rules should have regard to the proposed new format of bills of costs, if my recommendations in chapter 45 below are accepted. When the rules for costs management are being drafted, it will also be necessary to amend the rules in respect of costs capping. There must be harmony between both sets of rules, even though costs capping and costs management are separate concepts. In particular, in my view, the requirement for "exceptional circumstances" will have to be removed from section 23A.1 of the Costs PD.

7.19   Any set of costs management rules will have to make provision for the four elements referred to in paragraph 1.4 above. In so far as possible, the rules should build upon what is already within the CPR. For example, rule 35.4(4) (as recently amended) would naturally form part of any set of costs management rules, without the need for further amendment.[128]

7.20   <u>The future.</u> At a later stage the question of making costs management mandatory in certain categories of litigation or certain courts should be re-considered in the light of experience.

7.21   <u>Pre-action costs management.</u> In some areas of litigation, costs management post-issue comes too late in the day. By the time that the judge comes to close the stable door, the horse has already bolted. Indeed, there is a danger that parties may seek to circumvent post-issue controls upon recoverable costs by pushing work back into the pre-issue period. If excessive work is done pre-issue, the costs (though recoverable) may turn out to be unnecessary, for example because liability is not disputed. This argument has been pressed upon me with particular force in relation to clinical negligence, where claimants sometimes run up substantial costs before a letter of claim is sent. In my view some form of costs management will need to be developed whereby the court, on an ex parte application by telephone or on paper, approves further expenditure once a certain level of costs is reached. In chapter 23 above I suggest a procedure for pre-issue costs management in respect of clinical negligence cases. I propose that this procedure be piloted, as set out in chapter 23. Once we have some feedback from that pilot, consideration should be given to developing a more general procedure for pre-issue costs management in the light of experience. Although the form of any rules governing pre-issue costs management will be a matter for future consultation, I have no doubt that, in principle, such a procedure will be necessary if litigation costs are going to be kept proportionate. Primary legislation will be required, in order to enable the Civil Procedure Rule Committee (the "Rule Committee") to make rules in respect of pre-issue costs management.

(iv) The effect of re-defining proportionality

7.22   <u>Proposal in chapter 3.</u> In chapter 3 above I propose a definition of "proportionality", which would come into play on those occasions when an assessment of "reasonable" costs results in an excessive figure.[129] In essence proportionality trumps reasonableness. If the recommendation in chapter 3 is accepted, this will introduce a new dimension to costs management.

7.23   <u>The new dimension.</u> The judge carrying out costs management will not only scrutinise the reasonableness of each party's budget, but also stand back and consider whether the total sums on each side are "proportionate" in accordance with the new definition. If the total figures are not proportionate, then the judge will only approve budget figures for each party which are proportionate.[130] Thereafter both parties, if they choose to press on, will be litigating in part at their own expense.[131]

---

[128] As amended with effect from 1st October 2009, rule 35.4(4) provides: *"The court may limit the amount of a party's expert's fees and expenses that may be recovered from any other party."*

[129] This brief summary is no more than a signpost. The reader is referred back to chapter 3 above for a full discussion of proportionality.

[130] This approach will meet some of the concerns expressed by Professor Adrian Zuckerman in his article *"Lord Justice Jackson's Review of Civil Litigation Costs – Preliminary Report (2009)"* (2009) 28 C.J.Q. 435 at 442 – 446.

[131] Unless the conduct of the paying party causes a more generous assessment of costs to be appropriate at the end of the case.

7.24   The interaction between chapter 3 and this chapter is important. It would not be right for costs management to be carried out solely on the basis of reasonableness and then for the proportionality provision to come into play for the first time at the final assessment of costs.

8. RECOMMENDATIONS

8.1   I make the following recommendations:

(i)   The linked disciplines of costs budgeting and costs management should be included in CPD training for those solicitors and barristers who undertake civil litigation.

(ii)   Costs budgeting and costs management should be included in the training offered by the JSB to judges who sit in the civil courts.

(iii)   Rules should set out a standard costs management procedure, which judges would have a discretion to adopt if and when they see fit, either of their own motion or upon application by one of the parties.

(iv)   Primary legislation should enable the Rule Committee to make rules for pre-issue costs management.

8.2   My recommendations in respect of piloting pre-issue costs management are set out in chapter 23 above.

CHAPTER 41. PART 36 OFFERS

INDEX

1. INTRODUCTION

1.1   The introduction of Part 36 of the Civil Procedure Rules. Before April 1999 there was a procedure for defendants to make payments into court, with costs sanctions for claimants who pressed on and failed to do better at trial. However, there was no procedure in the rules for claimants' offers and there were no incentives for defendants to accept such offers. One of Lord Woolf's reforms was to introduce Part 36 of the Civil Procedure Rules ("Part 36"), whereby either party could make a settlement offer to the other party or parties. This procedure is backed up by a scheme of penalties and rewards, in order to encourage the making of reasonable settlement offers and the acceptance of such offers. Part 36 has been amended from time to time by the Civil Procedure Rule Committee in the light of experience. In particular, substantial revisions were made to Part 36 with effect from 6th April 2007.

1.2   General success of Part 36. Part 36 has generally been regarded as a success, even by those who are otherwise critical of the Woolf reforms. In April 2000 a survey of the FTSE 100 companies revealed that 90% of respondents believed that the Woolf reforms would encourage earlier settlement of disputes. This was seen as the key benefit of those reforms.[132] A survey of lawyers conducted by Morin for the Centre for Effective Dispute Resolution ("CEDR") in April 2000 showed a high level of overall satisfaction with the Woolf reforms, in particular with Part 36.[133] Evaluations by the Lord Chancellor's Department in 2001 and 2002 came to similar conclusions.[134]

1.3   Similar views about the general success of Part 36 have been expressed during the present Costs Review. For example, one substantial firm of solicitors in Sheffield, on behalf of one of its clients, writes:

---

[132] See "*Impact of the Woolf Reforms One Year On*", April 2000, page 7. This was a survey commissioned by Wragge & Co and prepared by City Research Group.

[133] See "*The CEDR civil Justice Audit*", April 2000, in particular at pages 44-45. This is available online at http://www.cedr.co.uk/library/articles/CJAreport.pdf.

[134] See "*Emerging Findings – an early evaluation of the Civil Justice Reforms*", March 2001, and "*Further Findings – A continuing evaluation of the Civil Justice Reforms*", August 2002, available online at http://www.dca.gov.uk/civil/emerge/emerge.htm and http://www.dca.gov.uk/civil/reform/ffreform.htm respectively.

"The introduction of Part 36 offers has been a widely successful change introduced by the CPR. Part 36 offers encourage settlement. In practice it has become standard for claimants and defendants to make Part 36 offers."

1.4   Two possible areas for reform.   Despite the positive effects of Part 36, there are two areas where it is suggested that further reform would be beneficial.   These are:

(i)   the interpretation of "advantageous" in rule 36.14(1); and

(ii)   the rewards for a claimant whose offer is not beaten.

1.5   One way costs shifting.   A separate issue for consideration will be how Part 36 should operate in those areas where one way costs shifting is introduced.

2. THE INTERPRETATION OF "ADVANTAGEOUS" IN RULE 36.14(1)

2.1   Rule 36.14(1).   Rule 36.14(1) (as amended with effect from 6th April 2007) provides:

"This rule applies where upon judgment being entered –

(a)   a claimant fails to obtain a judgment more advantageous than a defendant's Part 36 offer; or

(b)   judgment against the defendant is at least as advantageous to the claimant as the proposals contained in a claimant's Part 36 offer."

2.2   The Court of Appeal's interpretation of rule 36.14(1).   In *Carver v BAA plc* [2008] EWCA Civ 412; [2009] 1 WLR 113 ("*Carver*") the claimant in a personal injuries case beat the defendant's Part 36 offer by £51.   The trial judge held that, having regard to all the consequences of going to trial, it could not be said that the final outcome (although £51 higher) was "more advantageous" than accepting the defendant's offer made a year previously.   The Court of Appeal upheld that decision. Ward LJ, with whom Rix and Keene LJJ agreed, observed that "more advantageous" is an open-textured phrase.   He added, at paragraphs 30 to 32:

"It permits a more wide-ranging review of all the facts and circumstances of the case in deciding whether the judgment, which is the fruit of the litigation, was worth the fight.

The answer must, in my judgment, take account of the modern approach to litigation. The Civil Procedure Rules, and Part 36 in particular, encourage both sides to make offers to settle. Compromise is seen as an object worthy of promotion for compromise is better than contest, both for the litigants concerned, for the court and for the administration of justice as a whole. Litigation is time consuming and it comes at a cost, emotional as well as financial. Those are, therefore, appropriate factors to take into account in deciding whether the battle was worth it. Money is not the sole governing criterion.

It follows that Judge Knight was correct in looking at the case broadly. He was entitled to take into account that the extra £51 gained was more than off set by the irrecoverable cost incurred by the claimant in continuing to contest the case for as long as she did. He was entitled to take into account the added stress to her as she waited for the trial and the stress of the trial process itself.

-421-

No reasonable litigant would have embarked upon this campaign for a gain of £51."

The principles stated by the Court of Appeal in *Carver* are of general application; they are not confined to personal injuries litigation: see *Multiplex Constructions (UK) Ltd v Cleveland Bridge UK Ltd* (No. 7) [2008] EWHC 2280 (TCC) at [70] – [71]. It should be noted that in *Morgan v UPS* [2008] EWCA Civ 1476 the Court of Appeal distinguished *Carver* on the facts. The principles, however, remain as stated in *Carver*.

2.3   Preliminary Report. In PR paragraph 46.6.4 I referred to concerns which had been expressed about the effects of *Carver* and calls for its reversal by rule change. The essential complaint was that *Carver* introduced an unwelcome element of uncertainty, and that parties needed to be better able to predict the effect of settlement offers.

2.4   Comments during Phase 2. The overwhelming majority of respondents during Phase 2 agreed with the criticisms of *Carver* in the Preliminary Report. A firm of solicitors in Manchester writes:

> "The decision of the Court of Appeal in *Carver v BAA Plc*...has introduced an element of uncertainty in the Part 36 regime. The advantage of making a Part 36 offer had previously been certainty. If a claimant obtained a judgment more advantageous than the offer, the claimant would be entitled to receive (subject to the court's discretion) the enhanced benefits under Part 36. In monetary terms, this should translate to the claimant equalling or "beating" the offer by whatever margin. The *Carver* decision now provides that the courts will look at a wider range of factors when looking at whether the judgment is "more advantageous". This has had a detrimental effect on Part 36. We are of the view that this decision should be reversed."

A large commercial law firm in Leeds expresses similar views.

2.5   A large international firm of solicitors writes:

> "We agree that *BAA v Carver*...should be reversed. We can understand the judiciary's desire for as much discretion as possible in order to enable them to do what they consider to be the right thing in each case. However, discretion inevitably creates uncertainty and, as a result, offers parties issues about which to argue thereby generating satellite litigation and further costs. A black letter rule has many virtues."

2.6   A two partner firm of solicitors in Brixton, specialising in housing and personal injury claims, writes:

> "We absolutely agree with paragraph 6.4[135] that the uncertainty introduced into Part 36 by the case of *BAA v Carver* should be reversed."

2.7   A firm of solicitors with offices across the south of England, which does a wide range of civil litigation (including claimant and defendant personal injuries work) writes:

---

[135] This is a reference to PR paragraph 46.6.4.

"We would add to this list the reversal of the *Carver v BAA Plc*...ruling by the Court of Appeal that has obscured the clarity that was inherent in the earlier version of Part 36 of the Civil Procedure Rules 1998. *Carver* has also depressed the level of damages that many claimants' representatives and their ATE[136] insurers feel confident of negotiating: because of the costs risk. This can result in settlements below the proper entitlement."

2.8　The comments quoted above are typical of many other responses received during Phase 2. Although there were some defenders of *Carver* and the present interpretation of rule 36.14(1), they were few in number. No convincing arguments have been advanced to rebut the arguments set out in the preceding four paragraphs.

2.9　Conclusion. I confirm my provisional view expressed in the Preliminary Report[137] that *Carver* introduces an unwelcome degree of uncertainty into the Part 36 regime and also that it tends to depress the level of settlements. I recommend that the effect of *Carver* should be reversed either judicially (if an early opportunity arises) or by rule change. It should be made clear that in any purely monetary case "more advantageous" in rule 36.14(1)(a) means better in financial terms by any amount, however small.

3.　REWARDS FOR A CLAIMANT WHOSE OFFER IS NOT BEATEN

(i)　The present rules

3.1　Rule 36.14(3). Rule 36.14(3) provides:

"Subject to paragraph (6), where rule 36.14(1)(b) applies, the court will, unless it considers it unjust to do so, order that the claimant is entitled to –

(a)　interest on the whole or part of any sum of money (excluding interest) awarded at a rate not exceeding 10% above base rate for some or all of the period starting with the date on which the relevant period expired;

(b)　his costs on the indemnity basis from the date on which the relevant period expired; and

(c)　interest on those costs at a rate not exceeding 10% above base rate."

3.2　Rules 36.14(4) to (6). Rule 36.14(4) sets out the circumstances which the court will take into account[138] in considering whether it would be unjust to make the orders referred to in rule 36.14(2)[139] and (3). Rule 36.14(5) provides that, where the court awards interest on the same sum both under rule 36.14 and under any other power, the total rate of interest on that sum must not exceeded 10% above base rate. Rule 36.14(6) sets out the circumstances in which rule 35.14 (2) and (3) do not apply to a Part 36 offer.[140]

---

[136] After-the-event.
[137] PR paragraph 46.6.4.
[138] The circumstances are: (a) the terms of any Part 36 offer; (b) the stage in proceedings when any Part 36 offer was made, including in particular how long before the trial started the offer was made; (c) the information available to the parties at the time when the Part 36 offer was made; and (d) the conduct of the parties with regarding to the giving or refusing to give information for the purposes of enabling the offer to be made or evaluated.
[139] Rule 36.14(2) sets out the consequences of a claimant failing to beat a defendant's offer.
[140] The circumstances are: (a) where a Part 36 offer has been withdrawn; (b) where a Part 36 offer has been changed so that its terms are less advantageous to the offeree, and the offeree has beaten the less advantageous offer; and (c) where a Part 36 offer is made less than 21 days before trial, unless the court has abridged the relevant period.

3.3   Definitions. In this section of chapter 41 I shall use the phrase "adequate offer" to mean an offer which (a) one party makes, (b) the other party does not accept and (c) is at least as good (from the point of view of the rejecting party) as the result which the rejecting party achieves at trial.

(ii) Comments during Phase 2

3.4   General tenor. Although the procedure for claimants' offers was generally welcomed, many respondents regretted that claimants' offers had much less "teeth" than defendants' offers. A claimant's failure to beat a Part 36 offer can have dramatic consequences, sometimes wiping out the entirety of damages recovered. On the other hand, a defendant's failure to beat the claimant's offer has much milder effects and (it is said) even these are quite often reduced by the exercise of judicial discretion. A group of claimant clinical negligence solicitors urged this view upon me at a meeting held on 12th June 2009. They contended that there must be a hard financial penalty for failure to beat a claimant's offer. This would provide a real incentive for claimants to make reasonable offers. It would also provide a real incentive for defendants to accept such offers.

3.5   National law firm. A national law firm, based in Manchester, specialising in personal injury, clinical negligence and commercial litigation writes:

> "We note the comments throughout the Review that Pt 36 generally works well. We agree that it often does, but our experience is that a stronger sanction would encourage earlier settlement of more cases...
>
> The risks imposed by Part 36 offers are currently significantly tilted in favour of defendants because claimants risk paying all future costs in cases where offers are well pitched and not accepted. The risks are significant and, in our experience, weigh heavily on claimants.
>
> The risks to defendants are somewhat lighter. Indemnity costs actually cause little fear to defendants because they know that in cases they lose, they will usually meet 80 – 90% of costs in any event. Even when indemnity costs come into play, they know that the burden of increased costs will be limited and it is often in their interests to fight on in the hope that they can drag damages down...
>
> We would believe that if the costs sanctions were more evenly balanced, cases would settle earlier. For example if defendants failed to beat Pt 36 offers and had to pay a 50% uplift on costs incurred thereafter, they would pay more attention to offers made which would encourage settlement. At first sight, such an uplift seems excessive but, in PI / CN cases the risks to the claimant are that their damages are effectively wiped out by costs if they misjudge an offer. At the minute, for defendants the costs risk is outweighed by the benefit of dragging a case out and hoping that weariness will lead the claimant to accept a low offer of damages and if the defendant faced the same sort of risks that a claimant did, they would take note of Part 36 offers."

3.6   Trade Union view. A number of trade unions favour strengthening the effect of claimant offers. Unison (the largest trade union serving the public sector) writes:

> "In fact if further settlement incentives are proposed these should in our view relate to making sure defendants act reasonably in accepting Part 36 claimant offers. This could be readily achieved by attaching greater claimant benefits

like greater enhanced damages and higher costs sanctions should that offer be exceeded in court. This would be most beneficial, giving claimants Part 36 offers more teeth – something considered by Woolf many years ago but not implemented."

3.7   Unite (the UK's largest trade union) notes that Lord Woolf recommended much tougher interest penalties for defendants who failed to beat claimant offers. It states:

> "Unite would favour the use of increasing the compensation by this or similar means in a number of situations, including where insurers behave unreasonably and as a reward for being reasonable in relation to offers."

3.8   <u>Association of Her Majesty's District Judges.</u> As noted in chapter 19 above, the Association of Her Majesty's District Judges has proposed that there should be an uplift on damages of 10% in cases where the claimant recovers damages equal to or greater than the claimant's offer.

(iii) Assessment

3.9   <u>Analysis.</u>   This is another area where the original, and very sensible, recommendations of Lord Woolf were never implemented. In most, but not all,[141] cases the defendant's weapons from the armoury of Part 36 are more powerful than the claimant's weapons. The consequences which follow when a defendant rejects the claimant's adequate offer are less devastating than the consequences which follow when a claimant fails to beat the defendant's offer. As the law now stands, the claimant is insufficiently rewarded and the defendant is insufficiently penalised, when the claimant has made an adequate offer.

3.10   <u>Remedy.</u>   In my view, the claimant's reward for making an adequate offer should be increased. The proposal of the Association of Her Majesty's District Judges is the best way forward, namely that there should be an uplift of 10% on damages awarded. Nevertheless, in respect of higher value claims, say over £500,000, there may be a case for scaling down the uplift. If my proposal is accepted in principle, this could be the subject of further consultation.

3.11   <u>What to do where the relief claimed is non-monetary.</u>   In some litigation the principal relief, or even the sole relief, sought is non-monetary, for example an injunction or a declaration. It would be wrong if the claimants in such cases did not enjoy the same rewards for having made adequate offers as other claimants whose claims are purely financial. In my view, the only way to avoid such an inequitable situation arising is for the court to ascribe a value to any non-monetary relief which is awarded. This is not an impossible task. District judges regularly have regard to the approximate value of non-monetary relief, when deciding upon allocation of cases to tracks.

3.12   <u>Proposal.</u>   The judge should make a broad assessment of the value of any non-monetary relief awarded, on the basis of the evidence which the judge has received at trial. The judge should then take 10% of that figure (in addition to 10% of any financial relief awarded) as the appropriate uplift in a case where the claimant has made an adequate offer. This exercise should be carried out summarily when the judge is dealing with costs at the end of the case. Appeals against that assessment

---

[141] There are some exceptional cases where the claimant's reward for an effective offer is greater than the defendant's reward: see *AF v BG* [2009] EWCA Civ 757 at [14].

should be firmly discouraged, unless (a) the judge has erred in principle and (b) the extent of his or her error is significant.[142]

3.13   Draft rule. I therefore propose that there should be added to rule 36.14(3) the following sub-paragraph:

> "(d)   an additional sum comprising 10% of (i) the damages or other sum awarded and (ii) the financial value, as summarily assessed by the court on the basis of the evidence given at trial, of any non-monetary relief awarded."

3.14   If thought appropriate, provision could be added for scaling down the uplift in respect of higher value cases. The rules should, in any event, enable the court to award less than 10% uplift in cases where there are good reasons to take this course.

3.15   Benefits of the proposed reform. I believe that there are three benefits to be gained from the proposed reform. The first benefit is that there will be a more level playing field as between claimants and defendants. The second benefit is that more cases will settle early. Defendants will be less willing to press on to trial, when claimants have made reasonable offers. The third benefit is that in those cases which do go to trial, despite the claimant having made an adequate offer, the claimant will recover a significantly larger sum.

3.16   Importance of the third benefit. The third benefit is important, because of the proposals which I make in chapter 10 above in respect of conditional fee agreements ("CFAs"). If those proposals are implemented, claimants in successful cases on CFAs will have to pay success fees to their lawyers, but will not recover the success fees from the other side. As can be seen from chapter 2 above and from the tables in appendix 1 to this report, in cases which settle early the CFA success fees are generally modest and can be met by claimants out of their damages.[143] It is cases that go to trial which generate the largest success fees. The claimants in those cases now will be able to increase substantially their financial recovery by making well judged offers. The various rewards and gains which the claimant will make[144] should enable him to pay the success fee, and still be no worse off than he is under the present regime of recoverable success fees.

3.17   Conclusion. The reforms to Part 36 advocated in this chapter constitute a further justification for the central proposal of this report, which is contained in chapter 10 above, namely that CFA success fees should cease to be recoverable under costs orders.

---

[142] I.e. there is a significant difference between (a) 10% of the figure which the judge actually assessed as the value of the non-monetary relief and (b) 10% of the figure which the judge ought to have assessed.

[143] Those damages will be enhanced by 10%, which should be more than adequate in the majority of cases to cover the success fees.

[144] The claimant receives (i) a 10% increase in general damages in all cases, as proposed in chapter 10 above; (ii) a 10% increase in all damages (both general and special damages) as a reward for having made an adequate offer; and (iii) enhanced interest on damages under CPR rule 36.14(3)(a). All these extra funds should be sufficient to meet a success fee which, in personal injury cases, will be capped at 25% of damages, excluding damages referable to future loss (as proposed in chapter 10 above). The lawyers will also be sufficiently rewarded. They will receive (i) a success fee (capped at 25% of damages); (ii) indemnity costs under CPR rule 36.14(3)(b); and (iii) enhanced interest on costs under rule 36.14(3)(c).

4. HOW PART 36 WILL OPERATE IN AREAS WHERE THERE IS QUALIFED ONE WAY COSTS SHIFTING

4.1 In earlier chapters I have proposed that there be qualified one way costs shifting in claims for personal injuries, judicial review, defamation and related cases.

4.2 Although chapter 19 above is specifically focused upon personal injuries litigation, the proposals in paragraph 4.10 of that chapter are equally applicable to all types of case for which qualified one way costs shifting may be introduced. If a claimant fails to accept a defendant's adequate offer under CPR Part 36, the claimant will forfeit or (depending upon the circumstances) substantially forfeit the benefits of one way costs shifting. The proposed regime of one way costs shifting is "qualified" because in appropriate circumstances the protection falls away.

4.3 In the event that qualified one way costs shifting is introduced as proposed in earlier chapters, no amendment will be required to CPR Part 36 in order to provide incentives for claimants to accept adequate Part 36 offers. The present wording of rule 36.14(2) is sufficient.

5. RECOMMENDATIONS

5.1 I make the following recommendations:

(i) The effect of *Carver v BAA plc* [2008] EWCA Civ 412; [2009] 1 WLR 113 should be reversed.

(ii) Where a defendant rejects a claimant's offer, but fails to do better at trial, the claimant's recovery should be enhanced by 10%.

CHAPTER 42. COURTS ADMINISTRATION

INDEX

1. INTRODUCTION

1.1   Background. An issue that emerged during Phase 2 of the Costs Review was the effect of courts administration on the conduct (and cost) of civil litigation. Although many court users are pleased or satisfied with the level of service they receive from the courts, there are also many others who have encountered less than satisfactory performance which has led to the need to perform work that should not be necessary (with an attendant cost). Concerns about these matters have been expressed during Phase 2 both at meetings and in written submissions. By way of illustration I set out below an extract from one such submission:

"At the present time, whilst the Court Service usually does the best it can, a considerable portion of the costs incurred in litigation can be attributed to;

- delays and inconsistencies of service from the courts;

- telephones not being answered or being answered by staff who are not trained to deal with the query;

- continuous adjournments, sometimes to a new hearing several months later;

- delays in dealing with post, some courts operating with a backlog of several weeks.

General examples

Files go missing, papers do not make it to the right file, there is insufficient time to hear a matter and it is adjourned, there are insufficient Judges available so the matter is adjourned, the Judge does not feel he can hear the claim and so it is adjourned and the adjourned date, due to the number of cases in the system, is sometimes several months down the line.

Certain courts asked firms to stop sending hard copy letters as confirmation of faxes to try and reduce the amount of post received (as they were struggling to deal with it), but when chased for a response the courts could not find copies of the faxes. Firms were then sending a fax and telephoning to confirm receipt, which took longer and incurred more costs than simply posting a hard copy of the fax.

Another more recent example is a court which did not have the ability to receive an email attaching urgent copy documentation for a hearing, so a large fax had to be sent instead and the court said it would charge for each page over a certain length.

It is not practicable to contact some courts by telephone as you either telephone, and the telephone continues to ring (with no message facility), or the line is continually engaged."

A related concern is the level of court fees that are now payable in civil litigation, particularly for small to medium size claims. The Law Society's submission made the point that *"There have been considerable increases in court fees in recent years but this has not produced any noticeable improvements in the courts' services"*.

1.2   Professor Dame Hazel Genn expressed concerns about lack of resources for the civil courts in her 2008 Hamlyn lectures. In her first lecture she stated:

"The annual reports of Designated Civil Judges provide considerable evidence of the declining standards in county courts, both in terms of the fabric of the buildings, the pressures on the judiciary, and inadequate standards of administrative support. Having spent a large amount of time over the past 20 years hanging around courts and tribunals I can confirm the sorry state of the courts. When I talk of the crumbling of civil justice I speak as someone who enters the court buildings through the front door with the punters and I walk the public corridors. I have personally witnessed the decline. Terrible IT. Stressed admin staff. Too few books for Judges. Judges having to wander down to waiting rooms to get their next case because there is no one else to do it. Cases listed for 5 minutes. This is not about lawyers fees. This is about the resources allocated to the courts. The public areas of some civil courts are run down and squalid. They remind me of the worst to be found in NHS hospitals. But the courts are not outpatients' departments. They are sites of justice. They must have authority and legitimacy for which they have to command public confidence and respect."

1.3   Courts administration and the costs of civil litigation. My terms of reference do not specifically direct me to consider the management of the courts and their allocation of resources. Nor am I specifically asked to address issues relating to the "customer satisfaction" of court users. Nevertheless, it is clear enough that the costs of civil litigation are affected by the efficiency of the administration of the courts themselves. I should in this Final Report at least touch upon improvements to court administration that are likely to lead to greater cost efficiencies for end users.

1.4   The extent of the problem. Of course, anecdotal evidence has limitations, insofar as it paints a picture of a general malaise in the administration of the courts. In my own experience as a TCC judge, the administration of cases by court staff was generally very good, and court staff were able to adapt effectively to changes in administration, such as those brought about with the advent of e-working.[145] I have heard similar feedback about other courts and their efficient, hard-working staff. It is principally the county courts which have attracted the criticisms of court users (including the examples given above)[146] and even of district judges themselves. At least 95% of civil litigation is conducted through the county courts,[147] and it is primarily upon those courts that I will focus.

---

[145] See chapter 43 below.
[146] The Law Society's submission to me in Phase 2 stated that *"Experienced solicitors practising in a number of county courts and district registries estimate that 10-15% of litigators' time is spent on unnecessary work required by the court"*.
[147] PR paragraph 5.5.2.

2.1   General observations. There may be many reasons why the administration of some cases goes awry. Human error is one. Lack of familiarity with case administration, resulting from a high turnover of staff at certain courts, could be another. A third explanation may be that court staff are so overburdened with administration that they are unable to cope with the volume of cases passing through the courts. A criticism repeatedly mentioned to me is a perceived underfunding of the county courts, resulting in an inability to recruit sufficient numbers of staff and to invest in the long-overdue IT procurement.

2.2   HMCS[148] Review. On 17th September 2009 I met with Peter Risk, HMCS South West Regional Director, to discuss the difficulties in the administration of county court cases. Mr Risk has over 35 years of experience in courts administration at centres around England and Wales, including in London, the Midlands, Wales and most recently the South West. In his experience, the efficiency of courts administration was variable. He believes there are two reasons for this:

(i)   The first is turnover of staff. Courts that are well administered tend to have long-term staff who are familiar with procedures, whereas those courts with a higher turnover of staff face greater difficulties. Attracting and retaining skilful court staff depends upon a number of factors including geographical and economic ones. For example, in some regions where wages and salaries are generally lower, working in courts administration on the salaries paid by HMCS may be an attractive career option. The position may be different in other areas such as London, where there is a more transient population and a higher cost of living.

(ii)   Secondly, the majority of the time of court staff is spent processing documents that will not, or are unlikely to, involve judicial input. Undefended debt collection cases and attachment of earnings proceedings are prime examples of such work. The time that court staff spend on these matters reduces the time they have available to work upon cases that will be contested, and which require the involvement of a judge.

2.3   I can see the force of these observations. I understand that proposals are being considered by HMCS to address these matters. Some of the possible measures to improve court efficiency are mentioned below.

3. MEASURES TO IMPROVE EFFICIENCY

3.1   Removal of routine matters from frontline court staff. If routine matters that do not, or are unlikely to, require the involvement of a judge are removed from frontline court staff, such staff will be better able to focus upon administering cases that require a decision from the court. This should lead to an improvement in the quality of administration of cases (with concomitant costs savings to the parties). Routine matters (such as undefended debt claims and enforcement proceedings) that are removed from frontline court staff could be addressed by "back office" staff at bulk processing centres around the country ("regional centres"). HMCS' bulk centre at the Northampton County Court (which processes "online" and other claims submitted to it electronically) provides an example of how routine cases can be managed without ever requiring the intervention of a judge or court staff. If regional centres were to be located in areas that could attract long-term staff, who are or will

---

[148] Her Majesty's Courts Service.

become skilled in the processing of routine proceedings, that should lead to the delivery of a prompt and accurate service to court users (which in turn will lead to costs savings to parties).

3.2   If such measures were to be adopted, consideration could be given as to whether most claims should be issued and processed at regional centres, only to be transferred to a local court / hearing centre if defended and therefore in need of case management by and, possibly, trial before a judge. Most county court proceedings are of a routine nature, requiring no significant judicial input. I anticipate that litigants would prefer to issue such proceedings online at a regional centre. Nevertheless, it would in my view be wrong to compel everyone to issue proceedings at regional centres. Litigants who wish to issue claims in person at their local county court and to pay fees at the counter should be free to do so.

3.3   Whilst defended cases would have to be transferred to a county court, there are occasions under the present Civil Procedure Rules 1998 when even an undefended case, proceeding through the bulk centre, requires a judicial decision to be made in respect of it. At the moment, at Northampton, such files are sent to a number of deputy district judges who deal with the box work in their own time. Whilst this system works well, it creates both expense and delay. I understand that the Ministry of Justice, HMCS and the Association of Her Majesty's District Judges are beginning to look at what routine work that presently requires the attention of a district judge could be delegated to members of the HMCS staff and thus not have to be sent off to a deputy district judge for consideration. As I say in paragraph 3.6 below, I broadly support that initiative although it would also require the approval of the Civil Procedure Rule Committee.

3.4   <u>Increased use of technology.</u> County courts at the moment are "paper mountains". Although facilities exist in some courts to allow documents to be received by email, the vast majority of work for court administrative staff involves receiving and processing paper documents, and communicating with the parties in documentary form. Money is also handled without taking advantage of modern technology for processing payments (e.g. credit and debit cards), meaning that court staff often spend considerable time in processing cheques and similar forms of payment. In chapter 43 below I outline some of the measures that could be taken to improve the IT systems in the courts. If these measures were to be implemented, the paper mountains at the county courts (and other courts) could be significantly reduced. This should give court staff greater time to focus on the administration of cases. It must be accepted, of course, that IT does not necessarily provide a panacea to the overburdening of court staff. It is possible to be overwhelmed by emails instead of paper.[149]

3.5   <u>Docketing.</u> In Chapter 39 above I discussed the possibility of increased docketing in certain courts, including the county courts. The clear message from Phase 2 was that court users are in favour of the docketing of the more complex, document-heavy or technically specialised cases to specific judges, in so far as this is practicable.[150] It seems to me that a possible incidental benefit of docketing cases to specific judges is that those judges will then take greater responsibility for "their" cases, and be on hand to address glitches that may arise in administration, e.g. if documents are lost or application notices are misfiled. This, in turn, could lead to the more efficient conduct of court proceedings, and lower costs to the parties.

---

[149] As I have, on occasion, experienced during the course of this Costs Review.
[150] And does not itself add to delay if (say) the specific judge is away from his or her court.

3.6 <u>Increased delegation to proper officers.</u> There is already a pilot underway (CPR PD51B) whereby in certain situations, such as a party failing to file an Allocation Questionnaire, the appropriate notice (in that instance a notice requiring the Allocation Questionnaire to be filed within seven days from service of the notice) is drawn up by a member of the HMCS staff without reference to a judge. I understand from district judges that a fair amount of box work comprises similar very routine matters which could readily be delegated to proper officers. Obviously if a problem emerges in any given case, it can be referred upwards to a district judge. The benefits of increased delegation are threefold. First, the time of district judges will be freed up to deal more serious matters. Secondly, increased responsibility for proper officers may assist in making a long term career in the county court service more attractive. Thirdly, some proper officers could be located at regional centres, thus enabling more work to be dealt with effectively at those locations. The details of any scheme for delegating work from district judges to proper officers would need to be worked out with care. A number of informal delegation protocols have been put into effect in different regions. In my view, this matter should be put on a proper and formal basis. I understand that discussions are presently underway between the judiciary and the administration in this regard.

3.7 <u>Listing of fast track cases.</u> I am told that it is the practice in some regions to list fast track trials in all county courts on the same day, e.g. Thursday or Friday. The advantage of this practice is that if one court has more settlements than expected and another court has fewer settlements than expected, cases can be passed between one court and another without the need to take any trial out of the list. I am also told that this practice has declined in some regions. In my view, it makes good sense for different county courts in the same region to list fast track trials on the same day. This is a matter of detail which I draw to the attention of HMCS, but do not make the subject of a specific recommendation.

4. CONCLUSION AND RECOMMENDATIONS

4.1 <u>Conclusion.</u> Shortcomings in court administration, particularly in the county courts, drive up the costs of litigation. In any package of reforms to promote access to justice at proportionate costs, these matters cannot be ignored. I therefore support the current initiatives to improve court administration by making structural changes. These structural changes must be focused upon improving the standard of service delivered to court users, not upon saving costs. The civil courts are already self-financing.[151]

4.2 <u>General approach.</u> In summary:

(i) I would broadly support measures to remove routine cases (especially in the county courts) that do not require the decision of a judge from frontline court administration staff, and for those cases to be processed at regional centres. If this were done, it would free-up much of the time of court staff to deal with "real" cases that require the decision of a judge, and deliver a higher quality of service to court users (with attendant costs benefits).

(ii) The increased use of IT in the courts should also assist in reducing the "paper mountains" faced by frontline court staff, which in turn should free-up their time to focus upon case administration.

---

[151] See chapter 1 above.

(iii)   The increased use of docketing (in so far as practicable) may encourage judges to take a hands-on approach to the administration of "their" cases, resulting in smoother running of cases and associated costs benefits to the parties.

4.3   Matters concerning IT and the extent to which docketing is practicable are discussed in other chapters.

4.4   <u>Recommendations.</u>   The specific recommendations which I make in this chapter are:

(i)   Most county court cases should be issued at regional centres, where the staff will be skilled in processing routine proceedings. However, a facility to issue proceedings at all county courts must be retained.

(ii)   Only if cases are defended, should they be transferred to, or retained in, county courts, where the staff should be specifically trained for, and focused upon, the administration of contested cases.

(iii)   The Association of District Judges and HMCS should together draw up a scheme for the increased delegation of routine box work from district judges to proper officers within the court service.

CHAPTER 43. INFORMATION TECHNOLOGY

INDEX

1. INTRODUCTION

1.1   An effective information technology ("IT") system in the courts is essential to proper case management. The courts need up to date IT, in order (a) to process cases and (b) to communicate effectively with the outside world.

1.2   <u>Lord Woolf's recommendations.</u> In proposing an active case management role for the courts, Lord Woolf emphasised the importance of introducing effective IT systems: see chapter 13 of his interim report and chapter 21 of his final report.

1.3   Thirteen years have now elapsed since Lord Woolf published his final report. Ten years have elapsed since the introduction of the Civil Procedure Rules (the "CPR"). The courts still do not have an IT system which is adequate for the delivery of civil justice at proportionate cost. Instead we have a patchwork quilt of different IT systems which have evolved without proper co-ordination.

1.4   The IT systems currently existing within our civil courts compare unfavourably with those existing overseas. I shall briefly describe the IT systems in some other jurisdictions, before returning to our own problems.

2. IT SYSTEMS IN SOME OTHER JURISDICTIONS

(i) Austria

2.1   <u>Use of electronic filing.</u> The Austrian courts have supported the electronic filing of court documents since 1986. Now virtually every court transaction from filing a claim to final judgment can be performed online, with documents being digitally signed and authenticated.

2.2   <u>Mandatory for parties with professional representation.</u> It is compulsory for all parties who are professionally represented to file their court documents using the electronic system.[152]   Practitioners are given authentication details and their

---

[152] It is possible to apply to the court for an exemption from this requirement, if the costs of scanning and administering voluminous hard-copy evidence would outweigh the benefits.

electronic signature is required to certify that scanned documents are exact copies of the originals. Whenever a document is filed electronically, the other parties receive an automatic notification by email. The parties are entitled to see hard copies of any scanned documents.

2.3   <u>Unrepresented persons cannot use the electronic system.</u> Litigants in person are not able to file their court documents using the electronic system as only practitioners have the necessary authentication details. Litigants in person are therefore still required to file hard copies of their documents in the traditional way. However, this is a rarer occurrence than in England and Wales as the Austrian legal system requires parties to be represented for most cases.

2.4   <u>Use of documents at trial.</u> Paper copies of documents are still used in the courtroom at trial. However, any participant can choose to read the electronic version online if they have the necessary equipment to do so.

(ii) Singapore

2.5   Singapore moved to an electronic filing system in 2001 and it is now mandatory for parties to file court documents in Portable Document Format ("PDF"). The parties access the electronic system using their National Registration Identity Cards. The court provides a service to scan paper documents and convert them into PDF and 15% of documents are first added to the system in this way.

2.6   Parties are also encouraged to exchange documents in the PDF format. However, there is less use of technology for efficient document management internally within law firms.

(iii) Australia

2.7   <u>eFiling.</u> The Federal Court of Australia has an electronic filing system whereby litigants or legal representatives can lodge applications and other Court documents using the Federal Court's website. The website includes a step by step guide to lodging documents as well as a facility for paying filing fees by credit card.

2.8   <u>eCourtroom.</u>   There is also a facility whereby parties and their legal representatives can participate in a virtual courtroom. The Court may receive submissions and affidavit evidence from the parties electronically and the relevant docket Judge can give directions and make orders as if the parties were in a normal courtroom.

2.9   <u>eCase Administration.</u> The Federal Court also has a third electronic service whereby practitioners or parties can communicate with court staff on case related issues in a secure environment.   Only parties to the matter or their legal representatives have access to this service. The electronic system has a "reminder" function which enables court staff to set a reminder date for the system automatically to send an email to all parties where required, for example on issues relating to compliance.

2.10   <u>Recent developments.</u> In January 2009 a new Practice Note came into force.[153] This Practice Note applies in cases (a) involving a significant number of documents and (b) in which the use of technology in the management of documents

---

[153] It has since been superseded by Practice Note CM6 – Electronic Technology in Litigation (25th September 2009), but the new Practice Note is along similar lines to the January 2009 Practice Note.

and the conduct of proceedings would help to facilitate the quick, inexpensive and efficient resolution of the matter. In such cases, the Court will expect the parties to use technology efficiently and effectively in preparation for, and in the conduct of, the trial.

3. THE IT REQUIREMENTS OF THE CIVIL COURTS IN THE 21st CENTURY

3.1   The civil courts need an IT system which has the following capabilities:

(i)   Electronic filing for claim forms, statements of case, witness statements, expert reports and other documents lodged.

(ii)   The ability to maintain all documents lodged by the parties to a case or created by the court in a single electronic bundle relating to that case.

(iii)   The electronic bundle for each case should be accessible to the parties, court staff and the judge by means of an extranet with unique password.

(iv)   Digital signature technology to authenticate documents and correspondence sent by parties to the court or to each other.[154]

(v)   A facility for online payment of court fees and all other payments into court.

(vi)   Scanning equipment at all courts, so that parties without IT equipment can lodge documents at court.

(vii)   A national database on which the electronic bundles for each case are held (so that cases or hearings can be transferred from one court to another, without any need for transport of papers).

4. WHAT WE HAVE AT THE MOMENT

4.1   A patchwork quilt. At present, there is a plethora of different IT systems operating or being developed in the civil courts of England and Wales. These systems have been installed individually over a long period of time and they are not all compatible with one another. There had been plans to introduce a holistic electronic system across England and Wales, known as the Electronic Filing and Document Management ("EFDM") project, and while EFDM was in development other projects were postponed or cancelled. However, the EFDM project was halted for lack of funding in late 2008. I am advised by the Ministry of Justice (the "MoJ") that this does not preclude it being reinstated in the future, if funds become available.

4.2   The main IT systems currently in place in the civil courts are the following:

(i)   LINK: This was a project to install IT equipment and connections into the courts. That network is now in place in all courts and HMCS[155] offices.

(ii)   COINs: A case management system launched in 1997 for what is now the Administrative Court and it allows electronic records of cases to be kept. The application runs on an x.gsi network (accredited to government confidential criteria). COINs has inbuilt functionality that includes the creation and storage of documents against the case record, barcode scanning, a suite of

---

[154] There are issues to resolve in respect of digital signature technology, for example because lawyers may entrust their usernames and passwords to their secretaries. These issues lie beyond the scope of the civil justice Costs Review.
[155] Her Majesty's Courts Service.

management information reports and a listing diary. The application can be adapted to allow for changes in jurisdiction including, recently, the regionalisation of the Administrative Court.

(iii) <u>Possession Claims Online ("PCOL") and Money Claims Online ("MCOL"):</u> Electronic systems which allow litigants to issue simple, straightforward claims for possession or monetary claims online. The scope of PCOL and MCOL ends once a claim is defended, at which point the cases are printed and transferred to the traditional court system.

(iv) <u>Claims Production Centre:</u> Also known as the County Courts Bulk Centre ("CCBC"). This is a facility attached to Northampton County Court for the filing of vast numbers of straightforward claims. It has been in place since 1991 and it is mainly used by credit card providers to issue debt proceedings.

(v) <u>CaseMan:</u>[156] An electronic case management system which was designed to replace manual record cards in the county courts. Every event in a case can be recorded onto CaseMan and this allows court staff and judges to quickly review the status and history of any given case. There is no centralised database and each county court has its own system with only a partial link between them. CaseMan does not integrate well with other systems,[157] particularly Microsoft Windows applications such as Word and Outlook.

(vi) <u>eDiary:</u> An electronic diary and scheduling system which has been deployed across the county courts. It has been criticised as being limited to each county court, although the courts are able to view one another's diaries.

(vii) <u>JCIS:</u> A version of COINs developed for the Judicial Committee of the Privy Council. It is being replaced by the new Supreme Court software (see below).

(viii) <u>New Supreme Court software:</u> Developed by external consultants. I am told that it is not designed to integrate with any existing court IT system.

(ix) <u>SUPs:</u> The Service Upgrade Project started in 2003 with a plan for it to be installed in all civil courts. SUPs is a replacement for CaseMan and FamilyMan. It began national roll out on 21st September 2009. It is intended to provide a national database of court records, together with a range of case management, word processing, enforce

ement and other functions. It is aimed at improving the underlying IT infrastructure across the courts and providing a foundation for an electronic filing and document management system.

(x) <u>InterCOMM:</u> Also known as the Commercial Court IT project ("CCIT"). The first phase of this project, an electronic case management and listing system for internal use by court staff, was launched in 2005. The second phase of the project was to extend the system to court users but this was cancelled in favour of the EFDM project.

(xi) <u>Electronic working:</u> Could be considered the spiritual successor to EFDM. Electronic working (generally known as "e-working") provides an electronic filing system to court users and an electronic case file for judges and court staff plus the listing component from CCIT. It can be described as being fully end-to-end covering all transactions between parties, court staff and judges. So far e-working seems to have been successful, integrating reasonably well with other software such as Microsoft Windows applications. However, at the time of writing it is confined to the Commercial Court and the Technology and Construction Court (the "TCC").

---

[156] A similar system to CaseMan, known as FamilyMan, is used in divorce and care proceedings.
[157] Such as are generally operated by court users.

4.3   I am told that there are a number of other bespoke IT systems operating within the Royal Courts of Justice ("RCJ") complex. These include High Court Forms (a variation of CaseMan) and Bacchus (a legacy system used in the Bankruptcy and Companies Court). Both of these systems, in so far as they apply to jurisdictions which will be accommodated in the Rolls Building, are in scope for replacement by e-working.

5. PROPOSALS FOR THE FUTURE IN RESPECT OF IT SYSTEMS

5.1   <u>Need for strategic oversight.</u> First and foremost there needs to be a single body, comprised of active and well informed members, which will exercise strategic oversight over all IT systems which are installed in the civil courts. Both the practitioners to whom I have spoken and MoJ officials agree that there is need for such a body. In a subsequent note to me, however, the MoJ made the point that such a body could only be advisory, because the final decisions involve the expenditure of public money. I accept that qualification. However, the recommendations of such a body should carry considerable authority.

5.2   One possibility is that the Information Technology and the Courts Committee ("ITAC") could take on this role. In that event the judge who chairs ITAC would need to be released from part of his or her sitting commitments, so that he or she could chair regular meetings of ITAC and be kept closely informed of all looming IT issues. Alternatively, some other body could be established to exercise strategic oversight over all IT projects. Mr Justice Mann (the Judge in Charge of Modernisation and IT) has read this chapter in draft and agrees that there needs to be a more effective body to provide judicial oversight of IT projects, but he doubts that ITAC is the body to do this.

5.3   <u>Development teams for individual projects.</u> One reason for the success of the e-working system installed at the TCC and Commercial Court is that both a judge and practitioner were embedded in the development team. I recommend that this practice should be followed in future developments teams for specific IT projects.

5.4   <u>Extension of e-working.</u> The cancellation of EFDM was a serious blow. It leaves the vast majority of civil courts without any prospect of a centralised system of electronic case administration. The e-working system installed at the TCC and Commercial Court has realised the concepts espoused by the EFDM project, but it is currently planned to be available only for the jurisdictions to be accommodated in the new Rolls Building.[158] Thus it will be extended to the Chancery Division, including the Bankruptcy and Companies Court. I strongly recommend that e-working should be extended to the rest of the High Court in London, in particular the Queen's Bench Division. It should also be extended to the Senior Courts Costs Office ("SCCO").[159] This would produce a significant rationalisation of the IT systems currently in place across the RCJ. If the recommendation made in chapter 45 below for revising the format of bills of costs is accepted,[160] the SCCO will need IT facilities to receive and deal with bills of costs electronically.

---

[158] E-working was demonstrated to future users of the Rolls Building at an e-working Awareness Workshop on 20th October 2009. My judicial assistant attended the workshop and reports that there was general enthusiasm for the project, although certain technical issues were in the process of being identified and overcome.
[159] Formerly the Supreme Court Costs Office.
[160] See chapter 45 below, paragraphs 5.4 to 5.8.

5.5   Once e-working has been introduced across the High Court in London, I recommend that it should be rolled out across all county courts and district registries across England and Wales. This would achieve the objectives of EFDM before that project was cancelled. Mr Justice Ramsey has recently drawn attention to the success of e-working at the London TCC and has urged that it be introduced to TCC courts at regional centres outside London.[161] The MoJ advises, and of course I accept, that e-working would require substantial adaptation for use in the county courts.

5.6   Costs involved. I am informed by the MoJ that the costs of installing e-working in the Commercial Court (including initial development costs) and its integration with CCIT were about £2m. The estimated costs of installing e-working in TCC, Chancery Division and Bankruptcy and Companies Court are approximately £4.5m. The costs of installing e-working across the rest of the High Court in London have not yet been determined.

5.7   No estimates have been obtained for the costs of extending e-working across all civil courts in England and Wales. Nor have the benefits been quantified. On the other hand, in my view it is self evident that the introduction of e-working or a similar system across all civil courts will lead to substantial savings in civil litigation costs. Indeed, this was the logic behind the proposal for EFDM (which would have been taken forward this year but for lack of funding).

5.8   Once e-working is fully installed in all Rolls Building jurisdictions the annual maintenance cost is estimated at £240,000. There are no figures available for maintenance costs relating to any national deployment.

5.9   Costs savings to be made in the future. Once effective IT systems have been introduced into all civil courts, HMCS will be able to pursue business change strategies that will deliver substantial savings in staffing and non-pay costs such as postage, stationery and storage. This will require corporate management oversight via the Civil Business Modernisation programme that ties together business change and IT system development and allows for enabling costs in infrastructure, training and organisational restructuring.

5.10   Security issues. One potential barrier to the jurisdiction-wide installation of e-working is security. The civil courts in England and Wales currently operate on the gsi network which imposes extremely strict security and assurance standards. This creates both financial and practical difficulties. For example, a party cannot submit documents by attending court with documents on electronic media, such as a USB stick, since the devices to read their documents are disabled on all court computers.[162]

5.11   One can see why such stringent security requirements are valid and necessary for users such as GCHQ,[163] SOCA[164] and the Cabinet Office, since the information that these bodies seek to protect is government information, much of which is extremely sensitive. However, in the civil justice system the information in question does not belong to the government, but to the parties. Furthermore, some of the information may reach the public domain as the case proceeds.

---

[161] See "*Electronic working in the TCC, is it e-working?*", PLC Construction., 21st October 2009 available online at http://construction.practicallaw.com/blog/construction/plc/?p=261.
[162] The MoJ tells me that this is to prevent the introduction of malicious code into the network.
[163] Government Communications Headquarters.
[164] The Serious Organised Crime Agency.

5.12   The current paper-based system is not totally secure. Bundles of documents do not have passwords, post does not come encrypted from pre-authorised postal workers, nor are they backed up.   Court files are vulnerable to unauthorised interception, theft, destruction, duplication and modification.   Information transmitted through e-working should not be any less secure than information transmitted on paper. Furthermore, similar systems to e-working already exist in the private sector (online banking for example) and they are considered to be sufficiently secure.

5.13   My view is that consideration should be given to establishing an IT network for the courts which is separate from, and therefore not constrained by, the requirements of, the gsi system. Although a high level of security should undoubtedly remain, it should be proportionate to the information requiring protection.[165]

5.14   The focus of the present review is upon the costs of civil justice. The question whether there should be a separate IT network for the courts is only relevant to my inquiry, in that it might contribute to reducing the overall costs of civil litigation. However, it is right to note that this question gives rise to wider issues, which are for others to consider. The MoJ takes the view that a separate IT network for the courts would be unduly expensive and would be vulnerable to attacks. Mr Justice Mann, commenting on an earlier draft of this chapter writes:

> "I also very strongly support the suggestion that a court network should be established independently of the gsi. There are frequent examples of how the rigorous security requirements of the gsi get in the way of sensible working practices, and I consider it is contrary to the reasonable requirements of the court service and the judiciary to have to labour under the full rigour of gsi.
>
> ...
>
> A proliferation of networks is not desirable, and gateways into the gsi (which would have to exist) can cause problems, but a less rigorously controlled network is likely to reap benefits in terms of usability. I would add that there are many judges who think a separate requirement is required on constitutional grounds, but again I do not think it is appropriate to develop that point."

Mr Justice Ramsey, who has been closely involved in introducing e-working to the TCC, also endorses the proposal that there should be a court network separate from the gsi network.

5.15   Whether the creation of a separate IT network for the courts (a) is the right way to proceed and (b) would create a material reduction in litigation costs are serious questions, which should not be brushed aside.   My recommendation in relation to this issue is that serious consideration should be given to the question whether a separate IT network for the courts should be created. This is exactly the sort of question that should be addressed by the oversight body proposed in paragraph 5.1 above.

5.16   Impact of possible reforms to the county courts. In chapter 42 above I discuss possible reforms to the county courts. The effect of these reforms (if implemented) would be that many of the current routine functions would be transferred from

---

[165] A higher level of security should still remain for some cases: for example, family cases or price sensitive judgments. I am advised that proper security could be achieved by use of encryption.

county courts to back offices in suitable locations, leaving smaller numbers of staff in the county courts who would service contested cases or cases requiring hearings. If these reforms are implemented, the county courts would become more focused organisations. This may reduce the burden and cost of equipping all county courts with effective IT systems of the kind described above.

6. PROPOSALS IN RESPECT OF RELATED MATTERS

6.1 <u>Training.</u> A concomitant of the above recommendations is that judges and court staff must receive proper training. Legal practitioners must receive proper training. Likewise law firms and barristers chambers must ensure that their staff are properly trained.[166] Law firms must also be willing to adapt their procedures. For example, at the present time relatively few firms of solicitors are willing to accept service by email.

6.2 <u>Amendments to CPR.</u> The introduction of effective IT into the courts will necessitate a number of amendments to the CPR, practice directions and court forms. That drafting exercise will accompany, and will be consequential upon, the introduction of effective IT systems across the civil courts. Since this is self-evident, I do not make it the subject of a separate recommendation. I place on record, however, that at the time of drafting this chapter (December 2009) a practice direction to facilitate electronic working is being drawn up. The draft practice direction, which is currently emerging, seems to me to be eminently sensible.

7. RECOMMENDATIONS

7.1 I make the following recommendations:

(i) A suitable body should be appointed to exercise strategic oversight over all IT systems which are installed in the civil courts.

(ii) Judges and practitioners should be included in future development teams for individual court IT projects.

(iii) E-working should be extended to the rest of the High Court in London, in particular the Queen's Bench Division and also to the SCCO.

(iv) Once e-working has been introduced across the High Court in London, it should be rolled out (suitably adapted) across all county courts and district registries in England and Wales.

(v) Consideration should be given to establishing an IT network for the courts which is separate from, and therefore not constrained by the security requirements of, the gsi system. This network should have its own appropriate level of security.

(vi) Judges and court staff should receive proper training in relation to court IT systems. Likewise legal practitioners and their staff should be properly trained in relation to court IT systems and should be willing to adapt their procedures.

---

[166] This may be less of a problem for the younger generation of lawyers than for my own generation.

REVIEW OF
CIVIL LITIGATION COSTS

PART 7. ASSESSMENT OF COSTS

CHAPTER 44. SUMMARY ASSESSMENT

INDEX

1. INTRODUCTION

1.1   Chapter 52 of the Preliminary Report outlines the procedure for summary assessment of costs under CPR rule 44.7. The chapter identifies a number of benefits and drawbacks of the current position. Three possible options are then put forward for consideration:

(i)   Option 1: make no change to the present rules governing summary assessment.

(ii)   Option 2: abolish the summary assessment procedure and instead encourage judges to order interim payments on account of costs, alternatively provisional assessments.

(iii)   Option 3: restructure the summary assessment procedure.

1.2   Comments during Phase 2 were also invited on the issues of guideline hourly rates for solicitors ("GHRs").

1.3 <u>Abbreviations.</u> In this chapter I refer to the Costs Practice Direction as the "Costs PD". I refer to the Advisory Committee on Civil Costs as the "ACCC".

1.4 <u>The circumstances in which the court carries out summary assessment of costs.</u> The circumstances in which the court makes a summary assessment of costs are set out in Costs PD paragraph 13.2.[1]

2. DEBATE DURING PHASE 2

(i) Summary assessment procedure

(a) Costs assessment seminar

2.1 <u>The seminar.</u> The issue of summary assessment was discussed at the seminar on the assessment of costs co-hosted by the Senior Courts Costs Office[2] Costs Practitioners Group and Reed Smith LLP on 30th July 2009 (the "costs assessment seminar"). The general tenor at that meeting was towards option 3. Particular support was expressed for the summary assessment procedure in respect of interim hearings. One district judge thought that the format of summary assessment should be retained but more detail on costs provided. Another district judge agreed that more detail was needed, especially in fast track trials. A third district judge noted that judges and recorders now had experience of doing summary assessments in practice and as a result they were improving. The Senior Costs Judge noted that judges at all levels are reluctant to conduct summary assessments. A chancery barrister said that summary assessment worked in the county courts where it was undertaken by district judges. However, it should not be operated at High Court level: barristers would need to be educated and High Court judges are reluctant to carry out summary assessments. The Senior Costs Judge suggested that some cases in the High Court and the Court of Appeal are so complex and so high value that summary assessment of costs is not practicable. One district judge stated that for a summary assessment at the end of a trial, the parties should give more information than they do at present. In particular, there should be a break down and explanation of the documents item.

2.2 <u>The consensus of opinion.</u> The consensus which emerged at the seminar was that summary assessment works well in the county court. However, in the Court of Appeal, the High Court and the specialist courts, judges should only do summary assessment if they feel comfortable in doing so. Otherwise, in those courts judges should order detailed assessment together with an interim payment on account of costs. Where judges in those courts undertake summary assessments, they may either do so orally or, alternatively, give their decisions in writing. Practitioners reported that the approach of giving decisions on summary assessment in writing worked well. There was general support for the proposition that more information should be given for the purposes of summary assessments at the end of trials.

(b) Written submissions

2.3 <u>Professional Negligence Bar Association.</u> The Professional Negligence Bar Association (the "PNBA") is one of the few respondents to express unqualified support for the current summary assessment procedure in its Phase 2 submission. In the PNBA's view, "*summary assessment has been one of the more successful*

---

[1] See PR paragraph 52.1.3.
[2] Formerly the Supreme Court Costs Office.

innovations of the CPR”. The PNBA considers that there is much less “*unproductive interlocutory skirmishing*” than before, because litigants fear immediate costs orders as a consequence of making unreasonable applications. However, the PNBA acknowledges that its experience of summary assessment is largely confined to interim hearings and suggests that, if there is widespread dissatisfaction with the results of summary assessments following fast track trials, the answer may be to limit summary assessment to interlocutory hearings. The PNBA expresses concern about abolishing the procedure altogether:

> “We consider that abolition would be a retrograde step. There is real benefit in early final determination of the sum payable under costs orders. The danger with larger interim payments is that, instead of a single heavily contested summary assessment hearing, there would be a heavily contested hearing to determine the level of the interim payment (presumably requiring the expense of the preparation of some form of statement of costs or bill of costs) and then a heavily contested detailed assessment hearing at a later stage.
>
> There would be not dissimilar drawbacks if summary assessment were to be replaced by provisional assessment of the costs.”

2.4   Law Society. The Law Society believes that summary assessment has broadly worked well and it is one of the successes of Lord Woolf's reforms. Judges tend to take a pragmatic view by deducting a certain amount from the successful party's statement of costs, thereby achieving “*rough justice*” for the parties. The Law Society does not propose a case for reform of the summary assessment procedure. The system has its faults but it works, in that it provides a “*broad-brush*” approach which does not cause significant injustice to either side. A more fundamental question is to ask how summary assessment may be accommodated within a system of costs management.

2.5   Support for abolition. A handful of submissions received during Phase 2 support abolition of the summary assessment procedure. The Forum of Complex Injury Solicitors shares the concerns identified in PR chapter 52 as to consistency and the expertise of assessing judges and favours the replacement of summary assessment with an order for an interim payment on account of costs. A firm of claimant personal injury solicitors considers that summary assessments following a fast track trial work most unfairly for the claimant. Its experience is that judges arbitrarily slash its costs without any adequate investigation or reason. The judge is usually tired at the end of the day and just wants to approach matters on a “*broad-brush*” approach. The firm suggests that the judge should simply order an amount on account. It believes that most cases would then settle without the need for detailed assessment.

2.6   Manchester Law Society. Although the Manchester Law Society prefers restructuring the summary assessment procedure, a significant number of its members favour option 2, in particular the alternative suggestion for the judge to make a provisional assessment of the costs. However, 75% is too high a value. There is also a concern that it may be unfair in that a party which thinks that it should do slightly better may be deterred from pursuing an award for the legitimate balance by the fear of having to bear the costs of a full detailed assessment. If option 3 is favoured, the Manchester Law Society considers that it should become compulsory for parties to break down some of the items in the statement of costs (namely work done on documents and “attendance on others”) and to state specifically the costs of preparing the statement.

2.7   Similar dissatisfaction with the current Form N260[3] is also expressed by a number of other respondents who favour a restructuring of the summary assessment procedure. Criticisms are that it is too simple and has a bad layout. Suggestions for improvement include the following:

(i)   The CPR should be amended so as to require Form N260 to be accompanied by appropriate certificates signed by a partner (as required for bills for detailed assessment).

(ii)   The form should be revised so as to constitute a "*halfway house*" between the current Form N260 and the bill for detailed assessment, with a more detailed bill but contained within two or three pages.

(iii)   A schedule should be included detailing time spent considering and preparing documents, with a brief narrative to describe the work done by the solicitors pre and post proceedings.

2.8   <u>Association of Personal Injury Lawyers.</u> The Association of Personal Injury Lawyers ("APIL") considers that summary assessment on interim hearings is working adequately. However, with respect to fast track trials, summary assessment is unsatisfactory. Lack of costs knowledge by both counsel and the hearing judge can be a disadvantage to both claimants and defendants. It is essential that adequate training on costs is provided for the judiciary. APIL believes that further work should be done to develop the idea of an early interim payment on account of costs post trial. It recommends that, on conclusion of a fast track trial the judge should make an interim award on base costs to the successful party, to be paid within 14 days of the conclusion of the hearing. Either party would then have the option of applying for detailed assessment once an interim payment has been made. The claimant could apply if he thought that the overall settlement proposed by the defendant, taking into account the interim payment, was insufficient. The defendant would have such an option if they thought that the payment was excessive and the claimant had decided to accept it in full and final settlement. This would allow defendants to continue to make appropriate costs challenges but in the meantime would also provide prompt payment to the claimant's solicitor for work done. APIL considers that this is likely to lead to a narrowing of the issues that eventually come before the court.

2.9   <u>Firms of solicitors.</u> One firm of solicitors which conducts exclusively claimant personal injury work favours option 3, restructuring. Summary assessments should remain limited to fast track cases and multi-track trials lasting less than one day. Although, summary assessment can work well and avoid unnecessary costs associated with detailed assessment, there are some difficulties with the current position. Summary assessment procedures are often rushed and proper time should be allocated to deal with costs. Some judges only occasionally hear civil trials and, when conducting summary assessments, treat costs as they would in a criminal case (with the concept of additional liabilities being treated as somewhat foreign). Training should be provided and judges should be able to request assistance if the assessment is not within their experience. The firm of solicitors believes that summary assessment at the end of a trial is not appropriate where costs are awarded in whole on in part on the indemnity basis. Costs should be disclosed earlier (24 hours before the date of the hearing is too late).

2.10   Another firm which conducts mainly claimant personal injury, claimant clinical negligence and claimant and defendant commercial litigation, considers that the summary assessment procedure following interim applications appears to be

_____

[3] The format for statements of costs for summary assessment: see PR paragraph 52.1.5.

working well. However, some change is needed to summary assessments conducted at the end of fast track trials or disposal hearings. When costs are summarily assessed at the end of a trial or disposal hearing, district judges are all too keen to slash the time claimed in costs schedules whilst providing very little explanation. This is often due to lack of information, both in the form N260 and counsel's argument. The firm contrasts this to its experience of detailed assessments, where its time is reduced very little. It considers that the summary assessment procedure should be restructured in the following way:

> "We agree with this suggestion that judges should be encouraged to consider summary assessment only where they have sufficient expertise, where time is available to conduct the assessment properly and where all those involved in the summary assessment have the necessary information to support the judge in his decision making."

2.11   Liability insurer. The view of one liability insurer is that although the amounts allowed on summary assessment may "*noticeably exceed*" the amounts that would be allowed on a detailed assessment of the same costs, the process of summary assessment remains desirable in order to avoid the additional layer of costs of detailed assessment. The insurer would not support the abolition of summary assessment and the introduction of payments on account as an alternative. However, the process of summary assessment could be improved in two ways: (a) by increasing the amount of costs training given to judges and (b) by allocating a proper amount of time to the process of summary assessment.

2.12   Judiciary. Members of the judiciary who address the issue of summary assessment in their submissions are in favour of option 3, restructuring. One judge notes that although summary assessment has been much criticised, its advantages outweigh its disadvantages. Inconsistency is inevitable: to most of those members of the judiciary who come from the Bar, costs have been a "*closed book*"; even amongst those judges who were solicitors, there is no uniformity because (inevitably) some people are more generous than others. The procedure is necessarily robust, but that does not make it automatically unfair. Summary assessment has the advantage of immediacy and there is an obvious cash flow advantage to the receiving party. Detailed assessment on the other hand is laborious and complicated. The judge does, however, consider that there should be a mandatory requirement for a payment on account (except where the paying party is legally aided) unless there is a good reason not to make an order. A deputy district judge states that the single most worrying aspect of summary assessments is the "*inability to scrutinise, within the confines of the summary assessment, claims of time spent that have every appearance of being unreasonable i.e. too high*". She suggests that where the judge attempting to conduct a summary assessment concludes that the bill is disproportionate and that the scrutiny required cannot be undertaken in the time available, the bill should be referred for detailed assessment with an order that no costs be allowed to the receiving party in respect of the costs of the assessment.

2.13   The Liverpool District Judges consider that the summary assessment of costs works well and results in considerable savings of costs that would arise from detailed assessment. The vast majority of hearings in the civil courts are dealt with by district judges, all of whom have long experience either in practice or on the bench of summary assessments. The Liverpool District Judges recognise that there are some judges on the circuit bench or higher who do not have the same experience and are less comfortable with summary assessments, so some variation may be required. They suggest that consideration be given to the procedure which has been adopted in Liverpool:

"In Liverpool a situation has arisen where all Circuit Judges undertake summary assessment, but even the more experienced have difficulties with specific costs issues in some cases. In such a case they assess those parts of the costs with which they are comfortable but refer the more difficult (usually technical) issues to one of the Regional Costs Judges, who determine that/those issues effectively by an informal detailed assessment, listed before them directly by order of the Trial Judge without reference to the usual commencement procedure set out in Part 47. This procedure is not, strictly, in accordance with the rules but it works and the parties accept it."

(ii) Guideline hourly rates

2.14   Association of British Insurers.   The Association of British Insurers (the "ABI") expresses the view in its Phase 2 submission that current GHRs are *"disproportionate, support excessive referral fees and are an unnecessary drain on all policyholders, business and local authorities"*. This is particularly the case in personal injury cases. The ABI recently commissioned a consultancy firm (a) to undertake an independent assessment of the market for personal injury solicitors; (b) to compare marketing costs across different sectors; and (c) to assess whether reducing GHRs could have serious implications for access to justice. The consultancy firm concluded that, unlike in normal competitive markets where marketing costs are subject to constraints imposed by consumer behaviour, in the personal injury claims market this constraint does not exist because claimants are protected from the costs incurred by their own solicitor. This is likely to lead to marketing costs that are significantly higher. Marketing costs incurred by solicitors are much higher than in a broad range of other sectors. A reduction in hourly rates for claimant personal injury solicitors would reduce the amount spent on marketing but this is *"unlikely to have a significant impact on access to justice because it will still be profitable to find claimants even at a much lower hourly rate"*. The ABI believes that these findings support the case for reducing the hourly rates for claimant personal injury solicitors.

2.15   Firms of solicitors. A number of solicitors' firms address the issue of hourly rates in their submissions. One firm which specialises in, amongst other areas of law, personal injury, considers that arguments that claimants' solicitors' costs are excessive and disproportionate is *"specious"*. The ways in which claimant and defendant costs operate are not analogous in any way. Defendant solicitors take on volume work which comes in on a regular basis; they are paid whether they win or lose. They take cases on at a later stage, when decisions can be made on liability and quantum. This is not the case for claimant solicitors, who have very little information at the outset and have to carry out investigations and incur expenses before assessing whether there are reasonable prospects of success. A solicitor who specialises in personal injury and other insurance-related litigation on behalf of defendants and insurers, on the other hand, sees no good reason why claimant solicitors should be paid at a higher rate than defendant solicitors. The fact that a claimant's solicitor must fund a number of unsuccessful cases in addition to the successful ones is supposed to be reflected in the success fee, not the charging rate. Defendant solicitors are obliged to charge what the market can stand, whereas there is no discernable market pressure on claimant solicitors. What is needed is either a regulation limiting the recoverable charging rate or an Advisory Committee on Civil Costs[4] which actually reduces charging rates.

2.16   A national law firm which operates in a number of areas of civil litigation, including insurance, also laments the disparity between claimant and defendant

---

[4] As to which see PR paragraphs 52.2.6 to 52.2.12.

costs. It disagrees with the suggestion at PR paragraph 10.10.2 that insurance solicitors are bound to charge less than claimant solicitors. It argues that defendant solicitors have to prospect for work in the same way as claimant solicitors. Very often there is more for insurance solicitors to do in preparing a case, particularly in terms of disclosure and witnesses. Although insurance solicitors have educated clients, they do require lengthy explanation of the issues because they may wish to contribute to the strategy of the case and be in a position to give instructions. The firm's experience is that an insurance lawyer's investment of time is at least as high as that of a claimant. Another firm of solicitors which does a lot of defendant clinical negligence work states that claimant solicitors in clinical negligence cases regularly claim rates which exceed the GHRs on the basis that the complexity of clinical negligence justifies an enhanced rate. This is not always disputed by the costs masters. The firm does not consider that clinical negligence is really more complex than most other types of litigation when dealt with by someone who specialises in that work. It sees no justification in the argument that claimant solicitors should be entitled to exceptional rates, particularly when contrasted with defendant hourly rates which represent the "true" market. A City of London firm can claim in excess of £800 per hour if acting on a clinical negligence case under a CFA with a 100% success fee. This is about £600 more than a defendant lawyer doing the same work. The firm suggests two possible options for reform:

(i)   Establish a more robust generic GHR based on actual costs and appropriate uplift. Relevant factors would include geographical location and type of case, as well as the value of damages or whether the case is standard or exceptional.

(ii)   The same exercise as (i) above but with specific reference to clinical negligence cases. An additional adjustment could be made to take into account the value of the claim.

2.17   Liverpool District Judges. The Liverpool District Judges accept that more research is needed in order to determine what the appropriate GHRs should be. There has been a tendency to increase rates each year broadly in line with inflation, without reference to a solicitor's overheads and profit margins. A proper evaluation of the actual costs to solicitors and barristers of carrying out their instructions is needed. As regards solicitors, there may be merit in returning to the old A and B formula.[5] There should also be greater clarity of the basis upon which barristers' fees are charged.

3. ANALYSIS

(i) Summary assessment procedure

(a) Procedure to be followed

3.1   The way forward. Of the three options canvassed in the Preliminary Report, I am quite satisfied that option 3 is the proper way forward. Summary assessment is a valuable tool which has made a substantial contribution to civil procedure, not least by deterring frivolous applications and reducing the need for detailed assessment proceedings. The summary assessment procedure should be retained and improvements should be made in order to meet the criticisms which have been expressed during Phases 1 and 2 of the Costs Review.

---

[5] As to which see PR paragraph 52.2.1.

3.2   In chapter 40 above I have recommended that all judges should receive effective training in relation to costs budgeting and costs management. An incidental benefit of this training should be an increase in the skill of all judges at carrying out summary assessments.

3.3   <u>Fast track trials.</u> If my recommendations for fixing costs in the fast track are accepted, then the amount of costs due will be agreed between the parties in most cases; where the amount is not agreed, the summary assessment of costs will be relatively straightforward and should be undertaken at the end of the trial. Cases will be few and far between where it is appropriate to direct a detailed assessment of costs in a fast track case.

3.4   <u>Interim applications.</u> Bearing in mind what was said at the costs assessment seminar and also the contents of the written submissions, I am satisfied that in the county court summary assessments of costs at the end of interim applications are generally working well. However, in the Court of Appeal, the High Court and the specialist courts not all judges feel comfortable about summarily assessing costs at the end of "heavy" applications. I recommend that if any judge in the Court of Appeal, the High Court or the specialist courts feels that he or she lacks the time or the expertise to assess the costs of an interim application, then the judge should direct a detailed assessment of those costs, whilst at the same time ordering a substantial interim payment in respect of costs. If the interim payment is well judged, it is highly likely that the assessment proceedings will be resolved at an early stage. Before taking this fall back course, the judge should first consider whether he or she would be able to deliver a competent summary assessment of costs on paper, if necessary after receiving further written submissions form the parties. Hopefully the number of judges who feel that they lack expertise to assess costs at the end of an interim application will decrease in number over the next few years.

3.5   <u>Multi-track trials.</u> The Costs PD provides that the trial judge will generally assess the costs of an action if the trial is concluded within a day: see Costs PD paragraph 13.2(2). On the evidence, sometimes this works well and sometimes it does not. I recommend that if any judge feels that he or she lacks the time or the expertise to assess the costs of an action, the trial of which has concluded within a day, then the judge should direct a detailed assessment of those costs, whilst at the same time ordering a substantial interim payment in respect of costs. Before taking this fall back course, the judge should first consider whether he or she would be able to deliver a competent summary assessment of costs on paper, if necessary after receiving further written submissions form the parties.

<u>(b) Information available for summary assessments</u>

3.6   <u>At the end of interim applications.</u> Form N260 is, in my view, generally sufficient for the purpose of assessing the costs of an interim application. The work, the value of which is being assessed, all relates to an application which the court has just determined. In most cases it is not hugely difficult for the judge to consider the extent to which the work and the disbursements set out in Form N260 were reasonable.

3.7   <u>At the end of trials and appeals.</u> In respect of summary assessments at the end of a trial or appeal, I consider that Form N260 provides insufficient information. The court is assessing not only costs related to the trial or appeal, but also the costs of the whole pre-trial process. In the short term, I recommend that a revised and more informative version of Form N260 be prepared for use in connection with summary assessments at the end of trial. In the long term, the course which I recommend is that set out in the next chapter. A new software system should be developed, which will be capable of generating bills of costs at different levels of generality. An intermediate level of generality should be used for the purpose of assisting the court to carry out summary assessment of costs.

(ii) Guideline hourly rates

3.8   As explained in the Preliminary Report, the existing GHRs have been issued solely for the purpose of summary assessment of costs: see PR chapter 52, section 2. In the next chapter I shall consider whether the GHRs or some variant of them should apply to detailed assessments. The issue for consideration now is whether the GHRs or the procedure by which they are drawn up requires reform.

3.9   GHRs should be set by Costs Council. As stated in chapter 6 above, the level of GHRs is a critical element in the civil justice system. For the reasons set out in that chapter, in my view the proper body to review and revise the GHRs is a Costs Council. Proposals for how the Costs Council should be constituted and operate are set out in chapter 6.

3.10   Robust decisions required. If my recommendation in chapter 6 is accepted, the Costs Council will have to make some robust decisions in order to redress existing anomalies. These decisions should include the following:

(i)   Is there any justification for paying "City" rates to firms of solicitors which choose to set up in the City of London but are not doing "City" work? In my view, "City" rates should only be paid for heavy commercial work. Defamation, clinical negligence and similar work should not be remunerated at rates above London 2.

(ii)   What reductions should there be in hourly rates for personal injury work, if referral fees are banned or capped, as recommended in chapter 20 above. I accept that firms will incur marketing costs, possibly at the rate of about £200 per case. But the present level of referral fees has grossly distorted the costs of personal injuries litigation.

(iii)   If one takes defendant hourly rates as representing reasonable rates set by the market in certain areas of civil litigation, what factors justify higher rates for claimant solicitors and what allowance should be made for those factors?

3.11   I do not in this report set out a proposed set of GHRs. That would be usurping what is presently the function of the ACCC. Instead I recommend[6] a new mechanism for setting GHRs and draw attention to some of the factors which must be taken into account.

3.12   Principles upon which GHRs should be set. One of the first tasks of the Costs Council will be to formulate the principles upon which GHR are set. I suggest that the aim of the GHR should be to reflect market rates for the level of work being undertaken.[7] These would be the rates which an intelligent purchaser with time to shop around for the best deal would negotiate.

3.13   How GHRs should be used in summary assessments. The GHRs are blended rates, unlike the old "A" and "B" rates which were formerly used.[8] Therefore, as their

---

[6] In chapter 6 above.

[7] In relation to hourly rates for clinical negligence, see chapter 23 above paragraphs 6.12 to 6.14.

[8] See PR paragraph 52.2.1.

name suggests, the GHRs can only be guidelines or starting points. The judge doing the summary assessment should move up or down from those rates, as appropriate.

4. RECOMMENDATIONS

4.1   I make the following recommendations:

(i)   If any judge at the end of a hearing within Costs PD paragraph 13.2 considers that he or she lacks the time or the expertise to assess costs summarily (either at that hearing or on paper afterwards), then the judge should order a substantial payment on account of costs and direct detailed assessment.

(ii)   A revised and more informative version of Form N260 should be prepared for use in connection with summary assessments at the end of trials or appeals.

4.2   My recommendations in respect of the Costs Council are set out in chapter 6 above. They are not repeated in this chapter.

CHAPTER 45. DETAILED ASSESSMENT

INDEX

1. INTRODUCTION

1.1   Preliminary Report. In chapter 53 of the Preliminary Report I outlined the present procedure for detailed assessment, the concerns about that procedure and possible options for reform.

1.2   Abbreviations. In this chapter I refer to the Costs Practice Direction as the "Costs PD". I refer to the Senior Courts Costs Office[9] as the "SCCO". I use the term "costs judge" to cover both costs judges at the SCCO and regional costs judges outside London. I use the term "costs officer" to mean an authorised court officer, i.e. a civil servant who has been authorised by the Lord Chancellor to assess costs. I use the abbreviation "PP" for paying party and "RP" for receiving party. I use the abbreviation "GHRs" for guideline hourly rates for solicitors.

2. COSTS ASSESSMENT SEMINAR

2.1   The seminar. The Seminar on Assessment of Costs (the "costs assessment seminar") was held on 30th July 2009. It was hosted by the Senior Courts Costs Office Costs Practitioners Group and Reed Smith LLP. The seminar was well attended by practitioners and judges who are expert in the field. The seminar was chaired by Costs Judge John O'Hare. Most of the seminar was devoted to detailed assessment, rather than summary assessment. I shall now summarise the views which were expressed on specific topics.

(i) Detailed bills of costs

2.2   Bill format. The present format of bills did not attract favourable comment. The concerns expressed include the following. The bill is expensive and cumbersome to draw. It does not make use of the available technology. It is not easy for the reader of a bill to digest its import. The bill does not contain all necessary

---

[9] Formerly the Supreme Court Costs Office.

information. For example, a bare statement that Miss X spent 10 hours interviewing witnesses is insufficient. The bill should state the reasons why this was done.

2.3   <u>Documents item.</u>   This is generally the most contentious item, upon which large sums turn. Bills usually give insufficient information to enable the reader or the costs judge to determine how much time was properly spent in considering and dealing with documents. A bill ought to make it plain what time was spent on documents in relation to each issue in the case: for example, "special damages involved issues A, B and C and we spent x hours on issue A ..." etc. Document items in the bill should be divided into topics.

2.4   <u>Mismatch between time recording and bills.</u>   Most people record the time which they spend, e.g. eight hours on documents, but not what they were doing in that time. Solicitors should capture the relevant information on their time recording systems, as work proceeds. There should be codes for different tasks.

2.5   <u>Voting.</u>   I took a vote on the comments concerning bills of costs, as summarised in the three preceding paragraphs. There were 41 votes in agreement with those comments, two votes in disagreement and six abstentions.

2.6   <u>Working group set up.</u>   In view of the degree of unanimity about the shortcomings of bills of costs, I set up a working group to consider possible revisions to the format for bills of costs. Following the setting up of the working party, some practitioners and judges suggested that the new form of bill of costs could be based upon the budget form used in the Birmingham costs management pilot.[10]   The working group agreed to consider this.

(ii) Events after the bill of costs

2.7   <u>Points of dispute and points of reply.</u>   Points of dispute are said to be over-long, therefore expensive to read and expensive to reply to. Points of reply are similarly prolix. Both of these pleadings are in large measure formulaic and are built up from standard paragraphs held by solicitors on their databases. In addition, there are lengthy passages in the points of dispute and the points of reply dealing with time spent on documents. It would be better if both the points of dispute and the points of reply concentrated on the reasoning of the bill, not the detailed items. It was suggested that points of dispute should focus on matters of substance in a bill. They should, where practical, deal with items compendiously, rather than repeat the same objection time and again.

2.8   <u>Active case management of detailed assessment proceedings.</u>   Active case management is welcomed. Some costs judges list directions hearings in substantial assessment proceedings and this is regarded as beneficial.

2.9   <u>Provisional assessment.</u>   The proposal for provisional assessment set out in PR paragraph 53.4.9 was discussed. It was pointed out that this would add to the workload of costs judges and costs officers. However, the majority view (supported by Senior Costs Judge Peter Hurst) was that this reform would be beneficial. In the straw poll at the end of this discussion, there were 38 votes in favour of provisional assessment and four against. As to the upper limit for provisional assessment, a regional costs judge proposed £50,000, whereas others proposed £25,000. Again I took a straw poll. There were 28 votes for £50,000 and 24 votes for £25,000.

---

[10] As to which, see chapter 40 above.

2.10   <u>Preliminary issues.</u>   Preliminary issues are regarded as an effective means to cut through detailed assessments.   For example, hourly rates and similar matters could be decided first, leaving other matters to be agreed or, in default of agreement, determined at a separate hearing.   Indeed, such preliminary issue hearings are already common in the SCCO.

2.11   <u>Costs of detailed assessment offers and settlement offers.</u>   Views differed as to whether the presumption should remain that PP pays the costs of detailed assessment proceedings or, alternatively, costs should be at large.   One suggestion was that RP should recover its costs of the assessment proceedings if it recovered a specified proportion (e.g. two thirds or possibly 80%) of the sum claimed.   Another view was that RP should recover its costs of the assessment proceedings, unless it failed to beat an effective offer.   This discussion was inconclusive and no consensus emerged.   The Senior Costs Judge stated that the present rules allow some discretion. On occasions he awards to RP only part of its costs or, indeed, makes no order for costs in respect of the assessment proceedings.

2.12   A number of speakers were opposed to the general rule in Costs PD paragraph 46.1 that an effective offer by PP must be made within 14 days of service of the notice of commencement.   It was proposed that PP should be able to make an effective offer at any stage of proceedings and that RP should have 21 days for acceptance of such an offer.   At the end of this discussion I took a straw poll.   There were 47 votes in favour of removing the "14 day rule" and allowing 21 days for acceptance of any offer.   There were three votes against this proposal and four abstentions.

3. WORKING GROUP REPORT

3.1   The working group focused principally upon the "documents" item in bills. The gist of the working group's report is as follows.   The documents item is set out in a schedule, which sometimes exceeds 50 pages in length.   Such a schedule creates difficulties both for PP and for the costs judge.   It is not easy to identify the time spent on any specific task, especially if that task is spread over several days.

3.2   The working group proposes that the documents item should be broken down into convenient sub-headings, with the relevant work carried out shown under each sub-heading.   An example of such a breakdown is appended to the working group's report.

3.3   The working group is concerned about the undue length of narrative at the start of some bills.   It recommends that practitioners should be reminded of the requirement in Costs PD paragraph 4.5(1) that the background information included in the bill should set out: "*a brief description of the proceedings up to the date of the notice of commencemen*t".

4. WRITTEN SUBMISSIONS

4.1   There was a wide range of views expressed in the written submissions and numerous suggestions for reform were put forward.   Unsurprisingly, many of the submissions traversed the same matters as the costs assessment seminar.   I shall focus upon just some of the submissions.

4.2   <u>Judges.</u>   The Association of Her Majesty's District Judges states that whenever an order for costs is made, the court should always order a payment on account. The Association proposes that the bill of costs should simply be a duplicate of the solicitors' time record; that PP should be compelled to make an offer when serving points of dispute; that there should be published GHRs for detailed assessments. The Association is opposed to provisional assessment on two grounds: first, this would involve additional work for both court staff and district judges; secondly, the process would add little to summary assessment.

4.3 An experienced designated civil judge has sent in detailed comments, the gist of which is as follows. The system of time recording in six minute units is open to abuse and is abused. The merger of "A" and "B" rates into single GHRs has led to a significant increase in recoverable costs. The culture of the profession has changed. Fee earners are given high targets for chargeable hours. This leads to aggressive time recording and sometimes gross exaggeration. Orders for payments on account of costs should be mandatory. Detailed assessment proceedings should be effectively managed, in order to narrow the issues.

4.4 <u>Association of Law Costs Draftsmen.</u> The Association of Law Costs Draftsmen (the "ALCD") states that points of dispute should be short and to-the-point; indeed they can be dispensed with in low value cases (below £20,000) unless there is some specific point to be raised. The ALCD opposes the increasing use of directions in detailed assessment proceedings. It considers that compulsory offers would not be appropriate. Instead the court should take a tougher line with PPs which make no offers or unreasonably low offers. The Part 36 procedure should be encouraged within assessment proceedings. The ALCD supports my proposal[11] that time for appealing should run from the end of the final hearing, not from the date of the decision which is challenged. The ALCD supports the proposal for provisional assessment, which was originally put forward in the ALCD's Phase 1 submission. In relation to hourly rates, the ALCD favours a return to the "A" and "B" rates. The ALCD has reservations about the current GHRs for summary assessment and does not believe that these should be used for detailed assessment.

4.5 <u>Law Society.</u> The Law Society notes that, if the costs management proposals set out in the Preliminary Report are accepted, it would seem that detailed assessment will have a place only in the context of cases where RP's costs significantly exceed the budget. The Law Society would support this. The Law Society agrees with the concerns about the present detailed assessment procedure expressed in PR chapter 53. It identifies particular problems as being the length of points of dispute, the significant cost of preparing the bill and the lack of effective IT for the SCCO.

4.6 <u>Manchester Law Society.</u> The Manchester Law Society is critical of the GHRs for commercial litigation, which are generally much lower than the actual rates charged. The Society is concerned that hourly rates allowed for commercial work in Manchester are substantially lower than the hourly rates allowed in the Commercial Court in London. The Society does not consider that the present level of differential can be justified. One consequence is that commercial litigation, which would otherwise be brought in Manchester, is issued in London. This is to the detriment of the Manchester courts and the local Bar.

4.7 <u>Chester and North Wales Law Society.</u> The Chester and North Wales Law Society, adopting the submissions of a firm of solicitors in that area, believes that

---

[11] PR paragraph 53.4.8.

assessments would be speeded up and made less costly if challenges based on the indemnity principle were abolished.[12]

4.8   London Solicitors Litigation Association. The London Solicitors Litigation Association (the "LSLA") believes that the Part 36 procedure, suitably adapted, should be incorporated into assessment proceedings. The LSLA favours simplifying and streamlining bills of costs. It also favours making greater use of modern technology. The LSLA states

> "Given that amongst solicitors the exchange of documents electronically has become increasingly common, electronic transfer of information with the Court is a natural development. However, clearly the issue of compatibility arises which will first, require the SCCO to be equipped with a system that can accept the electronic transmission of bills and, secondly, will require firms of solicitors to operate systems which will be able to interface with the SCCO system. It would also be hoped that such developments would not preclude the submission of paper bills to the SCCO."

4.9   The LSLA supports the proposal that time for appealing should run from the end of the final hearing. It also supports the proposal for provisional assessment, provided that the points of dispute are provided to the costs officer. In relation to hourly rates, the LSLA opposes reverting to the "A" and "B" principle, as this would make assessment proceedings more complex and lengthy. The present system, despite its faults, gives a measure of certainty. The LSLA believes that the same hourly rates should apply to detailed assessment as apply to summary assessment. There is no reason or purpose for applying a different rate to work done which is to be summarily assessed.

4.10   Commercial Litigation Association. The Commercial Litigation Association ("CLAN") believes that detailed assessment will become less common if costs management is adopted. CLAN agrees with the various concerns expressed in PR chapter 53 and supports the reforms proposed in that chapter. CLAN emphasises that proper IT must be provided to the courts, so that assessment proceedings can be conducted in an effective manner.

4.11   Association of Personal Injury Lawyers. The Association of Personal Injury Lawyers ("APIL") believes that a "Part 36 style rule with sanctions" should be introduced into CPR Part 47; both parties should be free to make successive offers, although PP should be required to make one mandatory offer at the points of dispute stage. The rules should discourage technical challenges. APIL commends the approach of the Multi-Track Code,[13] which requires technical challenges to the enforceability of the retainer to be made within 28 days of the letter of claim. APIL believes that the form of bills of costs is anachronistic and supports reforms to improve and update the bill format. In order to reduce the length of points of dispute, there should be a ban on including quotations from case law.

4.12   Forum of Complex Injury Solicitors. The Forum of Complex Injury Solicitors ("FOCIS") supports the proposals for compulsory offers and putting back the date from which time for appealing runs. FOCIS also supports the proposal for provisional assessments, pointing out that these are commonplace in legal aid and work reasonably well. It opposes returning to "A" and "B" rates.

---

[12] As to which, see chapter 5 above.
[13] As to which, see chapter 22 above.

4.13   Other submissions. A number of firms of solicitors or individual practitioners sent in helpful submissions. These included some additional points which merit mention. One proposal is for a new rule that no firm of solicitors can claim the cost of more than two people attending a hearing, save with an express direction from the judge at that hearing. One firm is concerned that some bills of costs are not merely inaccurate, but "clearly fraudulent". It argues that further verification for the content of bills should be provided and that the rules in relation to disclosure in detailed assessment proceedings should be reviewed.

4.14   One costs draftsman argues that the court should reject any bill which does not comply with the Costs PD. He also expresses concern that, in his view, too many unqualified members of staff are being allowed the Grade C and, occasionally, even the Grade B charging rates.

5. ANALYSIS

(i) Fast track cases

5.1   Profit costs. If my recommendations for fixing all costs in the fast track are accepted, the need for detailed assessments in the fast track will largely be eliminated. I say "largely" rather than totally, because the regime proposed envisages certain exceptions, as discussed in chapter 15 above. In those exceptional cases the procedure for assessing costs should be in accordance with my proposals for the multi-track.

5.2   Disbursements. Certain disbursements in fast track cases will not be the subject of fixed costs. If the parties are unable to agree these disbursements, there should be a procedure whereby the disputed items can be referred to the court with submissions in writing, so that the costs judge or district judge can deal with the matter on the papers without a hearing. This should be a final decision (not a provisional assessment), although it would be subject to appeal in the usual way. The judge should have power to list the matter for oral argument, if an issue arises which merits oral argument.

(ii) Multi-track cases

(a) Bill of costs

5.3   The three requirements. There are three requirements which have to be satisfied:

(i)   The bill must provide more transparent explanation than is currently provided, about what work was done in the various time periods and why.

(ii)   The bill must provide a user-friendly synopsis of the work done, how long it took and why. This is in contrast to bills in the present format, which are turgid to read and present no clear overall picture.

(iii)   The bill must be inexpensive to prepare. This is in contrast to the present bills, which typically cost many thousands of pounds to assemble.

5.4   How to meet those requirements. In my view, modern technology provides the solution. Time recording systems must capture relevant information as work proceeds. The bill format must be compatible with existing time recording systems, so that at any given point in a piece of litigation a bill of costs can be generated automatically. Such a bill of costs must contain the necessary explanatory material, which is currently lacking from the bills prepared for detailed assessment. Crucially, the costs software must be capable of presenting the bill at different levels of generality. This will enable the solicitor to provide either (a) a user-friendly synopsis or (b) a detailed bill with all the information and explanation needed for a detailed assessment or (c) an intermediate document somewhere between (a) and (b). The software must provide for work which is not chargeable or work which is written off to be allocated to a separate file.

5.5   Armed with such a software system, solicitors should be able to produce up-to-date costs information for the client or schedules of costs for summary assessment at whatever level of generality may be required. Also, at the end of the case, the solicitors will be able to produce a detailed bill of costs, which can be used either for negotiating costs with the other side or for a detailed assessment hearing.

5.6   I therefore recommend that work should be put in hand to develop existing software systems, so that they can (a) capture relevant information as work proceeds and (b) automatically generate bills of costs at whatever level of generality may be required. Two of my assessors, Senior Costs Judge Peter Hurst and Jeremy Morgan QC, have discussed the possibility of such software being developed with a firm of law costs consultants. The current proposals are that a bill should be presented in the order "phase, task, activity".[14] According to these proposals, the bill is divided into five "phases": (1) case assessment, advice and administration; (2) pleadings and interim applications; (3) disclosure; (4) trial preparation and trial; and (5) detailed assessment. Each phase is then broken down to identify different tasks. A summary sheet lists the profit costs and disbursements in respect of each task in each phase. In the body of the bill itself, each task in each phase is set out in chronological order, with an indication of the time spent and the amount claimed. A bill in this form could easily be transmitted in electronic form, provided that all those involved had compatible IT software. If bills were to be prepared along the lines suggested, and dealt with electronically, there would potentially be large savings in time and costs. One advantage of the proposed system is that costs information can be extracted at different levels of generality. The electronic formatting of bills should, in principle, provide greater transparency.

5.7   I readily accept that developing new software will be expensive. However, if successful, it will generate major savings. The huge costs of drafting bills of costs will be avoided. The suggestion made by the Association of Her Majesty's District Judges (viz that a print out of the solicitors' time record be used for detailed assessment) will not be adopted directly, but my proposal is a variant of that suggestion. The resulting bills will be easy to read and digest, thus meeting many of the concerns expressed during Phase 2. The work done on documents (often the largest item in any bill) will become intelligible. This will give effect to the very sensible advice given by the working group. Furthermore the software will be able to generate (a) simple schedules of costs for the purpose of summary assessment or (b) detailed bills for the purposes of negotiation or detailed assessment at the end of a case. The court must have IT systems capable of receiving bills in electronic format.

5.8   The long term aim. Consideration should also be given to developing a single software system which can generate both cost budgets and bills of costs. The

---

[14] The three-tiered structure of the scheme is based on the Uniform Task-Based Management System adopted by many US firms and by a limited but growing number of solicitors in this country who have US corporate clients. This is a budgeting and billing system designed to provide clients and law firms with useful standardised costs information on legal services. It is set out in the Codeset available on the American Bar Association website at http://www.abanet.org/litigation/utbms/.

ultimate aim must be to harmonise the procedures and systems which will be used for costs budgeting, costs management, summary assessment and detailed assessment.

(b) Procedures for detailed assessment

5.9   The recommendations which I make in respect of a new format for bills of costs and concomitant software, if accepted, will take some time to develop. I shall now focus on reforms to detailed assessment procedure, which ought to be made in the near future, irrespective of whether the wider proposals in respect of bill format and software are accepted. Having considered the views expressed at the costs assessment seminar and the numerous written submissions received, I propose a package of reforms to the costs assessment procedure, as set out in the following paragraphs.

5.10   Interim payments. The Costs PD should provide that whenever the court makes an order for costs to be assessed, the court shall also order an interim payment on account of costs, unless there is good reason not to do so. It would be going too far for the rules to make an order for interim payment automatic. For example, there may be doubt about the right to any further costs or there may be a real prospect of a set off at a later stage.

5.11   Points of dispute and points of reply. Both points of dispute and points of reply need to be shorter and more focused. The practice of quoting passages from well known judgments should be abandoned. The practice of repeatedly using familiar formulae, in Homeric style, should also be abandoned. The pleaders on both sides should set out their contentions relevant to the instant cases clearly and concisely. There should be no need to plead to every individual item in a bill of costs, nor to reply to every paragraph in the points of dispute.

5.12   In order to achieve the required approach to points of dispute and points of reply I propose that sections 35 and 39 of the Costs PD be amended as set out in appendix 10 to this report.

5.13   Compulsory offers. PP should be required to make an offer when it serves its points of dispute. The offer may be contained in the points of dispute or in a separate document. The sum offered may be more or less than the amount of the interim payment ordered by the court.

5.14   Offers. The Part 36 procedure should apply to detailed assessment proceedings. The "14 day" provision in Costs PD paragraph 46.1 should be repealed.

5.15   Costs of detailed assessment proceedings. The default position should remain as set out in CPR rule 47.18. However, if PP makes an offer which RP fails beat, then the normal consequence should be that RP pays PP's costs after the date when the offer expired. Likewise RP should be rewarded for making a sufficient offer, which PP rejects. The reward should be enhanced interest and indemnity costs in respect of the assessment proceedings.

5.16   Time for appeal. Time for appeal should start to run from the conclusion of the final hearing, unless the court orders otherwise. There will be some occasions when it would be appropriate for the court to order otherwise. For example, it may be sensible for an appeal against a decision on preliminary issues to proceed before the full detailed assessment takes place.

5.17   Provisional assessment. The proposals for provisional assessment should be piloted for a year in respect of bills up to £25,000. The pilot rules should provide that where a party elects to proceed to an oral hearing, it will have to pay both sides' costs, if it does not do better than the provisional assessment by a defined percentage (possibly 10%). It would be sensible to defer this pilot until after the proposed fixed costs regime for the fast track has been introduced (if my recommendations in that regard are accepted).[15] I suggest that that this pilot be carried out at one of the larger civil justice centres outside London,[16] possibly at Manchester or Liverpool. The decision whether to introduce provisional assessment at all court centres and, if so, up to what level of bill, should be taken in the light of the results of that pilot. The crucial issues to be monitored during the pilot are:

(i)   What demands provisional assessment makes upon the resources of the court.

(ii)   How many provisional assessments are accepted by the parties and how many are taken further.

(iii)   What costs savings are achieved by the parties as a result of provisional assessment.

5.18   Success fees. No success fees under conditional fee agreements should be recoverable against the opposing party in respect of detailed assessment proceedings.[17]

5.19   Guideline hourly rates. GHRs should be set which are applicable to both summary assessment and detailed assessment. I do not advocate returning to the former "A" and "B" rates, because these engender uncertainty and debate.

5.20   The present GHRs are applicable only to summary assessment.[18] If the new GHRs are to be given the formal status of guidelines in relation to detailed assessment, they will assume greater importance than the present GHRs. Accordingly, I have recommended in chapter 6 above that the GHRs should be set and reviewed by a Costs Council.

5.21   My comments about GHRs in chapter 44 above at paragraphs 3.8 to 3.13 are repeated.

5.22   Commercial litigation in Manchester. The concerns raised by the Manchester Law Society must be a matter for the Costs Council to consider (if my recommendation for the creation of such a body is accepted).[19]

6. RECOMMENDATIONS

6.1   I make the following recommendations:

(i)   A new format of bills of costs should be devised, which will be more informative and capable of yielding information at different levels of generality.

---

[15] As to which, see chapter 15 above.
[16] The number of bills below £25,000 is likely to be much larger at a civil justice centre outside London than at the SCCO.
[17] See chapter 10 above, paragraph 5.25.
[18] However, they are often referred to at detailed assessment hearings.
[19] See chapter 6 above.

(ii)   Software should be developed which will (a) be used for time recording and capturing relevant information and (b) automatically generate schedules for summary assessment or bills for detailed assessment as and when required. The long term aim must be to harmonise the procedures and systems which will be used for costs budgeting, costs management, summary assessment and detailed assessment.

(iii)   A package of measures to improve detailed assessment proceedings should be adopted, as set out in section 5 of this chapter.

(iv)   The proposals for provisional assessment should be piloted for one year at a civil justice centre outside London in respect of bills up to £25,000.

PART 8. CONCLUSION

CHAPTER 46. CONCLUDING REMARKS

This report, which must be read in conjunction with the Preliminary Report, sets out my opinion on the issues raised by the terms of reference. As stated in the foreword, the recommendations are interlocking. If the Government and the Civil Procedure Rule Committee see fit to implement these reforms, I believe that they will promote access to justice for all parties (both claimant and defendant) at proportionate cost.

RECOMMENDATIONS

Unless otherwise stated, all abbreviations and defined terms used in these recommendations are included in the glossary.

CHAPTER 3. PROPORTIONATE COSTS.

1   "Proportionate costs" should be defined in the CPR by reference to sums in issue, value of non-monetary relief, complexity of litigation, conduct and any wider factors, such as reputation or public importance; and the test of proportionality should be applied on a global basis.

CHAPTER 4. THE CAUSES OF DISPROPORTIONATE COSTS AND HOW THEY SHOULD BE TACKLED WHILST PROMOTING ACCESS TO JUSTICE

2   When striking the balance between the need for predictability and the need for simplicity, the Rule Committee, the MoJ drafting team and the authors of practice directions, protocols and court guides should accord higher priority in future to the goal of simplicity.

3   There should be no further increases in civil court fees, save for increases which are in line with the Retail Price Index rate of inflation. All receipts from civil court fees should be ploughed back into the civil justice system.

CHAPTER 5. INDEMNITY PRINCIPLE

4   The common law indemnity principle should be abrogated.

CHAPTER 6. COSTS COUNCIL

5   The ACCC should be disbanded and a Costs Council should be established.

CHAPTER 8. BEFORE-THE-EVENT INSURANCE

6   Positive efforts should be made to encourage the take up of BTE insurance by SMEs in respect of business disputes and by householders as an add-on to household insurance policies.

CHAPTER 9. AFTER-THE-EVENT INSURANCE

7   Section 29 of the Access to Justice Act 1999 and all rules made pursuant to that provision should be repealed.

8   Those categories of litigants who merit protection against adverse costs liability on policy grounds should be given the benefit of qualified one way costs shifting.

CHAPTER 10. CONDITIONAL FEE AGREEMENTS

9   Section 58A(6) of the Courts and Legal Services Act 1990 and all rules made pursuant to that provision should be repealed.

10   The level of general damages for personal injuries, nuisance and all other civil wrongs to individuals should be increased by 10%.

CHAPTER 11. THIRD PARTY FUNDING

11 A satisfactory voluntary code, to which all litigation funders subscribe, should be drawn up. This code should contain effective capital adequacy requirements and should place appropriate restrictions upon funders' ability to withdraw support for ongoing litigation.

12 The question whether there should be statutory regulation of third party funders by the FSA ought to be re-visited if and when the third party funding market expands.

13 Third party funders should potentially be liable for the full amount of adverse costs, subject to the discretion of the judge.

CHAPTER 12. CONTINGENCY FEES

14 Both solicitors and counsel should be permitted to enter into contingency fee agreements with their clients. However, costs should be recoverable against opposing parties on the conventional basis and not by reference to the contingency fee.

15 Contingency fee agreements should be properly regulated and they should not be valid unless the client has received independent advice.

CHAPTER 13. CLAF OR SLAS

16 Financial modelling should be undertaken to ascertain the viability of one or more CLAFs or a SLAS, after and subject to, any decisions announced by Government in respect of the other recommendations of this report.

CHAPTER 14. LITIGANTS IN PERSON

17 The prescribed rate of £9.25 per hour recoverable by litigants in person should be increased to £20 per hour. The prescribed rate should be subject to periodic review.

CHAPTER 15. FIXED COSTS IN THE FAST TRACK

18 The recoverable costs of cases in the fast track should be fixed, as detailed in chapter 15.

CHAPTER 19. ONE WAY COSTS SHIFTING

19 A regime of qualified one way costs shifting, as detailed in chapter 19, should be introduced for personal injury cases.

CHAPTER 20. REFERRAL FEES

20 The payment of referral fees for personal injury claims should be banned.

CHAPTER 21. ASSESSMENT OF GENERAL DAMAGES FOR PAIN, SUFFERING AND LOSS OF AMENITY

21 A working group should be set up to establish a uniform calibration for all software systems used in assessment of damages for pain, suffering and loss of amenity, consequential upon personal injury, up to £10,000. That

calibration should accord as nearly as possible with the awards of general damages that would be made by the courts.

CHAPTER 22. PERSONAL INJURIES LITIGATION: PROCESS AND PROCEDURE

22   The new process being developed by the MoJ for low value RTA claims should be monitored to ensure that the costs savings achieved are not negated by satellite litigation and avoidance behaviour.

23   There should be discussions between claimant and defendant representatives, under the aegis of the CJC, in order to develop a streamlined process for all fast track personal injury cases which fall outside the MoJ's new process.

24   The effect of MROs upon the costs of personal injuries litigation should be kept under close scrutiny.

25   Direct communication should always be permitted between a solicitor and any medical expert whom an MRO instructs on behalf of that solicitor.

CHAPTER 23. CLINICAL NEGLIGENCE

26   There should be financial penalties for any health authority which, without good reason, fails to provide copies of medical records requested in accordance with the Pre-Action Protocol for the Resolution of Clinical Disputes.

27   The time for the defendant to respond to a letter of claim should be increased from three months to four months. Any letter of claim sent to an NHS Trust or ISTC should be copied to the NHSLA.

28   In respect of any claim (other than a frivolous claim) where the NHSLA is proposing to deny liability, the NHSLA should obtain independent expert evidence on liability and causation during the four month period allowed for the response letter.

29   The NHSLA, the MDU, the MPS and similar bodies should each nominate an experienced and senior officer to whom claimant solicitors should, after the event, report egregious cases of defendant lawyers failing to address the issues.

30   The protocol should provide a limited period for settlement negotiations where the defendant offers to settle without formal admission of liability.

31   Case management directions for clinical negligence cases should be harmonised across England and Wales.

32   Costs management for clinical negligence cases should be piloted.

33   Regulations should be drawn up in order to implement the NHS Redress Act 2006.

CHAPTER 24. IP LITIGATION

34   Consideration should be given by the Patents Court judges and the IPCUC to the question whether the Patents Court and Patents County Court Guide should be amended to include any of the proposals set out in paragraph 2.5 of chapter 24.

35   The proposals in the IPCUC Working Group's final report for reforming the PCC should be implemented.

36 After reformation of the PCC, the Guide should be amended to give clear guidance on the requirements for statements of case, illustrated by model pleadings annexed to the Guide.

37 There should be a small claims track in the PCC for IP claims with a monetary value of less than £5,000 and a fast track for IP claims with a monetary value of between £5,000 and £25,000.

38 One or more district judges, deputy district judges or recorders with specialist patent experience should be available to sit in the PCC, in order to deal with small claims and fast track cases.

39 There should be consultation with court users, practitioners and judges, in order to ascertain whether there is support either for (a) an IP pre-action protocol or (b) the Guide to give guidance regarding pre-action conduct.

CHAPTER 25. SMALL BUSINESS DISPUTES

40 A High Court judge should be appointed as judge in charge of the Mercantile Courts.

41 A single court guide should be drawn up for all Mercantile Courts.

42 Consideration should be given to devising a special streamlined procedure for business disputes of lower value.

43 HMCS should prepare a guide in respect of "small business disputes" for the assistance of business people who wish to deal with such disputes themselves without the assistance of lawyers, either by mediation or on the small claims track.

CHAPTER 26. HOUSING

44 The Government should reconsider undertaking a simplification of substantive housing law, as proposed by the Law Commission in 2003, 2006 and 2008.

45 Where a landlord could use PCOL to issue possession proceedings but chooses to issue manually, he should only be able to recover an amount equal to the PCOL issue fee.

46 The Pre-Action Protocol for Possession Claims based on Rent Arrears should be amended in order to set out what steps should be taken by landlords, so as to comply with their obligations under ECHR article 8.

47 Paragraph 24.2 of the Part 52 practice direction should be amended in order to set out what categories of documents should be lodged by the respondent in homelessness appeals and when these should be lodged.

48 Consultation should be carried out on the proposal that where a housing claim is settled in favour of a legally aided party, that party should have the right to ask the court to determine which party should pay the costs of the proceedings.

CHAPTER 27. LARGE COMMERCIAL CLAIMS

49 After 18 months, the question whether section D6 of the Admiralty & Commercial Courts Guide ought to be repealed or amended should be reconsidered in the light of experience.

50   Sections D4 and D8 of the Admiralty & Commercial Courts Guide should be amended to permit more frequent allocation of appropriate cases to designated judges.

CHAPTER 28. CHANCERY LITIGATION

51   CPR Part 8 should be amended to enable the court to assign a case to the fast track at any time.

52   The amount of costs deductible from a trust fund or estate should be set at a proportionate level at an early stage of litigation. Whether the balance of costs should be paid by the party who incurred them or by some other party should be determined by the judge.

53   Practice Direction B supplementing CPR Part 64 should be amended to provide that, save in exceptional cases, all *Beddoe* applications will be dealt with on paper.

54   A suitable body of tax experts should become an "approved regulator" within section 20 of the Legal Services Act 2007.

55   Part 6 of the Costs Practice Direction should be amended to require parties in Part 8 proceedings to lodge costs estimates 14 days after the acknowledgment of service (if any) has been filed.

56   A scheme of benchmark costs should be implemented for bankruptcy petitions and winding up petitions.

57   Costs management procedures should be developed in order to control the costs of more complex insolvency proceedings.

58   The Law Society and the ChBA should set up a working group in order to consider the remaining chancery issues raised by the Preliminary Report.

CHAPTER 29. TECHNOLOGY AND CONSTRUCTION COURT LITIGATION

59   Section 5 of the TCC Guide should be amended to draw attention to the power of the court to disallow costs in respect of pleadings or witness statements which contain extensive irrelevant or peripheral material.

60   Paragraphs 14.4.1 and 14.4.2 of the TCC Guide should be amended, so that they are focused upon key issues rather than all issues in the case.

61   The CPR should be amended so that appropriate TCC cases can be allocated to the fast track. Section 68(1)(a) of the Senior Courts Act 1981 should be amended, so that district judges of appropriate experience may be authorised to manage and try fast track TCC cases.

62   Mediation should be promoted with particular vigour for those low value construction cases in which conventional negotiation is unsuccessful.

CHAPTER 30. JUDICIAL REVIEW

63   Qualified one way costs shifting should be introduced for judicial review claims.

64   If the defendant settles a judicial review claim after issue and the claimant has complied with the protocol, the normal order should be that the defendant do pay the claimant's costs.

CHAPTER 32. DEFAMATION AND RELATED PROCEEDINGS

65   If recoverability of success fees and ATE insurance premiums is abolished:

      (i)   The general level of damages for defamation and breach of privacy claims should be increased by 10%.

      (ii)   A regime of qualified one way costs shifting should be introduced.

66   Paragraph 3.3 of the Pre-Action Protocol for Defamation should be amended to read as follows:

    "The Claimant should identify in the Letter of Claim the meaning(s) he/she attributes to the words complained of."

67   The question whether to retain trial by jury in defamation cases should be reconsidered.

CHAPTER 33. COLLECTIVE ACTIONS

68   The starting point or default position in collective actions should be (a) in personal injury actions, qualified one way costs shifting and (b) in all other actions, two way costs shifting. At the certification stage, the judge may direct that a different costs regime shall operate.

69   Rule 9.01(4) of the Solicitors' Code of Conduct 2007 should be amended, so as to permit the third party funding of collective personal injury claims.

CHAPTER 34. APPEALS

70   There should be a separate review of the procedures and costs rules for appeals, after decisions have been reached in relation to the recommendations in this report concerning first instance litigation.

71   Pending that review, appellate courts should have a discretionary power, upon granting permission to appeal or receiving an appeal from a no-costs jurisdiction, to order (a) that each side should bear its own costs of the appeal or (b) that the recoverable costs should be capped at a specified sum.

CHAPTER 35. PRE-ACTION PROTOCOLS

72   The Pre-Action Protocol for Construction and Engineering Disputes should be amended, so that (a) it is less prescriptive and (b) the costs (or at least the recoverable costs) of complying with that protocol are reduced. The need for that protocol should be reviewed by TCC judges, practitioners and court users after 2011.

73   The general protocol, contained in Sections III and IV of the Practice Direction – Pre-Action Conduct, should be repealed.

74   Annex B to the Practice Direction – Pre-Action Conduct should be incorporated into a new specific protocol for debt claims.

CHAPTER 36. ALTERNATIVE DISPUTE RESOLUTION

75   There should be a serious campaign (a) to ensure that all litigation lawyers and judges are properly informed about the benefits which ADR can bring and (b) to alert the public and small businesses to the benefits of ADR.

76   An authoritative handbook should be prepared, explaining clearly and concisely what ADR is and giving details of all reputable providers of mediation. This should be the standard handbook for use at all JSB seminars and CPD training sessions concerning mediation.

CHAPTER 37. DISCLOSURE

77   E-disclosure as a topic should form a substantial part of (a) CPD for solicitors and barristers who will have to deal with e-disclosure in practice and (b) the training of judges who will have to deal with e-disclosure on the bench.

78   A new CPR rule 31.5A should be drafted to adopt the menu option in relation to (a) large commercial and similar claims and (b) any case where the costs of standard disclosure are likely to be disproportionate. Personal injury claims and clinical negligence claims should be excluded from the provisions of rule 31.5A.

CHAPTER 38. WITNESS STATEMENTS AND EXPERTS

79   CPR Part 35 or its accompanying practice direction should be amended in order to require that a party seeking permission to adduce expert evidence do furnish an estimate of the costs of that evidence to the court.

80   The procedure developed in Australia, known as "concurrent evidence" should be piloted in cases where all parties consent. If the results of the pilot are positive, consideration should be given to amending CPR Part 35 to provide for use of that procedure in appropriate cases.

CHAPTER 39. CASE MANAGEMENT

81   Measures should be taken to promote the assignment of cases to designated judges with relevant expertise.

82   A menu of standard paragraphs for case management directions for each type of case of common occurrence should be prepared and made available to all district judges both in hard copy and online in amendable form.

83   CMCs and PTRs should either (a) be used as occasions for effective case management or (b) be dispensed with and replaced by directions on paper. Where such interim hearings are held, the judge should have proper time for pre-reading.

84   In multi-track cases the entire timetable for the action, including trial date or trial window, should be drawn up at as early a stage as is practicable.

85   Pre-action applications should be permitted in respect of breaches of pre-action protocols.

86   The courts should be less tolerant than hitherto of unjustified delays and breaches of orders. This change of emphasis should be signalled by amendment of CPR rule 3.9. If and in so far as it is possible, courts should monitor the progress of the parties in order to secure compliance with orders and pre-empt the need for sanctions.

87   The Master of the Rolls should designate two lords justices, at least one of whom will so far as possible be a member of any constitution of the civil division of the Court of Appeal, which is called upon to consider issues concerning the interpretation or application of the CPR.

88   Consideration should be given to the possibility of the Court of Appeal sitting with an experienced district judge as assessor when case management issues arise.

CHAPTER 40. COSTS MANAGEMENT

89   The linked disciplines of costs budgeting and costs management should be included in CPD training for those solicitors and barristers who undertake civil litigation.

90   Costs budgeting and costs management should be included in the training offered by the JSB to judges who sit in the civil courts.

91   Rules should set out a standard costs management procedure, which judges would have a discretion to adopt if and when they see fit, either of their own motion or upon application by one of the parties.

92   Primary legislation should enable the Civil Procedure Rule Committee to make rules for pre-issue costs management.

CHAPTER 41. PART 36 OFFERS

93   The effect of *Carver v BAA plc* [2008] EWCA Civ 412; [2009] 1 WLR 113 should be reversed.

94   Where a defendant rejects a claimant's offer, but fails to do better at trial, the claimant's recovery should be enhanced by 10%.

CHAPTER 42. COURTS ADMINISTRATION

95   Most county court cases should be issued at regional centres, where the staff will be skilled in processing routine proceedings. However, a facility to issue proceedings at all county courts must be retained.

96   Only if cases are defended, should they be transferred to, or retained in, county courts, where the staff should be specifically trained for, and focused upon, the administration of contested cases.

97   The Association of District Judges and HMCS should together draw up a scheme for the increased delegation of routine box work from district judges to proper officers within the court service.

CHAPTER 43. INFORMATION TECHNOLOGY

98   A suitable body should be appointed to exercise strategic oversight over all IT systems which are installed in the civil courts.

99   Judges and practitioners should be included in future development teams for individual court IT projects.

100   E-working should be extended to the rest of the High Court in London, in particular the Queen's Bench Division and also to the SCCO.

101   Once e-working has been introduced across the High Court in London, it should be rolled out (suitably adapted) across all county courts and district registries in England and Wales.

102   Consideration should be given to establishing an IT network for the courts which is separate from, and therefore not constrained by the security

requirements of, the gsi system. This network should have its own appropriate level of security.

103   Judges and court staff should receive proper training in relation to court IT systems. Likewise legal practitioners and their staff should be properly trained in relation to court IT systems and should be willing to adapt their procedures.

CHAPTER 44. SUMMARY ASSESSMENT

104   If any judge at the end of a hearing within Costs PD paragraph 13.2 considers that he or she lacks the time or the expertise to assess costs summarily (either at that hearing or on paper afterwards), then the judge should order a substantial payment on account of costs and direct detailed assessment.

105   A revised and more informative version of Form N260 should be prepared for use in connection with summary assessments at the end of trials or appeals.

CHAPTER 45. DETAILED ASSESSMENT

106   A new format of bills of costs should be devised, which will be more informative and capable of yielding information at different levels of generality.

107   Software should be developed which will (a) be used for time recording and capturing relevant information and (b) automatically generate schedules for summary assessment or bills for detailed assessment as and when required. The long term aim must be to harmonise the procedures and systems which will be used for costs budgeting, costs management, summary assessment and detailed assessment.

108   A package of measures to improve detailed assessment proceedings should be adopted, as set out in section 5 of chapter 45.

109   The proposals for provisional assessment should be piloted for one year at a civil justice centre outside London in respect of bills up to £25,000.

PRIMARY LEGISLATION REQUIRED

1   Such legislation as is necessary to abrogate the common law indemnity principle.

2   Repeal of section 29 of the Access to Justice Act 1999.

3   Repeal of section 58A(6) of the Courts and Legal Services Act 1990.

4   Legislation to permit the regulation of contingency fee agreements for civil litigation.

5   Legislation to permit pre-action applications in respect of breaches of pre-action protocols.

6   Legislation to permit pre-action costs management by the court.

7   Legislation to permit the proposed reconstitution of the Patents County Court.

8   Section 68(1) of the Senior Courts Act 1981 should be amended to permit district judges to be nominated to sit in the Technology and Construction Court for the purpose of hearing fast track cases.

9   Legislation to permit the amendment of CPR Part 36 as proposed in chapter41.

Other recommendations in this report could be dealt with either by rule change or by primary legislation.

ANNEX 1. SUBMISSIONS RECEIVED BETWEEN 31ST JANUARY AND 8TH MAY 2009

4-5 Gray's Inn Square

5 Raymond Buildings

Allianz ProzessFinanz GmbH

Berrymans Lace Mawer

Browne Jacobson LLP

ClientEarth

Dr Clive Leveson

Hempsons Solicitors

Hill Dickinson LLP

Medical Defence Union

Morgan Cole Solicitors

Mr John Mitchell, SMART Club

Mr Peter Edwards

Ms Philippa Jessel

Plexus Law, a division of Parabis Law LLP

Potter Rees Solicitors

Russell Jones & Walker

Shoosmiths

Smith Jones Solicitors

Stewarts Law LLP

Walker Morris Solicitors

ANNEX 2. SUBMISSIONS RECEIVED AFTER 8ᵀᴴ MAY 2009

12 King's Bench Walk

Abbey Legal Protection

ABI (Association of British Insurers)

ABTA (Association of British Travel Agents)

Accidents Direct UK Ltd

Ace European Group Ltd

ACSG (Accident Compensation Solicitors Group)

Addleshaw Goddard LLP

Alan Tunkel, member of the Bar Council CLAF Group

ALCD (Association of Law Costs Draftsmen)

Alexander Learmonth, New Square Chambers

Allen & Overy LLP

Allianz Legal Protection

AMRO (Association of Medical Reporting Organisations)

Andrew Petchey, Howell-Jones LLP

Andrew Ritchie QC, 9 Gough Square

Andrew Scott, Beachcroft LLP

Anthony Gold Solicitors

Anthony Speight QC, 4 Pump Court

APIL (Association of Personal Injury Lawyers)

ARAG

Ashurst LLP

Association of Her Majesty's District Judges

Association of Northern Mediators

Aviva Insurance UK Ltd

AvMA (Action against Medical Accidents)

AXA Insurance

Bakers Personal Injury Solicitors

Bar Council CFA Panel (a Remuneration Committee Sub-Committee)

Bar Council CLAF group

Bar Council Sub-Committee on Civil Legal Aid

Bar Council Young Barristers' Committee

Barlow Lyde & Gilbert LLP

Beachcroft LLP

Beachcroft LLP, Clinical Risk Group

Berrymans Lace Mawer LLP

Bevan Brittan LLP

Bioindustry Association

Birmingham City Council Legal and Democratic Services

Birmingham Law Society Dispute Resolution Committee

Bond Pearce LLP, Dispute Resolution Department

Bond Pearce LLP, Personal Injury Department

Brachers Solicitors LLP

Bristol Mercantile Court Users' Committee

British Airways Plc

Browne Jacobson LLP

CAJE (Coalition for Access to Justice for the Environment)

Cambridge House Law Centre

CAP (Claims Against Professionals)

Capsticks LLP

Cardiff Civil Justice Centre District Judges

Carol Scudamore, Tollers LLP

CEDR (Centre for Effective Dispute Resolution)

Chancery Bar Association

Chandler Ray Solicitors

Chester and North Wales Law Society

Chris Ennis, Davis Langdon LLP

Chris Tagg, Bobbetts Mackan

Christopher Semken, New Square Chambers

City of London Law Society Intellectual Property Committee

City of London Law Society Litigation Committee

Civil Court Users Association

Civil Justice Council

Claims Standards Council

Claire Parkinson, Reynards Solicitors

CLAN (Commercial Litigation Association)

Clarke Willmott LL

Clerksroom

ClientEarth

Clifford Chance LLP

CMS Cameron McKenna LLP

Cobden House Chambers

COMBAR (Commercial Bar Association)

Commercial Court Users' Committee Sub-Committee

Commercial Litigators Forum

Communication Workers Union

Confederation of British Industry

Consumer Focus

Co-operative Financial Services

Council of Circuit Judges Civil Committee

CSC Computer Sciences Ltd

DAS Legal Expenses Insurance Company

Dean Talbot, Ross Aldridge LLP

Deans Court Chambers

Deloitte LLP

Derrick Smethurst, Russell & Russell Solicitors

District Judge Cawood, Portsmouth Combined Court Centre

District Judge Guy Baddeley, Birmingham Civil Justice Centre

District Judge MacKenzie, Worcester Combined Court

District Judge Robert Hill, Scarborough County Court

District Judge Roger Britton, Bristol County Court

District Judge Simon Middleton, Bodmin County Court

Doughty Street Chambers, Housing and Social Welfare Department

Dr Richard Bloore

Dr Deirdre Dwyer, Faculty of Law, University of Oxford

Dr Eleanor Harries

Ecclesiastical Insurance Group and Everatt & Co. Solicitors

Edwin Coe LLP

Elite Insurance Company Ltd

Elizabeth Morrison, Solicitor and Deputy District Judge (Civil)

Employment Law Barristers Association

Epiq Systems Limited

Equerry Advisers Limited and Equerry Litigation Funding Limited

European Justice Forum

Fentons Solicitors LLP

FirstAssist Legal Protection

Fisher Meredith LLP

FOCIS (Forum of Complex Injury Solicitors)

FOIL (Forum of Insurance Lawyers)

Fortis Insurance Ltd

Foundation for Information Policy Research

Franks & Co Limited

Freshfields Bruckhaus Deringer LLP

FSB (Federation of Small Businesses)

Fulbright & Jaworski International LLP

Gadsby Wicks Solicitors

Gail Hince, Reynards Solicitors

GC100 Group

General Council of the Bar

George Ide LLP

Gibbs Wyatt Stone

Glenys Hunt, Leeds Lloyd Whitely Solicitors

GMB - Britain's General Union

Gordon Exall, Zenith Chambers

Greenwoods Solicitors

Guy Adams, St. John's Chambers

Halliwells LLP

Hammonds LLP

Harbour Litigation Funding

Hardwicke Building, Public Law Department

Hart Brown Solicitors

Herbert Smith LLP

Hill Dickinson LLP

His Honour Judge Richard Holman, Designated Civil Judge, Manchester

HLPA (Housing Law Practitioners Association)

HM Revenue & Customs

Hodge Jones & Allen LLP

Hugh James Solicitors

ILEX (Institute of Legal Executives)

IM Litigation Funding Ltd

Insurance Services Office Ltd

Intellectual Property Court Users' Committee

Intellectual Property Lawyers Association

International Underwriting Association of London Ltd

Iram Akhtar, Ministry of Justice

Irwin Mitchell LLP

JLT Law, a division of Jardine Lloyd Thompson UK Ltd

John Baron MP

John Morris Collins, Zenith Chambers

John Ross Martyn, New Square Chambers

John Simmonds, Registrar in Bankruptcy of the High Court

Jolyon Holden, Holden & Co Solicitors

Jon Grunewald, Watmores Solicitors

K&L Gates LLP

Keating Chambers

Kennedys LLP

Keoghs LLP

Kerry Bretherton, Hardwicke Building

Keystone Legal Benefits Ltd and Bastion Insurance Company Limited

KPMG LLP UK Forensic Accounting

Kremers Solicitors Ltd

Laurence Beck, Accident Advice Helpline

Law Society of England and Wales

Legal Aid Practitioners Group

Legal Services Commission

LEIG (Legal Expenses Insurance Group)

Leigh Day & Co, Clinical Negligence Department

Leigh Day & Co, Environmental Claims Department

Leigh Day & Co, Judicial Review Department

Leigh Day & Co, Personal Injury Department

Liberty

Litigation Funders' Alliance

Liverpool District Judges

Liverpool Victoria Insurance Company

LMA (Lloyd's Market Association)

London Common Law and Commercial Bar Association

Lord Justice Dyson

Lovells LLP

LSLA (London Solicitors Litigation Association)

Manchester Law Society

Manchester Mercantile Court Users' Committee

Martin Horan, Financial & Legal Insurance Company Ltd

Martin Scott, Walker Morris Solicitors

Mason Hayes Solicitors

MASS (Motor Accident Solicitors Society)

Master Jonathan Winegarten, Chief Chancery Master

Mayer Brown, Litigation and Dispute Resolution Department

McCann Fitzgerald LLP

MDU (Medical Defence Union)

Messrs Paul Hattori and Craig Kersey

Messrs Qasim Nawaz and Tim Wallis

MIB (Motor Insurers' Bureau)

Michael Fordham QC and Jessica Boyd, Blackstone Chambers

Mitsui Sumitomo Insurance Underwriting at Lloyd's Ltd

MLA (Media Lawyers Association)

Moore Blatch Resolve LLP

Morgan Cole Solicitors

Morrison Spowart Solicitors

MPS (Medical Protection Society)

Mr Alan Nicholson and Ms Christina Nicholson

Mr Chris Dale

Mr Francis Miller

Mr Geoffrey Moralee

Mr James Bowers

Mr Jim Diamond

Mr Justice David Steel

Mr Michael Cook

Mr Mike O'Dwyer

Mr Paul Simpson LLB BA

Mr Peter Thompson QC

Mr Richard Ross

Mr Robert Asbury

Mr Stuart M. Speiser

Mr Terence Vaughan

Mrs Joanne Ewart

Mrs Pauline Hodgetts

Ms Jenny Newall and Ms Norma Kay

Munich Re Group

Nabarro LLP

Nabarro LLP on behalf of Persimmon Homes Ltd

Nabarro LLP on behalf of the Department of Energy & Climate Change Coal Liabilities Unit

National Accident Helpline

NHSLA (National Health Service Litigation Authority)

Nicholas Crewe, member of the Association of Law Costs Draftsman

North Eastern Circuit Personal Injury Bar

North Insurance Management Ltd (North of England P&I Association Ltd)

Northern Circuit Commercial Bar Association

Norton Rose LLP

NUT (National Union of Teachers)

OIM Underwriting Ltd

Oliver & Co Solicitors

Oriel Chambers' Civil Practitioners

Pannone LLP

Parabis Law LLP

Pattinson & Brewer

Paul Randolph, Lamb Building

Paul Simms, Citilegal International Ltd

PBA (Property Bar Association)

PIBA (Personal Injuries Bar Association)

PNBA (Professional Negligence Bar Association)

PNLA (Professional Negligence Lawyers Association)

Powell Forster Solicitors

Premex Group

Premier Medical Group

PricewaterhouseCoopers LLP Forensic Services

Professor Dominic Regan

Professor Michael Zander QC

Prospect Union for Professionals

Public Law Project

QBE Insurance (Europe) Limited

RBS Insurance

Richard Buxton Solicitors

Richard Schaverien, Howlett Clarke Solicitors

Richard Sheehan, Commercial Litigation Funding Limited

Robert Smart, DLA Piper UK LLP

Roger Bartlett, 5 St. Andrew's Hill

Rowlands Solicitors LLP

Royal & Sun Alliance Insurance plc

Russell Jones & Walker Solicitors

SABIP (Strategic Advisory Board for Intellectual Property Policy)

Schillings Lawyers

Shadbolt LLP

Shelter

Shoosmiths LLP

Simmons & Simmons LLP

Simon Edwards, 39 Essex Street

Simon Hargreaves QC, Keating Chambers

Simon Read, Zenith Chambers

Sir Henry Brooke

Sir Stephen Oliver QC

SMART Evaluate

Society for Computers and Law (SCL)

Squire & Co Solicitors

Stephen Cottrell, 1 Temple Gardens

Stevens & Bolton LLP

Stewarts Law LLP

Stuart Brown QC, Parklane Plowden

Surrey Law Society

TECBAR (Technology and Construction Bar Association)

Technology and Construction Court High Court Judges

TeCSA (Technology and Construction Solicitors Association)

Temple Legal Protection

Tesco plc

The Honourable Robert McClelland MP, Attorney-General for Australia

The Judge

Thomas & Meighen

Thompsons Solicitors

Thompsons Solicitors and Bond Pearce Solicitors

Thorneycroft Solicitors Ltd

Thring Townsend Lee & Pembertons

Tollers LLP

Tony Willoughby, Rouse Legal

Trading Standards Institute

Trust Mediation Ltd

TUC (Trades Union Congress)

Tuckers Solicitors

UKELA (United Kingdom Environmental Lawyers Association)

UNISON

Unite the Union

United States Chamber of Commerce Institute for Legal Reform

USDAW (Union of Shop, Distributive and Allied Workers)

Vince Neicho, Allen & Overy LLP

Walker Smith Way Solicitors

Ward Hadaway Solicitors

Weightmans LLP

Welsh Health Legal Services

Welwyn Hatfield Borough Council

Williamson and Soden

Xerces LLP on behalf of NFU Mutual

Young Legal Aid Lawyers

Zurich Insurance plc

ANNEX 3. CONFERENCES, SEMINARS AND MEETINGS ATTENDED DURING PHASE 2

11th May 2009	Meeting with judges at the Birmingham Civil Justice Centre
12th May 2009	Meeting with Lord Woolf
14th May 2009	Sweet & Maxwell conference on CFA law
14th May 2009	Seminar and panel discussion regarding class actions (Herbert Smith LLP)
18th May 2009	Meeting with Pinsent Masons to discuss costs budgeting
19th May 2009	Giving evidence to the Culture, Media and Sport Select Committee
20th May 2009	Meeting with representatives of the Federation of Small Businesses
20th May 2009	Meeting with Sir Henry Brooke
22nd May 2009	Meeting with US judges Paul Grimm and John Facciola (accompanied by HH Judge Simon Brown QC and Mr Chris Dale)
22nd May 2009	Meeting with clinical negligence defence organisations (National Health Service Litigation Authority, Medical Defence Union and Medical Protection Society) and panel solicitors (hosted by Weightmans LLP)
26th May 2009	Meeting with Birmingham user groups of the Technology and Construction Court and the Mercantile Court
27th May 2009	Meeting with the Association of Litigation Professional Support (hosted by White & Case LLP)
27th May 2009	Meeting with representatives of the Surrey Law Society
9th June 2009	Commercial Litigation Association Annual Conference: "Practical Challenges for Modern Commercial Litigators"
9th June 2009	Ark Group e-disclosure 2009 seminar
10th June 2009	Forum of Insurance Lawyers ("FOIL") Annual Seminar: "From new business structures to new costs rules – are you ready for the change?"
11th June 2009	IBC Legal's 5th Annual Professional Negligence & Liability Forum

11th June 2009	Meeting with Barlow Lyde and & Gilbert practitioners and clients
12th June 2009	Meeting with clinical negligence claimant practitioners (hosted by Irwin Mitchell)
15th June 2009	Manchester Law Society 8th Annual Civil Costs Conference: "Jackson Review Special"
16th June 2009	Civil Procedure Seminar Series: Costs, Oxford Law Faculty, University College Oxford
18th June 2009	Experienced practitioners' meeting to discuss issues relating to disclosure
19th June 2009	Public seminar in Cardiff
22nd June 2009	Meeting with e-disclosure providers (hosted by 4 Pump Court)
22nd June 2009	Hamlyn seminar
23rd June 2009	Commercial Litigation Funding Conference 2009: "The New Landscape" (hosted by No5 Chambers)
24th June 2009	Meeting with Trades Union Congress legal officers
24th June 2009	Meeting with practitioners and clients of a City firm
25th June 2009	Professional Negligence Lawyers Association conference: "Professional Liability in the Credit Crunch"
26th June 2009	Public seminar in Birmingham
29th June 2009	Demonstration of insurer softwares and discussion with Association of Personal Injury Lawyers ("APIL"), Motor Accident Solicitors Society ("MASS"), FOIL and insurers regarding calibrated PI damages software
29th June 2009	Meeting with Herbert Smith LLP practitioners and clients
30th June 2009	Meeting with John Baron MP and Dr Anthony Barton
30th June 2009	Meeting with practitioners and clients of CMS Cameron McKenna LLP
2nd July 2009	Claims Standards Council Claims Conference
2nd July 2009	Meeting with Manchester Judges
3rd July 2009	Public seminar in Manchester
6th – 7th July 2009	International Conference on Litigation Costs and Funding, Centre for Socio-Legal Studies and Institute of European and Comparative Law, University of Oxford

8th July 2009	Meeting with Andrew Frazer of the Ministry of Justice
9th July 2009	Meeting with the Civil Justice Committee of the Law Society
9th July 2009	Centre of Construction Law afternoon conference 2009: "Projects in distress & Economic justice" (hosted by King's College London)
10th July 2009	Public seminar in London
13th July 2009	Meeting with Norton Rose LLP practitioners and clients
13th July 2009	Meeting with the Honourable Mr Justice Andrew Smith
13th July 2009	Commercial litigators seminar (hosted by Freshfields Bruckhaus Deringer LLP)
16th July 2009	Meeting with the costs sub-committee of the Commercial Court users' group
17th July 2009	Meeting with the Legal Services Board
20th July 2009	Meeting with the Strategic Advisory Board for Intellectual Property policy
20th July 2009	Informal seminar 1: After-the-event insurance, success fees and conditional fee agreements (hosted by Reynolds Porter Chamberlain)
21st July 2009	Informal seminar 2: CLAFs, SLASs and contingency fees (hosted by the Chartered Institute of Arbitrators)
21st July 2009	Meeting with Farrer & Co media practitioners and media clients
22nd July 2009	Predictable costs scoping meeting (hosted by the Civil Justice Council) (first part only)
22nd July 2009	Informal seminar 3: Fixed costs (a) in the fast track and (b) above the fast track (hosted by Eversheds LLP)
23rd July 2009	Meeting with the Legal Expenses Insurance Group including representatives of DAS Legal Expenses Insurance Company Ltd, Elite Insurance Company and Helphire Automotive Division
23rd July 2009	Meeting with Tesco plc
23rd July 2009	Meeting with Trust Mediation Ltd
23rd July 2009	Meeting with the Civil Mediation Council
23rd July 2009	Meeting with Gadsby Wicks Solicitors

23rd July 2009	Meeting with the Coalition for Access to Justice for the Environment including representatives of Greenpeace, the Environmental Law Foundation, WWF-UK and Friends of the Earth
23rd July 2009	Meeting with APIL
23rd July 2009	Meetings with MASS
24th July 2009	Informal seminar 4: Chancery litigation (hosted by Clifford Chance LLP)
27th July 2009	Informal seminar 5: Judicial review and environmental claims (hosted by Herbert Smith LLP)
28th July 2009	Informal seminar 6: Business disputes involving SMEs (hosted by Holman Fenwick Willan LLP)
29th July 2009	Informal seminar 7: Case management and cost management (hosted by Mayer Brown International LLP)
30th July 2009	Informal seminar 8: The assessment of the costs (co-hosted by the Supreme Court Costs Office Costs Practitioners' Group and Reed Smith LLP)

Table 1: Table summarising PR appendix 1: CFA cases won by claimant, total costs and damages paid

	Number of cases	Total damages	Total costs paid to claimant (less VAT)	Base profit costs	Success fee	Counsel fee	Counsel success fee	ATE premium	Other disbursements	Total claimant costs plus damages	Total claimant costs as a percentage of damages
Total for all CFA cases	159	£926,906.58	£1,461,362.39	£565,632.25	£480,560.08	£97,738.88	£84,712.12	£889,713.48	£156,157.56	£2,388,268.97	158%
Average for all CFA cases		£5,829.60	£9,190.96	£3,557.44	£3,022.39	£614.71	£532.78	£5,595.68	£982.12	£15,020.56	158%

All cases which include a success fee for either solicitor or counsel are assumed to be CFA cases.
Cases with no monetary damages awarded have been excluded from this calculation.

Table 2: Table summarising PR appendix 1: Non-CFA cases won by claimant, total costs and damages paid

	Number of cases	Total damages	Total costs paid to claimant (less VAT)	Profit costs	Counsel fee	Other disbursements	Total claimant costs plus damages	Total claimant costs as a percentage of damages
Total for all Non-CFA cases	214	£1,934,396.33	£981,448.23	£723,199.99	£102,486.62	£155,761.62	£2,915,844.56	51%
Average for all Non-CFA cases		£9,039.24	£4,586.21	£3,379.44	£478.91	£727.86	£13,625.44	51%

All cases which include a success fee for either solicitor or counsel are assumed to be CFA cases and have therefore been excluded from this calculation.
Cases with no monetary damages awarded have been excluded from this calculation.

Appendix 1: Tables for chapter 2

Table 3: Table summarising PR appendix 1: Cases won by defendant or where defendant gets costs paid

	Number of cases	Total costs paid to defendant (less VAT)	Profit costs	Counsel fee	Other disbursements
Total for all cases	84	£344,826.97	£237,558.87	£84,689.50	£22,578.60
Average per case		£4,105.08	£2,828.08	£1,008.21	£268.79

These cases include 82 claims where the defendant is assumed to have won and two cases relating to defence costs where part 36 offers were not beaten. NB - Judgment set aside cases have not been included in these cases as it was considered that including such cases would skew the results too much.

Table 4: Table summarising PR appendix 1: Cases won by defendant (or where defendant gets costs paid) and where claimant's claimed damages are quantified

	Number of cases	Damages claimed by claimants	Total costs paid to defendant (less VAT)	Profit costs	Counsel fee	Other disbursements	Total defendant costs as a percentage of damages
Total for all cases	58	£1,385,109	£208,043.62	£152,176.02	£46,257.00	£9,610.60	15%
Average per case		£23,881.19	£3,586.96	£2,623.72	£797.53	£165.70	15%

These cases include all cases where damages claimed were quantified as "£x" or "not exceeding £x". I have excluded cases where (a) damages were not quantified or (b) damages "exceeding £x" were claimed. One counterclaim case was excluded from these figures.
These cases include 56 claims where the defendant is assumed to have won and two cases relating to defence costs where part 36 offers were not beaten.

Table 5: Table summarising PR appendix 2: CFA cases won by claimant, total costs and damages paid

	Number of cases	Total damages	Total costs paid to claimant (less VAT)	Base profit costs	Success fee	Counsel fee	Counsel success fee	ATE premium	Other disbursements	Total claimant costs plus damages	Total claimant costs as a percentage of damages
Total for all CFA cases	16	£85,337.00	£173,014.30	£60,496.00	£57,920.00	£14,086.00	£9,334.30	£7,556.00	£23,622.00	£258,351.30	203%
Average for all CFA cases		£5,333.56	£10,813.39	£3,781.00	£3,620.00	£880.38	£583.39	£472.25	£1,476.38	£16,146.96	203%

All cases which include a success fee for either solicitor or counsel are assumed to be CFA cases.
Cases with no monetary damages awarded have been excluded from this calculation.

Table 6: Table summarising PR appendix 2: non-CFA cases won by claimant, total costs and damages paid

	Number of cases	Total damages	Total costs paid to claimant (less VAT)	Profit costs	Counsel fee	Other disbursements	Total claimant costs plus damages	Total claimant costs as a percentage of damages
Total for all Non-CFA cases	35	£432,608.00	£239,527.00	£152,680.00	£55,690.00	£31,157.00	£672,135.00	55%
Average for all Non-CFA cases		£12,360.23	£6,843.63	£4,362.29	£1,591.14	£890.20	£19,203.86	55%

Cases with no monetary damages awarded have been excluded from this calculation.
All cases which include a success fee for either solicitor or counsel are assumed to be CFA cases and have therefore been excluded from this calculation.

Table 7: Table summarising PR appendix 8: CFA cases won by claimant, total costs and damages paid

	Number of cases	Total damages	Total costs paid to claimant (less VAT)	Base profit costs	Success fee	Counsel fee	Counsel success fee	Other disbursements	Total claimant costs plus damages	Total claimant costs as a percentage of damages
Total for all CFA cases	15	£107,387.00	£190,260.27	£80,118.00	£50,616.27	£15,804.00	£1,197.00	£42,525.00	£297,647.27	17%
Average for all CFA cases		£7,159.13	£12,684.02	£5,341.20	£3,374.42	£1,053.60	£79.80	£2,835.00	£19,843.15	177%

All cases which include a success fee for either solicitor or counsel are assumed to be CFA cases.
Cases with no monetary damages awarded have been excluded from this calculation.
In this survey, ATE premiums were treated as disbursements see PR paragraph 11.2.12.

Table 8: Table summarising PR appendix 8: Non-CFA cases won by claimant, total costs and damages paid

	Number of cases	Total damages	Total costs paid to claimant (less VAT)	Profit costs	Counsel fee	Other disbursements	Total claimant costs plus damages	Total claimant costs as a percentage of damages
Total for all Non-CFA cases	61	£660,198.00	£310,515.00	£218,417.00	£37,957.00	£54,141.00	£970,713.00	47%
Average for all Non-CFA cases		£10,822.92	£5,090.41	£3,580.61	£622.25	£887.56	£15,913.33	47%

All cases which include a success fee for either solicitor or counsel are assumed to be CFA cases and have therefore been excluded from this calculation.
Cases with no monetary damages awarded have been excluded from this calculation.

Table 9: Table summarising PR appendix 8: Cases won by defendant or where defendant gets costs paid

	Number of cases	Total costs paid to defendant (less VAT)	Profit costs	Success fee	Counsel fee	Counsel success fee	Other disbursements
Total for all cases	23	£93,056.00	£58,385.00	£5,130.00	£23,150.00	£0.00	£6,391.00
Average per case		£4,045.91	£2,538.48	£223.04	£1,006.52	£0.00	£277.87

These cases include 18 claims where the defendant is assumed to have won and five counterclaims. One of the counterclaims included a success fee paid to the solicitor. NB - Judgement set aside cases have not been included in these cases as it was considered that including such cases would skew the results too much.

Appendix 1: Tables for chapter 2

Table 10: Table summarising PR appendix 18: CFA cases won by claimant, total costs and damages paid

	Number of cases	Total damages	Total costs paid to claimant (less VAT)	Base profit costs	Success fee	Counsel fee	Counsel success fee	ATE premium	Other disbursements	Total claimant costs plus damages	Total claimant costs as a percentage of damages
Total for all CFA cases	494	£2,951,438.62	£1,746,535.97	£1,108,214.37	£231,874.58	£25,790.08	£3,288.69	£142,221.63	£224,379.19	£4,697,974.59	59%
Total for CFA cases settled pre-issue	415	£2,111,739.30	£1,078,194.72	£681,846.92	£135,736.68	£6,393.17	£260.15	£106,197.69	£141,808.24	£3,189,934.02	51%
Total for CFA cases settled post-issue pre-trial	78	£835,359.32	£656,290.09	£422,389.95	£93,154.77	£19,074.41	£3,028.54	£35,131.44	£78,695.42	£1,491,649.41	79%
Total for CFA cases gone to trial or appeal	1	£4,340.00	£12,051.16	£3,977.50	£2,983.13	£322.50	£0.00	£892.50	£3,875.53	£16,391.16	278%

	Total damages	Total costs paid to claimant (less VAT)	Base profit costs	Success fee	Counsel fee	Counsel success fee	ATE premium	Other disbursements	Total claimant costs plus damages	Total claimant costs as a percentage of damages
Average for CFA cases	£5,974.57	£3,535.50	£2,243.35	£469.38	£52.21	£6.66	£287.90	£454.21	£9,510.07	59%
Average for CFA cases settled pre-issue	£5,088.53	£2,598.06	£1,643.00	£327.08	£15.41	£0.63	£255.90	£341.71	£7,686.59	51%
Average for CFA cases settled post-issue pre-trial	£10,709.73	£8,413.98	£5,415.26	£1,194.29	£244.54	£38.83	£450.40	£1,008.92	£19,123.71	79%
CFA case gone to trial or appeal	£4,340.00	£12,051.16	£3,977.50	£2,983.13	£322.50	£0.00	£892.50	£3,875.53	£16,391.16	278%

All cases which had a success fee either claimed or allowed were assumed to be CFA cases. Cases 51,52, 153 and 328 had no success fees recorded but had claimed for success fees. There are 46 cases out of the 495 non-CFA cases where ATE premiums were recorded but no success fees. The insurer which supplied the data regards these 46 cases as anomalous and queries whether the data have been captured correctly. I have decided to exclude these 46 cases from the present analysis.

Table 11: Table summarising PR appendix 18: Non-CFA, no ATE premium cases won by claimant, total costs and damages paid

	Number of cases	Total damages	Total costs paid to claimant (less VAT)	Profit costs	Success fee	Counsel fee	Counsel success fee	ATE premium	Other disbursements	Total claimant costs plus damages	Total claimant costs as a percentage of damages
Total for all non-CFA, no ATE premium cases	449	£ 3,101,668.90	£ 1,207,712.04	£ 963,836.06	£ -	£ 39,935.89	£ -	£ -	£ 169,736.46	£ 4,309,380.94	39%
Total for non-CFA, no ATE premium cases settled pre-issue	356	£ 1,596,364.21	£ 647,113.28	£ 548,220.38	£ -	£ 4,959.25	£ -	£ -	£ 90,864.48	£ 2,243,477.49	41%
Total for non-CFA, no ATE premium cases settled post-issue pre-trial	92	£ 1,503,298.79	£ 555,122.28	£ 412,392.20	£ -	£ 34,277.51	£ -	£ -	£ 78,164.98	£ 2,058,421.07	37%
Total for non-CFA, no ATE premium cases gone to trial or appeal	1	£ 2,005.90	£ 5,476.48	£ 3,223.48	£ -	£ 699.13	£ -	£ -	£ 707.00	£ 7,482.38	273%

	Total damages	Total costs paid to claimant (less VAT)	Profit costs	Success fee	Counsel fee	Counsel success fee	ATE premium	Other disbursements	Total claimant costs plus damages	Total claimant costs as a percentage of damages
Average for non-CFA, no ATE premium cases	£ 6,907.95	£ 2,689.78	£ 2,146.63	£ -	£ 88.94	£ -	£ -	£ 378.03	£ 9,597.73	39%
Average for non-CFA, no ATE premium cases settled pre-issue	£ 4,484.17	£ 1,817.73	£ 1,539.94	£ -	£ 13.93	£ -	£ -	£ 255.24	£ 6,301.90	41%
Average for non-CFA, no ATE premium cases settled post-issue pre-trial	£ 16,340.20	£ 6,033.94	£ 4,482.52	£ -	£ 372.58	£ -	£ -	£ 849.62	£ 22,374.14	37%
Non-CFA, no ATE premium case gone to trial or appeal	£ 2,005.90	£ 5,476.48	£ 3,223.48	£ -	£ 699.13	£ -	£ -	£ 707.00	£ 7,482.38	273%

Table 12: Data from one liability insurer in respect of personal injury claims won by claimant in 2008

Damages value band	Volume settled	Average damages	Average own costs	Average third party costs	Combined costs
Motor personal injury					
£1,000 - £2,500	335	£1,825	£1,315	£3,647	£4,962
£2,501 - £5,000	400	£3,655	£1,495	£4,846	£6,341
£5,001 - £10,000	279	£7,254	£1,894	£7,264	£9,158
£10,001 - £15,000	84	£12,339	£2,970	£9,662	£12,632
£15,001 - £20,000	44	£18,000	£4,452	£11,120	£15,572
£20,001 - £25,000	26	£23,447	£8,123	£14,650	£22,773
Employer's liability / public liability					
£1,000 - £2,500	209	£1,775	£2,038	£6,809	£8,847
£2,501 - £5,000	208	£3,882	£2,000	£8,225	£10,225
£5,001 - £10,000	162	£7,340	£2,381	£9,856	£12,237
£10,001 - £15,000	85	£12,596	£4,388	£13,274	£17,662
£15,001 - £20,000	34	£17,547	£5,395	£18,965	£24,360
£20,001 - £25,000	29	£23,372	£4,005	£13,454	£17,459

Table 13: Table summarising low value claims in PR appendix 26: All fast track cases

	Number of cases	Total Damages	Total claimant costs (including VAT)	Base profit costs	Success Fee	ATE premium	Other disbursements	Total claimant costs plus damages	Total claimant costs as a percentage of damages
Total for Employers' Liability cases - Litigated	623	£3,515,819.51	£4,661,896.54	£2,853,477.06	£757,879.50	£351,627.43	£698,912.55	£8,177,716.05	133%
Total for Motor cases - Litigated	1646	£6,237,039.66	£7,245,560.32	£5,556,912.46	£225,205.72	£169,027.74	£1,294,414.40	£13,482,599.98	116%
Total for Occupational Health (Disease) – Litigated	57	£309,871.38	£478,053.87	£248,008.14	£129,463.53	£41,460.66	£59,121.54	£787,925.25	154%
Total for Public Liability cases – Litigated	380	£1,846,541.60	£3,153,722.60	£1,910,681.80	£581,582.40	£172,455.40	£489,003.00	£5,000,264.20	171%
Total for all litigated cases	2706	£11,909,272.15	£15,539,233.33	£10,569,079.46	£1,694,131.15	£734,571.23	£2,541,451.49	£27,448,505.48	130%

	Number of cases	Total Damages	Total claimant costs (including VAT)	Base profit costs	Success Fee	ATE premium	Other disbursements	Total claimant costs plus damages	Total claimant costs as a percentage of damages
Average for Employers' Liability cases - Litigated		£5,643.37	£7,482.98	£4,580.22	£1,216.50	£564.41	£1,121.85	£13,126.35	133%
Average for Motor cases - Litigated		£3,789.21	£4,411.98	£3,386.07	£136.82	£102.69	£786.40	£8,201.19	116%
Average for Occupational Health (Disease) - Litigated		£5,436.34	£8,386.91	£4,351.02	£2,271.29	£727.38	£1,037.22	£13,823.25	154%
Average for Public Liability cases - Litigated		£4,859.32	£8,299.27	£5,028.11	£1,530.48	£453.83	£1,286.85	£13,158.59	171%
Weighted average for all litigated cases		£4,401.06	£5,742.51	£3,905.79	£626.06	£271.46	£939.19	£10,143.57	130%

Table 13 (cont): Table summarising low value claims in PR appendix 26: All fast track cases

	Number of cases	Total Damages	Total claimant costs (including VAT)	Base profit costs	Success Fee	ATE premium	Other disbursements	Total claimant costs plus damages	Total claimant costs as a percentage of

-497-

	Number of cases	Total Damages	Total claimant costs (including VAT)	Base profit costs	Success Fee	ATE premium	Other disbursements	Total claimant costs plus damages	damages
Total for Employers' Liability cases - Non-litigated	1704	£8,340,193.92	£7,028,608.08	£4,613,774.84	£934,064.64	£691,449.12	£789,139.44	£15,368,802.00	84%
Total for Motor cases - Non-litigated	158	£1,619,520.54	£738,686.34	£559,896.70	£30,479.78	£18,841.50	£129,468.36	£2,358,206.88	46%
Total for Occupational Health (Disease) - Non-litigated	74	£273,398.92	£426,053.52	£206,851.46	£117,658.52	£60,018.44	£41,525.10	£699,452.44	156%
Total for Public Liability cases - Non-litigated	1476	£6,046,404.48	£6,491,403.72	£4,207,633.20	£1,080,756.72	£504,673.92	£698,339.88	£12,537,808.20	107%
Total for all non-litigated cases	3412	£16,279,517.86	£14,684,751.66	£9,588,336.24	£2,162,959.66	£1,274,982.98	£1,658,472.78	£30,964,269.52	90%

	Number of cases	Total Damages	Total claimant costs (including VAT)	Base profit costs	Success Fee	ATE premium	Other disbursements	Total claimant costs plus damages	Total claimant costs as a percentage of damages
Average for Employers' Liability cases - Non-litigated		£4,894.48	£4,124.77	£2,707.72	£548.16	£405.78	£463.11	£9,019.25	84%
Average for Motor cases - Non-litigated		£10,250.13	£4,675.23	£3,543.65	£192.91	£119.25	£819.42	£14,925.36	46%
Average for Occupational Health (Disease) - Non litigated		£3,694.58	£5,757.48	£2,795.29	£1,589.98	£811.06	£561.15	£9,452.06	156%
Average for Public Liability cases - Non-litigated		£4,096.48	£4,397.97	£2,850.70	£732.22	£341.92	£473.13	£8,494.45	107%
Weighted average for all non-litigated cases		£4,771.25	£4,303.85	£2,810.18	£633.93	£373.68	£486.07	£9,075.11	90%

Note – There are slight differences between the figures shown in this table and the figures in PR appendix 26 which appear to be due to rounding differences.

Table 14: Table summarising low value claims in PR appendix 26: Fast track cases with costs only proceedings (these are a subset of the non-litigated claims)

	Number of cases	Total Damages	Total claimant costs (including VAT)	Base profit costs	Success Fee	ATE premium	Other disbursements	Total claimant costs plus damages	Total claimant costs as a percentage of damages
Total for Employers' Liability cases - Non-litigated	233	£1,262,529.14	£1,297,910.19	£848,301.74	£173,000.17	£114,398.34	£162,209.94	£2,560,439.33	103%
Total for Motor cases - Non-litigated	42	£380,185.68	£273,501.48	£202,154.40	£12,382.44	£6,251.70	£52,712.94	£653,687.16	72%
Total for Occupational Health (Disease) - Non-litigated	15	£80,083.50	£94,917.00	£47,210.40	£28,154.70	£9,299.70	£10,252.20	£175,000.50	119%
Total for Public Liability cases - Non-litigated	259	£1,165,331.65	£1,597,146.81	£995,984.50	£298,173.75	£101,310.44	£201,678.12	£2,762,478.46	137%
Total for all costs only proceedings	549	£2,888,129.97	£3,263,475.48	£2,093,651.04	£511,711.06	£231,260.18	£426,853.20	£6,151,605.45	113%

	Number of cases	Total Damages	Total claimant costs (including VAT)	Base profit costs	Success Fee	ATE premium	Other disbursements	Total claimant costs plus damages	Total claimant costs as a percentage of damages
Average for Employers' Liability cases - Non-litigated		£5,418.58	£5,570.43	£3,640.78	£742.49	£490.98	£696.18	£10,989.01	103%
Average for Motor cases - Non-litigated		£9,052.04	£6,511.94	£4,813.20	£294.82	£148.85	£1,255.07	£15,563.98	72%
Average for Occupational Health (Disease) - Non litigated		£5,338.90	£6,327.80	£3,147.36	£1,876.98	£619.98	£683.48	£11,666.70	119%
Average for Public Liability cases - Non-litigated		£4,499.35	£6,166.59	£3,845.50	£1,151.25	£391.16	£778.68	£10,665.94	137%
Weighted average for all costs only proceedings		£5,260.71	£5,944.40	£3,813.46	£932.08	£421.24	£777.51	£11,205.11	113%

Appendix 1: Tables for chapter 2

Table 15: Table summarising low value claims in PR appendix 26: All PCR cases

	Number of cases	Total Damages	Total claimant costs (including VAT)	Base profit costs	Success Fee	ATE premium	Other disbursements	Total claimant costs plus damages	Total claimant costs as a percentage of damages
Total PCR Cases	3994	£11,338,127.26	£8,641,058.94	£6,406,695.52	£444,891.66	£526,568.96	£1,262,902.80	£19,979,186.20	76%
Total for all PCR cases	3994	£11,338,127.26	£8,641,058.94	£6,406,695.76	£444,891.66	£526,568.96	£1,262,902.80	£19,979,186.20	76%

	Number of cases	Total Damages	Total claimant costs (including VAT)	Base profit costs	Success Fee	ATE premium	Other disbursements	Total claimant costs plus damages	Total claimant costs as a percentage of damages
Average PCR cases		£2,838.79	£2,163.51	£1,604.08	£111.39	£131.84	£316.20	£5,002.30	76%
Average for all PCR cases		£2,838.79	£2,163.51	£1,604.08	£111.39	£131.84	£316.20	£5,002.30	76%

Note – There are slight differences between the figures shown in this table and the figures in PR appendix 26 which appear to be due to rounding differences.

Table 16: Table summarising low value claims in PR appendix 26: PCR cases with costs only proceedings (these are a subset of the total PCR claims)

	Number of cases	Total Damages	Total claimant costs (including VAT)	Base profit costs	Success Fee	ATE premium	Other disbursements	Total claimant costs plus damages	Total claimant costs as a percentage of damages
Total PCR cases	321	£758,930.67	£790,016.31	£541,180.32	£33,348.69	£42,311.01	£173,176.29	£1,548,946.98	104%
Total for all costs only proceedings	321	£758,930.67	£790,016.31	£541,180.32	£33,348.69	£42,311.01	£173,176.29	£1,548,946.98	104%

	Number of cases	Total Damages	Total claimant costs (including VAT)	Base profit costs	Success Fee	ATE premium	Other disbursements	Total claimant costs plus damages	Total claimant costs as a percentage of damages
Average PCR cases		£2,364.27	£2,461.11	£1,685.92	£103.89	£131.81	£539.49	£4,825.38	104%
Average for all costs only proceedings		£2,364.27	£2,461.11	£1,685.92	£103.89	£131.81	£539.49	£4,825.38	104%

Appendix 1: Tables for chapter 2

Table 17: Table summarising low value claims in PR appendix 26: PCR cases not including cases with costs only proceedings

	Number of cases	Total Damages	Total claimant costs (including VAT)	Base profit costs	Success Fee	ATE premium	Other disbursements	Total claimant costs plus damages	Total claimant costs as a percentage of damages
Total PCR cases	3673	£10,579,196.59	£7,851,042.63	£5,865,515.20	£411,542.97	£484,257.95	£1,089,726.51	£18,430,239.22	74%
Total for all costs only proceedings	3673	£10,579,196.59	£7,851,042.63	£5,865,515.20	£411,542.97	£484,257.95	£1,089,726.51	£18,430,239.22	74%

	Number of cases	Total Damages	Total claimant costs (including VAT)	Base profit costs	Success Fee	ATE premium	Other disbursements	Total claimant costs plus damages	Total claimant costs as a percentage of damages
Average PCR cases		£2,880.26	£2,137.50	£1,596.93	£112.05	£131.84	£296.69	£5,017.76	74%
Average for all costs only proceedings		£2,880.26	£2,137.50	£1,596.93	£112.05	£131.84	£296.69	£5,017.76	74%

Table 18: Table summarising high value claims in PR appendix 26: All high value multi-track cases

	Number of cases	Total Damages	Total claimant costs (including VAT)	Base profit costs	Success Fee	ATE premium	Other disbursements	Total claimant costs plus damages	Total claimant costs as a percentage of damages
Total for Employers' Liability cases - Litigated	45	£11,108,155.95	£1,758,523.05	£957,300.75	£312,529.50	£59,903.10	£428,789.70	£12,866,679.00	16%
Total for Motor cases - Litigated	42	£19,243,812.42	£1,600,063.08	£1,012,208.82	£158,473.14	£13,842.78	£415,538.34	£20,843,875.50	8%
Total for Public Liability cases - Litigated	10	£1,854,501.00	£306,363.40	£178,731.30	£21,474.50	£2,415.00	£103,742.60	£2,160,864.40	17%
Total for all litigated cases	97	£32,206,469.37	£3,664,949.53	£2,148,240.87	£492,477.14	£76,160.88	£948,070.64	£35,871,418.90	11%

	Number of cases	Total Damages	Total claimant costs (including VAT)	Base profit costs	Success Fee	ATE premium	Other disbursements	Total claimant costs plus damages	Total claimant costs as a percentage of damages
Average for Employers' Liability cases - Litigated		£246,847.91	£39,078.29	£21,273.35	£6,945.10	£1,331.18	£9,528.66	£285,926.20	16%
Average for Motor cases - Litigated		£458,186.01	£38,096.74	£24,100.21	£3,773.17	£329.59	£9,893.77	£496,282.75	8%
Average for Public Liability cases - Litigated		£185,450.10	£30,636.34	£17,873.13	£2,147.45	£241.50	£10,374.26	£216,086.44	17%
Weighted average for all litigated cases		£332,025.46	£37,782.98	£22,146.82	£5,077.08	£785.16	£9,773.92	£369,808.44	11%

Appendix 1: Tables for chapter 2

Table 18 (cont): Table summarising high value claims in PR appendix 26: All high value multi-track cases

	Number of cases	Total Damages	Total claimant costs (including VAT)	Base profit costs	Success Fee	ATE premium	Other disbursements	Total claimant costs plus damages	Total claimant costs as a percentage of damages
Total for Employers' Liability cases - Non-litigated	17	£3,413,140.66	£270,586.11	£177,164.99	£37,304.46	£12,981.71	£43,134.95	£3,683,726.77	8%
Total for Motor cases - Non-litigated	10	£1,442,370.50	£162,625.10	£124,604.20	£7,598.60	£1,668.90	£28,753.40	£1,604,995.60	11%
Total for Public Liability cases - Non-litigated	2	£230,000.00	£12,950.02	£10,015.78	£783.24	£0.00	£2,151.00	£242,950.02	6%
Total for all non-litigated cases	29	£5,085,511.16	£446,161.23	£311,784.97	£45,686.30	£14,650.61	£74,039.35	£5,531,672.39	9%

	Number of cases	Total Damages	Total claimant costs (including VAT)	Base profit costs	Success Fee	ATE premium	Other disbursements	Total claimant costs plus damages	Total claimant costs as a percentage of damages
Average for Employers' Liability cases - Non-litigated		£200,772.98	£15,916.83	£10,421.47	£2,194.38	£763.63	£2,537.35	£216,689.81	8%
Average for Motor cases - Non-litigated		£144,237.05	£16,262.51	£12,460.42	£759.86	£166.89	£2,875.34	£160,499.56	11%
Average for Public Liability cases - Non-litigated		£115,000.00	£6,475.01	£5,007.89	£391.62	£0.00	£1,075.50	£121,475.01	6%
Weighted average for all non-litigated cases		£175,362.45	£15,384.87	£10,751.20	£1,575.39	£505.19	£2,553.08	£190,747.32	9%

Note - The average '"Total claimant costs (plus VAT)" for Employers' liability cases in PR appendix 26 does not add up in the original appendix, the figure shown in this table is correct.

Table 19: Table summarising high value claims in PR appendix 26: High value multi-track cases with costs only proceedings (these are a subset of the non-litigated claims)

	Number of cases	Total Damages	Total claimant costs (including VAT)	Base profit costs	Success Fee	ATE premium	Other disbursements	Total claimant costs plus damages	Total claimant costs as a percentage of damages
Total for Employers' Liability cases - Non-litigated	6	£1,038,140.70	£91,624.56	£60,597.96	£13,961.16	£3,148.74	£13,916.70	£1,129,765.26	9%
Total for Motor cases - Non-litigated	2	£220,000.00	£24,675.02	£18,552.70	£1,753.02	£350.00	£4,019.30	£244,675.02	11%
Total for all costs only proceedings	8	£1,258,140.70	£116,299.58	£79,151.06	£15,714.18	£3,498.74	£17,936.00	£1,374,440.28	9%

	Number of cases	Total Damages	Total claimant costs (including VAT)	Base profit costs	Success Fee	ATE premium	Other disbursements	Total claimant costs plus damages	Total claimant costs as a percentage of damages
Average for Employers' Liability cases - Non-litigated		£173,023.45	£15,270.76	£10,099.66	£2,326.86	£524.79	£2,319.45	£188,294.21	9%
Average for Motor cases - Non-litigated		£110,000.00	£12,337.51	£9,276.35	£876.51	£175.00	£2,009.65	£122,337.51	11%
Weighted average for all costs only proceedings		£157,267.59	£14,537.45	£9,893.84	£1,964.27	£437.34	£2,242.00	£171,805.04	9%

-505-

Table 20: Table summarising medium value claims in PR appendix 26: All low value multi-track cases

	Number of cases	Total Damages	Total claimant costs (including VAT)	Base profit costs	Success Fee	ATE premium	Other disbursements	Total claimant costs plus damages	Total claimant costs as a percentage of damages
Total for Employers' Liability cases - Litigated	250	£9,597,860.00	£3,698,900.00	£2,249,342.50	£657,162.50	£155,445.00	£636,950.00	£13,296,760.00	39%
Total for Motor cases - Litigated	134	£4,653,346.98	£1,837,795.26	£1,303,793.20	£75,183.38	£26,804.02	£432,014.66	£6,491,142.24	39%
Total for Occupational Health (Disease) - Litigated	8	£310,016.16	£153,345.12	£78,269.28	£42,719.52	£5,064.64	£27,291.68	£463,361.28	49%
Total for Public Liability cases - Litigated	82	£2,525,868.14	£1,205,614.84	£730,303.48	£216,620.22	£27,425.72	£231,265.42	£3,731,482.98	48%
Total for all litigated cases	474	£17,087,091.28	£6,895,655.22	£4,361,709.46	£991,685.62	£214,739.38	£1,327,521.76	£23,982,746.50	40%

	Number of cases	Total Damages	Total claimant costs (including VAT)	Base profit costs	Success Fee	ATE premium	Other disbursements	Total claimant costs plus damages	Total claimant costs as a percentage of damages
Average for Employers' Liability cases - Litigated		£38,391.44	£14,795.60	£8,997.37	£2,628.65	£621.78	£2,547.80	£53,187.04	39%
Average for Motor cases - Litigated		£34,726.47	£13,714.89	£9,729.80	£561.07	£200.03	£3,223.99	£48,441.36	39%
Average for Occupational Health (Disease) - Litigated		£38,752.02	£19,168.14	£9,783.66	£5,339.94	£633.08	£3,411.46	£57,920.16	49%
Average for Public Liability cases - Litigated		£30,803.27	£14,702.62	£8,906.14	£2,641.71	£334.46	£2,820.31	£45,505.89	48%
Weighted average for all litigated cases		£36,048.72	£14,547.80	£9,201.91	£2,092.16	£453.04	£2,800.68	£50,596.51	40%

Table 20 (cont): Table summarising medium value claims in PR appendix 26: All low value multi-track cases

	Number of cases	Total Damages	Total claimant costs (including VAT)	Base profit costs	Success Fee	ATE premium	Other disbursements	Total claimant costs plus damages	Total claimant costs as a percentage of damages
Total for Employers' Liability cases - Non-litigated	247	£8,323,660.41	£1,825,273.19	£1,240,130.19	£242,148.92	£94,381.17	£248,612.91	£10,148,933.60	22%
Total for Motor cases - Non-litigated	124	£3,700,675.84	£764,024.76	£585,988.04	£31,102.92	£10,688.80	£136,245.00	£4,464,700.60	21%
Total for Occupational Health (Disease) - Non-litigated	5	£128,971.00	£29,274.95	£17,613.70	£6,289.65	£2,303.75	£3,067.85	£158,245.95	23%
Total for Public Liability cases - Non-litigated	97	£2,785,700.32	£648,428.51	£439,068.56	£101,833.51	£27,493.68	£80,032.76	£3,434,128.83	23%
Total for all non-litigated cases	473	£14,939,007.57	£3,267,001.41	£2,282,800.49	£381,375.00	£134,867.40	£467,958.52	£18,206,008.98	22%

	Number of cases	Total Damages	Total claimant costs (including VAT)	Base profit costs	Success Fee	ATE premium	Other disbursements	Total claimant costs plus damages	Total claimant costs as a percentage of damages
Average for Employers' Liability cases - Non-litigated		£33,699.03	£7,389.77	£5,020.77	£980.36	£382.11	£1,006.53	£41,088.80	22%
Average for Motor cases - Non-litigated		£29,844.16	£6,161.49	£4,725.71	£250.83	£86.20	£1,098.75	£36,005.65	21%
Average for Occupational Health (Disease) - Non litigated		£25,794.20	£5,854.99	£3,522.74	£1,257.93	£460.75	£613.57	£31,649.19	23%
Average for Public Liability cases - Non-litigated		£28,718.56	£6,684.83	£4,526.48	£1,049.83	£283.44	£825.08	£35,403.39	23%
Weighted average for all non-litigated cases		£31,583.53	£6,906.98	£4,826.22	£806.29	£285.13	£989.34	£38,490.51	22%

Note - There are slight differences between the figures shown in this table and the figures in PR appendix 26 which appear to be due to rounding differences.

Appendix 1: Tables for chapter 2

Table 21: Table summarising medium value claims in PR appendix 26: Low value multi-track cases with costs only proceedings (these are a subset of the non-litigated claims)

	Number of cases	Total Damages	Total claimant costs (including VAT)	Base profit costs	Success Fee	ATE premium	Other disbursements	Total claimant costs plus damages	Total claimant costs as a percentage of damages
Total for Employers' Liability cases - Non-litigated	81	£2,902,954.95	£761,557.95	£514,291.68	£103,152.69	£35,013.06	£109,100.52	£3,664,512.90	26%
Total for Motor cases - Non-litigated	27	£904,237.56	£249,962.22	£187,247.97	£6,904.71	£1,575.18	£54,234.36	£1,154,199.78	28%
Total for Occupational Health (Disease) - Non-litigated	1	£27,000.00	£9,125.00	£4,757.47	£2,378.73	£760.00	£1,228.80	£36,125.00	34%
Total for Public Liability cases - Non-litigated	36	£1,019,216.52	£275,416.56	£201,036.60	£35,915.76	£9,315.36	£29,148.84	£1,294,633.08	27%
Total for all costs only proceedings	145	£4,853,409.03	£1,296,061.73	£907,333.72	£148,351.89	£46,663.60	£193,712.52	£6,149,470.76	27%

	Number of cases	Total Damages	Total claimant costs (including VAT)	Base profit costs	Success Fee	ATE premium	Other disbursements	Total claimant costs plus damages	Total claimant costs as a percentage of damages
Average for Employers' Liability cases - Non-litigated		£35,838.95	£9,401.95	£6,349.28	£1,273.49	£432.26	£1,346.92	£45,240.90	26%
Average for Motor cases - Non-litigated		£33,490.28	£9,257.86	£6,935.11	£255.73	£58.34	£2,008.68	£42,748.14	28%
Average for Occupational Health (Disease) - Non litigated		£27,000.00	£9,125.00	£4,757.47	£2,378.73	£760.00	£1,228.80	£36,125.00	34%
Average for Public Liability cases - Non-litigated		£28,311.57	£7,650.46	£5,584.35	£997.66	£258.76	£809.69	£35,962.03	27%
Weighted average for all costs only proceedings		£33,471.79	£8,938.36	£6,257.47	£1,023.12	£321.82	£1,335.95	£42,410.14	27%

Table 22: Table summarising successful clinical negligence claims by funding type

Total	Number of cases	Total Damages	Total claimant costs	Total defendant costs	Total claimant costs plus damages	Total claimant costs as a percentage of damages	Claimant costs as a percentage of defendant costs
Funded by CFA	213	£19,171,504	£8,386,736	£2,039,122	£27,558,240	44%	411%
Funded by LSC	186	£46,059,695	£9,834,936	£4,665,401	£55,894,631	21%	211%
Self-funded	71	£1,560,820	£534,210	£249,471	£2,095,030	34%	214%
Funded by BTE insurance	40	£8,250,179	£1,909,909	£643,139	£10,160,088	23%	297%
Unknown	47	£1,932,305	£772,020	£268,642	£1,912,448	40%	287%
TOTAL	557	£76,974,504	£21,437,811	£7,865,774	£97,620,437	28%	273%

-509-

Table 23: Table summarising split of outcome by funding source

	Total (number of cases)	Nil damages	Percentage of cases with nil damages	Damages paid/structured settlement	Percentage of successful cases
Funded by CFA	306	93	30%	213	70%
Funded by LSC	306	120	39%	186	61%
Self-funded	142	71	50%	71	50%
Funded by BTE insurance	51	11	22%	40	78%
Unknown	195	148	76%	47	24%
TOTAL	1000	443	44%	557	56%

Table 24: Table summarising high value clinical negligence claims (including structured settlements) by funding type

	Number of cases	Total Damages	Total claimant costs	Total defendant costs	Total claimant costs plus damages	Total claimant costs as a percentage of damages	Claimant costs as a percentage of defendant costs
Funded by CFA	37	£15,783,384	£5,090,890	£1,274,115	£20,874,274	32%	400%
Funded by LSC	51	£42,692,900	£6,934,243	£3,505,587	£49,627,142	16%	198%
Self-funded	4	£755,547	£228,430	£97,529	£983,977	30%	234%
Funded by BTE insurance	10	£7,446,528	£1,468,090	£436,077	£8,914,618	20%	337%
Unknown	4	£1,071,636	£181,296	£102,092	£637,483	17%	178%
TOTAL	106	£67,749,994	£13,902,948	£5,415,400	£81,037,493	21%	257%

Table 25: Table summarising high value clinical negligence claims (excluding structured settlements) by funding type

	Number of cases	Total Damages	Total claimant costs	Total defendant costs	Total claimant costs plus damages	Total claimant costs as a percentage of damages	Claimant costs as a percentage of defendant costs
Funded by CFA	36	£13,289,901	£4,916,890	£1,208,294	£18,206,790	37%	407%
Funded by LSC	38	£26,767,216	£3,731,238	£1,922,103	£30,498,454	14%	194%
Self-funded	4	£755,547	£228,430	£97,529	£983,977	30%	234%
Funded by BTE insurance	10	£7,446,528	£1,468,090	£436,077	£8,914,618	20%	337%
Unknown	4	£1,071,636	£181,296	£102,092	£1,252,932	17%	178%
TOTAL	92	£49,330,827	£10,525,944	£3,766,095	£59,856,771	21%	279%

Table 26: Table summarising medium value clinical negligence claims by funding type

	Number of cases	Total Damages	Total claimant costs	Total defendant costs	Total claimant costs plus damages	Total claimant costs as a percentage of damages	Claimant costs as a percentage of defendant costs
Funded by CFA	50	£2,218,095	£1,660,529	£426,199	£3,878,624	75%	390%
Funded by LSC	55	£2,581,091	£1,847,589	£774,445	£4,428,680	72%	239%
Self-funded	10	£416,989	£123,400	£109,902	£540,389	30%	112%
Funded by BTE insurance	10	£599,401	£210,634	£128,025	£810,035	35%	165%
Unknown	13	£551,270	£262,641	£68,388	£637,483	48%	384%
TOTAL	138	£6,366,846	£4,104,793	£1,506,959	£10,295,210	64%	272%

Table 27: Table summarising low value clinical negligence claims by funding type

	Number of cases	Total Damages	Total claimant costs	Total defendant costs	Total claimant costs plus damages	Total claimant costs as a percentage of damages	Claimant costs as a percentage of defendant costs
Funded by CFA	126	£1,170,025	£1,635,318	£338,808	£2,805,343	140%	483%
Funded by LSC	80	£785,704	£1,053,104	£385,369	£1,838,809	134%	273%
Self-funded	57	£388,284	£182,380	£42,040	£570,664	47%	434%
Funded by BTE insurance	20	£204,250	£231,185	£79,036	£435,435	113%	293%
Unknown	30	£309,400	£328,083	£98,163	£637,483	106%	284%
TOTAL	313	£2,857,664	£3,430,070	£943,416	£6,287,733	120%	364%

Table 28: Table summarising PR appendix 17: CFA cases won by claimant, total costs and damages paid

	Number of cases	Total damages	Costs paid to claimant	Total claimant costs plus damages	Total claimant costs as a percentage of damages	Defendants' costs incurred	Defendants' costs as a percentage of damages paid
Total for all CFA cases	27	£1,961,750.00	£6,160,551.00	£8,122,301.00	314%	£2,452,259	125%
Total for CFA cases settled	22	£1,820,750.00	£4,363,632.00	£6,184,382.00	240%	£1,184,921	65%
Total for CFA cases won at trial	2	£115,000.00	£1,746,381.00	£1,861,381.00	1519%	£1,259,824	1095%
Total for CFA cases - Offer of Amends	3	£26,000.00	£50,538.00	£76,538.00	194%	£7,514	29%

	Total damages	Costs paid to claimant	Total claimant costs plus damages	Total claimant costs as a percentage of damages	Defendants' costs incurred	Defendants' costs as a percentage of damages paid
Average for all CFA cases	£72,657.41	£228,168.56	£300,825.96	314%	£90,824	125%
Average for CFA cases settled	£82,761.36	£198,346.91	£281,108.27	240%	£53,860	65%
Average for CFA cases won at trial	£57,500.00	£873,190.50	£930,690.50	1519%	£629,912	1095%
Average for CFA cases - Offer of Amends	£8,666.67	£16,846.00	£25,512.67	194%	£2,505	29%

Cases where damages were included within costs paid have been excluded from this calculation.
In cases where the claimant is not VAT registered VAT will be included in the claimant costs.

Table 29: Table summarising PR appendix 17: Non-CFA cases won by claimant, total costs and damages paid

	Number of cases	Total damages	Costs paid to claimant	Total claimant costs plus damages	Total claimant costs as a percentage of damages	Defendants' costs incurred	Defendants' costs as a percentage of damages paid
Total for all non-CFA cases	120	£1,129,467.00	£3,346,498.00	£4,475,965.00	296%	£2,355,153	209%
Total for non-CFA cases settled	118	£1,039,467.00	£2,896,498.00	£3,935,965.00	279%	£1,932,902	186%
Total for non-CFA cases won at trial	1	£60,000.00	£420,000.00	£480,000.00	700%	£416,177	694%
Total for non-CFA cases - Offer of Amends	1	£30,000.00	£30,000.00	£60,000.00	100%	£6,074	20%

	Total damages	Costs paid to claimant	Total claimant costs plus damages	Total claimant costs as a percentage of damages	Defendants' costs incurred	Defendants' costs as a percentage of damages paid
Average for all non-CFA cases	£9,412.23	£27,887.48	£37,299.71	296%	£19,626	209%
Average for non-CFA cases settled	£8,809.04	£24,546.59	£33,355.64	279%	£16,381	186%
Average for non-CFA cases won at trial	£60,000.00	£420,000.00	£480,000.00	700%	£416,177	694%
Average for non-CFA cases - Offer of Amends	£30,000.00	£30,000.00	£60,000.00	100%	£6,074	20%

Cases where damages were included within costs paid have been excluded from this calculation.
In cases where the claimant is not VAT registered, VAT will be included in these figures.

Table 30: Table summarising PR appendix 17: CFA cases (excluding case 1) won by claimant, total costs and damages paid

	Number of cases	Total damages	Costs paid to claimant	Total claimant costs plus damages	Total claimant costs as a percentage of damages	Defendants' costs incurred	Defendants' costs as a percentage of damages paid
Total for all CFA cases	26	£1,846,750.00	£4,127,406.00	£5,974,156.00	223%	£1,894,509	103%
Total for CFA cases settled	21	£1,705,750.00	£2,330,487.00	£4,036,237.00	137%	£627,171	37%
Total for CFA cases won at trial	2	£115,000.00	£1,746,381.00	£1,861,381.00	1519%	£1,259,824	1095%
Total for CFA cases - Offer of Amends	3	£26,000.00	£50,538.00	£76,538.00	194%	£7,514	29%

	Total damages	Costs paid to claimant	Total claimant costs plus damages	Total claimant costs as a percentage of damages	Defendants' costs incurred	Defendants' costs as a percentage of damages paid
Average for all CFA cases	£71,028.85	£158,746.38	£229,775.23	223%	£72,866	103%
Average for CFA cases settled	£81,226.19	£110,975.57	£192,201.76	137%	£29,865	37%
Average for CFA cases won at trial	£57,500.00	£873,190.50	£930,690.50	1519%	£629,912	1095%
Average for CFA cases - Offer of Amends	£8,666.67	£16,846.00	£25,512.67	194%	£2,505	29%

Cases where damages were included within costs paid have been excluded from this calculation.
In cases where the claimant is not VAT registered, VAT will be included in these figures.
Case 1 has been excluded from this calculation as the claimant costs of £2.03m and defendant costs of £557k with damages of £115k skewed the results.

-517-

Table 31: Table summarising PR appendix 17: Non-CFA cases (excluding case 2) won by claimant, total costs and damages paid

	Number of cases	Total damages	Costs paid to claimant	Total claimant costs plus damages	Total claimant costs as a percentage of damages	Defendants' costs incurred	Defendants' costs as a percentage of damages paid
Total for all non-CFA cases	119	£1,024,467.00	£1,646,498.00	£2,670,965.00	161%	£916,173	89%
Total for non-CFA cases settled	117	£934,467.00	£1,196,498.00	£2,130,965.00	128%	£493,922	53%
Total for non-CFA cases won at trial	1	£60,000.00	£420,000.00	£480,000.00	700%	£416,177	694%
Total for non-CFA cases - Offer of Amends	1	£30,000.00	£30,000.00	£60,000.00	100%	£6,074	20%

	Total damages	Costs paid to claimant	Total claimant costs plus damages	Total claimant costs as a percentage of damages	Defendants' costs incurred	Defendants' costs as a percentage of damages paid
Average for all non-CFA cases	£8,608.97	£13,836.12	£22,445.08	161%	£7,699	89%
Average for non-CFA cases settled	£7,986.90	£10,226.48	£18,213.38	128%	£4,222	53%
Average for non-CFA cases won at trial	£60,000.00	£420,000.00	£480,000.00	700%	£416,177	694%
Average for non-CFA cases - Offer of Amends	£30,000.00	£30,000.00	£60,000.00	100%	£6,074	20%

Cases where damages were included within costs paid have been excluded from this calculation.
In cases where the claimant is not VAT registered, VAT will be included in these figures.
Case 2 has been excluded from this calculation as the claimant costs of £1.7m and defendant costs of £1.43m with damages of £105k skewed the results.

Table 32: Table summarising PR appendix 17: CFA cases won by claimant, total costs and damages paid. Cases with no defendants' costs removed

	Number of cases	Total damages	Costs paid to claimant	Total claimant costs plus damages	Total claimant costs as a percentage of damages	Defendants' costs incurred	Defendants' costs as a percentage of damages paid
Total for all CFA cases	21	£1,889,500.00	£6,116,768.00	£8,006,268.00	324%	£2,452,259	130%
Total for CFA cases settled	17	£1,754,500.00	£4,322,149.00	£6,076,649.00	246%	£1,184,921	68%
Total for CFA cases won at trial	2	£115,000.00	£1,746,381.00	£1,861,381.00	1519%	£1,259,824	1095%
Total for CFA cases - Offer of Amends	2	£20,000.00	£48,238.00	£68,238.00	241%	£7,514	38%

	Total damages	Costs paid to claimant	Total claimant costs plus damages	Total claimant costs as a percentage of damages	Defendants' costs incurred	Defendants' costs as a percentage of damages paid
Average for all CFA cases	£89,976.19	£291,274.67	£381,250.86	324%	£116,774	130%
Average for CFA cases settled	£103,205.88	£254,244.06	£357,449.94	246%	£69,701	68%
Average for CFA cases won at trial	£57,500.00	£873,190.50	£930,690.50	1519%	£629,912	1095%
Average for CFA cases - Offer of Amends	£10,000.00	£24,119.00	£34,119.00	241%	£3,757	38%

Cases where damages were included within costs paid have been excluded from this calculation.
In cases where the claimant is not VAT registered VAT will be included in the claimant costs.
Cases which did not show any defendants' costs have been removed from this calculation as all defence costs would have been incurred in-house.

Appendix 1: Tables for chapter 2

Table 33: Table summarising PR appendix 17: Non-CFA cases won by claimant, total costs and damages paid. Cases with no defendants' costs removed

	Number of cases	Total damages	Costs paid to claimant	Total claimant costs plus damages	Total claimant costs as a percentage of damages	Defendants' costs incurred	Defendants' costs as a percentage of damages paid
Total for all non-CFA cases	48	£842,217.00	£3,058,419.00	£3,900,636.00	363%	£2,355,153	280%
Total for non-CFA cases settled	46	£752,217.00	£2,608,419.00	£3,360,636.00	347%	£1,932,902	257%
Total for non-CFA cases won at trial	1	£60,000.00	£420,000.00	£480,000.00	700%	£416,177	694%
Total for non-CFA cases - Offer of Amends	1	£30,000.00	£30,000.00	£60,000.00	100%	£6,074	20%

	Total damages	Costs paid to claimant	Total claimant costs plus damages	Total claimant costs as a percentage of damages	Defendants' costs incurred	Defendants' costs as a percentage of damages paid
Average for all non-CFA cases	£17,546.19	£63,717.06	£3,900,636.00	363%	£49,066	280%
Average for non-CFA cases settled	£16,352.54	£56,704.76	£3,360,636.00	347%	£42,020	257%
Average for non-CFA cases won at trial	£60,000.00	£420,000.00	£480,000.00	700%	£416,177	694%
Average for non-CFA cases - Offer of Amends	£30,000.00	£30,000.00	£60,000.00	100%	£6,074	20%

Cases where damages were included within costs paid have been excluded from this calculation.
In cases where the claimant is not VAT registered, VAT will be included in these figures.
Cases which did not show any defendants' costs have been removed from this calculation as all defence costs would have been incurred in-house.

Table 34: Table summarising PR appendix 17: CFA cases (excluding case 1) won by claimant, total costs and damages paid. Cases with no defendants' costs removed

	Number of cases	Total damages	Costs paid to claimant	Total claimant costs plus damages	Total claimant costs as a percentage of damages	Defendants' costs incurred	Defendants' costs as a percentage of damages paid
Total for all CFA cases	20	£1,774,500.00	£4,083,623.00	£5,858,123.00	230%	£1,894,509	107%
Total for CFA cases settled	16	£1,639,500.00	£2,289,004.00	£3,928,504.00	140%	£627,171	38%
Total for CFA cases won at trial	2	£115,000.00	£1,746,381.00	£1,861,381.00	1519%	£1,259,824	1095%
Total for CFA cases - Offer of Amends	2	£20,000.00	£48,238.00	£68,238.00	241%	£7,514	38%

	Total damages	Costs paid to claimant	Total claimant costs plus damages	Total claimant costs as a percentage of damages	Defendants' costs incurred	Defendants' costs as a percentage of damages paid
Average for all CFA cases	£88,725.00	£204,181.15	£292,906.15	230%	£94,725	107%
Average for CFA cases settled	£102,468.75	£143,062.75	£245,531.50	140%	£39,198	38%
Average for CFA cases won at trial	£57,500.00	£873,190.50	£930,690.50	1519%	£629,912	1095%
Average for CFA cases - Offer of Amends	£10,000.00	£24,119.00	£34,119.00	241%	£3,757	38%

Cases where damages were included within costs paid have been excluded from this calculation.
In cases where the claimant is not VAT registered, VAT will be included in these figures.
Case 1 has been excluded from this calculation as the claimant costs of £2.03m and defendant costs of £557k with damages of £115k skewed the results.
Cases which did not show any defendants' costs have been removed from this calculation as all defence costs would have been incurred in-house.

Appendix 1: Tables for chapter 2

Table 35: Table summarising PR appendix 17: Non-CFA cases (excluding case 2) won by claimant, total costs and damages paid. Cases with no defendants' costs removed

	Number of cases	Total damages	Costs paid to claimant	Total claimant costs plus damages	Total claimant costs as a percentage of damages	Defendants' costs incurred	Defendants' costs as a percentage of damages paid
Total for all non-CFA cases	47	£737,217.00	£1,358,419.00	£2,095,636.00	184%	£916,173	124%
Total for non-CFA cases settled	45	£647,217.00	£908,419.00	£1,555,636.00	140%	£493,922	76%
Total for non-CFA cases won at trial	1	£60,000.00	£420,000.00	£480,000.00	700%	£416,177	694%
Total for non-CFA cases - Offer of Amends	1	£30,000.00	£30,000.00	£60,000.00	100%	£6,074	20%

	Total damages	Costs paid to claimant	Total claimant costs plus damages	Total claimant costs as a percentage of damages	Defendants' costs incurred	Defendants' costs as a percentage of damages paid
Average for all non-CFA cases	£15,685.47	£28,902.53	£44,588.00	184%	£19,493	124%
Average for non-CFA cases settled	£14,382.60	£20,187.09	£34,569.69	140%	£10,976	76%
Average for non-CFA cases won at trial	£60,000.00	£420,000.00	£480,000.00	700%	£416,177	694%
Average for non-CFA cases - Offer of Amends	£30,000.00	£30,000.00	£60,000.00	100%	£6,074	20%

Cases where damages were included within costs paid have been excluded from this calculation.
In cases where the claimant is not VAT registered, VAT will be included in these figures.
Case 2 has been excluded from this calculation as the claimant costs of £1.7m and defendant costs of £1.43m with damages of £105k skewed the results.
Cases which did not show any defendants' costs have been removed from this calculation as all defence costs would have been incurred in-house.

Table 36: Table summarising claims settled where damages paid by Treasury Solicitor to claimant funded by CFA or ATE

	Total costs	Base profit costs	Success fee	Counsel fee	Counsel success fee	ATE insurance premiums	Other disbursements	VAT
Total Claimed	£1,089,165.71	£436,612.33	£305,276.69	£53,439.33	£10,460.82	£26,037.00	£125,946.11	£131,393.43
Total Settled	£799,574.21	£388,948.39	£155,684.37	£37,930.88	£8,979.26	£24,394.50	£87,178.77	£96,458.04
Percentage	73.41%	89.08%	51.00%	70.98%	85.84%	93.69%	69.22%	73.41%

Based on 38 settled cases between July and October 2009.
Success fee settled figures based on Treasury Solicitor estimate of reasonable success fee.

Sample Reference	Status	Damages Paid £	Defence Costs Paid £	Claimant Costs Paid £	% Claimant Costs of Damages	Claimant Funding
1	Closed - Nil Damages	0	11,607	0	-	Legal Services Commission
2	Structured Settlement with Reverse Indemnity	720,817	102,946	186,968	26%	Legal Services Commission
3	Closed - Structured Settlement	861,437	73,698	97,500	11%	Legal Services Commission
4	Settled - Damages Paid	4,200,000	85,541	218,000	5%	Legal Services Commission
5	Settled - Damages Paid	20,000	12,657	16,000	80%	Unknown
6	Settled - Damages Paid	4,000	9,899	4,462	112%	Unknown
7	Settled - Damages Paid	900,000	42,816	161,000	18%	Legal Services Commission
8	Settled - Damages Paid	500,000	50,645	75,000	15%	Legal Services Commission
9	Structured Settlement	248,000	67,784	92,500	37%	Legal Services Commission
10	Settled - Damages Paid	40,000	11,490	21,000	53%	Legal Services Commission
11	Closed - Nil Damages	0	199,376	0	-	Legal Services Commission
12	Settled - Damages Paid	75,000	20,805	40,000	53%	Legal Services Commission
13	Settled - Damages Paid	69,000	22,316	45,900	67%	Legal Services Commission
14	Settled - Damages Paid	2,070,711	158,451	274,150	13%	Legal Services Commission
15	Closed - Nil Damages	0	21,410	0	-	Legal Services Commission
16	Closed - Nil Damages	0	2,495	0	-	Unknown
17	Structured Settlement	1,145,475	213,737	303,013	26%	Legal Services Commission
18	Settled - Damages Paid	100,000	78,637	120,520	121%	Legal Services Commission
19	Settled - Damages Paid	1,625,000	77,814	113,708	7%	Legal Services Commission
20	Closed - Nil Damages	0	19,954	0	-	Legal Services Commission
21	Closed - Nil Damages	0	11,725	0	-	Unknown
22	Settled - Damages Paid	301,636	47,098	86,800	29%	Unknown
23	Settled - Damages Paid	135,000	13,538	33,746	25%	Unknown
24	Settled - Damages Paid	30,000	18,965	47,503	158%	Legal Services Commission
25	Closed - Nil Damages	0	7,137	0	-	Legal Services Commission
26	Closed - Nil Damages	0	1,790	0	-	Legal Services Commission
27	Settled - Damages Paid	126,000	52,080	69,000	55%	Conditional Fee Arrangement
28	Closed - Nil Damages	0	10,928	0	-	Legal Services Commission
29	Settled - Damages Paid	2,259,122	51,982	163,500	7%	Legal Services Commission
30	Structured Settlement	1,116,657	171,623	269,476	24%	Legal Services Commission
31	Settled - Damages Paid	240,000	41,479	88,000	37%	Legal Services Commission
32	Settled - Damages Paid	54,991	24,847	60,000	109%	Legal Services Commission
33	Settled - Damages Paid	506,350	177,026	315,000	62%	Legal Services Commission
34	Closed - Nil Damages	0	2,030	0	-	Legal Services Commission
35	Settled - Damages Paid	120,000	13,359	32,400	27%	Legal Services Commission
36	Settled - Damages Paid	1,006,885	53,802	42,000	4%	Legal Services Commission
37	Closed - Structured Settlement	717,013	59,417	335,000	47%	Legal Services Commission
38	Closed - Nil Damages	0	24,858	0	-	Legal Services Commission
39	Settled - Damages Paid	6,000	1,558	6,750	113%	Unknown
40	Closed - Nil Damages	0	32,873	0	-	Legal Services Commission
41	Structured Settlement	1,878,159	105,493	233,000	12%	Legal Services Commission
42	Closed - Nil Damages	0	16,283	11,759	-	Legal Services Commission
43	Settled - Damages Paid	2,612,621	124,074	225,362	9%	Legal Services Commission
44	Closed - Nil Damages	0	3,452	0	-	Legal Services Commission
45	Settled - Damages Paid	110,000	17,594	22,899	21%	Legal Services Commission
46	Settled - Damages Paid	15,696	16,445	20,763	132%	Legal Services Commission
47	Settled - Damages Paid	60,600	13,458	20,690	34%	Legal Services Commission
48	Settled - Damages Paid	200,000	4,099	31,000	16%	Legal Services Commission
49	Closed - Nil Damages	0	1,447	0	-	Legal Services Commission
50	Closed - Nil Damages	0	7,507	0	-	Conditional Fee Arrangement
51	Settled - Damages Paid	30,000	22,019	21,000	70%	Legal Services Commission
52	Settled - Damages Paid	2,734,915	102,523	245,000	9%	Legal Services Commission
53	Structured Settlement	616,512	122,243	155,850	25%	Legal Services Commission
54	Settled - Damages Paid	690,000	47,132	70,000	10%	BTE Insurance
55	Closed - Nil Damages	0	5,131	0	-	Unknown
56	Settled - Damages Paid	2,500,000	85,723	590,000	24%	BTE Insurance
57	Settled - Damages Paid	2,250,000	246,335	401,150	18%	Legal Services Commission
58	Settled - Damages Paid	110,400	44,006	80,000	72%	Legal Services Commission
59	Closed - Nil Damages	0	10,101	0	-	Legal Services Commission
60	Settled - Damages Paid	494,429	73,649	115,000	23%	Conditional Fee Arrangement
61	Settled - Damages Paid	35,000	54,912	60,000	171%	Legal Services Commission
62	Settled - Damages Paid	25,000	15,615	28,729	115%	Unknown
63	Settled - Damages Paid	450,000	37,117	112,500	25%	Conditional Fee Arrangement
64	Closed - Nil Damages	0	28,646	0	-	Legal Services Commission
65	Closed - Nil Damages	0	0	0	-	Unknown
66	Structured Settlement	1,882,313	112,162	255,000	14%	Legal Services Commission
67	Settled - Damages Paid	115,000	10,734	17,430	15%	Self Funded
68	Settled - Damages Paid	300,000	61,179	50,000	17%	Legal Services Commission
69	Settled - Damages Paid	99,516	13,196	26,000	26%	Legal Services Commission
70	Settled - Damages Paid	10,721	11,848	21,824	204%	Legal Services Commission
71	Settled - Damages Paid	2,720	7,158	21,453	789%	Legal Services Commission
72	Settled - Damages Paid	1,241,443	90,268	242,940	20%	BTE Insurance
73	Closed - Nil Damages	0	0	0	-	Unknown
74	Structured Settlement with Reverse Indemnity	2,796,081	150,400	293,198	10%	Legal Services Commission
75	Settled - Damages Paid	27,600	11,002	20,000	72%	Legal Services Commission
76	Closed - Nil Damages	0	0	0	-	Self Funded
77	Settled - Damages Paid	40,000	25,835	32,750	82%	BTE Insurance
78	Closed - Nil Damages	0	60,105	0	-	Legal Services Commission
79	Settled - Damages Paid	700,000	49,192	240,000	34%	Conditional Fee Arrangement
80	Closed - Nil Damages	0	6,417	0	-	Unknown
81	Closed - Nil Damages	0	0	0	-	Legal Services Commission
82	Settled - Damages Paid	11,250	1,863	26,332	234%	Legal Services Commission
83	Closed - Nil Damages	0	10,486	0	-	Legal Services Commission
84	Settled - Damages Paid	125,547	59,551	80,500	64%	Self Funded

Sample Reference	Status	Damages Paid £	Defence Costs Paid £	Claimant Costs Paid £	% Claimant Costs of Damages	Claimant Funding
85	Closed - Nil Damages	0	21,439	0	-	Legal Services Commission
86	Settled - Damages Paid	49,401	7,709	13,750	28%	BTE Insurance
87	Settled - Damages Paid	458,752	36,205	112,500	25%	Conditional Fee Arrangement
88	Settled - Damages Paid	78,632	26,676	60,000	76%	Legal Services Commission
89	Settled - Damages Paid	1,100,000	49,725	245,000	22%	Conditional Fee Arrangement
90	Settled - Damages Paid	90,000	20,326	76,500	85%	Legal Services Commission
91	Settled - Damages Paid	66,000	10,560	20,441	31%	Legal Services Commission
92	Settled - Damages Paid	1,400	8,636	7,844	560%	Legal Services Commission
93	Settled - Damages Paid	25,000	11,325	20,389	82%	Legal Services Commission
94	Settled - Damages Paid	2,080	10,294	22,153	1065%	Legal Services Commission
95	Settled - Damages Paid	37,500	10,115	21,697	58%	Legal Services Commission
96	Settled - Damages Paid	23,500	16,131	44,500	189%	Conditional Fee Arrangement
97	Settled - Damages Paid	10,000	37,386	66,093	661%	Conditional Fee Arrangement
98	Settled - Damages Paid	1,016,049	103,998	480,000	47%	Conditional Fee Arrangement
99	Settled - Damages Paid	22,500	1,278	15,000	67%	Conditional Fee Arrangement
100	Settled - Damages Paid	53,129	1,641	14,750	28%	Unknown
101	Settled - Damages Paid	1,075,000	76,497	325,298	30%	Conditional Fee Arrangement
102	Closed - Nil Damages	0	0	0	-	Legal Services Commission
103	Closed - Nil Damages	0	3,476	0	-	Conditional Fee Arrangement
104	Settled - Damages Paid	280,000	22,504	120,000	43%	Self Funded
105	Settled - Damages Paid	7,500	31,953	59,273	790%	Conditional Fee Arrangement
106	Closed - Nil Damages	0	13,800	0	-	Legal Services Commission
107	Settled - Damages Paid	137,000	18,962	33,000	24%	Legal Services Commission
108	Closed - Nil Damages	0	0	0	-	Unknown
109	Settled - Damages Paid	150,000	22,520	83,500	56%	BTE Insurance
110	Settled - Damages Paid	117,500	18,395	25,000	21%	Legal Services Commission
111	Settled - Damages Paid	40,000	16,268	12,500	31%	Self Funded
112	Closed - Nil Damages	0	8,671	0	-	Conditional Fee Arrangement
113	Settled - Damages Paid	175,000	15,976	57,000	33%	Legal Services Commission
114	Settled - Damages Paid	45,000	33,347	45,450	101%	Legal Services Commission
115	Settled - Damages Paid	129,871	25,679	72,500	56%	Legal Services Commission
116	Closed - Nil Damages	0	24,838	0	-	Conditional Fee Arrangement
117	Settled - Damages Paid	50,000	20,280	56,850	114%	Conditional Fee Arrangement
118	Settled - Damages Paid	65,000	9,405	26,000	40%	BTE Insurance
119	Settled - Damages Paid	4,500	347	10,500	233%	Unknown
120	Closed - Nil Damages	0	9,158	0	-	Legal Services Commission
121	Settled - Damages Paid	15,000	10,409	27,000	180%	Legal Services Commission
122	Closed - Nil Damages	0	10,486	0	-	Legal Services Commission
123	Closed - Nil Damages	0	3,174	0	-	Unknown
124	Closed - Nil Damages	0	0	0	-	Unknown
125	Settled - Damages Paid	1,500,000	132,216	523,341	35%	Conditional Fee Arrangement
126	Closed - Nil Damages	0	36,459	0	-	Legal Services Commission
127	Settled - Damages Paid	20,000	20,181	55,000	275%	Legal Services Commission
128	Settled - Damages Paid	50,000	8,978	38,500	77%	Unknown
129	Settled - Damages Paid	550,000	41,858	70,000	13%	Legal Services Commission
130	Settled - Damages Paid	28,000	6,855	11,500	41%	Legal Services Commission
131	Settled - Damages Paid	10,000	654	27,750	278%	Conditional Fee Arrangement
132	Settled - Damages Paid	550,000	22,638	60,000	11%	Legal Services Commission
133	Settled - Damages Paid	156,000	47,477	72,000	46%	Legal Services Commission
134	Structured Settlement	1,793,946	208,222	633,000	35%	Legal Services Commission
135	Settled - Damages Paid	30,500	16,039	21,673	71%	Legal Services Commission
136	Settled - Damages Paid	5,800	13,587	12,337	213%	Legal Services Commission
137	Settled - Damages Paid	20,000	9,521	16,500	83%	Unknown
138	Closed - Nil Damages	0	1,626	0	-	Legal Services Commission
139	Settled - Damages Paid	321,115	54,713	102,500	32%	Legal Services Commission
140	Settled - Damages Paid	375,000	27,524	86,500	23%	Conditional Fee Arrangement
141	Settled - Damages Paid	21,000	306	20,000	95%	Conditional Fee Arrangement
142	Settled - Damages Paid	25,000	24,847	43,000	172%	Legal Services Commission
143	Settled - Damages Paid	120,000	16,001	65,000	54%	Conditional Fee Arrangement
144	Closed - Nil Damages	0	45,856	0	-	Legal Services Commission
145	Settled - Damages Paid	650,000	23,421	165,000	25%	Conditional Fee Arrangement
146	Settled - Damages Paid	160,000	26,988	78,000	49%	Legal Services Commission
147	Settled - Damages Paid	11,000	197	5,925	54%	Legal Services Commission
148	Structured Settlement	407,171	128,363	153,750	38%	Legal Services Commission
149	Closed - Nil Damages	0	0	0	-	Legal Services Commission
150	Closed - Nil Damages	0	1,800	0	-	Legal Services Commission
151	Settled - Damages Paid	20,000	10,825	31,000	155%	Unknown
152	Settled - Damages Paid	8,400	524	10,719	128%	Legal Services Commission
153	Settled - Damages Paid	32,017	28,840	37,000	116%	Legal Services Commission
154	Closed - Nil Damages	0	32,781	0	-	Legal Services Commission
155	Closed - Nil Damages	0	414	0	-	Unknown
156	Settled - Damages Paid	47,500	4,309	36,000	76%	Legal Services Commission
157	Closed - Nil Damages	0	2,487	0	-	Legal Services Commission
158	Settled - Damages Paid	25,000	1,354	26,500	106%	Legal Services Commission
159	Closed - Nil Damages	0	38,767	0	-	BTE Insurance
160	Settled - Damages Paid	300,000	78,839	345,000	115%	Conditional Fee Arrangement
161	Settled - Damages Paid	100,000	17,033	74,000	74%	Conditional Fee Arrangement
162	Closed - Nil Damages	0	19,087	0	-	Conditional Fee Arrangement
163	Settled - Damages Paid	42,166	12,566	19,000	45%	Conditional Fee Arrangement
164	Settled - Damages Paid	85,000	22,695	55,000	65%	BTE Insurance
165	Settled - Damages Paid	14,000	350	0	0%	Legal Services Commission
166	Settled - Damages Paid	20,000	16,458	44,250	221%	Legal Services Commission
167	Settled - Damages Paid	10,000	5,092	16,123	161%	Unknown
168	Settled - Damages Paid	35,000	14,891	34,500	99%	Legal Services Commission

Sample Reference	Status	Damages Paid £	Defence Costs Paid £	Claimant Costs Paid £	% Claimant Costs of Damages	Claimant Funding
169	Closed - Nil Damages	0	0	0	-	Conditional Fee Arrangement
170	Closed - Nil Damages	0	13,760	0	-	Legal Services Commission
171	Closed - Nil Damages	0	0	0	-	Conditional Fee Arrangement
172	Settled - Damages Paid	15,000	840	30,000	200%	Legal Services Commission
173	Settled - Damages Paid	50,000	9,342	60,000	120%	Unknown
174	Closed - Nil Damages	0	0	0	-	Legal Services Commission
175	Settled - Damages Paid	32,000	18,491	38,750	121%	Legal Services Commission
176	Settled - Damages Paid	7,500	5,596	12,250	163%	BTE Insurance
177	Settled - Damages Paid	90,000	14,876	60,000	67%	Legal Services Commission
178	Settled - Damages Paid	5,000	16,416	17,500	350%	Legal Services Commission
179	Closed - Nil Damages	0	225	0	-	Conditional Fee Arrangement
180	Closed - Nil Damages	0	1,179	0	-	Legal Services Commission
181	Settled - Damages Paid	7,000	20,012	33,500	479%	Legal Services Commission
182	Settled - Damages Paid	135,000	8,341	29,000	21%	Unknown
183	Settled - Damages Paid	7,500	295	19,500	260%	Legal Services Commission
184	Settled - Damages Paid	12,000	10,736	50,000	417%	Conditional Fee Arrangement
185	Settled - Damages Paid	10,000	7,249	12,000	120%	BTE Insurance
186	Settled - Damages Paid	25,000	291	14,600	58%	Legal Services Commission
187	Settled - Damages Paid	10,000	6,522	6,125	61%	Legal Services Commission
188	Settled - Damages Paid	40,000	15,434	63,000	158%	Conditional Fee Arrangement
189	Settled - Damages Paid	10,000	8,035	24,000	240%	Legal Services Commission
190	Settled - Damages Paid	150,000	18,755	50,000	33%	Conditional Fee Arrangement
191	Settled - Damages Paid	203,491	24,916	59,000	29%	Legal Services Commission
192	Settled - Damages Paid	40,000	1,272	12,500	31%	Legal Services Commission
193	Closed - Nil Damages	0	1,280	0	-	Self Funded
194	Settled - Damages Paid	1,550,000	74,221	195,000	13%	BTE Insurance
195	Settled - Damages Paid	4,250	0	5,500	129%	Conditional Fee Arrangement
196	Settled - Damages Paid	16,000	24,984	55,000	344%	BTE Insurance
197	Settled - Damages Paid	8,000	4,944	12,690	159%	Legal Services Commission
198	Closed - Nil Damages	0	0	0	-	Legal Services Commission
199	Closed - Nil Damages	0	16,282	0	-	Legal Services Commission
200	Settled - Damages Paid	18,000	1,298	16,000	89%	Conditional Fee Arrangement
201	Settled - Damages Paid	125,000	43,802	243,000	194%	Conditional Fee Arrangement
202	Settled - Damages Paid	4,000	5,166	3,750	94%	Conditional Fee Arrangement
203	Settled - Damages Paid	12,500	15,737	20,000	160%	Legal Services Commission
204	Closed - Nil Damages	0	6,750	0	-	Legal Services Commission
205	Settled - Damages Paid	760,000	64,452	520,000	68%	Conditional Fee Arrangement
206	Settled - Damages Paid	10,000	114	9,500	95%	Funding Details Requested
207	Closed - Nil Damages	0	0	0	-	Legal Services Commission
208	Closed - Nil Damages	0	13,463	0	-	BTE Insurance
209	Closed - Nil Damages	0	61,162	0	-	Conditional Fee Arrangement
210	Closed - Nil Damages	0	0	0	-	Legal Services Commission
211	Settled - Damages Paid	35,000	12,567	18,033	52%	Legal Services Commission
212	Settled - Damages Paid	75,000	45,556	26,000	35%	Self Funded
213	Settled - Damages Paid	70,000	18,924	15,000	21%	Self Funded
214	Settled - Damages Paid	250,000	23,232	66,500	27%	Conditional Fee Arrangement
215	Settled - Damages Paid	23,713	4,560	23,000	97%	Legal Services Commission
216	Settled - Damages Paid	7,000	4,014	14,400	206%	Legal Services Commission
217	Settled - Damages Paid	12,500	6,204	28,588	229%	Conditional Fee Arrangement
218	Closed - Nil Damages	0	14,426	0	-	Legal Services Commission
219	Settled - Damages Paid	45,000	14,136	28,904	64%	Legal Services Commission
220	Settled - Damages Paid	85,000	2,028	22,057	26%	Legal Services Commission
221	Settled - Damages Paid	2,500	7,578	2,290	92%	Conditional Fee Arrangement
222	Settled - Damages Paid	500,000	33,114	31,750	6%	Unknown
223	Settled - Damages Paid	200,000	9,866	30,000	15%	Conditional Fee Arrangement
224	Settled - Damages Paid	57,500	3,083	12,375	22%	Legal Services Commission
225	Settled - Damages Paid	100,000	39,714	67,000	67%	Legal Services Commission
226	Settled - Damages Paid	65,000	22,617	44,000	68%	Legal Services Commission
227	Settled - Damages Paid	12,500	9	15,800	126%	Legal Services Commission
228	Settled - Damages Paid	10,000	1,650	20,000	200%	Self Funded
229	Settled - Damages Paid	170,000	18,065	170,000	100%	Conditional Fee Arrangement
230	Closed - Nil Damages	0	0	0	-	Self Funded
231	Closed - Nil Damages	0	0	0	-	Funding Details Requested
232	Closed - Nil Damages	0	11,147	0	-	Legal Services Commission
233	Closed - Nil Damages	0	2,283	0	-	Legal Services Commission
234	Settled - Damages Paid	19,000	4,019	9,950	52%	Self Funded
235	Settled - Damages Paid	12,000	20,362	15,750	131%	Legal Services Commission
236	Settled - Damages Paid	21,000	13,686	20,842	99%	Legal Services Commission
237	Settled - Damages Paid	28,500	28,290	57,500	202%	Legal Services Commission
238	Settled - Damages Paid	710,000	46,629	145,000	20%	Conditional Fee Arrangement
239	Settled - Damages Paid	15,000	8,104	21,000	140%	Conditional Fee Arrangement
240	Settled - Damages Paid	25,000	9,799	14,000	56%	Unknown
241	Settled - Damages Paid	8,500	303	11,800	139%	BTE Insurance
242	Closed - Nil Damages	0	20,790	0	-	Legal Services Commission
243	Settled - Damages Paid	262,500	12,990	37,500	14%	Conditional Fee Arrangement
244	Closed - Nil Damages	0	15,764	0	-	Conditional Fee Arrangement
245	Closed - Nil Damages	0	49,713	0	-	Legal Services Commission
246	Settled - Damages Paid	45,000	8,968	26,000	58%	Legal Services Commission
247	Settled - Damages Paid	50,000	36,337	140,000	280%	Legal Services Commission
248	Closed - Nil Damages	0	0	40	-	Legal Services Commission
249	Settled - Damages Paid	15,100	0	9,250	61%	Conditional Fee Arrangement
250	Settled - Damages Paid	6,000	4,955	10,000	167%	Legal Services Commission
251	Closed - Nil Damages	0	24,070	0	-	Self Funded
252	Settled - Damages Paid	50,000	6,536	37,500	75%	Conditional Fee Arrangement

Sample Reference	Status	Damages Paid £	Defence Costs Paid £	Claimant Costs Paid £	% Claimant Costs of Damages	Claimant Funding
253	Settled - Damages Paid	1,500	12,888	5,500	367%	Self Funded
254	Settled - Damages Paid	125,000	29,933	20,750	17%	Legal Services Commission
255	Settled - Damages Paid	120,000	13,669	45,000	38%	Legal Services Commission
256	Settled - Damages Paid	80,000	19,668	31,000	39%	BTE Insurance
257	Settled - Damages Paid	11,500	772	20,000	174%	Conditional Fee Arrangement
258	Settled - Damages Paid	60,000	10,701	51,839	86%	Conditional Fee Arrangement
259	Closed - Nil Damages	0	0	0	-	Unknown
260	Settled - Damages Paid	225,000	16,252	51,739	23%	Conditional Fee Arrangement
261	Settled - Damages Paid	40,000	27,493	46,050	115%	Legal Services Commission
262	Closed - Nil Damages	0	0	0	-	Unknown
263	Settled - Damages Paid	25,000	16,599	41,000	164%	Conditional Fee Arrangement
264	Closed - Nil Damages	0	0	32	-	Conditional Fee Arrangement
265	Settled - Damages Paid	50,000	11,189	54,500	109%	Legal Services Commission
266	Settled - Damages Paid	25,000	25,339	112,500	450%	Conditional Fee Arrangement
267	Settled - Damages Paid	1,000	0	700	70%	Unknown
268	Settled - Damages Paid	2,000	3,276	8,500	425%	Conditional Fee Arrangement
269	Settled - Damages Paid	7,000	0	8,000	114%	Unknown
270	Settled - Damages Paid	22,500	15,458	52,500	233%	Conditional Fee Arrangement
271	Closed - Nil Damages	0	0	0	-	Legal Services Commission
272	Settled - Damages Paid	10,000	921	12,500	125%	Conditional Fee Arrangement
273	Closed - Nil Damages	0	6,944	0	-	Unknown
274	Settled - Damages Paid	200,000	27,323	50,150	25%	BTE Insurance
275	Settled - Damages Paid	192,352	36,327	32,750	17%	Conditional Fee Arrangement
276	Settled - Damages Paid	43,750	5,349	16,750	38%	Conditional Fee Arrangement
277	Closed - Nil Damages	0	13,031	0	-	Self Funded
278	Settled - Damages Paid	12,500	842	23,900	191%	Conditional Fee Arrangement
279	Closed - Nil Damages	0	0	0	-	Legal Services Commission
280	Settled - Damages Paid	4,000	4,101	3,813	95%	Legal Services Commission
281	Closed - Nil Damages	0	0	0	-	Self Funded
282	Settled - Damages Paid	750,000	28,581	55,000	7%	Legal Services Commission
283	Settled - Damages Paid	4,500	2,226	13,000	289%	Legal Services Commission
284	Settled - Damages Paid	10,000	289	4,750	48%	Conditional Fee Arrangement
285	Settled - Damages Paid	45,000	22,934	31,000	69%	Legal Services Commission
286	Settled - Damages Paid	1,500	500	6,500	433%	Conditional Fee Arrangement
287	Settled - Damages Paid	10,000	5,524	13,500	135%	Unknown
288	Settled - Damages Paid	20,000	396	24,000	120%	Conditional Fee Arrangement
289	Settled - Damages Paid	35,000	143	14,250	41%	BTE Insurance
290	Closed - Nil Damages	0	0	0	-	Unknown
291	Settled - Damages Paid	1,000	5,593	6,750	675%	BTE Insurance
292	Closed - Nil Damages	0	0	0	-	BTE Insurance
293	Settled - Damages Paid	5,000	0	0	0%	Self Funded
294	Closed - Nil Damages	0	0	0	-	Unknown
295	Settled - Damages Paid	16,000	11,496	19,500	122%	Legal Services Commission
296	Settled - Damages Paid	24,000	565	7,000	29%	Legal Services Commission
297	Closed - Nil Damages	0	2,961	0	-	Self Funded
298	Closed - Nil Damages	0	0	0	-	Unknown
299	Closed - Nil Damages	0	19,117	0	-	Legal Services Commission
300	Closed - Nil Damages	0	0	0	-	Unknown
301	Settled - Damages Paid	100,000	8,212	33,000	33%	Legal Services Commission
302	Closed - Nil Damages	0	0	0	-	Legal Services Commission
303	Settled - Damages Paid	2,500	746	12,728	509%	Conditional Fee Arrangement
304	Settled - Damages Paid	5,500	85	5,900	107%	Legal Services Commission
305	Settled - Damages Paid	52,500	25,515	17,250	33%	Conditional Fee Arrangement
306	Settled - Damages Paid	125,621	10,369	65,000	52%	Conditional Fee Arrangement
307	Settled - Damages Paid	7,500	10,319	16,500	220%	Legal Services Commission
308	Settled - Damages Paid	40,000	6,263	27,500	69%	Conditional Fee Arrangement
309	Settled - Damages Paid	22,000	6,810	12,000	55%	Legal Services Commission
310	Settled - Damages Paid	87,000	13,361	94,000	108%	Conditional Fee Arrangement
311	Settled - Damages Paid	37,500	386	18,500	49%	Unknown
312	Settled - Damages Paid	15,000	4,834	14,500	97%	Conditional Fee Arrangement
313	Closed - Nil Damages	0	8,246	175	-	Legal Services Commission
314	Settled - Damages Paid	6,000	4,895	8,950	149%	Legal Services Commission
315	Closed - Nil Damages	0	0	0	-	Legal Services Commission
316	Settled - Damages Paid	142,500	13,973	32,761	23%	Conditional Fee Arrangement
317	Settled - Damages Paid	110,000	12,308	47,695	43%	Conditional Fee Arrangement
318	Settled - Damages Paid	5,000	11,232	5,705	114%	Conditional Fee Arrangement
319	Settled - Damages Paid	3,500	3,164	11,636	332%	Legal Services Commission
320	Settled - Damages Paid	6,500	10,500	39,002	600%	Conditional Fee Arrangement
321	Settled - Damages Paid	550,000	28,754	56,500	10%	BTE Insurance
322	Settled - Damages Paid	27,788	3,922	22,000	79%	Conditional Fee Arrangement
323	Closed - Nil Damages	0	0	0	-	Self Funded
324	Settled - Damages Paid	62,500	15,194	56,000	90%	Conditional Fee Arrangement
325	Closed - Nil Damages	0	1,864	0	-	Conditional Fee Arrangement
326	Closed - Nil Damages	0	10,483	0	-	Legal Services Commission
327	Settled - Damages Paid	10,000	299	9,000	90%	Conditional Fee Arrangement
328	Settled - Damages Paid	110,000	12,857	50,000	45%	Conditional Fee Arrangement
329	Settled - Damages Paid	71,252	30,969	56,000	79%	Legal Services Commission
330	Closed - Nil Damages	0	4,142	0	-	BTE Insurance
331	Settled - Damages Paid	35,000	540	19,500	56%	Conditional Fee Arrangement
332	Closed - Nil Damages	0	0	0	-	Conditional Fee Arrangement
333	Settled - Damages Paid	15,000	673	11,500	77%	Conditional Fee Arrangement
334	Settled - Damages Paid	80,000	549	24,500	31%	Unknown
335	Settled - Damages Paid	15,000	657	20,000	133%	Unknown
336	Settled - Damages Paid	5,000	7,851	14,000	280%	Conditional Fee Arrangement

Appendix 2: 1,000 clinical negligence cases closed or settled by the NHSLA in the period from 1st April 2008 to 31st March 2009

Sample Reference	Status	Damages Paid £	Defence Costs Paid £	Claimant Costs Paid £	% Claimant Costs of Damages	Claimant Funding
337	Settled - Damages Paid	20,000	22,704	36,000	180%	Conditional Fee Arrangement
338	Settled - Damages Paid	60,000	2,593	62,953	105%	Conditional Fee Arrangement
339	Settled - Damages Paid	7,500	17,250	22,500	300%	Legal Services Commission
340	Closed - Nil Damages	0	4,266	0	-	Conditional Fee Arrangement
341	Settled - Damages Paid	25,000	3,776	20,000	80%	Legal Services Commission
342	Settled - Damages Paid	16,000	0	13,308	83%	Legal Services Commission
343	Settled - Damages Paid	5,000	5,458	9,000	180%	Conditional Fee Arrangement
344	Settled - Damages Paid	45,000	19,639	0	0%	Conditional Fee Arrangement
345	Settled - Damages Paid	80,000	522	47,450	59%	Conditional Fee Arrangement
346	Closed - Nil Damages	0	0	0	-	Legal Services Commission
347	Closed - Nil Damages	0	0	0	-	Unknown
348	Closed - Nil Damages	0	199	0	-	Legal Services Commission
349	Closed - Nil Damages	0	0	0	-	Conditional Fee Arrangement
350	Settled - Damages Paid	30,000	968	18,500	62%	Conditional Fee Arrangement
351	Closed - Nil Damages	0	0	0	-	Unknown
352	Settled - Damages Paid	150,000	19,941	58,000	39%	Conditional Fee Arrangement
353	Settled - Damages Paid	92,500	21,180	0	0%	BTE Insurance
354	Closed - Nil Damages	0	13,241	0	-	Conditional Fee Arrangement
355	Settled - Damages Paid	7,500	4,354	10,500	140%	Self Funded
356	Settled - Damages Paid	75,000	7,490	12,750	17%	BTE Insurance
357	Settled - Damages Paid	27,500	3,650	21,635	79%	Conditional Fee Arrangement
358	Settled - Damages Paid	17,500	368	13,500	77%	Conditional Fee Arrangement
359	Settled - Damages Paid	7,500	190	7,500	100%	Conditional Fee Arrangement
360	Settled - Damages Paid	7,000	9,667	17,500	250%	Legal Services Commission
361	Settled - Damages Paid	350,000	9,472	35,000	10%	Legal Services Commission
362	Closed - Nil Damages	0	0	0	-	Funding Details Requested
363	Settled - Damages Paid	25,000	3,523	18,250	73%	Legal Services Commission
364	Closed - Nil Damages	0	0	0	-	Unknown
365	Closed - Nil Damages	0	0	0	-	BTE Insurance
366	Settled - Damages Paid	30,000	25,569	75,000	250%	Conditional Fee Arrangement
367	Closed - Nil Damages	0	3,575	0	-	Conditional Fee Arrangement
368	Settled - Damages Paid	2,000	155	4,500	225%	Conditional Fee Arrangement
369	Settled - Damages Paid	3,500	73	3,660	105%	Self Funded
370	Closed - Nil Damages	0	0	0	-	Conditional Fee Arrangement
371	Settled - Damages Paid	1,500	744	5,222	348%	Conditional Fee Arrangement
372	Settled - Damages Paid	60,000	535	14,000	23%	Conditional Fee Arrangement
373	Settled - Damages Paid	19,500	3,330	16,000	82%	Conditional Fee Arrangement
374	Closed - Nil Damages	0	0	100	-	Unknown
375	Closed - Nil Damages	0	0	0	-	Funding Details Requested
376	Closed - Nil Damages	0	0	0	-	Conditional Fee Arrangement
377	Closed - Nil Damages	0	8,050	0	-	Self Funded
378	Settled - Damages Paid	20,000	7,205	11,101	56%	Legal Services Commission
379	Settled - Damages Paid	20,000	9,241	25,428	127%	BTE Insurance
380	Closed - Nil Damages	0	0	0	-	Unknown
381	Settled - Damages Paid	251,233	44,496	80,000	32%	Legal Services Commission
382	Settled - Damages Paid	42,045	492	16,500	39%	Self Funded
383	Settled - Damages Paid	3,000	0	0	0%	Self Funded
384	Settled - Damages Paid	200,000	30,540	72,500	36%	Conditional Fee Arrangement
385	Closed - Nil Damages	0	13,869	0	-	Legal Services Commission
386	Settled - Damages Paid	5,000	160	9,500	190%	Legal Services Commission
387	Settled - Damages Paid	19,500	1,042	18,500	95%	Legal Services Commission
388	Settled - Damages Paid	50,000	18,547	18,000	36%	Conditional Fee Arrangement
389	Settled - Damages Paid	10,000	0	8,500	85%	Self Funded
390	Settled - Damages Paid	10,000	11,538	13,750	138%	Legal Services Commission
391	Closed - Nil Damages	0	0	0	-	Unknown
392	Closed - Nil Damages	0	0	0	-	Funding Details Requested
393	Settled - Damages Paid	20,000	20,371	16,500	83%	Unknown
394	Closed - Nil Damages	0	0	0	-	Unknown
395	Closed - Nil Damages	0	15,337	0	-	Legal Services Commission
396	Settled - Damages Paid	15,000	162	7,500	50%	Conditional Fee Arrangement
397	Settled - Damages Paid	50,000	11,837	20,500	41%	Legal Services Commission
398	Settled - Damages Paid	5,000	6,138	18,000	360%	Conditional Fee Arrangement
399	Settled - Damages Paid	50,000	21,420	50,000	100%	Legal Services Commission
400	Closed - Nil Damages	0	0	0	-	Funding Details Requested
401	Settled - Damages Paid	2,000	300	6,000	300%	Conditional Fee Arrangement
402	Closed - Nil Damages	0	4,864	0	-	Legal Services Commission
403	Settled - Damages Paid	17,500	0	7,625	44%	BTE Insurance
404	Settled - Damages Paid	45,000	4,785	10,000	22%	Legal Services Commission
405	Settled - Damages Paid	190,000	9,673	40,000	21%	BTE Insurance
406	Closed - Nil Damages	0	0	0	-	Conditional Fee Arrangement
407	Settled - Damages Paid	30,000	6,860	23,500	78%	Legal Services Commission
408	Closed - Nil Damages	0	3,690	0	-	Self Funded
409	Settled - Damages Paid	45,000	9,483	50,000	111%	Conditional Fee Arrangement
410	Settled - Damages Paid	10,000	7,370	20,000	200%	Conditional Fee Arrangement
411	Closed - Nil Damages	0	2,126	0	-	Legal Services Commission
412	Closed - Nil Damages	0	0	0	-	BTE Insurance
413	Closed - Nil Damages	0	0	0	-	Unknown
414	Closed - Nil Damages	0	0	0	-	Conditional Fee Arrangement
415	Settled - Damages Paid	27,000	8,839	44,500	165%	Conditional Fee Arrangement
416	Settled - Damages Paid	225,000	25,862	109,000	48%	BTE Insurance
417	Settled - Damages Paid	16,093	8,904	8,450	53%	Legal Services Commission
418	Closed - Nil Damages	0	0	0	-	Funding Details Requested
419	Settled - Damages Paid	50,000	16,788	18,000	36%	Legal Services Commission
420	Settled - Damages Paid	1,000	52	3,500	350%	Self Funded

Sample Reference	Status	Damages Paid £	Defence Costs Paid £	Claimant Costs Paid £	% Claimant Costs of Damages	Claimant Funding
421	Settled - Damages Paid	25,000	7,635	48,652	195%	Conditional Fee Arrangement
422	Closed - Nil Damages	0	0	0	-	Unknown
423	Settled - Damages Paid	45,000	5,871	33,500	74%	Conditional Fee Arrangement
424	Settled - Damages Paid	175,000	16,057	39,000	22%	Legal Services Commission
425	Settled - Damages Paid	5,000	1,500	0	0%	Self Funded
426	Settled - Damages Paid	10,500	4,459	28,500	271%	Conditional Fee Arrangement
427	Settled - Damages Paid	70,000	16,662	78,000	111%	Conditional Fee Arrangement
428	Settled - Damages Paid	40,000	-109	15,881	40%	Conditional Fee Arrangement
429	Settled - Damages Paid	3,000	575	8,750	292%	Conditional Fee Arrangement
430	Settled - Damages Paid	17,500	3,243	17,000	97%	Legal Services Commission
431	Settled - Damages Paid	20,000	0	7,522	38%	Self Funded
432	Settled - Damages Paid	1,500	0	1,000	67%	Conditional Fee Arrangement
433	Closed - Nil Damages	0	31,492	0	-	Legal Services Commission
434	Settled - Damages Paid	15,300	860	7,750	51%	Legal Services Commission
435	Settled - Damages Paid	7,000	159	9,750	139%	Legal Services Commission
436	Structured Settlement	2,493,483	65,821	174,000	7%	Conditional Fee Arrangement
437	Settled - Damages Paid	4,000	7,422	11,500	288%	Legal Services Commission
438	Structured Settlement with Reverse Indemnity	1,742,103	67,394	194,750	11%	Legal Services Commission
439	Closed - Nil Damages	0	0	0	-	Conditional Fee Arrangement
440	Closed - Nil Damages	0	0	0	-	Unknown
441	Closed - Nil Damages	0	0	0	-	Unknown
442	Closed - Nil Damages	0	0	0	-	Legal Services Commission
443	Closed - Nil Damages	0	0	0	-	Unknown
444	Settled - Damages Paid	50,000	11,503	18,000	36%	Conditional Fee Arrangement
445	Settled - Damages Paid	20,000	201	7,750	39%	BTE Insurance
446	Closed - Nil Damages	0	0	0	-	Conditional Fee Arrangement
447	Closed - Nil Damages	0	0	0	-	Unknown
448	Settled - Damages Paid	20,000	540	5,900	30%	Conditional Fee Arrangement
449	Settled - Damages Paid	6,000	1,193	22,000	367%	Conditional Fee Arrangement
450	Settled - Damages Paid	4,250	0	0	0%	Self Funded
451	Settled - Damages Paid	10,800	5,355	11,025	102%	BTE Insurance
452	Settled - Damages Paid	10,000	9,454	14,750	148%	Conditional Fee Arrangement
453	Closed - Nil Damages	0	0	0	-	Self Funded
454	Settled - Damages Paid	25,000	6,236	25,000	100%	Conditional Fee Arrangement
455	Closed - Nil Damages	0	0	0	-	Conditional Fee Arrangement
456	Settled - Damages Paid	3,000	88	3,580	119%	Self Funded
457	Settled - Damages Paid	100,000	0	18,800	19%	Legal Services Commission
458	Settled - Damages Paid	16,500	337	17,524	106%	Conditional Fee Arrangement
459	Settled - Damages Paid	10,000	63	4,550	46%	Conditional Fee Arrangement
460	Closed - Nil Damages	0	0	0	-	Conditional Fee Arrangement
461	Settled - Damages Paid	5,000	6,255	18,600	372%	Legal Services Commission
462	Settled - Damages Paid	7,000	5,834	6,250	89%	Unknown
463	Closed - Nil Damages	0	0	0	-	Unknown
464	Closed - Nil Damages	0	0	0	-	Conditional Fee Arrangement
465	Settled - Damages Paid	4,000	243	7,500	188%	Legal Services Commission
466	Closed - Nil Damages	0	5,151	0	-	Legal Services Commission
467	Settled - Damages Paid	9,000	165	12,100	134%	Legal Services Commission
468	Settled - Damages Paid	7,000	7,285	6,231	89%	Unknown
469	Settled - Damages Paid	30,000	1,525	14,750	49%	Legal Services Commission
470	Closed - Nil Damages	0	0	0	-	Conditional Fee Arrangement
471	Closed - Nil Damages	0	1,394	0	-	Unknown
472	Settled - Damages Paid	4,250	5,453	16,500	388%	Conditional Fee Arrangement
473	Closed - Nil Damages	0	3,368	0	-	Legal Services Commission
474	Settled - Damages Paid	7,500	3,235	14,100	188%	Conditional Fee Arrangement
475	Closed - Nil Damages	0	0	0	-	Unknown
476	Settled - Damages Paid	15,000	96	9,125	61%	Legal Services Commission
477	Settled - Damages Paid	1,250	1,193	2,200	176%	Funding Details Requested
478	Settled - Damages Paid	23,000	6,357	8,500	37%	BTE Insurance
479	Settled - Damages Paid	20,083	121	9,000	45%	Legal Services Commission
480	Closed - Nil Damages	0	3,302	0	-	Self Funded
481	Closed - Nil Damages	0	2,622	0	-	Legal Services Commission
482	Settled - Damages Paid	20,000	8,540	25,750	129%	Conditional Fee Arrangement
483	Closed - Nil Damages	0	0	0	-	Self Funded
484	Closed - Nil Damages	0	0	0	-	Legal Services Commission
485	Settled - Damages Paid	35,151	788	15,000	43%	Self Funded
486	Settled - Damages Paid	40,000	12,111	50,000	125%	Conditional Fee Arrangement
487	Settled - Damages Paid	14,000	448	12,000	86%	Conditional Fee Arrangement
488	Closed - Nil Damages	0	0	0	-	Conditional Fee Arrangement
489	Settled - Damages Paid	42,500	6,202	12,500	29%	BTE Insurance
490	Settled - Damages Paid	10,000	7,926	19,600	196%	Legal Services Commission
491	Settled - Damages Paid	16,500	5,807	14,500	88%	Legal Services Commission
492	Closed - Nil Damages	0	0	0	-	Legal Services Commission
493	Settled - Damages Paid	3,500	0	8,000	229%	Conditional Fee Arrangement
494	Settled - Damages Paid	40,000	11,611	40,000	100%	Conditional Fee Arrangement
495	Settled - Damages Paid	10,000	604	13,500	135%	Conditional Fee Arrangement
496	Settled - Damages Paid	70,268	5,210	16,000	23%	Conditional Fee Arrangement
497	Settled - Damages Paid	30,000	1,094	30,250	101%	Legal Services Commission
498	Closed - Nil Damages	0	0	0	-	Conditional Fee Arrangement
499	Closed - Nil Damages	0	0	0	-	Legal Services Commission
500	Settled - Damages Paid	7,000	66	2,850	41%	Legal Services Commission
501	Settled - Damages Paid	6,000	1,738	3,900	65%	Unknown
502	Settled - Damages Paid	17,500	615	25,500	146%	Conditional Fee Arrangement
503	Settled - Damages Paid	2,500	0	11,697	468%	Legal Services Commission
504	Closed - Nil Damages	0	1,411	0	-	Conditional Fee Arrangement

Sample Reference	Status	Damages Paid £	Defence Costs Paid £	Claimant Costs Paid £	% Claimant Costs of Damages	Claimant Funding
505	Closed - Nil Damages	0	2,701	0	-	Legal Services Commission
506	Closed - Nil Damages	0	1,048	0	-	Unknown
507	Settled - Damages Paid	9,000	341	8,011	89%	BTE Insurance
508	Settled - Damages Paid	150,085	24,601	31,000	21%	BTE Insurance
509	Settled - Damages Paid	5,000	220	0	0%	Self Funded
510	Closed - Nil Damages	0	672	0	-	Unknown
511	Closed - Nil Damages	0	4,687	0	-	Conditional Fee Arrangement
512	Settled - Damages Paid	7,500	262	6,350	85%	Legal Services Commission
513	Closed - Nil Damages	0	0	0	-	Conditional Fee Arrangement
514	Closed - Nil Damages	0	0	0	-	Conditional Fee Arrangement
515	Settled - Damages Paid	11,500	534	21,750	189%	Unknown
516	Closed - Nil Damages	0	0	0	-	Unknown
517	Settled - Damages Paid	5,000	2,824	32,000	640%	Conditional Fee Arrangement
518	Settled - Damages Paid	4,000	136	7,700	193%	Legal Services Commission
519	Settled - Damages Paid	2,400	64	3,400	142%	Self Funded
520	Settled - Damages Paid	40,000	1,712	35,941	90%	Legal Services Commission
521	Closed - Nil Damages	0	0	0	-	Unknown
522	Closed - Nil Damages	0	0	0	-	Conditional Fee Arrangement
523	Closed - Nil Damages	0	4,966	0	-	Legal Services Commission
524	Closed - Nil Damages	0	29,735	0	-	Self Funded
525	Settled - Damages Paid	45,000	7,964	40,000	89%	Conditional Fee Arrangement
526	Settled - Damages Paid	20,000	5,429	10,500	53%	Legal Services Commission
527	Settled - Damages Paid	65,000	6	6,600	10%	Conditional Fee Arrangement
528	Closed - Nil Damages	0	0	0	-	Legal Services Commission
529	Settled - Damages Paid	25,000	8,257	7,000	28%	Legal Services Commission
530	Settled - Damages Paid	3,500	237	5,500	157%	Legal Services Commission
531	Settled - Damages Paid	5,000	644	12,750	255%	Funding Details Requested
532	Closed - Nil Damages	0	18,823	0	-	Legal Services Commission
533	Settled - Damages Paid	16,000	0	0	0%	Unknown
534	Settled - Damages Paid	15,000	0	0	0%	Self Funded
535	Closed - Nil Damages	0	24,665	0	-	Legal Services Commission
536	Settled - Damages Paid	4,000	388	15,000	375%	Conditional Fee Arrangement
537	Closed - Nil Damages	0	0	0	-	Conditional Fee Arrangement
538	Settled - Damages Paid	30,068	14,533	14,000	47%	Self Funded
539	Settled - Damages Paid	30,000	9,714	35,000	117%	Conditional Fee Arrangement
540	Settled - Damages Paid	4,000	345	16,000	400%	Funding Details Requested
541	Settled - Damages Paid	30,225	0	0	0%	Self Funded
542	Closed - Nil Damages	0	1,704	0	-	Conditional Fee Arrangement
543	Closed - Nil Damages	0	0	0	-	Unknown
544	Closed - Nil Damages	0	0	0	-	Legal Services Commission
545	Settled - Damages Paid	20,000	50	16,300	82%	Conditional Fee Arrangement
546	Closed - Nil Damages	0	2,720	0	-	Self Funded
547	Settled - Damages Paid	12,000	167	6,000	50%	Self Funded
548	Closed - Nil Damages	0	2,309	0	-	Legal Services Commission
549	Settled - Damages Paid	2,500	255	5,000	200%	Conditional Fee Arrangement
550	Settled - Damages Paid	150,000	9,281	26,000	17%	Conditional Fee Arrangement
551	Closed - Nil Damages	0	0	0	-	Unknown
552	Settled - Damages Paid	50,000	171	6,000	12%	Unknown
553	Closed - Nil Damages	0	3,877	0	-	Conditional Fee Arrangement
554	Closed - Nil Damages	0	0	0	-	Conditional Fee Arrangement
555	Settled - Damages Paid	3,000	730	9,950	332%	Conditional Fee Arrangement
556	Settled - Damages Paid	150,000	1,667	80,000	53%	Conditional Fee Arrangement
557	Closed - Nil Damages	0	0	0	-	Legal Services Commission
558	Closed - Nil Damages	0	5,608	0	-	Legal Services Commission
559	Settled - Damages Paid	1,000	3,305	10,500	1050%	Conditional Fee Arrangement
560	Settled - Damages Paid	4,200	253	6,600	157%	Legal Services Commission
561	Settled - Damages Paid	22,500	5,667	17,918	80%	Conditional Fee Arrangement
562	Closed - Nil Damages	0	0	0	-	Funding Details Requested
563	Closed - Nil Damages	0	0	0	-	Unknown
564	Settled - Damages Paid	25,000	906	16,000	64%	Conditional Fee Arrangement
565	Settled - Damages Paid	9,000	85	2,438	27%	Self Funded
566	Settled - Damages Paid	7,500	157	9,000	120%	Legal Services Commission
567	Settled - Damages Paid	21,000	307	7,250	35%	Conditional Fee Arrangement
568	Settled - Damages Paid	40,000	8,687	13,637	34%	Legal Services Commission
569	Closed - Nil Damages	0	0	0	-	Legal Services Commission
570	Closed - Nil Damages	0	3,203	0	-	Conditional Fee Arrangement
571	Closed - Nil Damages	0	0	0	-	Unknown
572	Settled - Damages Paid	16,000	5,384	29,000	181%	Conditional Fee Arrangement
573	Settled - Damages Paid	20,000	202	16,000	80%	Conditional Fee Arrangement
574	Closed - Nil Damages	0	0	0	-	Self Funded
575	Closed - Nil Damages	0	0	0	-	BTE Insurance
576	Closed - Nil Damages	0	0	0	-	Conditional Fee Arrangement
577	Settled - Damages Paid	22,500	439	17,500	78%	Conditional Fee Arrangement
578	Closed - Nil Damages	0	3,579	0	-	Unknown
579	Closed - Nil Damages	0	0	0	-	Self Funded
580	Settled - Damages Paid	45,000	9,934	32,000	71%	Conditional Fee Arrangement
581	Settled - Damages Paid	20,000	1,076	8,350	42%	Conditional Fee Arrangement
582	Closed - Nil Damages	0	0	0	-	Unknown
583	Closed - Nil Damages	0	0	0	-	Conditional Fee Arrangement
584	Settled - Damages Paid	9,000	1,234	7,221	80%	BTE Insurance
585	Closed - Nil Damages	0	9,050	0	-	Legal Services Commission
586	Closed - Nil Damages	0	0	0	-	Conditional Fee Arrangement
587	Settled - Damages Paid	500	0	2,100	420%	BTE Insurance
588	Closed - Nil Damages	0	0	0	-	Conditional Fee Arrangement

Sample Reference	Status	Damages Paid £	Defence Costs Paid £	Claimant Costs Paid £	% Claimant Costs of Damages	Claimant Funding
589	Settled - Damages Paid	4,000	131	8,883	222%	Conditional Fee Arrangement
590	Closed - Nil Damages	0	0	0	-	Self Funded
591	Settled - Damages Paid	1,000	930	5,500	550%	Conditional Fee Arrangement
592	Settled - Damages Paid	2,000	96	4,025	201%	Conditional Fee Arrangement
593	Closed - Nil Damages	0	0	0	-	Conditional Fee Arrangement
594	Closed - Nil Damages	0	1,108	0	-	Legal Services Commission
595	Closed - Nil Damages	0	1,040	0	-	Funding Details Requested
596	Closed - Nil Damages	0	0	0	-	Conditional Fee Arrangement
597	Closed - Nil Damages	0	0	0	-	Conditional Fee Arrangement
598	Settled - Damages Paid	2,000	0	500	25%	Self Funded
599	Settled - Damages Paid	15,000	1,537	9,000	60%	Legal Services Commission
600	Settled - Damages Paid	4,000	199	16,450	411%	Conditional Fee Arrangement
601	Settled - Damages Paid	1,000	136	5,900	590%	Legal Services Commission
602	Closed - Nil Damages	0	0	0	-	Unknown
603	Settled - Damages Paid	10,000	1,422	20,560	206%	Conditional Fee Arrangement
604	Settled - Damages Paid	8,500	0	6,000	71%	Unknown
605	Settled - Damages Paid	60,000	1,276	17,300	29%	Conditional Fee Arrangement
606	Settled - Damages Paid	8,500	605	10,258	121%	Legal Services Commission
607	Settled - Damages Paid	40,000	348	26,500	66%	Legal Services Commission
608	Closed - Nil Damages	0	0	0	-	Self Funded
609	Settled - Damages Paid	50,000	7,384	12,150	24%	Conditional Fee Arrangement
610	Closed - Nil Damages	0	0	0	-	Self Funded
611	Settled - Damages Paid	25,000	8,004	24,000	96%	Unknown
612	Settled - Damages Paid	129,197	3,795	61,146	47%	Conditional Fee Arrangement
613	Closed - Nil Damages	0	0	0	-	Self Funded
614	Closed - Nil Damages	0	0	0	-	Unknown
615	Settled - Damages Paid	27,500	3,378	13,125	48%	Conditional Fee Arrangement
616	Settled - Damages Paid	12,000	0	4,500	38%	Self Funded
617	Closed - Nil Damages	0	0	0	-	Unknown
618	Closed - Nil Damages	0	0	0	-	Unknown
619	Closed - Nil Damages	0	0	0	-	Unknown
620	Closed - Nil Damages	0	0	0	-	Unknown
621	Closed - Nil Damages	0	0	0	-	Conditional Fee Arrangement
622	Settled - Damages Paid	39,983	271	15,250	38%	Legal Services Commission
623	Settled - Damages Paid	350,000	3,004	50,000	14%	Legal Services Commission
624	Settled - Damages Paid	15,000	5,000	4,550	30%	Conditional Fee Arrangement
625	Settled - Damages Paid	100,000	12,102	59,160	59%	Conditional Fee Arrangement
626	Closed - Nil Damages	0	0	0	-	Unknown
627	Closed - Nil Damages	0	0	0	-	Legal Services Commission
628	Closed - Nil Damages	0	5,777	0	-	Legal Services Commission
629	Settled - Damages Paid	20,000	90	9,300	47%	BTE Insurance
630	Closed - Nil Damages	0	0	0	-	Funding Details Requested
631	Settled - Damages Paid	60,000	8,518	33,750	56%	Conditional Fee Arrangement
632	Settled - Damages Paid	3,000	84	4,000	133%	Legal Services Commission
633	Settled - Damages Paid	27,500	555	15,000	55%	Conditional Fee Arrangement
634	Settled - Damages Paid	75,000	668	44,000	59%	Legal Services Commission
635	Closed - Nil Damages	0	0	0	-	Legal Services Commission
636	Settled - Damages Paid	55,000	2,401	36,041	66%	Conditional Fee Arrangement
637	Settled - Damages Paid	8,250	249	6,925	84%	Self Funded
638	Closed - Nil Damages	0	0	0	-	Self Funded
639	Settled - Damages Paid	17,000	60	6,000	35%	Self Funded
640	Closed - Nil Damages	0	0	0	-	Legal Services Commission
641	Closed - Nil Damages	0	0	0	-	Conditional Fee Arrangement
642	Settled - Damages Paid	35,000	7,698	12,634	36%	BTE Insurance
643	Settled - Damages Paid	30,000	6,647	8,501	28%	Conditional Fee Arrangement
644	Settled - Damages Paid	10,000	5,733	25,000	250%	BTE Insurance
645	Settled - Damages Paid	11,000	1,044	26,500	241%	Conditional Fee Arrangement
646	Closed - Nil Damages	0	8,663	0	-	Legal Services Commission
647	Settled - Damages Paid	1,300	240	5,063	389%	Conditional Fee Arrangement
648	Closed - Nil Damages	0	0	0	-	Unknown
649	Settled - Damages Paid	2,000	0	4,100	205%	Self Funded
650	Closed - Nil Damages	0	0	0	-	Unknown
651	Closed - Nil Damages	0	0	0	-	Legal Services Commission
652	Settled - Damages Paid	2,500	2,076	7,125	285%	Legal Services Commission
653	Closed - Nil Damages	0	0	0	-	Conditional Fee Arrangement
654	Closed - Nil Damages	0	0	0	-	Conditional Fee Arrangement
655	Settled - Damages Paid	1,500	140	8,000	533%	Conditional Fee Arrangement
656	Closed - Nil Damages	0	0	0	-	Unknown
657	Closed - Nil Damages	0	0	0	-	Legal Services Commission
658	Settled - Damages Paid	312,500	8,302	0	0%	Conditional Fee Arrangement
659	Closed - Nil Damages	0	0	0	-	Conditional Fee Arrangement
660	Closed - Nil Damages	0	0	0	-	Funding Details Requested
661	Settled - Damages Paid	35,000	227	15,800	45%	Unknown
662	Settled - Damages Paid	8,500	8,509	15,000	176%	Conditional Fee Arrangement
663	Closed - Nil Damages	0	0	0	-	Unknown
664	Closed - Nil Damages	0	1,461	0	-	Legal Services Commission
665	Settled - Damages Paid	15,000	261	15,884	106%	Self Funded
666	Settled - Damages Paid	25,123	2,599	21,150	84%	Conditional Fee Arrangement
667	Closed - Nil Damages	0	0	0	-	Self Funded
668	Settled - Damages Paid	50,641	10,717	0	0%	Unknown
669	Settled - Damages Paid	10,000	2,031	21,000	210%	Conditional Fee Arrangement
670	Settled - Damages Paid	3,000	334	5,324	177%	Conditional Fee Arrangement
671	Settled - Damages Paid	7,000	172	3,650	52%	Conditional Fee Arrangement
672	Closed - Nil Damages	0	0	0	-	Unknown

Sample Reference	Status	Damages Paid £	Defence Costs Paid £	Claimant Costs Paid £	% Claimant Costs of Damages	Claimant Funding
673	Closed - Nil Damages	0	0	0	-	Funding Details Requested
674	Closed - Nil Damages	0	0	0	-	Unknown
675	Closed - Nil Damages	0	0	0	-	Unknown
676	Settled - Damages Paid	5,000	1,728	5,000	100%	Conditional Fee Arrangement
677	Closed - Nil Damages	0	4,165	0	-	Legal Services Commission
678	Closed - Nil Damages	0	836	0	-	Legal Services Commission
679	Closed - Nil Damages	0	0	0	-	Legal Services Commission
680	Settled - Damages Paid	1,000	0	944	94%	Legal Services Commission
681	Closed - Nil Damages	0	0	0	-	Legal Services Commission
682	Settled - Damages Paid	3,750	285	4,000	107%	BTE Insurance
683	Settled - Damages Paid	9,000	761	11,000	122%	Legal Services Commission
684	Closed - Nil Damages	0	0	0	-	Conditional Fee Arrangement
685	Closed - Nil Damages	0	0	0	-	Funding Details Requested
686	Closed - Nil Damages	0	0	0	-	Unknown
687	Settled - Damages Paid	2,000	232	4,075	204%	Conditional Fee Arrangement
688	Closed - Nil Damages	0	3,761	0	-	Conditional Fee Arrangement
689	Settled - Damages Paid	18,000	11	2,250	13%	Legal Services Commission
690	Closed - Nil Damages	0	0	0	-	Legal Services Commission
691	Closed - Nil Damages	0	0	0	-	Legal Services Commission
692	Closed - Nil Damages	0	333	0	-	Conditional Fee Arrangement
693	Closed - Nil Damages	0	0	0	-	Unknown
694	Closed - Nil Damages	0	0	0	-	Self Funded
695	Closed - Nil Damages	0	0	0	-	Conditional Fee Arrangement
696	Closed - Nil Damages	0	0	0	-	Funding Details Requested
697	Closed - Nil Damages	0	0	0	-	Funding Details Requested
698	Closed - Nil Damages	0	0	0	-	Self Funded
699	Closed - Nil Damages	0	0	0	-	Legal Services Commission
700	Closed - Nil Damages	0	0	0	-	Unknown
701	Closed - Nil Damages	0	0	0	-	BTE Insurance
702	Settled - Damages Paid	3,000	260	12,000	400%	Self Funded
703	Settled - Damages Paid	5,000	7,772	0	0%	Self Funded
704	Closed - Nil Damages	0	0	0	-	Self Funded
705	Closed - Nil Damages	0	2,400	0	-	Conditional Fee Arrangement
706	Settled - Damages Paid	5,000	4,169	5,000	100%	Conditional Fee Arrangement
707	Closed - Nil Damages	0	0	0	-	Funding Details Requested
708	Settled - Damages Paid	6,000	0	0	0%	Self Funded
709	Settled - Damages Paid	2,000	0	0	0%	Self Funded
710	Settled - Damages Paid	4,000	116	5,000	125%	BTE Insurance
711	Closed - Nil Damages	0	0	0	-	Self Funded
712	Settled - Damages Paid	5,500	45	3,300	60%	Conditional Fee Arrangement
713	Closed - Nil Damages	0	0	0	-	Conditional Fee Arrangement
714	Closed - Nil Damages	0	0	0	-	Conditional Fee Arrangement
715	Settled - Damages Paid	13,000	68	5,350	41%	Self Funded
716	Settled - Damages Paid	3,750	0	5,305	141%	Conditional Fee Arrangement
717	Closed - Nil Damages	0	32	0	-	Conditional Fee Arrangement
718	Settled - Damages Paid	5,000	478	7,719	154%	Conditional Fee Arrangement
719	Closed - Nil Damages	0	0	0	-	Unknown
720	Settled - Damages Paid	7,500	61	2,700	36%	Conditional Fee Arrangement
721	Settled - Damages Paid	5,000	358	6,000	120%	Conditional Fee Arrangement
722	Closed - Nil Damages	0	0	0	-	Self Funded
723	Closed - Nil Damages	0	0	0	-	Conditional Fee Arrangement
724	Settled - Damages Paid	15,000	0	1,670	11%	Self Funded
725	Closed - Nil Damages	0	0	0	-	Self Funded
726	Closed - Nil Damages	0	0	0	-	Self Funded
727	Closed - Nil Damages	0	0	0	-	Conditional Fee Arrangement
728	Settled - Damages Paid	6,250	89	5,200	83%	Conditional Fee Arrangement
729	Closed - Nil Damages	0	0	0	-	Self Funded
730	Settled - Damages Paid	30,000	7,967	10,000	33%	Conditional Fee Arrangement
731	Settled - Damages Paid	7,500	165	4,000	53%	BTE Insurance
732	Settled - Damages Paid	22,500	365	10,000	44%	Conditional Fee Arrangement
733	Settled - Damages Paid	10,000	0	940	9%	Self Funded
734	Closed - Nil Damages	0	0	0	-	Unknown
735	Closed - Nil Damages	0	0	0	-	Conditional Fee Arrangement
736	Closed - Nil Damages	0	0	0	-	Funding Details Requested
737	Closed - Nil Damages	0	0	0	-	Conditional Fee Arrangement
738	Settled - Damages Paid	25,000	0	12,800	51%	Self Funded
739	Closed - Nil Damages	0	0	0	-	Funding Details Requested
740	Settled - Damages Paid	1,000	0	1,763	176%	Self Funded
741	Settled - Damages Paid	5,000	2,223	11,500	230%	Legal Services Commission
742	Closed - Nil Damages	0	0	0	-	Legal Services Commission
743	Settled - Damages Paid	2,500	243	4,500	180%	Conditional Fee Arrangement
744	Closed - Nil Damages	0	0	0	-	Conditional Fee Arrangement
745	Settled - Damages Paid	6,000	327	6,400	107%	Funding Details Requested
746	Closed - Nil Damages	0	0	0	-	Funding Details Requested
747	Closed - Nil Damages	0	0	0	-	Conditional Fee Arrangement
748	Settled - Damages Paid	18,500	0	0	0%	Self Funded
749	Closed - Nil Damages	0	0	0	-	Self Funded
750	Closed - Nil Damages	0	0	0	-	Unknown
751	Closed - Nil Damages	0	0	0	-	Conditional Fee Arrangement
752	Closed - Nil Damages	0	0	0	-	Unknown
753	Closed - Nil Damages	0	0	0	-	Legal Services Commission
754	Closed - Nil Damages	0	0	0	-	Conditional Fee Arrangement
755	Settled - Damages Paid	12,500	632	13,500	108%	Legal Services Commission
756	Settled - Damages Paid	8,000	988	16,500	206%	Conditional Fee Arrangement

Sample Reference	Status	Damages Paid £	Defence Costs Paid £	Claimant Costs Paid £	% Claimant Costs of Damages	Claimant Funding
757	Settled - Damages Paid	1,000	0	1,118	112%	Self Funded
758	Closed - Nil Damages	0	0	0	-	Legal Services Commission
759	Closed - Nil Damages	0	0	0	-	Unknown
760	Settled - Damages Paid	80	0	0	0%	Self Funded
761	Closed - Nil Damages	0	0	0	-	Legal Services Commission
762	Closed - Nil Damages	0	0	0	-	Unknown
763	Closed - Nil Damages	0	0	0	-	Funding Details Requested
764	Closed - Nil Damages	0	0	0	-	Funding Details Requested
765	Closed - Nil Damages	0	0	0	-	BTE Insurance
766	Closed - Nil Damages	0	0	0	-	Unknown
767	Closed - Nil Damages	0	0	0	-	Conditional Fee Arrangement
768	Closed - Nil Damages	0	0	0	-	Funding Details Requested
769	Closed - Nil Damages	0	0	0	-	Unknown
770	Closed - Nil Damages	0	0	0	-	Funding Details Requested
771	Closed - Nil Damages	0	0	0	-	Conditional Fee Arrangement
772	Closed - Nil Damages	0	0	0	-	Unknown
773	Closed - Nil Damages	0	0	0	-	Unknown
774	Closed - Nil Damages	0	0	0	-	Conditional Fee Arrangement
775	Settled - Damages Paid	2,500	194	5,750	230%	Conditional Fee Arrangement
776	Settled - Damages Paid	75,000	2,604	22,500	30%	Conditional Fee Arrangement
777	Settled - Damages Paid	17,500	485	31,000	177%	Conditional Fee Arrangement
778	Closed - Nil Damages	0	0	0	-	Unknown
779	Settled - Damages Paid	5,000	30	1,750	35%	Conditional Fee Arrangement
780	Closed - Nil Damages	0	0	0	-	Legal Services Commission
781	Closed - Nil Damages	0	0	0	-	Conditional Fee Arrangement
782	Closed - Nil Damages	0	0	0	-	Self Funded
783	Closed - Nil Damages	0	0	0	-	Conditional Fee Arrangement
784	Closed - Nil Damages	0	0	0	-	Self Funded
785	Settled - Damages Paid	3,000	485	5,700	190%	Conditional Fee Arrangement
786	Settled - Damages Paid	22,000	808	16,000	73%	Conditional Fee Arrangement
787	Closed - Nil Damages	0	0	0	-	Unknown
788	Closed - Nil Damages	0	0	0	-	Conditional Fee Arrangement
789	Closed - Nil Damages	0	2,666	0	-	Legal Services Commission
790	Closed - Nil Damages	0	0	0	-	Unknown
791	Settled - Damages Paid	850	0	0	0%	Self Funded
792	Closed - Nil Damages	0	0	0	-	Funding Details Requested
793	Settled - Damages Paid	18,000	186	9,550	53%	Conditional Fee Arrangement
794	Settled - Damages Paid	6,500	471	7,750	119%	Conditional Fee Arrangement
795	Closed - Nil Damages	0	0	0	-	Self Funded
796	Closed - Nil Damages	0	0	0	-	Legal Services Commission
797	Closed - Nil Damages	0	0	0	-	Legal Services Commission
798	Closed - Nil Damages	0	0	0	-	Conditional Fee Arrangement
799	Closed - Nil Damages	0	0	0	-	Unknown
800	Closed - Nil Damages	0	0	0	-	Unknown
801	Closed - Nil Damages	0	0	0	-	Unknown
802	Closed - Nil Damages	0	0	0	-	Unknown
803	Closed - Nil Damages	0	0	0	-	Unknown
804	Settled - Damages Paid	7,250	349	4,500	62%	Conditional Fee Arrangement
805	Closed - Nil Damages	0	0	0	-	Self Funded
806	Closed - Nil Damages	0	0	0	-	Conditional Fee Arrangement
807	Closed - Nil Damages	0	0	0	-	Self Funded
808	Closed - Nil Damages	0	0	0	-	Conditional Fee Arrangement
809	Closed - Nil Damages	0	0	0	-	Conditional Fee Arrangement
810	Closed - Nil Damages	0	0	0	-	Conditional Fee Arrangement
811	Settled - Damages Paid	3,500	676	3,450	99%	Conditional Fee Arrangement
812	Settled - Damages Paid	12,000	0	4,850	40%	Conditional Fee Arrangement
813	Closed - Nil Damages	0	0	0	-	Self Funded
814	Closed - Nil Damages	0	0	0	-	Unknown
815	Closed - Nil Damages	0	0	0	-	BTE Insurance
816	Closed - Nil Damages	0	0	0	-	Unknown
817	Closed - Nil Damages	0	0	0	-	Self Funded
818	Settled - Damages Paid	4,650	371	5,384	116%	Funding Details Requested
819	Settled - Damages Paid	15,000	228	7,000	47%	Conditional Fee Arrangement
820	Closed - Nil Damages	0	0	0	-	Legal Services Commission
821	Closed - Nil Damages	0	-44	0	-	Conditional Fee Arrangement
822	Closed - Nil Damages	0	0	0	-	Funding Details Requested
823	Closed - Nil Damages	0	0	0	-	Legal Services Commission
824	Settled - Damages Paid	12,000	0	9,636	80%	Conditional Fee Arrangement
825	Settled - Damages Paid	2,500	151	3,406	136%	Legal Services Commission
826	Settled - Damages Paid	10,000	89	2,800	28%	Legal Services Commission
827	Closed - Nil Damages	0	0	0	-	Legal Services Commission
828	Closed - Nil Damages	0	0	0	-	Self Funded
829	Closed - Nil Damages	0	0	0	-	Unknown
830	Closed - Nil Damages	0	0	0	-	Self Funded
831	Settled - Damages Paid	95,000	4,869	21,000	22%	Legal Services Commission
832	Settled - Damages Paid	3,500	191	4,600	131%	Conditional Fee Arrangement
833	Closed - Nil Damages	0	0	0	-	Conditional Fee Arrangement
834	Settled - Damages Paid	15,000	404	7,000	47%	Unknown
835	Closed - Nil Damages	0	0	0	-	Unknown
836	Closed - Nil Damages	0	0	0	-	Unknown
837	Closed - Nil Damages	0	0	0	-	Self Funded
838	Settled - Damages Paid	3,000	0	5,500	183%	Conditional Fee Arrangement
839	Closed - Nil Damages	0	0	0	-	Funding Details Requested
840	Closed - Nil Damages	0	0	0	-	Legal Services Commission

Sample Reference	Status	Damages Paid £	Defence Costs Paid £	Claimant Costs Paid £	% Claimant Costs of Damages	Claimant Funding
841	Closed - Nil Damages	0	0	0	-	Self Funded
842	Closed - Nil Damages	0	0	0	-	Funding Details Requested
843	Closed - Nil Damages	0	0	0	-	Self Funded
844	Settled - Damages Paid	5,000	28	3,000	60%	Legal Services Commission
845	Closed - Nil Damages	0	0	0	-	Funding Details Requested
846	Closed - Nil Damages	0	0	0	-	Legal Services Commission
847	Closed - Nil Damages	0	0	0	-	Self Funded
848	Settled - Damages Paid	10,000	539	4,500	45%	Conditional Fee Arrangement
849	Settled - Damages Paid	15,000	362	8,500	57%	Unknown
850	Settled - Damages Paid	10,000	146	4,809	48%	Legal Services Commission
851	Settled - Damages Paid	7,000	619	5,350	76%	Conditional Fee Arrangement
852	Settled - Damages Paid	1,200	6,194	1,225	102%	BTE Insurance
853	Settled - Damages Paid	2,500	88	3,726	149%	Legal Services Commission
854	Settled - Damages Paid	4,000	0	7,850	196%	Conditional Fee Arrangement
855	Closed - Nil Damages	0	0	0	-	Unknown
856	Closed - Nil Damages	0	0	0	-	Self Funded
857	Settled - Damages Paid	40,000	2,959	15,500	39%	Unknown
858	Closed - Nil Damages	0	0	0	-	Funding Details Requested
859	Closed - Nil Damages	0	0	0	-	Self Funded
860	Settled - Damages Paid	100,000	9,293	60,000	60%	Conditional Fee Arrangement
861	Settled - Damages Paid	3,500	0	2,925	84%	Conditional Fee Arrangement
862	Closed - Nil Damages	0	0	0	-	Conditional Fee Arrangement
863	Settled - Damages Paid	7,500	1,467	19,000	253%	Conditional Fee Arrangement
864	Settled - Damages Paid	6,500	0	1,000	15%	Self Funded
865	Settled - Damages Paid	15,000	616	36,331	242%	Unknown
866	Closed - Nil Damages	0	0	0	-	Self Funded
867	Closed - Nil Damages	0	0	0	-	Funding Details Requested
868	Settled - Damages Paid	40,000	9,249	16,250	41%	Conditional Fee Arrangement
869	Closed - Nil Damages	0	0	0	-	Self Funded
870	Settled - Damages Paid	5,500	0	0	0%	Self Funded
871	Settled - Damages Paid	30,000	0	2,362	8%	Unknown
872	Settled - Damages Paid	5,000	0	0	0%	Self Funded
873	Closed - Nil Damages	0	0	0	-	Self Funded
874	Closed - Nil Damages	0	0	0	-	Unknown
875	Settled - Damages Paid	9,250	205	6,350	69%	Legal Services Commission
876	Settled - Damages Paid	15,000	651	13,000	87%	Conditional Fee Arrangement
877	Settled - Damages Paid	5,000	0	7,200	144%	BTE Insurance
878	Closed - Nil Damages	0	0	0	-	Unknown
879	Settled - Damages Paid	22,755	3,778	7,750	34%	Self Funded
880	Settled - Damages Paid	15,000	940	11,500	77%	Unknown
881	Closed - Nil Damages	0	0	0	-	Legal Services Commission
882	Closed - Nil Damages	0	0	0	-	Legal Services Commission
883	Closed - Nil Damages	0	0	0	-	Legal Services Commission
884	Settled - Damages Paid	35,000	6,105	11,600	33%	Self Funded
885	Closed - Nil Damages	0	0	0	-	Unknown
886	Settled - Damages Paid	235,000	4,741	10,500	4%	Self Funded
887	Settled - Damages Paid	2,500	0	1,000	40%	Self Funded
888	Closed - Nil Damages	0	0	0	-	Funding Details Requested
889	Closed - Nil Damages	0	0	0	-	Unknown
890	Settled - Damages Paid	10,000	2,642	7,000	70%	Conditional Fee Arrangement
891	Settled - Damages Paid	7,000	6,413	10,250	146%	Conditional Fee Arrangement
892	Closed - Nil Damages	0	0	0	-	Legal Services Commission
893	Settled - Damages Paid	250	0	0	0%	Self Funded
894	Closed - Nil Damages	0	0	0	-	Self Funded
895	Closed - Nil Damages	0	0	0	-	Unknown
896	Settled - Damages Paid	17,500	397	5,000	29%	Conditional Fee Arrangement
897	Closed - Nil Damages	0	0	0	-	Self Funded
898	Settled - Damages Paid	20,000	1,006	8,000	40%	Funding Details Requested
899	Settled - Damages Paid	3,000	2,391	1,659	55%	Self Funded
900	Closed - Nil Damages	0	0	0	-	Conditional Fee Arrangement
901	Closed - Nil Damages	0	415	0	-	Self Funded
902	Closed - Nil Damages	0	0	0	-	Legal Services Commission
903	Closed - Nil Damages	0	0	0	-	Legal Services Commission
904	Closed - Nil Damages	0	851	0	-	Conditional Fee Arrangement
905	Settled - Damages Paid	3,000	0	3,000	100%	Conditional Fee Arrangement
906	Closed - Nil Damages	0	1,212	0	-	Self Funded
907	Settled - Damages Paid	1,000	0	0	0%	Self Funded
908	Settled - Damages Paid	1,100	0	1,000	91%	Conditional Fee Arrangement
909	Closed - Nil Damages	0	0	0	-	Conditional Fee Arrangement
910	Closed - Nil Damages	0	0	0	-	Legal Services Commission
911	Closed - Nil Damages	0	0	0	-	Unknown
912	Closed - Nil Damages	0	0	0	-	Unknown
913	Closed - Nil Damages	0	0	0	-	Legal Services Commission
914	Closed - Nil Damages	0	0	0	-	Self Funded
915	Closed - Nil Damages	0	0	0	-	Self Funded
916	Settled - Damages Paid	1,000	0	0	0%	Self Funded
917	Closed - Nil Damages	0	0	0	-	Legal Services Commission
918	Closed - Nil Damages	0	0	0	-	Funding Details Requested
919	Settled - Damages Paid	34,500	7,236	0	0%	Self Funded
920	Closed - Nil Damages	0	0	0	-	Unknown
921	Settled - Damages Paid	3,125	528	2,000	64%	Conditional Fee Arrangement
922	Closed - Nil Damages	0	0	0	-	Funding Details Requested
923	Closed - Nil Damages	0	0	0	-	Conditional Fee Arrangement
924	Settled - Damages Paid	750	0	0	0%	Self Funded

Sample Reference	Status	Damages Paid £	Defence Costs Paid £	Claimant Costs Paid £	% Claimant Costs of Damages	Claimant Funding
925	Settled - Damages Paid	10,000	43	3,100	31%	Self Funded
926	Closed - Nil Damages	0	0	0	-	Conditional Fee Arrangement
927	Closed - Nil Damages	0	350	0	-	Self Funded
928	Settled - Damages Paid	10,000	328	13,250	133%	Self Funded
929	Closed - Nil Damages	0	0	0	-	Self Funded
930	Closed - Nil Damages	0	0	0	-	Conditional Fee Arrangement
931	Closed - Nil Damages	0	0	0	-	Conditional Fee Arrangement
932	Closed - Nil Damages	0	0	0	-	Self Funded
933	Closed - Nil Damages	0	0	0	-	Funding Details Requested
934	Settled - Damages Paid	5,000	78	3,500	70%	Conditional Fee Arrangement
935	Closed - Nil Damages	0	0	0	-	Self Funded
936	Closed - Nil Damages	0	0	0	-	Unknown
937	Settled - Damages Paid	27,500	425	13,400	49%	Conditional Fee Arrangement
938	Closed - Nil Damages	0	0	0	-	Unknown
939	Settled - Damages Paid	6,000	0	2,429	40%	Self Funded
940	Settled - Damages Paid	2,000	54	3,950	198%	Conditional Fee Arrangement
941	Closed - Nil Damages	0	0	0	-	Unknown
942	Closed - Nil Damages	0	0	0	-	Legal Services Commission
943	Settled - Damages Paid	2,500	0	1,500	60%	Conditional Fee Arrangement
944	Closed - Nil Damages	0	0	0	-	Legal Services Commission
945	Closed - Nil Damages	0	0	0	-	Funding Details Requested
946	Settled - Damages Paid	19,400	2,984	15,000	77%	Conditional Fee Arrangement
947	Closed - Nil Damages	0	0	0	-	Legal Services Commission
948	Closed - Nil Damages	0	0	0	-	Funding Details Requested
949	Closed - Nil Damages	0	0	0	-	Self Funded
950	Closed - Nil Damages	0	0	0	-	Conditional Fee Arrangement
951	Closed - Nil Damages	0	0	0	-	Funding Details Requested
952	Closed - Nil Damages	0	0	0	-	Funding Details Requested
953	Settled - Damages Paid	7,500	0	3,000	40%	Conditional Fee Arrangement
954	Closed - Nil Damages	0	0	0	-	Unknown
955	Closed - Nil Damages	0	0	0	-	Funding Details Requested
956	Closed - Nil Damages	0	0	0	-	Self Funded
957	Closed - Nil Damages	0	0	0	-	Funding Details Requested
958	Closed - Nil Damages	0	0	0	-	Funding Details Requested
959	Closed - Nil Damages	0	0	0	-	Conditional Fee Arrangement
960	Closed - Nil Damages	0	0	0	-	Legal Services Commission
961	Closed - Nil Damages	0	0	0	-	Funding Details Requested
962	Closed - Nil Damages	0	0	0	-	Funding Details Requested
963	Closed - Nil Damages	0	0	0	-	Self Funded
964	Settled - Damages Paid	1,500	0	0	0%	Self Funded
965	Closed - Nil Damages	0	0	0	-	Self Funded
966	Closed - Nil Damages	0	0	0	-	Funding Details Requested
967	Closed - Nil Damages	0	0	0	-	Unknown
968	Closed - Nil Damages	0	0	0	-	Legal Services Commission
969	Closed - Nil Damages	0	0	0	-	Conditional Fee Arrangement
970	Settled - Damages Paid	5,000	0	5,500	110%	Conditional Fee Arrangement
971	Settled - Damages Paid	2,500	0	2,070	83%	Self Funded
972	Settled - Damages Paid	5,000	0	350	7%	Funding Details Requested
973	Closed - Nil Damages	0	0	0	-	Funding Details Requested
974	Closed - Nil Damages	0	0	0	-	Conditional Fee Arrangement
975	Closed - Nil Damages	0	0	0	-	Unknown
976	Closed - Nil Damages	0	0	0	-	Legal Services Commission
977	Settled - Damages Paid	12,500	1,673	4,000	32%	Self Funded
978	Closed - Nil Damages	0	0	0	-	Funding Details Requested
979	Settled - Damages Paid	1,000	0	0	0%	Self Funded
980	Closed - Nil Damages	0	0	0	-	Self Funded
981	Settled - Damages Paid	793	0	0	0%	Self Funded
982	Closed - Nil Damages	0	2,524	0	-	BTE Insurance
983	Closed - Nil Damages	0	0	0	-	Funding Details Requested
984	Closed - Nil Damages	0	0	0	-	Self Funded
985	Closed - Nil Damages	0	0	0	-	Self Funded
986	Settled - Damages Paid	1,750	275	4,012	229%	Conditional Fee Arrangement
987	Closed - Nil Damages	0	0	0	-	Self Funded
988	Closed - Nil Damages	0	0	0	-	Unknown
989	Settled - Damages Paid	15,500	0	0	0%	Self Funded
990	Closed - Nil Damages	0	0	0	-	Self Funded
991	Settled - Damages Paid	7,500	607	6,750	90%	Conditional Fee Arrangement
992	Closed - Nil Damages	0	0	0	-	Unknown
993	Closed - Nil Damages	0	0	0	-	Self Funded
994	Settled - Damages Paid	1,000	0	0	0%	Self Funded
995	Settled - Damages Paid	2,000	0	5,300	265%	Legal Services Commission
996	Settled - Damages Paid	11,406	0	823	7%	Self Funded
997	Closed - Nil Damages	0	0	0	-	Funding Details Requested
998	Closed - Nil Damages	0	0	0	-	Unknown
999	Closed - Nil Damages	0	0	0	-	Self Funded
1000	Closed - Nil Damages	0	926	0	-	Conditional Fee Arrangement
	TOTAL	**76,974,504**	**9,230,707**	**21,449,916**		

Appendix 3: 15 large intellectual property cases settled or taken to first instance trial in the period from 1999 to 2007

Summary of costs to first instance judgment or earlier settlement (this may not show total costs)

These tables show adjusted total costs. Current hourly rates have been applied to the time recorded. Disbursements have been scaled according to inflation.

These tables show cumulative costs of all work done up to the completion of a certain event. They do not show the specific costs of the event.

The order of events has been standardised across all cases. Where the standardised order does not match the actual order the total costs appear to go down. Costs did not go down; for such cases, the table shows the events in the wrong order.

Where there are nil costs for both the claim form and defence, this is normally because the firm took over the case from another firm after these events.

Cost to event

Cost to event	Case 1	Case 2	Case 3	Case 4	Case 5	Case 6	Case 7	Case 8	Case 9	Case 10	Case 11	Case 12	Case 13	Case 14	Case 15	MIN (>0)	MAX	AVG (>0)
IP	Patents	Patents	Patents	Patents	Trade marks	Patents	Designs	Patents	Patents	Patents	Trade marks	Patents	Patents	Patents	Patents			
Party represented	Claimant	Claimant	Claimant	Claimant	Claimant	Defendant	Claimant	Defendant	Defendant	Claimant	Claimant	Defendant	Claimant	Claimant	Defendant			
Year	1999	2003	2000	2000	2002	2001	2003	2003	2004	2004	2004	2005	2004	2007	2007			
Claim Form/POC/POI	£ -	£ 39,298.94	£ 80,000.08	£ 14,636.71	£ 31,864.17	£ 31,492.68	£ 62,533.44	£ -	£ -	£ 7,943.80	£ 77,529.18	£ -	£ 19,602.08	£ 47,248.81	£ -	£ 7,943.80	£ 80,000.08	£ 41,214.99
Defence/CC/GOI	£ -	£ 53,336.81	£ 94,213.71	£ 28,326.83	£ 180,436.97	£ 60,963.52	Data missing	£ -	£ 58,226.00	£ 11,030.80	Data missing	£ 21,159.22	£ 33,990.45	£ 80,997.49	£ 74,236.39	£ 11,030.80	£ 180,436.97	£ 63,356.20
Reply and defence to CC	£ 227,307.09	£ 66,458.71	£ 124,394.49	£ 55,660.64	£ 276,949.63	£ 80,682.22	£ 144,282.84	£ 10,474.44	£ 70,258.10	£ 17,802.60	Data missing	£ 32,908.35	£ 37,473.45	none	£ 85,970.08	£ 17,802.60	£ 276,949.63	£ 101,679.02
Disclosure/PD	£ 119,765.69	£ 233,904.92	£ 242,153.67	none	£ 277,776.03	Data missing	£ 249,866.71	£ 117,316.75	£ 373,950.86	£ 107,870.81	£ 433,258.46	£ 43,399.22	£ 135,708.36	none	£ 581,725.36	£ 10,474.44	£ 581,725.36	£ 234,154.54
Witness statements	£ 493,378.66	£ 289,923.82	£ 624,121.05	none	£ 463,831.51	Data missing	£ 531,062.38	£ 219,207.35	£ 464,528.51	£ 331,044.63	£ 578,993.68	£ 21,159.22	£ 169,699.93	£ 256,954.53	£ 1,147,248.50	£ 21,159.22	£ 1,147,248.50	£ 422,251.01
Expert report	£ 468,880.16	£ 306,425.42	£ 895,973.62	none	none	£ 205,697.43	£ 648,478.02	£ 317,945.25	£ 507,126.58	none	£ 578,993.68	none	£ 237,077.60	£ 602,128.54	£ 1,522,183.39	£ 205,697.43	£ 1,522,183.39	£ 546,797.63
Start of trial	£ 502,039.66	£ 361,309.32	£ 1,063,342.27	£ 237,736.68	£ 422,488.71	£ 299,298.82	£ 754,405.52	£ 347,228.55	£ 655,732.04	none	£ 772,985.51	£ 128,908.64	£ 298,534.00	£ 864,092.97	none	£ 128,908.64	£ 1,063,342.27	£ 513,755.34
End of trial	£ 619,406.62	£ 376,788.72	£ 1,104,128.17	£ 237,736.68	£ 485,916.11	£ 309,221.12	£ 878,422.82	none	£ 712,327.99	none	£ 815,406.11	£ 163,803.27	£ 323,153.20	£ 1,030,718.76	£ 1,540,933.29	£ 163,803.27	£ 1,540,933.29	£ 569,558.32
Settlement	none	£ 422,081.50	none	none	none	none	none	none	none	none	none	none	none	none	none	£ 422,081.50	£ 422,081.50	£ 871,430.58
Judgment	£ 646,261.47	none	£ 1,121,864.33	£ 242,127.48	£ 522,654.11	£ 383,739.90	£ 1,202,026.67	£ 408,932.15	£ 783,007.09	£ 651,276.95	£ 893,733.48	£ 196,957.23	£ 346,802.30	£ 1,088,726.72	none	£ 196,957.23	£ 1,202,026.67	£ 653,069.41

% of costs to event

% of costs to event	Case 1	Case 2	Case 3	Case 4	Case 5	Case 6	Case 7	Case 8	Case 9	Case 10	Case 11	Case 12	Case 13	Case 14	Case 15	MIN (>0)	MAX	AVG (>0)
Claim Form/POC/POI	0%	9%	7%	6%	6%	8%	5%	0%	0%	1%	9%	0%	6%	4%	0%	1%	9%	6%
Defence/CC/GOI	0%	13%	8%	12%	35%	16%	Data missing	0%	7%	2%	Data missing	11%	10%	7%	5%	2%	35%	11%
Reply and defence to CC	35%	16%	11%	23%	53%	21%	12%	3%	9%	3%	Data missing	17%	11%	none	6%	3%	53%	18%
Disclosure/PD	19%	55%	22%	none	53%	Data missing	21%	29%	48%	17%	48%	22%	39%	none	38%	11%	55%	32%
Witness statements	76%	69%	56%	none	89%	Data missing	44%	54%	59%	51%	65%	11%	49%	24%	74%	11%	89%	53%
Expert report	73%	73%	80%	none	none	54%	54%	78%	65%	57%	65%	none	68%	55%	99%	54%	99%	66%
Start of trial	78%	86%	95%	98%	81%	78%	63%	85%	84%	none	86%	65%	86%	79%	none	63%	98%	81%
End of trial	96%	89%	98%	98%	93%	81%	73%	none	91%	none	91%	83%	93%	95%	100%	73%	98%	90%
Settlement	none	100%	none	none	none	none	none	none	none	none	none	none	none	none	none	100%	100%	100%
Judgment	100%	none	100%	100%	100%	100%	100%	100%	100%	none	100%	100%	100%	100%	none	100%	100%	100%

Weeks to event

Weeks to event	Case 1	Case 2	Case 3	Case 4	Case 5	Case 6	Case 7	Case 8	Case 9	Case 10	Case 11	Case 12	Case 13	Case 14	Case 15	MIN	MAX	AVG
Claim Form/POC/POI	0	0	0	0	0	0	0	0	0	0	0	0	0	0	0		0	0
Defence/CC/GOI	11	9	6	11	55	3	Data missing	8	12	9	Data missing	5	9	8	12	3	55	12
Reply and defence to CC	75	12	9	19	64	5	12	13	15	11	Data missing	8	11	none	15	5	75	21
Disclosure/PD	69	28	19	none	64	Data missing	32	16	52	29	39	13	44	none	43	5	69	37
Witness statements	104	32	58	none	71	Data missing	52	25	60	55	59	5	59	24	58	5	104	51
Expert report	104	33	67	none	none	19	58	28	62	57	59	none	69	57	64	19	104	56
Start of trial	105	37	72	53	69	24	60	31	68	none	64	28	77	66	none	24	105	58
End of trial	106	37	73	53	71	25	64	32	69	none	65	30	78	67	64	25	106	59
Settlement	none	37	none	none	none	none	none	none	none	none	none	none	none	none	none	37	64	54
Judgment	111	none	86	53	79	39	86	44	79	62	67	36	82	72	none	36	111	70

	Case 1	Case 2	Case 3	Case 4	Case 5	Case 6	Case 7	Case 8	Case 9	Case 10	Case 11	Case 12	Case 13	Case 14	Case 15	MIN	MAX	AVG
Monthly average cost	£ 25,297.35	£ 49,566.06	£ 56,680.24	£ 19,849.89	£ 28,745.98	£ 42,752.56	£ 60,730.30	£ 40,382.05	£ 43,065.39	£ 45,641.91	£ 57,959.28	£ 23,771.64	£ 18,376.29	£ 65,701.63	£ 104,614.92	£ 18,376.29	£ 104,614.92	£ 45,542.37

APPENDIX 4. PARTICIPANTS IN THE FACILITATIVE MEETINGS ON FIXED COSTS HOSTED BY THE CIVIL JUSTICE COUNCIL

Allianz Insurance plc
Anthony Gold Solicitors
Association of British Insurers
Association of Local Authority Risk Managers
Association of Personal Injury Lawyers
Atherton Godfrey
Aviva plc
AXA
Bar Council
Berrymans Lace Mawer LLP
Birmingham City Council
Bolton Council
Bristol City Council
Browne Jacobson LLP
Cambridge House Law Centre
Carpenters Law
Cloisters Chambers
Colemans - CTTS Solicitors
Cs2 Lawyers
Forum of Insurance Lawyers
Garden Court Chambers
Glaisyers Solicitors LLP
Gough Sqaure
Hackney Homes
Hansen Palomares Solicitors
Hodge Jones & Allen
Housing Law Practitioners Association
Irwin Mitchell LLP
Jaggards
Lambeth Law Centre
Law Society
Marsons Solicitors
Ministry of Justice (observer)
Morrish Solicitors
Motor Accident Solicitors Society
Motor Insurers' Bureau
Osbornes
Personal Injuries Bar Association
RBS Insurance
Russell Jones & Walker Solicitors
Thompsons Solicitors
UNISON
Unite the Union
Walker Smith Way Solicitors
Weightmans LLP
Westminster University
Wirral Borough Council
Zurich Insurance

Appendix 4: List of those who participated in the facilitative meetings concerning fast track fixed costs

Appendix 5: Fixed costs matrix for fast track personal injury claims

TABLE A – FIXED COSTS

	MoJ RTA Claims Process					Pre Issue			Post Issue			
	Pre issue £1,000-£10,000	Pre issue £1,000-£10,000	Issued £1,000-£10,000	Issued £1,000-£10,000	Issued £1,000-£10,000	Pre issue £1,000-£5,000	Pre Issue £5,001-£10,000	Pre Issue £10,001-£25,000	Issued – Post issue Pre Allocation	Issued – Post allocation pre listing	Issued – Post listing pre trial	Trial – Advocacy Fee (Plus column 11)
	1	2	3	4	5	6	7	8	9	10	11	12
	Stage 1 - Notification leads to Admission of Liability	Stage 2 - Liability admitted, med rep obtained	Stage 3 - Settled pre hearing	Stage 3 - Assessment Hearing (paper)	Stage 3 - Assessment Hearing (Oral)	Case Settles before Issue	Case Settles before Issue	Case Settles before Issue				
Road Traffic Accident												
Fixed Costs	£400	£1,200	£1,450*	£1,450	£1,700 (including £250 advocate)	£800 + 20% of Damages	£1,800 +15% of Damages over £5k	£2,500 + 10% of Damages over £10k	£1,750 + 20% of Damages	£2,450 + 20% of Damages	£3,200 + 20% of Damages	£485 (to £3,000) £690 (£3-10,000) £1,035 (£10-15,000) £1,650 (£15,000+)
Escape	na	na	na	na	na	+ 20%	+ 20%	+ 20%	+ 20%	+ 20%	+ 20%	na
Success Fee	12.5%	12.5%	12.5%**	100%**	100%***	12.5%	12.5%	12.5%	12.5%	12.5%	12.5%	100%***
Employers Liability Accident												
Fixed Costs	na	na	na	na	na	£1,550 + 17.5% of Damages	£2,425 +12.5% of Damages over £5k	£3,050 + 10% of Damages over £10k	£3,175 + 20% of Damages	£3,875 + 25% of Damages	£4,775 + 30% of Damages	£485 (to £3,000) £690 (£3-10,000) £1,035 (£10-15,000) £1,650 (£15,000+)
Escape	na	na	na	na	na	+ 20%	+ 20%	+ 20%	+ 20%	+ 20%	+ 20%	na
Success Fee	na	na	na	na	na	25%	25%	25%	25%	25%	25%	100%***
Public Liability Accident												
Fixed Costs	na	na	na	na	na	£1,550 + 17.5% of Damages	£2,425 +10% of Damages over £5k	£2,925 + 10% of Damages over £10k	£3,000 + 17.5% of Damages	£3,600 + 22.5% of Damages	£4,300 + 27.5% of Damages	£485 (to £3,000) £690 (£3-10,000) £1,035 (£10-15,000) £1,650 (£15,000+)
Escape	na	na	na	na	na	+ 20%	+ 20%	+ 20%	+ 20%	+ 20%	+ 20%	na
Success Fee	na	na	na	na	na	45%	45%	45%	45%	45%	45%	100%***

Legend:

Existing CPR Parts 45 and 46

MoJ RTA Claims Process

Proposed Fixed Costs

Notes:

1. All Fixed Cost figures are cumulative across stages, although payments are made at the end of each stage in the MoJ RTA Claims Process (save children claims)
2. An additional £150 is paid for advice on quantum and £500 for an approval hearing (contested/uncontested) at Stage 3 in children's cases in the MoJ RTA Claims Process
3. Defendants' costs are fixed at Stage 3 only in the MoJ RTA Claims Process
4. Base fees - in all cases increased by 12.5% where London firm
5. Success fees - in all non-trial EL cases are 27.5% for membership organisations

* Stage 3 costs are only payable where settlement is higher than the defendant's Stage 2 offer
** Of Stage 3 costs only
*** Of all Base Costs

TABLE B – FIXED COSTS WITH DISCOUNTS FOR EARLY ADMISSION OF LIABILITY

	MoJ RTA Claims Process					Pre Issue			Post Issue			
	Pre issue £1,000-£10,000 **1**	Pre issue £1,000-£10,000 **2**	Issued £1,000-£10,000 **3**	Issued £1,000-£10,000 **4**	Issued £1,000-£10,000 **5**	Pre issue £1,000-£5,000 **6**	Pre Issue £5,001-£10,000 **7**	Pre Issue £10,001-£25,000 **8**	Issued – Post issue Pre Allocation **9**	Issued – Post allocation pre listing **10**	Issued – Post listing pre trial **11**	Trial - Advocacy Fee (Plus column 11) **12**
	Stage 1 - Notification leads to Admission of Liability	Stage 2 – Liability admitted, med rep obtained	Stage 3 – Settled pre hearing	Stage 3 – Assessment Hearing (paper)	Stage 3 – Assessment Hearing (Oral)	Case Settles before Issue	Case Settles before Issue	Case Settles before Issue				
Road Traffic Accident												
Fixed Costs	£400	£1,200	£1,450*	£1,450	£1,700 (including £250 advocate)	£800 +20% of Damages	£1,800 +15% of Damages over £5k	£2,550 +10% of Damages over £10k	£1,800 +20% of Damages	£2,500 +20% of Damages	£3,250 +20% of Damages	£485 (to £3,000) £690 (£3-10,000) £1,035 (£10-15,000) £1,650 (£15,000+)
Escape	na	na	na	na	na	+20%	+20%	+20%	+20%	+20%	+20%	na
Success Fee	12.5%	12.5%	12.5%*	100%**	100%**	12.5%	12.5%	12.5%	12.5%	12.5%	12.5%	100%***
Employers Liability Accident												
Fixed Costs	na	na	na	na	na	£1,600 +17.5% of Damages	£2,475 +12.5% of Damages over £5k	£3,100 +10% of Damages over £10k	£3,225 +20% of Damages	£3,925 +25% of Damages	£4,825 +30% of Damages	£485 (to £3,000) £690 (£3-10,000) £1,035 (£10-15,000) £1,650 (£15,000+)
Escape	na	na	na	na	na	+20%	+20%	+20%	+20%	+20%	+20%	na
Success Fee	na	na	na	na	na	25%	25%	25%	25%	25%	25%	100%***
Public Liability Accident												
Fixed Costs	na	na	na	na	na	£1,600 +17.5% of Damages	£2,475 +10% of Damages over £5k	£2,975 +10% of Damages over £10k	£3,050 +17.5% of Damages	£3,650 +22.5% of Damages	£4,350 +27.5% of Damages	£485 (to £3,000) £690 (£3-10,000) £1,035 (£10-15,000) £1,650 (£15,000+)
Escape	na	na	na	na	na	+20%	+20%	+20%	+20%	+20%	+20%	na
Success Fee	na	na	na	na	na	45%	45%	45%	45%	45%	45%	100%***

Legend:

Existing CPR Parts 45 and 46 — Proposed Fixed Costs

MoJ RTA Claims Process

Notes:

1. If an admission of liability is made within the protocol period, £250 will be deducted from the proposed Fixed Costs if the case settles pre-issue, and £500 will be deducted if the case concludes post-issue (incl at trial)
2. All Fixed Cost figures are cumulative across stages, although payments are made at the end of each stage in the MoJ RTA Claims Process (save children claims)
3. An additional £150 is paid for advice on quantum and £500 for an approval hearing (contested/uncontested) at Stage 3 in children's cases in the MoJ RTA Claims Process
4. Defendants' costs are fixed at Stage 3 only in the MoJ RTA Claims Process
5. Base fees - in all cases increased by 12.5% where London firm
6. Success fees - in all non-trial EL cases are 27.5% for membership organisations

* Stage 3 costs are only payable where settlement is higher than the defendant's Stage 2 offer
** Of Stage 3 costs only
*** Of all Base Costs

Appendix 5: Fixed costs matrix for fast track personal injury claims

APPENDIX 6. POST-ISSUE COSTS BUDGET QUESTIONNAIRE FOR CLINICAL NEGLIGENCE CASES

IN THE HIGH COURT OF JUSTICE   **Claim No.**
QUEEN'S BENCH DIVISION
BETWEEN

Claimant

And

Defendant

DRAFT /

CLAIMANT'S COST BUDGET QUESTIONNAIRE FOR USE IN CLINICAL NEGLIGENCE CASES

To be sent to the Claimant's solicitors as soon as possible after the issue of proceedings or transfer-in

This completed form is to be submitted by e.mail direct to the assigned Master by [date]

Address:
[ ]   master.yoxall@judiciary.gsi.gov.uk
[ ]   master.roberts@judiciay.gsi.gov.uk

A copy of this questionnaire in Word will be provided by the Master by e.mail on request.

The Court will set a budget for the Claimant's *base* costs (including disbursements such as fees for counsel and experts) up to and including trial (or to such other stage as may be appropriate) upon consideration of: [1] the answers to this questionnaire; [2] any supporting statement by the Claimant's solicitor; and [3] submissions made at any Budget Hearing conducted by the Master.

The solicitor's supporting statement must not exceed 3 pages (1.5 spacing).

Upon receipt of the completed questionnaire the Master will either set a cost budget (giving an option to request a Budget Hearing) or list a Budget Hearing.

A Budget Hearing (if any) will be listed for no more than 10 minutes. It will usually be held by telephone. The hearing will be inquisitorial. The hearing will be without notice to the Defendant.

A copy of the completed questionnaire, the supporting statement (if any) and the Cost Budget Order must be served by the Claimant on the Defendant within 7 days of the order (or with the claim form if that is yet to be served).

Should the Defendant wish to vary the Cost Budget Order, he may apply for such an order by application on notice. (The Defendant must apply within 7 days of service of the order if represented by solicitors. If unrepresented at the time of service, such an application must be made within 14 days). The Defendant's application must be supported by an estimate of his own costs and any supporting statement must not exceed 3 pages (1.5 spacing). On issue of the application the Master will list a Budget Hearing. Such applications will be discouraged by the Masters. An adversarial, cost generating hearing is to be avoided if at all possible.

The Order made by the Master will be in the following terms.

UPON reading the Claimant's cost budgeting questionnaire
[AND UPON hearing the solicitor for the Claimant]
IT IS ORDERED that

1.   *The Claimant's budget for base costs and disbursements up to and including trial [or to such other stage the court considers appropriate] is set at £   , excluding VAT.*

2.   *Should there be a change in circumstances, the Claimant may apply to the Master (without notice to the Defendant) to reduce or enlarge the base costs budget.*

3   *The Defendant may apply to vary this order within 7/14 days of service of the order.*

4.   *Costs in case.*

5.   *The Claimant is to serve a sealed copy of this order, and a copy of the completed questionnaire and any supporting statement submitted with the questionnaire by   [or with the claim form].*

6.   *If this order was made without a hearing the Claimant may apply (by e.mail) for a Budget Hearing.*

Dated etc

THE QUESTIONNAIRE

1. What is the value of the claim?	£
2. How is the claim funded? *Please tick*	Private: [ ] CFA: [ ] Public funding [ ]
3. How much documentation is there in the case?	Number of pages (approx): Lever arch files:
4. What is your estimate of base _costs incurred_ to date? *Do NOT provide the estimate in Precedent H form at this stage. Please simply state the figure.*	£
5. What are the hourly rates and experience of those engaged on this case?	£ p/h (with [ ] years post qualification experience) £ £
6. How many witnesses of fact will be relied upon?	[ ] In respect of breach of duty and causation; [ ] In respect of quantum, condition and prognosis.
7. What are the disciplines of the experts you propose to rely upon (subject to permission)?	4.1 **Joint experts** *Please list* 4.2 **Experts in respect of breach of duty and causation** *Please list* 4.3 **Experts in respect of quantum, condition and prognosis** *Please list*
8. What is your estimate of counsel(s) brief fee and daily refresher for the trial?	£
9. What is your time estimate for the length of trial?	[ ] days on a trial of a preliminary issue on breach of duty and causation? [ ] days on a whole trial.

10. What is your estimate of _future_ base costs up to and including trial?	£ on a trial of a preliminary issue on breach of duty and causation; £ on a whole trial.
11. What budget of base costs up to and including trial do you propose?	£ for a trial of a preliminary issue on breach of duty and causation; £ for a whole trial.
12. Do you wish to provide a statement in support of your budget figure?	_**Please annex any statement to the completed questionnaire.**_ _The statement must be not more than 3 sides long (1.5 spacing)._

DRAFT   30/11/09

APPENDIX 7. PRE-ISSUE COSTS BUDGET QUESTIONNAIRE FOR CLINICAL NEGLIGENCE CASES

Dated etc

Case No. HQ

THE QUESTIONNAIRE

1. What is the value of the claim?	£
2. How is the claim funded? *Please tick*	Private: [ ] CFA: [ ] Public funding [ ]
3. How much documentation is there in the case?	Number of pages (approx): Lever arch files:
4. What is your estimate of base _costs incurred_ to date? *Do NOT provide the estimate in Precedent H form at this stage. Please simply state the figure.*	£
5. What are the hourly rates and experience of those engaged on this case?	£ p/h (with [ ] years post qualification experience) £ £
6. How many witnesses of fact will be relied upon?	[ ] In respect of breach of duty and causation; [ ] In respect of quantum, condition and prognosis.
7. What are the disciplines of the experts you propose to rely upon?	4.1 <u>Joint experts</u> *Please list* 4.2 <u>**Experts in respect of breach of duty and causation**</u> *Please list* 4.3 <u>**Experts in respect of quantum, condition and prognosis**</u> *Please list*

8. What is your estimate of _future_ base costs up to and including issue?	£ on a trial of a preliminary issue on breach of duty and causation; £ on a whole trial.

DRAFT   30/11/09

PETITIONER'S STATEMENT OF COSTS
(Bankruptcy petition – standard [fixed] [benchmark] costs
LONDON 1

Registrar/District Judge

In the
Court
Case reference

Case Title

	profit costs	Disbursements
Preparation: to include taking instructions, preparing statutory demand, attendances on client, the debtor, the process server, the court, supporting creditor(s) etc	£1100.00	
Process server's fee		£160.00
Drafting/issuing petition and witness statement in support	£175.00	
Search fee		£5.00
Court fee		£190.00
[Deposit		£430.00]
Process server's fee		£160.00
Attendance at first hearing	£225.00	
Sub Total	£1,500.00	£945.00
Add		
[application for substituted service and court fee	£225.00	£30.00]
[Per further adjournment	£225.00	]
[application to extend time and court fee	£30.00	£30.00]
Amount of VAT claimed:		
On solicitors fees		£
On other expenses		£
GRAND TOTAL		£

The above costs do not exceed the costs which the Petitioner is liable to pay in respect of the work which this schedule covers and where the actual costs are less than the [fixed] [benchmark] costs the lower figure has been claimed

Dated   Signed

                                  Name of firm of solicitors
                                  [partner] for the Petitioner

PETITIONER'S STATEMENT OF COSTS
(Bankruptcy petition – standard [fixed] [benchmark] costs
NATIONAL 1

Registrar/District Judge

In the
Court
Case reference

Case Title

	profit costs	Disbursements
Preparation: to include taking instructions, preparing statutory demand, attendances on client, the debtor, the process server, the court, supporting creditor(s) etc	£725.00	
Process server's fee		£160.00
Drafting/issuing petition and witness statement in support	£125.00	
Search fee		£5.00
Court fee		£190.00
[Deposit		£430.00]
Process server's fee		£160.00
Attendance at first hearing	£160.00	
Sub Total	£1,010.00	£945.00
Add		
[application for substituted service and court fee	£160.00	£30.00]
[Per further adjournment	£130.00	]
[application to extend time and court fee	£30.00	£30.00]
Amount of VAT claimed:		
On solicitors fees		£
On other expenses		£
GRAND TOTAL		£

The above costs do not exceed the costs which the Petitioner is liable to pay in respect of the work which this schedule covers and where the actual costs are less than the [fixed] [benchmark] costs the lower figure has been claimed

Dated   Signed

Name of firm of solicitors
[partner] for the Petitioner

-547-

Appendix 8: Four sample petitioners' statements of costs proposed by the insolvency proceedings fixed costs working group

PETITIONER'S STATEMENT OF COSTS
(Winding up Petition – standard [fixed] [benchmark] costs
LONDON 1

Registrar/District Judge

In the	
	Court
Case reference	

Case Title

	profit costs	Disbursements
Preparation: to include taking instructions, attendances on client, the company, the process server, the court, supporting creditor(s) etc	£1,000.00	
Preparing statutory demand (if appropriate)	£110.00	
Company search fee		£4.00
Court search fee		£5.00
Process server's fee (demand)		£80.00
Drafting/issuing petition and witness statement in support	£110.00	
Court fee		£195.00
[Deposit		£715.00]
Process server's fee		£80.00
Advertisement		£75.00
Counsel's fee		£50.00
Sub Total	£1,220.00	£1204.00
Add		
[Per further adjournment: solicitor or counsel	£225.00	£50.00]
Amount of VAT claimed:		
On solicitors fees		£
On other expenses		£
GRAND TOTAL		£

The above costs do not exceed the costs which the Petitioner is liable to pay in respect of the work which this schedule covers and where the actual costs are less than the [fixed] [benchmark] costs the lower figure has been claimed

Dated   Signed

                                    Name of firm of solicitors
                                    [partner] for the Petitioner

Registrar/District Judge

In the	
	Court
Case reference	

Case Title

	Profit costs	Disbursements
Preparation: to include taking instructions, attendances on client, the company, the process server, the court, supporting creditor(s) etc	£725.00	
Preparing statutory demand (if appropriate)	£80.00	
Company search fee		£4.00
Court search fee		£5.00
Process server's fee (demand)		£80.00
Drafting/issuing petition and witness statement in support	£80.00	
Court fee		£195.00
[Deposit		£715.00]
Process server's fee		£80.00
Advertisement		£75.00
Counsel's fee		£50.00
Sub Total	£885.00	£1204.00
Add		
[Per further adjournment: solicitor or counsel	£160.00	£50.00]
Amount of VAT claimed:		
On solicitors fees		£
On other expenses		£
GRAND TOTAL		£

The above costs do not exceed the costs which the Petitioner is liable to pay in respect of the work which this schedule covers and where the actual costs are less than the [fixed] [benchmark] costs the lower figure has been claimed

Dated   Signed

                            Name of firm of solicitors
                            [partner] for the Petitioner

APPENDIX 9. TEMPLATE BUDGET FORM FOR BIRMINGHAM COSTS MANAGEMENT PILOT

Claimant / Defendant's estimate of costs dated [ ]

In the: [to be completed]
Parties: [to be completed]
Claim number: [to be completed]

Work done / to be done	Assumptions [to be completed as appropriate]	Disbursements	Profit Costs	Total
Pre-action costs		£0.00	£0.00	£0.00
Issue / pleadings		£0.00	£0.00	£0.00
CMC		£0.00	£0.00	£0.00
Disclosure		£0.00	£0.00	£0.00
Witness statements		£0.00	£0.00	£0.00
Expert reports		£0.00	£0.00	£0.00
PTR		£0.00	£0.00	£0.00
Trial preparation		£0.00	£0.00	£0.00
Trial		£0.00	£0.00	£0.00
Settlement discussions		£0.00	£0.00	£0.00
Contingent cost A: [explanation]		£0.00	£0.00	£0.00
Contingent cost B: [explanation]		£0.00	£0.00	£0.00
Contingent cost C: [explanation]		£0.00	£0.00	£0.00
[Insert additional contingent rows as required]				
GRAND TOTAL (including both incurred costs and estimated costs)				£0.00

comprising incurred costs of:

and estimated costs of:

Assumed into the costs of each stage should be the time costs for (a) attendance on own client (b) correspondence with the other party and (c) the general project and strategy

A breakdown of the above figures is found on the following pages.

This estimate **excludes**:
VAT [if applicable]
Costs of detailed assessment
Success fee [delete if no CFA]
ATE insurance premium [delete if no ATE insurance]
Other [to be completed as appropriate]

APPENDIX 9. TEMPLATE BUDGET FORM FOR BIRMINGHAM COSTS MANAGEMENT PILOT

Claimant / Defendant's estimate of costs dated [ ]

In the: [to be completed]
Parties: [to be completed]
Claim number: [to be completed]

Delete as applicable:	RATE (per hour)	Pre-action costs (Incurred / estimated)		Issue / pleadings (Incurred / estimated)		CMC (Incurred / estimated)		Disclosure (Incurred / estimated)		Witness statements (Incurred / estimated)	
		Hours	Total	Hours	Total	Hours	Total	Hours	Total	Hours	Total
Solicitors' time costs [descriptions to be amended as applicable to retainer]											
Partner			£0.00		£0.00		£0.00		£0.00		£0.00
Senior associate			£0.00		£0.00		£0.00		£0.00		£0.00
Mid level associate			£0.00		£0.00		£0.00		£0.00		£0.00
Junior associate			£0.00		£0.00		£0.00		£0.00		£0.00
Trainee			£0.00		£0.00		£0.00		£0.00		£0.00
Paralegal			£0.00		£0.00		£0.00		£0.00		£0.00
Expert's costs											
Fees											
Disbursements											
Counsel's fees [indicate seniority]											
Leading counsel			£0.00		£0.00		£0.00		£0.00		£0.00
Junior counsel			£0.00		£0.00		£0.00		£0.00		£0.00
Court fees											
Disbursements											
Explanation of disbursements [details to be completed]											
Total		0	£0.00	0	£0.00	0	£0.00	0	£0.00	0	£0.00

Appendix 9: Template budget form for Birmingham costs management pilot

APPENDIX 9. TEMPLATE BUDGET FORM FOR BIRMINGHAM COSTS MANAGEMENT PILOT

Claimant / Defendant's estimate of costs dated [ ]

In the: [to be completed]
Parties: [to be completed]
Claim number: [to be completed]

Delete as applicable:	RATE (per hour)	Expert reports		PTR		Trial preparation		Trial		Settlement (negotiation / mediation)		Contingent cost A: [explanation e.g. application for a freezing injunction]	
		Incurred / estimated		Incurred / estimated		Incurred / estimated		Incurred / estimated		Incurred / estimated		Incurred / estimated	
		Hours	Total	Hours	Total	Hours	Total	Hours	Total	Hours	Total	Hours	Total
Solicitors' time costs [descriptions to be amended as applicable to retainer]													
Partner			£0.00		£0.00		£0.00		£0.00		£0.00		£0.00
Senior associate			£0.00		£0.00		£0.00		£0.00		£0.00		£0.00
Mid level associate			£0.00		£0.00		£0.00		£0.00		£0.00		£0.00
Junior associate			£0.00		£0.00		£0.00		£0.00		£0.00		£0.00
Trainee			£0.00		£0.00		£0.00		£0.00		£0.00		£0.00
Paralegal			£0.00		£0.00		£0.00		£0.00		£0.00		£0.00
Expert's costs													
Fees													
Disbursements													
Counsel's fees [indicate seniority]													
Leading counsel			£0.00		£0.00		£0.00		£0.00		£0.00		£0.00
Junior counsel			£0.00		£0.00		£0.00		£0.00		£0.00		£0.00
Court fees													
Disbursements													
Explanation of disbursements [details to be completed]													
Total		0	£0.00	0	£0.00	0	£0.00	0	£0.00	0	£0.00	0	£0.00

In the: [to be completed]
Parties: [to be completed]
Claim number: [to be completed]

Claimant / Defendant's estimate of costs dated [ ]

Delete as applicable:	RATE (per hour)	Incurred / estimated		Incurred / estimated	
		Contingent cost B: [explanation e.g. amending pleadings]		Contingent cost C: [explanation e.g. specific disclosure application inc. hearing]	
		Hours	Total	Hours	Total
Solicitors' time costs [descriptions to be amended as applicable to retainer]					
Partner			£0.00		£0.00
Senior associate			£0.00		£0.00
Mid level associate			£0.00		£0.00
Junior associate			£0.00		£0.00
Trainee			£0.00		£0.00
Paralegal			£0.00		£0.00
Expert's costs					
Fees					
Disbursements					
Counsel's fees					
Leading counsel			£0.00		£0.00
Junior counsel			£0.00		£0.00
Court fees					
Disbursements					
Explanation of disbursements [details to be completed]					
Total		0	£0.00	0	£0.00

Appendix 9: Template budget form for Birmingham costs management pilot

APPENDIX 10. PROPOSED AMENDMENTS TO SECTIONS 35 AND 39 OF THE COSTS PRACTICE DIRECTION

1. SECTION 35 OF THE COSTS PRACTICE DIRECTION

Section 35 of the Costs Practice Direction concerns points of dispute and the consequence of not serving under CPR rule 47.9.

The Practice Direction, so far as relevant, presently states:

"35.2   Points of dispute should be short and to the point and should follow as closely as possible Precedent G of the Schedule of Costs Precedents annexed to this Practice Direction.

35.3   Points of dispute must –

(1)   identify each item in the bill of costs which is disputed,

(2)   in each case, state concisely the nature and grounds of dispute,

(3)   where practicable suggest a figure to be allowed for each item in respect of which a reduction is sought, and

(4)   be signed by the party serving them, or his solicitor."

Suggested Amended Practice Direction:

"35.2   Points of dispute have in the past become too long and repetitive. Points of dispute should be short and to the point. The points should identify any points of principle, as well as any specific items, but once a point has been made it should not be repeated in respect of subsequent items in the bill. Points of dispute should follow the amended Precedent G of the Schedule of Costs Precedents annexed to this Practice Direction.

35.3   Points of dispute must -

(1)   identify any general points or points of principle which require decision before the individual items in the bill are addressed, and

(2)   identify specific points stating concisely the nature and grounds of dispute. Once the point has been made it should not be repeated but the item numbers, where the point arises, should be inserted in the left hand box as shown in the amended Precedent G.

2. SECTION 39 OF THE COSTS PRACTICE DIRECTION

Section 39 of the Costs Practice Direction deals with the optional reply under CPR rule 47.13.

The Practice Direction, so far as relevant, presently states:

"39.1

(1)   Where the receiving party wishes to serve a reply, he must also serve a copy on every other party to the detailed assessment proceedings. The time for doing so is within 21 days after service of the points of dispute.

(2)   A reply means:

    (i)   a separate document prepared by the receiving party; or

    (ii)   his written comments added to the points of dispute.

(3)   A reply must be signed by the party serving it or his solicitor."

It is suggested that a further paragraph be added to this section:

"(4)   Where replies are served these should be limited to replies to points of principle and concessions only. A simple rejection of the paying party's points of dispute is of no assistance to the court."

SCHEDULE OF COSTS PRECEDENTS
PRECEDENT G

IN THE HIGH COURT OF JUSTICE   2000 B 9999

QUEEN'S BENCH DIVISION

OXBRIDGE DISTRICT REGISTRY

B E T W E E N

WX

Claimant

- and -

YZ

Defendan

POINTS OF DISPUTE SERVED BY THE DEFENDANT

Item	Dispute	Claimant's Comments
General point	Base rates claimed for the assistant solicitor and other fee earners are excessive. Reduce to £158 and £116 respectively plus VAT.	
Point of principle	The claimant was at the time a child/protected person/insolvent and did not have the capacity to authorise the solicitors to bring these proceedings.	
(5)	The ATE premium claimed is excessive. Reduce to £400.	
(6), (12), (17), (23), (29), (32)	(i) The number of conferences with counsel is excessive and should be reduced to 3 in total (9 hours). (ii) There is no need for two fee earners to attend each conference. Limit to one assistant solicitor in each case.	
(42)	The claim for timed attendances on claimant (schedule 1) is excessive. Reduce to 4 hours.	
(47)	The total claim for work done on documents by the assistant solicitor is excessive. A reasonable allowance in respect of documents concerning court and counsel is 8 hours, for documents concerning witnesses and the expert	

	witness 6.5 hours, for work done on arithmetic 2.25 hours and for other documents 5.5 hours. Reduce to 22.25 hours.	
(50)	The time claimed for preparing and checking the bill is excessive. Reduce solicitor's time to 0.5 hours and reduce the costs draftsman's time to three hours.	
(51)	The success fee claimed is excessive. Reduce to 25%.	

Served on .... [date] by ....[name] [solicitors for] the Defendant.